Sixth edition

Marketing Across Cultures

Jean-Claude Usunier

Julie Anne Lee

PEARSON

Harlow, England • London • New York • Boston • San Francisco • Toronto • Sydney
Auckland • Singapore • Hong Kong • Tokyo • Seoul • Taipei • New Delhi
Cape Town • São Paulo • Mexico City • Madrid • Amsterdam • Munich • Paris • Milan

PEARSON EDUCATION LIMITED
Edinburgh Gate
Harlow CM20 2JE
United Kingdom
Tel: +44 (0)1279 623623
Web: www.pearson.com/uk

_____

First published 1992 (print)
Second edition published 1996 (print)
Third edition published 2000 (print)
Fourth edition published 2005 (print)
Fifth edition published 2009 (print)
Sixth edition published 2013 (print and electronic)

ISBN: 978-0-273-75773-3 (print)
       978-0-273-75776-4 (PDF)
       978-0-273-78102-8 (eText)

British Library Cataloguing-in-Publication Data
A catalogue record for the print edition is available from the British Library

Library of Congress Cataloging-in-Publication Data
Usunier, Jean-Claude.
   Marketing across cultures / Jean-Claude Usunier, Julie Anne Lee. -- 6th ed.
      p. cm.
   ISBN 978-0-273-75773-3 (pbk.)
   1. Export marketing--Social aspects.   2. International business enterprises--Social
aspects.   3. Intercultural communication.   4. Marketing--Cross-cultural studies.
I. Lee, Julie Anne.   II. Title.
   HF1416.U85 2013
   658.8'4--dc23

                                                                2012030139

10 9 8 7 6 5 4 3 2 1
17 16 15 14 13

Print edition typeset in 10/12pt Minion by 35
Print edition printed and bound in Gosport, UK, by Ashford Colour Press Ltd

NOTE THAT ANY PAGE CROSS REFERENCES REFER TO THE PRINT EDITION

Brief contents

Introduction: marketing in the global villages   xiii
Acknowledgements   xvii

Part 1 The cultural variable in international marketing   1

Introduction to Part 1   2
1 The cultural process   4
2 Cultural dynamics 1: time and space   25
3 Cultural dynamics 2: interactions and behaviours   47
4 Language, culture and communication   68

Part 2 The integration of local consumption in a global marketing environment   99

Introduction to Part 2   100
5 Cross-cultural consumer behaviour   102
6 Local consumers and the globalization of consumption   131
7 Cross-cultural market research   184

Part 3 Marketing decisions for the intercultural environment   217

Introduction to Part 3   218
8 Intercultural marketing strategy   220
9 Product strategy: physical, service and symbolic attributes   251
10 The critical role of price in relational exchange   290
11 International distribution and sales promotion   316

Part 4 Intercultural marketing communications   339

Introduction to Part 4   340
12 Branding: managing meaning   342
13 Intercultural marketing communications 1: advertising   372
14 Intercultural marketing communications 2: personal selling,
   networking and public relations   428

Author index   465
Subject index   468

Contents

Introduction: marketing in the global villages   xiii
Acknowledgements   xvii

Part 1   The cultural variable in international marketing   1

Introduction to Part 1   2

1   The cultural process   4

1.1   Defining culture   4
1.2   Elements of culture   6
1.3   Culture and nationality   10
1.4   Culture, competence and stereotypes   15
1.5   Ethnocentrism and self-reference criteria   17

Questions   20
References   21

Appendix 1: Teaching materials   23
A1.1   *Critical incident*: An old lady from Malaysia   23
A1.2   *Critical incident*: The parable   23
A1.3   *Reading*: Body rituals among the Naciremas   24

Appendix reference   24

2   Cultural dynamics 1: time and space   25

2.1   A model of action based on cultural assumptions   26
2.2   Time: cross-cultural variability   27
2.3   Space territoriality   31
2.4   Concept of the self and others   35
2.5   Chronically and situationally accessible cultural norms   39

Questions   40
References   41

Appendix 2: Teaching materials   42
A2.1   *Cross-cultural scenario*: Inshallah   42
A2.2   *Cross-cultural interaction*: Engineering a decision   42
A2.3   *Cross-cultural interaction*: Opening a medical office in Saudi Arabia   43

A2.4   *Reading*: Language and time patterns – the Bantu case   44
A2.5   *Exercise*: World picture test   45

Appendix references   46

3 Cultural dynamics 2: interactions and behaviours   47

3.1   Models of interaction   47
3.2   Culture-based attitudes towards action   55
3.3   Cultural assumptions and actual behaviour   62

Questions   63
References   64

Appendix 3: Teaching materials   65
A3.1   *Critical incident*: An American in Vietnam   65
A3.2   Rationales for Section A2.1 (cross-cultural scenario) and
        Sections A2.2 and A2.3 (cross-cultural interaction)   65

Appendix references   67

4 Language, culture and communication   68

4.1   Verbal communication: the role of context   69
4.2   Non-verbal communication   74
4.3   Language shaping our world views   77
4.4   The Internet: communication in cyberspace   81
4.5   Improving communication effectiveness in international business 82

Questions   85
References   86

Appendix 4: Teaching materials   88
A4.1   *Exercise*: Multicultural class   88
A4.2   *Exercise*: I 'love' cake   88
A4.3   *Case*: Longcloud – languages in cyberspace   88
A4.4   *Case*: Supreme Canning   93
A4.5   *Critical incident*: Scandinavian Tools Company   95

Appendix references   97

Part 2 The integration of local consumption in a global marketing environment   99

Introduction to Part 2   100

5 Cross-cultural consumer behaviour   102

5.1   Culture and consumer behaviour   103
5.2   The influence of culture on selected aspects of consumer behaviour 107
5.3   Investigating the cross-cultural applicability of consumer behaviour
        concepts   111

5.4   Ethnic consumption   114
5.5   Marketing as an exchange of meanings   116

Questions   118
References   118

Appendix 5: Teaching materials   121
A5.1   *Exercise*: 'Dichter's consumption motives'   121
A5.2   *Exercise*: Investigating the cross-cultural applicability of a consumer
        complaint scale   122
A5.3   *Case*: Mobile phones in the European Union   122
A5.4   *Exercise*: Cross-cultural consumer behaviour and the
        standardization/adaptation of service offers   128
A5.5   *Exercise*: Multi-domestic versus global   128

Appendix references   129

6   Local consumers and the globalization of consumption   131

6.1   Free trade doctrine and the denial of cultural variety in consumers' tastes   132
6.2   The global convergence of consumption patterns   134
6.3   The emergence of a global consumer culture   136
6.4   Local products and consumption experiences   139
6.5   Local consumer cultures and resistance to change   145
6.6   Emergent patterns of mixed local/global consumer behaviour   148

Questions   151
References   152

Appendix 6: Teaching materials   155
A6.1   *Case*: Setting the stage – Disneyland Resort Paris   155
A6.2   *Case*: Papa Ingvar's worries   160
A6.3   *Case*: McDonald's – a global cultural icon?   165

Appendix references   178

7   Cross-cultural market research   184

7.1   Local marketing institutions and infrastructures   185
7.2   Equivalence in cross-cultural research   188
7.3   Translation equivalence   192
7.4   Measure equivalence   195
7.5   Comparability of samples   199
7.6   Data-collection equivalence   201
7.7   Researching internationally   205
7.8   Conclusion   206

Questions   207
References   208

Appendix 7: Teaching materials   211
A7.1   *Case*: Mobile phones in the European Union   211
A7.2   *Exercise*: Hair shampoo questionnaire   211

Appendix reference   216

Part 3 Marketing decisions for the intercultural environment   217

Introduction to Part 3   218

8 Intercultural marketing strategy   220

8.1	Cost arguments and global strategies	221
8.2	The globalization of competition	227
8.3	Globalization of international marketing strategies	228
8.4	Market segments	231
8.5	Conclusion	235

Questions   235
References   236

Appendix 8: Teaching materials   238
A8.1	*Case*: Bollywood: selling Indian movies in the West	238
A8.2	*Case*: Muslim Cola: cola wars or cola crusades?	242
A8.3	*Case*: Odol	244
A8.4	*Exercise*: Dangerous Enchantment	246

Appendix references   248

9 Product strategy: physical, service and symbolic attributes   251

9.1	Adaptation or standardization of product attributes	252
9.2	Physical attributes	254
9.3	Service attributes	259
9.4	Symbolic attributes	264

Questions   268
References   268

Appendix 9: Teaching materials   271
A9.1	*Case*: Movies worldwide	271
A9.2	*Case*: Fast food – Halal or Haram?	277

Appendix references   286

10 The critical role of price in relational exchange   290

10.1	Price as a signal conveying meaning	291
10.2	Bargaining	291
10.3	Price and consumer evaluations	294
10.4	International price tactics	298
10.5	Market situations, competition and price agreements	304
10.6	Managing prices in highly regulated environments	307

Questions   309
References   309

Appendix 10: Teaching materials   312

A10.1 *Case*: Saito Importing Company 312
A10.2 *Case*: Riva International 313
A10.3 *Case*: Taman SA 315
A10.4 *Case*: AIDS – global ethics and the pricing of AIDS drugs 315

Appendix reference 315

11 International distribution and sales promotion 316

11.1 Criteria for choosing foreign distribution channels 316
11.2 Role of distribution as a 'cultural filter' 321
11.3 Direct marketing and the Internet 323
11.4 Sales promotion: other customs, other manners 326

Questions 329
References 330

Appendix 11: Teaching materials 333
A11.1 *Case*: ComputerLand in Japan 333
A11.2 *Case*: Virtual beehive – online marketing of US honey 334

Appendix references 338

Part 4 Intercultural marketing communications 339

Introduction to Part 4 340

12 Branding: managing meaning 342

12.1 National images diffused by product origin and brand name 343
12.2 Consumer product evaluation according to country of origin 345
12.3 National, international and global brands 349

Questions 359
References 360

Appendix 12: Teaching materials 365
A12.1 *Exercise*: Interpreting symbolic attributes 365
A12.2 *Case*: Soshi Sumsin Ltd 365
A12.3 *Case*: Derivados de Leche SA 367
A12.4 *Case*: K21-tech: B2B or B2C brands for computer components? 369

Appendix references 371

13 Intercultural marketing communications 1: advertising 372

13.1 Influence of culture on attitudes towards advertising 375
13.2 Culture and advertising strategy 377
13.3 Culture and advertising execution 380
13.4 Media worldwide: technological advances and cultural convergence 389
13.5 The globalization of advertising 392

Questions 396
References 397

Appendix 13: Teaching materials   403
A13.1 *Case*: Brand USA – selling Uncle Sam like Uncle Ben's   403
A13.2 *Case*: Excel and the Italian advertising campaign   407
A13.3 *Exercise*: Borovets – a Bulgarian ski resort   409
A13.4 *Exercise*: Slogans and colloquial speech   410
A13.5 *Case*: Mexicom designs a public health communication campaign
       for Mexico   411

Appendix references   425

**14 Intercultural marketing communications 2: personal
     selling, networking and public relations**   **428**
14.1 Intercultural commerce   428
14.2 Networks in business markets   435
14.3 Buyer–seller interactions   436
14.4 Sales force management in a cross-cultural perspective   438
14.5 Public relations across cultures   442
14.6 Bribery: facts   444
14.7 Bribery: ethical aspects   446

Questions   451
References   452

Appendix 14: Teaching materials   455
A14.1 *Case*: When international buyers and sellers disagree   455
A14.2 *Case*: Setco of Spain   456
A14.3 *Case*: Union Carbide at Bhopal   457
A14.4 *Case*: The *Brenzy nouveau* has arrived!   460
A14.5 *Case*: Bielrohr AG   462

Author index   465
Subject index   468

Introduction
Marketing in the global villages

Classical consumer marketing textbooks generally emphasize world markets and are often cross-border extensions of American marketing thought, blatantly ignoring people, languages and cultures and implicitly arguing in favour of uniformity. By contrast, large multinational companies, such as Mars, Pepsi-Cola, L'Oréal or Nestlé, do not in fact follow the traditional textbook recipes: their practice is always much more adaptive to, and respectful of, local contexts. Further, the relatively recent financial shockwaves have left much of the developed world with very low or non-existent growth. This has prompted companies to examine seriously the potential for growth into emerging and developing nations. However, these markets have very different consumers, with very different interests, preferences, purchasing patterns and price sensitivities, very different competitive environments and very different marketing infrastructure.[1]

This text offers a different approach to global marketing, based on the recognition of diversity in world markets and on local consumer knowledge and marketing practices. We invite the reader to undertake an exercise in decentering. We try to break out of our 'Francocentric' and 'Aussie-centric' boxes, in much the same way as Gorn[2] invites us to break out of 'North American boxes'. Understanding international diversity[a] in consumer behaviour and marketing management becomes the central teaching objective for an international marketing textbook.

This text adopts an intercultural approach to international marketing; this has two main dimensions:

1. *Comparing* national marketing systems and local commercial customs in various countries, with the aim of emphasizing what is country specific and what is universal, or at least regional. Such an approach is essential for the preparation and implementation of marketing strategies in different national contexts.

2. Studying *interactions* between business people, buyers and sellers (and their companies), who have different national/cultural backgrounds. This intercultural view extends this to include the interactions between consumers from different backgrounds and products (their physical and symbolic attributes, as well as the messages surrounding them). Thus, interaction is meant in a broad sense: not only between people, but also between people and messages, and people and products. In this book, commerce is emphasized as much as marketing. When the word *commerce* is used in this text, it refers to the complex dimensions of business relationships entwined with interpersonal relations.

The basic assumption behind this book is that culture penetrates our inner being subconsciously and at a deep level. World cultures share many common features. Nevertheless, when common elements are combined they all display a unique style, *vis-à-vis* kinship patterns, education systems, valuation of the individual and the group, emphasis on economic activities, friendship patterns, time-related organization patterns, the criteria for aesthetic appreciation, and so on. The examples that are used in this book are by their very nature eclectic. We have chosen examples that seem to be the most striking and pertinent.

This book does not try to describe cultures exhaustively, or from an insider's point of view. What we have attempted to provide for the reader is *a method for dealing with intercultural situations in international marketing*. The underlying postulate of this book is that international marketing relationships have to be built on solid foundations. Transaction costs in international trade are high: only a stable and firmly established link between business people can enable them to overcome disagreements and conflicts of interest. In international marketing it is advisable to be very methodical and long-term oriented, to select a limited number of partners and opportunities, and to develop them to their fullest extent.

Changes in the sixth edition

The sixth edition has been extensively rewritten. The order of chapters and sections within chapters has changed to improve the readability and flow of ideas. The dramatic increase in the number of cross-cultural and international marketing studies published in the last few years has seen many of the original research findings extended to other cultures, other contexts and integrated with other theories and ideas. Rather than include details of each study, we have summarized the results to present a more cohesive picture (where possible) and referenced examples of the research in the area.

The world is going through a dramatic period of change. These changes include a shift in global power from the West to the East, rising prosperity and growth of the global middle class, especially in emerging economies, increased urbanization and aging of the population and increasing concerns about social and environmental issues.[3] As such, the website links have been extended to encourage the reader to search the Internet for relevant up-to-the-moment information.

Target audience

This book is designed for instructors and students who consider global diversity as an asset and an opportunity, rather than a liability or a threat, and who find pleasure in discovering new ways of life and experiencing the challenge of cultural differences in world markets. *Marketing Across Cultures* is particularly useful and relevant in the case of multicultural, multilingual, and multinational classes, institutions and/or countries. This book is to be proposed as a primary textbook for those instructors who want to emphasize culture, sales, negotiations, and a cross-cultural approach to consumer behaviour and market research, and as a secondary text for other IM instructors who want to follow a more traditional approach to international marketing.

The sixth edition has been written for:

- senior undergraduate students who have already studied a marketing management course;
- postgraduate students (MBA in particular) for a cross-cultural/international marketing elective course;
- research students who have an in-depth interest in cultural and comparative aspects of International Business and Global Marketing; and
- senior executives who wish to develop culturally sensitive approaches to global marketing strategy.

For instructors

Additional materials are available for instructors who adopt the text at **www.pearsoned.co.uk/usunierlee**:

- Electronic forms of all cases with hyperlinks to the cited website for additional information.
- An instructor's manual with pedagogical guidance, answers to the end-of-chapter questions and teaching notes for all cases.
- PowerPoint slides for each chapter.
- A test bank for each chapter.
- Some additional cases and exercises.

All correspondence should be sent to the following email: **marketingacrosscultures@gmail.com**

Outline

- Part 1, comprising the first four chapters, is devoted to the cultural variable. These chapters try to define it, to delineate the components of culture, and finally to emphasize its dynamic nature. [Chapter 4 on language, culture and communication issues, was previously at the start of Part 4, and has been extensively rewritten and integrated into this section.]
- Part 2 deals with the globalization of markets, which is *the* central issue in international marketing; Chapters 5 and 6 examine consumer behaviour, taking both a local and a global perspective, while Chapter 7 deals with local and regional marketing environments, especially research.
- Part 3 presents the general impact of globalization on international marketing strategies (Chapter 8), with special emphasis on a key issue for product strategy, namely, the dilemma between adaptation

Table I.1 The impact of cultural differences on selected aspects of marketing

Area of marketing	Cultural differences influence . . .	Chapter
Consumer behaviour	Cross-cultural consumer attitudes and decision making	5
	Local consumers and global consumption	6
Market research	Equivalence and methods in cross-national market surveys	7
Marketing strategy	Global versus locally customized marketing strategies	8
Targeting segments	Cross-border vs. country clustering	8
Product	Adaptation or standardization of product attributes	9
Price	Bargaining rituals/Price–quality evaluations/Price strategies towards consumers, competitors and suppliers	10
Distribution	Channel style and service, producer–distributor relationships	11
Brand image	Brand and country-of-origin evaluations by consumers	12
Advertising	Tailoring messages to local audiences' cultural traits	13
Personal selling	Selling styles, sales force management, networking and public relations, bribery and ethical issues in an international context	14

and standardization (Chapter 9). In Chapters 10 and 11, which concern price policies and the choice of distribution channels, emphasis has been deliberately placed on the culture-based approaches to such decisions.

■ Part 4 presents marketing communications in an intercultural environment. It starts with Chapter 12, which deals with the complex management of meanings related to brand names for international markets and to country-of-origin images. The next two chapters deal with advertising issues, personal selling, public relations, and bribery and ethical issues in international marketing. Table I.1 presents a summary of the basic contents of Chapters 5 to 14, linking culture to marketing issues.

This book is written from both a European and Australasian viewpoint with many examples relating to these two areas of the world. As with all international marketing texts, this one is not universal. It may be perceived as being less pragmatically written and less issue-oriented than most. Statements may sometimes be classed as value judgements, since they are not always supported by empirical evidence, as is the case in American textbooks. Therefore, this

book may sometimes seem unusual to native English-speaking readers. We regard this approach as part of the message of the book: it is more contextual, and therefore less explicit.

Each chapter concludes with questions and is followed by an appendix comprising some or all of the following: cases, exercises and critical incidents. In addition, many interesting links, cases and exercises have been included on the book's website (**www. hec.unil.ch/jusunier/teaching/index.htm**) and in the instructor's manual. Since different national versions of this book have been published (Dutch, English, French and German), it may be used in cross-cultural training settings.

Note

a. Here, 'diversity' is not meant in its American sense with a strong anti-discrimination stance (reported for instance by Litvin[4]), but rather in its simplest meaning of 'state or quality of being different or varied', with no value judgement about whether 'diversity' is good or bad. In fact, it is neither good nor bad, as shown by Lian and Oneal[5] through a cross-national study linking cultural diversity to economic development for 98 countries over the 1960–1985 period.

References

1. Douglas, Susan P. and C. Samuel Craig (2011), 'Convergence and Divergence: Developing a Semiglobal Marketing Strategy, *Journal of International Marketing*, 19(1), 82–101.
2. Gorn, Gerald J. (1997), 'Breaking out of the North American box', in Merrie Brucks and Debbie McInnis (eds), *Advances in Consumer Research*, vol. 24, Association for Consumer Research: Provo, UT, pp. 6–7.
3. Euromonitor (2011), 'In Focus: The Biggest Global Trends Influencing Consumer Markets', downloaded 11 Feb 2012: http://www.euromonitor.com.
4. Litvin, Deborah R. (1997), 'The Discourse of Diversity: From Biology to Management', *Organization*, 4(2), 187–209.
5. Lian, Brad and John R. Oneal (1997), 'Cultural Diversity and Economic Development: A Cross-national Study of 98 Countries, 1960–1985', *Economic Development and Cultural Change*, 46(1), 61–77.

Acknowledgements

Authors' acknowledgements

We wish to acknowledge the help of the academic institutions that have provided us with the opportunity to teach and research international marketing over the last ten years. We are also indebted to many colleagues for their ideas and assistance and for encouraging us to put more and more emphasis on the cultural dimension of international marketing. We would also like to thank senior editor Thomas Sigel for his support and Peter Hooper, Aylene Rogers and Colin Reed at Pearson Education who have been instrumental in the production of this book, as well as Saskia Faulk for her great contribution in writing new cases. We accept responsibility for any errors and shortcomings.

Publisher's acknowledgements

We are grateful to the following for permission to reproduce copyright material:

Figures

Figure 3.1 from Motivation, leadership and organization: do American theories apply abroad? *Organizational Dynamics*, Summer, 42–63 (Hofstede, G. 1980), copyright © 1980, reprinted with permission from Elsevier; Figure 3.2 from Understanding culture: theory, research and application *Psychology Press* (Schwartz, S. H. 2009) pp. 127–150, Culture matters: national value cultures, sources and consequences. In C.-Y. Chiu, Y. Y. Hong, S. Shavitt, & R. S. Wyer, Jr. (eds), republished with permission of Taylor & Francis Group LLC – Books; Figure 13.2 from Coordinating international advertising, *Journal of Marketing*, 42(1), January, pp. 28–34, American Marketing Association (Peebles, D. M., Ryans, J. K. Jr and Vernon, I. R. 1978); Figure 14.2 from *Marketing,*

Principles and Practice, Pitman (Adcock, Dennis, Bradfield, Ray, Halborg, Al and Ross, Caroline 1993), copyright © Pearson Education Limited 1993.

Tables

Table 5.5 from International Telecommunication Union (2010); Table 7.2 adapted from *Consumer Behavior*, 4th ed, John Wiley & Sons Limited (Samuel, Craig C. and Douglas, Susan P. 2001), copyright © John Wiley & Sons Limited, reprinted with permission; Table 7.4 from Verbal rating scales for multinational research, *European Research*, March, p. 76 (Pras, Bernard and Angelmar, Reinhard 1978), copyright © March 1978 by ESOMAR® – The World Association of Research Professionals (this article first appeared in European Research, published by ESOMAR®); Table 9.1 from Integrating adaptation and standardisation in international marketing: the adaptstand modelling process, *Journal of Marketing Management*, 19, 283–305 (Vrontis, Demetris 2003), copyright © Westburn Publishers Ltd, reprinted by permission of Taylor & Francis Ltd, www.tandfonline.com on behalf of The Westburn Publishers Ltd.; Table 12.3 adapted from Linguistic distinction among top brand names, *Journal of Advertising Research*, 27(4), pp. 39–44 (Vanden Bergh, Bruce, Adler, Keith and Oliver, Lauren 1987); Table 13.1 after Solomon, Norman (2002) from Branding new and improved wars, *Fairness and Accuracy in Reporting* (FAIR), 29 October and Seiminski, Gregory (1995), The art of naming operations, *Parameters*, pp. 81–98, reprinted with permission.

Text

Case Studies A2.1 and A3.2 from *The Cultural Dimension of International Business*, 5th edn (Ferraro, Gary P.), copyright © 2006, reproduced by permission of Pearson Education, Inc., Upper Saddle River, NJ; Case Studies A2.2, A2.3 and A3.2 from *Intercultural*

Interactions: A Practical Guide, Sage (Brislin, Richard W., Kushner, Kenneth, Cherrie, Craig and Yong, Mahealani 1986), republished with permission of Sage Publications Inc. Books, permission conveyed through Copyright Clearance Center, Inc.; Case Study A2.4 from *Management Interculturel: Modes et Modèles*, Economica (Usunier, Jean-Claude and Napoléon-Biguma, Constantin 1991) Gauthey Franck and Dominique Xardel (eds); Box 4.1 from *Beyond Culture*, Doubleday (Edward T. Hall 1976), copyright © 1976, 1981 by Edward T. Hall. Used by permission of Doubleday, a division of Random House, Inc.; Box 4.3 from The silent language in overseas business, *Harvard Business Review*, May–June, 87–96 (Edward T. Hall 1960); Case Studies 4.3, A5.3, A6.1, A6.2, A6.3, A8.1, A8.2, A9.1, A11.2, A13.1, 13.5 and Box A9.2 from Saskia Faulk and Jean-Claude Usunier, 2011, The Institute of Research in Management of the University of Lausanne, Saskia Faulk and Jean-Claude Usunier prepared this case solely to provide material for class discussion. The authors do not intend to illustrate either effective or ineffective handling of a business situation. The authors may have disguised certain names and other identifying information to protect confidentiality; Case Studies A4.4 and A10.1 from *International Marketing and Export Management*, Pearson Education (Duerr, Mitsuko Saito 1989) 85–7, Gerald Albaum and Jesper Strandskov and Edwin Duerr and Laurence Dowd (eds), reprinted and electronically reproduced by permission of Pearson Education, Inc., Upper Saddle River, New Jersey; Case Study A5.1 from *Consumer Behavior: Buying, Having and Being*, 4th ed, Pearson Education (Solomon, Michael R. 1999); Box 6.5 from *Business of Europe: Managing Change*, Sage (Steele, Murray 1991), European Brewing Industry, Roland Calori and Peter Lawrence (eds), reproduced by permission of Sage Publications, London, Los Angeles, New Delhi and Singapore, copyright © Sage Publications, 1991; Box 7.3 from Is Schwartz's Value Survey interval scaled and does it really matter? *Journal of Cross-Cultural Psychology*, 41(1), pp. 76–86 (Lee, Julie Anne and Soutar, Geoffrey N. 2010), copyright © 2010 by Sage Publications, reprinted by permission of Sage Publications; Box 7.4 from Qualitative research in developing countries, *Journal of Market Research Society*, 24(2), pp. 90–1 (Goodyear, Mary 1982); Box 8.2 from Hollensen, Svend (1991), Shift of market servicing organization in international markets: a Danish case study, Harald Vestergaard (ed.), An Enlarged Europe in the Global Economy, *Proceedings of the 17th Annual Conference of the European International Business Association*, Copenhagen Business School: Copenhagen, pp. 732–42; Exercise A8.4 from *Dangerous Enchantment*, Harlequin (Mather, Anne 1966), permission to reproduce text granted by Harlequin Books S.A.; Box 10.2 from *The Protestant Ethic and the Spirit of Capitalism*, Charles Scribner's Sons (Weber, Max 1958), by permission of Oxford University Press, USA; Case Studies A12.2 and A12.3 adapted from *Marketing in the International Environment*, 2nd ed., Pearson Education (Cundiff, E. W. and Hilger, M. T. 1988) pp. 440–42, © 1988, electronically reproduced by permission of Pearson Education, Inc., Upper Saddle River, New Jersey; Case Study 13.2 from *International Marketing Review*, Emerald Group Publishing Limited (Luqmani, Musshtaq, Yavas, Ugur and Quraeshi, Zahir 1989) pp. 61–4; Box 14.4 from *L'argent Noir*, Librarie Artheme Fayard (Péan, Pierre 1988).

Photographs

1 Corbis; 99 Getty Images; 339 Reuters: Amit Dave.

Cover images: *Front:* Copyright 2010 Thomson Reuters

In some instances we have been unable to trace the owners of copyright material, and we would appreciate any information that would enable us to do so.

Part 1 The cultural variable in international marketing

Introduction to Part 1

In an increasingly global world where barriers to trade and international exchange constantly diminish, cultural differences remain the single most enduring factor to influence marketing strategies. Part 1 of this book introduces key concepts in cultural studies that influence our understanding of local markets and the design of international marketing strategies.

Chapter 1 presents the basic elements of culture and introduces ways in which culture impacts international marketing. It provides a discussion of seminal definitions and major aspects of culture, including language and social institutions. It introduces the sources of culture and discusses the limitations in viewing culture as nationality. This chapter also highlights how culture affects the development of skills, and discusses stereotypes, ethnocentrism and our self-reference criteria. The objective of Chapter 1 is to enable readers to understand how their own cultural conditioning colours their interpretation of others. The end-of-chapter teaching materials are designed to reinforce this.

Chapter 2 introduces the cultural dynamics of time and space. These basic cultural assumptions impact many aspects of material culture, such as the sense of ownership, preference for durability, and so on. The chapter begins with a model of action, based on cultural assumptions, which influences individual decision making. It then examines cross-cultural variability in perceptions of time and space. It also looks at the way we 'borrow' or integrate foreign items and customs into our societies. The last section examines intercultural hostility towards unknown people, including prejudices and negative stereotypes.

Chapter 3 explains how cultural assumptions influence human interactions. It examines how people define who they are and who others are, which is basic to any culture. A series of issues are then examined including how people differ in their attitudes towards action, how they relate thinking to action, how they deal with desires and feelings, and how they cope with rules. This chapter ends with an examination of how cultural assumptions shape actual behaviour.

Chapter 4 focuses on communication, which is never language-free. It discusses how language, both verbal and non-verbal, shapes our world views, inasmuch as the words we use and the way we assemble them in speech correspond to particular assumptions and experiences about the world in which we live. This can lead to ethnocentrism, which is a spontaneous tendency to refer to our own beliefs and values when interpreting situations and trying to make sense out of experience. Stereotyping is another way to reduce unfamiliarity by oversimplifying foreign traits. Therefore, it comes as no surprise that misunderstandings in intercultural communication are quite frequent. The last section in this Chapter explains how to avoid cultural misunderstandings and improve communication effectiveness in international business, especially when using interpreters.

1

The cultural process

Culture has taken a more, rather than less, prominent place in marketing in the twenty-first century. Market growth in affluent, well-developed countries has slowed, and attention has turned toward emerging markets, where the potential is enormous. In many emerging economies, attention is moving from the most affluent – and arguably, the most global – members of society to the growing middle class. However, we know relatively little about how to compete effectively in these markets.

In fact, our understanding of other cultures is often very limited, forcing us to rely on rather shallow or stereotyped ideas. Accordingly, international marketers often resort to using country or nation-states as primary segmentation bases, because borders are easily definable. However, few nations are homogeneous, and many have distinct ethnic, linguistic and religious groups that need to be considered. Culture is complex.

Understanding what is influenced by culture is also more complicated than may initially be expected. While international marketing necessarily gives a prominent place to culture, not everything is culturally driven. Individual behaviour is influenced, but not determined, by culture, as it is only one of the many layers that influence behaviour. However, the influence of culture is difficult to isolate, as it may be hard to recognize from within and to understand from without.

In this chapter we focus on the cultural process and the elements of culture that are likely to impact international business operations. To do this, we explore the following:

1. cultural definitions;
2. the elements of culture, including language, institutions, material productions and symbolic productions and how they fit together to form a coherent culture;
3. the relationship between culture and nationality;
4. the relationship between culture, competence and stereotypes; and
5. self-shock, ethnocentrism and overcoming self-reference criteria.

1.1

Defining culture

In French, the word *culture* was defined by Emile Littré in his nineteenth-century dictionary as 'cultivation', meaning to grow, in terms of farming activity. The abstract sense of the word probably originated in Germany where the word *kultur* was used as early as the eighteenth century to refer to civilization. In the Anglo-Saxon world the abstract notion of culture, as cultivation of the mind, came into widespread use at the beginning of the twentieth century. Today, culture is still often defined in terms of the cultivation of the mind. For instance, the *Oxford English Dictionary*'s first definition of culture[1] is 'the arts and other manifestations of human intellectual achievement'. The second definition is more relevant to this book, as the shared 'ideas, customs, and social behavior of a particular people or society'. However, these are both rather narrow definitions of culture.

Website link 1.1

Search for alternative definitions of culture, such as the one provided by the Centre for Advanced Research on Language Acquisition (CARLA): http://www.carla.umn.edu/culture/definitions.html.

Back in 1945, Ralph Linton (p. 21)[2] suggested a somewhat broader definition of culture:

A culture is the configuration of learned behaviour and results of behaviour whose component elements are shared and transmitted by the members of a particular society.

His emphasis on behaviour is compatible with Clifford Geertz's[3] view of culture as the control mechanisms of society (i.e., the plans, recipes, rules and instructions for behaviour), without which people would have difficulty living together. This emphasizes the usefulness of culture to society and to the individual, in that everyday tasks are simplified by the unwritten rules we understand through participation in our society. These unwritten cultural 'rules' lead us to feel that our own cultural norms are *naturally right* and that other different cultural norms are unnatural or strange. For instance, we all know the generally acceptable *right* time to eat dinner or to go to sleep based on our cultural norms, which makes these small everyday decisions relatively easy. However, what is considered to be the *right* time for these activities differs dramatically by culture and subcultures. The inclusion of subcultures highlights the fact that multiple normative solutions to social problems are available in all cultures, but as Kluckhohn and Strodtbeck[4] argue in the next section, the solutions are differentially preferred.

Particular solutions to universal problems

Kluckhohn and Strodtbeck argue that humans share biological traits and characteristics that lead to a preference for certain solutions to universal problems in society, which are reflected in our cultural values. They argue this on the basis of three assumptions (p. 10):

1. '. . . there is a limited number of common human problems for which all peoples at all times must find some solution.'

2. 'While there is a variability in solutions of all the problems, it is neither limitless nor random but is definitely variable within a range of possible solutions.'
3. '. . . all alternatives of all solutions are present in all societies at all times, but are differentially preferred. Every society has, in addition to its dominant profile of value orientations, numerous variant or substitute profiles.'[4]

Similarly, Malinowski described *preferred solutions* to the biological state of hunger, as being dependent on the rules and principles of shared culture (p. 75):

Cultural determination is a familiar fact as regards hunger or appetite, in short the readiness to eat. Limitations of what is regarded as palatable, admissible, ethical; the magical religious, hygienic and social taboos on quality, raw materials, and preparation of food; the habitual routine establishing the time and the type of appetite – all these could be exemplified from our civilization, from the rules and principles of Judaism, or Islam, Brahmanism or Shintoism, as well as from every primitive culture.[5]

Website link 1.2

Search for more information about Malinowski, who championed the modern ethnographic method of long-term fieldwork in the Trobriand Islands from 1915 to 1918, such as on the following website: http://www.csiss.org/classics/content/98.

How culture links the individual to society

While it is important to understand the role that culture plays in the smooth functioning of society and individuals within society, it is also important to understand that individuals have a role in the evolution of their culture. According to Linton (p. 15):

Actually, the role of the individual with respect to society is a double one. Under ordinary circumstances, the more perfect his conditioning and consequent integration into the social structure, the more effective his contribution to the smooth functioning of the whole and the surer his rewards. However, societies have to exist and function in an ever-changing world. The unparalleled ability of our species to adjust to changing conditions and to develop ever more effective responses to familiar ones rests upon the residue of individuality which survives in every one of us after society and culture have done their utmost. As a simple unit in the social organism, the individual perpetuates the status quo.[2]

Linton also emphasizes the limits to the cultural programming that society can impose on an individual (p. 14):

No matter how carefully the individual has been trained or how successful his conditioning has been, he remains a distinct organism with his own needs and with capacities for independent thought, feeling and action. Moreover he retains a considerable degree of individuality.[2]

Clearly, individuals are not simply *programmed* by their culture, as they are free to adopt or adapt the commonly accepted norms of their culture to suit their needs.

We will see this in the many social representations referred to throughout this book, as they are at the intersection of the psychological/individual and social/collective levels. Social representations are forms of operational knowledge, which help us to categorize and interpret circumstances, phenomena, individuals and theories and enable us to make daily decisions. They are constantly updated through our behaviour and social activities, or as a result of the media, public opinion polls, news summaries, court decisions and legal penalties. While social representations are held by individuals, they vary across societies. If we consider Goodenough's definition of culture, as a set of beliefs or standards, shared by a group of people, which help the individual decide what is, what can be, how to feel, what to do and how to go about doing it (i.e., our operational or operating culture),[6] we can see that there is no reason for culture to be equated with the whole of one particular country or even society. Goodenough's view of operational culture (i.e., shared by those who must cooperate on a task within a given group) is consistent with differing social representations. While social representations are less profound than the basic cultural orientations (e.g., individualism, collectivism and others discussed in Chapters 3 and 4), as they alter within shorter time spans (10 to 20 years versus centuries), they are still important as they are more suited to the urgent need for collective and individual adaptation to reality than cultural orientations.

It is also important to note that many people operate in more than one culture or subculture, including international business professionals, immigrants, bilinguals, and even teenagers who may switch between their parent and peer cultures. While Goodenough assumes that an individual can choose the culture in which to interact at any given moment or in any given situation, there is a growing body of research that illustrates the pervasiveness of environmental cues that seem to elicit a subconscious switch in operational culture. For instance, researchers have found culturally compatible differences in the way bilinguals respond to the same survey, written in different languages (e.g., Mandarin versus English). Similar differences in response have been found in bicultural individuals (e.g., those who have lived in different countries), when different cues are presented that prime or make one culture more salient, including:

- culturally common symbols (e.g., American flag versus Chinese dragon);
- famous people (e.g., Marilyn Monroe versus a Chinese opera singer);
- landmarks (e.g., the Capitol Building versus the Great Wall); and even
- popular cartoons (e.g., *Superman* versus *Stone Monkey*).[7]

This illustrates the importance of the operational culture in the interpretation of what is *right* for a given situation.

1.2

Elements of culture

A culture must be relatively coherent, so that the sum of its elements reinforces the knowledge, beliefs and values that are useful to its continuation. The four major elements of culture include:

1. language;
2. institutions;
3. material productions; and
4. symbolic productions.

Each of these is discussed below; however, there are many overlaps in influence, as a cultural item may belong to one or more of these four elements of culture simultaneously. For instance, music is a language, an institution, an artistic production and also a symbolic element.

Language as an element of culture

Language is an important element of culture, as it is the primary mechanism for sharing and transmitting information between members of a particular society. However, it is also claimed that the language we learn in our native community shapes and structures our world view and our social behaviour, as it influences how we select issues, solve problems and act.[8] As a linguist and anthropologist, Benjamin Lee Whorf – a chemical engineer working for a fire insurance company – spent his spare time tracing the origins and grammar of American Indian languages.[8] He is the author of a seminal, and quite controversial, hypothesis – often referred to as the Whorfian hypothesis or Whorf–Sapir hypothesis – which contends that the structure of language has a significant influence on perception and categorization. Although the Whorfian hypothesis has been criticized by many linguists, it remains a fundamental metaphor, though not a fully validated scientific theory. As such, some aspects of this theory have been incorporated, either explicitly or implicitly, in various parts of this book, especially in Chapter 2, which considers the Whorf–Sapir hypothesis in more detail, as well as broader issues of communication, including context and non-verbal cues. Further consideration is also given to this hypothesis in other chapters, where language and linguistic issues are prominent, such as cross-cultural market research (Chapter 7), branding (Chapter 12), and intercultural marketing communication (Chapters 13 and 14).

Website link 1.3

Search for information about languages around the world, such Ethnologue and the Santa Fe Institutes' Evolution of Human Language site: http://www.ethnologue.org.

Institutions as an element of culture

Institutional elements are the 'spine' of the cultural process that links the individual to the group. Institutions include the family, as well as political institutions, or any kind of social organization that encourages an individual to comply with rules in exchange for various rewards (e.g., being fed, loved, paid, and so on). These rules are not static and individuals may also act as a proactive agent of change within an institution, in a similar way to Linton's arguments in the previous section.

Institutions organize people into groups. While there are many different ways in which an institution can organize people, there are likely to be certain culturally preferred solutions to this problem. For instance, some cultures prefer to organize people into groups that are stable, such as family lineage and gender, whereas others prefer to organize them into more transient groupings, such as their occupation or those with common interests.

BOX 1.1

Language groups

While there are about 6000 languages,[9] many of them are only spoken by a relatively small number of people. The three largest language groups (including dialects), are as follows:

- Chinese languages spoken in 31 countries by 1219 million people;
- Spanish languages spoken in 44 countries by 329 million people; and

- English languages spoken in 112 countries by 328 million people.[10]

However, these are not the only languages that should be considered in business, as 389 (6 per cent of the world's languages) are spoken by more than one million people, or almost 94 per cent, of the population.

Malinowski[5] compiled a list of seven universal principles around which institutions are formed across cultures:

1. The principle of *reproduction* integrates people around blood relationships and marriage as an established contractual framework.
2. The principle of *territoriality* integrates people around common interests dictated by neighbourhood and vicinity.
3. The principle of *physiology* integrates people around their sex, age, and physical traits or defects. This includes the sexual division of labour, sex roles, the relationship patterns between age groups, and the way minority members of the community are treated.
4. The principle of *spontaneous tendency to join together* integrates people around common goals. This includes various kinds of associations, such as primitive secret societies, clubs, artistic societies, etc.
5. The principle of *occupational and professional activities* integrates people around labour divisions and expertise. In modern societies, this includes industry organizations, trade unions, courts, the police, the army, educational institutions and religious bodies.
6. The principle of *hierarchy* integrates people around rank and status, including the nobility, the middle class and slaves, or more generally any kind of social class system or caste system.
7. The principle of *totality* integrates diverse elements into a reasonably coherent whole. The political process (e.g., feudal, democratic, theocratic, dictatorial, etc.) expresses the need for totality.

It is easy to see that individuals belong to more than one level of institution, as each in isolation provides only a limited picture of how a culture operates. To gain a more complete picture, some researchers examine multi-level relationships between institutions and values at the individual level. One such database is the World Values Survey, which tracks basic values and beliefs of various publics within and across countries.

Website link 1.4

Visit the World Values Survey website to learn more about values and cultural changes in societies all over the world: http://www.worldvaluessurvey.org.

Material productions as an element of culture

The products or outputs of our society also transmit, reproduce, update and improve the knowledge and skills in society.

Primary productions that are elements of culture are varied. They include:

- artistic productions, such as music and art;
- intellectual productions, such as articles and books;
- physical productions, such as factories, tools and machinery, as well as the products we consume (e.g., food, clothing, ornaments); and
- service productions, such as banks, communication, media and education.

All of these productions serve as output and also inputs into our culture.

However, the quantity and quality of productions should not be confused with *civilization*, as indicated by the German word *kultur*. Material consumption and wealth do not necessarily equate with cultural sophistication, and cultural attitudes toward material goods vary enormously. For example, Kumar[11] discusses the differing world views in India and China. The Indian world view, based on Brahmanism, has the goal of inner spirituality. It emphasizes spirituality over achievement and does not place a high value on wealth, acquisition or production. Conversely, the Chinese world view is based on Confucian Pragmatism with the goal being harmonious social order. It emphasizes meritocracy and hard work, focusing on action in the material, rather than the spiritual world. Thus, what constitutes success is coloured by our culture.

Symbolic productions as an element of culture

Symbolic and sacred elements of culture determine the relationship between the physical and the metaphysical world. In some cultures, the metaphysical world is present in everyday life, whereas it is denied in other cultures. Cultures, through religious and moral beliefs, often define whether there is life after death and, if so, what kind. The scientific movement, especially at the end of the nineteenth century, seemed close to pushing back the boundaries of the metaphysical world. Nowadays most scientists recognize that the

BOX 1.2

Religion and diets

The world's population is approximately distributed among the following religious categories, many of which follow complex dietary practices, some of which are listed as follows:

- 33 per cent are Christian. The Christian faith has relatively few food restrictions, although some refrain from eating meat – fish is usually okay – on Fridays.
- 22 per cent are Muslim. The Muslim faith specifies *Halal* dietary rules. These rules prohibit the consumption of pork, carnivorous animals, sea animals without fins or scales, and any meat that is not prepared in the *Halal* way. Alcohol is not permitted, including products that use alcohol (e.g., vanilla extracts which can be less than 50 per cent alcohol). No food from dawn to sunset during the holy month of Ramadan; however, pregnant women, women who are menstruating, children, and the sick are exempt.

- 14 per cent are Hindu. The Hindu faith prohibits beef, as the cow is considered sacred; Many Hindus are also vegetarian.
- 7 per cent are Buddhist. Strict Buddhists are vegetarians.
- Less than 1 per cent are Sikh, Jewish, or Baha'i. The Sikh faith has relatively few food restrictions, although many are vegetarians. The Jewish faith has a complex set of food practices, which include Kosher preparation. Many foods are prohibited or restricted, including pork, animals which have split hooves and chew the cud (e.g., sheep and cows), and shellfish. Also, meat and dairy should not be eaten together. The Baha'i faith has no dietary restrictions, although the consumption of alcohol and drugs is prohibited.
- 11 per cent are other religions.
- 9 per cent are non-religious.
- 2 per cent are Atheists.

(Source: CIA, *The World Factbook*[12] and the *Butlers Guild*.[13])

metaphysical question will never be fully resolved by knowledge. What is of interest to us is not the answers to these questions, but how moral and religious assumptions in various cultures impact on individual and group behaviour.

Culture and religion often seem entangled, with noticeable differences between cultures that hold different religious beliefs. Box 1.2 illustrates the sometimes complicated food restrictions that vary greatly between people who follow different faiths. Where societies are relatively homogeneous, these differences can quite dramatically influence a culture, including many aspects of business and marketing.

Website link 1.5

Search for information on religions of the world, such as the Tony Blair Faith Foundation site, which includes a selection of videos that explore the topic of religious identities: http://www.fgi-tbff.org/ or http://www.religionfacts.com/.

Traditional societies have always been more consciously involved in symbolic thought and behaviour than modern societies. Since less is *explained*, more must be *related*. For example: Why does the sun shine every day? Should its disappearance be considered ominous? What should be done to satisfy it, so that it goes on spreading its generous rays on the fields and rivers? The bloody ritual sacrifices in the pre-Columbian civilizations were heavily charged with symbolic content, where human sacrifices were dedicated to the sun. However, we should not overlook symbolic thought in Western societies, where Friday the 13th, black cats, and walking under a ladder can all be considered to bring bad luck. Seemingly harmless beliefs such as these often have a relatively large impact on business. For example, the Stress Management Center and Phobia Institute estimated that over US$700 million is lost in businesses each Friday 13th, as many people prefer to stay home on this symbolic day.[14] It is a common mistake to believe that the symbolic dimension has largely disappeared in modern life.

Symbols are not only related to religious and metaphysical matters; they also extend into everyday life. Symbols, such as road signs, wedding rings, McDonald's golden arches, or skull and crossbones, are prolific and useful, as they convey a significant amount of information instantly. In each case these symbols are objects that convey something more than the material object itself. Consequently, the interpretation of a symbol is strongly culture bound.

Throughout the book we illustrate the strength of the symbolic dimension, especially in marketing communication, where the symbolisms of colour, shape, labels, brand name, and so on are commonly used to convey additional information about products and services. We also discuss the meaning of numbers in several sections, including consumer behaviour, marketing research and pricing, as there is a growing body of evidence that marketers need to be very aware of the use of auspicious (e.g., 8 in China) and suspicious (e.g., 4 in China and 9 in Japan) numbers, especially in Asia.

Culture as a collective fingerprint and cultural superiority

Culture is a collective fingerprint of our identity. It is made up of a *coherent* set of elements that complement rather than contradict each other. Such individual elements of culture do not exist in isolation and cannot easily be taken out of their context. Further, there are no objectively *good* or *bad* elements of a particular cultural group; it all depends on your subjective view.

Cultures may be evaluated and ranked, but only on the basis of evidence related to a set of *culturally determined criteria* for very specific activities. Some people may make better warriors, others have finer aesthetic judgement, yet others are more musically gifted. However, these elements belong to a *coherent* culture. Comparisons might delude us into thinking we could select the best from each culture and arrive at 'ideal' combinations. However, it is not quite this easy. For instance, a joke about Europeans goes something like this: 'Heaven is where the cooks are French, the mechanics are German, the policemen are English, the lovers are Italian, and it is all organized by the Swiss. Hell is where the policemen are German, the mechanics are French, the cooks are British, the

lovers are Swiss, and it is all organized by the Italians.' While this joke is definitely stereotypical, it does capture some information about long-established cultural capabilities. As such, it serves to remind us how difficult it would be to take what we consider to be the best traits from each culture, while rejecting what we consider to be the worst. Any attempt to combine the best of several cultures would eventually turn out to be a disaster, because *coherence* is needed at the highest level (corresponding to *identity* at the individual level).

1.3

Culture and nationality

Nationality is a relatively easy way to divide individuals into larger groups. However, the relationship between nationality and culture is unclear. While a commonly shared culture is important in building modern nation-states, it is more fundamental at the community level. As soon as nation-states began to emerge, they struggled against local particularisms, such as dialects and customs. Conflicts in large countries are often based on conflicts between cultural subgroups, including the War of Secession in the United States, the rivalry between the English and the Scots in the United Kingdom, the progressive elimination of local powers in the highly centralized French state, and today's struggles between different religious groups in the Middle East and other Asian countries. Each of these conflicts relates to distinctive differences in cultural elements, including language, values, religion, and concepts of freedom.

Businesses must be especially wary of equating culture directly with nation-state, as effective communication is crucial to the marketing process. There is a long list of very good reasons to avoid this, including the following:

1. A country's culture can only be defined by reference to other countries' cultures. India is a country culture in comparison with Italy or Germany, but the Indian subcontinent is made up of highly diversified ethnic and religious groups including Muslims, Hindus and Sikhs, and with over 20 principal languages.
2. Many nation-states are explicitly multicultural. For instance, Switzerland has four official languages,

including German, French, Italian and Rumantsch, which are spoken to differing extents in different regions of the country. The Swiss political system, established more than seven centuries ago, helps people to successfully manage the complex trade-off between compliance with local cultural peculiarities and a common attitude towards anything that is not Swiss.

3. Political decisions, especially during the last century, have imposed the formation of new nation-states, particularly through the processes of colonization and decolonization. The borders of these new states, sometimes straight lines on a map, were often set with little regard for cultural realities. Many significant national cultures, such as that of the Kurds (split between the Iraqis, the Syrians, the Turks and the Iranians) have never been accorded the right to a territory or a state.

Sources of culture

The national element is seldom the main source of culture when regarded from an *operational culture* perspective. Figure 1.1 depicts the basic sources of cultural background at the level of the individual. These sources combine to form cultural frames at the individual level, where a medical researcher, or computer hardware specialist, whatever their nationality, share a common specialized education, common interests, and largely the same professional culture. This professional culture is developed through common training, working for similar companies, reading the same publications worldwide and contributing to research where international cross-cultural comparability of purely scientific methods and results is fundamental.

Figure 1.1 Sources of culture

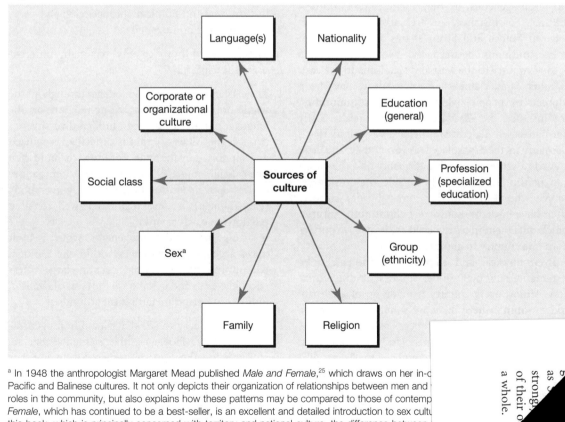

[a] In 1948 the anthropologist Margaret Mead published *Male and Female*,[25] which draws on her in-d Pacific and Balinese cultures. It not only depicts their organization of relationships between men and roles in the community, but also explains how these patterns may be compared to those of contemp *Female*, which has continued to be a best-seller, is an excellent and detailed introduction to sex cultu this book, which is principally concerned with territory and national culture, the difference between i in fact the most basic cultural distinction.

Similarly, social class may be a distinctive source of culture, to a greater or lesser degree, depending on the country. In France and England, where there are traditions of accepted birth inequalities and a strong historical orientation, social class is a very distinctive source of culture and the way one speaks immediately reveals one's social class. However, in the United States, Australia, Japan and the Scandinavian countries, this is not as marked. Social class, like gender, is not a territory-based source of culture. In this case, social classes can be transcended.

The sense of belonging to an important ethnic group may override the feeling of belonging to a particular nation-state. The Tamil population in Sri Lanka, which makes up about 20 per cent of the total Sri Lankan population, is mostly centred around Jaffna in the north of the island. It is strongly linked with the large Tamil community in southern India (numbering 55 million), which supports them in their claim for autonomy within their nation-state.

Nations that border other countries are rarely fully homogeneous, as they include 'cross-border' cultures. For instance, the area around the border between France and Spain shares a culture which offers continuity between the two countries: the Basque country to the west and Catalonia to the east. In other cases, elements of each culture have been adopted by people living in border communities. For instance, the Alsatians in France speak mostly German-based dialects and behave very similarly to Germans in the workplace; however, they also lean towards a sense of French nationality and the adoption of the French lifestyle outside the workplace. People who belong to these cross-border cultures often have in-depth knowledge about both cultures, which puts them in a privileged position as exporters from one country to another.

Even physical and climatic conditions can be systematic, although subtle, sources of differentiation. Almost every country is made up of a 'North' and a 'South', where there are somewhat noticeable cultural and lifestyle differences, as least to those within the country. This appears to be the case, even in relatively homogeneous countries that share linguistic, ethnic, religious and institutional views, such as Sweden, However, this difference may not be as ly perceived by foreigners, who are more aware wn differences from Swedes and Sweden as

Cultural homogeneity and relevant segmentation

Firms often find it difficult to decide how to segment international markets, with some targeting transnational ethnic segments, others targeting national segments, and others targeting cross-border regional segments. While Chapter 8 examines the issues around global versus regional marketing strategies, and considers segmentation bases in more detail, a review of the cultural literature can help to identify important information about potential groupings.

While homogeneity clearly favours the emergence of a coherent culture in a nation-state, few countries are truly homogeneous, especially when different types of homogeneity are considered, such as:

1. linguistic homogeneity;
2. religious homogeneity;
3. ethnic homogeneity;
4. climatic homogeneity;
5. geographical homogeneity;
6. institutional and political homogeneity; and
7. social/income homogeneity.

In fact, the word 'homogeneity' has many different meanings, including:

1. The existence of a uniform modality throughout the whole population (e.g., only one religion, or one language) or at the very least limited diversity.
2. An accepted diversity that is officially recognized and supported by the State. For instance, more than one official language in common use, being more or less spoken and/or understood by everybody (e.g., Canada), or several different well-accepted religions (e.g., Germany).
3. A strong 'perceived homogeneity', which is built upon acceptable differences within the national community, such as people accepting large differences in wealth and income, on the basis of fatalism, indifference or on metaphysical grounds.

From this, it is easy to see that global homogenization is unlikely. However, the elements that tie subcultures together can strengthen nationality. For instance, Sweden is culturally more homogeneous than the United States, and as such might be expected to hold a stronger national identity, but in reality it is the United States that has a stronger national identity than Sweden.[15]

The concept of national culture

National culture relies on the concept of within-country homogeneity and between-country differences. As such, it is primarily a starting point for uncovering cultural differences between countries. Several different national culture frameworks report a wide range of countries scores or positions, on a relatively small number of conceptually complex constructs, including those by Geert Hofstede,[16] the World Values Survey,[17] Shalom Schwartz,[18] the GLOBE[19] and Fons Trompenaars.[20] To date, Hofstede's original framework has been used most extensively to investigate a wide range of business issues, including many aspects of marketing. This framework initially derived four dimensions of national culture (individualism/collectivism, power distance, masculinity/femininity and uncertainty avoidance) from a large study of IBM employees, and later, Hofstede and colleagues[21] added a fifth (long-term/short-term orientation) based on the work on Michael Bond and colleagues[22] and then a sixth (indulgence/restraint) based on the work of Michael Minkov[23] and the World Values Survey. These and other dimensions of national culture are described in more detail in the following chapters and referred to throughout the book, as a relatively large body of cross-cultural work relates these dimensions to phenomenon of interest to marketers. However, we need to keep in mind that national culture scores only offer a broad brushstroke of information. Further, they can be difficult to interpret, as a moderate score at the national level could represent a pervasive moderate level of importance, or a great deal of variability in the population.

In reality, culture has many levels or layers, which more often correspond to linguistic, ethnic, religious or even organizational entities than to nation-states. National culture is too general to avoid the traps of cliché and stereotype; however, it is useful, in that it is difficult for anyone to understand the nuances of multiple cultures. Thus, despite its limitations, the concept of national culture can still be an interesting Pandora's box.

Website link 1.6

Search for information on national cultural dimensions, such as those from Geert Hofstede. Try comparing your home country to a country you would like to visit: **http://geert-hofstede.com/countries.html**.

One of the important questions around culture is how it influences individuals. Some believe that culture has a distinct imprint on individuals, in that personality traits exist for which the average individual in one culture scores significantly higher (or lower) than those belonging to another culture. This corresponds to the idea of national character or, more precisely, the concept of a modal personality. The modal personality approach largely grew out of enquiries as to why certain people are more violent, more aggressive, more domineering, and collectively more prone than others to declare war on foreign nations or to organize and implement genocide. These questions stemmed from the Second World War, especially the Nuremberg trials. Numerous empirical studies have been undertaken, particularly during the 1950s and 1960s, to examine the process of forming a national character (e.g., examining child-rearing practices, education systems, and the socialisation process of children). The results neither prove nor disprove the existence of national character.

Others favour the idea that personality traits are largely free from the influence of culture. According to Linton (pp. 14–15),[2] the individual's 'integration into society and culture goes no deeper than his learned responses, and although in the adult the greater part of what we call the personality, there is still a good deal of the individual left over'. The question of whether personality is modal (culture-bound) or culture-free is not just academic. In Linton's view, individuals may have personalities quite separate from their cultural background. From a 'national character' perspective, one would expect to meet people with an average personality that reflects their culture. Obviously, this is not the case.

National character and educational practices

In order to study how national character is formed, education systems and child-rearing practices may be observed, especially in the early years (up to the age of five or six). Key elements of personality develop during this time, due to feeding and nourishing, weaning, personal hygiene and toilet training, the degree and modes of socialization into various parts of the community (with other children, with adults, with the opposite sex), the demands and prohibitions imposed on small children, and finally the reward/ sanction systems, all of which orientate behaviour.[4]

Formal education has a role in cultural transmission, as well as the teaching of academic knowledge and skills. This can take various forms, including hidden or implicit socialization aspects. For instance, in addition to teaching language skills, the stories in commonly used texts often convey cultural messages, such as those found by Imada, to be consistent with the individualist or collectivist tendencies in the US and Japan (pp. 11–12):[24]

American stories provide a role model who is a strong, distinctive individual, capable of achieving what he or she really wants, whereas Japanese stories teach children to be kind, considerate, an altruistic member of the group, and to recognize the importance of friendship . . . American stories contained more features that reflect individualistic cognitive styles, such as taking a first-person perspective, focusing on success, making dispositional and self-serving attributions, and emphasizing happiness, than did Japanese stories. In contrast, Japanese stories contained more features that reflect collectivistic cognitive styles, such as taking a third-person perspective, focusing on failure, making situational and self-critical attribution, and balancing happiness and sadness, than did American stories.

School systems also reinforce appropriate behaviour. For instance, Margaret Mead's[25] view is that the United States 'adolescent peer culture' is shaped by education systems that favour diffuse, depersonalized authority where children need to have their own strong inner moral control. As adults, the cheerful, easy-going, informal Americans are often jokingly referred to by in many other countries as resembling big children. This is in stark contrast with Amy Chua's description of the Chinese Tiger Mother, an extract of which is described in Box 1.3.

BOX 1.3

Extract from the *Battle Hymn of the Tiger Mother*

'A lot of people wonder how Chinese parents raise such stereotypically successful kids. They wonder what these parents do to produce so many math whizzes and music prodigies, what it's like inside the family, and whether they could do it too. Well, I can tell them, because I've done it. Here are some things my daughters, Sophia and Louisa, were never allowed to do:

- attend a sleepover;
- have a playdate;
- be in a school play;
- complain about not being in a school play;
- watch TV or play computer games;
- choose their own extracurricular activities;
- get any grade less than an A;
- not be the No. 1 student in every subject except gym and drama;
- play any instrument other than the piano or violin;
- not play the piano or violin.

I'm using the term 'Chinese mother' loosely. I know some Korean, Indian, Jamaican, Irish and Ghanaian parents who qualify too. Conversely, I know some mothers of Chinese heritage, almost always born in the West, who are not Chinese mothers, by choice or otherwise. I'm also using the term 'Western parents' loosely. Western parents come in all varieties.

All the same, even when Western parents think they're being strict, they usually don't come close to being Chinese mothers. For example, my Western friends who consider themselves strict make their children practice their instruments 30 minutes every day. An hour at most. For a Chinese mother, the first hour is the easy part. It's hours two and three that get tough.'. . .

Western parents try to respect their children's individuality, encouraging them to pursue their true passions, supporting their choices, and providing positive reinforcement and a nurturing environment. By contrast, the Chinese believe that the best way to protect their children is by preparing them for the future, letting them see what they're capable of, and arming them with skills, work habits and inner confidence that no one can ever take away.'

(Source: Amy Chua, pp. 3–4.[26] Amy Chua is a Professor of Law at Yale Law School. Visit Amy Chua's website: http://amychua.com/.)

1.4

Culture, competence and stereotypes

Early research on the intellectual abilities of non-European people classified the thought patterns of primitives as 'pre-logical'. Little by little this somewhat extreme attitude, that 'primitives' could never understand things as we do ('we' being the modern, Westernized people of European origin), has given way to a more reasonable position. We now know that scores on intelligence quotient (IQ) tests are relative to the type of questions asked and the situations evoked in the verbal part of the test (reading, memorization and understanding of texts). Even quantitative aspects of IQ tests (i.e., mathematics, geometry, statistics, logic), require a familiarity with handling abstract and mathematical signs. There is no test that is universally relevant, in that it encompasses all the possible facets of human intelligence, or offers total objectivity in the experimental and empirical methods used to evaluate them. Definitions of intelligence are culturally contingent, and as such, IQ scores differ across cultures in predictable ways. While intelligence tests can have practical benefits, IQ scores should be interpreted cautiously when tests devised by one culture are administered to people from other cultures.

Website link 1.7

Why not try a free web-based IQ test?:
http://www.ifreeiqtest.com/.

Skills and our environment

The environment in which we live influences our perceptions, beliefs, attitudes and behaviour. For instance, there are clear differences in people's perception of visual illusions that are attributed to their physical environment. Figure 1.2 depicts two equal lines; however, line 'a' had to be almost 1/5 longer than line 'b' before American students perceived them as equal, whereas people from the Kalahari accurately perceived their equality.[27] This difference is attributed to exposure to recurrent features of our physical environment, with the emphasis on straight

Figure 1.2 Müller-Lyer illusion

(Source: Segall et al.[27])

lines and sharp angles in a constructed environment and more rounded and curvilinear shapes in a more natural setting.[15]

Our physical environment also influences our culture. Some cultures are considered to be more work orientated and more efficient when it comes to producing material goods, which has often explained by environmental factors, such as climate. Box 1.4 contains the beginning of Montesquieu's theory of climates.[28] While the physiological explanations are scarcely credible now, it is nevertheless a starting point for the north/south climatic stereotype. The question is: do some countries/climates tend to harden (or soften) people, with the result that they become more (or less) inclined towards activities of war, commerce or industry, and more (or less) efficient in pursuing these activities? For instance, a hot climate may directly influence culture, by physically discouraging effort and action, or indirectly influence culture through adaptation to climatic conditions, such as the development of air conditioners and heaters. If climate has both a direct and an indirect influence, via progressive genetic adaptation and/or cultural traits acquired through education and socialization, then air conditioning may be necessary but not enough to counter climatic differences. For instance, climate has been found to have an indirect effect on a country's competitiveness, as temperate countries are more likely to overpay their workers, relative to their standing on the worldwide ladder of wealth.[29]

Stereotypes

While our cultural or normative knowledge helps us to make sense of the world, stereotypes serve as simplified intellectual representations of other people; however, they also tend to promote our differences, which can make them dangerous. Michel Droit, in his book *Chez les Mangeurs D'Hommes* (*The Man Eaters*), exposes the stereotype of the sorcerer in primitive societies. He describes the people of Papua New Guinea through the eyes of civilized observers

BOX 1.4

Of the difference of men in different climates

A cold air[a] constringes the extremities of the external fibres of the body; this increases their elasticity, and favors the return of the blood from the extreme parts to the heart. It contracts[b] those very fibres; consequently, it increases also their force and elasticity. People are therefore more vigorous in cold climates. Here the action of the heart and the reaction of the extremities of the fibres are better performed, the temperature of the humors is greater, the blood moves freer towards the heart, and reciprocally, the heart has more power. This superiority of strength must produce various effects; for instance, a greater boldness, that is, more courage; a greater sense of superiority, that is, more frankness, less suspicion, policy, and cunning. In short, this must be productive of very different tempers. Put a man into a close warm place, and, for the reasons above given, he will feel a great faintness. If, under this circumstance, you propose a bold enterprise to him, I believe you will find him very little disposed towards it: his present weakness will throw him into a despondency; he will be afraid of every thing, being in a state of total incapacity. The inhabitants of warm countries are, like old men, timorous; the people in cold countries are, like young men, brave. If we reflect on the late[c] wars, (which are more recent in our memory, and in which we can better distinguish some particular effects, that escape us at a greater distance of time), we shall find that the northern people, transplanted into southern regions,[d] did not perform such exploits as their countrymen who, fighting in their own climate, possessed their full vigor and courage.

[a] This appears even in the countenance: in cold weather people look thinner.
[b] We know it shortens iron.
[c] Those for the succession to the Spanish monarchy.
[d] For instance in Spain.

(Source: Montesquieu, pp. 224–5.[27])

who are necessarily their ideological enemies (Droit, p. 124, J.-C. Usunier translation):

Armed with tamed snakes which they use to execute their victims, with poisons, enchanted prayers and medicinal herbs known only to them, sorcerers, through well-organized propaganda and strong co-operative solidarity, let entire populations live in fear and sometimes in terror of their 'nepou', that is their evil powers.[30]

This does not necessarily mean that Michel Droit's description of the sorcerer is false. He reveals part of reality, but also ignores how the sorcerer is an integral part of Papuan communities.

Similarly, when the French perceive Americans as being arrogant and tough in business, and the British as insincere, it is likely that this stereotypical oversimplification also has an emotional function as self-defence against a difference that provokes anxiety.[31] American arrogance is, in fact, related to a different hierarchy of values, where professional relations are centred on the task at hand or the object of discussion to the exclusion of personal relations with the other party.

Stereotypes are often used to capture the salient traits of a 'foreign' national character, as could be seen in the stereotypical joke in Section 1.2. However, they are seldom very accurate, as Soutar and colleagues[32] found when they asked experienced Australian and Japanese international businesspeople to estimate the most important values of their own culture, as well as those of other culture. For instance, Japanese business people reported that their relationships with others was the most important value listed, whereas Australian businesspeople felt this was much less important to the Japanese than other values, such as being well respected, having a sense of belonging and security.[32] Further, stereotypes differ quite dramatically across cultures, as can be seen in Box 1.5, which shows how French people are viewed (at least stereotypically) by people from other nations.

Finally, Yoshida (p. 1)[33] relates an amusing anecdote of a European professor who assigned students from different nationalities to submit a report on elephants. Stereotypical submissions included: 'A philosophical analysis of the existence of the elephant' from a German

BOX 1.5

Stereotypes of the French

How various nationalities perceive the French:

The Germans: Pretentious and offhand. Fashionable, womanizing, frivolous, fickle, well-mannered, resourceful.

The British: Nationalistic, chauvinistic, intransigent, centralist, dependent on the state, polite but not open-minded, humourless, short-tempered.

The Dutch: Cultured, fond of good living, fidgety, talkative, not very serious, feelings of superiority.

The Spanish: Pretentious, early sleepers, cold and distant, hypocritical, impolite, patronizing, hard working.

The Swedish: In-built superiority complex, scornful, boastful, talkative, immoral, dirty, neo-colonialists, disorganized, cultured gastronomy, suffocating hierarchy.

The Finns: Xenophobic, superficial, scornful, chauvinistic, courteous, romantic, enjoying life, patriotic, chaotic.

The Americans: Chauvinistic, well-mannered. Combination of good food and good conversation, Paris. Curious about foreign people, pretentious, talkative, pleasant, intelligent.

The Russians: Talkative, self-satisfied, lazy. Luxury, inequality, culture. Pleasant, intelligent, resourceful.

The North Africans: Fairly racist, a little stingy, reasonably honest. Good education and good food. Selfish.

The Asians: Exhibitionist, indiscreet. Reticent in making friends. Bureaucracy and red tape.

The Black Africans: Racist, honest, lacking respect for elders and betters. At odds with themselves and nature. Not spontaneously hospitable.

(Source: Gruère and Morel, p. 51.[34])

---

student, 'How to raise an elephant in your backyard for money and fun without risk of litigation' from an American student, 'A comparative analysis of elephant studies in foreign countries, particularly Europe and America: what the Elephant thinks of us Japanese' from a Japanese student, and a Chinese student simply submitted a recipe.

Website link 1.8

Search for blogs about stereotypes from different perspectives:
http://en.wordpress.com/tag/stereotype/.

1.5

Ethnocentrism and self-reference criteria

Living according to one's culture in daily life is almost an unconscious action. The cost of adopting the cultural norms in your own culture is minimal; however,

the costs, in terms of the amount of effort associated with the identification and adoption of the traits of another culture are much higher. This is clear in the difficulties encountered by immigrants, even those who have immigrated voluntarily.

Culture-shock and self-shock

Self-shock extends the concept of culture-shock, which is considered to be a reaction to difference, to a reaction to differences with and within the self.[35] When people from different cultures meet, such as expatriate managers meeting local executives or international sellers meeting local buyers, the interaction can create uncertainty. At first it may seem that the basic problem is simply reducing uncertainty by 'getting to know the other'. But as Alder (p. 18)[36] describes, there is in fact a 'progressive unfolding of the self' in an intercultural encounter, which can be attributed to 'a set of intensive and evocative situations in which the individual perceives and experiences other people in a distinctly new manner and, as a consequence, experiences new facets and dimensions of existence'.

Facing foreigners may disturb our personal identity or self-image through the 'mirror effect' – that is, self-image is constructed from our perceptions of others' voiced opinions and behavioural responses to us. Our ability to maintain an enduring self-concept relies on 'the resemblance and continuity of the image and the sense that others have of us' (p. 13).[37] In a mono-cultural setting, 'self-image' is built unconsciously based on reflections of known others. However, in an intercultural setting where the 'mirror' is foreign, maintaining our personal identity can be problematic as it: (1) is unconscious, (2) requires sound intercultural understanding, and (3) requires good communication skills.

The root of 'self-shock' lies in the relationship between the ego (that is, personal identity), personal behaviour, and the 'other' (as the 'other' actually is, and as the 'other' is perceived by the ego). Self-shock results from a deep imbalance between the need to confirm personal identity and the ability to do so. The intercultural self-shock situation increases the need to reinforce our personal identity, while at the same time resulting in a loss of ability to satisfy this need. This often results in a self-defence mechanism to avoid the painful double constraint of self-shock which leads to abrupt stereotypical judgements about foreigners. For instance, Gauthey (p. 64)[38] cites a general manager of a software company, a subsidiary of a French advertising and communications group, who says: 'I can't stand the English, and when I go to London, I never leave the airport.' This attitude is clearly defensive: in refusing to leave the airport, he remains on neutral international ground, refusing to run the risk of being confronted by the image that the English will have of him.

Ethnocentrism and self-reference criterion

The concept of ethnocentrism was first introduced by G.A. Sumner[39] more than 80 years ago, to distinguish between *ingroups* (those groups with which an individual identifies) and *outgroups* (those regarded as antithetical to the *ingroup*). Sumner defined ethnocentrism as a tendency for people to perceive their own group as the centre and to scale and rate outgroups with reference to their own group. In its most extreme form, ethnocentrism relates to beliefs about

the superiority of ones' own culture, which may lead to lack of interest in, and even contempt for, the culture of other groups.[40]

In a less extreme form, it relates to the natural tendency of people to refer their own standards, including the symbols, values and ways of thinking of their own ethnic or national group and to judge others according to these norms. James Lee[41] termed this tendency as our Self-Reference Criterion (SRC). He argued that we all have an automatic and unconscious tendency to refer to our own thought framework – which is mainly tied to our national culture – to interpret situations, evaluate people, communicate, negotiate or decide which attitude to take. This framework is generally modelled by ethnocentrism, which is also discussed in Chapter 10 in relation to country-of-origin effects.

Ethnocentric SRC tendencies can be reduced or eliminated with some effort. Lee[41] suggests the following steps in order to try to correct the decisional bias related to our SRC, when dealing with international operations:

1. Define the problem or the objectives, as would be done according to the customs, behavioural standards and ways of thinking of the decision maker's country.
2. Similarly, define the problem or the objectives as would be done according to the customs, behavioural standards and ways of thinking of the foreign country.
3. Isolate the influence of the self-reference criterion on the problem, and identify the extent to which it complicates the decision-making problem.
4. Redefine the problem (and often the objectives), without the bias related to the SRC and then find the solutions and make decisions that fit with the cultural context of the foreign market.

The first two points are illustrated in the following situation. People are standing in line at an amusement park, such as Disneyland, where there are some very popular attractions. In the original context in the US, discipline with respect to queues is strong. They are usually well organized and there are even tangible indications for this (e.g., yellow lines on the ground indicating where people should stop to queue, tape or bars that are visibly present to help form queues). In the foreign context of France, where there is a developed sense of 'free-for-all' and less of a habit of organized queues (combined with a resistance to anything that seems too socially structured), discipline with respect to queues cannot be assumed. If Americans in France rely on their SRC criteria, they are likely to become rapidly frustrated. However, if they redefine the problem and objectives outside their SRC, they may be better placed to find an amicable solution to overcome the problem. However, this depiction of the SRC includes some degree of naivety and inadequacy, as it assumes that a culture's mysteries can be easily understood.

Cultural expertise is a complex reality. Sometimes neither marketing experts from the home (in total ignorance) nor host (through lack of consciousness of their own culture) countries are capable of the diagnosis required to correct the decisional bias related to our SRC, especially in steps 3 and 4. Further, removing the bias effect using the SRC approach does not always result in immediate outcomes. Billikopf,[42] who was tutored on Russian culture and talked to interpreters about appropriate behaviour in various situations, describes his first trip to Russia. On one of these occasions the interpreter explained that a gentleman must always be courteous to ladies, such as pouring her *limonad*. Later, he tried to use this reasoning when he offered his host's wife a banana. When she smiled and said yes without reaching for one, he picked one for her and peeled it half way before he handed it to her. His host's smile told him he had done the right thing. On a later trip he was informed that: 'In Russian, when a man peels a banana for a lady it means he has a romantic interest in her' (p. 1).[42] Billikopf further cautions that generalizations about eye-contact, personal space, touch and interest in participation, especially based on faulty observation, can be dangerous.

It is important to realize that even those who immerse themselves in another culture do not fully understand the nuances, as they are often conditioned throughout childhood. As Gauthey (p. 63)[38] states: 'It seems a thousand times easier to stay attached to our own values and to transfer onto the foreigner the responsibility to change his point of view than to decenter ourselves, that is to leave our system of reference and put ourselves in the place of the other.'

Racism

Racism is often confused with cultural hostility. Racism precedes cultural hostility, but cultural hostility does not necessarily imply racism. People may be hostile to those from another culture without being a racist. There is a theory behind racism: that, because of their race (i.e., physiology), some human beings are inferior in terms of intelligence, creative abilities, moral sense, or some other factor. The theories of Gobineau and Hitler's *Mein Kampf* are writings that clearly developed and propagated racist views.

Website link 1.9

Hitler is known as the consummate all-time terrorist – learn more through his memoir, *Mein Kampf*: http://www.roadtopeace.org/index.php?itemid=125.

Cultural hostility

In contrast to racism, cultural hostility does not imply prior prejudices as to who is inferior or superior according to race or culture. Culture is part of a person's heritage. There is a strong affective dimension, when a person's cultural values are threatened. This emotional response may result from:

1. Simple interactions with people whose cultural values are quite different. This may lead to feelings of unease, difficulty in communication and lack of empathy. A defensive response may develop, in terms of minor and unconscious cultural hostility.
2. Collective reactions to groups that are culturally different. Cases are so numerous worldwide that it would need many pages to list them exhaustively. A few examples include Transylvanian Hungarians and Romanians, people in ex-Yugoslavia, Armenians of High Karabakh and Azeris of the Azerbaijan enclave in Soviet Armenia; Walloons and Flemings in Belgium; Protestant and Catholic communities in Ulster. *Identity is a matter of culture rather than race.*

It is not only territorial conflicts but also economic competition that may cause cultural hostility, especially when combined with cultural differences. For instance, some negative feelings toward the Japanese in the United States were generated by media about the large trade imbalance, combined with culturally based Japanese protectionism. Despite the large trade imbalance with China, there seems to be less economic animosity, thank, to lower levels of protectionism.

Cultural hostility directed at successful nations is often a fairly ambiguous feeling, where admiration and envy for the other's achievements go along with contempt for many traits of the envied people and an unwillingness to understand the root causes of the other's success. This may also result in naive copies of selected cultural artefacts as magical ways of becoming stronger: in *Robinson Crusoe* savages were about to eat Man Friday in order to gain his qualities.

Chapter 4 of this book further examines the mechanism of cultural hostility, which is sometimes increased by language and communication problems. Intercultural misunderstandings may stem from a lack of competency in the other's language, or from the natural tendency to adopt defensive stereotypes. This often results in a snowballing cultural hostility.

Questions

1. In light of the definitions of culture given in this chapter, is it possible for a culture to disappear? Why, or why not? Give an example.

2. A common problem, across cultures, is to attract/be attractive for potential partners. Discuss how, in Kluckhohn and Strodtbeck's terms, there is a range of possible solutions, and how they are differentially preferred across societies. Outline possible consequences for marketing.

3. Discuss the case of multi-language/multi-religion countries (e.g., India, Canada, Switzerland). How can people in these countries share a common culture? Are there any identifiable segments of culture within these countries?

4. Discuss the role of education (at home, at school and elsewhere) in the transmission of culture.

5. What is a *national character* and how is it useful to marketers?

6. Can you describe at least one circumstance when you had an ethnocentric attitude? If you find it hard, can you explain why?

7. Discuss the following statements from Gannon (1994, pp. 5 and 68) on stereotyping:

'Many Germans, for instance, do not like to converse much during their meals. Germans will ordinarily begin their meals by taking a sip of beer or soda and then picking up and holding knives and forks throughout the meal, putting them down only when they are finished eating. For many Germans eating is a serious business that is not to be disturbed by trivial comments and animated conversation.'

'Germans also frequent the symphony on a regular basis; the former West Germany with its population of 62 million boasts approximately 80 symphony orchestras . . . This societal and cultural love of music has produced some of the finest composers of classical symphonic music. In fact, many experts agree that the classical symphony reached its highest level of attainment and maturity in the works of Haydn and Mozart.'[43]

References

1. Oxford Dictionary Online, retrieved 14 July 2011 from http://oxforddictionaries.com/definition/culture.
2. Linton, Ralph (1945), *The Cultural Background of Personality*. New York: Appleton-Century.
3. Geertz, C. (1973), *The Interpretation of Cultures*: Selected Essays. New York: Basic Books.
4. Kluckhohn, Florence R. and Frederick L. Strodtbeck (1961), *Variations in Value Orientations*. Westport, CT: Greenwood Press.
5. Malinowski, Bronislaw (1944), *A Scientific Theory of Culture and Other Essays*. Chapel Hill, NC: University of North Carolina Press.
6. Goodenough, Ward H. (1971), *Culture, Language and Society*. Reading, MA: Modular Publications, 7, Addison-Wesley.
7. Hong, Y., Morris, M. W., Chiu, C. and Benet-Martínez, V. (2000), 'Multicultural Minds: A Dynamic Constructivist Approach to Culture and Cognition', *American Psychologist*, 55 (7), 709–20.
8. Carroll, John B. (1956), *Language, Thought and Reality: Selected Writings of Benjamin Lee Whorf*. Cambridge, MA: MIT.
9. Santa Fe Institute, *Evolution of Human Languages*, retrieved 13 Jan 2012 from http://ehl.santafe.edu/intro1.htm.
10. Lewis, M. Paul (ed.) (2009), *Ethnologue: Languages of the World, Sixteenth edition*, ebook retrieved 11 Jan 2012 from http://www.ethnologue.com/.
11. Kumar, Rajesh (2000), 'Confucian Pragmatism vs Brahmanical Idealism: Understanding the Divergent Roots of Indian and Chinese Economic Performance', *Journal of Asian Business*, 16 (2), 49–69.
12. *CIA Factbook*, retrieved 13 Jan 2010 from http://www.cia.gov/library/publications/the-world-factbook/geos/xx.html.
13. *Butlers Guild*, retrieved 13 Jan 2010 from http://www.butlersguild.com.
14. *Friday the 13th Means Millions in Lost Business Productivity*, retrieved 22 July 2011 from http://www.cnbc.com/id/38691586/Friday_the_13th_Means_Millions_in_Lost_Business_Productivity.
15. Keillor, Bruce D. and G. Thomas M. Hult (1999), 'A Five-Country Study of National Identity: Implications for International Marketing Research and Practice', *International Marketing Review*, 16 (1), 65–82.
16. Hofstede, G. (2001), *Culture's Consequences* (2nd edn). Thousand Oaks, CA: Sage.
17. Inglehart, R. (1997), *Modernization and Postmodernization: Cultural, Economic, and Political Change in 43 Societies*. Princeton, NJ: Princeton University Press.
18. Schwartz, S. H. (2009), *Culture Matters: National Value Cultures, Sources and Consequences*. In C.-Y. Chiu, Y. Y. Hong, S. Shavitt and R. S. Wyer Jr (eds), *Problems and Solutions in Cross-cultural Theory, Research and Application*. New York: Psychology Press.
19. House, R. J., Hanges, P. J., Javidan, M., Dorfman, P. and Gupta, V. (eds) (2004), *Cultures, Leadership, and Organizations: GLOBE Study of 62 Societies*. Newbury Park, CA: Sage.
20. Smith, P. B., Dugan, S. and Trompenaars, F. (1996), 'National Culture and the Values of Organizational Employees: A Dimensional Analysis Across 43 Nations', *Journal of Cross-Cultural Psychology*, 27 (2), 231–64.
21. Hofstede, G., G. J. Hofstede and M. Minkov (2010), *Cultures and Organizations: Software of the mind*, 3rd edn. McGraw Hill: New York.
22. Chinese Culture Connection (1987), 'Chinese Values and the Search for Culture-free Dimensions of Culture', *Journal of Cross-Cultural Psychology*, 18 (2), 143–64.
23. Minkov, M. (2007), *What Makes us Different and Similar: A New Interpretation of the World Values Survey and Other Cross-cultural Data*. Sofia, Bulgaria: Klasika I Stil.
24. Imada, Toshie (2012), 'Cultural Narratives of Individualism and Collectivism: A Content Analysis of Textbook Stories in the United States and Japan', *Journal of Cross-Cultural Psychology*, 4 (4), 576–91.
25. Mead, Margaret (1948), *Male and Female*. New York: William Morrow.
26. Chua, Amy (2011), *Battle Hymn of the Tiger Mother*. Penguin Press, USA.
27. Segall, Marshall H., Pierre R. Dasen, John W. Berry and Ype H. Poortinga (1990), *Human Behavior in Global Perspective*. New York: Pergamon.
28. Montesquieu, Charles de (1748), *The Spirit of Laws* (Thomas Nugent, Trans.) (6th edn). Dublin: McKenzie and Moore.
29. Van De Vliert, Evert (2003), 'Thermoclimate, Culture, and Poverty as Country-level Roots of Workers' Wages', *Journal of International Business Studies*, 34 (1), 40–52.
30. Droit, Michel (1952), *Chez les mangeurs d'hommes*. Paris: La Table Ronde.
31. Gauthey, Franck and Dominique Xardel (1990), *Le Management Interculturel*. Paris: Collection 'Que Sais-Je?'
32. Soutar, Geoffrey N., Richard Grainger and Pamela Hedges (1999), 'Australian and Japanese Value Stereotypes: A Two Country Study', *Journal of International Business Studies*, 30 (1), 203–16.
33. Yoshida, Susumu (2000), 'Can the West Understand the East? And Vice-versa? Issues of Cross-Cultural Communication', *Management Japan*, 33, 1–13.
34. Gruère, Jean-Pierre and Pierre Morel (1991), *Cadres Français Et Communications Interculturelles*. Paris: Eyrolles.

35. Zaharna, R. S. (1989), 'Self Shock: The Double-binding Challenge of Identity', *International Journal of Intercultural Relations*, 13 (4), 501–26.

36. Adler, Peter S. (1975), 'The Transitional Experience: An Alternative View of Culture Shock', *Journal of Humanistic Psychology*, 15, 13–23.

37. Erikson, Erik (1950), *Childhood and Society*. New York: Norton.

38. Gauthey, Franck (1989), 'Gérer les Différences dans L'entreprise Internationale', *Intercultures*, 6 (April), 59–66.

39. Sumner, G. A. (1906), *Folk Ways*. New York: Ginn Custom Publishing.

40. Levine, Robert A. and Donald T. Campbell (1972), *Ethnocentrism: Theories of Conflicts, Ethnic Attitudes, and Group Behavior*. New York: John Wiley.

41. Lee, James A. (1966), 'Cultural Analysis in Overseas Operations', *Harvard Business Review* (March–April), 106–11.

42. Billikopf Encina, Gregorio (1999), 'Cultural Differences?', retrieved 18 Jan 2012 from www.cnr.berkeley.edu/ucce50/ag-labor/7article/article01.htm.

43. Gannon, Marin J. (1994), *Understanding Global Cultures: Metaphorical Journeys Through 17 Countries*, Thousands Oaks, CA: Sage Publications.

Teaching materials

A1.1 Critical incident

An old lady from Malaysia

The frail, old, almost totally blind lady appeared at every clinic session and sat on the dirt floor enjoying the activity. She was dirty and dishevelled, and obviously had very little, even by Malaysian kampong (local village) standards.

One day the visiting nurse happened upon this woman in her kampong. She lived by herself in a rundown shack about 10 by 10 feet [3 × 3 m]. When questioned how she obtained her food, she said she was often hungry, as she only received food when she worked for others – pounding rice, looking after the children, and the like.

The nurse sought to obtain help for the woman. It was finally resolved that she would receive a small pension from the Department of Welfare which would be ample for her needs.

At each weekly clinic, the woman continued to appear. She had become a centre of attention, laughed and joked freely, and obviously enjoyed her increased prestige. No change was noted in her physical status, however. She continued to wear the same dirty black dress and looked no better fed.

The nurse asked one of the rural health nurses to find out if the woman needed help in getting to a shop to buy the goods she seemed so sorely in need of.

In squatting near the woman, the rural health nurse noted a wad of bills in the woman's pocket. 'Wah,' she said, 'It is all here. You have spent nothing. Why is that?'

The woman laughed and then explained: 'I am saving it all for my funeral.'

(Source: Weeks *et al.*, pp. 24–5.[1])

A1.2 Critical incident

The parable

The leader tells the following parable to the group, illustrating with rough chalkboard drawings if desired:

Rosemary is a girl of about 21 years of age. For several months she has been engaged to a young man – let's call him Geoffrey. The problem she faces is that between her and her betrothed there lies a river. No ordinary river mind you, but a deep, wide river infested with hungry crocodiles.

Rosemary ponders how she can cross the river. She thinks of a man she knows who has a boat. We'll call him Sinbad. So she approaches Sinbad, asking him to take her across. He replies, 'Yes, I'll take you across if you'll spend the night with me.' Shocked at this offer, she turns to another acquaintance, a certain Frederick, and tells him her story. Frederick responds by saying, 'Yes, Rosemary, I understand your problem – but – it's your problem, not mine.' Rosemary decides to return to Sinbad, spends the night with him, and in the morning he takes her across the river.

Her reunion with Geoffrey is warm. But on the evening before they are to be married, Rosemary feels compelled to tell Geoffrey how she succeeded in getting across the river. Geoffrey responds by saying, 'I wouldn't marry you if you were the last woman on earth.'

Finally, at her wit's end, Rosemary turns to our last character, Dennis. Dennis listens to her story and says, 'Well, Rosemary, I don't love you . . . but I will marry you.' And that's all we know of the story.

(Source: Weeks *et al.*, pp. 24–5.[1])

Discussion guide

1. Before any discussion, participants should be asked to write down individually on a piece of paper the characters of whose behaviour they most approve, plus a sentence or two explaining their first choice.
2. Participants may be split into small groups of four or five, to share their views and raise relevant issues.
3. The discussion should centre on the cultural relativity of values and their relation to one's own cultural background.

A1.3 Reading

Body rituals among the Naciremas

Website link A1.1

Text for this reading is located on the book website: **www.pearsoned.co.uk/usunierlee**.

Appendix reference

1. Weeks, William H., Paul B. Pedersen and Richard W. Brislin (1987), *A Manual of Structured Experiences for Cross-Cultural Learning*. Yarmouth, ME: Intercultural Press.

2

Cultural dynamics 1: time and space

If we adopt Selma Lagerlöf's definition of culture as 'what remains when that which has been learned is entirely forgotten' (my translation of the aphorism attributed to Selma Lagerlöf by Karl Petit, p. 100) from Karl Petit,[1] culture may appear to be a vague and practically limited concept. Its main use would be as a 'synthesis variable': an explanation that serves as a last resort. It would also serve as an explanatory variable for residuals, when other explanations are unsuccessful. However, Lagerlöf's definition usefully identifies two basic elements of cultural dynamics at the individual level:

1. Culture is learned.
2. Culture is forgotten, in the sense that we cease to be conscious of its existence as a learned behaviour.

Yet culture remains present throughout our daily activities. Culture represents our adaptation to reality, based on complex interactions between values, attitudes and behavioural assumptions. Cultural differences arise from preferences for solutions to common human problems, which form cultural norms in society. Despite changes to our natural and social environments, which expose our culture to new solutions, cultural preferences have strong roots and cultural change is relatively slow, with the gaps between cultures appearing to be fairly stable[2,3] However, cultural norms serve as constraints and opportunities rather than dictating how individuals act. Culture is normative rather than deterministic. As such, cultural frameworks and theories provide a valuable starting point to understand the impact of culture as a cohesive whole. This information can then be modified based on additional information about individuals and specific situations, which may interact to influence behaviour.

In this chapter we describe different cultural solutions to the universal problems of how to deal with time, space and concepts of the self and others. Rather than focus on one particular cultural theory, we integrate dimensions proposed in commonly cited cultural theories, such as those proposed by Hall,[4,5,6,7] Hofstede,[2] Inglehart,[8] Kluckhohn and Strodtbeck.[9] Schwartz,[10] House,[11] and Trompenaars.[12] While we give some country-specific illustrations where a particular solution is likely to be considered obviously 'right' or fluent with the countries' culture, it is important to remember that *alternative solutions* are available in any society. The objective here is not to classify countries or cultures, but rather to expose the reader to a set of learned assumptions that explain how cultural norms differ and to present readers with the opportunity to contrast these differences with their own learned cultural assumptions to enhance cross-cultural learning.

Cross-cultural learning involves examining different cultural 'mindsets' which contain culturally-congruent content, procedures and goals.[13] While it is possible to develop cultural awareness from reading materials written from a culturally alien perspective, it takes conscious, deliberative, reflective thinking to examine and understand both your own and the other cultures' perspectives. Cultural assumptions are not completely in the realm of *Unbewußtsein* (unconsciousness, deep-seated and inaccessible); they are rather in the realm of *Unterbewußtsein*, which is located at a subconscious level, where interaction and self-questioning can reveal them. As such, exposure to different cultural solutions, along with a concerted effort to understand, compare and contrast them in a non-evaluative manner, can lead to a deeper level of cultural understanding.

In Section 2.1 we propose a model of action based on different cultural assumptions. These cultural assumptions (depicted in Figure 2.1) are described in this and the next chapter. We then discuss major cultural assumptions around the concepts of time (Section 2.2), space (Section 2.3) and self and others (Section 2.4). Finally, in Section 2.5 we highlight culture as both a chronically and situationally accessible, multi-level, multi-layered construct.

2.1

A model of action based on cultural assumptions

Figure 2.1 presents a model of action that illustrates how basic cultural assumptions in three major areas (time, space and the concept of the self and others)

influence interaction models, which shape our attitudes towards action and, in turn, our actions (further discussed in Chapter 3). These basic cultural assumptions are statements about the nature of reality, in response to a set of fundamental human problems. These assumptions give communities a framework for evaluating solutions to these fundamental problems, combining a cognitive dimension (*what people think*), an affective dimension (*what people like*) and a directive dimension (*what people do*).

As discussed in Chapter 1, while every society faces a common set of problems, different histories and emphases in these societies result in divergent dominant solutions. In this chapter, we combined Kluckhohn and Strodtbeck's approach[9] with those adopted by other authors[2,6,10] to indicate where differences in cultural influences are likely to exist. These are presented in five tables, including different assumptions around our conceptions of time (Table 2.1),

Figure 2.1 A model of cultural dynamics

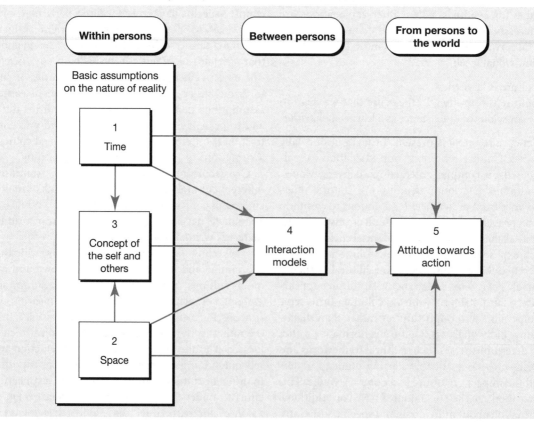

space (Table 2.2), and the concepts of self and others (Table 2.3), as well as interaction models (Table 3.1) and attitudes towards action in (Table 3.4), presented in Chapter 3.

Each of the five tables highlights common problems, important solutions and dominant differences across cultures. This leads to a detailed inventory of basic differences in cultural assumptions that influence inter-actions, which will be described in detail in Chapter 3 and throughout the book, as we highlight the impact of culture on specific areas of international marketing. In subsequent chapters, cultural assumptions are used to explain elements of consumer behaviour (Chapter 5), market research (Chapter 7), marketing management (Chapters 8 to 11) and marketing communications (Chapters 12 to 14).

Figure 2.1 provides a guide to the current chapter. Our exploration starts with the cultural variability in the concept of time.

2.2 Time: cross-cultural variability

A universal perception of time seems indisputable, and so is rarely questioned. However, from a cross-cultural perspective, time may well be the area of greatest difference, because (1) assumptions are very deep-seated and (2) formally, we hold a common model of clock-based time, which is normatively perceived as being linear, continuous and economic. However, our assumptions around the concept of time and its importance have a strong influence on how we function socially. Our assumptions around time provide a common framework for activities and help to synchronize individual human behaviour and events over time. Our time orientation influences many marketing concepts, such as the product life cycle, sales forecasting and the planning of new product launches.[14]

Dimensions of time orientations

Many of the commonly cited cultural theories include time-related orientations. Some focus on perceptions of the flow of time (e.g., Hall's monochromic and poly-chromic task orientation[4-7] and Trompenaars' time dimension as being linear versus holistic[12]), whereas others focus on the temporal focus in society (e.g., Kluckhohn and Strodtbeck's past, present and future orientations,[9] the Chinese Cultural Connection's Confucian Work Dynamism[14] (termed Long Term Orientation by Hofstede[2]). Table 2.1 integrates and builds on these time-related cultural assumptions and describes the contrasting or archetypical differences that correspond to four common time related problems, as subsequently discussed.

Economicity of time

The first time-related problem in Table 2.1 relates to the extent to which time is regarded as a scarce and tangible resource. Western countries (e.g., the United States, Australia and most of Western Europe) are often representative of the 'time-is-money' culture, where time is seen as an economic good. Since time is perceived as a scarce resource, people should try to allocate it in the most economically optimal way. This results in people using their time as 'wisely' as possible in scheduling or establishing timetables and deadlines. Measurement of parking meter time by units of 7.5 minutes or sport performance by the hundredths of a second is typical of precisely measured

Table 2.1 Time-related cultural differences

Basic problem/Cultural orientations	Contrasts across cultures
1. Is time money? Economicity of time	■ Time is regarded as a scarce resource. ■ Time is plentiful and indefinitely available.
2. How to schedule tasks?	
(a) Monochronic	■ Only one task is undertaken at a time, following a preset schedule.
(b) Polychronic	■ Multiple tasks undertaken simultaneously and appointment times, if any, are flexible. Time is less important than the situational context.
3. Is time a continuous line?	
(a) Linearity	■ Time is seen as linear, separate blocks.
(b) Cyclicity	■ Time is cyclical, with daily, yearly and seasonal cycles.
4. How should we emphasize past, present and future?	
Temporal focus (a) towards the past	■ The past is important. Resources must be spent on teaching history and building museums. Oral and written traditions are important. Roots are implanted in the past and no plant can survive without its roots.
(b) towards the present	■ Live in the 'here and now'. Although not always enjoyable, the present must be accepted for what it is: the only true reality.
(c) towards the future	■ Plan for the future. Prepare for the long term; appreciate achievements (e.g., science). The future is inevitably 'bigger and better'.

economic time with direct and explicit financial consequences. Economic time norms tend to be very strict regarding time schedules, appointments, dates and durations. Appointments are likely to be scheduled with a starting and an ending time.

The economicity of time influences attitudes towards money, as well as the monetary value of time, both of which are important to marketing.[15,16] In cultures with a strong economic time, products are created to 'save time' and services are based on blocks of time, including bank loans and life insurance policies. Buyer–seller interactions are also heavily influenced by the economicity of time, including the waiting process, communication style and efficiency of service.

Website link 2.4

Search for information about how cultures deal with economic or non-economic time perceptions. This website shows how Disney World is making queues go faster: http://www.gizmodo.com.au/2010/12/how-disney-world-is-making-queues-go-faster/.

Monochronic versus polychronic use of time

Take a moment to think about yourself. Would you prefer, for example, to read this paper while completing other tasks? Or, would you prefer to read the paper from beginning to end and then move on to another task? (p. 155)[17]

This is an example of the second time related problem in Table 2.1, which relates to task scheduling. Edward Hall described two extreme task scheduling behaviours, which he termed monochronism (M-time) and polychronism (P-time).[6] M-time individuals prefer to do one thing at a time and tend to adhere to preset schedules. When confronted by a dilemma (e.g., a discussion with someone that lasts longer than planned), M-time people will politely stop the conversation in order to keep to their schedule. In M-time societies, not only the start of a meeting but also its finish is often planned. Conversely, P-time individuals do several things at the same time, easily modify preset schedules, and seldom experience time as 'wasted'. P-time may seem quite chaotic to M-time people: 'There is no recognized order as to who is to be served next, no queue or numbers indicating who has been waiting the longest' (Hall, p. 47).[6]

P-time people are more committed to relationships than to schedules. When confronted with a situation where a discussion with someone lasts longer than planned, they prefer to go on talking or working after preset hours rather than keep to a schedule, if they have one.

The PERT (Programme Evaluation and Review Technique) method is an example from a typical M-time 'agenda culture'. PERT explicitly aims to reduce polychronic tasks (even when they take place simultaneously!) to provide a monochronic solution (the critical path). Management methods, originating in Western cultures, favour monochronic task organization. They clearly devalue polychronic tendencies, which tend to make plans and schedules difficult. When it comes to delays and being 'on time', precise monochronic systems give priority to meeting dates and commitments to schedules.[18,19]

Cultural assumptions around M- or P-time are important for understanding buyer–seller interactions, as they tend to promote very different expectations. This is also important for scheduling in almost every aspect of business, including completion times, deliveries and promotional campaigns, where differing expectations can be calamitous.

David Palmer and David Schoorman[20] integrated Hall's M- and P-time with the economicity of time to distinguish three dimensions:

1. *Time use preference (M- vs. P-time)*: The extent to which people prefer to engage in multiple tasks simultaneously.
2. *Context (low vs. high)*: The extent of context needed to effectively communicate. M-time is associated with low context communication, conveying only explicit meaning in messages. P-time is associated with high context communication, where the information that surrounds an event, as well as many indirectly meaningful cues, are needed to correctly interpret the message. High and low context messages are explained in detail in Chapter 4.
3. *Time tangibility (economicity)*: The extent to which time is viewed as a commodity that can be bought, sold, saved, spent or wasted.

Palmer and Schoorman suggest that these three dimensions interact to produce eight types of individual temporality. In a survey of 258 middle and senior executives from 25 nations – although most were Americans – they found most executives to be Type A

(44 per cent), being polyphasic, time urgent and low context; or M1 (32 per cent), being monochronic, time urgent and low context. Other patterns are likely to form with different samples from different cultures. This illustrates the importance of understanding the interaction between time use, cultural factors, and individual preferences, as the work environment and personality (extroversion) both appear to add to our understanding of cultures influence on time orientations.[21]

Linearity (L) versus cyclicity (C) of time
The third time-related problem in Table 2.1 relates to the continuity of time. A strong economic view of time, combined with monochronism, emphasizes a linear time line, where time is viewed as being a line with a point – the present – at the centre. Each portion of the line can be cut into slices, which are supposed to have a certain value.

Basic religious beliefs play a key role in supporting such a linear view of time. Christianity, and other monotheistic religions, have a one-shot interpretation of worldly existence. Only on the final judgement day will Christians know if they are to be granted eternal life. However, the Asian religions, including Hinduism and Buddhism, assume that on the death of the body, the soul is born again in another body. The belief in regular reincarnation, until a pure soul is allowed to escape the cycle and go to *nirvana*, radically changes the nature of time in a specific life. This is not 'all the time I have got', it is simply one of my 'times' across several lives. For most Asians, cyclicity is central in their pattern of time. *Nirvana* is the final release from the cycle of reincarnation. It is attained by extinction of all desires and individual existence, culminating in absolute blessedness (in Buddhism), or in absorption into Brahman (in Hinduism). Naturally, patience is on the side of the people believing in cyclical reincarnation of the soul. For Christians, it is more urgent to achieve, because their souls are given only one worldly life. But, as the New Testament puts it clearly, those who do right, even in the very last moment, will be considered favourably.

Another element that favours a cyclical view of time is the degree of emphasis put on the natural rhythms of years and seasons, the sun and the moon. This concept contrasts so-called 'modern' with 'traditional' societies, in so far as 'modern' means technology, mastering nature and, to a certain extent, the loss of nature-related reference points. Despite this, highly developed societies such as the Japanese are known for having maintained a strong orientation to nature. The floral art of *ikebana* and the emphasis on maintaining a contact with nature, even in highly urban environments, are testimonies to their attachment to the natural rhythms of nature. Even within a country, the relationship to nature influences the model of time adopted by urban as compared with rural people.

Elements of cyclicity of time have three main origins: (1) religious assumptions about reincarnation of the soul; (2) natural rhythms of years, seasons and days; and (3) the social division of time periods, which is more arbitrary, less natural and 'given', than we assume. Time is naturally both linear and cyclical.

Temporal orientations: past, present, future

The fourth time-related problem in Table 2.1 relates to the temporal focus of human life. As stated by Kluckhohn and Strodtbeck[9] (pp. 13–15):

The possible cultural interpretations of temporal focus of human life break easily into the three point range of past, present and future . . . Spanish-Americans, who have been described as taking the view that man is a victim of natural forces, are also a people who place the present time alternative in first position . . . Many modern European countries . . . have strong leanings to a past orientation . . . Americans, more strongly than most people of the world, place an emphasis upon the future – a future which is anticipated to be 'bigger and better'.

Societies differ in whether the extent to which the focus is on the past, present or future, as typified by the following:[9]

- Past-oriented people emphasize the past in explaining where we are now. They tend to value the preservation and maintenance of tradition, including restoration of old buildings, investment in museums and the value of teaching history at school. Many European and some Asian cultures tend to be past oriented.
- Present-oriented people focus on the 'here and now', believing that the past is over and the future is uncertain, theoretical and difficult to imagine. They accommodate changes in beliefs and traditions; however, religion may play an important role in pushing people towards a present orientation, especially if it emphasizes that only God decides the future. Arabic–Muslim culture has been described as fatalistic and short-term oriented.[22] As stated by Harris and Moran (p. 474):

Who controls time? A Western belief is that one controls his own time. Arabs believe that their time is controlled, to a certain extent, by an outside force – namely Allah – therefore the Arabs become very fatalistic in their view of time . . . Most Arabs are not clockwatchers, nor are they planners of time.[23]

- Future-oriented people focus on planning for a bigger and better tomorrow. They tend to find ways to replace the old and delay immediate gratification to invest in the future. An example of this is the millions of Americans who start a savings account for their child's education when s/he is born. Future-oriented societies will tend to invest in science or technology. Americans and some Asian cultures are considered future oriented.

While these orientations tend to differentiate cultures, they are also related to individual characteristics and traits.[24] For instance, older people tend to be more past oriented, whereas younger people tend to be more present or future oriented. Furthermore, societies undergoing change may underplay their basic temporal orientation during this period.

Website link 2.5

Search for information about how languages reflect and shape our conception of time, such as this weblink about how time flies in the Andes: **http://www.guardian.co.uk/science/2005/feb/24/4.**

Important differences in temporal orientations were also found in the Chinese Value Survey (CVS), which purposefully introduced an Eastern bias to counter the historical Western bias in value surveys.[14] The CVS proposed a Confucian Work Dynamism, which corresponds to a future orientation on one hand and a past and present orientation on the other. Later, Hofstede (p. 359)[2] referred to this as Long Term Orientation (LTO) versus Short Term Orientation (STO):

Long Term Orientation stands for the fostering of virtues oriented towards future rewards, in particular, perseverance and thrift. Its opposite pole, Short Term Orientation, stands for the fostering of virtues related to the past and present, in particular, respect for tradition, preservation of 'face' and fulfilling social obligations.

In this case, an LTO is future oriented, emphasizing long-term virtues such as frugality, perseverance, savings and investing, whereas an STO emphasizes short-term virtues. Short-term virtues can correspond to the past (i.e., respect for tradition and fulfilment of social obligations) or present (i.e., immediate gratification, including social consumption and spending). LTO scores are strongly correlated with national economic growth and have been used to explain the dramatic growth of the East Asian economies in the latter part of the twentieth century.[2] Many Asian countries (e.g., Hong Kong, Japan and South Korea) score quite high on LTO, whereas most Western countries (e.g., Australia, Germany, USA and UK) and developing nations (e.g., Pakistan and West Africa) score much lower.

including our social and physical spaces. *Territoriality* (discussed in Chapter 1) is an organizing principle that can be used to form groups, based on family ties or common characteristics including education, religion and professional associations. Territoriality also extends to our physical environment, including responsibility toward the natural environment.

Many of the commonly cited cultural theories include space territoriality dimensions. These are mostly related to the territoriality of group membership (e.g., Kluckhohn and Strodtbeck[9]) and our use of space (e.g., Hall[4]), which are related Kluckhohn and Strodtbeck's[9] activity orientation. Table 2.2 integrates and builds on these space-related cultural assumptions and describes the contrasting or archetypical differences that correspond to four common space-related problems, as subsequently discussed.

2.3
Space territoriality

People are territorial by nature. They must define who has ownership and control over certain spaces,

Personalization versus depersonalization

The first space-related problem in Table 2.2 focuses on whether people are categorized by who they are (personalization) or what they do (depersonalization).

Table 2.2 **Space-related cultural differences**

Basic problem/Cultural orientations	Contrasts across cultures
1. Are people insiders or outsiders, based on what people do or on what they are?	
(a) Personalization	■ What you can do, depends on who you are (i.e., *being*).
(b) Depersonalization	■ What you do is more important than who you are.
2. What are the rights and obligations of group membership?	
(a) Ingroup orientation	■ Belonging to ingroups (i.e., family, tribe, clan and nation) includes important rights and obligations that are unlikely to be accorded to outgroup members.
(b) Outgroup orientation	■ Assumes all people have equal rights, even distant others.
3. How can membership be gained?	
(a) Concrete territoriality	■ Ingroup *being* orientation based on who the person is (e.g., birth); unlikely to be acquired by outgroup adults.
(b) Abstract territoriality	■ Outgroup *doing* orientation based on what the person does (e.g., skills).
4. How to deal with physical space?	
(a) Group cultures with close physical contact	■ Tendency to live near to one another, and to be undisturbed by such intimacy.
(b) Individualistic cultures prefer private space	■ The need for private space around one's body, and to dislike intrusion into this space.

Personalization means that assumptions about what a person can *do* depend on who the person *is*. Since not all is prima facie visible, it will be necessary to spend time to understand who this person is. Personalization is evident in cultures with a strong *being* orientation.

A '*being*' orientation emphasizes belonging, based on shared predetermined characteristics, including those you:

1. are born into, such as gender, family, social class, ethnic background, religion, or nationality; and
2. currently belong to, such as age (young versus older people) and marital status.

A strong *being* orientation assumes that who the person *is*, naturally, legitimately and forcefully, influences the roles, power and capacities he or she has in society. A typical causal chain in a *being* orientation is: she is a woman, thus she belongs to the group of people in charge of reproduction and nurturing roles, thus she cannot work outside the home. There is a strong link between a *being* orientation and the concept of the self and others, which helps translate this concept into interaction models.

A strong *being* emphasis is often indicated by what people call themselves and others. In many traditional societies, language designates people by a term meaning 'human being'. For the Bantu people, the word 'Bantu' actually means human being. This, more or less, emphasizes that others are not *real* human beings. Without going so far, the Japanese language also divides 'we' and 'they'. Japanese people call themselves *Nihonjin* and foreigners *Gaijin* (those from the outside). Similarly, Pakistanis in the UK call themselves *Apney* (our own people) and white English *Gorey*.[25]

In contrast, depersonalization means that predetermined personal characteristics (e.g., extended family, social class, ethnic background, religion, gender and age) are less important than what you do (e.g., abilities, talents and education). Here, less time is spent discovering who a person is, especially if time is strongly economic, as it is not necessary to know who a person *is* in order to decide what this person can *do*. Depersonalization is evident in cultures with a *doing* orientation.

A strong *doing* orientation assumes that what people are *does not* naturally, or legitimately, influence the roles, power and capabilities people have in

society. What is important is what people can achieve, given their individual talents and abilities. In the purest version of the *doing* orientation, even character and personality would be considered as unimportant in what individuals can achieve. Tasks are viewed as standard and people as interchangeable. Deeds are separated from emotions and *doing* belongs to a world of its own, radically separated from the *being*.

Ingroup/outgroup orientation

The second space-related problem in Table 2.2 focuses on the rights and responsibilities toward members of our group. Who people consider as their group depends on their ingroup or outgroup orientation, which is related to individualism/collectivism (further discussed in Chapter 3). The concept of ingroup and outgroup is quite complex, as it involves patterns of kin-based loyalty and obligation. It also considers the natural relationship between the *being* orientation and the emphasis on group belonging, which has to do with natural law and the right of people to occupy a certain territory.

Who is a member of the ingroup?
The largest possible ingroups are nations. Benefits related to nationality are strongly space-related, including the right to live, work and enjoy citizenship of a definite territory. In some countries, legitimacy is primarily based on your ancestry, where nationality may be legally based on *jus sanguinis* (law of the blood) and only granted if at least one parent is a national. In other countries (e.g., Australia, France, the UK and the USA), nationality is legally based on *jus soli* (law of the soil) and is also granted to all those born in the country. This delineates different ways of defining the content of an ingroup (in this case a national group): on the one hand, people emphasize blood and kin; on the other, they do not.

The family is the smallest and most basic ingroup unit. Strong ingroup orientation is most often accompanied by a rhetoric based on family relationships, with a dominant father (outside oriented), a protective mother (inside oriented) and sisters and brothers, alternately considered as rivals within the ingroup (because they are competing for parents' love, affection and preference) and allies in comparison with the outgroup (because they share the same fundamental identity; they *are* of the same kin). The family space is the house and surrounding land, which is private but not closed to outsiders, who may enter under definite conditions.

In contrast, outgroup orientation is based on the assumption of the fundamental unity of mankind, beyond the borders of ingroup spaces (e.g., family, religious and national groups). All individuals are seen as having equal rights and there is a responsibility to care for those who are weaker. Rules are universal and expected to apply to everyone in the same manner. In outgroup-oriented society, people would be expected to report a perpetrator of a crime to authorities, regardless of whether the person was a close family member or not.

While these two orientations are roughly opposed, they are not complete opposites. Even within societies we find some variability in the application of ingroup or outgroup mindsets, depending on the situation. Oyserman[26] (p. 182) termed this 'culture as situated cognition' to recognize the impact of 'social contexts, human artefacts, physical spaces, tasks, and language, on [the] accessible cultural mindset'. In the previous example, members of a strong outgroup culture are, on average, more likely to see laws as universally applicable even to their close family; however, ingroup alternatives are also *available*, if they are made salient and relevant to the situation.

What does membership involve in terms of rights and obligations?

Ingroup bonds involve relationships of loyalty that do not extend beyond the borders of the ingroup space. Loyalty can be based on kinship or patronage (an extended form of kinship based on symbolic adoption or taking another's child as one's own). Ingroup loyalty is based on allegiance, even in the face of conflicts with other members of the ingroup or when experiencing unfair treatment from the most powerful members. Loyalty is fundamentally non-reciprocal: people do not expect other ingroup members' loyalty because they are loyal themselves. There are no time constraints on loyalty: one may wait for 50 years to be rewarded for loyalty or one may never be rewarded.

Strong ingroup orientation increases an insider's loyalty, but simultaneously decreases the feeling of obligation towards outsiders. Morality is space related. It might, for instance, be considered as perfectly virtuous to lie to or steal from people to whom no loyalty is owed. The Mafia is a good illustration of an ingroup-oriented society. Morality is based on a set of values favouring strict loyalty, treason being punished by a death sentence, and yet the godfather who has ordered it goes to the burial ceremony because he still 'loves' the betrayer.

Ingroup orientation partly explains behavioural relativity. Some national groups have a reputation for their compliant behaviour at home – where rules are strictly enforced – and for 'looser' conduct abroad. Outside their ingroup, they no longer feel the need to observe the rules that apply at home. They do not need to respect outgroup rules, even those similar to their ingroups, since outsiders do not deserve loyalty or respect.

Ingroup or outgroup orientation has a deep influence on the system of ethics and morality in a society. Outgroup orientation values universal rules, applied to everybody. Human rights ethics are a typical feature of outgroup orientation. Objectivity and reciprocity are preferred over loyalty. Loyalty is not to the group, not to people, but to the rules and values that govern the society as a whole. This relates to personalization (people orientation) versus depersonalization (rule orientation), as discussed previously. The depersonalized approach in outgroup-oriented cultures leads to a greater sensitivity to the problems of human beings far away from their own space.

These differences have a major impact on cross-cultural consumer behaviour, in terms of product ownership and usage (discussed further in Chapter 5) and international business, in terms of the information needed to understand the connections between people and how contracts are made and honoured (discussed further in Chapter 14).

Concrete versus abstract territoriality

The third space related problem in Table 2.2 focuses on how group membership can be obtained. If people are very territorial, it is important to know how to gain access to them, even as an external partner, such as a business partner in a joint venture or strategic alliance.

Group membership may be gained on the basis of either concrete or abstract territoriality. The type of territoriality is largely dependent on the combination of ingroup/outgroup and the *being/doing* divides.

1. When ingroup and *being* orientation are strong, membership is generally gained on the basis of *concrete territoriality*.
2. When outgroup and *doing* orientation are strong, membership is based on *abstract territoriality*.

Ingroup membership based on *concrete territoriality* requires characteristics that cannot be acquired by outgroup adults. Here, ingroup criteria are most likely to be related to birth, socialization (i.e., in the same village or country) and education (i.e., same school system). In cases where it is impossible to gain membership, one should behave as a friendly but realistic outsider. Building a warm and reliable friendship can provide a sense of security in ingroup societies, as such conversations should be contextualized, beginning with an exchange of information about family. However, outsiders often, too quickly, view cultures with an ingroup/*being* orientation as being narrow-minded, provincial and hostile towards foreigners.

Membership-based *abstract territoriality* corresponds largely to Western *doing* cultures, where an outgroup orientation is valued. What people have *done* up to now is indicated by their resumé. An interview guide in countries where affirmative action compliance is important may consider it discriminatory to enquire about an applicant's age, citizenship, marital status, and birthplace. This information is not only legitimate in *being* cultures, it is essential to ascertain who the applicant *is*. Abstract territoriality is mostly based on professional achievements, evidenced by diplomas, membership of professional bodies, being an alumnus of a prestigious university, and so on. The epitome of abstract territoriality is represented by *insider* trading laws, which considered the use of a natural ingroup advantage to be evil.

Business school graduates or those holding the title of doctor in Germany belong to abstract territoriality groups, as they are based on *doing* and competence rather than *being*. In this model, it is assumed that access to membership is organized on a non-discriminatory and objective basis and that it is in the interest of society as a whole because the 'best people' are doing the 'appropriate job'. However, even in a *doing* framework, relational competence never disappears in favour of pure professional competence. Managing relationships is still an important part of the *doing* competences.

Paradoxically, when abstract territoriality is very strong, it largely recreates primitive ingroup behaviour, but based on different criteria. Even the world of academia, which is very outgroup oriented in terms of gender, nationality, religion and age, is very ingroup oriented when it comes to doctoral degrees and the journals where people publish.

Group membership assumptions are important for many aspects of international marketing, especially as a foreign firm in a national competitive environment. For instance, foreign firms entering Africa and Middle Eastern countries may have difficulties making public relations contacts, dealing with staffing issues, and handling situations involving business ethics. Foreign firms with an outgroup orientation often have a difficult time understanding the issues surrounding the favouring of one party over another on the ground of personal relationship, which is standard practice for ingroup-oriented people. In fact, these actions are often viewed as corruption by outgroup-oriented people.

Physical space

The final space related problem in Table 2.2 focuses on how physical space is viewed, including possessiveness, control and authority over physical space. The 'language of space' is culturally determined. Individuals refer to culturally based rules concerning space, such as the codes concerning social distance. For example, how far should one stand from other people in order to respect their area of private space? Edward Hall[4] developed the concept of 'proxemics': the study of human use of space as a specialized elaboration of culture. In Western cultures, there are three primary zones of space: the intimate zone (0–45cm; 0 to 18 inches), the personal zone (0.45–1m; 18 inches to 3 feet), and the social zone (1–2m; 3 to 6 feet). Touch can occur for Westerners in the intimate and personal zones, but sensory involvement and communication is less intense in the social zone.

The following physical space assumptions differ across cultures:

1. What are the sizes of the three zones? To what extent do they overlap?
2. Who is allowed to enter these zones of physical space?

3. What is considered adequate sensory exchange within definite interpersonal distances?

The last question is important in marketing terms, as our sense of physical space mixes with culturally determined sensory codes, based on sight, sound, touch and smell, to give meaning to product characteristics. For instance, some Western countries, such as Australia, UK, and the USA, focus on a suppression of personal odours in public spaces, which has created a mass market for room deodorizers, antiperspirants, mouthwashes and deodorants. Although smell suppression is globally 'modern', it is not clear whether it will remain so in the future, with people striving for a more natural expression of themselves.

The list of basic space-related cultural assumptions in Table 2.2 is not exhaustive. Some other aspects need to be considered. For instance, the availability of inhabitable physical space and the density of population vary greatly across countries, with profound impact on material culture. Population density increases the importance of an assumption that 'smaller is better' or 'bigger is better'. It also influences how towns are organized and how urban and rural landscapes are integrated and interrelated and how transportation is developed.

Website link 2.6

Search for information on proxemics, such as this weblink about whether level of personal space is acceptable in America. Take the elevator test: **http://www.everythingesl.net/inservices/ proxemics_elevator.php**.

2.4

Concept of the self and others

The concept of the self and others deals with how the organization of a society is internalized by people and reflected in the view we have of ourselves in relation to others. It is largely about people within a society responding positively and unconsciously to membership. People make assumptions about the hows and whys of their membership in society, even though they are largely unaware of it. These assumptions differ from one society to another.

Many of the commonly cited cultural theories include concept of self and other. These are related to cultural assumptions about human nature (e.g., Kluckhohn and Strodtbeck[9]), how we appraise others (e.g., Kluckhohn and Strodtbeck's[9] activity orientation), and whether we are likely to hold an interdependent or independent self-construal (e.g., Markus and Kitayama[27]). Table 2.3 integrates and builds on these cultural assumptions and describes the contrasting or archetypical differences that correspond to four common relational problems, as subsequently discussed.

How we view ourselves and others has major implications in the area of consumer behaviour, as our possessions are meaningful reflectors of our identities. We ascribe meaning to what we buy and consume, as we strive to assert, complete, or attain our 'ideal' self through our possessions.[28] These issues are further discussed in Chapter 5, which focuses on cross-cultural consumer behaviour.

Is human nature good or bad?

The first problem in Table 2.3 focuses on how we treat new people for the first time, which depends on our understanding of human nature: basically good or bad. This influences our views of strangers, as well as the concept of friendship. If we assume human nature is basically good, we have a friendly and open-minded attitude towards people we do not know. When visiting the United States or Australia, Europeans are often amazed by how well they are received. It is clear that Australians have a strong positive belief about new people, who are assumed to be good. Such an attitude has a functional side in relatively new countries. However, these attitudes are not without bias. Twentieth-century films of the 'Western' genre often contrasted 'bad' Indians and 'good' European settlers. This mixed form of human nature orientation is fairly straightforward: 'civilized' = good; 'uncivilized' (Indians, gamblers, desperadoes) = bad.

In contrast, first contact with the Latin Europeans and South Americans can be more difficult. The novels of Colombian writer Gabriel García Márquez are typical of the view that human nature is basically bad (e.g., *One Hundred Years of Solitude* and *Love in the Time of Cholera*). Trust should only be given to those who are known to be trustworthy.

Table 2.3 Concepts of the self and others

Basic problem/Cultural orientations	Contrasts across cultures
1. How should we assess strangers?	
(a) Human nature basically good	■ Unknown people are considered favourably.
(b) Human nature basically bad	■ Unknown people are treated with suspicion.
2. Who should be considered trustworthy, reliable? How do we assess characteristics?	
(a) Perceptions of age	■ Older (younger) people are viewed favourably.
(b) Gender	■ Genders differ in capabilities and roles, or not.
(c) Social class	■ The emphasis placed on social class attributed to wealth or birth.
3. Appraising oneself: To give the correct appearance one should display	
(a) Low/high self-esteem	■ Shy and modest versus extrovert or even arrogant.
(b) Low/high potency	■ Power should be hidden versus shown.
(c) Low/high activity	■ Busy people or unoccupied/idle people are well regarded.
4. Relating the individual to the group	
(a) Independence	■ The individual, as an autonomous independent entity is the basic unit in society.
(b) Interdependence	■ People are an integral part of their group, which is the basic unit in society.

Website link 2.7

Learn more about Gabriel García Márquez, one of the world's greatest authors: http://www.themodernword.com/gabo/index.html.

In reality, assumptions about human nature are of a dialectic nature – that is, the apparent contradiction between the two assumptions is resolved at a higher level of thinking. They would read more as:

■ Human nature is basically good, but . . .
■ Human nature is basically bad, but . . .
■ Human nature lies somewhere between good and bad, and . . .

The two sides of each basic assumption coexist in most religions, which strive to improve individuals, especially through the social morals they develop. However, individuals still need culturally based reference points for evaluating others.

The dynamics of friendship involves assumptions about human nature. If human nature is assumed to be good, then friendship develops quickly, but often quite superficially. Since most people are supposed to be basically good, it is not as necessary to select a small group of 'true' friends. In contrast, when it is assumed that human nature is generally bad, friendship develops more slowly owing to initial distrust. Fewer, but deeper friendships will develop. A strong circle of friends may be a protective barrier against a society perceived as unfriendly, if not hostile. While human nature orientation is not directly related to action, it is related to marketing through collaboration, competition and the messages we create, which often depict things such as bad versus good characters.

How do we appraise others?

The second problem in Table 2.3 focuses on cultural assumptions around how we judge others in many different areas of our lives, including making friends, choosing business partners, and targeting potential customers. Apart from personality traits, which we judge by intuition, we also use many available clues, such as age, gender and behaviour. This information about what people *are* in society indicates what they are allowed to *do*, depending on our culture.

We automatically appraise others by their associated socio-demographic characteristics (e.g., age, gender, social class), which helps us to judge their conduct in particular roles (the perfect partner, businessman, child, etc.). *Ideal* role models are depicted in books, films, television series, and many other cultural artefacts that convey subliminal normative messages. For instance, we have an abundance of identification possibilities from films, such as *Harry Potter*, *Spiderman*, and Robert Neville in *I am Legend*. We constantly receive messages on how to behave from these and other common sources of information in our society. Heroes are desirable role models, even though we know that these characters are fictional.

Gender is probably the most important cultural difference from the demographic information, because of the definite roles and self-concepts imposed on boys and girls by their culture. In *Male and Female*, Margaret Mead (pp. 7–8) says:

In every known society, mankind has elaborated the biological division of labour into forms often very remotely related to the original biological differences that provided the original clues. Upon the contrast in bodily form, men have built analogies between sun and moon, night and day, goodness and evil, strength and tenderness, steadfastness and fickleness, endurance and vulnerability. Sometimes one quality has been assigned to one sex, sometimes to the other ... Some people think of women as too weak to work out of doors, others regard women as the appropriate bearers of heavy burdens ... some religions, including our European traditional religions, have assigned women an inferior role in the religious hierarchy, others have built their whole symbolic relationship with the supernatural world upon male imitations of the natural function of women. In some cultures women are regarded as sieves through whom the best guarded secrets will sift; in others it is the men who are the gossips.[29]

(Copyright © 1949 by Margaret Mead. Reprinted by permission of HarperCollins Publishers.)

The place of women in society has changed greatly over the last century. Some basic rights, such as voting, were long denied to women; though the place of a woman is still very different from that of a man in certain places. In many countries women are largely dependent on men, mostly on an economic basis. In some Muslim countries such as Saudi Arabia, women are not allowed to work outside the home, and are often not permitted to go outside alone; however, they may be able to shop in designated family times, when single women are allowed, but not single men. Interestingly, Dubai has introduced pink taxis, which are driven by and can only be ridden by women. Worldwide differences in the self-concept of women, and the concept of women held by men, are striking.

> **Website link 2.8**
>
> Search for interesting information about the place of women in society, such as these weblinks about Saudi women driving: **http://www.telegraph.co.uk/news/worldnews/middleeast/saudiarabia/8582308/Saudi-women-defy-driving-ban.html**. **http://www.telegraph.co.uk/motoring/news/8930168/Allowing-women-drivers-in-Saudi-Arabia-will-be-end-of-virginity.html**.

Youth may be associated with inexperience, doubtful character and lack of seriousness, or, by way of contrast, with open-mindedness, creativity, and the ability to change things and to undertake new ventures. Naturally, both sets of qualities are found in young people of all cultures. What is more interesting is how certain cultures, like Japan and Africa, place a higher value on older people, while others, like the United States and Australia, value younger people in society. This divergence may be related to the qualities typically found in the more highly valued age group being implicitly perceived as more congruent and favourable for the overall development of the society.

An emphasis on age is associated with some of the cultural orientations discussed in Chapter 4, as well as the dominant family models in a particular society. Parental authority and structure tends to be weaker in nuclear than extended families, which influences perceptions about the relationship between age and competence. 'Modern culture' tends to value younger people, as they are better able to adapt to very rapid change. This influence is seen in TV advertising that revolves around beautiful young, rough and ready young boys or yuppie-like professionals. In contrast, 'traditional cultures' see elders as a source of wisdom and guidance for the community and as a consequence their age is more highly valued.

All societies place people in particular strata, such as *social classes and castes*, but the criteria are often different. In economically oriented societies they may divide people into the 'haves' and the 'have-nots', but other criteria may be based on birth or education, even in the absence of obvious wealth or income. For instance, in many newer Western countries social class is based on wealth. In others, such as India, it is based on birth. In India, castes – a special order of social stratification – include four major hereditary classes into which the Hindu society is divided: the *Brahman* (priestly class), *Kshatriya* (warrior class), *Vaisya* (merchant and peasant classes) and *Sudra* (labour class), which are generally not transcended. In China, social class is something in between, in that it does not belong to an individual but extends to his or her family.[30]

Like many other elements of the concept of the self and others, social class is important for consumer behaviour, as people express their real or imagined class differences by what they buy and use. In countries where the emphasis on class is strong, people in higher classes see themselves as *being substantially different* from those in lower classes. This can extend to speaking the language differently (or even a different language), prohibiting interclass marriages, and distinguishing oneself by specific tastes and lifestyles.

Further, certain societies, such as Ethiopia, the Philipines, Thailand and China,[31] tend to emphasize the importance of context when they appraise others. At the country level, Owe and colleagues[31] found that 'contextualism' scores (i.e., the importance of knowing contextual information, such as the family, group membership, and place, to understanding people), positively predicted ingroup favouritism, differentiated trust between in- and out-groups and corruption.

Website link 2.9

Search for information about caste systems, such as this in-depth analysis of the Hindu caste system: http://www.hinduwebsite.com/hinduism/h_caste.asp.

How do we judge ourselves?

The third problem in Table 2.3 focuses on cultural assumptions around how we judge ourselves. People hold a certain view of themselves, which is subconsciously chosen to be culturally appropriate to their ingroup. Three main areas of cultural contrasts may be identified: self-esteem, perceived potency and perceived activity.[32]

1. Personal self-esteem can be low or high according to whether we think of ourselves as good or not so good. Low self-esteem is usually accompanied by modest and self-effacing behaviour, whereas higher self-esteem is accompanied by more assertiveness and self-assured behaviour. People from Asian cultures, where there is more emphasis on the group than the individual, often display behaviours related to lower self-esteem. This does not mean that they deserve less esteem, but rather that each assumes that they deserve less *as an individual*. In many Asian cultures, self-esteem is more likely to be related to interpersonal situations, whereas in Western cultures it is more likely to be associated with feeling superior or proud.

2. In cultures where potency is high, individuals tend to view themselves as powerful and capable of accomplishing almost any task. The French proverb '*Impossible n'est pas français*' (Translation: 'There's no such thing as can't') is a typical high perceived-potency saying.

3. In cultures where the appropriate level of personal activity is seen as high, people will more often boast about being 'workaholics', they will work more weekends, and generally be more satisfied with overworking. In contrast, when the appropriate image of the self is based on a low level of activity, as in the Hindu case, people will focus on fewer hours spent in the office, low involvement in work-related issues, and having time available for pure inactivity.

These three dimensions interact, so that people who are low on self-esteem, perceived power and perceived activity feel powerless and often accept the world as it is. Conversely, people with high self-esteem, perceived power and perceived activity are more likely to be overconfident and take on difficult tasks, even to the extent of failure.

Website link 2.10

Search for information on work-life balance, such as this weblink, which ranks the top 23 countries: http://www.theatlantic.com/business/archive/2012/01/the-23-best-countries-for-work-life-balance-we-are-number-23/250830/#fullscreen.

How do we relate the individual to the group?

The fourth problem in Table 2.3 focuses on how we relate individuals to the group. The boundaries between people, and the groups they belong to, are important to all societies for ensuring smooth and efficient functioning. The concepts of individualism and collectivism, which are discussed in detail in Chapter 4, are relevant here, as they involved differences in self-concept content and the focus of relationships. In individualist cultures, people: a) usually see themselves as autonomous and independent; b) are motivated by their own preferences, needs and rights; and c) give priority to their personal goals and emphasize a rational analysis of their relationships with others.[33] In collectivist cultures, people: a) usually see themselves as an integral part of one or more collectives or ingroups, such as family and co-workers; b) are motivated by norms and duties imposed by the ingroup; c) give priority to the goals of the ingroup; and d) try to emphasize their connectedness with the ingroup.[33]

On the basis of the cultural dimensions of individualism and collectivism, Markus and Kitayama[27] identified two predominant types of self-concept that focus on how the individual is related to the group: *independent* and *interdependent*. Those with a predominantly *independent* self-concept see themselves and others as having significant dispositional attributes that are detached from context, whereas those with a predominantly *interdependent* self-concept see themselves in 'relation-to-other' (p. 225).[27] Those with an *independent* self-concept emphasize '(a) internal abilities, thoughts, and feelings; (b) being unique and expressing the self; (c) realizing internal attributes and promoting one's own goals; and (d) being direct in communication' and those with an *interdependent* self-concept emphasize '(a) external, public features such as status, roles, and relationships, (b) belonging and fitting in, (c) occupying one's proper place and engaging in appropriate action, and (d) being indirect in communication and reading others' minds' (p. 581).[34]

2.5 Chronically and situationally accessible cultural norms

A relatively large body of work examines cultural influences as fixed or as situational, especially in relation to the constructs of individualism and collectivism. Oyserman and colleagues[26] provide evidence that individualism and collectivism are, indeed, both fixed, in terms of being normatively, chronically accessible to people in these cultures, and also situational, in that an *individualist* or *collectivist mindset* can be primed within a culture. From a situated perspective, Oyserman (p. 182) argues that 'describing a society as individualistic simply means that members of this society are, on average, more likely to construe situations as being "about" things centralized and valued in individualism; describing a society as collectivistic means that members of this society are, on average, more likely to construe situations as being "about" things centralized and valued in collectivism.'[26] Cultural or country level differences are due to this normative knowledge being chronically accessible (available in memory) that make this solution feel obvious, fluent or right. However, since *both solutions* are available to people across societies, contextual information can influence which mindset feels right in the situation.

Culture as a chronically accessible construct has been supported by a very large number of studies, which compare differences across countries, as will be described throughout this book. Culture as a situationally accessible construct has also been supported by a growing number of studies that use priming (i.e., small situational cues) to change the accessibility of this normative information (see Oyserman for a review[26]). As these priming studies help to understand the processes by which cultural assumptions influence behaviour, they will be examined in more detail in Chapter 5 when we discuss consumer behaviour.

Situational accessibility does not mean that cultural norms have less influence, but it does give us a better understanding of the ecological fallacy, where the existence of individual-level relationships is assumed, based on culture-level findings.[2]

Questions

1. Discuss cultural variation in the solutions that have been found across societies to the four common problems listed below:
   (a) How to secure oneself (to feel secure, subjectively, and to protect oneself, objectively) against unforeseeable negative events (a grave illness, an accident, etc.).
   (b) How to treat the oldest in the community when they can no longer work.
   (c) Who should have access to education, on what criteria, and how should its cost be financed, given that the resources available for education, private and public, are not infinite? To what extent should education be given to *all* members of a particular society, irrespective of their age, social class and personal capacities? On which bases should access to education be organized?
   (d) How should couples, the basic unit for the reproduction of the species, be formed? What role should love, common ethnic or social belonging, age or (even) sex, play in such a process?

2. Discuss the marketing implications of differing cultural solutions to points (a) and (b) in question 1, in terms of the existence of certain products or services, provided by the market, the state or mutual bodies, organized within the family group or by a traditional community.

3. What is the influence of space availability (mostly determined by population density in a definite country or area) on material culture? Give examples.

4. Indicate how the following products and services are 'loaded' with time, in terms of time used in consumption, time-saving device, durability, waiting time, seasonality, time projections in the past and the future, etc. (as an example, Box 7.1 describes the time load in life insurance policies):
   (a) a dishwashing machine;
   (b) a haircut;
   (c) obtaining cash from your bank;
   (d) spending two-week vacations at *Club Méditerranée*;
   (e) fresh orange juice versus dried orange juice (i.e., concentrated powder).

5. How would you expect consumer behaviour to vary across cultures for the five products/services above? (Cite one example per case.)

6. You try to park your car. A sign indicates that parking in this area is limited to 15 minutes. Another sign reads: 'Long-term parking, 300 metres'. What do these explicit signs suggest concerning temporal culture in this country?

7. Define what would be the most important criteria for recruitment in a *being*-oriented society as compared with a *doing*-oriented society.

8. In most countries, police and judiciary positions are subject to a condition of nationality (being a national is a requirement for entering the service) whereas in universities and research centres positions are open to applicants regardless of their nationality. Why?

9. Find examples of cultural borrowing (in everyday life, in the press, in people's behaviour, in work as well as leisure activities, the arts, etc.).

10. Try to elaborate on the following assertion: 'The usual traffic in marketing and business texts is that this generally starts with the American text and this is then translated into other languages or sometimes used in the original version.' What are the problems likely to be encountered by non-US educators and practitioners when using such materials? On the other hand, what are the advantages of using them?

References

1. Petit, Karl (1960), *Dictionnaire des Citations*, Paris: Marabout: Verviers.
2. Hofstede, Geert (2001), *Culture's Consequences* (2nd edn). Thousand Oaks, CA: Sage
3. de Mooij, Marieke and Geert, Hofstede (2011), 'Cross-Cultural Consumer Behavior: A Review of Research Findings', *Journal of International Consumer Marketing*, 23 (3–4), 181–92.
4. Hall, Edward T. (1959), *The Silent Language*. New York: Doubleday.
5. Hall, Edward T. (1966), *The Hidden Dimension*. New York: Doubleday.
6. Hall, Edward T. (1976), *Beyond Culture*. Garden City, NY: Anchor Press/Doubleday.
7. Hall, Edward T. (1983), *The Dance of Life*. New York: Anchor Press/Doubleday.
8. Inglehart, R. (1997), *Modernization and Postmodernization: Cultural, Economic, and Political Change in 43 Societies*. Princeton, NJ: Princeton University Press.
9. Kluckhohn, Florence R. and Frederick L. Strodtbeck (1961), *Variations in Value Orientations*. Westport, CT: Greenwood Press.
10. Schwartz, Shalom (2004), 'Beyond individualism/collectivism: New cultural dimensions of values', in U. Kim, H. C. Triandis, C. Kagitcibasi, S. C. Choi, and G. Yoon (eds), *Individualism and Collectivism: Theory, Method, and Applications*. Thousand Oaks, CA: Sage, pp. 85–119.
11. House, Robert J., P. J. Hanges, M. Javidan, P. W. Dorfman and V. Gupta (eds) (2004), *Culture, leadership, and organizations: the GLOBE study of 62 societies*. Thousand Oaks, CA: Sage.
12. Trompenaars, F. (1993), *Riding the Waves of Culture: Understanding Cultural Diversity in Business*. London: Economist Books.
13. Oyserman, D., N. Sorensen, R. Reber and S. X. Chen (2009), 'Connecting and Separating Mind-sets: Culture as Situated Cognition', *Journal of Personality and Social Psychology*, 97, 217–35.
14. Chinese Cultural Connection (1987), 'Chinese Values and the Search for Culture-free Dimensions of Culture', *Journal of Cross-Cultural Psychology*, 18, 143–74.
15. Jacoby, Jacob, George J. Szybillo and Carol K. Berning (1976), 'Time and Consumer Behavior: An Interdisciplinary Overview', *Journal of Consumer Research*, 2, 320–39.
16. Spears, Nancy, Lin Xiaohua and John C. Mowen (2001), 'Time Orientation in the United States, China, and Mexico: Measurement and Insights for Promotional Strategy', *Journal of International Consumer Marketing*, 13 (1), 57–75.
17. Hecht, T. D. and N. J. Allen (2005), 'Exploring Links between Polychronicity and Well-being from the Perspective of Person-job Fit: Does it Matter if you Prefer to do only One thing at a Time? *Organizational Behavior and Human Decision Processes*, 98, 155–78.
18. Usunier, Jean-Claude (1991), 'Business Time Perceptions and National Cultures: A Comparative Survey', *Management International Review*, 31 (3), 197–217.
19. Usunier, Jean-Claude (2003), 'The Role of Time in International Business Negotiations', in *International Business Negotiations*, Pervez N. Ghauri and Jean-Claude Usunier (eds) (2nd edn). Oxford: Elsevier.
20. Palmer, David K. and David F. Schoorman (1999), 'Unpackaging the Multiple Aspects of Time in Polychronicity', *Journal of Managerial Psychology*, 14 (3/4), 323.
21. König, Cornelius J. and Mary J. Waller (2010), 'Time for Reflection: A Critical Examination of Polychronicity', *Human Performance*, 23, 173–90.
22. Ferraro, Gary P. (1990), *The Cultural Dimension of International Business*. Englewood Cliffs, NJ: Prentice Hall.
23. Harris, Philip R. and Robert T. Moran (1987), *Managing Cultural Differences* (2nd edn). Houston, TX: Gulf Publishing Company.
24. Usunier, Jean-Claude and Pierre Valette-Florence (1994), 'Perceptual Time Patterns ("Time Styles"): A Psychometric Scale', *Time and Society*, 3 (2), 219–41.
25. Chapman, Malcom and Ahmad Jamal (1997), 'Acculturation: Cross Cultural Consumer Perceptions and the Symbolism of Domestic Space', *Advances in Consumer Research*, 24, 138–43.
26. Oyserman, D. (2011), 'Culture as Situated Cognition: Cultural Mindsets, Cultural Fluency, and Meaning Making', *European Review of Social Psychology*, 22, 164–214.
27. Markus, Hazel Rose and Shinobu Kitayama (1991), 'Culture and the Self: Implications for Cognition, Emotion and Motivation', *Psychological Review*, 98 (2), 224–53.
28. Belk, Russel W. (1988), 'Possessions and the Extended Self', *Journal of Consumer Research*, 5, 139–68.
29. Mead, Margaret (1948), *Male and Female*. New York: William Morrow.
30. Wong, Nancy and Aaron Ahuvia (1995), 'From Tofu to Caviar: Conspicuous Consumption, Materialism and Self-Concepts in East-Asian and Western Cultures', in *Proceedings of the Second Conference on the Cultural Dimension of International Marketing*. Odense, 68–89.
31. Owe, Ellinor *et al.* (in press), 'Contextualism as an Important Facet of Individualism-Collectivism: Personhood Beliefs Across 37 National Groups', *Journal of Cross-Cultural Psychology*, first published on 31 January 2012 as doi:10.1177/0022022111430255.
32. Triandis, Harry C. (1983), 'Dimensions of Cultural Variation as Parameters of Organizational Theories', *International Studies of Management and Organization*, XII (4), 139–69.
33. Triandis, Harry C. (1995), *Individualism and Collectivism*. Boulder, CO: Westview.
34. Singelis, Theodore M. (1994), 'The Measurement of Independent and Interdependent Self-construals', *Personality and Social Psychology Bulletin*, 20 (5), 580–91.

Appendix 2

Teaching materials

A2.1 Cross-cultural scenario

Inshallah

Stefan Phillips, a manager for a large US airline, was transferred to Dhahran, Saudi Arabia, to set up a new office. Although Stefan had had several other extended overseas assignments in Paris and Brussels, he was not well prepared for working in the Arab world. At the end of his first week Stefan came home in a state of near total frustration. As he sat at the dinner table that night he told his wife how exasperating it had been to work with the local employees, who, he claimed, seemed to take no responsibility for anything. Whenever something went wrong they would simply say '*Inshallah*' ('If God wills it'). Coming from a culture which sees no problem as insoluble, Stefan could not understand how the local employees could be so passive about job-related problems. 'If I hear one more *inshallah*,' he told his wife, 'I'll go crazy.'

Question

What might you tell Stefan to help him better understand the cultural realities of Saudi Arabia?

(Source: Ferraro, p. 118.[1] Ferraro, Gary, *The Cultural Dimensions of International Business*, 5th edn, © 2006; reproduced by permission of Pearson Education, Inc., Upper Saddle River, NJ.)

A2.2 Cross-cultural interaction

Engineering a decision

Mr Legrand is a French engineer who works for a Japanese company in France. One day the general manager, Mr Tanaka, calls him into his office to discuss a new project in the Middle East. He tells Mr Legrand that the company is very pleased with his dedicated work and would like him to act as chief engineer for the project. It would mean two to three years away from home, but his family would be able to accompany him and there would be considerable personal financial benefits to the position – and, of course, he would be performing a valuable service to the company. Mr Legrand thanks Mr Tanaka for the confidence he has in him but says he will have to discuss it with his wife before deciding. Two days later he returns and tells Mr Tanaka that both he and his wife do not like the thought of leaving France and so he does not want to accept the position. Mr Tanaka says nothing but is somewhat dumbfounded by his decision.

Question

Why is Mr Tanaka so bewildered by Mr Legrand's decision?

1. He believes it is foolish for Mr Legrand to refuse all the financial benefits that go with the position.

2. He cannot accept that Mr Legrand should take any notice of his wife's opinion in the matter.

3. He believes Mr Legrand is possibly trying to bluff him into offering greater incentives to accept the offer.

4. He feels it is not appropriate for Mr Legrand to place his personal inclinations above those of his role as an employee of the company.

(Source: Brislin *et al.*, p. 158.[2] Republished with permission of Sage Publications Inc. Books, from *Intercultural Interactions: A Practical Guide*, Richard W. Brislin, Kenneth Cushner, Craig Cherrie and Mahealani Young, 2nd ed, copyright © 1986; permission conveyed through Copyright Clearance Center, Inc.)

A2.3 Cross-cultural interaction

Opening a medical office in Saudi Arabia

Dr Tom McDivern, a physician from New York City, was offered a two-year assignment to practise medicine in a growing urban centre in Saudi Arabia. Many of the residents in the area he was assigned to were recent immigrants from the much smaller outlying rural areas.

Because Western medicine was relatively unknown to many of these people, one of Dr McDivern's main responsibilities was to introduce himself and his services to those in the community. A meeting at a local school was organized for that specific purpose. Many people turned out. Tom's presentation went well. Some local residents also presented their experiences with Western medicine so others could hear the value of using his service. Some of Tom's office staff were also present to make appointments for those interested in seeing him when his doors opened one week later. The meeting was an obvious success. His opening day was booked solid.

When that day finally arrived, Tom was anxious to greet his first patients. Thirty minutes had passed, however, and neither of his first two patients had arrived. He was beginning to worry about the future of his practice while wondering where his patients were.

Questions

What is the major cause of Tom's worries?

1. Although in Tom's mind and by his standards his presentation was a success, people actually only made appointments so as not to hurt his feelings. They really had no intention of using his services, as modern medicine is so foreign to their past experiences.

2. Given the time lag between sign-up and the actual day of the appointment, people had time to rethink their decision. They had just changed their minds.

3. Units of time differ between Arabs and Americans. Whereas to Tom his patients were very late, the Arab patient could still arrive and be on time.

4. Tom's patients were seeing their own traditional healers from their own culture; after that, they could go on to see this new doctor, Tom.

(Source: Brislin *et al.*, pp. 160–1.[2] Republished with permission of Sage Publications Inc. Books, from *Intercultural Interactions: A Practical Guide*, Richard W. Brislin, Kenneth Cushner, Craig Cherrie and Mahealani Young, 2nd ed, copyright © 1986; permission conveyed through Copyright Clearance Center, Inc.)

A2.4 Reading

Language and time patterns – the Bantu case

Cultural and linguistic unity of the Bantu area

The Bantu area spreads along the southern side of a line that starts from Douala, Cameroon, by the Atlantic Ocean, and finishes at the mouth of the Tana river in the Indian Ocean. It divides northern and southern Africa. The Bantu area covers most of the southern cone of this continent.

These wide territories (several million square kilometres) are occupied by Bantu people, with the limited exception of some other small ethnic groups. The cultural unity of this people has been established on the basis of common linguistic features. As early as the middle of the nineteenth century, W. Bleek (quoted by Kadima and Lumwanu[3]) had recognized that Bantu languages shared common lexical elements and many grammatical forms. In taking Bleek's work one stage further, anthropologists, historians and linguists have tried to identify the common social and cultural traits which allow a particular area to be classified as Bantu.

Alexis Kagame[4] for instance, has studied Bantu linguistic systems, especially their underlying structures. He has collated what he terms 'compared Bantu philosophy'. The convergence of authors when describing the conception of time in Bantu cultures is quite marked.

The unification of time and space

At the heart of the Bantu's intuition of time lies the postulate of a very close relation between time and space. Within this postulate none of these basic dimensions of reality exist without the others. Alexis Kagame[4] reveals this conceptual link.

Ontologically, Bantu culture puts whatever may be conceived or said into one of four categories:

1. The being – of intelligence (man).
2. The being – without intelligence (thing).
3. The being – as localizer (be it place or date).
4. The being – modal (incidentality, or modification of the being).

The major assumption made by Kagame is that translation of Bantu words in metaphysical categories is possible. He therefore translates *ha-ntu* as the being-localizer. This common word expresses the unity of space (place) and time (date). In the Bantu language this term means both the 'there' of locus and the 'now' of time. It is an indivisible localizer, both spatial and temporal.

The localizing prefix *ha-*, which forms *ha-ntu*, and its variants *pa-ntu* and *ka-ntu* are found in the eastern zone of the Bantu territory. Its equivalent in the western zone is *va*, whereas it is *go* in the south-eastern part of the Bantu area. The idea of unification between space and time in Bantu languages is shared by Emil Pearson,[5] who has lived in the south-east of Angola since the 1920s. He writes in his book *People of the Aurora* (p. 75):

In the Ngangela language there is no word, as far as I know, for 'time' as a continuous, flowing passage of events or the lack of same. Time is experiential or objective, that is, it is that which is meaningful to the person or thing which experiences it. *Time and space are cognate incidents of eternity.* The same word is used for both 'time' and 'space' (the latter in the sense of 'distance').

'*Ntunda*' can either express meaningful time or meaningful space. For example: '*Ntunda kua i li*' – 'There is some distance'; and '*Ntunda i na hiti*' – 'Time has passed'. The related verb '*Simbula*', means 'delay', the thought being of awaiting 'meaningful time'. To the European the African may seem to be idling away useful time, whereas the latter, according to his philosophy, is awaiting experiential time, the time that is right for accomplishing his objective. 'Time' is locative, something that is virtually concrete, not something abstract. The locatives '*Ha*', '*Ku*' and '*Mu*' are used for expressing 'time' as well as 'place'. Example: '*Ha Katete*' – 'In the beginning' (as to either time or place); '*Ku lutue*' can mean either 'in front' or 'in the future'. '*Mu nima*' can mean 'behind' as to place, or 'after' as to time.

Bantu time experience

Two significant points sharply contrast the way Bantus experience time with the Western way of experiencing it within a technological environment. First, Bantus have no theoretical substantive to designate time as an entity *per se*, which can be quantified and measured. Second, for Bantus, the temporal dimension is intrinsic to the event itself. It is not an abstraction as in most Occidental developed cultures. To these cultures it appears as a content which flows regularly from the past to the future, through the present; a flow in which everything moves at the same speed, being 'in time'. For Bantu people time has no real value, no meaning, without the occurrence of an event which will serve as a 'marker'. The intuition of time only becomes effective when an action or an event happens: warriors' expedition, arrival of the train, rainfall, starvation on the increase. Time then becomes individualized. It is drawn out of anonymity. It is not anybody's time which would be abstractedly defined. It is concrete time concerning people I know. Instead of considering time as a straight railway track, where events may happen successively, it will only be spoken of as 'the time of this . . .' or 'the time of that . . .', or time which is favourable for this and that. That is why, on many occasions, there is no point in giving dates, that is to refer oneself to ideal time coordinates. History is not a series of dates, but a link between various events. Everything possesses its own internal time. Each event occurs at its own time.

(Source: Usunier and Napoleon-Biguma, pp. 95–114.[6] Reproduced with the kind permission of the publisher and the co-author.)

A2.5 Exercise

World picture test

Objective

To clarify participants' understanding of countries and cultures of the world through their knowledge of geography.

- *Participants*: Three or more persons. Facilitator.
- *Materials*: Paper and pens.
- *Setting*: No special requirements.
- *Time*: At least 30 minutes to one hour.

Procedure

1. Each participant is given a sheet of paper and a pen and asked to:
   (a) draw a map of the world as best they can within a five-minute time period;
   (b) name as many of the countries as they can;

(c) mark any country they have visited for a week or longer;

(d) exchange papers with other members of the group and discuss what differences are evidenced in what the other person put into their drawing and/or left out of the drawing.

2. Discuss the following points:

(a) Does a person's awareness of the shape of a country reveal that person's awareness of the shape of the culture?

(b) When a person leaves out a country, what does this mean?

(c) When a person leaves out a continent, what does this mean?

(d) What country did the person place in the centre of the map and what does that mean?

(e) When a person draws a country out of place in relation to other countries, what does this mean?

(f) Were they better acquainted with countries they had visited?

(g) When the person objects violently to doing the drawing, what does that mean?

(h) How well did persons draw home countries of other group members?

(i) What do the persons plan to do as a result of what they learned in this exercise?

(Source: Weeks *et al.*, pp. 107–8.[7])

Appendix references

1. Ferraro, Gary P. (1990), *The Cultural Dimension of International Business.* Englewood Cliffs, NJ: Prentice Hall.

2. Brislin, Richard W., Kenneth Kushner, Craig Cherrie and Mahealani Yong (1986), *Intercultural Interactions: A Practical Guide.* Newbury Park, CA: Sage.

3. Kadima, K. and F. Lumwanu (1989), 'Aires linguistiques à l'intérieur du monde Bantu: Aspects généraux et innovations, dialectologie et classifications', in Théophile Obenga (ed.), *Les Peuples Bantu, migrations, expansion et identité culturelle.* Paris: Editions L'Harmattan, 63–75.

4. Kagame, Alexis (1975), 'Aperception Empirique du Temps et Conception de L'histoire dans la Pensée Bantu', in *Les Cultures et le Temps.* Paris: Payot/Unesco.

5. Pearson, Emil (1977), *People of the Aurora.* San Diego, CA: Beta Books.

6. Usunier, Jean-Claude and Constantin Napoléon-Biguma (1991), 'Gestion Culturelle Du Temps: Le Cas Bantou', in *Management Interculturel: Modes et Modèles*, Gauthey Franck and Dominique Xardel (eds), Paris: Economica.

7. Weeks, William H., Paul B. Pedersen and Richard W. Brislin (1987), *A Manual of Structured Experiences for Crosscultural Learning.* Yarmouth, ME: Intercultural Press.

3

Cultural dynamics 2: interactions and behaviours

The cover picture of an issue of *Fortune* magazine relating to management styles shows an American with oriental eyes attempting to eat a hamburger using chopsticks. This metaphor illustrates the fluency of culture and how difficult it is to transpose elements of one culture onto another. As discussed in Chapters 1 and 2, human culture depicts a cohesive set of solutions to basic universal problems. The range of solutions to these basic human problems can be broken down into a set of basic cultural assumptions; however, it must be remembered that the different cultural assumptions do not develop in isolation.

Figure 2.1 in Chapter 2 illustrated the basic cultural assumptions related to cultural models of time, space, and concepts of self and others. This chapter focuses on the second half of the model of cultural dynamics, and examines the cultural assumptions that influence how people interact (Section 3.1) and what leads to action, including attitudes (Section 3.2), information (Section 3.3), feelings (Section 3.4) and rules (Section 3.5). This material is organized around common problems (explained in the Table 3.1) that directly relate to Figure 2.1. The final section in the chapter (Section 3.6) discusses how basic cultural assumptions translate into everyday behaviour.

cultural theories, such as those by Hall,[1] Hofstede,[2] Inglehart,[3] Kluckhohn and Strodtbeck,[4] Schwartz,[5] House[6] and Trompenaars[7] propose a range of possible interaction models. However, only a few of these have obtained large datasets that allow the world's main national cultures to be compared (e.g., over 100,000 respondents for Hofstede,[2] 99,000 for the World Values Survey,[3] 55,000 for Schwartz,[8] 17,000 for the GLOBE project,[6] and 8,800 for Trompenaars and colleagues[9]). Of these, Hofstede's cultural dimensions are still by far the most commonly applied in the field of marketing, despite the growing popularity of the GLOBE project in management and Schwartz's cultural value orientations across a number of fields. While there have been criticisms of Hofstede's dimensions that we need to be aware of (such as being overly simplified, empirically driven, and based only on IBM employees[10]), the dimensions make sense for marketing and sales and, as such, have been studied extensively in international marketing and comparative consumer behaviour. Further, replications show that the dimensions are fairly stable, at least in terms of the distance between cultures.[2,11,12] Consequently, this book more often refers to evidence based on Hofstede's dimensions, but attempts to add some insights about other cultural orientations, where appropriate.

3.1

Models of interaction

In this chapter we describe different cultural solutions to universal problems related to how people interact within societies. Many of the more commonly cited

Website link 3.1

Search for comparisons on different dimensions of culture, such as those by Hofstede and the GLOBE: http://www.geert-hofstede.com/. http://www.grovewell.com/pub-GLOBE-intro.html.

Table 3.1 Interaction models

Cultural orientations	Contrasts across cultures
1) The nature of relations between people; boundaries between people and the group	
(a) Individualism	■ People are largely autonomous and motivated by personal preferences, needs and rights.
(b) Collectivism	■ People are motivated by norms and duties imposed by the ingroup and give priority to ingroup over individual goals.
2) Equality or inequality in interpersonal interactions	
(a) High power distance	■ Hierarchy is strong and power is centralized at the top.
(b) Low power distance	■ Power is more equally distributed and superior and subordinates have a sense of equality.
3) Interacting with others or for others	
(a) Masculinity/mastery	■ Assertiveness and personal achievement are favoured.
(b) Femininity/harmony	■ Caring for others, adopting nurturing roles and emphasizing quality of life is more important.
4) Dealing with uncertainty	
(a) Strong uncertainty avoidance	■ Ambiguous situations are avoided; uncertainty reducing rules and procedures are seen as a necessity.
(b) Weak uncertainty avoidance	■ Ambiguity does not create the same level of anxiety; uncertainty is seen as an opportunity.
Developing appropriate communication with others	
(a) High context	■ Communication is more diffuse and the meaning of a message is derived from the context and knowledge of the speaker.
(b) Low context	■ Communication concentrates on specific issues and the meaning of a message is literal and explicit.

Table 3.1 describes the main cultural assumptions that relate to interactions between people and lists the contrasting or archetypal differences that are considered culturally appropriate interaction models in particular societies. The impact of these dimensions of national culture has been examined on a wide range of issues; with those relevant to marketing being reviewed throughout this book.[2,11,13] Each of these assumptions is briefly discussed in the following sections.

Relations between people and the group: individualism and collectivism

The first problem in Table 3.1 relates to the nature of relations between people and the boundaries between

the person and group. Solutions to this problem are described by the dimensions of *individualism* and *collectivism* (e.g., Hofstede,[2] and the GLOBE Project[6]). Hofstede (p. 225) describes these dimensions as follows:[2]

Individualism stands for a society in which the ties between individuals are loose: everyone is expected to look after him/herself and her/his immediate family only. Collectivism stands for a society in which people from birth onwards are integrated into strong, cohesive in-groups, which throughout people's lifetime continue to protect them in exchange for unquestioning loyalty.

Schwartz (p. 129) also refers to the relationship between the individual and group in his *autonomy–embeddedness* dimension: people in autonomous cultures are encouraged to 'cultivate and express their own preferences, feelings, ideas, and abilities, and to find meaning in their own uniqueness', whereas embedded cultures expect people to obtain meaning in life 'through social relationships, through identifying with the group, participating in its shared way of life, and striving toward its shared goals'.[8] Schwartz argued that individuals in cultures that are high in embeddedness and low in autonomy socialize their children to be obedient and hardworking and discourage imagination in order to reinforce tradition and conformity values.

In individualistic societies, people are expected to take care of their own and their immediate family's needs. Relationships are said to be rational, or based on the concept of reciprocity, where an individual who gives something to another expects some sort of return within a reasonable time span. In contrast, in collectivist countries, the social structure is stronger, with people clearly distinguishing between members of the ingroup and members of the outgroup. Relationships are said to be relational, in that people expect their group to care for them in exchange for unwavering loyalty.

These dimensions refer to concepts of the self and others (assumptions located *within* persons, as discussed in Chapter 2), as well as to a model of interaction *between* people. This is explicitly recognized by the GLOBE Project, which identified these two aspects as *institutional-collectivism* (i.e., how institutions encourage and reward collective action) and *ingroup-collectivism* (i.e., the degree to which individuals express pride, loyalty and cohesiveness in their group). People in countries that are higher in individualism are usually more self-sufficient and less dependent on others. On average, they are more likely to own and use private gardens rather than using

public parks for gathering, have dogs and cats that eat pet food, have insurance, and perform do-it-yourself activities, such as painting and home carpentry.[2] Across wealthy nations, individualism is related to higher car ownership per 1000 people.[13]

Recently, variation across individualist and collectivist societies has also been recognized in terms of hierarchical relationship, leading to horizontal (emphasizing equality) and vertical (emphasizing hierarchy) dimensions of individualism and collectivism.[14] Shavitt and colleagues[15] describe the differences as follows:

1. In vertical individualist societies, people are concerned with distinguishing themselves from others to improve their standing.
2. In horizontal individualist societies, people are concerned with expressing uniqueness and self-reliance.
3. In vertical collectivist societies, people are concerned with enhancing the cohesion and status of their ingroup and complying with authorities.
4. In horizontal collectivist societies, people are concerned with sociability and interdependence.

Table 3.2 outlines the hierarchical and status motivations behind these dimensions. Shavitt and colleagues[15] detail several areas in which this combination of values is likely to have a significant influence, including how people respond to others and how they respond to the marketing mix, especially advertising message appeal and effectiveness.

Equality or inequality: power distance

The second problem in Table 3.1 relates to the legitimacy of inequality, in terms of an unequal distribution of power. It is shown as much by the

Table 3.2 Hierarchical dimensions of individualism and collectivism

	Horizontal	Vertical
Individualism	Independent self-concept See self at same level as others (e.g., Sweden, Denmark, Australia)	Independent self-concept See self within a hierarchy (e.g., USA, Great Britain, France)
Collectivism	Interdependent self-concept See self at same level as others (e.g., Israeli kibbutz)	Interdependent self-concept See self within a hierarchy (e.g., Korea, Japan, India)

behavioural values of superiors who display their power and exercise it, as by the behavioural values of subordinates who wait for their superiors to show their status and power, and are uncomfortable if they do not.[2] Families in high power distance societies tend to teach children obedience and respect for parents and older relatives, whereas families in low power distance societies are more egalitarian and tend to treat children as equals. In high power distance societies, superiors and subordinates feel separated from each other. It is not easy to meet and talk with higher ranking people, and the real power tends to be very much concentrated at the top. In contrast, in low power distance societies, members of the organization tend to feel equal, and close to each other in their daily work relationships. They cope with situations of higher hierarchical distance by delegating power.[2]

There is some overlap between Hofstede's power distance and Schwartz's hierarchy-egalitarianism dimensions, as Schwartz's hierarchy construct also focuses on unequal distribution of power. However, the conceptualisation of egalitarianism is broader, as it stresses a greater recognition of all humans as moral equals that leads to a concern for the welfare of all people. Cultures high on hierarchy expect individuals to adhere to rigid rules designed to ensure smooth societal functioning, and tend to value social power, authority, humility, and wealth. Cultures high on egalitarianism acknowledge the importance of interpersonal cooperation to ensure individual and collective success, and tend to value equality, social justice, responsibility, help and honesty. Hierarchical cultures have large power distance, whereas egalitarian cultures tend toward a small power distance.

Interacting with or for others: masculinity and femininity

The third problem in Table 3.1 relates to whether we interact *with* others or *for* others. The assumptions behind the masculinity/femininity divide are different: should we help people (at the risk of their being weakened by a lack of personal effort) or should we not (at the risk, for them, of being even worse off)? This dimension roughly corresponds to the dominant gender role patterns: male/assertive and the female/nurturing roles. On average, men tend to score high on one extreme and women on the other, *across*

societies, but there are also significant differences *between* societies.

In masculine societies the emphasis is on assertiveness, money, showing off possessions and caring less about the welfare of others. Generally, there is a stronger role differentiation between males and females, but both boys and girls learn to be assertive and ambitious. In masculine societies, people are likely to be more possession oriented, and achievement is demonstrated by status brands and jewellery.[13] People in masculine societies (whether individualist like the US or collectivist like Japan) admire the strong.

In feminine societies the emphasis is on nurturing roles, interdependence between people and caring *for* others (who are seen as worth caring for, because they are temporarily weak). Generally, there is less gender role differentiation and both boys and girls learn to be modest and to sympathize with the underdog. In feminine societies the welfare system is highly developed, education is largely free and easily accessible, and there is openness about admitting to problems, such as in northern European countries. People in trouble are shown patience and hope. In feminine societies people are more likely to share both large and small decisions, such as the choice of main car and everyday food shopping, and to purchase less expensive watches and jewellery.[11]

Schwartz's mastery construct also emphasizes assertiveness and ambition, but contrasts this to harmony with the social and natural environment, rather than femininity.[8] However, these constructs show little empirical overlap, as the mastery–harmony dimension regulates how individuals relate to others and their environment.[8] Cultures that are high on mastery encourage individuals to develop and hone their skills, using them to direct and change the environment, as well as personal and group goals, whereas cultures that are high on harmony encourage individuals to understand and appreciate their environment in its current state.

Uncertainty avoidance

The fourth problem in Table 3.1 relates to how we deal with uncertainty. There are basically two ways. Societies high in uncertainty avoidance assume that uncertainty is bad and everything in society must aim to reduce it. Organizations in these societies promote stable careers and produce rules and procedures to reduce ambiguity. People in these cultures tend to be better groomed as a way of organizing their world and prefer purity in food, as evidenced by higher consumption of mineral water.[11] In contrast, societies low in uncertainty avoidance assume that people have to deal with uncertainty, because it is inevitable. The future is by definition unknown, but it can be speculated, and people and institutions can deal with likely outcomes. People in these cultures tend to be more innovative and entrepreneurial.[16]

Uncertainty avoidance should not be confused with risk avoidance. Hofstede notes that risk is more specific than uncertainty and is often expressed as a probability that a specific outcome will occur, whereas uncertainty is a situation in which anything can

happen. In fact, some people may engage in risky behaviour in order to reduce ambiguities, 'such as starting a fight with a potential opponent rather than sitting back and waiting' (p. 148).[2]

Website link 3.2

A comprehensive resource for business etiquette around the world can be found at: http://www.cyborlink.com/besite.

Table 3.3 shows the scores for 53 countries/regions on each of Hofstede's dimensions. Figure 3.1 presents a diagrammatic map of countries when individualism and power distance are combined. This combination of cultural dimensions illustrates patterns or clusters

Figure 3.1 A map of 53 countries ranked on power distance and individualism indices

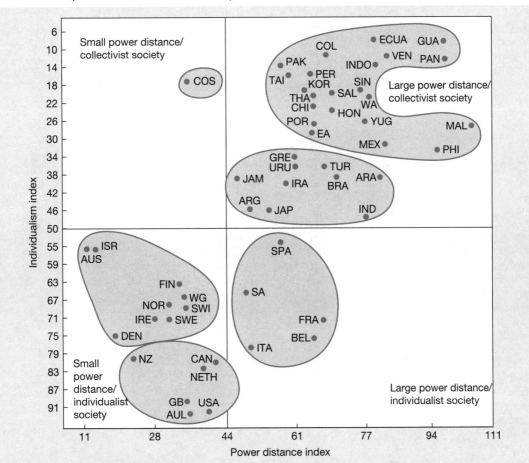

(Source: Hofstede, 1980.[2] Reprinted from Motivation, leadership, and organization: do American theories apply abroad? Summer, Geert Hofstede, *Organizational Dynamics*, pp. 42–63, copyright © 1980, with permission from Elsevier.)

Table 3.3 Values of Hofstede's cultural dimensions for 53 countries or regions

Country/region	Dimensions				
	Power distance	Uncertainty avoidance	Individualism	Masculinity	Long-/short-term orientation
Arab countries[a]	80	68	38	53	–
Argentina	49	86	46	56	–
Australia	36	51	90	61	31
Austria	11	70	55	79	31
Belgium	65	94	75	54	38
Brazil	69	76	38	49	65
Canada	39	48	80	52	23
Chile	63	86	23	28	–
Colombia	67	80	13	64	–
Costa Rica	35	86	15	21	–
Denmark	18	23	74	16	46
East African region[b]	64	52	27	41	25
Ecuador	78	67	8	63	–
Finland	33	59	63	26	41
France	68	86	71	43	39
Great Britain	35	35	89	66	25
Greece	60	112	35	57	–
Guatemala	96	101	6	37	–
Hong Kong	68	29	25	57	96
India	77	40	48	56	61
Indonesia	78	48	14	46	–
Iran	58	59	41	43	–
Ireland	28	35	70	68	43
Israel	13	81	54	47	–
Italy	50	75	76	70	34
Jamaica	45	13	39	68	–
Japan	54	92	46	95	80
Malaysia	104	36	26	50	–
Mexico	81	82	30	69	–
Netherlands	38	53	80	14	44
New Zealand	22	49	79	58	30
Norway	31	50	69	8	44
Pakistan	55	70	14	50	0
Panama	95	86	11	44	–
Peru	64	87	16	42	–
Philippines	94	44	32	64	19
Portugal	63	104	27	31	30
Salvador	66	94	19	40	–
Singapore	74	8	20	48	48
South Africa	49	49	65	63	–
South Korea	60	85	18	39	75
Spain	57	86	51	42	19
Sweden	31	29	71	5	33
Switzerland	34	58	68	70	40
Taiwan	58	69	17	45	87
Thailand	64	64	20	34	56
Turkey	66	85	37	45	–
United States	40	46	91	62	29

Table 3.3 (*cont'd*)

Country/region	Dimensions				
	Power distance	Uncertainty avoidance	Individualism	Masculinity	Long-/short-term orientation
Uruguay	61	100	36	38	–
Venezuela	81	76	12	73	–
West African region[c]	77	54	20	46	16
West Germany	35	65	67	66	31
Yugoslavia	76	88	27	21	–
Overall mean	57	65	43	49	39
Standard deviation	22	24	25	18	22

[a] Saudi Arabia, Egypt, United Arab Emirates, Iraq, Kuwait, Lebanon and Libya.
[b] Ethiopia, Kenya, Tanzania and Zambia.
[c] Ghana, Nigeria and Sierra Leone.
(Source: Hofstede, 2001. © Geert Hofstede B.V.; quoted with permission.[2])

of countries that have a common history, such as the northern European cluster or the Anglo-Saxon cluster.

As shown in Figure 3.1, there is a relationship between individualism and power distance in societies. Those countries that are higher in collectivism also tend to be higher in power distance and those higher in individualism also tend to be lower in power distance.

Schwartz[8] also presented a two-dimensional representation of the cultural distance between 77 cultural groups, using all seven dimensions. In this map (see Figure 3.2), the arrows indicate the direction of increasing scores for each of the seven dimensions. This map illustrates distinct regional differences, with Western Europe being higher in egalitarianism and

Figure 3.2 Schwartz map

(Source: Republished with permission of Taylor & Francis Group LLC – Books, from *Understanding Culture: Theory, Research, and Application*, S. H. Schwartz, Psychology Press, copyright © 2009; permission conveyed through Copyright Clearance Center, Inc.)

autonomy. In contrast, the Middle East, Sub-Saharan African, and both South and Southeast Asia were higher in embeddedness and hierarchy.

The cultural relativity of management theories

Hofstede first raised concerns about the cultural relativity of management theories.[17] Management theories are rooted in the cultural context in which they were developed. Any simple direct transfer is problematic. For instance, Abraham Maslow's hierarchy of needs[18] and McClelland's theory of the achievement motive[19] are directly related to two dimensions of US culture: strong masculinity and individualism. People are motivated in an overtly conscious manner by extrinsic factors and the rewards that result from their actions. In contrast, Freudian theory, which has not been greatly applied by US management theorists, sees the individual as driven by the internal and largely unconscious interaction between the id, ego and superego. The superego (unconscious inner pilot) criticizes the thoughts and acts of the ego (conscious self-concept), which tries to control the id (unconscious forces). According to Hofstede,[17] Austria, the birthplace of Sigmund Freud and his theories, scores significantly higher than the US on uncertainty avoidance and lower on individualism. Freud's superego acts as an internalized, uncertainty-absorbing device. This may explain why motivation is more related to internalized social values.

Clashes in dominant solutions

Multinational and global companies need to consider the impact of culture, as cultural norms influence a wide range of work preferences, including perceptions for authority, leadership styles, fairness, interpersonal relationships, communication, and expectations of the organisation, and many other aspects of business. In terms of fairness perceptions, people in individualist cultures prefer equity-based rules in the distribution of rewards and punishments, whereas those in collectivist cultures tend to prefer equality rules (equal compensation regardless of effort) in individualist cultures. People compare their rewards for work against others in the same market. Extrinsic rewards

(e.g., bonuses, gifts, holidays, monetary incentives) are often more highly valued in masculine, individualistic countries, where there is also lower uncertainty avoidance. In contrast, intrinsic rewards are more valued in societies that are more feminine, and/or more collectivist, and/or with higher uncertainty avoidance. Further, the gap between CEO and worker pay is positively related to power distance and negatively related to individualism.[20] However, Hofstede's dimensions provide less explanation of the differences in CEO pay across countries, as other market-based factors exert a strong influence, such as legal regulations, ownership types and market-factors.

Differences in dominant solutions to problems within organizations are also evident. For instance, students of various nationalities were asked to write a diagnosis and solution to a conflict between the sales and product development departments. The French sought a solution from the chairperson, emphasizing hierarchy in problem-solving. The Germans saw the problem as the absence of formal rules and written procedures. The English saw the problem as a lack of interpersonal communication. According to Hofstede (p. 60),[2] 'the implicit model of the organization for most French was a pyramid (both centralized and formal); for German a well-oiled machine (formalized, but not centralized); and for most British a village market (neither formalized, nor centralized)'.

Organizational structures are also related to culture. In a matrix organization, for instance, there is a double hierarchical linkage (e.g., with a product division at the regional level and a subsidiary general manager at the country level). This structure is not accepted well by either the French or Germans. For the French, it violates the principle of unity of command. For the Germans, it thwarts their need for organizational clarity and is not acceptable unless individual roles inside the organization can be unambiguously defined.

Self-reliance versus dependence

Being self-reliant or ingroup dependent naturally involves assumptions about the self, as discussed in Chapter 2. For example, valuing elders in the community will tend to decrease the legitimacy of independence among younger age groups. Similarly, traditional sex roles promote the dependence of women.

Table 3.4 Self-reliance versus dependence

Hofstede's dimension	Influence on self-reliance/dependence
Individualism	■ Increases self-reliance
Power distance	■ Promotes dependence
Masculinity	■ Increases self-reliance
Uncertainty avoidance	■ Promotes dependence
Long-term orientation	■ Promotes dependence

Even social class may encourage dependence, where people in higher social classes behave patronizingly towards those in lower classes. People in collectivist cultures, especially those with higher power distance, often prefer more structured roles, with clearer directions and expect more paternalistic, caring supervisory relationships.

Self-reliant people find motivation and control within themselves, whereas dependent people need to find outside support, motivation and control. As summarized in Table 3.4, low power distance and uncertainty avoidance combined with high individualism and masculinity will be related to more self-reliance (e.g., the US and Australia) – that is, high power distance promotes dependence, whereas low power distance does not. The most extreme contrast to this is Latin countries, such as Chile, Portugal or Brazil (see Table 3.3).

Two assumptions are central in developing either self-reliance or dependence among individuals. The first basic issue is whether people have an external or an internal locus of control, as people with an internal locus of control have more self-reliance because they believe in their ability to manage their own world.[21]

Website link 3.3

Find out where you fall on the locus of control personality dimension by taking this quick and free online survey: **http://www.psych.uncc.edu/pagoolka/LocusofControl-intro.html**.

The second issue in relation to self-reliance versus dependence is the kind of family role that a particular culture favours. In Latin societies, the parent–child relationship is a very strong underlying model for interaction. Even in situations which are normally assumed to be between equals, people may unconsciously and spontaneously act in parent–child roles. For instance, in conflicts a superior will easily fall into the role of a 'critical' parent – in the terms of Eric Berne's transactional analysis[22,23] – leaving their counterparts to behave in the role of a 'compliant child' by obeying, or a 'rebel child', by leaving. Where parent–child roles underlie models of interaction, many relationships will be in the realm of dependence. Generally, functional relationships will be based on filial dependence, whereas dysfunctional relationships will develop from conflicting roles.

For people who come from societies where self-reliance is standard behaviour, it is extremely irritating not to be treated as an adult, with equal rights and obligations. Many aspects of the French culture favour dependence, with the major exception of a strong individualist orientation. This results in a pattern of varying dependence, where people constantly play a game of dispute and reconciliation in teamwork and true self-reliance can only be fostered by creative activity and/or working independently.

3.2 Culture-based attitudes towards action

This section draws together a wide range of differences in cultural assumptions to illustrate how these norms influence action and attitudes toward action. Cultural assumptions are reflected in both limited and complex action; however, the influence in actions that do not involve problem solving (e.g., repetitive and routine tasks) tends to be more remote, such as purchasing the toothpaste your parents bought. Non-routine tasks that require a more complex course of action are more directly influenced by cultural assumptions, because they:

1. Must be based on a clear sense of purpose (why act?).
2. Involve a largely unpredictable future, including elements of uncertainty and risk.
3. Need input from past experiences.
4. Imply the need to balance collective and individual interests.
5. Need to relate the hand to the brain, the heart and the mouth.

Expressed metaphorically, action (hand), in a cross-cultural perspective, can hardly be separated from how people think (brain), how they relate their wishes and desires to actions (located somewhere between brain, heart and mouth), and how they mix feelings (located clearly in the heart for most cultures) with deeds. Table 3.5 details the main differences across cultures in terms of attitudes towards action.

Most marketing and managerial action involves non-routine tasks that incorporate the elements listed above. This can be problematic in an international setting, as most interpretive clues are based on an individual's or organization's own cultural assumptions. Basic cultural assumptions, and combinations of these, have an influence on the way we cognitively evaluate real-world situations and issues. The following section

Table 3.5 Attitudes towards action

Basic problem/cultural orientations	Contrasts across cultures
1. Why act?	
(a) Doing/mastery	■ Nothing is impossible. It is unconscionable when one does nothing ('master of destiny').
(b) Being/subjugation to nature	■ Fate is responsible for most actions; we should not try to thwart it. One must accept their destiny ('subjugation').
2. What is action?	
(a) 'Speech' orientation	■ Speech is action. There are many paths to successful action.
(b) 'Deed' orientation	■ Speech is separate from action (do, not talk). There is a clear sequencing of the steps for successful action.
3. How to relate thinking to action?	
(a) Ideologism	■ *Take* decisions from a range of solutions. Thinking patterns, style of speech and actions selected within the context of broad ideological principles (religious, political, social, legal, etc.).
(b) Pragmatism	■ *Make* decisions by problem solving. Precise issues must be addressed and a practical attitude is favoured to achieve concrete results.
(c) Intellectual styles	■ Differences in assigning a dominant role to theory (Teutonic style), empirical evidence (Saxonic style), speech (Gallic style), or modesty and virtue (Nipponic style) in assessing truthful propositions for action.
4. How to relate wishes and desires to action?	
(a) 'Wishful thinking' orientation (WT)	■ Emphasize enthusiasm, imagination of the future.
(b) Non-WT	■ Emphasize the principle of reality. Desires and wishes are checked objectively against constraints of the real world.
5. How to relate feelings to action?	
(a) Affective (A)	■ People believe that mixing feelings and actions is legitimate and useful.
(b) Neutral (N)	■ People separate feelings from actions. They separate friendship from business.
6. How to deal with rules?	
(a) Practical rules	■ Rules are made and respected, discussed and implemented quite strictly.
(b) Ideal rules	■ There is discrepancy between the 'ideal' rules and what people actually do. Exploring and bypassing rules is an accepted practice.

illustrates the ways in which we all construct our reality, within our native cultural community.

Why act?

The first problem in Table 3.5 examines the cultural influences on assumptions around the value of 'acting'. Not everyone is preoccupied with doing, acting, being efficient and achieving tangible results that can be appraised by others. From an existential point of view this preoccupation with 'doing' is not really justified. In the long term, we will all be dead.

Montesquieu's 1748 description of the Indians and Thais as *indolent nations* in *The Spirit of Laws* (pp. 228–9), illustrates a 'being' orientation:

The Indians believe that repose and non-existence are the foundations of all things, and the end in which they terminate. Hence they consider entire inaction as the most perfect of all states, and the object of their desires. To the supreme Being they give the title of immoveable. The inhabitants of Siam (Thailand) believe that their utmost happiness consists in not being obliged to animate a machine or to give motion to a body.[24]

Not only are the Indians and Siamese (the Thai people) more 'being' oriented, they also have a quite different view of their relationship with nature from Westerners (i.e., subjugation to nature rather than mastery over nature). As noted previously, their religions include belief in reincarnation. Upon the death of the body, the soul transmigrates or is born again in another body. Life therefore is not seen as 'one shot', but more as a cyclical phenomenon. This puts less pressure on people to be 'doing' oriented and means there is more inducement to *be* blameless and virtuous, since it is these factors that will influence the status of further reincarnations. Inaction is one of the surest ways to lead a blameless life. While this orientation helps the individual to cope with reality, it may be less helpful for the complexities of living in a larger social system.[25]

Both being and doing orientations have their merits and it is obviously difficult to find supportive evidence as to whether we are reincarnated or not. Thus, it is more interesting to investigate the consequences for action. When Kumar (p. 59)[25] discusses the consequences of Brahmanism in India, he points out that the emphasis on 'thought' (being) over 'action' (doing) means that implementation receives less attention: there is 'an emphasis on developing grandiose schemes without concern for implementation at all'.

Fatalism is a belief that directly influences action, not necessarily in terms of acting less, but rather in terms of acting *differently*. It clearly posits the locus of control as being outside, in the metaphysical environment. It also provides convenient explanations for unpredictable events, which allow people to resume activity quickly after major catastrophes (earthquakes, fires, car accidents). Fatalism makes mourning easier and facilitates the acceptance of strongly negative personal events, such as a bankruptcy.

Website link 3.4

How does a determinist cross the street? **http://www. naturalism.org/fatalism.htm#How%20Determinists.**

What is action?

The second problem in Table 3.5 focuses on cultural assumptions around what constitutes 'acting'. Some cultures tend to classify words, speeches and, more generally, acts of communication as 'deeds'. In many cultures, there are popular sayings that effectively condemn speech on the basis that it is not real action ('do, not talk'). In the real world, life is more complicated. Communications are a category of act, and their potential influence on others is beyond doubt. But whether communication is considered as being significantly related to action differs across cultures.

The word 'poetry' comes from the Greek word *poio*, a verb meaning to 'make', to 'produce', to 'build'. This sheds some light on judgements of the usefulness of poetry based on different cultural assumptions. On one hand, poetry is seen as distinctly distant from action in the real world. On the other, poetry is seen as a direct source of inspiration for action. Indeed if a 'classical' model of action is assumed (i.e., one that is culturally European/Western based), the following sequence is expected to occur:

1. analysis of the problem and the issues at stake;
2. gathering of relevant information;
3. listing and evaluating possible solutions;
4. selecting the 'best' decision;

5. implementation: while the decision tends to be more individualized, the implementation process involves individual and collective action from diverse agents; and

6. appraisal of the outcome, control of the difference between target and actual outcomes, and feedback to a previous step in the sequence.

This sequence can be easily criticized as culturally non-universal. Even if we were to accept that this sequence is true, or in fact anything was 'true', it would still involve a great deal of cultural relativity. The Japanese have no word for decision making, and action/decision/control processes are viewed as implementation issues.[26] This leads to the Japanese first consulting each one of a large group of people at various levels in the organization, who all comment on how to do something (not necessarily on why).

How to relate thinking to action?

The third problem in Table 3.5 focuses on cultural assumptions around the relationship between thinking and 'acting'. In relating thinking to action, we need to consider:

1. Whether solutions are *taken* from a range of possible actions, or *made* deductively?
2. What information is relevant for action? Broadly, do *the parts always represent the whole*, or narrowly, *focus is the key to relevance* when acting.
3. What is the basis for *correct action*: (a) data; (b) theory; (c) personal conviction; (d) virtue because it is morally correct to think and do so?

Ideologists versus pragmatists

If future partners do not share common 'mental schemes', it is difficult for them to solve problems together. For instance, buyer and seller agreements will be easier if they share a joint view of the world, especially on the following points:

1. What is the relevant information for action?
2. How should this information be sought, evaluated and fed into the decision-making process?

Ideologists will use a wide body of ideas, Marxism or liberalism, for instance, that provide them with a formal and coherent description of the world. In an ideologist framework, every event is supposed to carry meaning. Typically, ideologists will *take* decisions – that is, pick a solution from a range of possible decisions (which are located outside the person who decides).

Conversely, pragmatists first consider the diversity of real-world situations, and then derive principles inductively. Reality is seen as a series of independent and concrete problems to be solved. The issues will make complete sense when related to practical, precise and even down-to-earth decisions. Typically, pragmatists will *make* decisions, that is, they will both decide and implement them. Decisions are enacted, not selected.

Triandis[27] suggests that complex traditional societies will tend to be ideologist, whereas pluralistic societies or cultures experiencing rapid social change will tend to be pragmatist. This distinction may also be traced back to the difference between the legal systems of *common law* (e.g., Australia, UK and US) and of *code law* (e.g., French, German and Italian). Whereas the common law favours legal precedents set by the courts and past rulings (cases), code law favours laws and general texts that are intended to build an all-inclusive system (or code) of written rules of law. Codes aim to formulate general principles that embody the entire set of particular cases.

The ideologist orientation, which is found in southern and eastern Europe, leads negotiators to focus on a set of principles before any detailed discussion on specific clauses of the contract. They have a tendency to prefer globalized negotiations in which all the issues are gathered in a 'package deal'.

The pragmatist orientation, which is found in northern Europe and most former UK colonies, leads negotiators to define problems of limited scope, then solve them one after the other. They tend to concentrate their thinking on supportable facts (e.g., deeds, not words; evidence, not opinions; figures, not value judgements) and are willing to reach practical decisions.

Communication may be difficult when partners do not share the same mental scheme. The most unlikely situation for success is an ideologist-oriented contractor/supplier who tries to sell to a pragmatist-oriented owner/buyer. The ideologist will see the pragmatist as being overly interested in trivial details, too practical, and incapable of looking at issues from a higher standpoint. Pragmatists will resent ideologists for being too theoretical, lacking practical sense, and being concerned with issues that are too broad to lead to implementable decisions.

What information is relevant for action? How should it be used?

The dimensions of ideologism and pragmatism are not mutually exclusive. For instance, it would be a mistake to consider Americans as pure pragmatists with no leaning towards ideology. They are pragmatic in that they identify problems clearly and precisely as 'issues' and collect evidence systematically. Their attitude is matter of fact. To be 'down to earth' is a positive expression, whereas its French equivalent is often pejorative. But they are also somewhat ideological in their free-market/individual oriented view of the world. This view is generally accepted without question, and also enshrined in their Constitution, anti-trust legislation and corporate law. It is therefore somewhat irrelevant to debate practical matters as an ideologist would. Ideology is rarely present on a daily basis when information directly relevant to action is gathered or discussed. Thus, they are more likely to be conscious of pragmatic considerations when ideology and ideas are the object of debate.

In international business negotiations, there is often a discussion of principles, which may lead to a substantive outcome. The fundamental skill of diplomats (who are, in many respects, experts in matters of culture) is to obtain the acceptance and underwriting of basic principles by their counterparts, the effectiveness of which is only apparent at a later date.

Dealing with desires and feelings

The fourth and fifth problems in Table 3.5 focus on cultural assumptions relating to our subjective reality and the role of emotions in public life. In Freudian terms, management is based on the principle of reality, and not on the principle of pleasure. Therefore, there is little interest in examining an individual's desires and feelings, which are considered to be purely subjective. However, in a cross-cultural perspective, desires and feelings are important. People have different ways of relating their actions to their desires and feelings. In this section, we discuss 'wishful thinking' (WT) orientation and affective versus neutral cultures.

How to relate wishes and desires to action?

Words and deeds may be classified in two separate categories or combined. They may be in opposition to each other, in that words are empty or hollow, or complementary, in that words influence and sometimes cause others to act. Most acts of authority are only words.

An important issue for cultural action styles is the problematic link between what one says and what one does. WT is based on, first, thinking, then, saying, how one wants things to be, not how they are. Since nobody knows exactly how things will be in the future, a non-WT-oriented person will try to say how he or she realistically thinks they will be, not how he or she wants them to be. WT is more inhibited in a culture that clearly divides words from deeds (do what you say, say what you do).

Where speech is considered an action, WT may become necessary to galvanize people towards an ideal and improbable future. WT is more prevalent in present-oriented cultures, as people do not worry so much about the future. WT is a convenient way to escape from the constraints of longer-term realities by focusing on the here and now. It dodges problems to be solved, and hides divergences and possible conflicts, at least in the short term.

WT is related to any action that deals with the future and with potential reality, including the listing of prices, bidding and negotiations, the management of delivery delays, attitudes towards new projects, and advertising campaigns where arguments may 'explain why' the audience should be convinced by the message.

> **Website link 3.5**
>
> Search for information about wishful thinking in American business: http://www.american.com/archive/2008/january-february-magazine-contents/the-dangers-of-wishful-thinking.

Affective versus neutral cultures

The contrast between affective and affectively neutral cultures is described by Trompenaars (p. 63):[7] 'Members of cultures which are affectively neutral do not telegraph their feelings but keep them carefully controlled and subdued. Neutral cultures are not necessarily cold or unfeeling, nor are they emotionally constipated or repressed.' Trompenaars classified countries on the basis of individuals' self-reported willingness to express their feelings openly if they felt upset about something at work. The highest neutrality was for the Japanese (83 per cent), followed by (the former West) Germany (75 per cent) and the United Kingdom (71 per cent). The Dutch (55 per cent) and Americans (40 per cent) expressed their emotions more easily. Finally, Italy (29 per cent) and France (34 per cent) were clearly more affective cultures, with more people agreeing they would express their feelings openly.[7]

The contrast between affective and neutral cultures is closely related to the being/doing divide in basic cultural assumptions and to dependence in the models of interaction. If people are strictly *doing* oriented they tend to disregard expressions of *being*. Feelings and affectivity are seen as *being* in the purely personal and private, individual domain. Thus, Anglo-Saxon and many East-Asian cultures tend to suppress these feelings and view their direct expression as inappropriate for effective interaction.

Extremes in either affective or neutral cultural orientations are problematic. On one hand, overly suppressed emotions and feelings can lead to flawed interaction and few results. People may discover quite late that personal antipathy is a major hurdle to interaction. On the other hand, open expression of emotion may cause offence and undue delays.

The feelings/action issue is important for the choice of partners to improve communications in marketing negotiations, managing sales personnel, establishing relationships with foreign distribution channels, or preparing locally appropriate advertising materials. Every culture has certain codes and rituals that allow for a compromise between the two extreme positions. What varies is the starting assumption:

1. Expressing emotions is legitimate and useful for action (affective cultures).
2. Expressing emotions needs to be separated from action (neutral cultures).

It needs, however, to be refined, by the addition of two further caveats. First, as emphasized by Trompenaars,[7] people have no fewer emotions in neutral cultures than in affective cultures; perhaps the contrary is true. If feelings and emotions are contained, they may build up and result in hidden negative feelings. Second, the influence of culture should not be overstated, as there is high variability in individuals' personality traits and interactions. More is universal than culture-specific in the area of feelings and emotions. Chapter 4 on language, culture and communication explores the issue of affectivity versus neutrality in more detail.

Coping with rules

The sixth and final problem in Table 3.5 is how to deal with rules. While this may seem to be straightforward, the way in which rules are interpreted is culturally bound.

Rules and basic assumptions

A rule is an authoritative regulation or direction concerning method or procedure. Rules are formalized norms that generally comprise a scale of sanctions according to the gravity of the breach. Rules can be made which are respected, discussed and implemented quite explicitly, or there may be a discrepancy between ideal rules and what people actually do, leading them to behaviour involving the exploring and bypassing of rules.

Some typical indicators of rule-related behaviour include how people deal with speed limits, traffic lights, queuing at banks or bus stations, filling out income statements, and so on. A naive interpretation of rules would be that they are made to be respected. The real function of rules is more complex. Written rules are fairly standard across cultures; it is the way we react to them that differs. Rules need to be interpreted on the basis of our cultural assumptions and interaction models (see Table 3.6):

1. A positive human nature orientation (HNO) leads to rules where sanctions are small and often positively reinforced; with a reward for respecting the rule being preferred to a penalty. People are trusted to respect rules and they are seen to gain benefit from them. Conversely, a negative HNO leads to rules where sanctions are high and severe enforcement is carried out. People cannot be trusted to respect rules, as human nature is seen as opportunistic and basically bad. There is no faith in objectivity.

2. The level of power distance in a particular society has an influence on both the design of rules and their implementation.[2] Low power distance results in people having input, in some way, to the design of rules. It also leads to rules being applied with a sense of fairness and equity to everybody, including those with more power in the society. In contrast, high power distance results in people being subject to rules that are designed and imposed by others. Furthermore, these rules apply more stringently to those with less power in society. The most powerful people are seen as being beyond the reach of rules that are designed to control 'ordinary people'.

3. Strong ingroup orientation (see Chapter 2) often leads to the syndrome that rules are 'applicable only here'. Rules do not need to be followed when outside their community.

4. The emphasis on guilt (*inner feeling* of responsibility for committing an offence) versus shame (a painful *emotion, directed to the outside*, resulting from an awareness of having done something dishonourable as a group member) influences behaviour toward rules, as well as the punishments and rewards associated with them.

Table 3.6 presents four stereotypical rule types and their relationship with HNO and power distance. In this case, the HNO assumption must be understood in a comparative way between the ruler and the ruled: 'good' means that the ruled view themselves as 'better' than or equal to the ruler; 'bad' means that the ruled view themselves as 'as bad' as or 'even worse' than their rulers.

Types of rules and rule-related behaviour

Anglo-rules, including those of northern European countries, are basically 'pragmatic' rules. People generally comply with the rule out of a sense of responsibility built on positive motivation. Rules are understood as helping society to work more smoothly and efficiently and everyone is supposed to benefit from their being respected. In this picture, people are universally at ease with their rules; even if they sometimes break them (nobody is perfect).

'Challengeable rules' are found in many parts of southern Europe (e.g., Italy and France) and South America (e.g., Brazil), where power distance is reasonably high and ordinary people view themselves as having a better nature than those at the top. Since rules are mostly directed at the population from the top, without 'instructions for use', people are expected to investigate the extent to which rules can be transgressed. The only way to explore a new rule is to breach it discreetly, in order to know whether it is intended to be applied seriously, or whether it is simply one more empty threat that is neither enforced nor respected.

'Mechanical rules' are found in the German or Swiss case. They are made democratically because power distance is low, but there is distrust of people. Sanctions are explicit and implemented fairly literally. Respect for rules has a fairly mechanical and automatic side: they are applied literally.

The final stereotypical case is found in many developing with high power distance and negative assumptions as to the nature of human beings, powerful or not. Rules are often very strict, formal and somewhat unrealistic. Chapter 10 develops the example of foreign exchange control systems, which lead to bypassing rules by over- or under-invoicing. Oppressive rules oblige people to bypass the law and encourage rulers towards corrupt behaviour, in that they can implement un-implementable rules with some leniency in exchange for a bribe. Oppressive rules lead to a high discrepancy between what people

Table 3.6 Type of rules and behaviour according to HNO and power distance

		Power distance	
		Low	High
Human nature orientation	Good	Pragmatic rules (responsible compliance)	Challengeable rules (exploring behaviour)
	Bad	Mechanical rules (automatic compliance)	Oppressive rules (bypassing behaviour)

say they will do and what they actually do. This leads to a sort of systematic social schizophrenia, where we might see police changing money in the illegal parallel exchange market. Official rules can be complicated by opportunistic behaviour and the level of difficulty in obeying them. It is relatively easy to see local patterns of dealing with rules in any country. An examination of the basic rules relating to the functioning of society, such as traffic, queuing, and taxation, will quickly illustrate how rules are actually implemented.

People who favour universal rules are characterized by an inner compliance dynamic based on guilt, that is, self-reproach caused by an inner feeling that one is responsible for a wrong or offence. The moral punishment is to a large extent internalized within the psyche as in the Freudian concept of *Schuld* (in German: debt, fault, culpability). Conversely, people who favour relative rules are characterized by an external compliance dynamic. In this case it has to do with losing face, having one's honour threatened, and risking rejection by the ingroup members. Local rules are territory bound and concern breach of loyalty to the ingroup.

Adopting a more open view of how people attribute meaning to rules makes sense for a large array of international marketing issues. Consumer behaviour is influenced by, rules on waiting, attitudes towards queuing, theft from stores by consumer or sales staff, the attention paid by consumers to instructions for use (e.g., pharmaceuticals and food), the attitude towards filling in market research questionnaires, giving truthful information. In fact, any ethical issue that involves social responsibility of manufacturers, service providers or consumers have to be examined with a view to their cross-cultural relativity.

3.3

Cultural assumptions and actual behaviour

As previously explained, all societies face common problems, and although there is a dominant solution, alternatives are always present. These alternatives can combine in a dialectic way. Japanese people are often depicted as collectivist and the Americans as individualist, but there are limits to this distinction. Who is more humane, more personal and more sensitive in interpersonal relations, more attentive and under-

standing than the average Japanese person? Who cares more about the wider community than the average American, whose objective is to 'socialize in the community'? In the United States the word 'community' is used extensively. Indeed Americans and Japanese share a common problem: that of combining individual actions and collective undertakings.[4]

This problem may be solved only by a process which is essentially dialectic. In any society there exists a dominant cultural assumption about what the *first* priority should be: either the individual (as in the United States), or the group (as in Japan) is the basic survival unit. Then come the secondary cultural assumptions, which complement the basic assumption. In the US the community is where people integrate to build a common society, and their reciprocal links should be strictly and explicitly codified. In Japan, the utmost level of sensitivity must be developed in interpersonal relations, so that the working of the group is kept as smooth as possible.

The basic cultural assumptions described in the previous sections are in fact deep-rooted beliefs that generate basic values. Indirectly they guide our daily behaviour, but they may also clash with it. By their very nature, they are subconscious, as is the process by which they shape our interaction with others and our conduct. However, there is some leeway for other sources of influence. For instance, we use social representations to make decisions. We are influenced by other values and other standards of demeanour, such as work rules, company codes of conduct, lifestyles or friendship patterns which work closer to the surface than basic cultural assumptions. These standards of demeanour help people to manage adjustments in the short term. They change over much shorter periods of time (10 or 20 years) than basic cultural assumptions (probably formed over centuries). This leads us to question the extent to which less profound levels of culture influence people, such as corporate culture or educational culture.

Multinational companies (MNCs) offer their employees many opportunities for intercultural exchange and, therefore, we might expect the values shared by executives in MNCs to converge. In order to grasp differences in cognitive styles, Laurent asked managers of different nationalities to indicate their agreement or disagreement with the following statement (p. 86):[28] 'It is important for a manager to have at hand precise answers to most of the questions that his subordinates may raise about their work.' Only 10 per cent of Swedes agreed, in contrast, 66 per cent of Italians and 53 per cent of French believe managers should have precise answers to most of their subordinates' questions. Most Anglo-Saxon and northern European people tend to see managers as problem solvers, whereas Latin and Asian people see them more as *experts*. These differences were observed in people working in their home country. In a later study Laurent[29] asked the same question of executives who had been working for a long time in MNCs where teams had been built up from a large number of different nationalities. We might expect a decrease in the differences between national groups of managers, but the situation is exactly the opposite. When a corporate culture tries to shape a manager's (or even an employee's) daily behaviour, it may look as if it succeeds (because people are concerned about their job and career), but it only scratches the surface. Moreover, since this is forced upon them, not only does it fail to change basic cultural assumptions, but even reinforces them.

Does this mean that international experience has no effect on managers? It is more likely that international experience will influence our 'current view' of the way the business world works than the basic cultural assumptions that guide our behaviour. For instance, a study of Japanese and Korean managers' views on marketing tactics found the importance of brand names and superior product design were more similar in firms that had a high level of internationalization than those whose focus was domestic.[30] Thus, changes occur in the realm of organizational learning, rather than in our fundamental cultural assumptions.[31]

Questions

1. What do you think the cultural roots to personal modesty might be?

2. Which examples would you suggest to exemplify American individualism?

3. In many countries there is an institution called 'parliamentary democracy'. On which basic cultural values is it based, in your opinion? Is there a relationship between the development of marketing and parliamentary democracy?

4. Given country scores on Hofstede's five dimensions, what do you expect would be the problems encountered by a typical boss from country X in managing a typical employee from country Y (even at the risk of some stereotyping and sweeping generalizations)?
   (a) An American boss managing Japanese subordinates.
   (b) A Japanese boss managing French subordinates.
   (c) A French boss managing Swedish subordinates.
   (d) A Swedish boss managing Japanese subordinates.

5. A conversation is in progress between a British manager and a French manager concerning a common (large) project. The project is at a very early stage (examining its feasibility, setting deadlines for construction, planning of steps in building process, etc.). The Frenchman is very enthusiastic and argues: 'Let's go, we can do it; *impossible n'est pas français!*' ['impossible is not a French word']. The Englishman feels somewhat uneasy about the turn of the conversation. Why?

6. Are there Japanese individualists? Why?

7. A sign indicates: 'Parking time limited to 10 minutes. Be fair.' Which views of time and rules does this reveal? Try to imagine signs with different information for people who have a different approach to rules.

References

1. Hall, Edward T. (1959), *The Silent Language*. New York: Doubleday.
2. Hofstede, Geert (2001), *Culture's Consequences* (2nd edn). Thousand Oaks, CA: Sage Publications.
3. Inglehart, R. (1997), *Modernization and Postmodernization: Cultural, Economic, and Political Change in 43 Societies*. Princeton, NJ: Princeton University Press.
4. Kluckhohn, Florence R. and Frederick L. Strodtbeck (1961), *Variations in Value Orientations*. Westport, CT: Greenwood Press.
5. Schwartz, Shalom (2004), 'Beyond individualism/collectivism: New cultural dimensions of values', in U. Kim, H. C. Triandis, C. Kagitcibasi, S. C. Choi, and G. Yoon (eds), *Individualism and Collectivism: Theory, Method, and Applications*. Thousand Oaks, CA: Sage, pp. 85–119.
6. House, Robert J., P. J. Hanges, M. Javidan, P. W. Dorfman and V. Gupta (eds) (2004), *Culture, Leadership, and Organizations: The GLOBE Study of 62 Societies*. Thousand Oaks, CA: Sage.
7. Trompenaars, F. (1993), *Riding the Waves of Culture: Understanding Cultural Diversity in Business*. London: Economist Books.
8. Schwartz, S. H. (2009), 'Culture matters: National value cultures, sources and consequences', in C.-Y. Chiu, Y. Y. Hong, S. Shavitt and R. S. Wyer, Jr. (eds), *Understanding Culture: Theory, Research and Application*. New York: Psychology Press, pp. 127–50.
9. Smith, P. B., S. Dugan and F. Trompenaars (1996), 'National Culture and the Values of Organizational Employees: A Dimensional Analysis across 43 Nations', *Journal of Cross-Cultural Psychology*, 27 (2), 231–64.
10. McSweeney, B. (2002), 'Hofstede's Model of National Cultural Differences and their Consequences: A Triumph of Faith – A Failure of Analysis', *Human Relations*, 55, 89–118.
11. de Mooij, Marieke and Geert Hofstede (2002), 'Convergence and Divergence in Consumer Behavior: Implications for International Retailing', *Journal of Retailing*, 78 (1), 67–9.
12. Søndergaard, Michael (1994), 'Hofstede's Consequences: A Study of Reviews, Citations and Replications', *Organization Studies*, 15 (3), 447–56.
13. de Mooij, Marieke and Geert Hofstede (2011), 'Cross-Cultural Consumer Behavior: A Review of Research Findings', *Journal of International Consumer Marketing*, 23, 3–4, 181–92.
14. Singelis, Theodore M., Harry C. Triandis, Dharm P. S. Bhawuk, and Michele J. Gelfand (1995), 'Horizontal and Vertical Dimensions of Individualism and Collectivism: A Theoretical and Measurement Refinement', *Cross-Cultural Research: The Journal of Comparative Social Science*, 29 (3), 240–75.
15. Shavitt, Sharon, Ashok K. Lalwani, Jing Zhang, and Carlos J. Torelli (2006), 'The Horizontal/Vertical Distinction in Cross-Cultural Consumer Research', *Journal of Consumer Psychology*, 16 (4), 325–56.
16. Steenkamp, Jan-Benedict E. M., Frenkel ter Hofstede, and Michel Wedel (1999), 'A Cross-National Investigation into the Individual and National Cultural Antecedents of Consumer Innovativeness', *Journal of Marketing*, 63 (April), 55–69.
17. Hofstede, Geert (1980), 'Motivation, Leadership and Organization: Do American Theories Apply Abroad?', *Organizational Dynamics* (Summer), 42–63.
18. Maslow, A. H. (1954), *Motivation and Personality*. New York: Harper.
19. McClelland, D., J. Atkinson, J. Clark and E. Lowell (1953), *The Achievement Motive*. New York: Appleton-Century-Crofts.
20. Grenness, Tor (2011), 'The impact of national cultures on DEO compensation and salary gaps between CEOs and manufacturing workers', *Compensation & Benefits Review*, 43 (2), 100–108.
21. Rotter, Julian B. (1966), 'Generalized Expectancies for Internal Versus External Control of Reinforcement', *Psychological Monographs*, 80 (1), 1–28.
22. Berne, Eric (1961), *Transactional Analysis in Psychotherapy*. New York: Grove Press.
23. Berne, Eric (1964), *Games People Play*. New York: Grove Press.
24. Montesquieu, Charles de (1748), *The Spirit of Laws* (Thomas Nugent, Trans.) (6th edn). Dublin: McKenzie and Moore.
25. Kumar, Rajesh (2000), 'Confucian Pragmatism Vs. Brahmanical Idealism: Understanding the Divergent Roots of Indian and Chinese Economic Performance', *Journal of Asian Business*, 16 (2), 49–69.
26. Lazer, William, Shoji Murata, and Hiroshi Kosaka (1985), 'Japanese Marketing: Towards a Better Understanding', *Journal of Marketing*, 49 (Spring), 69–81.
27. Triandis, Harry C. (1983), 'Dimensions of Cultural Variation as Parameters of Organizational Theories', *International Studies of Management and Organization*, XII (4), 139–69.
28. Laurent, André (1983), 'The Cultural Diversity of Western Conceptions of Management', *International Studies of Management and Organization*, XII (1–2), 75–96.
29. Laurent, André (1989), 'Cultural Shock', in *European Foundation for Management Development Annual Conference*. Marseille.
30. Lee, Jangho, Thomas W. Roehl, and Soonkyoo Choe (2000), 'What Makes Management Style Similar and Distinct across Borders? Growth, Experience and Culture in Korean and Japanese Firms', *Journal of International Business Studies*, 31 (4), 631–52.
31. Kim, Daniel H. (1993), 'The Link between Individual and Organizational Learning', *Sloan Management Review*, 36 (1), 37–50.

Appendix 3

Teaching materials

A3.1 Critical incident

An American in Vietnam

An American in Vietnam recalls an illuminating story told him by a Vietnamese who complained about a lack of understanding between the two allies. They were discussing the fate of a province chief named Vong, once hailed by the Americans as the best province chief in Vietnam. Vong was accused of embezzling some 300,000 American dollars earmarked for an airstrip, and was tried and sentenced to be executed. It seemed a harsh sentence, considering the corruption prevalent at the time, and the American asked the Vietnamese if he agreed.

'No', the Vietnamese said, 'Vong should be executed because he's a stupid man.'

'Stupid? Because he got caught?' the American asked.

The Vietnamese shook his head impatiently. 'No, no, not because he took the money', he said. 'That is not important. But you know what this stupid man did? He pacified six more hamlets than his quota. This caused the general who gave him the quota to lose face, and that is stupid.'

The perplexed American said, 'In America, he'd get a medal for exceeding his quota.' The Vietnamese shook his head and said, 'You Americans will never understand the Vietnamese.'

Question

What aspects of the incident are significant in describing the difference in opinion between these two persons?

(Source: Weeks *et al.*, p. 22.¹)

A3.2 Rationales for Section A2.1 (cross-cultural scenario) and Sections A2.2 and A2.3 (cross-cultural interaction)

A2.1 Scenario: Inshallah

This scenario can best be understood by first appreciating the very different views in US culture and Saudi culture concerning 'locus of control'. In the US it is believed that, ultimately, people are responsible for their own destiny. If something goes wrong, it is believed, it is frequently possible for the individual to *do* something (that is, to change certain behaviour) to bring about the desired outcome. In Saudi Arabia, and indeed throughout the Arab world, people are taught from an early age that all things are subject to the direct will of Allah. All plans for the future (including, of course, business plans) are viewed with a sense of inevitability and will be realized only if God wills it. This is not to say that people in the Arab world would not work hard to help bring about the desired results. Rather, they believe that despite the effort, the desired ends will not happen unless God is willing. Perhaps Stefan would have been less frustrated if he had translated *inshallah* to mean 'if possible' or 'God willing' rather than as a knee-jerk response used to absolve oneself of all responsibility for one's actions.

(Source: Ferraro, p. 162.[2] Reproduced with permission.)

A2.2 Interaction: engineering a decision

1. There is little evidence for this in the story. While the financial benefits are relevant, to Mr Tanaka they are probably a minor consideration in the situation. Please choose another response.
2. It is quite probable that coming from a male-dominant Japanese society he does think it odd that Mr Legrand should mention his wife's opinion. However, the decision not to go to the Middle East also appears to be Mr Legrand's personal inclination so this does not fully account for Mr Tanaka's bewilderment. There is another explanation. Please choose again.
3. It is unlikely that Mr Tanaka would consider this. There are factors far removed from personal gain dominating his concern. Please choose again.
4. This is the most likely explanation. In Japanese and many other collectivist societies a person is defined much more as a collection of roles (parent, employee, servant, official) than by his or her individual identity. Therefore, fulfilling these roles to the best of one's ability is regarded as more important than one's personal inclinations. Thus, Mr Tanaka would see that Mr Legrand's responsibility as a company employee would be to accept the position whether or not he is personally happy about the idea. Mr Legrand's refusal is thus bewildering and makes him think that his belief in Mr Legrand's dedication has been completely misplaced. Mr Legrand, however, comes from a culture where individual freedoms are highly valued and so exercises his right to refuse the offer with little compunction. The cultural conflict thus resides in different strengths of values applied to the roles occupied by a person in the culture.

(Source: Brislin *et al.*, pp. 177–8.[3] Republished with permission of Sage Publications Inc. Books, from *Intercultural Interactions: A Practical Guide*, Richard W. Brislin, Kenneth Cushner, Craig Cherrie and Mahealani Young, 2nd ed, copyright © 1986; permission conveyed through Copyright Clearance Center, Inc.)

A2.3 Interaction: opening a medical office in Saudi Arabia

1. It is unlikely that people would sign up solely to satisfy a newcomer's feeling. There is a better explanation. Please select again.
2. If there is a considerable time lag between when a person makes a decision and the action upon it, it is possible that they may change their mind. However, there is no indication in the incident to support this. Please select another response.

3. Units of time reference differ markedly between Arab and American cultures. To an American, the major unit of time is five minutes. Fifteen minutes is a significant period of time. To an urban Arab, the unit of time that corresponds to our five-minute block is fifteen. Thus, when the Arab is 30 minutes late (by the clock), he is not even ten minutes late by his standards. This is the best answer. Tom's patients may still arrive.

4. While the patients may be seeing their own traditional healers, they would not necessarily do so in the strict sequence suggested by this alternative. There is a more precise explanation. Please choose again.

Appendix references

1. Weeks, William H., Paul B. Pedersen, and Richard W. Brislin (1987), *A Manual of Structured Experiences for Cross-Cultural Learning*. Yarmouth, ME: Intercultural Press.
2. Ferraro, Gary P. (1990), *The Cultural Dimension of International Business*. Englewood Cliffs, NJ: Prentice Hall.
3. Brislin, Richard W., Kenneth Kushner, Craig Cherrie and Mahealani Yong (1986), *Intercultural Interactions: A Practical Guide*. Newbury Park, CA: Sage.

4

Language, culture and communication

Language plays a central role in marketing communications when they take place in an international and multilingual context, since communication styles, as well as world views, are deeply influenced by the structure of languages. Communication can never be language-free and language is obviously a major component of culture. However, it is often under-emphasized in the international business literature, for several reasons:

1. Language seems to be translatable through dictionaries, professional translators and even online translators. Unfortunately, part of the message – that which is culturally unique – is lost in the translation process: as the Italian proverb says *traduttore, traditore*, literally translated as, 'translator, traitor'. Further, online translators lack the context of the message that gives it meaning, as will be elaborated in this chapter.
2. International business literature focuses on decision making and strategy formulation, rather than the implementation of decisions. The logic of the planning stage can overlook the significance of language and communication, as language is most important in the implementation phase where we interact with buyers, employees, colleagues and superiors.
3. An understandable Western bias, since English has traditionally been the *lingua franca* (the working language) of international business. Consequently, native speakers of English have no real motivation to learn foreign languages. There is much

more motivation for people from China, France, Germany, Italy and Japan to take the question of language seriously.

Fortunately, awareness is even more necessary than knowledge in relation to the impact of language and communication differences on international business. Given the variety of national and regional languages, one cannot expect to be able to speak and write them all. Even multilingual businesspeople will frequently be faced with language contexts in which they have little or no proficiency. What is needed then is awareness that large chunks of reality will always be partly hidden from non-native speakers. Accordingly, we focus on how linguistic/cultural groupings, through words or language structure, express a definite world view; *eine Weltanschauung* as the Germans express it.

In this chapter we review the main aspects of language and communication that have both a direct and an indirect impact on international business operations, including:

1. verbal communication styles and their relationship to contextual factors;
2. non-verbal communication, especially through gestures as well as eye and body language;
3. the way language shapes and reflects particular world views;
4. the Internet; and
5. ways of dealing with language differences in international business.

4.1

Verbal communication: the role of context

'Verbal' implies words and sentences and, in most of what follows, spoken discourse, rather than written communication, which is discussed in more detail in Chapter 13 when we focus on advertising. Verbal language is often thought to be quite explicit; however, the extent to which the actual words can contain the full message differs by cultures. Linguistic differences are often perceived to be one of the main causes of intercultural communication misunderstandings, though certainly not the only ones. Non-verbal communication, which helps us to understand the communication, is likely to exacerbate any misunderstandings.

A first major distinction in cross-cultural, language-based communication is whether the messages sent by the speaker are explicit: that is, can they be taken literally rather than interpreted 'in context'? Setting messages 'in context' would imply that what is literally said has to be in some way reinterpreted using various cues taken from the context, particularly the cultural background of the speaker. When differences in the coding/decoding process are ignored by communicators, they may persist throughout the whole interaction process. Instead of disappearing, they may become more marked when people are better acquainted with each other.

Language-based communication 'in context'

When we think about communicating, we first think of the verbal mode of communication. Phrases and words in a single language have – more or less – a precise meaning; or at least this is the necessary assumption for believing that a listener can receive a clear message from a speaker. This assumption allows us to avoid the time-consuming task of constantly verifying that the message received is the same message that was sent. However, effective communication incorporates several elements:

1. Even in an exchange that is primarily verbal, part of the message is non-verbal, including gestures, gesticulations and attitudes. It is important to know the extent that non-verbal/implicit messages *mix* with verbal/explicit messages.

2. Communication integrates feedback mechanisms to verify or improve the clarity of messages. In many cultures it is important to check the accuracy of the communication by multiple means, including repetition, paraphrases and interruptions.

3. In most cases communication is dependent on its context, including who says it and where and when it is said. Contextual factors may change what seems to be said literally.

The concept of context brings together the sum of mechanisms that allow the message to be understood in relation to the beliefs or standards shared by a group of people within a given culture. In his collection *The Snows of Kilimanjaro*, Ernest Hemingway[1] tells a story, entitled 'A Day's Wait', in which a young boy is told that he has a fever of 102°F (approximately 38.9°C), though he does not know that the temperature was measured on this scale. Since he had previously been in France, he thinks of the temperature as being on the Celsius temperature scale, and asks: 'About how long will it be before I die?' His mother does not understand his interpretation and explains that people do not die of a fever of 102. The young boy goes on arguing: 'I know they do. At school in France, the boys told me you can't live with 44 degrees. I've got 102.' Finally his mother understands that he has been waiting all day to die and she explains that, like kilometres and miles, temperature can be measured on different scales, and what is 37 degrees on one thermometer is 98 on another.[1] While almost all verbal messages involve some element of contextual information, cultures differ in the extent to which this information is central to understanding the message.

Cultural norms: High- to low-context

The emphasis on the role of context in cross-cultural communication was highlighted by Edward T. Hall, an American anthropologist (see Bluedorn,[2] for an interesting interview with Hall). Edward Hall (p. 79)[3] contrasted high-context and low-context cultures (see Box 4.1), in the following way:

A high-context (HC) communication or message is one in which most of the information is either in the physical context or internalized in the person, while very little is in the coded, explicit, transmitted part of the message.

A low-context (LC) communication is just the opposite; i.e., the mass of the information is vested in the explicit code.

This indicates that an understanding of who the other person is (e.g., age, gender, dress, social standing) may be important to understanding and decoding the actual verbal message. It also indicates that the location (e.g., workplace, home, over dinner) and type of conversation (e.g., with friends, an informal chat with colleagues, a formal business meeting, a serious negotiation, a sales pitch) may also influence the way the verbal message is decoded.

One notion that may help to understand differences in context-related communication styles is the distinction between specific and diffuse styles/ communication. In low-context cultures, people tend to focus on specific issues and address their counterpart in a specific role (as a buyer for instance); not necessarily impersonally, but with a specific view of what the other has to do. In high-context cultures people generally address broader issues and move more easily between different conceptions of their counterpart (as a private person, as a buyer, as a potential friend). While this type of communication can be considered diffuse in style, it should not be equated with 'confused', even though people from high-context cultures may at times appear complicated to those from low-context cultures.

In low-context cultures people favour explicit messages. These messages are almost 'digital', in that the message can be interpreted quite literally, such as 'I can offer you a price of $140 per package of 12, to be delivered in cases of 144 within five weeks.' In this case, anything other than the 'words' is less important to the message.

The Swiss, for instance, have a reputation for being explicit and low in context. This implies a great deal of precision in the verbal aspect of communication and consistency across contexts. For instance, in Switzerland a speed limit is interpreted literally as just that. A speed limit of 120 kilometres an hour on motorways means that when a driver is caught speeding by the police, a speedometer error of 6 per cent is allowed and then the fine is given in proportion to the speed violation. Similarly, if a patient arrives late for a doctor's appointment in certain Swiss cantons, he or she should pay a cash penalty and reschedule the appointment if the doctor is unavailable.

These examples should be taken for what they are; not as illustrations of an unhealthy preoccupation with punctuality, exactness and respect for rules, but as evidence of a tight social order, a highly organized social system that is costly to run, but is also beneficial. In the case of the health service, a Swiss doctor who has made a preliminary assessment over the phone with a patient will schedule their time together very precisely. If each party makes an effort to keep the appointment, the result is a genuine saving. The patient will also avoid a long period in the waiting room, exposed to the germs of the other patients.

In high-context cultures the actual 'words' convey less of the message, as most of the information is within the person or situation. People from high-context cultures use implicit messages; therefore, they cannot communicate effectively unless they have a fairly good understanding of their conversation partner. In Japan the manner of speaking shifts in register between more than 20 subtly different forms

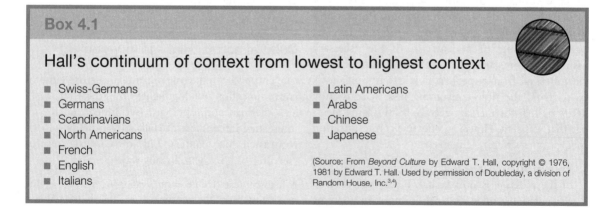

Box 4.1

Hall's continuum of context from lowest to highest context

- Swiss-Germans
- Germans
- Scandinavians
- North Americans
- French
- English
- Italians

- Latin Americans
- Arabs
- Chinese
- Japanese

(Source: From *Beyond Culture* by Edward T. Hall, copyright © 1976, 1981 by Edward T. Hall. Used by permission of Doubleday, a division of Random House, Inc.[3,4])

according to the age, sex and social position of the conversation partner, as well as the relative positions of the speakers in the social hierarchy (pupil/teacher, buyer/seller, employee/employer). Impersonal dealings (e.g., a person who comes for a day to discuss a contract rapidly gets to the heart of the matter, and uses the limited time available for discussion to focus on crucial matters) will make people from high-context cultures feel ill at ease and impede their conversation. People from high-context cultures tend to be more socially oriented, less confrontational, and more complacent about life than people from low-context cultures.[5]

Misunderstandings between cross-cultural communicators may be due to differences in opinion as to what is truly important. On the one hand, a person from a high-context, diffuse-communication culture will prefer spending some time chatting about life in general, with the very purpose of getting to know their negotiating partner. On the other hand, a person from a low-context, specific-communication culture will prefer to get straight down to business, with the aim of minimizing wasted time chatting about irrelevant matters.

There are also cultures that fall in the middle range, where people may alternate between an explicit/specific and an implicit/diffuse communication style. The UK and France have this tendency. The British practice of 'understatement' values complicity between people at the expense of clarity. French has often been considered a good language for diplomacy, because it can be alternately vague and precise, depending on the words and style chosen.

Empirical studies, especially qualitative research, generally support Hall's theory, although very few studies have examined more than one or two of the countries along the continuum of low- to high-

context described in Box 4.1. Despite this, small, but significant, differences in communication styles were found at the country level and larger effects were found when individual differences were taken into account. International business communication exposure and training may be one of the reasons for this, which may be especially important for those from low-context countries. High-context business communication is characterized by the following:

- a greater reliance on normative/cultural knowledge;
- a greater reliance on informal information and networks;
- a greater level of personal involvement; and
- more indirect message formation.[3]

The relationship between language and context

Contextuality of communication is partly related to whether the language itself expresses ideas and facts more or less explicitly. The Germanic (Germany, Switzerland and Austria), North American (Canada and the US) and Scandinavian cultures are all low-context, where people commonly use explicit communication. Both German and English languages allow for this, as they are precise and fairly context-free languages. This is especially true for 'international English'. The *lingua franca* of international business is context-free, rendering it impoverished, but at the same time precise. In contrast, Japanese is less precise than English or even French, as can be seen in Box 4.2. Personal pronouns are often not explicitly expressed in Japanese, and the number of tenses is much smaller, especially in comparison to French. In Japanese, both spoken words (that is,

---

Box 4.2

How to avoid saying 'no' in Japanese

Keiko Ueda[6] distinguishes 16 ways to avoid saying 'no' in Japanese, as the language does not have an explicit word for 'no'. The range of possible solutions varies from a vague 'no', to a vague and ambiguous 'yes', a mere silence, a counter-question, a tangential response, exiting (leaving), making an excuse such as sickness or a previous obligation, criticizing or refusing the question itself, saying 'No, but . . .' or 'Yes, but . . .', delaying answers ('We will write you a letter') and making apologies.

sounds) and written words (based on *kanji*, or pictographs) often have multiple meanings, so that the listener needs some kind of contextual clarification. Sometimes, Japanese people write the *kanji* (ideographs) briefly on their hand to make clear what they are saying.

Naturally it would be a mistake to say that certain languages are vague and others precise. The real world is more complex. All languages share a common objective; they have a common problem to solve, which is conveying meaning in an appropriate way from person to person. However, they achieve it differently, relying to varying degrees on precise words, structured grammar or, in contrast, on contextual indications of how ambiguous meanings should be made precise.

Website link 4.1

Search translation dictionaries, such as German to English, to examine the range of meanings associated with different verbs, like *absetzen*. Then search for words, such as the word *give*, in low-context countries, where we would expect fewer different definitions that can be used to define the context. Go to: **http://www.wordreference.com/**.

Cultural norms and communication styles

So far, the discussion has been mostly about low- and high-context types of communication and their relationship to precision in languages, as well as to the specificity or the diffuseness of the communication focus. However, verbal communication styles include a series of other elements, including the tone of voice, frequency and nature of conversational overlap, speed of speech, degree of apparent involvement in what one says, emphasis on talking versus emphasis on listening, as well as digressive and indirect speech styles. These are marked by cultural norms which implicitly define what is 'good' communication; 'good' meaning appropriate between members of the cultural community in so far as they share the same code.

There are at least three situations in which norms in cross-cultural communication are likely to be very different:

1. When communicators come from cultures that differ in their emphasis on the individual versus the group (see Chapters 2 and 3 for a more detailed explanation). In cultures where the emphasis is on the individual, the communication style is likely to focus on talking and self-assertion, whereas in cultures where the emphasis is on the group over the individual, a more modest, listening communication style is likely, all other things being equal (e.g., differences in personality characteristics).

2. When communicators rely on different norms to indicate interest or engagement in the conversation. The Latin style of interruption is a way of showing empathy and a shared interest in the topic. People from Latin cultures often find themselves speaking before others have finished their sentence. They believe that they are able to speak and listen at the same time. However, those from Anglo-Saxon and Nordic cultures often feel uncomfortable with these interruptions, regardless of their partner's intentions. These differences in communication styles reflect differing views of what is an appropriate interaction.

3. When communicators rely on different norms in their emphasis on talking versus listening. Latin cultures tend toward a 'two speakers' communication style, whereas the Japanese tend toward a 'two listeners' communication style. Japanese top executives often behave like a 'sphinx': they are almost pure listeners. Their role is to hear people, rather than speak. Consequently, Japanese supervisors often lack the public speaking skills expected in the West. In Japan silence is, in fact, valued as a full element of communication. It conveys messages, which, although implicit, may be interpreted through contextual factors.

These communication norms are often infused with positive or negative affect. For instance, silence may be experienced positively, as a moment for listening (especially to what is 'not said'), or negatively as a sign of possible loss of interaction, as a time-waster, or even as a sign of possible animosity on the part of the conversation partner. Many messages are included in silent communication, and, in general, Westerners tend to fear them much more than Asians. Similarly, conversational overlap may be seen as diluting the clarity of exchange, mere impoliteness, a lack of interest in what one says, or as childishness on the part of the overlapper. Conversely, it may be interpreted as a sign of empathy, a quick time-saving feedback, or even a necessary sign for pursuing the exchange.

As we hope to have shown, the rules for achieving 'good' communication are largely cultural or normative. The feeling that the flow of messages is going smoothly between two conversation partners is based on their ability to avoid a 'bad' communication, where messages would be altered or interrupted. The value judgement about 'good' or 'bad,' appropriate or inappropriate, is largely based on subconscious cultural standards. In a local setting people agree implicitly on the appropriate rules of communication. In an intercultural setting people have to allow themselves the informal opportunity to discuss and establish the rules of their communication (i.e.,

meta-communication). It is quite clearly a difficult task. Box 4.3 illustrates the substantial difficulties involved in clarifying the rules of communication about what friendship means and involves.

Communication rules can be especially sensitive when problems occur. For instance, Sugimoto[8] describes the two forms of apology in Japan, the *sunao* apology, which is a sort of gently submissive apology given with good grace; and a sincere form of apology, which is more from the heart. These apologies are codified in Japanese conduct manuals, which provide many readily usable apologetic expressions. In contrast, most Westerners tend to favour direct, spontaneous and unformulaic apologies, as sincerity is conveyed through original expression. A lack of understanding of the correct form of apology can dramatically change the intended meaning.

Box 4.3

The language of friendship

The American finds his friends next door and among those with whom he works. It has been noted that we take people up quickly and drop them just as quickly. Occasionally a friendship formed during school days will persist, but this is rare. For us (Americans) there are few well-defined rules governing the obligations of friendship. It is difficult to say at which point our friendship gives way to business opportunism or pressure from above. In this we differ from many other people in the world. As a general rule, in foreign countries friendships are not formed as quickly as in the United States, but go much deeper, last longer and involve real obligations. For example, it is important to stress that in the Middle East and Latin America your 'friends' will not let you down. The fact that they personally are feeling the pinch is never an excuse for failing their friends. They are supposed to look out for your interests. Friends and family around the world represent a sort of social insurance that would be difficult to find in the United States. We do not use friends to help us out of disaster as much as we do as a means of getting ahead – or, at least, of getting

the job done. The United States systems work by means of a series of closely tabulated favours and obligations carefully doled out where they will do the most good. And the least that we expect in exchange for a favour is gratitude.

The opposite is the case in India, where the friend's role is to 'sense' a person's need and to do something about it. The idea of reciprocity as we know it is unheard of. An American in India will have difficulty if he attempts to follow American friendship patterns. He gains nothing by extending himself on behalf of others, least of all gratitude, because the Indian assumes that what he does he does for the good of his own psyche. He will find it impossible to make friends quickly and is unlikely to allow sufficient time for friendships to ripen. He will also note that, as he gets to know people better, they may become more critical of him, a fact that he finds hard to take. What he does not know is that one sign of friendship in India is speaking one's mind.

(Source: Hall.[7] Reproduced with permission.)

4.2

Non-verbal communication

Much of what is exchanged in communication is implicit, rather than explicitly coded in the words expressed, which places non-verbal aspects largely within Edward Hall's 'context'.[3] The non-verbal aspects of communication, including the rules, rites and usage are culture-bound. For instance, Jordanians, as compared to Americans, make more eye contact, use a more direct body orientation and touch each other more often during their communications. Small differences, such as these, can impact perceptions of credibility and influence trust. Castillo and Mallard[9] found that Australian university students were more suspicious of Dutch actors using nonverbal behaviour that was inconsistent with Australian norms (e.g., more smiling, looking away and more hand movements) than those displaying normative behaviour; however, this bias in deception judgements was overcome when they were given culturally specific explanations prior to viewing the communication (such as, people from the Netherlands typically display more smiling, gaze aversion and hard/arm movements than Australians). Training in other cultures' specific non-verbal norms may significantly improve cross-cultural communication.

The non-verbal part of communication is largely within Hall's[3] 'context', which relies on the decoding of implicit messages. The elements of context can be separated into four components:

1. Non-verbal communication components (e.g., gestures, gesticulations, eye contact).
2. The analogical components of verbal messages (e.g., saying 'yes' in a way that makes it mean 'no', profuse thank you's that contain a meaning other than their 'digital' content precisely because of their excess).
3. Personal characteristics that are emitted unintentionally by the speakers (e.g., age, size, weight, sex, dress, status). All of these characteristics are encoded as part of the speakers' communication and decoded by the listener according to his or her own cultural programme.
4. Environmental components or the circumstances of the conversation (e.g., the type of place, atmosphere of the meeting, organization of the space, time frame).

Although all four of these components are processed together, this section focuses on the first aspect, non-verbal communication. However, we also recognize that analogical components, personal characteristics and the environment interact to produce culture-bound interpretations, as previously discussed. Box 4.4 lists a wide variety of non-verbal communication forms that have been examined in the literature. This list can serve as a starting place for examining your own interpretive frameworks.

Communication through gestures

Body language is an infinite source of differences and misunderstandings. The following account by Condon and Youssef[11] illustrates how a simple gesture can be understood to have a very different meaning from what was intended:

A professor who was of English origin and taught at the University of Cairo was sitting on his chair with his feet in front of him, the soles of his shoes facing toward his Egyptian students. A Muslim considers this to be an obvious insult. A student demonstration followed, and it was taken up by the newspapers, which denounced British arrogance and demanded the professor be sent back to his home country.

Website link 4.2

Search the Internet for differences in interpretation of hand gestures, such as this interesting video on cultural interpretations of body language on YouTube: http://www.youtube.com/watch?v= pxoB6MhmbIg&NR=1.

While most gestures have the potential to convey multiple meanings in intercultural settings, hand gestures are particularly problematic. The meaning of head gestures is also open to cultural difference. Moving the head from left to right is a sign of negation for most cultures; however it is a sign of affirmation for others, including India. In many Western countries patting a child on the head is a gesture of affection; however in Malaysia and many Islamic countries the head is considered to be the source of spiritual and intellectual activity and is therefore sacred.[12] As Box 4.5 shows, a simple piece of advice would be to avoid gesturing with the hand for fear of being

Box 4.4

Categories of non-verbal behaviour and specific behaviours

- **Smiling:** Smiling frequency and duration, extent of smile, facial agreement.
- **Eye contact:** Frequency, duration.
- **Raised brows:** Eyebrows raised/lowered.
- **Expressiveness:** Facial expressiveness, intensity of facial expression.
- **Nodding:** Nod frequency, nod rate.
- **Self-touch:** Duration, frequency of touching nose, lip, hand, face, head or hair.
- **Other-touch:** Hand on arm, shoulder, back, knee, or hand touch tendencies, touch duration, instrumental touch.
- **Hand/arm gestures:** Gesture and frequency.
- **Postural openness:** Legs open, folded, extended, arm wrap or clasped behind head, body position open/closed, making oneself look smaller or taller.
- **Postural relaxation:** Erect posture, lean backwards, relaxed posture, forward lean.

- **Body/leg shifting:** Movement frequency, leg re-crossing, shifting while listening or speaking.
- **Moving feet:** Position and movement of feet.
- **Distance:** Seated and standing distance to other.
- **Facing orientation:** Directness of orientation to interaction partner.
- **Vocal:** Pitch, loudness, animation, vocal tension.
- **Interruptions:** Interruption rate.
- **Overlaps:** Overlapping simultaneous speech.
- **Pausing/latency:** Response latency before speaking, frequency.
- **Filled pauses:** Use of sounds such as 'uh', pause frequency.
- **Speech errors:** Rate of verbal influency, speech errors.
- **Laughter:** Laughing frequency, relaxed laughter.
- **Rate of speech:** Rate of speech.

(Adapted from: Hall, Coats, Smith LeBeau.[10] Reproduced with permission.)

Box 4.5

Avoid gesturing with the hand, and yet . . .

In general, avoid gesturing with the hand. Many people take offence at being beckoned this way, or pointed at, even if only conversationally. In parts of Asia, gestures and even slight movements can make people nervous. If you jab your finger in the air or on a table to make a point, you might find that your movements have been so distracting that you have not made your point at all. Unintentionally, Americans come across as aggressive and pushy. Yet, in other parts of the world, particularly in Latin America or Italy, gesturing is important for self-expression, and the person who does not move a lot while talking comes across as bland or uninteresting. As always, watch what local people do. Or ask. While in England we once asked, 'How do you point out someone without pointing?' Our companion dropped a shoulder, raised his eyebrows and jerked his head to the side, as though tossing it in the direction he meant to point. Clear as day, he pointed without pointing.

(Source: Copeland and Griggs, p. 111.[13])

misunderstood, and remember to look around or even ask, as there are circumstances and places where hand gestures may be acceptable or even needed.

The manner of greeting people also differs greatly between cultures. While the French have the custom of shaking hands the first time they meet a person each day, most Anglo cultures (e.g., Australia, the USA, the UK) use this custom much less extensively. People from these cultures are surprised by this gesture, which is interpreted as excessive. However, surprisingly to the French, and many other cultures, some large stores in the USA (e.g., Walmart) employ 'greeters' at the entry/exit to their stores, where one of their main tasks is to welcome customers verbally and wish them a pleasant day. Similarly, in certain large Japanese department stores there are hostesses whose sole job is to bow to each customer who comes into the store. Anyone who has observed bowing rituals in Japanese railway stations or airports cannot help but be struck by their complexity, where the number, depth and synchronization are accurately codified. As Ferraro (p. 73)[14] emphasizes: 'In fact it is possible to tell the relative social status of the two communicators by the depth of their bows (the deeper the bow, the lower the status) ... The person of lower status is supposed to initiate the bow, and the person of higher status determines when the bow is completed.'

Physical contact and proxemics form another area of non-verbal communication, where large differences exist across cultures. Ferraro[14] offers a comprehensive description of the forms of non-verbal communication involving physical contact (e.g., kissing the cheek, lips, hand, or foot, taking a person by the arm, clasping the shoulders, pinching the cheek, shaking hands, tickling, stroking, patting). These gestures are subject to extremely varied codes of use, as they indicate differences in the realm of familiarity and appropriate sexual conduct. The kiss, regarded as normal between Russian men or Arab men, who may also hold hands in the streets, may appear shocking to Anglo-Saxons. Ferraro recounts his own experience while conducting anthropological field research in Kenya (pp. 85–6):

After several months of living and working with Kikuyu, I was walking through a village in Kiambu district with a local headman who had become a key informant and a close personal acquaintance. As we walked side by side my friend took my hand in his. Within less than 30 seconds my palm was perspiring all over his. Despite the fact that I knew cognitively that it was a perfectly legitimate Kikuyu gesture of friendship, my own cultural values (that is, that 'real men' don't hold hands) were so ingrained that it was impossible for me not to communicate to my friend that I was very uncomfortable.[14]

Different levels of physical contact between, and within, genders vary widely across cultures. For instance, the way in which men and women show their feelings for each other by kissing in public in some European cultures, such as France, may be shocking to other cultures, where this behaviour is seen as something that should be kept private. Similarly, men and women dancing in a closely intertwined position, as is often the case in social gatherings in Latin America, may seem indecent to some people from other cultures.

Facial expressions and communication with the eyes

Laughing and smiling, frowning and knitting one's brow are all communication. A smile can be a sign of satisfaction, of agreement, of embarrassment ... or even nothing at all. Certain cultures consider the spontaneous expression of attitudes and emotions by a facial expression to be normal, whereas in other cultures, particularly in Asia, it is more desirable not to show emotion. This has given rise to the impression of Asians as inscrutable and stoic. According to Morschbach (p. 308):

Self control, thought of as highly desirable in Japan, demands that a man of virtue will not show a negative emotion in his face when shocked or upset by sudden bad news; and, if successful, is lauded as *taizen jijaku to shite* (perfectly calm and collected) or *mayu hitotsu ugokasazu ni* (without even moving an eyebrow) ... The idea of an expression-less face in situations of great anxiety was strongly emphasized in the *bushido* (way of the warrior) which was the guide-line for samurai and the ideal for many others.[15]

Visual engagement, such as looking someone straight in the eyes, or, conversely, looking away, lowering the eyes, or turning them away when they meet someone else's, all have different meanings in different cultures. As Harris and colleagues[16] remarked, Arabs often look each other straight in the eyes because they believe that the eyes are the windows of the soul and that it is important to know the heart and soul of those one is working with. By contrast, Japanese children are taught in school not to look their teacher in the eyes, but to look at the level of the neck. When they become adults, it is considered a gesture of respect to lower their eyes in front of their superiors. Europeans have a tendency to look people straight in the eyes; like Americans and Australians, they tend to associate a lack of honesty with someone who looks away, and see it as potentially signalling an unfriendly, defiant, impersonal or inattentive attitude.

Dealing with unknown communication styles, especially non-verbal ones, is not an easy task. It is impossible to have an exhaustive knowledge of the full range of cultural interpretations of physical behaviour, gestures and contact, such as those listed in Box 4.4. It is difficult to behave correctly without extensive knowledge, as it must be recognized that part of the locally 'adequate' behaviour was learned in childhood, through rearing and education practices, and the learned physical demeanour is profoundly ingrained. However, it is clear that one can avoid major behavioural mistakes by researching the customs and norms of the specific cultures with which you are likely to interact. Awareness of differences allows us to *unlearn* or progressively discover the cultural relativity of our own verbal and non-verbal communication behaviour. The *unlearning process* is a condition for the learning process to begin.

Politeness and courtesy are especially important in intercultural communications. These social considerations are often conveyed by non-verbal elements of communication and, as such, are always high-context in any culture.[17] While there are some universal rules, such as not spitting at a person or slapping another's face, there are many more rules that are embedded in context, which varies across cultures. The word *courtesy* is derived from the word 'court', meaning the residence of a king or emperor. It emphasizes the kind of noble behaviour that enhances self-respect through the respect of others. Most languages have such a word. German, for instance, has the word *höflich* (polite), based on the German word for court, *hof*. However, it is important to note that foreigners are given latitude if they are ignorant of their customs, provided they are not arrogant and show consideration for their hosts. Modest, though firm, behaviour often facilitates the acceptance of cultural mistakes by the other party.

4.3
Language shaping our world views

As mentioned in Chapter 1, language interacts with our view of the world and, at least in part, conditions our experiences. This issue is especially important for advertisers, who need to describe consumer benefits, suggest product qualities and convince potential buyers, very rapidly, which is why international advertising is 'Whorfian', even if advertisers and their agencies are not conscious of it. Language in advertising is not only used to communicate the literal meaning; it is also used to convey a very rapid understanding or to evoke a mood or emotion. For example, life insurance advertising carries the implication of death, which may be taboo in certain cultures, or subject to the use of a particular vocabulary and subdued style. Advertising – especially when it comes to targets and strategies – is never as standardized as it may seem. For instance, a brand that is sold worldwide is not necessarily perceived as global in all countries. For example, although Coca-Cola is considered to be a global brand, it is often perceived as American in other countries. Despite this widespread perception, people still tend to interpret it through their own values and usage contexts. Cultural influences on advertising are discussed in much more detail in Chapter 13, as the language input in marketing communications is much more significant than it may seem at first glance.

Language influencing culture?

Does language shape culture, and therefore cultural behaviour, or does language simply reflect culture? In this section we provide examples that illustrate the ways in which language can shape and reflect different assumptions in terms of time, emotions and feelings, attitude to action, and social hierarchy, and how this is expressed in the colloquial phrases used in marketing communications.

The first proponent of the idea that language has a decisive influence on culture was the linguist Edward Sapir, who put forward that language influences thought and perception. In this view, language creates categories in our minds, which, in turn, directly influence the things we judge to be similar and those that *deserve* to be differentiated. Language influences our way of observing, describing, interacting and eventually constructing our reality or world view (*Weltanschauung*). Sapir (p. 214) writes:

The fact of the matter is that the real world is to a large extent unconsciously built up on the language habits of the group. No two languages are ever sufficiently similar as to be considered as representing the same social reality. The worlds in which different societies live are distinct worlds, not merely the same world with different labels attached.[18]

The linguist and anthropologist Benjamin Lee Whorf developed and extended Sapir's hypothesis, which contends that the structure of language has a significant influence on perception and categorization. However, the argument that language alone is responsible for these differences is rejected by most linguists. For example, the gender given to words is not necessarily indicative of a particular cultural meaning (e.g., the gender of the earth, the sun and the moon, or of vices and virtues); for most it often seems to reflect an arbitrary choice.

The language and culture causality debate, which is scientifically very complex, risks turning into a 'chicken and egg' argument. In a static scenario where an individual or a certain group has been educated in a homogeneous cultural environment, language is likely to influence world views and actions. However, the theory is less valid in a dynamic scenario where language changes from generation to generation or where people travel abroad. When people travel, they encounter opportunities to borrow language and culture. Interaction between language and culture is reciprocal, particularly in the light of cultural borrowing. Common sense reveals limitations to the Whorfian hypothesis, especially in relation to those who speak many languages, those who were raised in various linguistic and cultural environments, and those who share a strong national culture in spite of language differences, such as the Swiss.

There is a growing body of research that indicates that culture, rather than language alone, is responsible for differences in categorization. For instance, regardless of the language in which they were asked, bilingual Chinese categorized objects according to their *relationship* more often than European Americans, who more often categorized the same objects according to their category membership.[19] This appears to reflect the value that the cultures place on relationships versus the attributes of objects, as discussed in Chapter 3. However, it is clear that language is intertwined with culture. This relationship is illustrated in Box 4.6, which describes how languages reflect different patterns of time.

The view that language reflects culture can also be seen in the colloquialisms/metaphors and specificity of the words used to communicate the important aspects of culture. The dominant sport is often recognizable in the metaphors used in different countries, such as baseball in America ('it is in the ballpark' or

'he is in the big league now'), cricket in the UK ('on the back foot' or 'hit it for a six'). The natural environment also features strongly in metaphors, such as the Australia sayings 'beyond the black stump' (a long way away) or 'a kangaroo loose in the top paddock' (intellectually impaired), as well as the number of words that can be used for physical occurrences that demand precise description. For instance, there is a much larger number of terms for different types of snow in the Inuit language and other near Artic Circle languages, than in languages from warmer climates. Another example is the rich culinary vocabulary in France, where a preoccupation with good food is an element of society that strongly influences daily life.

Words that are missing from one language are often borrowed from other languages. This is especially so for introduced foods. For example, many commonly used 'English' words are borrowed from other cultures, including hamburger (German), pasta (Italian), tea (China) and Cabernet (French), but it is also the case for concepts that are borrowed from other cultures.

Website link 4.3

Search for words that might be borrowed. Here are ten words that you might think were from English: http://www.toptenz.net/top-10-words.php.

The vast majority of marketing text is written in English and translated into other languages.[20] It rarely happens the other way around. Holden illustrates the difficulties in translating these largely American concepts into languages such as Russian, where the product life cycle cannot be easily illustrated and segmentation is literally translated into '*segmentatsiya*', which means little to Russians. On the positive side, Holden (p. 88)[20] points out that scholars from non-English speaking countries 'acquire in effect two separate world-views about their academic discipline. But more than that . . . the experience of synthesising two professional world-views gives them, not necessarily a fully-fledged third world-view as such, but unquestionably new insights which would not have arisen without this experience-commingling process mediated through the knowledge of another foreign language.'

Business vocabulary from Western contexts is often difficult to translate into other languages, if

Box 4.6

Time patterns revealed by language

Representations of time are conveyed through the medium of language, as a means of communication and therefore collective action. Whorf comments about the Hopi language in the following terms:

After long and careful study and analysis, the Hopi language is seen to contain no words, grammatical forms, constructions or expressions, that refer directly to what we call 'time', or to past, present, and future, or to motion as kinematic rather than dynamic (i.e. as a continuous translation in space and time rather than as an exhibition of a dynamic effort in a certain process), or that even refer to space in such a way as to exclude that element of extension or existence that we call 'time', and so by implication leave a residue that could be referred to as 'time'. Hence, the Hopi language contains no reference to 'time', either implicit or explicit. (Carroll, pp. 57–8.[22])

The vocabulary of time reveals much about the linkage between language and cultural representations. For those who have doubts about the existence of differences in cultural representations of time that are revealed, conveyed and reproduced by language, the example of the English/US word 'deadline' is illustrative. A quick translation into French would give 'échéance [temporelle]' or 'délai de rigueur'[23] but would not render the intensity of this word. Taken literally, it seems to suggest something like 'beyond this (temporal) line, you will (there is a danger of) die (dying)'. It therefore gives a genuine notion of urgency to what was originally a very abstract notion (a point which has been agreed upon on a line of time). The word 'deadline' is used in French by many businesspeople as such (un deadline), even though it is not in the official dictionary, because it conveys a typically Anglo-American sense of urgency that French people do not find in their own language.

Language also reflects (and pre-shapes) how people envision the future. In some African languages (Kamba and Kikuyu), there are three future tenses which express (1) action in two to six months; (2) action that will take place immediately; and (3) action 'in the foreseeable future, after this or that event'. Commenting on the uses of these African tenses, M'biti (pp. 74–5) demonstrates how coherence and sophistication in the accurate use of the near future, are important to people.

You have these tenses before you: just try to imagine the tense into which you would translate passages of the New Testament concerning the Parousia of Our Lord Jesus Christ, or how you would teach eschatology . . . If you use tense no. 1, you are speaking about something that will take place in the next two to six months, or in any case within two years at most. If you use no. 2, you are referring to something that will take place in the immediate future, and if it does not take place you are exposed as a liar in people's eyes. Should you use no. 3 you are telling people that the event concerned will definitely take place, but when something else has happened first. In all these tenses, the event must be very near to the present moment: if, however, it lies in the far distant future – beyond the two-year limit – you are neither understood nor taken seriously.[24]

Levine[25] (pp. 48–9), conducting research on Brazilian versus US time, highlights the way concepts of punctuality are reflected in the language. He takes the example of the translation from English to Portuguese of a questionnaire containing the verb 'to wait':

Several of our questions were concerned with how long the respondent would wait for someone to arrive versus when they hoped the person would arrive versus when they actually expected the person would come. Unfortunately for us, it turns out that the terms to wait, to hope and to expect are all typically translated as the single verb *esperar* in Portuguese. In many ways our translation difficulties taught us more about Brazilian–Anglo differences in time conception than did the subjects' answers to the questions.[25]

There is a sort of continuum across languages in the accuracy of description of the waiting phenomenon (a fundamental issue in time experience!). French language, which lies somewhere between English and Portuguese in terms of temporal accuracy, uses two verbs: *attendre* (to wait) and *espérer* (to hope). 'To expect' has no direct equivalent in French and must be translated by a lengthy circumlocution (*compter sur l'arrivée de . . .*).

real equivalence of meaning is sought. Terms such as: 'empirical evidence', 'feedback', 'deadline', 'cognitive', 'emotional' and 'successful', can be problematic. Even such an elementary word as 'fact' contains a rather demanding content. In English, a fact must be an *established* piece of reality. In French, its equivalent, *fait*, is less demanding in terms of unanimously agreed-on reality (*les faits peuvent être discutés*, corresponding to a spirit of the facts being 'challenged' rather than just discussed). In German, a fact may be translated by *Tatsache*, *Wirklichkeit*, *Wahrheit* or *Tat* – it can mean equally a piece of 'reality', a piece of 'truth' or a piece of 'action'.

The following short passage caricatures the English way of acting:

This man is achievement and deadline oriented. He first reviews the issues at stake. Then he tries hard to gather data, to verify, measure. As much as possible he will bring hard facts, empirical evidence, not simple opinions. If and when his thoughts and his emotions are conflicting, he will choose to behave as a matter-of-fact and down-to-earth guy. Being individually rewarded, he is therefore eager to perform the task and complete the job. He (almost) always meets his schedule.

However, the difficulties in translating this text extend far beyond the purely lexical and grammatical. These problems correspond to what is often called the *spirit* of a language (in French, *le génie de la langue*). Far from being merely a linking of a chain of words, a language contains a series of stands taken on the nature of our relationship to reality. As an example, the English word 'business' is fairly positive, as it connotes being 'busy' and an emphasis on doing things (e.g., getting down to business); however, according to Fisher (p. 148) the meaning is much less positive in Spanish:

'In Spanish the word is 'negocio' . . . The key is the 'ocio' part of the word, which connotes leisure, serenity, time to enjoy and contemplate as the preferred human condition and circumstance. But when harsh reality forces one from one's 'ocio,' when it is negated, then one has to attend to 'negocio'. The subjective meaning is obviously much less positive than in English.'[21]

It is interesting to compare languages with respect to their *qualities* (i.e., which is better at expressing ideas, facts, or moods, than the others). For instance, the following compares the *qualities* of three major

western European languages (English, French and German):

■ German is stronger than English in the expression of abstractions. In German, word endings such as *-heit*, *-keit*, *-ung*, *-schaft*, *-tum* and *-nis* allow the 'abstractification' of concrete notions. English is not only less able to express pure concepts, it is also less prone to.

■ English is more action and more outward oriented, and takes the view that data-oriented and objective approaches allow a separation between internal feelings and external actions.

■ French expresses inner states more accurately, with an emphasis on emotions rather than pure thoughts, describing the self and others. This corresponds to a view that any action is related to affectivity.

Stereotypically, we could say that English is a language of action, French a language of emotions and German a language of thoughts. While it is possible and very desirable to remove language barriers, it is still difficult to understand the emphasis on actions, thoughts and emotions across these languages.

It is easy to see why language and cultural skills are becoming increasingly important for multinational firms. Replacement costs for a core employee who leaves an overseas post average US$1 million.[26] The most common reason given for leaving is the inability to adjust to cultural and language differences.

Language as a reflection of status, hierarchy and a vision of appropriate social relationships

The way we address other people is another example of how language shapes or reflects a social hierarchy. There is only one word used in English for 'you', which is said to reflect an emphasis on equality and informality between people. In contrast, the French are considered to be more formal, as they often use the formal *vous* for people they do not know very well instead of the informal *tu*, which they reserve for family and friends. The Germans use *du* (second person singular) in informal and personal settings and *Sie* (third person plural) in formal address. The Germans, like the Spaniards, have three forms of address: while the second person plural (*ihr*) has been lost in practice in German, but remains in Spanish.

4.4

The Internet: communication in cyberspace

The Internet is often thought of as a low-context medium; however, it is far from immune to language-based difficulties, such as those between high- and low-context cultures. As MacLeod (p. 37)[27] notes: 'Sentences written in Japanese need to be formal, whereas an informal tone is suitable for the U.S. Translation also throws up questions of length. Each page of English may need up to two pages in German. In some Asian languages, not only are the characters larger than in English, they also read from right to left.' These issues need to be overcome at the development stage of multilingual websites.

It is important for businesses to understand that high-context languages are the ones that are growing most rapidly on the Internet, including Chinese and Arabic (1,277 per cent and 2,501 per cent, respectively between 2000 and 2010).[29] The percentage of English language online has dropped from 49 per cent in September 2000 to 27 per cent in June 2010, with the next most common languages on the Internet being Chinese (23 per cent), Spanish (8 per cent) and Japanese (5 per cent).[29,30] This translated into 922 million users from Asia, 476 million from Europe and 272 from North American, in 2011.[31] Further, differences in penetration or percentage of users from each of these regions shows where future growth is likely to be: 78 per cent penetration in North America, 58 per cent in Europe and only 24 per cent in Asia.[32] Box 4.7 illustrates the influence of culture on B2B website design.

As we have discussed throughout this Chapter, language translation is a complex issue, which is further elaborated in Chapter 7 (research). However, there are some issues relatively unique to the Internet, including ensuring software can accept foreign language features, such as double-byte Asian characters and[32] overcoming the subtleties involved in ever-expanding translation dictionaries.[33] As a result, cost becomes more salient, as website translation can cost upwards of US$20,000 (for a website consisting of 100 pages). Software can only go so far, translation is still very much a human process.[34]

While it might seem enticing to use automatic translation on the Internet, there are still many problems with accuracy, as even error rates of 1 per cent can cause serious problems in international business. Lu[35] experimented with three of the available translation tools on the Web, which allow people to search the Internet in both English and Asian languages and to compose e-mail messages in your own language

---

Box 4.7

Culture and business-to-business (B2B) web site design

Business school students at a Western European university were asked to code a subset of 597 English version B2B web sites from 57 countries that differed in the importance of context: low-context (e.g., Germany, Sweden), low-medium-context (e.g., U.S.A., Belgium), medium-context (e.g., Italy, France), Medium-high-context (e.g., Turkey, Egypt) and High-context (e.g., China, India). They found that B2B websites from lower-context cultures were more likely to:[36]

1. be easy to find (search engines, company name and language accessibility);
2. be exciting and entertaining;
3. have user-friendly navigation (work well, guides visitors, easy to read, up to date);

4. include corporate information (distributors, newsletters, jobs, activities, references and financial);
5. include product information cues (information and links);
6. include transaction cues (prices, availability, tips for use and end use and product software); and
7. include two-way communication (customization, secure transactions and logistics).

They also found that B2B websites from countries higher in individualism, lower in power distance and higher in uncertainty avoidance, positively impacted many of these characteristics.[37]

(Sources: Usunier and Roulin[36]; Usunier, Roulin and Ivens[37].)

and send them in another. He found that homonyms – words with the same spelling that have multiple meanings – still cause errors for machine translators (p. 39): 'EWSurf misunderstood the name of the Japanese electronics giant Sony as a term of endearment for a male child, and missed the true meaning of an MP3 player. So visitors to Sony's website are exhorted in Chinese to "enjoy your son's digital new music . . . using an MP3 contestant".'[38] Similarly, the word *dog* may mean a four-legged mammal in a strictly lexical definition, but it may also be used as verb meaning to persistently pursue, or a bad investment, or an ugly person, or ruin (as in 'going to the dogs').[38]

Website link 4.4

Try Google's online translation tool to translate 'Let's go out for a business lunch' into Spanish, and then back-translate from the Spanish language version into English. Is it equivalent? Try some other phrases. **http://translate.google.com/**.

Finally, we cannot ignore the importance of e-mail communication, which lends itself to low-context communication, so that we need to be very conscious of the receiver's cultural background. For instance, a common practice in the US is to automatically address others by their first name. The same is true in Iceland and Canada, as well as Australia. In more formal countries, such as Germany, Austria, Switzerland and Sweden as well as many Asian countries, you would never address a new contact by their first name unless invited to do so. Further, in high-context countries it is important to allow the context to flow into the message. As Woodward (p. 15) quotes, Jeanne Poole, manager of international HRM benefits and systems for PQ Corp, argues that:

You should be very careful [in e-mails] not just start out in a cold business-like manner with some cultures . . . If I am dealing with the Dutch, I don't have to be so careful; I can just get right to the point in my e-mail. If, on the other hand, I am dealing with our Chinese or Latin American friends, I am always more careful about how I begin my message to them. I build up to the topic by saying things such as, 'I hope you are doing well. We haven't talked in a while. I just wanted to take a minute to chat with you about something that came up.'[39]

4.5

Improving communication effectiveness in international business

A 'reasonable' way to use the Whorfian hypothesis

One potential consequence of the Sapir–Whorf hypothesis, if you choose to subscribe to it, is that businesspeople from different cultures not only communicate in different ways, but also perceive, categorize and construct their realities differently. This supposes a 'state of alert' in communication, or a readiness to accept that words, even those that are translated with no apparent difficulty, offer only an illusion of sharing in the same vision of reality. Accordingly, it is advisable to retain as many foreign words as possible in their original form, in the following ways:

1. By recognizing the need to keep culturally unique concepts in the native language form to signal their uniqueness.
2. By questioning interpreters, or even one's foreign business partners, about the precise meaning of words or expressions in the context of a particular culture (see Sussman and Johnson[40] for a qualitative examination of the roles of interpreters).
3. By clearly identifying areas of shared meaning.

For instance, when examining contract clauses it is crucial to extricate the true meaning of each clause, starting from the perspective that the words used will never be exactly equivalent. This is true even in the case of a dictionary translation that seems to indicate (falsely) that an English term (e.g., *act of God)* has a strict equivalent (e.g., the French term *force majeure)*. A simple way of investigating the equivalence of terms is to take two language dictionaries and compare the translations in both directions and by discussing the potential similarities and differences between locals of each culture.

However paradoxical and provocative it may seem, it is sometimes more important to be understood than to understand, inasmuch as the *understanding* depends on the mindset of the observer, as well as on the object to be understood. It is often difficult to understand what is written by cultural insiders unless it has been in some way recalibrated in the linguistic background of the reader, which means more than simply translated.

It is not as important for international business people to have a full command of foreign languages, as it is to understand what is unique in the structure of the foreign language and some of its words. Consulting a basic grammar book and paying careful attention to specific words can be a good start. Very often authors of books on Japanese business customs or management style keep Japanese words as they are originally pronounced when they want to signal a culturally specific meaning. Sometimes words that partly bridge the cultural divide are forged. For instance, Boye de Mente (p. 261)[41] cites the Japanese word *nomination*, which is made up of the first part of the Japanese word *nomimasu* (to drink) and the last half of 'communication': 'This Japlish word refers to business conversations and socializing that takes place in bars, cabarets, and other drinking establishments, and is one of the institutionalized ways of "wisdom gathering" in Japan.'

International business people who want to avoid some of the problems with linguistic ethnocentrism should strive for linguistic polycentrism by trying to understand and use important original-language words, understanding meaningful elements in the grammar (such as gender, tenses and sentence construction), and trying to behave as 'explorers' of the meanings and world views expressed by different languages.

A final note for native English speakers

In assessing English as the *lingua franca* of international business, it is essential to consider two very distinct groups: native and non-native English speakers. For non-native English-speaking businesspeople, learning English and often one or two other languages is a must. For instance, the Swedes, Finns, Danes and Norwegians often speak three or four foreign languages: English, another Nordic language and French, German or Spanish. The situation is very different for native English speakers. Simon (p. 2)[42] observes: 'The US continues to be the only nation where you can graduate from college without having had one year of a foreign language.' Australia also falls into this category. Although regrettable, this is explainable. The US and Australia are vast, linguistically homogeneous countries where almost everyone speaks English. Australia is also geographically remote. The major city of Melbourne is around 3200 km from the nearest major non-English-speaking population centre (in Papua New Guinea). In Australia it is not necessary to learn foreign languages, whereas in Europe most large cities are located less than 200 miles (330 km) from a foreign-speaking region and learning one or more foreign languages is a real asset. Although the US is now the fourth-largest Spanish-speaking country in the world – more than half the population of Miami is of Spanish-speaking origin – Americans do not generally feel they have to learn Spanish. Rather, Hispanics have more need to learn English.

There are also differences in the amount of effort required to learn certain foreign languages, especially if it means learning different written characters, as well as different words and sentence structures. If an American or a European wants to really learn Japanese, a large number of new characters have to be learned, whereas if a Japanese person wants to learn the Roman alphabet there are far fewer characters. For the *gaijin* (non-Japanese) there are two syllabaries of about 100 characters each (*hiragana* and *katakana*, phonetic symbols) and about 1850 *kanjis* (ideographic symbols) to learn, whereas there are only 26 phonetic characters in the Roman alphabet for the Japanese to learn which is a considerably smaller task.

English speakers can usually find other English speakers during their travels, and they can count on their foreign business partners having – at least superficially – a good command of English. Furthermore, most English speakers are tolerant and lenient towards the mistakes of their non-native counterparts: 'international English' sometimes has little to do with real English grammar and words.

For all of the above reasons, native English speakers may appear to be somewhat lazy about foreign languages. This 'English-only' bias has, somewhat understandably, led to a systematic underestimation of the impact of language differences in the international business literature. Most international business textbooks do not include a single reference in a foreign language, unless there is an easily available translated version. Even many of the texts devoted to culture in international business do not have a single *truly* foreign reference – that is, from a foreign author in a foreign language, although some works by foreign authors are listed, when they have been published in

English. This is likely to cause a substantial bias, since translated authors are not read in their own linguistic contexts and foreign authors who have not been translated into English are not even considered. However, there are practical reasons for maintaining language homogeneity in sources, as the reader would not be able to find or to read these references.

What is unfortunate, however, is that native English speakers are at a disadvantage, although the opposite may appear to be true. The main disadvantage is that they will only have a limited understanding of the 'world view' and communication styles from non-English countries. Furthermore, many native English speakers cannot imagine what it means or is like to express oneself in a language with a low level of proficiency, unless they themselves have tried to learn and speak a foreign language. Thus, native English speakers have to develop an awareness of their competitive disadvantage in terms of language.

The message is not to simply learn foreign languages. It is more important to understand the consequences of languages being different. Absolute proficiency in many languages is not needed. International businesspeople do not have to be multilingual. They do, however, need to have an awareness of what language differences imply.

It is also important to remember that non-native English speakers may seem to have a good command of English, but they still have a world view that has been shaped by their native language and culture. Thus, proficient non-native English speakers may look the same, but be quite different. This may be especially true for northern Europeans. They may seem to be similar as their English pronunciation is generally good, but in reality they have a different mindset and a much greater proficiency for oral than for written communication, which can cause problems when the written details of business contracts are discussed.

Website link 4.5

Find some examples of misunderstandings caused by interpretation, like this one:
http://www.takingontobacco.org/intro/funny.html.

The following are some guidelines for effective communication in international business:

1. Start by accurately assessing possible intercultural obstacles, such as language and communication issues. Businesspeople frequently underestimate or even completely overlook intercultural communication problems, since they often share a professional culture with their foreign partner. They are also deceived by a misleading international context in which the communication might be interpreted as Western. For example:

   Obviously, the modern intensity of international interaction, especially in business and in technological, communication and educational fields, has produced something of an internationalized 'culture' which reduces the clash of cultural backgrounds and stereotyped images. Happily for us this *modus vivendi* is largely based on Western practices and even on the English language, so many otherwise 'foreign' counterparts are accommodating to the American style of negotiation. (p. 8)[43]

   Unfortunately, businesspeople who feel no need to adapt, especially as far as language is concerned, may believe that their counterpart feels the same. Similarities are often illusions, especially when foreigners seemingly share an 'international culture'. Those who adapt are aware of differences, whereas those who must be adapted to remain unaware.

2. Be aware that what is explicitly said is not necessarily what is implicitly meant. Spend time checking communication accuracy, especially when the stakes are high (orders, delivery dates, contractual involvement in general).

3. Learning other non-verbal communication styles may prove difficult. Deep cultural learning is hard for adults. It is better to aim for a state of alertness, so that one does not decode non-verbal messages erroneously, rather than trying to gain full command of different types of non-verbal communication.

4. In many cases interpreters serve a crucial purpose; they are transposers of meaning. They do not work 'like a dictionary', translating literally. However, they may translate better from one language to another than in the reverse direction, depending on their language abilities and on their relationships with the parties. It is necessary to make sure that they are loyal to the party who has hired them and it may be advisable to hire several interpreters when the business at stake justifies it.

5. Remember that parts of language simply cannot be translated, as they convey culture-specific

meaning. Translators may not be able to communicate the entire message. Always keep in mind the Italian adage, '*traduttore, traditore*' ('translator, traitor').

6. Develop a 'bomb squad' ability to defuse conflicts based on negative stereotypes. Misunderstandings in intercultural communication often snowball and interact with purely interest-based conflicts, resulting in lose–lose confrontations or an end to the negotiations.

7. Bear in mind that all this cannot be improvised; it has to be practised. Skills in intercultural business communication are a long-term investment rather than a way of resolving urgent problems. In medical terms, cultural understanding in business appears as the prevention rather than the cure. It is as important to help others to understand one's own culture as it is to understand their culture, which often involves 'wining and dining'. When business negotiations start with one side lacking even minimal knowledge of the partner's culture, relations will often turn sour. In this case, the only way to negotiate is to discuss on the substantive ground of 'business is business'.

Questions

1. Comment on the following sentences from Fisher (1988, p. 172):[21]

   It is the subjective meaning of words and expressions that needs to be captured. Time spent exploring why a given utterance does not translate well may be more productive for the one who is actually trying to communicate than concentrating on technical excellence.

2. Give examples of low-context versus high-context communication, explaining what is meant by low and high contexts.

3. Transform the following buyer's remark into low-context and high-context sentences: 'Your price is too high compared with that of the competitors.'

4. Why can the obvious showing of emotions be considered dangerous? Why do cultures vary in the degree of emotional restraint?

5. Consider the gender aspect of words in the following languages. In English, almost everything is neutral except persons and some animals, and exceptionally an object such as a ship. French has feminine and masculine but no neutral. In German, persons, objects and concepts can be feminine, masculine or neutral. For instance 'sun', 'earth' and 'moon' are all neutral words in English; in French they are respectively masculine (*le soleil*) and feminine (*la terre, la lune*); in German the same words are feminine (*die Sonne, die Erde*) and masculine (*der Mond*). Elaborate on the possible cultural meanings of attributing gender to words. To what extent can we speak of more or less 'sexualized' languages (I mean here 'sexualized' and not simply 'gendered')? Outline the limitations of such an interpretive approach.

6. In Japanese there are no articles either definite or indefinite. *Hon*, for instance, means 'the book', 'a book', 'the books' or 'books'. What does this imply for the Japanese when they want to express their thoughts?

7. Consider gift-giving practices as an element of communication. What are the main dimensions of gift-giving (consider the donor, the recipient, the size and nature of the gift, the circumstances and its meaning for either side)? How would cultural interpretations differ? Take into account the values involved. (You can base your discussion on elements found in articles about gift-giving.)

References

1. Hemingway, Ernest (1976), *The Snows of Kilimanjaro and Other Stories*. New York: Charles Scribner's and Sons.
2. Bluedorn, Allen C. (1998), 'An Interview with Anthropologist Edward T. Hall', *Journal of Management Inquiry*, 7 (2), 109–15.
3. Hall, Edward T. (1976), *Beyond Culture*. New York: Doubleday.
4. Hall, E. T. and M. R. Hall (1990), *Understanding Cultural Differences: Germans, French, and Americans*. Yarmouth, ME: Intercultural Press.
5. Kim, Donghoon, Yigang Pan and Heung Soo Park (1998), 'High Versus Low-context Culture: A Comparison of Chinese, Korean, and American Cultures', *Psychology and Marketing*, 15 (6), 507–21.
6. Ueda, Keiko (1974), 'Sixteen Ways to Avoid Saying "No" in Japan', in *Intercultural Encounters in Japan*, J. C. Condon and M. Saito (eds). Tokyo: Simul Press.
7. Hall, Edward T. (1960), 'The Silent Language in Overseas Business', *Harvard Business Review* (May–June), 87–96.
8. Sugimoto, Naomi (1998), 'Norms of Apology Depicted in U.S. American and Japanese Literature on Manners and Etiquette', *International Journal of Intercultural Relations*, 22 (3), 251–76.
9. Castillo, P. A. and D. Mallard (2012), 'Preventing Cross-cultural Bias in Deception Judgments: The Role of Expectancies about Nonverbal Behaviour', *Journal of Cross-Cultural Psychology*, Vol. 43, 967–78.
10. Hall, J. A., E. J. Coats and L. Smith LeBeau (2005), 'Nonverbal Behavior and the Vertical Dimension of Social Relations: A Meta-analysis', *Psychological Bulletin*, 131 (6), 898–924.
11. Condon, John C. and Youssef Fahti (1975), *Introduction to Intercultural Communication*. Indianapolis: Bobbs Merrill.
12. Harris, Philip R. and Robert T. Moran (1987), *Managing Cultural Differences* (2nd edn). Houston, TX: Gulf Publishing Company.
13. Copeland, Lennie and Lewis Griggs (1986), *Going International*. New York: Plume Books/New American Library.
14. Ferraro, Gary P. (1990), *The Cultural Dimension of International Business*. Englewood Cliffs, NJ: Prentice Hall.
15. Morschbach, Helmut (1982), 'Aspects of Non-verbal Communication in Japan', in *Intercultural Communication: A Reader*, Larry Samovar and R. E. Porter (eds). (3rd edn). Belmont, CA: Wadsworth.
16. Harris, Philip R., Robert T. Moran, and Sarah Moran (2004), *Managing Cultural Differences: Global Leadership Strategies for the 21st Century*. Oxford: Butterworth-Heinemann.
17. Morand, David A. (1996), 'Politeness as a Universal Variable in Cross-cultural Managerial Communication', *International Journal of Organizational Analysis*, 4 (1), 52–74.
18. Sapir, Edward (1929), 'The Status of Linguistics as a Science', *Language*, 5, 207–14.
19. Unsworth, S. J., C. R. Sears and P. M. Pexman (2005), 'Cultural Influences on Categorization Processes', *Journal of Cross-cultural Psychology*, 36 (6), 662–88.
20. Holden, Nigel (1998), 'Viewpoint: International Marketing Studies – Time to Break the English-Language StrangleHold?', *International Marketing Review*, 15 (2), 86–100.
21. Fisher, Glen (1988), *Mindsets*. Yarmouth, ME: Intercultural Press.
22. Carroll, John B. (1956), *Language, Thought and Reality: Selected Writings of Benjamin Lee Whorf*. Cambridge, MA: MIT.
23. Langenscheidt (1989), *Compact Dictionary French–English/English–French*. New York: Kenneth Urwin Publishers.
24. M'biti, John (1968), 'African Concept of Time', *Africa Theological Journal*, 1, 8–20.
25. Levine, Robert V. (1988), 'The Pace of Life across Cultures', in *The Social Psychology of Time*, Joseph E. McGrath (ed.). Newbury Park, CA: Sage Publications.
26. Howard, David (2001), 'Lost in Translation', *Ziff Davis Smart Business*, 14 (11), 44.
27. MacLeod, Marcia (2000), 'Language Barriers', *Supply Management*, 5 (14), 37–8.
28. Luna, David, Laura A. Peracchio, and Maria D. de Juan (2002), 'Cross-Cultural and Cognitive Aspects of Web Site Navigation', *Journal of the Academy of Marketing Science*, 30 (4), 397–410.
29. Anon (2011), 'Top Internet Languages used in the web', *Internet World Stats*. Retrieved 2011 from www.internetworldstats.com/stats7.htm.
30. Cutitta, Frank (2002), 'Language Matters', *Target Marketing*, 25 (2), 40–44.
31. Retrieved 8 August 2011 from http://www.internetworldstats.com/stats.htm
32. Yunker, John (2000), 'Going Global', *Pharmaceutical Executive*, 20 (7), 138–46.
33. Bisby, Adam (1999), 'Translation Tools Speak Globally', *Computer Dealer News*, 15 (15), 17.
34. Heuberger, Andres (2001), 'Manage Your Global WWW Brand', *World Trade*, 14 (11), 56–60.
35. Lu, Caixia (2001), 'Chinese, or Just Chinglish?', *Far Eastern Economic Review*, 164 (15), 39.
36. Usunier, Jean-Claude, Nicolas Roulin, and Björn Ivens (2009), 'Cultural, National, and Industry-Level Differences in B2B Web Site Design and Content,' *International Journal of Electronic Commerce*, 14 (2), pp. 41–87.

37. Usunier, Jean-Claude, Nicolas Roulin (2010), 'The Influence of High- and Low-Context Communication Styles on the Design, Content, and Language of Business-to-Business Web Sites', *Journal of Business Communication*, 47 (2), pp. 189–227 (with Nicolas Roulin).

38. Castellucio, Michael (1999), 'Hey, Can Anybody Read This?', *Strategic Finance*, 81 (1), 63–64.

39. Woodward, Nancy Hatch (1999), 'Do You Speak Internet?', *HR Magazine*, 44 (4), 12–16.

40. Sussman, Lyle and Denise Johnson (1996), 'Dynamics of the Interpreter's Role: Implications for International Executives', *Journal of Language for International Business*, 7 (2), 1–14.

41. de Mente, Boye (1990), *How to Do Business with the Japanese*. Chicago, IL: NTC Books.

42. Simon, Paul (1980), *The Tongue Tied American*. New York: Continuum Press.

43. Fisher, Glen (1980), *International Negotiation: A Cross-cultural Perspective*. Yarmouth, ME: Intercultural Press.

Appendix 4

Teaching materials

A4.1 Exercise

Multicultural class

Look at the person seated next to you in class, or anyone with whom you have frequent interaction. Then select somebody originating from a foreign culture. List three examples of non-verbal communication that she or he uses, describe them accurately and decode their meaning. Now ask this person to look at you and do the same. Then work together and compare both interpretations and try to understand why meaning was shared or, possibly, not shared.

(This exercise can be implemented only with a good degree of cultural diversity within the student group.)

A4.2 Exercise

I 'love' cake

Start from the English verb 'to like' and find its equivalents in French, German and Spanish. Do not hesitate to translate them back into English in order to detect differences in meaning. Include in your search some basic etymological grounds (e.g., *gusto* in Spanish is based on the word for 'taste'). What differences in terms of world views are suggested by the different conceptual dimensions of 'liking' (preference, affective, pleasure, love, enjoyment, eating/ingesting, etc.) and their attributions to people, things or situations? Suggest possible consequences for international marketing and advertising strategies.

A4.3 Case

Longcloud – languages in cyberspace

Language is a steed that carries one into a far country. – Arabic proverb

In the Spring of 2012, brushing through green pastures in her rugged truck, Longcloud marketing director Sarah Elder mused over what she would say at this afternoon's meeting. Longcloud Lamb was a young company, specializing in chilled and frozen New Zealand lamb and goat products with a difference: it was organic and exceeded animal welfare stipulations in major export markets. Already with five established export partners in the USA and Japan, and 32 regular customers in the area, Sarah and her colleagues were pleasantly surprised by the phenomenal demand growth in only seven years of operations. Accelerated global growth for Longcloud was now imperative, to recoup costs of the recent acquisition of new lands, 42 per cent more stock, and an updated processing plant with EU and USDA certification and Halal capability.

Given that the company managed current wholesale customers in export markets using an e-commerce platform, it seemed obvious that a better website was the answer. In addition, the latest processing and shipping technology made it possible to send chilled cuts to smaller export customers on an individual basis. Most New Zealand exporters were beefing up their sites too. However, Canadian-born Sarah had been surprised that most were English-only. Longcloud aimed to capture certain European markets for organic chilled lamb and goat products, as well as niche markets around the world, such as organic restaurants, schools, and religious and non-profit organizations. The lamb meat cuts market was global, and interest in organic meats was a growing phenomenon. First in interest for organic lamb was the European Union, primarily Britain, France and Germany, followed by the US. Then, there were smaller markets throughout North Africa, the Middle East, and India, many with a particular interest in Longcloud's Halal capacity. There was a growing interest for organic goat meat in fragmented Latin American markets, also.

'Because we must differentiate ourselves from mainstream chilled lamb producers, we need to demonstrate our difference in our communications materials. What better way than to talk to customers and prospects in their own language?' Sarah would argue later that day in the meeting. Her colleagues then made a chorus of objections, such as 'The fact that Longcloud is organic is difference enough, we don't need to bother with languages', and 'Translating is so costly, can't we just put one of those *Altavista Babelfish* translation icons on each page? How are you going to decide which languages to use anyways?' Jumping into the fray, general manager Linden Carmody stated, 'Fine, so we publish our multilingual site, but all we can speak is bad French . . . so what happens to our customer relationship beyond on-site ordering and payments? Right, and what about e-mails, how will we understand and answer them?' Each one had a point, Sarah conceded. However, it was well established that customers appreciated the ease of conducting business in their own languages, at least for most of the transactions. Especially if Longcloud was to be dealing with niche markets, she opined, a more personalized approach would be necessary. She believed that was the case even if just two other languages were used, such as French for the ten or more countries that speak the language and seek organic lamb, and Arabic for countries with a Halal market and some organic sensitivities. With potentially wider and more diverse business contacts around the world, Sarah argued further, Longcloud's medium-term goal to grow its own tanned organic lambskin and organic wool products businesses was more likely to be realized. In the website language debate Longcloud was not alone: innumerable companies and organizations faced the same problem, and could find no easy solution.

According to *Global Reach*, more than 63 per cent of people accessing the Internet do not do so in English. In the last few years, Chinese has become almost as important as English, counting for 22.6 per cent of the global Internet usage in 2010.[1] Indeed, the number of Chinese-speaking Internet users has grown 1227 per cent over the last 10 years.[2] In 2000 an study by *Vilaweb* found that 68.39 per cent of web pages were in English, followed by Japanese (5.85 per cent), German (5.77 per cent) and Chinese (3.87 per cent).[3] Estimates are now complicated by the fact that many websites have multiple language versions, but approximately 30 per cent of websites are in English. Indeed, as more regions get access to the Internet, the ratio of English to Non-English websites decreases ever more.[4] There are manifold difficulties of estimating language use on web pages, especially since more and more websites are becoming multilingual. It is, however, clear that English does not dominate the Web anymore was the case at the beginning of the decade. English is still the dominant language used in the Web in terms of the number of Internet users by language with 27.3 per cent of the world total number of Internet users followed by Chinese with 22.6 per cent and Spanish with 7.8 per cent.[5] Table 4.1 below illustrates the ranking of languages by number of speakers. China has one of the world's fastest-growing online populations. By the end of the year 2009 the China Internet population had reached 384 million, growing by 29 per cent compared to the end of 2008.[6] German, Japanese and French appear to be relatively present on the Internet. However, the languages themselves do not have a correspondingly large population of first language speakers, as is clear from Table 4.1. French, for instance, is spoken by 64 million as a first language. But by about 130 million people as a first or a second language. Similarly English is spoken by 508 million people when non-native speakers are considered.[7]

Table 4.1 Ranking of languages according to number of first-language speakers

Language	Principal countries or regions spoken	Estimated speakers in millions
Chinese	China, Taiwan, the diaspora	1,213
Spanish	Latin America, Spain	329
English	Australasia, North America, South Africa, British Isles	328
Arabic	Middle East, North Africa	221
Hindi/Urdu	Indian subcontinent, the diaspora	182
Bengali	Indian subcontinent	181
Portuguese	Angola, Brazil, Mozambique, Portugal	178
Russian	Russia	144
Japanese	Japan	122
German	Germany	90.3

(Source: *Ethnologue*: *Languages of the World*, 16th edn, Dallas, USA, 2009. Retrieved 18 May 2011 from: http://www.ethnologue.com/ethno_docs/distribution.asp?by=size.[8])

According to *Internet World* Stats,[8] 1.966 billion people worldwide had access to Internet at the end of 2010. This compares with the 580 million at the same time in 2002. Within the decade from 2000 to 2010, the African continent had the fastest growth, increasing the number of Internet users by 2,357 per cent, including countries like Angola, Congo or Somalia that had growth percentages of over 45,000 per cent, to be compared to the worldwide growth of 444 per cent over the same period. China had the largest number online at 420 million users, followed by the US (239 million), Japan (99 million), India (81 million) and Brazil (72 million).

In terms of online access populations, Asia has become the leader in the last decade, before Europe and the North American continent. In Table 4.2 below, percentages of online access in terms of percentages of the total online population are listed by continents and the most important countries within these continents (see Table 4.2).

Table 4.2 Share of world online population

Country or region	Share of world online population (percent)
Asia	42
Europe	24
North America	14
Latin America	10
Africa	6
Middle East	3
Oceania / Australia	1

(Source: *Internet World* Stats, June 2010.[8])

The role of e-commerce

Global online retail sales reached USD 348.6 billion in 2009. However, e-commerce still accounts for only 2.5 per cent of global retail sales on a basis. The percentage of online buyers dramatically varies from country to country, ranging form a high 70 per cent in Australia or the Netherlands to a low 7 per cent in India or 19 per cent in Brazil, with intermediate situations such as China with 37 per cent and Spain with 31 per cent, (2009 figures).[9] The growth of global e-commerce presupposes the participation of a diverse language base, and the adaptation of e-commerce platforms to linguistic and cultural conditions. Many multinational corporations have websites that are entirely in English, however, and the number of major global businesses who have adapted their sites is growing slowly.

How to adapt a website – more than just a translation

When adapting software to local contexts, the following elements need to be considered: language, literacy and culture. For organizations looking to adapt their message locally around the globe, the same elements are pertinent in website and e-commerce platforms design. Apart from translations, which alone may account for half the localization costs for software, the choice of language or dialect may be critical. Should one select an 'official language' to the detriment of a language spoken unofficially by large numbers of the target audience? Elements of website design that need to be adapted according to the culture of the target audience include colours used, text versus graphics, a 'busy' screen versus a minimalist one, animations, symbols and icons.[10] Currently, there are software facilities for dealing with cultural variations in number formats, sort orders, and times and dates formats. At this time, technology is not well prepared to implement non-Gregorian calendar types. The correct and locally adapted use of proper names is also problematic.[11]

Which language?

When deciding which languages to use in adapting a regionally targeted website, certain social and economic factors should be considered independently of the number of speakers of the languages under consideration. Predominant among these are literacy, language use, and access. Indian languages are a case in point. India, with one billion people, has two official languages: English and Hindi. There are 18 major languages and 418 other languages spoken by 10,000 or more people.[12] First, there may be a large number of speakers for some languages, but the corresponding literacy rate may be quite low. Where this is the case, the complexity of the language used and the share of online graphics may reflect this. In addition, it is now possible to integrate speech or speech recognition systems (currently only available for the world's 'main' languages) on the site's capabilities.[13]

Second, many people around the world are accustomed to using languages other than their own for business or general communication purposes. As in many developing countries, some Indians may feel uneasy conducting business in any other language but English, yet they may feel similar unease communicating at home in English. The user's website language of preference may depend on whether the Internet is accessed from home or from work. English may be more acceptable for work-access, while a local language may be preferable for use from the home computer. For this reason, the company with international ambitions needs to determine the likely point of access for its target audiences.

Third, access to the Internet may be uneven. For instance, raw Internet access numbers may be low in some rural areas, yet one entrepreneur with a computer and Internet access may allow many others to access the net using the most basic equipment, in exchange for a user fee. Internet access may in this case be higher than initially assumed. Similarly, when looking at the size of the Internet audience in targeted nations, one should be wary of dismissing a small audience, such as the 0.1 per cent of Nigerians online. That small percentage represents 100,000 of the country's most affluent, and most likely the same people who make major decisions in government and its bureaucracies.[14]

Complicating the issue of adapting (or not) to a locally understood language are social factors that have imbued English with status, as the language of preference for business in some countries. At the same time, there are fierce debates over the use and even the survival of some Indian languages.[15] One should not assume that English is generally a safe choice: it is vital to gauge the attitudes of the target audience towards the language, because in some regions there may be historical or political reasons for polite hostility towards those who use English.

Those who decide to localize their websites should be aware of several software complexities involved in online publishing of non-Roman scripts, including Arabic, Bengali, Greek, Thai and Hebrew that have only recently been addressed. One of the problems caused by fonts online is the correct use of diacritics, the accents placed above and below letters – small symbols that can often change the meaning of a word depending on its orientation. These are used in some Nordic languages, Greek, French, Turkish, and some Eastern European languages, to name only a few. The directionality of symbols is another issue. The fact that numerals are ordered from left to right in Arabic and Hebrew scripts which themselves are oriented from right to left, is another example of of online font problems.[16] In addition, some non-Latin scripts require two bits in processing which complicates encoding and may considerably slow down an e-commerce site. The first program to address these problems was produced by the Unicode Consortium, with the goal of eventually codifying all characters produced by humans, anywhere and at any time in history. Currently in its fourth version, the Unicode Standard addresses issues like vertical script (as in East Asian languages) or the right-left orientation of Semitic scripts. Although there are other means of dealing with language representation, the Unicode Consortium has developed the only system to be accepted by the International Standards Organization, as well as the most widely used code within html format. The entire text of Unicode 4.0 is available at **http://www.unicode.com**, as well as useful guidance and information.

Questions

1. Assess in which ways culture, religion and language may influence foreign marketing operations in the organic meat business. Does it differ whether marketing and sales are implemented through traditional marketing or by e-commerce?

2. Investigate the possibility of using automatic translation programmes for non-English-speaking visitors of a website. For this, you can make your own trials on websites which offer free sample translation, such as **http://translate.google.com**, **http://www.freetranslation.com/**, **http://www.softissimo.com/** or **http://www.linguatec.de/news.en.shtml**.

3. Assess the approximate cost of developing a different language version of an English-based website.

4. Should Longcloud develop its website in languages other than English? If yes, which language(s)? Argue about the pros and cons of such decisions.

Saskia Faulk and Jean-Claude Usunier prepared this case solely to provide material for class discussion. The authors do not intend to illustrate either effective or ineffective handling of a business situation. The authors may have disguised certain names and other identifying information to protect confidentiality.

Version: (A) 2011-05-18

A4.4 Case

Supreme Canning

The Supreme Canning Company (the true name of the company is disguised) is an independent US packer of tomato products (whole peeled tomatoes, chopped tomatoes, katsup, paste, pizza and other sauces, and tomatoes and zucchini). The company is located in California. Although it produces some cans with its own brand label, much of its output is canned for others and their brand names and labels put on the cans. It produces shelf-size cans for eventual sale at retail, gallon-size cans for use by restaurants and industrial users, and 55-gallon drums for use by others for repacking or further processing. Its annual processing capacity is in excess of 100,000 tons of tomatoes (processed during an operating season of approximately three months).

The California canning industry had suffered from heavy competition from abroad and inadequate local demand. A somewhat increasing domestic demand for speciality tomato products, especially pizza and other sauces, was not adequate to absorb increasing imports. The high value of the US dollar had made it difficult for US companies to sell abroad. Excess capacity and the resulting depressed prices had led to bankruptcy for a number of Californian canners. With the decline of the value of the dollar and the efforts of Japan to reduce its trade barriers and increase imports, it appeared that Supreme Canning Company might be able to get into the Japanese market. An inquiry received from a foodpacker and distributor in Japan indicated interest from that side. The Japanese firm produced and distributed a large number of products, was well known in Japan, and was much larger than the US company.

Since Supreme Canning Company did not have well-known brand names of its own, the company was interested in acting as a large-scale supplier of products made to customer specifications for use by the customer or distribution under the customer's label. Thus, the inquiry from Japan was most welcome.

The Japanese company invited senior executives of the American firm to visit its production facilities and offices in Japan. Both the president and chairman of the board of Supreme Canning Company had a four-day visit with the executives of the company in Japan. The president of the US company, who had some knowledge of Japanese business practice from studies at Stanford University and from his widespread reading, attempted to act as a guide to Japanese business practice. The chairman of the board had little knowledge of Japan, and viewed himself as a decisive man of action. Although there were a few minor misunderstandings, the visit was concluded successfully and the Americans invited the Japanese to visit their plant in California for four days.

The Japanese indicated their interest in the signing of a mutual letter of cooperation. The American chairman of the board was not interested in this, but rather wanted some specific agreements and contracts. As the time for the Japanese visit to the US drew near, the Japanese indicated that their president would not be able to come. Some senior executives would be able to meet, but they would only be able to spend two days instead of four. The vice-chairman of the board of the California company wrote asking why the Japanese were not going to send their president, and inquiring why they could not spend four days instead of two, 'as we did in Japan'. The letter was frank and direct. The tone was that of a person talking to an equal, but not with any great deal of politeness. The Japanese company decided to cancel the visit, and no further negotiations or serious contacts were made.

Some months later, a local businessman of Japanese extraction asked the president of Supreme Canning Company if some representatives of another (and even larger) Japanese food products producer and distributor could visit the plant. Four Japanese showed up along with the local businessman, who acted as interpreter and go-between. The three middle-aged Japanese produced their *meishi* (business cards) and introduced themselves. Each spoke some English. The older man did not present a card and was not introduced. When the president of the American company asked who he was, the go-between said, 'He's just one of the company's directors'. The visit concluded without discussion of any business possibilities, but this was to be expected in an initial visit from Japanese businessmen.

Supreme's president later found out the family name of the unknown visitor and immediately recognized it as being that of the president of the Japanese company. He assumed that the president of the Japanese company had come but had hidden the fact. He felt that he had been taken advantage of. He telephoned the go-between and told him that he never wanted anyone from that company in his plant again. From a description of the unknown visitor, a consultant to the company realized that the visitor was not the president of the Japanese company. Rather, it was the semi-retired father of the president. The father retained a position on the board of directors and maintained an active interest in company activities, but was not active in day-to-day affairs. Unlike his son who was fluent in English, he spoke only Japanese.

(Source: Albaum, Gerald; Strandskov, Jesper; Duerr, Edwin, International Marketing and Export Management, 3rd Ed., copyright © 1998, pp. 85–87. Reprinted and Electronically reproduced by permission of Pearson Education, Inc., Upper Saddle River, New Jersey.[17])

Questions

1. Was the chairman of the American company wrong for not having found out in advance about Japanese business practices? Why did he not do so? (Answer the same questions in relation to the Japanese companies and US business practices.)

2. What are the principal cultural mistakes made (a) by the Americans from the Japanese perspective, and (b) by the Japanese from the American perspective?

3. What should the president of the American company do now?

A4.5 Critical incident

Scandinavian Tools Company

A major Swedish company that specialized in metal tools and factory equipment had created a French subsidiary a few years ago, based in Lyons, France. This plant was at first supplied with inputs (speciality steels, high-speed steels for blades and saws, etc.) from Sweden. It mostly produced and sold for the French markets and for exports to southern European markets, namely Italy, Spain and Portugal. The drive and energy for creating this new venture came from a young Swedish executive, Bo Svensson. Svensson had spent part of his time as a student, and then as a young engineer, in France. Thereafter he had been in a position to convince the top management of this large Swedish multinational company to launch a new subsidiary in France.

Svensson was very enthusiastic about France. He liked the country very much and had learnt the language, which he spoke fluently with a slight northern European accent. In the rush to start the new company everything went smoothly. Svensson, who was chief executive officer of the French venture, knew how to secure customers and make them loyal; he also knew how to deal with the headquarters in Sweden. The market was growing quickly and competition was not particularly fierce. At the beginning, products were made in Sweden and then exported to France, where Svensson and the subsidiary dealt with marketing and distribution.

After a few years demand began to swell, so the parent company in Sweden decided to build a production plant in France. Machines and factory equipment for the new plant came from Sweden, and the factory was quickly operating at normal capacity. Svensson then hired a vice-president for administration, André Ribaud, an ambitious young executive, also in his thirties, with a law background. The two men got on well together, although their backgrounds and personal profiles were quite different. They shared the work and responsibilities: Svensson was in charge of relations with headquarters, marketing and the monitoring of financial performance; as plant manager, Ribaud was in charge of production operations, human resource management, cost accounting, monitoring cost prices and delivery delays.

After a few years it appeared that Svensson felt more and more relaxed in his job. Quite independent in his profitable subsidiary of (at that time) 200 employees located in a place remote from Sweden, he was able to have a very flexible timetable. He was also very free with personal expenses, which he was entitled to have reimbursed by the subsidiary: he simply had to sign his own expenses receipts. Svensson did not hesitate to use this facility: he did not make a clear distinction between his own money and the company's. Svensson gradually got into the habit of abusing company-paid personal expenses. Ribaud was shocked. Svensson even went so far as to have the expenses of his mistress paid by the subsidiary.

Meanwhile, Ribaud was still working as efficiently as during the initial years. Growth had been impressive. Starting with a few employees in a two-room office in Lyons, the subsidiary had grown to a dynamic medium-sized company with more than 500 people on the payroll; Scandinavian Tools France had bought two plants from competitors. Following these changes, Ribaud's responsibilities quickly increased. He had involved himself completely and passionately with the company. He knew each member of staff personally and was respected by them.

Over time the relationship between the two men had considerably worsened. Svensson saw that Ribaud was winning more and more influence and power inside the company, and was well known by the customers. He felt jealous of him and tried his best to make Ribaud's life in the company difficult. Ribaud, on the other hand, increasingly resented the excessive expenses and the catty remarks of his boss, for whom he no longer felt any esteem. Svensson was a complex, energetic and whimsical character. His charisma and stamina had enabled him to seduce the French clients as well as the management staff at the headquarters in Sweden. The excellent financial performance of the French subsidiary had enabled him to retain the confidence of his superiors, who were also Swedish compatriots. They had trust in his management talents and therefore they allowed him a large degree of freedom. He had also established friendships with some of the senior directors at headquarters, especially with the director in charge of public relations. Svensson was well known at headquarters level, and he understood company 'politics' quite well.

After 15 years of almost steady growth, the market was reaching the stage of maturity. With the removal of borders within the EU, there were many acquisitions by large European and American competitors. The French subsidiary had lost some of its profitability. The middle managers were complaining to Ribaud about Svensson's lack of interest in the subsidiary and his mismanagement. Everybody believed that emergency decisions had to be taken before the situation got even worse. But Svensson turned a deaf ear to their complaints and remained unwilling to enter into discussion with either Ribaud or the other executives. The French were also amazed, and somewhat shocked, to see that there was no reaction from headquarters. It looked as if headquarters had little interest in the destiny of the French subsidiary. People at headquarters still seemed to have confidence in Svensson, who knew how to make them feel secure.

Ribaud did not feel comfortable in this situation. He felt that the financial balance of the subsidiary was threatened and that one factory would probably have to close in the near future. It also seemed to him that the interests of Swedish shareholders were not being adequately taken into account. Relations between Svensson and Ribaud were so damaged that Svensson was convinced that Ribaud was plotting against him. Svensson therefore systematically took a contradictory stance to Ribaud, at the risk of making inappropriate decisions that could possibly lead the subsidiary almost to the brink of bankruptcy.

Each time Ribaud brought up these problems during meetings with people from head-quarters, Svensson abruptly interrupted him, shifting from English to Swedish in order to keep him out of the conversation. Under heavy pressure from some of the executives of the subsidiary who were about to resign and leave the company, Ribaud felt obliged to react. He had tried, during visits by members of the Swedish headquarters, to give them, indirectly, an idea of the situation, but he got the impression that he was not being heard. They had their own image of the chief executive officer which was clearly different.

In desperation, Ribaud decided to send an official note to the top management in Stockholm, in which he told them that he would be obliged to resign if nothing was done to put an end to the present disorder. He tried to write it as objectively as possible in a matter-of-fact style, citing evidence and hard facts. This was not an easy task, since objectivity may prove difficult in such circumstances and, moreover, he was denouncing his boss, which is never very pleasant. He called one of the members of the top management in Stockholm whom he knew a little better than the others, explained about the letter and sent him a copy.

Question

What answer could he expect?

Appendix references

1. Anonymous (2010), 'Global Internet Usage by Language', *Wikipedia.org*, 11 April 2011. Retrieved 18 May 2011 from http://en.wikipedia.org/wiki/Global_Internet_usage.
2. Internet World Stats (2000–2010), 'Top Ten Internet Languages Used in the Web' 30 June 2010. Retrieved 18 May 2011 from: http://www.internetworldstats.com/stats7.htm.
3. Pastore, Michael (2000), 'Web pages by language', 5 July 2000. Retrieved 18 May 2011 from http://www.clickz.com/clickz/stats/1697080/web-pages-language.
4. Jack Welde (2011), 'How many websites are not in English?', 26 February 2011. Retrieved 18 May 2011 from http://www.quora.com/How-many-websites-percentage-or-absolute-numbers-are-not-in-english.
5. See 'Internet world users by language, Top 10 Languages', *Internet World Stats*, retrieved 24 May 2011 from http://www.internetworldstats.com/stats7.htm.
6. Reuters (2010), 'China Internet Population Hits 384 Million', Reuters, 15 January 2010. Retrieved 18 May 2011 from: http://www.reuters.com/article/2010/01/15/china-internet-idUSTOE60E06S20100115.
7. See http://listverse.com/2008/06/26/top-10-most-spoken-languages-in-the-world/, retrieved 24 May 2011.
8. Internet World Stats (2010), *World Internet Usage Statistics*, 30 June 2010. Retrieved 18 May 2011 from http://www.internetworldstats.com/stats.htm.
9. IMAP, *Retail Industry Global Report – 2010*, retrieved 24 May 2011 from http://www.imap.com/imap/media/resources/IMAPRetailReport8_23CB9AA9C6EBB.pdf.
10. Kang, Kyeong Soon and Brian Corbett (2001), 'Effectiveness of graphical components in web site e-commerce application: A cultural perspective', *Electronic Journal of Information Systems in Developing Countries*, 2001, Vol. 7, No. 2. Retrieved 18 May 2011 from http://www.ejisdc.org/ojs2/index.php/ejisdc/article/viewFile/35/35.
11. Hall, Patrick A. V. (2002), 'Bridging the digital divide', *Electronic Journal of Information Systems in Developing Countries*, 2002, Vol. 8, No. 1. Retrieved 18 May 2011 from http://www.ejisdc.org/.
12. Choudhry, Amitav (2000), 'India bursting at the linguistic seams', *The UNESCO Courier*, April, 2000. Retrieved 18 May 2011 from http://www.unesco.org.
13. Hall, Patrick A. V. (2002), 'Bridging the digital divide', *Electronic Journal of Information Systems in Developing Countries*, 2002, Vol. 8, No. 1. Retrieved 18 May 2011 from http://www.ejisdc.org/.
14. International Federation of Red Cross and Red Crescent Societies (2001), *Communications Guide*, International Federation of Red Cross and Red Crescent Societies, 2001. Retrieved 18 May 2011 from http://www.ifrc.org.
15. Choudhry, Amitav (2000), 'India bursting at the linguistic seams', *The UNESCO Courier*, April, 2000. Retrieved 18 May 2011 from http://www.unesco.org.
16. Correll, Sharon (2003), 'Examples of Complex Rendering', Non-Roman Scripts Initiative, Summer Institute of Linguistics (SIL), 21 April 2003. Retrieved 18 May 2011 from http://scripts.sil.org.
17. Duerr, Mitsuko Saito (1989), 'Supreme Canning', in *International Marketing and Export Management*, Gerald Albaum and Jesper Strandskov and Edwin Duerr and Laurence Dowd (eds). Reading, MA: Addison-Wesley.

Part 2　The integration of local consumption in a global marketing environment

Introduction to Part 2

Globalization has taken place at a rapid pace over the past half-century. The continuous expansion of cross-border marketing has been backed by the progressive elimination of barriers to trade, and the emergence of a global consumer culture. Although global convergence seems undeniable, some basic traits of local consumption experience are not converging. Further, the attractiveness of emerging economies, in terms of growth and sheer numbers, will serve to increase our exposure to consumer heterogeneity in global markets.

The general objective of Part 2 is to show how global and local patterns coexist in both consumer behaviour and marketing environments. The cross-cultural approach to international marketing that is presented in Chapters 5 to 7 should enable future international marketers to understand local consumer behaviour in its full complexity. This approach allows adaptation of the design and implementation of market research across national markets when research instruments and data collection procedures are not similarly understood and do not produce equivalent findings cross-nationally.

Quite often basic concepts have been developed in a specific cultural environment. In marketing, the major contributor has been the United States. As such, it is necessary to investigate whether the consumer behaviour concepts and theories can be applied across the borders of cultures without losing part of their relevance and explanatory power. Consequently, Chapter 5 explores the cross-cultural aspects of consumer behaviour theories. It starts by assessing how culture affects consumer behaviour and highlights its influence on selected concepts such as loyalty, involvement and dissatisfaction. The chapter also examines the topic of ethnic consumption. The last section in this chapter takes as its premise that marketing is based on exchanges of meanings between marketers and consumers. This perspective makes sense in international marketing since meaning is directly based on language, and linguistic diversity remains quite high cross-nationally.

The encounters between local consumers and increasingly globalized consumption items are complex, contradictory and sometimes problematic. Chapter 6 first explains how the trend to globalization has been ideologically supported over the past two centuries by the free trade doctrine and how this doctrine has tended to view products as commodities and to deny cross-national variety in consumers' tastes and consumption habits.

Analysis of global trends in consumption patterns shows some convergence at a broad, quantitative level: the utilitarian needs for reasonably priced, mass-produced products and services are drivers behind this fast-paced change. The emergence of a global consumer culture is based on increasing aspirations for a world-standard package of goods and services whose performance is highly predictable. However, the meaning attributed to products and consumption experiences remains to a large extent embedded in local contexts, that of shared habits within the cultural and linguistic groupings. Examples are given of increasingly global products, such as beer, which are locally reinterpreted and vested with specific meanings, which must be taken into account when designing marketing strategy. In some cases, local consumer cultures are strong enough to develop resistance to globalized consumption, if it is perceived as detrimental to local cultural and economic interests. In most cases, however, the emergent pattern is a mix of local and global consumer behaviour based on kaleidoscopic ways of assembling diverse consumption experiences and making sense of them in everyday life.

When market research takes place across borders, a number of survey instruments, such as questionnaires, scales, sampling techniques and interview techniques may not fit with the target contexts where data has to be collected. Chapter 7 describes the technicalities of cross-cultural market research – that is, the problems posed by the possible inequivalence of instruments and methods across research contexts. The chapter reviews equivalence issues, such as conceptual, functional, translation and measure equivalence, which are examined in successive sections and illustrated by real-life examples. The issue of samples and sampling procedures is addressed because of the need of international marketing decision makers for findings that can be consistently compared across cultures and markets. Chapter 7 also examines how local respondents may react to survey instruments and which sort of data biases result from their unfamiliarity with the chosen data-collection techniques. As a consequence, international research is often less technical than domestic research in terms of scientific survey instruments and needs more inputs of action research: this is illustrated in the last section with the example of the Japanese style of researching markets.

5

Cross-cultural consumer behaviour

'*Sehen Sie Mercedes mit anderen Augen. Die neue E-Klasse ist da*' says a Daimler-Benz poster for their new E-Class car ('Look at Mercedes with other eyes. The new E-Class arrives'). This chapter is all about 'looking with other eyes'. It deals with the influence of culture on consumer behaviour. Looking with the 'same eyes' means that theories, underlying models, concepts and views of what consumers are, what their motives are, and how they behave, are assumed to be universal. One may 'add glasses to the same eyes' so that what was previously invisible comes to light. But what Mercedes asks its potential consumers to do may be necessary: changing one's eyes in order to have a different perspective. Table 5.1 sums up four perspectives, starting from the view that both consumers (the object) and underlying consumer behaviour theories (the eyes) can be either universal or specific. When reading Table 5.1, it is important to note that no cell corresponds to a perspective that is better than any other; they are simply different perspectives.

As depicted in Table 5.1, the *global perspective*, in its purest form, is rarely found and may only make sense for specific classes of consumers, such as business people who travel worldwide, and their families ('the

global nomads'). However, the *global perspective* has been widely used to investigate international consumer behaviour, despite arguments against this practice.[1] As we will argue in Chapter 7, the cross-cultural applicability of consumer behaviour theories and concepts need to be investigated across international markets, as well as sub-cultural markets, such as different immigrant and ethnic groups.

The *imported perspective* is somewhat more reasonable and applicable where offerings are tailored to local markets and marketing environments, but basic underlying theories are not changed. Taking an imported perspective may enable the discovery of significant differences in consumer behaviour (CB) that require marketing adaptations. For instance, from a global perspective behavioural intentions models were assumed to be universally applicable: attitudes and expectations of important others influence intentions to perform a behaviour. Some insight can be gained from an imported perspective when the 'universal' relationships between these variables are examined at a cultural level: consumers in individualist cultures are more influenced by attitudes than they are the expectations of important others, while the

Table 5.1 Consumer behaviour in a cross-cultural perspective

		Consumer behaviour theories	
		Universal (etic)	Specific (emic)
Consumers	Universal	(1) Global perspective	(3) Ethnic consumption perspective
	Specific	(2) Imported perspective	(4) Cultural meaning perspective

reverse is true in collectivist cultures.[2–4] However, many aspects of consumer behaviour are not universal. In this case, further insight can be gained from the emic viewpoint, in terms of the ethnic consumption perspective or the cultural meaning perspective, which can uncover new constructs and new relationships between these constructs that leads to a better understanding of the behaviour. This is further explored in Section 5.1 which focuses on the influence of institutions, social conventions and habits or customs on consumer behaviour.

This chapter examines questions around the cross-cultural transportability of consumer behaviour theories. This is not to say that similarities do not exist between cultures. Commonalities are demonstrated by the success of products and services designed in perspectives 1 and 2. However, this does not mean that they could not have been even more successful. It is important to assess the cultural relativity of both consumers and the underlying models we apply, if we really want to understand cross-cultural consumer behaviour. Since both similarities and differences exist, it is important to know what one is looking for. This focus will guide the models that apply; those that let differences emerge or those that favour the discovery of similarities. This corresponds with the etic (universal) approach and the emic (specific) approaches.

Website link 5.1

Search for cross-cultural research from the emic and etic perspectives: **http://www.quirks.com/articles/a1995/19950102.aspx.**

Section 5.1 discusses the influence of some of the major cultural elements on consumer behaviour. It starts with the question of whether the hierarchy of needs applies cross-culturally. Not only whether people locate their needs at different levels in the hierarchy, across cultures, but also, whether the major assumptions in this model are valid across cultures. Then, the influence of institutions and social conventions are considered, including their relationship to decision-making. Then, both chronic and situational cultural mindsets are considered to illustrate how situational cues may affect what feels naturally right or fluid.

Section 5.2 examines the impact of culture on selected aspects of consumer behaviour. Table 5.2

provides a list of how culture can affect consumer decision-making. The table also suggests issues to be addressed in order to reach a better understanding of cultural differences in consumer behaviour. The final sections review how a selection of consumer behaviours are influenced by culture, including consumer involvement, cognitive styles, perceived risk and uncertainty and loyalty.

Section 5.3 further explores post-purchase dissatisfaction by analysing the transfer of consumer behaviour constructs across cultures. Marketers tend to apply consumer behaviour concepts in an ethnocentric manner, whereas they would learn more by focusing on a common problem: how do cultures solve a similar problem in a different way?

Section 5.4 examines the influences of ethnicity on consumption patterns. Ethnic consumption is a major area of cross-cultural consumer behaviour in two respects: (1) ethnic consumption has modified consumption patterns in countries opened to immigration; and (2) some ethnic products have reached world-class status by being adopted in most countries of the world, through migration and international travel.

Marketing is a process involving communication and exchange: consumers buy meanings as well as objects. Accordingly, Section 5.5 focuses on the way in which cultural background influences communication and exchange. Two examples are used to illustrate this: the role of emotions in Japanese marketing and the role of symbols in linking objects and persons in the Italian style of marketing.

5.1

Culture and consumer behaviour

Although consumer behaviour has strong universal components, its cultural variations cannot be ignored. Without presenting an exhaustive list, there are some essential points of cultural influence on consumer behaviour that are worth considering in some detail:

1. hierarchy of needs, which shape demand across product categories;
2. institutions, which influence consumer behaviour, given that most consumption is rooted in social life, a large part of which is institutionalized;
3. who makes decisions? and
4. the impact of cultural mindsets.

Hierarchy of needs

It is necessary to examine theories that appear to be universal from an etic perspective. Take, for instance, Maslow's[5] 'Hierarchy of Needs' which posits a hierarchical order of a set of basic universal needs. In this hierarchy, *physiological needs* must be satisfied first, as they are fundamental to survival. Then, *safety needs*, such as being sheltered and protected from dangers in the environment, emerge when physiological needs are satisfied. Then come what Maslow calls *social needs*, which include friendship and love relationships. Then come *esteem needs*, such as the desire for respect from others, which is supported by status-improving goods. Finally, when all other levels have been satisfied, is the need for *self-actualization*, encompassing the development of one's full potential as a human being.

However, culture influences this hierarchy on at least two levels. First, one of the basic axioms of Maslow's theory is not true in every culture: namely, that needs at a definite level must be satisfied in order for higher-order needs to appear. Second, similar kinds of needs may be satisfied in very different ways (products and consumption types).

Website link 5.2

Search for applications of Maslow's Hierarchy of Needs, such as this illustration of the television show 'Survivor': **http://www.bpsoutdoor.com/blog/?p=7**.

The level of economic development influences the satisfaction of our needs. In less developed economies, people usually focus on more basic survival needs. However, some cultures (e.g., Hindu) encourage the pursuit of self-actualization, the highest level (the satisfaction of which does not necessarily imply material consumption) and discourage the pursuit of lower-level needs. Here, the basic need for safety, including shelter and personal protection, is not satisfied according to the same criteria in different cultures. In certain developing countries people may deprive themselves of food in order to afford a refrigerator, thereby satisfying the social status and self-esteem need before satisfying their physical needs.[6]

The well-documented area of conspicuous consumption also contradicts the hierarchy of needs. As noted by Solomon (p. 426),[7] the term *conspicuous consumption* was coined by Veblen, who was initially inspired by anthropological studies of the Kwakiutl Indians:

These Indians had a ceremony called a potlach where the host showed off his wealth and gave extravagant presents to their guests. The more one gave away, the better one looked to the others. Sometimes, the host would use an even more radical strategy to flaunt his wealth. He would publicly destroy some of his property to demonstrate how much he had. This ritual was also used as a social weapon: Since guests were expected to reciprocate, a poorer rival could be humiliated by inviting him to a lavish potlach. The need to give away, even though he could not afford it, would essentially force the hapless guest into bankruptcy.[7]

A similar concept also exists in modern societies, especially in the context of fundraising, where appreciation banquets, luncheons and campaign parties present ritualized, symbolic gift-giving which induces participants into the social dynamics of philanthropy.[8] These examples suggest that consumer motivations are influenced by the dynamics of social life. Thus, one of the basic axioms of Maslow's theory is not supported across cultures; lower-level needs to not always need to be satisfied for the needs in the next level to appear. Although the order of need fulfilment may vary across cultures, the needs themselves are still strikingly consistent.

Institutions, social conventions, habits and customs

Institutions such as the State, the Church and Trade Unions influence the marketing environment, which in turn influences consumer behaviour. For example, the French Catholic hierarchy has generally been opposed to Sunday trading. In Germany trade unions strongly oppose an extension of store opening hours, which were restricted to be closed on Saturday afternoons and Sundays. The Federal government granted the states the authority to regulate shopping hours in 2006. These states maintained some restrictions in store opening hours, especially on Sundays. The result is that German consumers have a well-developed catalogue and home shopping market, and Internet shopping is growing quite rapidly.

Other products are institution-dependent: examples include marriage-related goods, such as a wedding dress, the products featured on wedding lists, or the many kinds of traditional gifts offered for specific occasions. One example is the initiative by a Parisian Catholic priest to take action against Halloween in favour of the next day, All Saints' Day (in honour of all the saints), traditionally an important holiday in France. In conjunction with the French Association of Bakers, a '*Gâteau de la Toussaint*' was developed to increase respect for the day of honouring the dead, thereby creating an institution-dependent product.

Website link 5.3

Search for information about the range of places that celebrate specific holidays, such as All Saints' Day: **http://www.timeanddate.com/holidays/common/all-saints-day**.

Of all the cultural conventions that structure daily life in the consumption domain, the most important is probably eating habits. According to Wilk (p. 327):[9] 'Food is both substance and symbol; providing both physical nourishment and a key form of communication that carries many kinds of meanings.' Cultural variations in eating habits include (also see Box 1.2 on dietary practices across different religions):

1. The number of meals consumed each day.
2. The standard duration and the position of meals in the daily schedule.
3. The composition of each meal. Servings may differ in size, comprise various types of food (local ingredients or cooking style) and differ in the nutritional content so that people can cope with long time periods without eating.
4. Beverages that accompany meals (water, coffee, tea, wine, beer, and so on) and their functional use as a refresher, energizer, coolant, or relaxer.
5. The social function, whether 'fuel' or daily 'social event'. Meals may be communal events where people entertain themselves by eating and chatting, or it may simply be a means of feeding oneself without any symbolic connotation.
6. The way it is put together. Is the food ready-made or is it prepared from basic ingredients? Does paid help prepare the meal? What is the cultural meaning of the meal being prepared by the wife or by her husband, for whom, in which particular situations?

The list of cultural variations in eating habits is endless, because nothing is more essential, more vital and at the same time more accurately defined by culture than eating habits. Eating habits should be considered as the whole process of purchasing food and beverages, cooking, tasting, and even commenting on them. For instance, Askegaard and Brunsø (p. 80)[10] report that 'cooking patterns in Singaporean families are definitely very different from the European ones. . . . the presence of a maid and the regular habit of dining out makes the "woman's task" more diffuse to define in terms of responsibility for the family's health and nutrition'. In other countries the solution is quite different. In the US, for instance, people prefer to buy 'ready-made' or pre-prepared foods, such as cookie dough, cake mix, and canned or dried soups. Of course, this type of food faces resistance from more traditional countries, where the housewife is expected to prepare meals from natural ingredients for her family.

Website link 5.4

Search for information on maid services in Singapore, such as this Expat guide: **http://www.expatsingapore.com/content/view/1174**.

Who makes decisions?

Most of the available marketing literature depicts individual consumers who make their own decisions. While this individual-centric conception remains at the heart of marketing research, there is a growing understanding that our decisions are strongly influenced by social factors. For example, Bagozzi's model of goal-directed behaviour encompasses multiple sources of social influence on an individual's intentions.[11] Further, Bagozzi and Lee (pp. 229–30)[12] describe the concept of social intentions, termed 'we-intentions to perform a group act . . . In this case a person plans to participate in a joint activity, but conceives of the activity less as individuals performing personal acts that contribute to a group performance than as a group action in which one is a member of the group'. In addition to the more traditional influence of expectations of important others, group norms and social identity also influence I- and We-intentions to different degrees across cultures.[12,13]

Two areas of marketing research can be used to examine group decisions: industrial marketing and family decision-making. Both literatures recognize that different people exert more or less influence depending on the importance of that decision to the group and individual. Generally, unimportant decisions are made by individuals, midrange decisions by a group, and very important decisions by a key decision maker.[14] For instance, across a range of Latin American countries, food and appliance decisions were mostly made by the wife, vacations, furniture, savings and insurance decisions were made jointly, and automobile selection was mostly made by the husband.[15] Both of these literatures also recognize that the final decision maker is not the only one to influence the decision; the role of different stakeholders needs to be examined across cultures.

In the consumer behaviour literature, the family is often seen as an interacting group of individuals, who influence each other in their decisions. Research usually focuses on one or two family members, almost always including the mother, who are asked about family purchasing decisions. Few studies view the family as an organic entity or single decision-making unit (as opposed to a casual collection of individuals who share information and some common interests and constraints). An organic view may help to uncover many social influences within the family group, which is more complex in studies that span cultures or countries.

The vast majority of the family decision-making literature has focused on Western families. Differences in influence have been found depending on factors, such as the product type, stage of the decision process, family member asked, the role structure within the family, spousal resources, and decision-making styles. However, social and cultural factors also impact this type of decision-making, with family structures varying across cultures. Rodman (pp. 63–5)[16] identified four stereotypical types of societies where the marital power is likely to differ:

1. *Patriarchy*: A high level of paternal authority across all levels of society (e.g., India).
2. *Modified Patriarchy*: Patriarchal family norms can differ by social class (e.g., Greece and Yugoslavia).
3. *Transitional Equalitarianism*: Equalitarian norms are replacing patriarchal norms, giving more normative flexibility, depending on personal resources (e.g., US).

4. *Equalitarianism*: Strong equalitarian values, where both husband and wife share power throughout all levels of society (e.g., Denmark and Sweden).

Family decision-making is also likely to differ across the individualism–collectivism and masculinity–femininity (described in Chapter 3) divide:[17]

■ Highly feminine individualist cultures, such as Denmark, Norway and Sweden, share social and economic responsibilities between men and women. They have overlapping gender roles, and high levels of equality and individual freedom.

■ Highly feminine collectivist cultures, such as Chile, South Korea and Thailand, also share social and economic responsibilities and have a high level of equality, but they have less individual freedom. In Thailand there are generally stronger family ties, more communication and family members have a greater influence on consumption behaviour than in Western families.

■ Highly masculine individualist cultures, such as Australia, Germany, the UK and the US, have large gender role differences, lower equality and a high level of individual freedom.

■ Highly masculine collectivist cultures, such as Hong Kong, Japan and Mexico, have large gender role differences, and lower levels of equality and individual freedom. Japanese mothers restrict their children's consumption, allowing less autonomy, while at the same time reporting a higher level of children's influence than American mothers who encourage the development of independent consumption relatively early.[18]

Another influence from collectivism is the role of the extended family. In the East, the extended family model has survived and it has a powerful influence on many purchase decisions. Even Chinese people, who may sometimes appear quite individualistically oriented when outside their national context, remain strongly bound by their family ties. Ikels (p. 30)[19] points out two factors that have reinforced family ties:

. . . first the traditional value of interdependence both between parents and children and among the masses as a whole has never been attacked; second, the economic conditions in China, and in rural China in particular, provide the elderly with opportunities to contribute to household income while at the same time making it impossible for them to go it alone.

Cultural mindsets

Consumers buy objects and services for the value they provide. In valuing things, consumers may attribute private and/or public meanings. Public meanings have been defined as the subjective meanings assigned to an object by outside observers (non-owners) of that object, or members of the society at large.[20] Public meanings emerge through socialization and participation in shared activities and are reinforced in social interchanges. Private meanings are the sum of the subjective meanings that an object holds for a particular individual. Some of the private meanings may derive from socially shared interpretations, but some of them are unique to the consumer because they are associated with private and even intimate experiences.

As discussed in Chapter 2, we argue that culture has a chronic and situational influence. This means that on average, culture provides information that is normatively useful to individuals. Cultural or country level differences are due to this normative knowledge being chronically accessible (available in memory), making the culturally preferred solution feel obvious, fluent or right. However, since a variety of potential *cultural solutions* (discussed in Chapters 2 and 3) are available to people across societies (although differentially preferred), contextual information can influence which cultural solution feels right in the situation, depending on the mindset that is made salient. That is, the appropriate cultural mindsets or self-construal can be primed by the context.

Oyserman[21] has extensively studied the effects of individualism and collectivism at the cultural or country level and also through priming (cues that make different cultural norms salient) individuals within or across countries. At the individual level, she and her colleagues have either reinforced the chronic cultural norms by providing culturally consistent cues (e.g., patriotic-themed or white plates at a BBQ) or reinforced situational norms by providing individualistic or collectivistic cues to make one or other mindset seem 'right' in the situation (e.g., using Chinese versus English language in Hong Kong). These situational mindsets then include relevant content, procedures and goals that indicate what the situation is 'about'.[21]

Two of the most studied mindsets relate to an *independent* (more common in individualist countries) or *interdependent* (more common in collectivist countries) self-construal.[22] When the independent self-concept is salient, individuals will naturally think about their identity as being separate and distinct, whereas when the interdependent self-construal is salient, individuals will naturally think about their identity as being connected with others. In this way, people in collectivist cultures are able to do tasks that require being distinct rather than connected when the situation requires it (e.g., excelling in an exam). Similarly, people in individualistic cultures are able to put others' goals ahead of their own when the situation requires it (e.g., helping their children).

The salience of an interdependent or independent self-construal has been found to influence many aspects of consumer behaviour, including reasons for purchase,[23] impulsive buying behaviour,[24] references for consumption symbols,[25] associations embedded in persuasion appeals,[26] the persuasion of approach and avoidance appeals,[25] and emotional appeals.[27] For instance, the independent self-construal is more strongly related to purchase reasons associated with uniqueness, while the interdependent self-construal is more strongly related to reasons associated with group affiliation.[23] In addition, Oyserman[21] provides further meta-analytic and experimental evidence that these cultural mindsets influence a wide range of attitudes and behaviours including the extent of focus on relationships, perceptions and memory, as well as the ability to focus on relevant, and ignore irrelevant information in complex tasks.

5.2

The influence of culture on selected aspects of consumer behaviour

Table 5.2 presents selected aspects of consumer behaviour that are influenced by cultural differences. This table is designed to be indicative, rather than exhaustive, as there has been a dramatic increase in the cross-cultural analysis of consumer behaviour and several reviews are available.[28,17] We focus on a selection of the relevant consumer behaviour literature, including consumer involvement, decision-making styles, perceived risk and loyalty. In the next section, we extend this discussion to post-purchase behaviours, focusing on consumer complaining.

Table 5.2 Possible impacts of cultural differences on selected aspects of consumer behaviour

Aspect of consumer behaviour	Impact of cultural differences: values involved/issues to be addressed	Section
Perception	Perception of shapes, colours and space varies across cultures.	2.3; 9.4
Motivation	Motivation to own, buy, spend, consume, show, share and/or give.	5.3
Learning and memory	Literacy levels. Memory as it is shaped by education. Familiarity with product classes shaped by education.	5.2; 5.3
Age	Do people know their exact age? Value of younger and older people in the society. Influence processes across age groups. How is purchasing power distributed across generations?	2.4
Mindsets and self-construals	Perceptions of self as distinct or a group member. Considerations of self versus other goals. Contextual norms that make a solution feel 'right'.	2.4; 2.5, 5.1
Group influence	Individualism/collectivism.	3.1, 5.2
	To what extent does one's group influence their attitudes and buying behaviour?	5.1
	How does consumer behaviour reflect the need to self-actualize individual identity or to manifest group belonging?	
Social class	Are social classes locally important?	3.1; 5.1
	Does consumption demonstrate social class belonging?	
	What type of products or services do social status-minded consumers buy? Are there exclusive shops?	
Gender roles	What is the division of labour? Who makes the decisions? Who shops? Are they the same person?	3.1; 3.2
Attitudes change	Resistance to change in consumer behaviour (possibly related to strong uncertainty avoidance, past orientation, and fatalism), especially when change could clash with local values and behaviour (e.g., resistance to fast food restaurants in France).	5.2
Decision-making	Family models (nuclear versus extended family).	5.1
	Involvement.	5.2
	Compulsive buying.	
Purchase	Loyalty.	5.2
	Environmental factors, especially legal and economic.	14.1, 14.6, 14.7
	Influence of others, including salespeople.	14.3
Post-purchase	Perceptions of product quality.	5.3; 9.1; 9.3; 10.3
	Consumer complaining behaviour.	5.3; 9.3
	Dissatisfaction/Consumerism.	5.3

Consumer involvement

Consumer involvement is generally a function of a person, a product or service and a situation.[29] Personal interests may vary, but situational factors, on the other hand, are likely to assume increased importance in Eastern as opposed to Western cultures. In Eastern cultures the extent of consumer involvement is likely to be higher for publicly consumed or shared products. Eastern consumers value social harmony and smooth family relationships (both nuclear and extended). Therefore, the social significance of a product is very important, because it may express status, gratitude, approval or disapproval. In contrast, involvement is likely to be lower when products are used for private consumption. In this case, consumers are likely to adopt a rather simple cognitive stance, favouring the physical functions of the product and being mostly concerned with price and quality.

Consumer cognitive styles

High-involvement purchase decisions are generally thought to have five stages: problem recognition, information search, alternative evaluations, purchase (perhaps) and post-purchase. (For habitual purchases and less-involving product decisions, these processes may have occurred in the past, even if they have been limited in terms of effort.) Each of these stages can be influenced by social and situational factors, including marketing stimuli (particularly advertising and sales promotion).

Consumer behaviour models have a rather linear, analytical and abstract style. Asian consumers tend to have a different cognitive style: the Chinese as well as the Japanese have a more synthetic, concrete and contextual orientation in their thought patterns.[30–33] Information acquisition on an attribute-by-attribute basis is not the dominant style of information processing employed by Asian consumers: information is processed in a more holistic way by choice alternative or some combination of attribute and choice alternative.[32]

This does not mean that Asians are less rational; on the contrary, they might be more rational in their purchasing. For instance, Chinese Confucian ideology promotes a long-term orientation which values perseverance and thrift.[17] This is likely to increase the prevalence of a more utilitarian shopping style, where price, quality and value are considered very important.[34] Further, Eastern collectivist consumers have been shown to engage in less impulsive buying than Western individualist consumers, despite having similar personal impulse tendencies.[24] Eastern consumers (as adults) learn to suppress their internal impulses in order to act appropriately in the situation. It seems that they are able to suppress their impulsiveness trait and act in a manner that is consistent with cultural norms.

Perceptions of risk and uncertainty

Perceived risk is an important consideration in the decision-making process, especially at the alternative (product or product category) evaluation stage.[35,36] Perceived risk can be broken into the psychological, financial, performance, physical, social and time or convenience risk.[37] In Western cultures, performance risk (whether the product performs as expected) has been suggested as a good measure of perceived risk as it is strongly related to overall perceptions of risk.[38] Performance risk may not be the most important type of risk in other cultures.

In Eastern cultures consumers may be more sensitive to social risk (because a purchaser may risk the loss of face in other people's eyes), than performance or financial risks. Their tight ingroup increases the importance of social expectations, whereas it decreases the importance of personal risk. People in collectivistic cultures are more risk-seeking in their financial choices than people in individualistic cultures.[39] This has been attributed to cushion theory, which suggests that social networks protect people if they take risks and 'fall'.[40]

In many developing nations physical risk has a low importance, because the mortality rate is high, and illness and death are accepted as part of this life, but perhaps not the next. The diminished importance of physical risk will influence the purchase of many products, including insurance, healthcare, food and transportation. In a country where road safety is not a high priority, we might see people sitting on the top of trains, or on chairs in the back of trucks, with no regard for safety issues. In this case, the more important risk associated with purchasing a car may be reliability: an engine breakdown may be seen as a disaster, because there is little or no available maintenance. These perceived risks are quite different from those experienced by the average purchaser of a car in a developed country.

It is important to note that risk is fundamentally different from uncertainty, although they have often been confused in the literature. Risk is quantifiable: it has an associated probability. Uncertainty has no associated probability; it is a situation in which anything can happen.[35] As Hofstede (p. 148)[17] points out, people may engage in risky behaviour in order to reduce ambiguity, 'such as starting a fight with a potential opponent rather than sitting back and waiting'. Consequently, they differentially influence consumer behaviour: perceptions of uncertainty increase information search, whereas perceptions of risk influence the evaluation of alternatives.[36]

Loyalty

Consumers can be loyal, repeating their purchases on a regular basis, buying the same brand or product, or buying at the same store or from the same catalogue or website. Loyal consumers prefer to be sure of what they buy. However, by doing this they reduce their opportunity to find other, and perhaps better, choices which could provide them with more value for their money. Disloyal consumers try new brands, shift from one brand to another when a new one is promoted, and take advantage of temporary price reductions. Disloyalty is the natural counterpart of loyalty (to a brand, a product, a store, etc.). What is culturally meaningful is to observe which one of these two opposite attitudes is considered as the legitimate, fundamental behaviour.

In the West *brand loyalty* is carefully surveyed, and demographics, lifestyles or situational variables are researched. Standard behaviour is assumed to be disloyal. Consumers are likely to switch brands to test competing products, thereby fostering price competition. It is standard behaviour to respond spontaneously to advertising and sales promotion, because consumers enjoy change more than stability. They seek more variety in their purchases.[41] Variety seeking has been linked to the need for uniqueness, which is more prevalent in Western cultures.[42] It is assumed that consumers are not rewarded for buying the same brand (i.e., 'brand loyal') and/or shopping in

the same store (i.e., 'store loyal'). A country's individualism score has been related to a greater propensity to buy brands they have never tried before.[28]

Loyalty is a key concept in collectivist cultures, which spreads from people to product, inasmuch as products are expressions of the self. There is an unusual level of single brand dominance in many Asian markets, with one brand accounting for 40–50 per cent of market share over quite a long period of time.[43] Consumers in collectivist societies have been shown to be more loyal on average for two reasons.[44] First, they tend to rely more on information found in their reference group – often by word-of-mouth communication – rather than on media information. Second, they tend to follow the group consensus until they are convinced that a new product is better. A rare examination of loyalty outside Western cultures reveals that consumers from China and South Korea tend to buy the same brands because these products fulfilled their experiential, social and function needs.[45]

While consumer satisfaction is related to loyalty, this relationship is stronger in individualistic societies, as well as those that have a higher level of uncertainty avoidance or masculinity (discussed in Chapter 3).[46] For example, consumers in New Zealand (NZ) and China were asked to reflect on a recent incident when they had seriously considered switching service providers (e.g., bank, insurance company, doctor, phone company, hairdresser). The most important factor for the NZ sample was confidence in the service provider (i.e., satisfaction and trust), whereas the most important consideration for the Chinese sample was time and effort (i.e., learning, switching and establishing a new relationship).[47] This illustrates the higher level of cost to switching in Eastern cultures. Not only is extra time required in developing a relationship with a new service provider, but extra time is also required in researching alternatives. The stronger reliance on word-of-mouth in Eastern cultures increases the effort required to gain the relevant information about alternatives.

It is necessary for marketing strategies to differ where consumers are fundamentally more loyal and less used to rational comparisons (such as price/quality cross-brand or cross-product comparisons), from those where consumers frequently shift brands. Uncertainty avoidance and collectivism are both positively related to loyalty, suggesting that companies entering markets with these characteristics will face more obstacles. Where consumers are more loyal, it may be necessary to build a loyal consumer base from scratch. Where consumers are less loyal, it may be more effective to persuade brand shifters to switch from other established brands, and then to try to turn the newly developed consumer base into a loyal one.[48] The extent of loyalty also has implications for brand equity. In South Korea the most important element of brand equity in apparel was loyalty, while perceptions of quality and familiarity were more important for Americans.[49]

5.3

Investigating the cross-cultural applicability of consumer behaviour concepts

Any element of consumer behaviour is filtered through cross-cultural lenses. For example, word-of-mouth communication is fairly universal: in any culture, people discuss and exchange information on their consumption experiences. People tend to seek information from acquaintances or online customer reviews when little relevant information is available (i.e., new films or new products), or when consumers have a low level of familiarity with a complex product (e.g., a new computer or smart phone). However, word-of-mouth communication is likely to be stronger in collectivist and ingroup-oriented societies, where outside information provided by an unknown other or marketer will be seen as less reliable than opinions from relatives and acquaintances.

The best solution for investigating cross-cultural applicability is always to start from the 'common problem' in Kluckhohn and Strodtbeck's terms.[50] For instance, why and how can consumers express dissatisfaction with products or services? The solution found in the consumer behaviour literature is based on the dominant normative solution in the West. Other alternatives must always be looked for, especially the alternative that the problem may not *have* a solution.

The example of consumer dissatisfaction

We can investigate the equivalence of consumer satisfaction and dissatisfaction by assessing the comparability of antecedent factors, formation processes and behavioural outcomes.[51]

1. What are the relevant antecedent factors that may differ? Do they include economic (e.g., buying power), temporal (e.g., time needed for purchase and consumption activities), cognitive (e.g., mental capacity available to understand and process information) and spatial (e.g., location of activities in terms of place and distance) differences, in terms of the way they are perceived and the criteria and processes used for allocation (e.g., a scarce resource in one country may not be scarce in another)? Are the categories and substitutability of these resources comparable? Are the contextual or situational influences, such as spatial aspects, social surroundings, and tasks comparable? For instance, in Chapter 2 we looked at the variability of time and space. Consumers are more likely to trade off or substitute time for money where time is considered an economic resource.

2. Are dissatisfaction formation processes the same, including ideal, expected, deserved and minimum tolerable product performance? Do consumers perceive discrepancies in the same way? For instance, in some countries, such as Mexico, consumers seem to rely more on perceptions, rather than the Western model of relying on confirmation or disconfirmation of their expectations.[51]

3. Will dissatisfaction influence action in the same way, such as repeat purchasing and switching behaviour? Some cultures have a higher social desirability bias and, as such, high reported satisfaction is unlikely to lead to the same level of repeat purchase as those from cultures with a lower social desirability bias.[52]

Attitudes towards consumerism vary across national contexts and so does the importance given to the consumer movement based on the following premises:

1. Is it legitimate for consumers to make their dissatisfaction known? In societies that experienced long periods of supply shortage this is not the case; complaints are useless.

2. Is it legitimate for consumers to force a producer, whose product is of dubious quality, to close down? In other words, is it right for consumers to cause innocent workers to lose their jobs?

3. Will complaining make any difference for the individual or for society?

These questions illustrate the problems associated with issues of consumer empowerment. The defence of individual consumers has consequences for society. Thus, expressing dissatisfaction frankly and openly may be considered appropriate.

In fact, normal practices in terms of returns and exchanges differ markedly around the world. In many countries, returns and exchanges are not possible, or only possible in very limited circumstances, such as in cases where products are unopened, have clear defects, and are accompanied by a receipt. Blodgett and colleagues (pp. 109–10) presented the following selection of customer comments about return policies and practices in different countries:[53]

Czech Republic: 'The policies toward returning products are similar to those applied in the USA. However, most retailers will not accept returned items . . . unless they are persuaded that you did not use the product "improperly" or in any way that is explicitly forbidden in the instructions for use.'

China: 'It is not common . . . for customers to return items that they are not satisfied with.'

Russia: 'The product can be returned if it was damaged/faulty and a customer kept purchase receipt and [had] service warranty (for example, with electronics) . . . Personal belongings such as apparel, cosmetics and beauty items, as well as leisure items (books, CDs', tapes etc.) could not be returned in any circumstances.'

Taiwan: 'It is usually not possible for customers to return an item in Taiwan.'

Kenya: 'You can not return a product once purchased and customers take their own risk. In my country customer relations is not very good . . .'

India: 'There is no customer empowerment. People realize that they are being "ripped off", but if everyone is a thief, what can the customer do.'

While returns may be limited by a lack of competition, social expectations and legislation, customer complaining should be less limited. However, there are dramatic differences across countries. Western consumers in general voice more dissatisfaction than Eastern consumers. Collectivist consumers, on the other hand, are less likely to voice a complaint directly and more likely to engage in negative word-of-mouth.[28] For example, South Koreans respond privately more often, including avoiding the firm's product, buying from another firm or telling others about their bad

experience, as compared to Americans who tend to discuss the problem with the manager, ask for the firm to fix it and believe that telling them will help them to do better in the future.[45]

Richins and Verhage (p. 203)[54] reported differences in American and Dutch consumers' beliefs about dissatisfaction with a product or a service:

Dutch consumers perceive more inconvenience and unpleasantness in making a complaint than do American consumers . . . Dutch consumers were less likely than Americans to feel a social responsibility to make complaints . . . Seemingly contradicting this finding, however, Dutch consumers are more likely than Americans to feel bothered if they don't make a complaint when they believe they should, a sort of guilt. Perhaps this seeming contradiction indicates that Dutch respondents tend to feel a personal rather than social obligation to make complaints.

The word *construct* relates to a concept that has several underlying dimensions, and may be measured quantitatively by identifying these various dimensions. The construct *consumer dissatisfaction and complaint behaviour* includes five different aspects of attitude towards complaining:[55]

1. beliefs about the effect experienced when one complains;
2. perceptions of the objective cost or trouble involved in making a complaint;
3. perception of retailer responsiveness to consumer complaints;
4. the extent to which consumer complaints are expected to benefit society at large; and
5. the perceived social appropriateness of making consumer complaints.

It is important to think about whether each of these aspects makes sense in the cross-cultural context. In the case of developing countries, micro-level (e.g., excessive prices, misleading advertising, lack of performance) and macro-level sources of consumer dissatisfaction (e.g., low income, inflation) may interact.[56] Cavusgil and Kaynak (p. 118)[56] argue that: 'In general micro-level sources appear to lead, over time, to a diffuse, latent discontent with the state of the marketplace; that is to macro-level dissatisfaction. Unsatisfactory experiences with specific products and services seem to be reflected in a disillusionment with all institutions in the society.' They argue that complaining behaviour does not have the same meaning if the buyer and seller know each other personally, as either acquaintances or relatives.

Looking with other eyes: questioning consumer behaviour

'Looking with other eyes' implies decentering yourself. For instance, the vast majority of European cars have manual gearboxes in contrast to American cars, which tend to have automatic gearboxes. Accordingly, since an automatic gearbox is not a standard feature of cars in Europe, consumers have to pay extra and wait a little longer to get an automatic car. Further, selling a car with an automatic gearbox in a European country may be difficult, since many Europeans consider automatic cars either as being reserved for people with disabilities or as a feature of luxury cars.

If we apply the perspectives from Table 5.1, the universal or global approach provides few clues for understanding the case of manual versus automatic gearboxes. The other perspectives provide many more insights by focusing on consumer specifics. In many countries, including most of Europe, there are limitations on the licensing of drivers of automatic cars, where those who obtain their licence in an automatic car are prohibited from driving a manual car. In contrast, US drivers are able to drive automatic and manual cars, as their licences do not specify which type of car was used in the test. In France almost everyone learns and takes their driving test in a manual car. The main exceptions are for drivers with disabilities. Thus, learning plays a key role in the resistance to change: having been educated on manual drive, they tend to stick to what they know. Second, many Europeans still believe that automatic gearbox cars have high fuel consumption (or poor gas mileage in US terms). Nowadays this is not true, since technology has progressed to the point where the difference is negligible, and in fact favours automatic cars in urban traffic conditions. Third, automatic vehicles are associated with high social status. Large and expensive cars are automatic more often than medium or small cars.

If we sum up on the basis of the perspectives presented in Table 5.1:

1. The *global perspective* assumes both universal theories and universal consumers. This perspective misses the specific consumer insights from the market.

2. The *imported perspective* assesses specific consumer insight assuming universal theory. This perspective allows the discovery of the social status and resistance to change arguments.

3. The *ethnic consumption perspective* applies specific theories but assumes consumers are universal. This perspective allows the researcher to identify a small 'ethnic' target, that of North American expatriates (although many of them love manual gearboxes, which to them look more sporty).

4. The *cultural meaning perspective* applies specific theories to specific consumers. This is the only perspective that reveals the symbolic argument (automatic being associated with disability), which is the major obstacle to selling the automatic car in Europe, even though they are much more comfortable to drive, and just as speedy and as fuel efficient as other cars.

Radical questioning

The application of 'different eyes' requires radical questioning. One way to question consumer behaviour cross-nationally is simply to examine motivations in each of these basic actions: to own, spend, save, buy, consume, display, share and give (see Table 5.2).

1. *Motivation to own* is based on the notion of ownership. The English verb 'to own' has no equivalent in Swahili, the dominant language in East Africa. Possession, that is, the rights of individuals over objects, is also much more limited in scope.

2. *Motivation to spend* may also be radically altered by negative views of money.

3. *Motivation to save* may be altered by a lack of future orientation, and the feeling that one should not bet on one's future.

4. *Motivation to buy* may be low when objects and material culture are not valued, which is independent of purchasing power, as in Hindu culture.

5. *Motivation to consume* may be largely hindered by a strong ecological stance, as in Denmark or Germany where sensitivity to environmental problems has practically eliminated plastic bottling in favour of reusable glass.

6. *Motivation to display* is naturally related to the self-construal and the prevailing pattern of property.

7. *Motivation to give* also varies across cultures. Giving rituals are widely practised in Japan, where the size of the gift is codified according to the type of social exchange. Gift-giving in Hong Kong, is embedded in sociocultural influences.[57] In other cultures, however, gift-giving practices may be less frequent, based on the view that it might embarrass the recipient, necessitate reciprocity, and ultimately lead to resentment if both participants feel obligated to participate in the ritual.

There have been many studies of gift-giving. One such study found that Korean and Americans have altruistic motivation more than 50 per cent of the time, but the number was higher for the American sample (86 per cent): Koreans more often gave out of obligation (17 per cent), self-interest (11 per cent), group conformity (7 per cent) and face-saving (5 per cent). Park (p. 580) cited a Korean respondent's thoughts about gift giving:

I do have a lot of occasions to give a gift for face saving. Because saving face is very important in social life, I should give a gift on those occasions in order not to lose face. But I can't afford them always. Actually, there are too many occasions to afford with my income. The most frequent gift occasions for face saving are weddings, funerals, New Year's Day and Choo Suk [Korean Thanksgiving]. When I receive a gift, I feel pressure to reciprocate sometime in the future. In fact, face saving gifts are not pleasant at all.[58]

Website link 5.5

Search for examples of business gift-giving etiquette in different cultures: **http://www.businessknowhow.com/growth/ccultural.htm**.

5.4

Ethnic consumption

Ethnicity as a thwarted ingroup orientation

Ethnic consumption is a strong component of modern consumption culture, reflecting the internationalization of lifestyles through migration and travel. Ethnic products have been popularized worldwide and ethnic food and restaurants are fast-growing segments in the food industry.

Ethnic consumption has a great deal to do with mixing consumption patterns of a heritage and settlement country in subcultural groups, such as immigrants, refugees and sojourners. One of the most influential models of migrants' adaptation and adjustment process is John W. Berry's bi-dimensional acculturation model.[59] This model is based on two orthogonal dimensions: heritage culture maintenance and settlement culture acquisition. These dimensions lead to four basic strategies:

1. *Assimilation* – Individual does not wish to maintain their heritage culture, but wishes to adopt the settlement culture.
2. *Integration* – Individual wishes to maintain their heritage culture and adopt the settlement culture.
3. *Separation* – Individual wishes to maintain their heritage culture, but does not wish to adopt the settlement culture.
4. *Marginalization* – Individual does not wish to maintain their heritage culture or adopt the settlement culture.

However, marginalization is considered the most problematic strategy, in that it rarely emerges and represents something different to the other three.

These strategies can be seen in the consumer behaviour of ethnic groups. Elements of heritage country maintenance can be seen in Ger and Østergaard's (p. 49) description of Turkish students in Denmark as more 'Turkish' than those who live in Turkey:

Some families brought the curtains from Turkey, thinking that the curtains in Odense were too simple. Their furniture reminded the Turkish author of the 1960s urban middle class furnishings in Turkey: chandeliers, then a symbol of wealth, a prominent buffet, and 'Turkish' crochéed covers hanging from the shelves. They displayed many knick-knacks – small decorative souvenirs, currently sold for tourists in Turkey . . . Several homes had Turkish flags. One male informant, who displayed such a flag, in addition to posters of the Turkish national anthem and Istanbul, rosary beads, a Turkish soccer team key chain, and a Koran, and who was wearing a small flag pin on his sweater, explained that the Danes always have flags in their houses. Unlike 'some who try to hide the fact that they are Turks', he wants everyone to know that he is Turkish. His e-mail messages end with 'We Love Turkey'.[60]

Similarly, elements of an *integration* strategy can be seen in Herbert Gans' (p. 184) description of the Italian immigrant culture's eating and consumption habits in a New York neighbourhood, which he calls 'West End':

Their actual diet, however, bears little resemblance to that of their Italian ancestors, for they have adopted American items that can be integrated into the overall tradition. For example, although their ancestors could not afford to eat meat, West Enders can, and they spend considerable sums on it. Typically American meats such as hot dogs, hamburger and steak are very popular indeed, but they are usually prepared with Italian spices, and accompanied by Italian side-dishes. The role of American culture is perhaps best illustrated by holiday fare. Turkey is eaten on Thanksgiving, but is preceded by a host of Italian antipastos, accompanied by Italian side-dishes, and followed by Italian desserts. This amalgamation of ethnic and American food is, of course, not exclusive to the West Enders, but can be found among all groups of foreign origin.[61]

Ethnic subcultures are based on shared beliefs and habits and the sense of belonging to a specific group of people, which is different from the society at large. Ingroup orientation is central to ethnicity, but to a large extent, the sense of belonging to the subcultural community is thwarted, because it is simultaneously necessary – and difficult – to identify with the values and behaviour of the dominant ingroup and the majority population. Hispanics in the US have to cope with this dilemma: they have to adjust to a predominantly WASP (White Anglo-Saxon Protestant) culture, while their basic assumptions, interaction models and sense of belonging would drive them towards the Hispanic community. However, this is not true of all communities within the US. For instance, in Miami, where according to the 2010 Census 65 per cent of people had at least some Hispanic or Latino descent, Americans from historically mainstream WASP backgrounds are expected to adjust to the 'mainstream' Hispanic culture. This may be more difficult for them, as Hispanic Americans made a voluntary decision to migrate and as such are more likely to accept that they may have to acquire their settlement culture. Many Americans from the historically mainstream WASP culture feel resentful and threatened with the high concentration of 'minority' groups.

Ethnicity is a matter of shared belief about a common ancestry. Bouchet's six main attributes of ethnic community are:[62]

1. a collective proper name;
2. a myth of common ancestry;
3. shared historical memories;

4. one or more differentiating elements of common culture (e.g., language);
5. an association with a specific homeland; and
6. a sense of solidarity.

People are more likely to identify with an ethnic group if it also has an emotional significance.[63] Behavioural involvement with an ethnic group includes speaking the language, eating cultural food and social interaction. These behaviours overlap with indicators of acculturation.

Acculturation (assimilation or integration) is likely to continue into the third or fourth generation. However, there is often resurgence of ethnic identity, as individuals search for their heritage. Therefore, it is wrong to equate consumers from a definite ethnic group to a specific market segment, which seeks specific products or service benefits; as noted in the section above it is more complex. The usefulness of observable ethnicity as a market-segmentation basis in international consumer marketing has been questioned.

Ethnic consumption should be considered as a complex reality, which marketers need to look at with quite an open mind. It gives birth to new ideas, such as the Chino-Latino cuisine, a fusion of Asian and Cuban cuisine to be found in New York, which has its roots in the Chinese immigration to Cuba in the early 1900s.[64]

Website link 5.6

Search for ethnic cuisines, such those listed on the following website: http://www.ctahr.hawaii.edu/new/CulturalCuisine/CulturalCuisine.htm.

When dealing with ethnic consumption, the following points must be kept in mind:

1. Translation or spelling mistakes or inadequate wordings may be resented as offending the group's honour. For instance, a *burrito* has been translated from Spanish as a *burrada*, which means 'big mistake'.[7] This results in minority groups feeling neglected because their language is misused, or at least not understood, or respected.
2. In ethnic behaviour, the status of membership, that is, the claim of being 'different' is central and may be pushed to its extreme. Smaller ingroups are stronger platforms for identification. The larger Hispanic category may be further broken into Mexicans, Puerto-Ricans, Cubans, etc.

3. The level of acculturation, or the degree to which people have learned the ways of the host culture, influences ethnic consumption. Age is also significant: older people and less-acculturated people tend to display stronger ethnic attitudes.

4. Identification needs are 'reversible', creating ambiguous and even contradictory demands. Most people belonging to ethnic communities strive for both integration into the society at large and maintenance of their specific cultural roots. In some areas of consumption, such as housing and furnishing, they may express their belonging to the larger national ingroup and in another area, such as food, they may maintain strong ethnic behaviour.

5.5

Marketing as an exchange of meanings

Consumers buy meanings and marketers communicate meanings through products and advertisements. Consumer goods are vehicles of cultural meanings and consumers choose and then make use of these cultural meanings. In order to understand this, however, we have to look with other eyes.[65] For instance, Penaloza (p. 373)[66] investigated the cultural meaning of the Old West in the United States, finding different meanings for whites and non-whites:

For whites, popular depictions of adventurous explorers, miners, and ranchers accompany those of land thieves, murderers, and forced religious converters. For Native Americans, popular depictions of hostile savages stand beside romantic naturalists and spiritualists, wealthy casino owners, and movement activists fighting ongoing battles for land, mineral, and water rights.

Marketing may be seen primarily as a process of exchange where communication, broadly defined, is central. Many of the meanings in marketing exchanges are culture based: they are intersubjectively shared by a social group.[67] Intersubjective sharing of meanings signifies that each person in the group knows that everyone else knows the cognitive schema. Therefore, in the process of exchange through buyer–seller relations, marketing communications or product consumption, interpretations are made spontaneously, as if they were obvious realities, and a great deal of

information in the process of marketing as exchange and communication need not be made explicit. For instance, Kragh and Djursaa (pp. 1314–15)[68] explored the meanings carried by Danish and English dining and living rooms in which participants viewed photographs from the other country:

The English respondents complain that Danish modernist rooms look old fashioned, . . . the English respondents also think the Danish rooms are boring and bare . . . Returning the compliment, the Danes complain that the English rooms are tasteless, and pinpoint the syntactical features which convey this message: they find them overdone, with too many flowers and patterns. In addition, they find the room composition odd, missing their sofa groups with coffee tables which are integral to Danish ideas of togetherness.

Culture may be considered as a sort of *meta-language* central to the marketing process when viewed as exchange and communication. It works as a type of *game rule*, implicitly indicating how people will interact in an exchange relationship, influencing their constraints and their leeway in behaviour and decisions. The attitudinal differences toward market research between the Americans and Japanese (Chapter 7) are a good example of this: what is the 'right' way (that is, legitimate or appropriate) to communicate with the market? What is the market (actual buyers versus potential consumers)? In each case, the objective is seemingly the same: to collect relevant information and market data, in order to decide on marketing strategies. Two examples illustrate the differences in marketing meta-communication: the role of emotions in Japanese marketing, and the emphasis on the symbolic relationship between person and object in the Italian style of marketing.

The role of emotions in Japanese marketing

There is wide range of books on Japanese marketing, which are unfortunately written only in Japanese *Kanji* and *Hiragana*, thereby limiting access for non-Japanese readers. But the Japanese provide details in English in the review of the largest Japanese advertising agency, *Dentsu Japan Marketing/Advertising*. Koichi Tanouchi, a professor of marketing at Hitotsubashi University, depicts the Japanese style of marketing as being fundamentally based on emotions and sensitivity.

He first insists, as many authors do, that Japan is oriented towards rice production, and is not a nation of hunters and gatherers. This means more collective organization and interpersonal sensitivity: the cultivation of rice requires the simultaneous flooding of paddy fields, which cannot be decided by an isolated landowner. This involves a strong collective solidarity, serious planning and individual tenacity. Tanouchi states that 'masculine' values are less developed in Japan than 'feminine' values, which is illustrated by the example of marital relationships in household and personal spending:

In Japan, the husband is supposed to hand all his income over to his wife. If he doesn't, he is criticized by people around him. If she complains about this to his boss in his business company, the boss is very likely to take the wife's side, and advise him to give all his salary to his wife and add that that is the best way to keep peace at home and that everyone else is doing so. The wife has the right to decide how much money her husband can have for daily lunch and coffee. Regularly, about once in a half year, Japanese newspapers carry a research report about the average amount of the money the average husbands get from their wives. Wives decide about their husbands' lunch money watching these figures (p. 78).[69]

Sensitivity and emotions seem to permeate most aspects of Japanese marketing.[69] This is evidenced by the high level of sensitivity and response to actual consumer needs and by the search for social harmony between producers and distributors. It is also prominent in Japanese sales force compensation arrangements, where collective reward systems are often used. They foster cooperation, avoid threatening individual competition and promote social harmony in the sales team.

The role of the symbolic link between object and person through the medium of design in Italian marketing

A specific Italian marketing style has emerged that is characterized by heavy emphasis, and corresponding financial commitment, devoted to product appearance and design. The product is intended to act as a link between producers–sellers and consumers–purchasers: both appreciate the aesthetic qualities of the object. The Italians concentrate on the style and functionality of the object, and its integration into the environment. The focal point is object symbolism and its fit with

---

Box 5.1

The functional form of the cigarette lighter

The stylized fluidity of the 'functional forms' testifies to the connotation of mental dynamics, the semblance of a lost relationship, in an attempt to reconstruct a purpose through the accumulation of signs. For example, a lighter in the shape of a pebble was successfully launched by advertising. The oblong, elliptic and asymmetrical form is 'highly functional', not because it provides a better light than another lighter, but because it fits exactly into the palm of the hand. 'The seas have polished it into the shape of the hand': it is an accomplished form. Its function is not to give a light, but to be easy to handle. Its form is, so to speak, predetermined by Nature (the sea) to be handled by man. This new purpose is the sole rhetoric of the lighter. The connotations are here twofold: as an industrial object, the cigarette lighter is supposed to recall one of the qualities of the handicraft object, the shape of which furthers the gesture and the body of man. Moreover the allusion to the sea brings us to the myth of Nature, itself cultured by man, which follows all his desires: the sea plays the cultural role of a polisher; it is the sublime handicraft of nature. As the stone rolled by the sea, furthered by the hand producing light, the cigarette lighter becomes a wonderful flint, a whole prehistoric and artisanate purpose comes into play in the very practical essence of an industrial object.

(Source: Baudrillard, pp. 82–3.[70] Author's translation.)

the meaning attributed to it by consumers, as such increasing importance is given to qualitative studies. The Italians are not alone in having an awareness of the symbolic meaning of possessions for consumers. But they incorporate it at a high level and make it an essential element of marketing strategies. Baudrillard described a 'system of objects' in 1968,[70] which was fairly successful in France, ultimately achieved real success in Italy, where he is regarded as a guru of marketing semiology (Box 5.1).

Finally, the other side of the poster mentioned at the start of this chapter says '*Bei Mercedes bleibt alles anders*' ('With Mercedes everything remains different'). In international marketing, where similarities abound, it is wise to examine specific differences in consumer behaviour with *different* eyes. This will provide a method of enquiry which favours the discovery of significant differences in how consumers behave across cultures and offers insights into the way consumers invest meaning into their purchases.

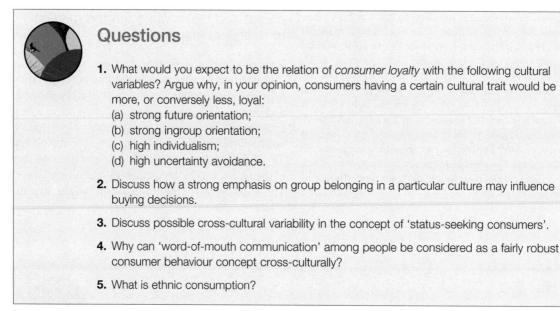

Questions

1. What would you expect to be the relation of *consumer loyalty* with the following cultural variables? Argue why, in your opinion, consumers having a certain cultural trait would be more, or conversely less, loyal:
   (a) strong future orientation;
   (b) strong ingroup orientation;
   (c) high individualism;
   (d) high uncertainty avoidance.

2. Discuss how a strong emphasis on group belonging in a particular culture may influence buying decisions.

3. Discuss possible cross-cultural variability in the concept of 'status-seeking consumers'.

4. Why can 'word-of-mouth communication' among people be considered as a fairly robust consumer behaviour concept cross-culturally?

5. What is ethnic consumption?

References

1. He, Y., M. A. Merz and D. A. Alden (2008), 'Diffusion of Measurement Invariance Assessment in Cross-national Empirical Marketing Research: Perspectives from the Literature and a Survey of Researchers', *Journal of International Marketing*, 16 (2), 64–83.
2. Bagozzi, Richard P., Nancy Wong, Shuzo Abe and Massimo Bergami (2000), 'Cultural and Situational Contingencies and the Theory of Reasoned Action: Application to Fast-food and Restaurant Consumption', *Journal of Consumer Psychology*, 9 (2), 97–106.
3. Lee, Julie Anne (2000), 'Adapting Triandis's Model of Subjective Culture and Social Behaviour Relations to Consumer Behaviour', *Journal of Consumer Psychology*, 9 (2), 117–26.
4. Lee, Chol and Robert T. Green (1991), 'Cross-cultural Examination of the Fishbein Behavioural Intentions Model', *Journal of International Business Studies*, 289–305.
5. Maslow, Abraham H. (1954), *Motivation and Personality*. New York: Harper and Row.
6. Belk, Russell W. (1988), 'Third World Consumer Culture', in *Research in Marketing*, E. Kumçu and A. Fuat Firat, (eds). Vol. 4. Greenwich, CT: JAI Press.
7. Solomon, Michael R. (1999), *Consumer Behavior* (4th edn). Upper Saddle River, NJ: Prentice Hall.
8. Hanson, John H. (1997), 'Power, Philanthropy, and Potlatch: What Tribal Exchange Rituals Can Tell Us About Giving', *Fund Raising Management*, 27 (12), 16–19.

9. Wilk, Richard (1995), 'Real Belizean Food: Building Local Identity in the Transnational Caribbean', in *Proceedings of the Second Conference on the Cultural Dimension of International Marketing*. Odense, 372–91.

10. Askegaard, Søren and Karen Brunsø (1999), 'Food-related Lifestyles in Singapore: Preliminary Testing of a Western Research Instrument in Southeast Asia', *Journal of Euromarketing*, 7 (4), 65–86.

11. Bagozzi, Richard P. (2000), 'On the Concept of Intentional Social Action in Consumer Behavior', *Journal of Consumer Research*, 27, 388–96.

12. Bagozzi, Richard P. and Kyu-Hyun Lee (2002), 'Multiple Routes for Social Influence: The Role of Compliance, Internalization and Social Identity', *Social Psychology Quarterly*, 65 (3), 226–47.

13. Lee, Julie Anne and Geoffrey Soutar (2004), 'Singaporeans I- and We-Intentions to Come to Australia', in *Australian and New Zealand Marketing Academy Conference (ANZMAC) Proceedings 2004*. Wellington, New Zealand: Victoria University.

14. Na, Woonbong, Youngseok Son, and Roger Marshall (2003), 'Purchase-role Structure in Korean Families: Revisited', *Psychology and Marketing*, 20 (1), 47–57.

15. Harcar, Talha and John E. Spillan (2006), 'Exploring Latin American Family Decision-Making Using Correspondence Analysis', *Journal of World Business*, 41 (3), 221–32.

16. Rodman, Hyman (1972), 'Marital Power and the Theory of Resources in Cultural Context', *Journal of Comparative Family Studies*, 3 (Spring), 50–69.

17. Hofstede, Geert (2001), *Culture Consequences*. Thousand Oaks, CA: Sage Publications.

18. Rose, Gregory M. (1999), 'Consumer Socialization, Parental Style, and Developement Timetables in the United States and Japan', *Journal of Marketing*, 63 (July), 105–19.

19. Ikels, C. (1983), *Aging and Adaption: Chinese in Hong Kong and the United States*. North Haven, CT: Archon Books.

20. Richins, Marsha (1994), 'Valuing Things: The Public and Private Meaning of Possessions', *Journal of Consumer Research*, 21 (3, December), 504–21.

21. Oyserman, D. (2011), 'Culture as Situated Cognition: Cultural Mindsets, Cultural Fluency, and Meaning Making', *European Review of Social Psychology*, 22, 164–214.

22. Markus, Hazel Rose and Shinobu Kitayama (1991), 'Culture and the Self: Implications for Cognition, Emotion and Motivation', *Psychological Review*, 98 (2), 224–53.

23. Lee, Julie Anne and Jacqueline J. Kacen (1999), 'The Relationship between Independent and Interdependent Self-Concepts and Reasons for Purchase', *Journal of Euro-Marketing*, 8 (1/2), 83–99.

24. Kacen, Jacqueline J. and Julie Anne Lee (2002), 'The Influence of Culture on Consumer Impulsive Buying Behavior', *Journal of Consumer Psychology*, 12 (2), 163–76.

25. Aaker, Jennifer L. and Bernd Schmitt (2001), 'Culture-Dependent Assimilation and Differentiation of the Self: Preference for Consumption Symbols in the United States and China', *Journal of Cross-Cultural Psychology*, 32, 561–76.

26. Aaker, Jennifer L. (2000), 'Accessibility or Diagnosticity? Disentangling the Influence of Culture on Persuasion Processes and Attitudes', *Journal of Consumer Research*, 26 (4), 340–57.

27. Aaker, Jennifer L. and Patti Williams (1998), 'Empathy Versus Pride: The Influence of Emotional Appeals across Cultures', *Journal of Consumer Research*, 25 (3), 241–61.

28. de Mooij, Marieke and Geert Hofsteded (2011), 'Cross-cultural consumer behaviour: A review of research findings', *Journal of International Consumer Marketing*, 23 (3–4), 181–92.

29. Engel, James F., Roger D. Blackwell and Paul W. Miniard (1993), *Consumer Behavior* (7th edn). Fort Worth, TX: The Dryden Press.

30. Yang, Chung-Fang (1989), 'Une Conception Du Comportement Du Consommateur Chinois', *Recherche et Applications en Marketing*, IV (1), 17–36.

31. Lazer, William, Shoji Murata and Hiroshi Kosaka (1985), 'Japanese Marketing: Towards a Better Understanding', *Journal of Marketing*, 49 (Spring), 69–81.

32. Liefeld, John P., Marjorie Wall and Louise A. Heslop (1999), 'Cross Cultural Comparison of Consumer Information Processing Styles', *Journal of Euro-Marketing*, 8 (1/2), 29–43.

33. Yau, Oliver H. M. (1988), 'Chinese Cultural Values: Their Dimensions and Marketing Implications', *European Journal of Marketing*, 22 (5), 44–57.

34. Zhou, Joyce, Mark Arnold, Arun Pereira and Jun Yu (2010), 'Chinese Consumer Decision-making Styles: A Comparison between the Coastal and Inland Regions, *Journal of Business Research*, 63, 45–51.

35. Quintal, Vanessa, Julie Anne Lee and Geoffrey N. Soutar (2010), 'Risk, Uncertainty and the Theory of Planned Behavior: A Tourism Example', *Tourism Management*, 31 (6), 797–805.

36. Quintal, Vanessa, Julie Anne Lee and Geoffrey N. Soutar (2010), 'Examining the Differential Impacts of Risk and Uncertainty Avoidance on Tourists' Information Search', *International Journal of Tourism Research*, 12 (4), 321–33.

37. Stone, Robert N. and Kjell Grønhaug (1993), 'Perceived Risk: Further Considerations for the Marketing Discipline', *European Journal of Marketing*, 27 (3), 372–94.

38. Mitchell, V. (1998), 'A Role for Consumer Risk Perceptions in Grocery Retailing', *British Food Journal*, 100 (4), 171–83.

39. Weber, E., C. Hsee, and J. Sokolowska (1998), 'What Folklore Tells Us About Risk and Risk Taking: Cross Cultural Comparisons of American, German and Chinese Proverbs', *Organizational Behavior and Human Decision Processes*, 75 (2), 170–86.

40. Weber, Elke U. and Christopher K. Hsee (2000), 'Culture and Individual Judgment and Decision Making', *Applied Psychology: An International Review*, 49 (1), 32–41.

41. Herrmann, Andreas and Mark Heitmann (2006), 'Providing More or Less? Accounting for Cultural Differences in Consumers' Preference for Variety', *International Marketing Review*, 23 (1), 7–24.

42. Drolet, A. (2002), 'Inherent Rule Variability in Consumer Choice: Changing Rules for Change's Sake', *Journal of Consumer Research*, 29 (3), 293–305.

43. Robinson, Chris (1996), 'Asian Cultures: The Marketing Consequences', *Journal of the Market Research Society*, 38 (1), 55–62.

44. Chiou, Jyh-Shen (1995), 'The Process of Social Influences on New Product Adoption and Retention in Individualistic Versus Collectivist Cultural Contexts', in *Proceedings of the Second Conference on the Cultural Dimension of International Marketing*. Odense, 107–27.

45. Kim, Jai-Ok, Sandra Forsythe, Quingliang Gu, and Sook Jae Moon (2002), 'Cross-Cultural Consumer Behavior, Needs and Purchase Behavior', *Journal of Consumer Marketing*, 19 (6), 481–502.

46. Zheng, Qiuying, Lin Mu, Tang Yao, Xiucheng Fan, (2011), 'Are Satisfied Customers Always Loyal? – A Meta-analytic Review and Assessment of Moderators of Customer Satisfaction-Loyalty Relationship', *Management and Service Science (MASS), 2011 International Conference*, pp. 1–4, 12–14 Aug. 2011. doi: 10.1109/ICMSS.2011.5998705.

47. Colgate, Mark, Vicky Thuy-Uyen Tong, Christina Kwai-Choi Lee, and John U. Farley (2007), 'Back from the Brink: Why Customers Stay', *Journal of Service Research*, 9 (3), 211–28.

48. Straughan, Robert D. and Nancy D. Albers-Miller (2001), 'An International Investigation of Cultural and Demographic Effects on Domestic Retail Loyalty', *International Marketing Review*, 18 (5), 521–41.

49. Jung, Jaehee and Eun-Young Sung (2008), 'Consumer-Based Brand Equity: Comparisons among Americans and South Koreans in the USA and South Koreans in Korea', *Journal of Fashion Marketing and Management*, 12 (1), 24.

50. Kluckhohn, Florence R. and Frederick L. Strodtbeck (1961), *Variations in Value Orientations*. Westport, CT: Greenwood Press.

51. Pons, Frank and Michel Laroche (2007), 'Cross-cultural Differences in Crowd Assessment', *Journal of Business Research*, 60 (3), 269–76.

52. Reynolds, Nina L. and Antonis Simintiras (2000), *Establishing Cross-National Equivalence of the Customer Satisfaction Construct*, EBMS Working Paper, 2000/7.

53. Blodgett, Jeffrey, Donna Hill and Aysen Bakir (2006), 'Cross-cultural Complaining Behavior? An Alternative Explanation', *Journal of Consumer Satisfaction, Dissatisfaction and Complaining Behavior*, 19, 103–17.

54. Richins, Marsha and Bronislaw J. Verhage (1985), 'Cross-cultural Differences in Consumer Attitudes and Their Implications for Complaint Management', *International Journal of Research in Marketing*, 2, 197–205.

55. Richins, Marsha (1983), 'Negative Word-of-mouth by Dissatisfied Consumers: A Pilot Study', *Journal of Marketing*, 47 (Winter), 68–78.

56. Cavusgil, Tamer S. and Erdener Kaynak (1984), 'Critical Issues in the Cross-cultural Measurement of Consumer Dissatisfaction: Developed Versus Ldc Practices', in *Comparative Marketing Systems*, Erdener Kaynak and Ronald Savitt (eds). New York: Praeger.

57. Joy, Annamma (2001), 'Gift Giving in Hong Kong and the Continuum of Social Ties', *Journal of Consumer Research*, 28, 239–56.

58. Park, Seong-Yeon (1998), 'A Comparison of Korean and American Gift-giving Behaviors', *Psychology and Marketing*, 15 (6), 577–93.

59. Berry, J. W., Uichol Kim, Thomas Minde and Doris Mok (1987), 'Comparative Study of Acculturation Stress', *International Migration Review*, 21, 491–511.

60. Ger, Güliz and Per Østergaard (1998), 'Constructing Immigrant Identities in Consumption: Appearance among the Turko-Danes', *Advances in Consumer Research*, 25, 48–52.

61. Gans, Herbert (1962), *The Urban Villagers*. New York: The Free Press.

62. Bouchet, Dominique (1995), 'Marketing and the Redefinition of Ethnicity', in *Marketing in a Multicultural World*, Janeen Arnold. Costa and Gary J. Bamossy (eds). Thousand Oaks, CA: Sage.

63. Tajfel, H. (1974), 'Social Identity and Intergroup Behavior', *Social Science Information*, 13 (2), 65–93.

64. Straus, Karen (1992), 'Go Hog Wild with Chino-Latino Pork Dishes', *Restaurants and Institutions*, 102 (19), 43–57.

65. McCracken, Grant (1991), 'Culture and Consumer Behaviour: An Anthropological Perspective', *Journal of the Market Research Society*, 32 (1), 3–11.

66. Penaloza, Lisa (2001), 'Consuming the American West: Animating Cultural Meaning and Memory at a Stock Show and Rodeo', *Journal of Consumer Research*, 28 (3), 369–98.

67. D'Andrade, Roy G. (1987), 'A Folk Model of the Mind', in *Cultural Models in Language and Thought*, Dorothy Quinn and Naomi Holland (eds). Cambridge: Cambridge University Press.

68. Kragh, Simon Ulrik and Malene Djursaa (2001), 'Product Syntax and Cross-cultural Marketing Strategies', *European Journal of Marketing*, 35 (11/12), 1301–19.

69. Tanouchi, Koichi (1983), 'Japanese-style Marketing Based on Sensitivity', *Dentsu Japan Marketing/ Advertising*, 23 (July), 77–81.

70. Baudrillard, Jean (1968), *Le Système Des Objets*. Paris: Gallimard.

Teaching materials

A5.1 Exercise

'Dichter's consumption motives'

Question

Discuss the cross-cultural variability of the major motives for consumption as identified by Ernest Dichter some 30 years ago. Choose five associations between motives and associated products for your discussion.

Motive	Associated products
Power, masculinity, virility	Power: sugary products and large breakfasts, bowling, electric trains, pistols, power tools.
	Masculinity, virility: coffee, red meat, heavy shoes, toy guns, buying fur coats for women, shaving with a razor.
Security	Ice-cream, full drawer of neatly ironed shirts, real plaster walls, home baking, hospital care.
Eroticism	Sweets, gloves, a man lighting a woman's cigarette.
Moral purity, cleanliness	White bread, cotton fabric, harsh household cleaning chemicals, bathing, oatmeal.
Social acceptance	Companionship: ice-cream (fun to share), coffee.
	Love and affection: toys, sugar and honey.
	Acceptance: soap, beauty products.
Individuality	Gourmet foods, foreign cars, cigarette holders, vodka, perfume, fountain pens.
Status	Scotch [whisky], ulcers, heart attacks, indigestion, carpets.
Femininity	Cakes and cookies, dolls, silk, tea, household curios.
Reward	Cigarettes, candy, alcohol, ice-cream, cookies.
Mastery over environment	Kitchen appliances, boats, sporting goods, cigarette lighters.
Disalienation (a desire to feel connectedness to things)	Home decorating, skiing, morning radio broadcasts.
Magic, mystery	Soups (have healing powers), paints (change the mood of a room), carbonated drinks (magical effervescent property), vodka (romantic history), unwrapping of gifts.

(Source: Solomon, p. 168. Solomon, Michael R., *Consumer Behavior: Buying, Having and Being*, 4th edn, © 1999, reproduced by permission of Pearson Education, Inc., Upper Saddle River, NJ.)

A5.2 Exercise

Investigating the cross-cultural applicability of a consumer complaint scale

A scale of consumer complaint behaviour (CCB) developed by Singh[1] is portrayed below. US respondents were asked to express their degree of agreement or disagreement on a six-point Likert scale on the items listed below (possible behavioural responses to dissatisfaction with a consumption experience). Factor analysis allowed three dimensions to be distinguished for CCB.

1. Voice CCB
   (a) Forget about the incident and do nothing.
   (b) Definitely complain to the store manager on your next trip.
   (c) Go back or call the repair shop immediately and ask them to take care of your problem.

2. Private CCB
   (a) Decide not to use that repair shop again.
   (b) Speak to your friends and relatives about your bad experience.
   (c) Convince your friends and relatives not to use that repair shop.

3. Third-party CCB
   (a) Complain to a consumer agency and ask them to make the repair shop take care of your problem.
   (b) Write a letter to the local newspaper about your bad experience.
   (c) Report to the consumer agency so that they can warn other consumers.
   (d) Take some legal action against the repair shop/manufacturer.

Question

Investigate the cross-cultural applicability of such a scale. Since you cannot do this with a full psychometric design, conduct your investigation mostly into the meaning, situations, institutions and behaviours depicted by the items.

A5.3 Case

Mobile phones in the European Union

In 2002 Jean-Michel Hubert, director of the French Telecoms Regulation Authority stated that the European mobile telecommunications were considered to be in a crisis. The main reason seemed to be a relatively saturated market and low average revenue per user (ARPU), at 29 euros in Europe versus 50 euros in the USA.[2] According to the Western European Mobile Forecasts and Analysis 2003–2008 report, the number of active subscribers was forecast to grow just 5 per cent per year to 309 million.[3] However, there are 553 million mobile subscribers in the European Union (EU) in October 2007,[4] an increase far beyond EU enlargment. Providing services at lower cost has become a challenge. Cuts in tariffs have stimulated growth, but ARPU has consequently stagnated or decreased. Across Africa the average revenue per user is $17.50 per month. In India, that figure drops to $10 a month. In Western Europe and the United States, the comparable number is nowadays close to $40.[5]

Mobile sector growth in the European Union is exponential. Average penetration is 112 per cent in October 2007 (see Table 5.3 for country data), whereas it is only 87 per cent for the United States and 84 per cent in Japan for the same period. The average penetration even increases to 119 per cent in the following year,[6] while it is 30 per cent in China and only 10 per cent in India, which are nevertheless expected to be the world's largest mobile markets by 2010.[7] In China growth is exponential but penetration is still relatively low, partly due to the size of the population. Penetration is dependent on age, being mainly driven by youths aged 13 to 18, for which penetration rate often reaches 90 per cent. In terms of new subscribers, the European market is near saturation. For an understanding of this phenomenon, one must look first at the issue of adoption and diffusion of new technology, and second at cultural differences among European countries. There are different competitive environments in each European country, with generally three to five mobile operators and a grand total of 100 country operators for Europe as a whole (among them many national subsidiaries of Europe-wide mobile operators such as Orange or Vodafone).[8] Price is an issue for mobile communication since it may be a relatively significant part of a person's budget, especially for young adults who do not yet earn their lives (see differences in price-mindedness across cultures in Section 10.3). Depending on country, prepaid mobile communication accounts for between 40 and 90 per cent (Italy and Malta) with an average 50 per cent for prepaid and 50 per cent for monthly paid. Design and aesthetic also matter for mobile handsets (see cross-cultural differences in aesthetics and perception of design in Section 8.4). Applications, mobile phones features, and content are important attributes for mobile phones users. Novelty orientation, innovative behaviour, and variety seeking also matter for mobile phones, since resistance to change may vary across cultures. Users also differ in terms of their sensitivity to disturbance caused to others when using a mobile phone in social settings.

Table 5.3 Mobile phone penetration in Europe[9] (2009)

Penetration	≥ 130%	115%–130%	100%–115%	<100%
Western Europe	Italy Luxemburg Germany Portugal Greece	Denmark Ireland Spain Finland UK	Sweden Belgium	France Malta
Eastern Europe	Estonia Lithuania Bulgaria Romania Czech Republic	Cyprus Hungary	Slovakia Poland Slovenia	Latvia Moldavia Albania

(Source: http://en.wikipedia.org/wiki/File:Europe_mobile_phone_penetration_map.png.)

Adoption of mobile phones

There is a popular theory behind the adoption of high-tech consumer equipment such as mobile phones – that is, the TAM (Technology Acceptance Model), with a considerable body of scientific literature in *Marketing and Information Technology* as well as *Management Information Systems*.[10,11] The key variables behind the user adoption of new IT technology are 'perceived usefulness' and 'perceived ease-of-use'. The more usefulness consumers perceive in the technological device and the less difficulty of use, the quicker they will adopt the new technology. A number of arguments can be made about different perceptions of mobile phones according to age, in terms of both 'perceived usefulness' and 'perceived ease-of-use'. Perceptions of usefulness may increase (or not) with new features being added to successive generations of mobile phones. For instance, one may wonder to what extent all features of 3G handsets are (or will be) really perceived as 'useful' (especially when their price is considered).

Other key variables in the TAM model are perceived behavioural control, perceived risk, and demographics (age, gender). Perceived risk for mobile phones may relate, for instance, to electromagnetic waves near the ear potentially causing brain tumours, a sensitive topic that still has not been medically proven. Perceived behavioural control is linked to the circum-stances of mobile phone use (e.g., car, restaurant, classroom, theatre, etc.) and involves safety issues and social concerns in situations where mobile phones can be perceived as rendering their users not in control of rather than in control of the device. Mobile operators can act to increase or emphasize factors that are favourable to the adoption of mobile phones and decrease those which are unfavourable. They may also segment markets according to demo-graphics (especially age, gender) or according to business vs. non-business use, this being relevant in terms of both adoption and use. Moreover, some segments are likely to be rather transnational (e.g., young users) and relatively culture-free.

The cultural roots of the European mobile phone predicament

Zbigniew Smoreda, sociologist at *France Telecom* and researcher on the Eurescom P903 study that examined mobile habits in nine countries, explains that overall, in countries like Denmark, Germany, and the UK, the primary reason for obtaining a mobile subscription was to keep one's life organized. For the French, the primary reason was to be available at all times. However, the most striking differences were found between urban and rural settings. The city user, whether in Copenhagen or Rome, is likely to use the phone often – perhaps partly due to the complications of city life, and partly due to age (they tend to be younger).[12] From an aesthetic perspective, Samsung handset designers speak of 'global localization' and the balance of 'reason and feeling' attributes that govern the design, then subsequently the marketing process[13] (see Table 5.4 below).

Table 5.4 Samsung's 'reason and feeling' attributes for mobile phone design

Region	Attribute: 'reason'	Attribute: 'feeling'
Asia	High tech	Cuteness
Europe	Minimal	Emotion
North America	Durable	Dynamic

(Source: Mark Delaney *et al.*, 'Global design and cultural identity', *Innovation* (Industrial Designers Society of America), Summer 2002.)

According to the Eurescom P903 study, Italians were the fastest adopters of the mobile telephone, quickly overtaking the Nordic countries where the standard was first launched. Italian youths take the credit for this; age being the 'most important factor for predicting the adoption of the mobile phone'.[14] It is not a cliché to say that Italians are talkative, according to Alessandra Bianchini, communications head at Italian mobile operator *Wind*, it is one of the reasons that mobile phones are ubiquitous in Italy. She goes on to say that another cliché about Italians – love of family – is another reason: the mobile phone is ideal for keeping in touch with relatives and friends. In fact, mobile technology was promoted more as a tool of communication rather than business from the outset in Italy. It is not a rare sight to see young Italians chatting on their phones, perched on the back of a scooter in the midst of city traffic – phones are used everywhere. In 2002 there were 50 million mobile numbers in Italy owned by 86 per cent of the population, and one-quarter of these had multiple subscriptions. The Netherlands, where 76.6 per cent of the population is a mobile user, presents a contrast to the Italian attitudes towards mobile use. In accordance with clichés about the Dutch, their use of the technology is economical: they are one of the least talkative on their mobile phones in Europe, partly due to concern over phone rates. According to Marc Gommers of mobile operator *Dutchtone*, another reason for this is the precision of the Dutch language that allows them to express themselves rapidly. There are also social norms that frown upon over-use of the phone in public; in restaurants they are banned, as they are in Denmark.[15] In France the lack of such social norms triggered increasing frustration about the inconsiderate use of mobile phones, inciting the government to legalize mobile phone jamming in public places – a measure agreed upon by 85 per cent of the population.[16]

According to a Gartner G2 report, 41 per cent of European adults use SMS, even more than those who use e-mail (30 per cent). That figure rises in Germany, where 43 per cent of adults prefer SMS to using e-mail (29 per cent).[17] Britons send more SMS than other Europeans (31 versus 26 per month on average). Europeans overall use SMS much more than Americans. Schuyler Brown of Euro RSCG Worldwide's S.T.A.R. (Strategic Trendspotting and Research) team believes that commuting and PC use determine SMS use. European teenagers tend to use public transport, an ideal situation for chatting via SMS, whereas American teens tend to drive to school and work. Likewise, the European teen spends more time in public spaces, where time can be spent sending and receiving SMS, compared with the American teen who is more likely to be stay at home, which is likely to be equipped with a PC, wide-screen TV, and game console, competitors for time and attention deviated to SMS in Europe.[18]

However, more theory is needed for looking at in-depth cultural differences, starting from the surface before digging deeper. Meaningful cultural differences in terms of mobile phone use can be discovered by looking at consumer behaviour *in context*. Such cultural differences are related *inter alia* to communication patterns, individualism–collectivism, language, time orientations (monochronism/polychronism),[19] and orientation to others. Key motivations for the use of a mobile phone are its freedom dimension, its significance in making communication with others easier, the pleasure of talking (i.e., oral culture favouring speaking over writing), and the need (or conversely, the fear) of being reachable always and everywhere: that is, a permanent social connection, at least with important others who know the mobile phone number. Mobile phones also involve the possibility of disturbing others (see proxemics, Section 2.3) and the sensitivity to perceived risk for one's health (see social representations, Section 1.5).

Mobile phones involve daily routines in reference to chronological time (Newtonian time). They save time (economic time) and enable immediate voice communication in order to relate to others (unorganized-time). Using mobile phones enables individuals to manage activities instantaneously, much like in a polychronic use of time. Differences in time orientation between France and Germany, and their influence on use of mobile phone have been shown to be significant.[20] An initial qualitative survey was set up in order to determine the main components of mobile communication behaviour through a focus group of twenty French mobile phone users. Three main dimensions appeared to be relevant for users: freedom, contact with others, and instantaneous behaviour. Interestingly, these dimensions are located on different levels. Freedom is a means-end interpretation of a value, contact with other people a social benefit, and instantaneous behaviour a functional benefit.

In France, two time-style dimensions, economic time and tenacity, had a significant influence on the general mobile communication attitude. The link between economicity and mobile communication attitude suggested that the French associate the use of a mobile phone with the capacity to organize their own lives and to save time. The French have been described as intellectually monochronic but behaviorally polychronic. Monochronism is more associated with tenacity than polychronism, explaining why tenacity in the French time style is negatively associated with the overall mobile communication attitude. In Germany, preference for quick return and non-organized time were found to have a significant influence on the overall mobile communication attitude. The positive link between preference for quick return and mobile communication attitude suggested that Germans associate the use of a mobile phone with instantaneous behaviour. The positive relationship between non-organized time and mobile communication indicate that mobile communication is also associated with flexible time and instantaneous behaviour. Paradoxically, the Germans, traditionally described as being monochronic and valuing organized time, positively associate mobile communication with free and spontaneous behaviour. These findings indicate that consumers are not sensitive to the same product benefits, depending on country and time style. French consumers mostly value the economicity aspect of using a mobile phone (saving time). The Germans put more value on mobile communication to get immediate gratification and to create space in their lives for unorganized time (increasing their freedom).

Third Generation (3G) applications

Mobile phone subscribers were expected to grow from two billion worldwide in 2005 to approximately 3.3 billion in 2010, representing annual growth of more than 10 per cent. The 3 billion mark was, however, reached in 2007,[21] mainly due to owners of multiple pre-paid SIM-cards as well as corporate clients in Europe and the United States. The forecast share of 3G subscribers should be more than 10 per cent in 2007, reaching 296 million.[22] In the European Union the average 3G penetration was 20 per cent in 2007. Regarding mobile applications in addition to voice and text messaging, there is interest in Europe in third-generation (3G or UMTS) capability for specific applications, such as information (including maps and directions, news, and financial), m-banking, and m-trading. Most of the year-on-year growth in phone sales is attributed to 'smart phones'. Figures surpass forecasts: there were 5.3 billion by the end of 2010 (see Table 5.5 below).[23]

Table 5.5 Key Global Telecom Indicators for the World Telecommunication Service Sector in 2010 (estimates)

	Global	Developed nations	Developing nations	Africa	Arab States	Asia & Pacific	CIS	Europe	The Americas
Mobile cellular subscriptions (millions)	5,282	1,436	3,846	333	282	2,649	364	741	880
Per 100 people	76.2%	116.1%	67.6%	41.4%	79.4%	67.8%	131.5%	120.0%	94.1%
Fixed telephone lines (millions)	1,197	506	691	13	33	549	74	249	262
Per 100 people	17.3%	40.9%	12.1%	1.6%	9.4%	14.0%	26.6%	40.3%	28.1%
Mobile broadband subscriptions (millions)	940	631	309	29	34	278	72	286	226
Per 100 people	13.6%	51.1%	5.4%	3.6%	9.7%	7.1%	25.9%	46.3%	24.2%
Fixed broadband subscriptions (millions)	555	304	251	1	8	223	24	148	145
per 100 people	8.0%	24.6%	4.4%	0.2%	2.3%	5.7%	8.7%	23.9%	15.5%

(Source: International Telecommunication Union, October 2010).

However, overall interest is tepid. A Taylor Nelson Sofres study of 7000 subscribers in 10 European countries found that Poland and Turkey were the most likely countries to adopt 3G, while 58 per cent of 'other' Europeans, and 66 per cent of Britons were 'not interested' in 3G phones. Britain, one of the most mature mobile markets in world, is mainly happy with 2G phones, and is not interested in going beyond pre-pay. A 2007 survey of British mobile phone users shows that 27 per cent sent a photo in the last 12 months, but only 15 per cent listened to an mp3, 12 per cent accessed the Internet, and 10 per cent downloaded ringtones. The use of other mobile applications is quite limited, with only 9 per cent sending a video clip, 6 per cent downloading music, 6 per cent paying for information, and a tiny 1 per cent watching TV.[24] The implication may be that Europeans are likely to keep their trusty old handsets, and only a minority will be interested in purchasing 3G phones.

In order to develop the 3G market, operators are seeking to increase non-voice revenue. Most of this revenue now comes from person-to-person messaging, and increasingly includes downloadable music and games.[25] Web logging (known as blogging) is now offered for mobile phone users whereby a personal webpage (known as a Foneblog by its Irish creator, **www.newbay.com**), complete with photos and even short videos, is created and may be viewed by other mobile phone users via WAP or a standard Web browser. Many games are already available, like Sweden's Botfighters game that combines SMS and Global Positioning Systems (GPS), informing players via SMS that they are approaching another player. The first to respond to the message receives extra 'life' game points. More simple games based on sports, driving, puzzle, and arcade formats are affordable and easy to procure. A realistic example of a phone game is the Finnish football team Helsinki PK-35 pay-per-shot game whereby their approximately 3000 fans may send text suggestions from their mobile phones for game strategy, including defence and substitutions.[26] If only mobile phone users could send text suggestions regarding strategy to their mobile operators, they could help these companies at a crossroads to navigate an uncertain future.

Questions

1. How can mobile operators, software designers and handset producers inspire Europeans to use their mobile phones for longer lengths of time and for more applications, especially in the context of smartphones?

2. Using the cultural differences highlighted in the case, explain how consumer behaviour for mobile phones may differ between one northern and one southern European country (your choice). Outline marketing strategies for second generation mobile communication targeted to northern and southern European countries that would take these differences into account.

3. What would you advise as a pan-European 3G marketing strategy for a mobile operator? Think in terms of the phenomenal success of Apple's I-phone and benchmark against most successful competitors in terms of 3G mobile phones in 2012.

Saskia Faulk and Jean-Claude Usunier wrote this case to provide material for class discussion. The authors do not intend to illustrate either effective or ineffective handling of a business situation. The authors may have disguised certain names and other identifying information to protect confidentiality.

A5.4 Exercise

Cross-cultural consumer behaviour and the standardization/adaptation of service offers

Based on a discussion of variations in consumer behaviour across countries, review arguments in favour of standardizing or adapting service operations in one or several of the following service industries:

- private banking;
- telecommunications;
- hairdresser;
- motor insurance;
- life insurance;
- hotels;
- haute cuisine restaurants;
- satellite launch.

You may distinguish different subsets of the service industry or different market segments within this service industry; consider two aspects in each industry:

1. whether the service and its characteristics are more or less standard worldwide;
2. whether consumer behaviour and especially the service encounter differs across domestic markets.

You may take into account the following issues in your discussion of the cross-cultural variability of service encounters and consumer behaviour:

- Does language have an influence on the service encounter?
- Does religion have an influence on attitudes towards the service and on the service encounter itself?
- Do time attitudes (waiting, long-term orientation, fatalism, linear vs. cyclical views of time, etc.) have an influence on the service encounter (pre-process, in-process, post-process)?
- Are there standards for this service industry? What is their reach?
- How does culture influence both the service customer and the service provider?

You may Google to get some additional insights on the issues above.

A5.5 Exercise

Multi-domestic versus global

For the following industries or products discuss to what extent:

1. a world **consumer** exists (in terms of tastes and preferences, consumption habits, social taboos, local regulations influencing consumer behaviour, differences related to language, consumer learning, etc.);

2. the **products or services** offered are themselves global (similar worldwide): you may distinguish major product types within the generic product (e.g., high-fermentation versus low-fermentation beer); and

3. the **industry** itself can be considered as global (players tend to be global ones and competition takes place on a global rather than multi-local basis).

- Airlines
- Beer
- Pharmaceuticals (ethical/prescription drugs)
- Pharmaceuticals (non-prescription/over-the-counter drugs)
- Tobacco (cigarettes, cigars, other tobacco-based products)
- Meat-based foods
- Automatic blood analysers
- Mail services (delivery of letters and parcels)
- Sheets and pillows
- Ski lifts
- Portable computers
- Writing instruments (you may distinguish between pencils, ball-point pens and fountain pens)
- Micro-chips
- Toilet tissues
- Washing machines (for cloth)
- Auditing services.

This exercise can be used in relation to Chapters 5 and 7 (where the concepts of multi-domestic and global markets are explained).

Appendix references

1. Singh, Jagdip (1988), 'Consumer Complaint Intentions and Behavior: Definitions and Taxonomical Issues', *Journal of Marketing*, 52 (January), 93–107.
2. Anonymous (2002), 'La téléphonie Européenne pour un recentrage sur le client', *Freesurf Actualité Hi Tech*, 21 November 2002.
3. Anonymous (2003) 'News', *Analysys News*, 26 March 2003. Retrieved 15 May 2011 from http://www.analysys.com/default.asp?Mode=article&iLeftArticle=1192.
4. Commission of the European Communities (2007), *Progess Report on the Single European Electronic Communications Market 2007* (all case information is based on this report, unless otherwise stated), source: http://ec.europa.eu/information_society/policy/ecomm/doc/library/annualreports/13th/SEC(2008)356DTSVol2final.pdf.
5. 'The Mobile Phone Megatrend: Exploring the New Frontier', 20 February 2007. Retrieved 15 May 2011 from: http://seekingalpha.com/article/27321-the-mobile-phone-megatrend-exploring-the-new-frontier.
6. Commission of the European Communities (2008), *Progress Report on the Single European Electronic Communications Market* (2008), source: http://eur-lex.europa.eu/LexUriServ/LexUriServ.do?uri=COM:2009:0140:FIN:EN:PDF.
7. Burns, Simon, 'China and India poised for stellar mobile growth', *Informatics*, 5 May 2010. Retrieved from: http://www.itnews.com.au/News/72764,china-and-india-poised-for-stellar-mobile-growth.aspx; see also: http://en.wikipedia.org/wiki/Mobile_phone.
8. For a complete list of the world's largest mobile network operators by number of subscribers see: http://en.wikipedia.org/wiki/List_of_mobile_network_operators.
9. Anonymous (2009), 'Europe Mobile Phone Penetration', 5 May 2011. Retrieved from: http://en.wikipedia.org/wiki/File:Europe_mobile_phone_penetration_map.png.
10. Davis, F. D., R. P. Bagozzi and P. R. Warshaw (1989), 'User Acceptance of Computer Technology: A Comparison of Two Theoretical Models', *Management Science*, 35 (8), 982–1003.

11. Venkatesh, Viswanath, Michael G. Morris, Gordon B. Davis and Fred D. Davis (2003), 'User Acceptance of Information Technology: Toward a Unified View', *MIS Quarterly*, 27 (3), 425–78.

12. Anonymous (2002) 'Européen et mobile', *ORANGE Magazine*, Spring, no.4, pp. 9–13.

13. Delaney, Mark, Jeff McFarland, Gee Hong Yoon, and Tom Hardy (2002) 'Global Design and Cultural Identity', *Innovation*, Summer 2002.

14. Eurescom (2001) 'c "ICT uses in everyday life"', *Eurescom P903 Newsletter*, p. 3, May 2001. Retrieved 15 May 2011 from http://www.eurescom.de/~ftproot/web-deliverables/public/P900-series/P903/p903_newsletter_may.pdf.

15. Anonymous (2002), 'Européen et mobile', *ORANGE Magazine*, Spring, no.4, pp. 9–13.

16. Ó hAnluain, Daithí (2002), 'They be jammin' in France', *Wired News*, 23 March 2002. Retrieved 15 May 2011 from http://www.wired.com/news/culture/0,1284,51273,00.html.

17. Gartner Group (2002), 'SMS bigger than email in Europe', *Nua Internet Surveys*, 5 November 2002. Retrieved 15 May 2011 from http://www.qlinks.net/quicklinks/stats12.htm.

18. Nahmany, Peggy (2003), 'Y RN'T WE N2 SMS?', *PR Newswire*, 12 February 2003.

19. Usunier, Jean-Claude and Pierre Valette-Florence (2007), 'The Time-Styles Scale: A Review of Developments and Replications over 15 years', *Time and Society*, 16 (2/3), 349–82.

20. Valette-Florence, Pierre, Jean-Claude Usunier and Jean-Marc Ferrandi (2001), 'Le temps des Consommateurs: Le cas du téléphone portable', *Revue Française de Gestion*, no. 132, January–February, 112–118 (English title: 'Consumer time: The case of mobile phones').

21. Anonymous, 'Global Mobile Phone Subscriptions to reach 4.5 billion by 2012', published March 2008. Retrieved 15 May 2011 from: http://www.cellular-news.com/story/29824.php.

22. Source: '3.3bn global mobile phone subscribers by 2010 – report'. Retrieved 15 May 2011 from http://www.dmeurope.com/default.asp?ArticleID=15236.

23. *Andy Favell, mobiThinking editor*, Global Mobile Statistics 2011: all quality mobile marketing research, mobile web stats, subscribers, ad revenue, usage, trends . . . , published March 2011. Retrieved 15 May 2011 from: http://mobithinking.com/stats-corner/global-mobile-statistics-2011-all-quality-mobile-marketing-research-mobile-web-stats-su#subscribers.

24. Anonymous (2007), 'Mobile Users Turned-off by Advanced Features,' *Cellular News*, 20 August 2007. Retrieved 15 May 2011 from http://www.cellular-news.com/story/25516.php.

25. Phillips, Leigh (2003), 'Messaging and entertainment services to boost mobile operator revenue and ARPU, report' *Europemedia.net*, 27 March 2003. Retrieved 17 May 2011 from http://www.analysys.com/default_acl.asp?Mode=article&iLeftArticle=5&m=&n=.

26. Laughlin, Kirk (2002), 'Revenue at Risk: Why are ARPUs Falling in North America, but Rising in Parts of Europe?', *America's Network*, 1 March 2002.

Local consumers and the globalization of consumption

The business world is going through a process of dramatic change and increased volatility.

According to *Euromonitor*, the five most important global trends in consumer markets are:[1]

1. A dramatic shift in global power from the West to the East, with China expected to be the world's largest economy by 2020, with over 20 per cent of the world's GDP (purchasing power parity).
2. Increasing concerns about social and environmental issues, focusing on the depletion of national resources and rapid growth in emerging economies.
3. Rising prosperity and growth of the global middle class, with consumer spending projected to increase by 32 per cent in emerging economies and 15 per cent in advanced economies (from 2010 to 2020).
4. Increased urbanization and aging of the population: one in every ten people will be over 65 and 70 per cent will live in urban areas by 2050.
5. Increased communication with 3.8 billion Internet users by 2020.

Each of these trends offers both opportunities and challenges for marketers from a wide range of organizations. As will be discussed in Chapter 8, international marketing used to focus primarily on how large firms from developed nations transferred their domestic know-how to other markets. However, the global trends listed above indicate the need to attend to a wider range of markets, with greater degrees of cultural and economic diversity. The traditional evolution of international expansion from national to international market entry (driven by the need for economies of scale), to local market expansion (driven by the need for economies of scope) and then, global rationalization (driven by the need for scale efficiencies), is entering a new phase, which will require a much greater understanding of local or regional markets.[2]

The growth of the middle class, especially in liberalizing emerging economics (e.g., China, India, Brazil, Indonesia and Turkey), and of the social network phenomenon, might be seen as an opportunity to target consumers who are increasingly sharing a common set of values, needs, habits and preferences. However, consumption habits and personal preferences across nations will always diverge. In Germany most homes do not have cupboards, because it is thought only poorer people have cupboards and not wardrobes. This way of thinking extends to Alsace, but stops in France and the Latin countries, where the convenience of both cupboards and wardrobes is recognized, and there is no implied socio-economic or class-related meaning. Nevertheless, iconic global brands, such as BMW, Godiva and Coca-Cola are thriving. As are iconic 'foreign' brands that can exploit their global capabilities, such as IKEA with its strong Swedish brand image.

We argue that it is the companies that are becoming increasingly global, rather than the consumers, who are still largely local. Consumption patterns may look like they are converging, but convergence is at the macroscopic level. Consumption patterns resemble Russian dolls, building up from home to city, from community to region, and from nation to globe.[3] It has become more important than ever to look closely at the unique elements of meaning local consumers invest in their products, services and consumption experiences.

In this chapter we discuss the three crucial assumptions behind globalization. The first aspect is demand, with the convergence of consumer behaviour and marketing environments at the macro level. The second aspect is supply and competition, with the shift away from domestic industries operating in national markets to global industries operating in world markets. The third aspect is the potential for cost reduction through the globalization of products and marketing offerings.

The first half of this chapter explores the justifications for globalization. First, we examine how traditional models of international trade have been strong drivers for globalization (Section 6.1). These traditional models ignore local consumers' tastes for local design and manufacture, and focus on utilitarian needs for generic products to justify worldwide similarity. As emerging markets become a key focus for growth, more attention needs to be paid to customers purchasing patterns, as well as competitive offerings. Second, we discuss the assumptions around the global convergence of consumption patterns (Section 6.2). Convergence happens at the macro level for generic product categories, but it is less evident at a micro level when we examine specific products and consumer behaviours. Third, we examine the emergence of a global consumer culture, based on 'modern cultural' values that may lead to a world standard package (Section 6.3).

The second half of this chapter explores the justifications for localization. We first examine products that are culture bound, and how goods and services and consumption experiences are infused with uniquely local meanings (Section 6.4). We then discuss consumer resistance to global products and consumption patterns which may threaten local interests (Section 6.5). Finally, we explore the kaleidoscopic patterns of local consumption in a globalizing world: that is, how consumers mix globalized products and local items in a grand *bricolage* (Section 6.6).

6.1

Free trade doctrine and the denial of cultural variety in consumers' tastes

Ricardo's hypothesis

Traditional international trade doctrine laid the foundations for the denial of culture in international

marketing. One of the seminal manuscripts on international trade is the seventh chapter of David Ricardo's *On the Principles of Political Economy and Taxation in 1817*,[4] which explains why countries and traders may benefit from developing international trade. Ricardo considers the case of two countries, England and Portugal, and two types of goods, wine and sheets. He posits *the law of comparative or relative advantage*, arguing that a country would benefit from international trade even when it is at a competitive disadvantage for both products. By trading internationally, each country finds a better exchange ratio for the goods than they can in their domestic market. By concentrating efforts and resources on products where they have a relative advantage, both countries increase their national and global welfare.

Though visionary, many implicit assumptions in Ricardo's theory are not clearly spelled out: (1) gains from trading internationally must offset transportation, customs duties and trading costs; (2) there are constant returns to scale; (3) products should be identical, or at least perceived as such by both consumers and merchants; (4) information must be easily available and efficient enough so that merchants in the two countries may be aware of the potential gains to be derived from international trade; and (5) there must be no other financial or government restriction or market barrier that limits international trade for these products.

The implicit assumption that products and consumers' tastes, habits and preferences are perfectly identical in two countries or the world is a difficult one. England produced almost no wine at the time and it is doubtful that British wine had the same physical characteristics, the same alcoholic content or the same taste as the Portuguese wine. English and the Portuguese tastes in bed linen were probably distinct enough (in terms of their fabrics and embroidery) to enable them to recognize clearly which were 'their' sheets. Furthermore, British beer was the drink of choice in pubs, whereas *vinho verde* ('green wine', or 'young wine') or *porto* ('port wine') were the favourite drinks of the Portuguese, often consumed while they listen to *fado* (guitar music). Ricardo, however, did not think of products as cultural artefacts. Only quantity and price matter. Exchange is purely economic: goods and services are commoditized, generic, indefinitely marketable and without cultural meaning.

Ricardo's theory came at the time of England's Corn Laws. He demonstrated that Britain should reduce its customs duties, thereby opening up its domestic market to foreign agricultural commodities – especially those from the colonies that were more cost competitive – and specialize in certain manufactured goods to be exported worldwide. It did not sufficiently acknowledge the human consequences, including rapid rural depopulation, social inequality, consumer frustration, stress, materialism, lack of self-sufficiency in food supplies, and threats to health and the environment.[5]

International trade theorists assume the inevitability of global change despite local consequences like job losses. However, the recent global economic downturn has seen this issue re-emerge, as many nations have increased protectionism to speed up recovery. Ernst & Young reported that 78 per cent of small- to medium-sized companies in Germany favoured protectionist measures to shelter them from the global recession.[6] Further, 'Buy domestic' campaigns have re-emerged, especially in countries affected by job losses and company bankruptcies.

Locally, people strongly defend their country and their cultural identity, which is largely thought of as embracing protectionism in international trade. This is illustrated in France by the *Lois Méline* introduced at the end of the nineteenth century out of a desire to protect French food supplies and French farmers, even though this meant higher costs for the consumer.

Website link 6.1

Search for changes in national policies and positions. Start before the global economic crisis, such as the summary of a US Democratic Party committee hearing considering the Bush administration's claim that outsourcing is good for the US economy: **http://dpc.senate.gov/hearings/hearing13/daly.pdf**.

Then, look at more recent information, such as President Obama's 2012 State of the Union address, which vows not to go back to an economy weakened by, among other things, outsourcing and bad debt: **http://www.whitehouse.gov/blog/2012/01/25/president-obama-state-union**.

In practice it is difficult to distinguish between protecting national/cultural interests (self-identity is enhanced by consumption) and protecting the interests of industries, which may deprive consumers of cheaper products, or even of the opportunity to buy particular products. Hence, there is a natural tendency to ignore culture or to consider it as an anecdotal variable, defending local, narrow interests rather than promoting global welfare. Historically, international business and international marketing perceived culture, in the 'modern' world, as an anecdote at best and a useless constraint at worst.[7] However, this argument relies on a macro-perspective rather than a multifaceted micro-examination of the 'modern' world.

The dismal treatment of diversity in global marketing

Traditionally, the global product philosophy lacked any consideration of meanings invested by local consumers. Instead, it conceived price as a universal concern, where low-cost arguments make sense. As advocated by Levitt,[7] and many other authors in the area of international marketing, we expected to see the emergence of global markets for standardized consumer products on a previously unimagined scale. In this world view, traditional differences in national tastes would disappear and local consumer preferences and national product standards would become 'vestiges of the past'. Consumers worldwide would look for good-quality/low-cost products, and global competitors would seek to standardize their offerings everywhere. Farewell diversity: we will not mourn your passing! However, homogenization has not happened, as this world view contains a number of flawed assumptions that are discussed in this and other chapters.

The first assumption concerns the strong ideology of 'standard' or utilitarian needs dominating consumption: people strive for a large quantity of fair-quality, low-cost products. Levitt rightly argued that low cost and high quality are not incompatible. However, this refers only to the quantitative definition of product quality, based on reliability, performance and durability. Here, quality is meant only in the sense of the word contained in the first of nine definitions given by *Collins English Dictionary* (p. 1325):[8]

'a distinguishing characteristic, property or attribute', this does not necessarily mean superior quality to other products. Quality in the sense of 'having or showing excellence or superiority' is only the ninth and last meaning in the dictionary.

The second assumption deals with the continuum between traditional and modern societies. In Western societies, 'traditional' and 'modern' are thought of as contradictions; however, this is too simplistic. Many Eastern collectivist societies, such as Japan, place a high value both on tradition and on modernization. They are modern in the technological sense, but their cultural assumptions are not Western, in the sense of having Western Europe or American values. The cultural assumption that 'modern' is more legitimate is highly questionable. It can lead people to imitate behaviour that is not necessarily appropriate to their own culture.

In the Western view, 'traditional' is of low value, as it is associated with the past, which is mostly seen as an impediment to effective action. This naive view of world diversity believes that we are all converging towards a 'modern' lifestyle marked by standard products and consumption patterns worldwide. There are, however, many non-utilitarian reasons for consumer behaviour; cultural diversity at the international level is a reality. Moreover, there are opportunities for companies that reject the 'consumption fordism' of globalization, to create differentiation and gain a competitive advantage. Over the past decade, even iconic global brands such as Coca-Cola repositioned their strategy to 'think locally and act locally'. Daft (p. 12), stated that:

Ours is a local business – we will think locally and act locally. We became one of the best marketers in the world because we understood that no one drinks 'globally'. Local people get thirsty, go to their local retailer, and buy locally made Coke. To think locally and act locally, we must push decision making and accountability to the local level . . . Understanding the local culture and acting on that understanding is paramount to success.[9]

More recently, firms worldwide are searching for growth opportunities in emerging markets (e.g., China, India, Brazil, Turkey, Mexico, the Philippines and Vietnam), which differ dramatically in terms of their cultural and economic environments. The growing middle class in these emerging economies will not simply be 'recipients' of excess production

from developed nations. Many of these emerging countries already have large domestic companies (with strong local knowledge and linkages) that are competitors for global companies. Further, opportunities exist beyond the middle classes, with the sheer number of people in rural China and India and low-income urban areas in Brazil and Mexico offering market potential, despite a small income of perhaps $1–$2 per day.[2] In this case marketers have a dual role to provide the needed products and services, as well as increase locals' ability to afford them. They need to overcome many challenges, including the design of product modifications and pricing strategies that appeal to locals, building innovative distribution systems, and creating meaningful promotional strategies. For instance, Project Shakti (Hindustan Unilever Ltd.) targeted and trained one woman in each village as a 'Shakti entrepreneur', providing a limited range of consumable products and a computer (which could also be rented to local children to help them learn English and computer skills) to simplify ordering.[2]

6.2

The global convergence of consumption patterns

The marketing environment

Some elements of our environment appear to be converging, at least at the macro level.

- The political environment worldwide has clearly moved towards a democratic system, despite continued political instability in many parts of the world and important exceptions.
- It is more and more difficult, given the powerful means of worldwide communication, through satellite television and the Internet, to block the access of citizens to information on what is happening in their own country and in the world. Very few countries restrict or attempt to control access to the Internet (e.g., China and Saudi Arabia).
- The general economic environment is converging to a certain extent, but there are major limitations in a number of areas that are important for marketing. While economic systems are converging

towards a market economy, the degree of poverty of a significant group of developing countries has been increasing over the years, whereas other emerging economies are experiencing rapid growth in discretionary income.

- Legal integration also has limits since legal traditions continue to differ greatly. Even in the European Union (EU), where integration is promoted, laws pertaining to marketing are regulated both at EU level and at the level of member states, which sometimes results in discrepancies and duplication.

- Marketing infrastructures are also converging, with standards of the marketing profession growing in consistency worldwide. Multinational companies have heavily influenced the widespread adoption of similar practices, even where they are adapted to local environments.

- Supply and competition are now largely globalized, with the progressive shift from domestic industries, operating in protected national markets, to global industries. For example, Li & Fung Ltd., a company based in Hong Kong, can source cotton from the US, send it to Pakistan to be dyed and knitted and then to Cambodia to be sewn.[10]

- Even marketing knowledge can be argued as converging, with American cultural premises that seem to have been adopted worldwide. However, a multitude of differences, both local and cultural, reflect differences in how marketing knowledge has been understood, sometimes misunderstood, and often transformed. Hence, management expectations about both consumers' responses and the performance of marketing tasks are not always supported, even in an environment to which they are apparently suited, due to a lack of awareness and understanding of the local marketing environment.

General convergence at the macro-level

There is also some evidence of macro-level convergence in consumption patterns. For example, there is significant demographic convergence in the European Union: (1) the age distribution – the population is growing older; (2) the size of households is decreasing; and (3) the proportion of immigrants is increasing, with higher concentrations in large cities.[11]

Convergence is also seen in the socio-cultural environment in terms of growing equality between men and women and increasing percentages of working women, while all over the EU, health and environmental concerns are on the rise. In Hofstede's terms,[12] there is a trend towards more *femininity*. Convergence in European consumer behaviour can be observed at a broad level. Services account for a larger part of the household budget and are the fastest-growing area of international trade.[13] Demand is growing for healthcare, environmentally friendly products and services, as well as fun and convenience products. However, Europe (EU and the rest of Europe) only accounts for a little over 10 per cent of the world's population, whereas Asia accounts for over 60 per cent.

Most of the empirical studies on globalization are synchronic in design; they study cross-national similarity in consumption patterns at a precise point in time. The most logical way to study the convergence process is, however, to examine how consumption changes over several time periods. A good illustration of long-term convergence in consumption figures is that of wine, traditionally a southern European drink, and beer, traditionally a northern European drink. Wine consumption has decreased and beer consumption has increased in the south (in France, Greece, Italy, Portugal and Spain), whereas the opposite pattern has evolved in the north (in Austria, Belgium, Denmark, Germany, Luxembourg and the UK), leading to macro-level convergence.[14] Also evident is a tendency towards drinks with lower alcohol content, stricter drink-driving laws and higher-quality products. Similarly, there is evidence of increasing macro-level similarity in cross-national consumption patterns in broad commodity categories, when a utility-maximizing framework is used.[14]

Numerous detailed examples are cited in support of the globalization of consumption behaviour. Beef consumption in Japan, traditionally a fish-eating country, has developed considerably, while there has been a rise in fish consumption in traditionally meat-eating countries.

Rather than discuss macro-level globalization, it makes more sense from an international marketing perspective to try to understand the nature of this phenomenon. With decreasing barriers to international trade over the last century (mostly in the past 50 years), consumers in most countries have access to a larger variety of goods. In this sense, globalization increases, rather than decreases, diversity for consumers.

Evidence of consumers' globalization at a micro-level

De Mooij and Hofstede (p. 62)[15] point out that: 'International marketers would like us to believe that in the "new Europe" with a single currency, consumers will become more similar, will increasingly eat the same food, wear jeans and cross-trainers, and watch the same television programs. Reality is likely to be different.'

Buying and consumption patterns in affluent countries appear to have, in fact, diverged as much as they have converged. Across 15 European countries, preference for new cars over second-hand cars depends more on culture than on wealth.[16] Today, consumers have more opportunities for choice and are often affected by social needs. As de Mooij (pp. 58–9) states:

Clothes satisfy a functional need, whereas fashion satisfies a social need. Some personal care products serve functional needs, but others serve social needs. A house serves a functional need and a home, a social need. Culture influences the type of house in which people live, how they relate to their homes, and how they tend to their homes. A car may satisfy a functional need, but the type of car for most people satisfies a social need. Social needs are culture-bound.[17]

At the micro-level, researchers find that culture influences consumption patterns, but that this influence differs by the product type, product/service category, situational factors, and reasons for purchase. For instance:

- Durable household and functional products vary more by culture than non-durable sensory and personal products.[18]
- Highly visible products, such as wristwatches, are more influenced by culture than consumer electronics.[19,20]
- Services, such as restaurants and air travel, are more influenced by culture than products, such as beer, jeans, soft drinks and stereos.[21]
- Situational factors differ by product type. For instance, the frequency, the time of day, where consumers shop, the length of shopping time and the reason all vary by culture for food, but not for clothing.[22]

- Reasons for purchase, such as maintenance, enjoyment and defence, differ by country.[23]

Many other examples of micro-level differences were elaborated on in Chapter 5.

Thus, at a micro-level, evidence about the globalization of consumer behaviour relating to specific products is somewhat inconclusive. Finding convincing proof of micro-level globalization is difficult, since testing for it would include such issues as the pace and process of globalization, the market segments involved and the geographically significant cultural areas.[24] The trend towards globalization depends partly on the specific aspect of consumer behaviour: whether buying behaviour, shopping behaviour, lifestyle, values, psychometrics and underlying attitudes, influence processes, including group influences and word-of-mouth. The use of culturally unique concepts and research instruments (largely Western) compresses differences, even when cross-cultural precautions are taken. Since the concepts and theories of marketing originated from the US culture, their full ability to capture local patterns of consumer behaviour is questionable.

6.3

The emergence of a global consumer culture

There are at least four ways to interpret global consumer culture: the proliferation of transnational corporations; the proliferation of global capitalism; global consumerism; and global consumption homogenization.[5] As there is no doubt that transnational corporations and capitalism have proliferated, this section will focus on global consumerism and later on global consumption homogenization.

Ger and Belk (p. 275)[5] define global consumerism as 'a widespread and unquenchable desire for material possessions'. It is a culture in which the majority of consumers avidly desire, and therefore try to acquire and display goods and services that are valued for non-utilitarian reasons such as status and novelty seeking as well as envy provocation.[25] The rise in most countries of large-scale, democratized consumption as a legitimate and positively valued human activity (unlike, say, war or monastic contemplation) has led to the emergence of a global consumer culture. This was illustrated by Prahalad and Lieberthal (p. 71): 'What is big and emerging in countries like China and India is a new consumer base consisting of hundreds of millions of people. Starved of choice for over 40 years, the rising middle class is hungry for consumer goods and a better quality of life and is ready to spend.'[26] It seems in every culture there is a culturally appropriate way to justify consumption. Even in countries where purchasing power does not really allow access to goods and services, Hollywood films, with an approximate market share of 90 per cent worldwide, have been a major driver of desires and aspirations, fuelling consumers' needs and envy. In many countries of the world, adding subtitles or dubbing movies is considerably less expensive than making them locally.

The world standard package and 'McDonaldized' consumption

A consumer culture guides people in defining their aspirations towards a certain set of possessions. The standard US 'package of goods' has developed into a world standard package that includes a car and a home with refrigerators, televisions and computers. The same holds true for services, since the fast-food restaurant has become part of the world standard package. Ritzer (p. 70) describes how strongly people identify with McDonald's around the world:

In Taipei, the Golden Arches have come to have more symbolic meaning than the local temple. In Seoul, people are passionate about McDonald's as well as their opposition to it. In Tokyo, Japanese boy scouts were reported to be pleasantly surprised when during a trip they discovered that there was a McDonald's in Chicago.[27]

In the emergence of a global consumer culture, a process dubbed the *McDonaldization* of society, the word 'standard' is central.[28] 'Standard' has three meanings: (1) the same for everybody; (2) the same everywhere in the world; (3) the same for all time. The paradoxical success of the 'Classic' Coca-Cola as against the 'new' Coca-Cola is an illustration of the last point. Standard also means that product quality remains the same unless new technological developments allow improvements which complement the previous attributes.

There are four elements in the McDonaldization process:[28]

1. *Efficiency*: The McDonaldized product or service in the 'Republic of Technology'[7] offers the optimum method for getting from one point (being hungry) to another (being fed). In contrast to traditional solutions, Fordist consumption values assembly-line organization and continuous processes: with the parking areas adjacent to the fast-food restaurant, a short walk to the counter, a limited menu for quick choice, finger food and speedy disposal of leftovers.

2. *Systematic quantification and calculation*: McDonald's offers more 'bang for the buck' and provides its customers with 'value' meals. Rational economic calculations based on the emphasis of price and the size/weight given for each ingredient extols the utilitarian view. In this model, quantity equals quality.

3. *Predictability*: Whether in Chicago, Los Angeles, Paris, Moscow or Tokyo, we find the same Big Mac and French Fries. Consumers find great comfort in this predictability which offers neither shocks nor surprises, and reduces perceived risk. There is not much surprise in the limited range of products offered, but we know that it will be consistent over time and place. Predictable food is based on predictable, often frozen, ingredients and corporate guidelines that detail every item of the fast-food outlet.

4. *Control through the substitution of non-human for human technology*: The system is operated so that there is limited human involvement in the whole production process: rules are fairly strict and automated systems (e.g., soft drinks or ice-cream dispensers) control the exact quantity, in line with point 2. This also facilitates predictability by reassuring customers about the service McDonald's delivers, in line with point 3.

The globalized consumption experience is only one part of the real world of consumption, but it plays a dominant role because it has been consistently and heavily portrayed as 'useful' and 'good for people'. It is also publicized somewhat inaccurately, since there is much more local adaptation, both in Coca-Cola and in McDonald's, than admitted by these global marketers. For instance, McDonald's has adapted elements of its menu to local tastes. In Japan there are Teriyaki burgers, as well as a 'Big America' menu which includes 'Broadway Burger' and a

'Beverly Hills Burger', in China bean sundaes, in Norway salmon burgers, and in Uruguay poached egg burgers. In addition, the same concept can mean something quite different when borrowed from another culture: 'The fast-food concept that fits the US fast lifestyle has adapted successfully to PRC's consumers' lifestyle, because less waiting and fast service do not mean to eat fast' (p. 92).[29] Almost a third of Ramanian Internet users shop online; however, over 80 per cent paid cash on delivery rather than using credit cards.

Website link 6.2

Search for indicators of cross-national financial purchasing power, such as the Big Mac index: http://www.economist.com/blogs/dailychart/2011/07/big-mac-index.

Globalization and 'modern' culture

The most debatable aspect of globalization is the belief that we are all converging towards a 'modern lifestyle'. This view of cross-cultural buyer behaviour involves three main assumptions: (1) modernity is a given, and technology is our path to a bigger and better future for all; (2) even if they differ externally, all societies, from traditional to developed, can be placed on a continuum of social change; and (3) the criterion for placing a society on the continuum is its degree of resistance to modern changes.[30]

Modern culture believes that scientific knowledge and technology are able to control nature and improve human existence. Even though it may be argued that we have already entered the postmodern era, most people still live in a modern era, marked by a strong belief in the achievements of science, its unlimited problem-solving capacity through technology and its exclusive contribution to global welfare.[31] Modernization is clear in Levitt's (p. 97)[7] view of globalization, where he criticizes multinational companies as being medieval (or pre-modern):

The multinational corporation knows a lot about a great many countries and congenially adapts to supposed differences. It willingly accepts vestigial national differences, not questioning the possibility of their transformation, not recognizing how the world is ready and eager for the benefit of modernity, especially when the price is right.

The multinational corporation accommodating mode to visible national differences is medieval.

Global values in modern culture emerge because consumers throughout the world inevitably have fairly similar responses to new technologies and product innovations. 'Modern' culture is characterized by:

1. an individualist orientation, supported by the exercise of purchasing power as a demonstration of individual freedom;
2. a strong emphasis on material achievements and materialistic values, that is, a doing/having rather than a being orientation;
3. a strongly economic, 'commoditized' time;
4. a tendency to discard the past in favour of a future orientation, while expressing some frustration at not living in the present as much as one would like; and
5. a fairly high degree of utilitarianism.

For instance, household equipment tends to individualize tasks, freeing people from both the constraints and the pleasures of communal life, in a mostly urban environment where families are nuclear and the extended family separated by large distances. An increased awareness of a clock-bound and universal time, at the expense of a local and nature-bound time, accompanies the enthusiasm for innovation and change. Modern culture posits a strong future orientation: consumers quickly dispose of perfectly functional products that are quickly obsolete (see Box 6.1). Various environmental concerns typify modern cultures, as countries become more polluted, the ozone layer is depleted, and global warming is an increasing cause for anxiety. Although Germany, with its *Grüne Punkt* (Green Point), still largely leads the environmental movement, the interest in 'green' products is growing worldwide. Notably, the interest is manifested in ways that are context appropriate. For instance, consumers in higher-density countries such as South Korea (approximately 500 people per square kilometre) give a higher priority to product disposability and biodegradability than consumers in Germany (with 235 people per square kilometre) or the USA (with 33 people per square kilometre).[32]

The controversial claim that the 'American way of life' has universal appeal and extends 'backward' to other nations is typical of the binary way of 'modern' thought, opposing concepts such as past/future, traditional/modern, true/false and rational/emotional.[33]

BOX 6.1

In Australia the local councils in some major cities collect household 'rubbish' that people place in their front yards, several times a year. People often begin to take out discarded objects weeks in advance to allow charities and others to pick up anything they might need. These piles often include a wide range of functional indoor and outdoor furniture, barbeques, and white goods (e.g., refrigerators, washing machines) that have been recently upgraded. Many people have furnished their entire house from these discards.

In fact, true globalization has to work both ways. US consumers will have to import genuine, unpasteurized, French *foie gras*, or crude milk cheese, which contains relatively harmless bacteria but also has real taste and consistency. Similarly, if globalization is to be less unidirectional, French consumers will have to develop a taste for peanut butter, American women will start wearing kimonos, and Australian men will swap their shorts and 'thongs' (in this case, thongs refer to a type of open rubber slipper for the feet!) for Bavarian *lederhosen*.

The emergence of a global 'modern' culture is often confused with the convergence of local cultures, leading to an incorrect description of globalization. A frequent mistake is to equate 'modern' with 'American'. While it is true that the US and US multinational companies have been the champions of 'modern' consumer goods (consumption Fordism) and services, globalization is not simply the worldwide extension of the 'American way of life'. The imitation of American solutions results mostly from borrowed answers to common worldwide challenges. American society values a pioneer spirit, is less resistant, and has fewer social impediments to change than more traditional societies. When the Japanese, French or Chinese change, it is not as a result of American pressure; they may simply 'borrow' some of their responses from the US (while often making the US scapegoats for the drawbacks of modernity).

Modern culture, with both high individualism and structured time patterns, implies a type of social organization centred on peer age segments. Girls give up their Barbie dolls between the ages of 12 and 13 because it would be inappropriate to play with dolls – even sophisticated ones – when they reach adolescence. Each age class increasingly has its own identity, its own way of doing things, membership is signalled through consumption, and the shared values and behaviours transcend national borders. There is also evidence that certain age groups, such as teenagers, are permitted a 'cultural time-out', where they are allowed, if not expected, to rebel against their cultural restraints. Later, when they join the workforce and start families they are expected to re-adopt culturally appropriate behaviour.

The increased adoption of modern culture cross-nationally is incorrectly interpreted as a sign of full convergence and as testimony to the progressive disappearance of local cultures. Significant elements of local cultures, such as language, writing systems, religions and relational patterns, stay visibly in the global landscape. While cultural differences rarely appear as the key explanation for behaviour, local cultures allow a deeper understanding of consumption in a specific context. Interpretation must be close to the local reality: for instance, drip/filter coffee taken 'to go' or enjoyed with a meal (as is common in the USA), is a widely different coffee-drinking experience from espresso enjoyed with friends at a local café in Europe or Australia. Local cultures do not really disappear; rather, a new layer of common culture is superimposed on them. The very fact that the Japanese and the Chinese are not willing to change their ideographic writing system, which from a purely utilitarian perspective makes little sense, demonstrates the very deep roots of local cultures.

6.4

Local products and consumption experiences

Not surprisingly, globalized Fordist consumption has a striking preference for 'culture-free' products and consumption situations. A different perspective on consumer behaviour centered on cultural meanings ascribed to things that may be useful, despite its limited use in international marketing texts. Many more insights can be gained by actually centering on a service, product or possession and how it is used in context than through the national character approach, based on limited universal variables and the design of cultural ideals (i.e., high versus low scores on common dimensions). For instance, Nguyen and Belk (p. 8) describe how traditional rites are selected and mixed with Western rights to construct a 'Vietnamese' wedding:[34]

The groom and I opened the tray of betel and areca. The groom picks two areca nuts, which are the symbols of husband and wife. I pick four leaves of betel, which represent the four virtues of women: công, dung, ngôn, hạnh (work, [beautiful] appearance, appropriate speech, and appropriate behavior). This is our Vietnamese traditional rituals. Betel and areca is unique to our culture.

They noted that the more traditional elements tend to be found in the wedding ceremony (lễ cư'ới), while the reception (tiệc cư'ới) is often more 'modern' (hiện đại), importing elements, such as 'cake-cutting' and 'champagne-pouring', yet presenting them as if they were local customs.

If consumer *culture* matters, then it is likely that consumers will invest more meaning in products and services that are more bound to cultural interpreta-tion. The question is therefore: what is more culture-free and what is more culture-bound, in terms of product and service categories on the one hand, and consumer behaviour on the other?

Culture-bound products

Culture bonds or connections arise in a number of ways, in relation to both the consumption situation and product attributes. Products that tend to be more culture-bound will be *richly* connected to the local cultural context in multiple ways, including the actual product and its production, as well as the shopping, purchasing, consumption and disposal environments. Furniture, for instance, will be more culture-bound than consumer electronics, as furniture often has a local style and a local manufacturing tradition, based on the availability of local materials. It is not only bought in shops and markets, but can be inherited or restored. Furniture is often shared with others, even on disposal. In contrast, consumer electronics are typically culture-free, as they are based on rapidly changing technology, where mass production can lead to dramatically lower prices. However, as noted in Box 6.3, there may still be local preferences in these relatively culture-free products, especially in terms of the price/feature trade-off. Fordist, no-frills electronic devices, such as the Personal Internet

---

BOX 6.2

Vietnam

The average annual disposable income in Vietnam was just $US819 in 2010. However, the growing middle class and expected increase in the average disposable income (74 per cent by 2020, in real terms) has seen increased competition in the local market. Despite this, domestic brands are rapidly growing in popularity. They are often relatively cheaper and more carefully address local needs. For instance, locally made mobile phones, such as An Binh Telecom Co's Q-Mobile are increasing in market share and volume sales, as they are relatively cheap (~$US19) and have the desired features, such as a camera with adequate memory and the ability to hold up to four sim cards. This growing competition has forced multinationals to lower their prices and to address local needs better.

Further, consumers in Vietnam are now exposed to the world stage. Traditional media are being replaced by Internet use, with 42 per cent of respondents from the four major cities reporting daily use. Television ownership is increasing rapidly, as are illegal satellite dishes, allowing Vietnamese to receive transmissions from other parts of Asia (e.g., Hong Kong, China, Indonesia, and Australia).

(Source: Based on information from the *Euromonitor*, 'Vietnam: Country Pulse'[35] and Nguyen and Belk.[34])

BOX 6.3

Time to wait

Market data were gathered for blood analysis equipment in several European countries (Germany, France, Italy, Spain and the United Kingdom) in hospital labs. Doctors were asked to rate the importance of time to results, which is a reason for adopting automatic blood analysis equipment allowing speedier outcomes. Responses reflect different degrees of preoccupation with time, Germans being the most concerned with short time to results (86 per cent of German labs mentioned this as a major factor in their buying decision), followed by the British (72 per cent), the French (67 per cent), the Spaniards (55 per cent), and the Italians (37 per cent). Thus, even for organizational purchasing, underlying cultural values are different.

Communicator, which was targeted at emerging markets in 2004, failed to achieve the expected sales and was taken off the market shortly after.

The local physical environment shapes the type, use and usefulness of many products. Products that are closely related to the local physical environment will be more culture-bound, as the physical environment influences the local material culture, which in turn is linked to climate, density of population, housing, flora and fauna, and so on. The absence of visible cattle rearing on most Japanese islands, except Hokkaido, distances Japanese people from dairy products. Japanese people find cheese, the most sophisticated dairy product, quite a strange food; cheese conveys little meaning except that of foreignness. Similarly, local ways of building are generally based on the availability of substitute building materials (e.g., wood, cement or stones), certain craft traditions (e.g., masonry versus carpentry), and constraints (e.g., earthquakes), which explain the dominance of local technical solutions. For instance, the use of steel in bridges and urban freeways is much higher in Japan than it is in Europe where bridges are mostly built with reinforced concrete. Similarly, wood is frequently used for housing construction in the United States, whereas it is quite marginal in Western Europe (except in Scandinavia) and Australia, where most people prefer houses built with clay bricks.

Language content is also a major art of the cultural content of a product, especially for genuinely cultural products (e.g., songs, soap operas, films and novels), as well as the written language used on or around a product, such as the packaging or brand name. For instance, the instructions for assembling IKEA furniture and Lego toys attempt to avoid complex multi-language explanations by using a series of basic pictures, which although sometimes confusing, are relatively more culture-free than written materials.

Culture bonds are strong for products or services that are consumed in a cultural and national context. The product or service, consciously or unconsciously, is more than a simple utilitarian purchase, resulting in a preference for products made in one's own country. This can be seen in the consumption of hot beverages throughout the world, with rituals around coffee and tea consumption taking on relatively unique forms internationally. In terms of product attributes, the use of local materials and production processes, recipes and craft techniques reinforce the perception of compatibility, if they are known as such by consumers.

Products that involve a *relationship to others*, in terms of displaying/showing or giving/sharing, are likely to be culture-bound, precisely because this relationship is culturally coded – that is, the social situation is likely to moderate the influence of culture. The same consumer may choose different brands depending on who is involved in the decision-making process or likely to use the product.[36-38] Conspicuous-consumption items, and more generally goods having a high signal value, are culture-bound. Whereas many luxury products are globally branded, the nature of their consumption is largely local, depending at least on concepts of the self and others.[39] Products that have been consumed as a part of life since childhood are often marked by locality. Peanut butter from the US and Vegemite from Australia are widely used local products which cannot be easily found in many countries and are not easily palatable in other cultures.

Complex products, such as films, are logically culture-bound, because they require a high level of interpretation and knowledge of the local context in order for the film to be fully understood and enjoyed. One of the reasons for the limited global success of most countries' films is that they rely on local cues which are not easily understood by different local audiences. However, the success of American movies is based on their low contextuality, simplified characters, reliance on the universal appeal of violence, love, and wealth, and their simple moral dichotomy, where good struggles against evil. Even so, many Hollywood films are modified during the dubbing process to add the appropriate local context. For instance, many of the jokes were changed in the German version of the animated movie *Aladdin* to make them more appealing and relevant to a German audience. Comedy, it seems, is largely culture-bound, the result of a sense of shared understanding.

The very *nature of the product* has some influence on the level of universality of needs. *Non-durables* seem to appeal more to tastes, habits and customs; therefore, they are more culture-bound. Clothing, confectionery, food and household cleaners are all culture-bound. While one could easily believe that industrial products are typically culture-free, this view is largely mistaken, because the contexts in which they are used, and the functionalities sought, depend on culture. The construction industry, for instance, is highly influenced by local cultural traditions, as well as the attitude towards time (short-term versus long-term orientation) and the perceived trade-off between the price and durability of equipment. In Europe the difference between national markets is considerable. For instance, clay water pipes are much more popular in Germany than France. While clay water pipes are two or three times more expensive than cast-iron pipes, they last much longer, well beyond the lifetime of those who buy them. The German local authorities and/or standard-setting bodies prefer a high investment cost/extended lifetime trade-off, whereas this timeframe is beyond the concern of French public decision makers. Furthermore, the major player in France for this kind of water pipe, Pont-à-Mousson founded in 1856, uses ductile cast iron, a solution it has promoted widely with the water utilities.

One framework for unravelling the degree and the nature of culture bonds for products is to undertake a 'cultural biography' of the goods surveyed.[40] Drawing on the analogy with the life of a person, the biography of an object allows one to understand how it ultimately nests itself within a cultural milieu. Kopytoff (p. 67) describes what a 'cultural biography' of a car in Africa might entail:

The biography of a car in Africa would reveal a wealth of cultural data: the way it was acquired, how and from whom the money was assembled to pay for it, the relationship of the seller to the buyer, the uses to which the car is regularly put, the identity of its most frequent passengers and of those who borrow it, the frequency of borrowing, the garages to which it is taken and the owner's relation to the mechanics, the movement of the car from hand to hand over the years, and in the end, when the car collapses, the final disposition of its remains. All of these details would reveal an entirely different biography from that of a middle-class American, or Navajo, or French peasant car.[40]

This type of analysis may uncover new interesting product uses, especially in lesser developed nations, where necessity dictates the conversion of products to maximize their use. Some culturally bound product uses include the use of car tyres to reinforce wells during the rainy season and the use of a telephone answering machine to check for power outages which may cause heat loss at a distant residence.[41]

Unique consumption experiences

Consumption is still largely a local reality. Far from being uniquely culture related, local reality also reflects the economy, climate and customs, and the mere fact that much of our life is still shared with others who have the same kind of 'local knowledge' in the Geertzian sense.[42] There are still huge differences in the pattern of household expenditures across developed and developing countries. Even in the EU, the percentages spent by households in various countries on food in general, and specifically vegetables, chocolate and cheese, still differ widely. Consumers attribute meaning to specific products and services in context, especially what it means to desire, to search, to evaluate, to purchase, to consume, to share, to give, to spend, and to dispose. Consumption experiences are full of social facts in interaction with other players in the market game: manufacturers, distributors, salespeople and also other consumers. Illustrations are given below.

Consumption and the environment

Cultural consumption involves how we see our environment, how nature and culture affect our perceptions and preferences. This is reflected in political regulation and standards, financial support to specific industries, as well as the local culture and level of environmental concern.[43] A simple comparison of usage shows that on average Germans are more likely to express their connection to the environment than the French. For instance, filters for drip-coffee machines are white in France and yellow-brown in Germany (*naturbraun*), paper handkerchiefs are generally white in France and yellow-brown in Germany and toilet paper, which is generally pink or white in France, is greyish in Germany. The Germans express their willingness to be environmentally friendly (*umweltfreundlich*) by purchasing paper-based products whose colour exhibits their genuinely 'recycled' nature – that is, not bleached with chlorine-based chemicals that are used to whiten the paper. The same holds true for German writing and copying paper, which, because of its greyish and irregular appearance, would be generally considered by most French as 'dirty' and of poor quality. The difference in consumer experience lies in the difference of *continuity* in the ecological concern. Germans feel the necessity to be nearer to nature because they live in a country about three times more densely populated than France and they insist on strong coherence between their words and their deeds. The two peoples seem to have different ways of reconciling nature and culture: Germans are often perceived stereotypically as natural, deep and aggressive, whereas the French are thought of as sophisticated. German culture finds its expression in love for nature and a preference for isolation, whereas French culture advocates social life and shows disdain for everything that is too nature oriented.[42] Further, the French have a strong preferences for the preservation of their cultural productions, which is seen in the number of geographically protected products they have applied for and been granted.[44]

Offering wine

Offering wine is a different experience in southern Europe from what it is in the United States, Japan or northern Europe. Hosts who receive wine from their guests have to decide whether to keep it for later, or to open it immediately to share it with their guests. In France, unless the host states that the wine is not suitable to accompany the meal, the received wine will be drunk with the guests; sharing is a must, and keeping the wine for oneself would imply that it may not be good enough to drink now. In many other countries it would be impolite to drink a gift with the giver, since it would mean the immediate destruction of a present that should be kept as a memory, at least for a time. The emphasis in each case is on different values: the sense of sharing on the one hand, and the sense of keeping a present as a memory of the donor on the other.

Habits, habitus and shared meaning

Culture may be viewed simply as shared habits and customs, and as shared meaning about how particular experiences are to be interpreted in context, rather than as a value system. This system of shared habits and interpretation is often incorporated into 'common sense' (shared meaning), which translates into French as 'good sense' (*bon sens*) with a clear value judgement, or into German as 'sound understanding' (*gesunder Menschenverstand*), showing that it is the appropriate solution. Habits are central in local consumer behaviour, because they limit options, simplify interpretation and assist in attitude formation at an almost automatic level. Habits mean we do not have to scan all possible alternatives all the time and they give us confidence in our decisions. But they are a largely overlooked element of consumer behaviour, probably because they are seen as passive decision making. However, many of our habits are grounded in our local culture, especially those we acquired by almost by osmosis from our parents and their parents before. Further, when our cognitive capacity is depleted or constrained, such as when we are emotionally aroused in terms of being angry or very happy, habitual behaviour is almost unavoidable.[45]

A Chinese proverb says that 'habit starts with the first time' and a Western proverb says that 'habit is second nature'. Culturally developed habits are often supported in child-rearing, schooling and education systems and the whole reward–sanction system that goes with our social surroundings. Habits are ways of doing that have been reinforced by authorization and gratification, so that once the programming is forgotten they appear to be legitimate. Three examples taken from diverse contexts may be used to illustrate this.

Kaffeetrinken

The German *Kaffeetrinken* is a traditional German form of enjoyment, organized mostly at weekends or holiday afternoons with family or friends, at home or in a *Konditorei* (pastry shop serving coffee and tea) or a restaurant, at about three or four o'clock. The special relationship of Germans to coffee, sweets and cakes (*Kuchen*) has much to do with happy hours experienced since childhood, when people relax in a somewhat constrained society with a deeply internalized pressure for conforming to rules.

British fire safety systems

The United Kingdom is one of the largest markets for fire safety equipment in the world; fire alarms outside buildings are intended to attract people's attention quickly in case of fire. The excessive fire safety instructions, in both public and private buildings, are striking for many foreigners. The tradition of using wood in building and the Great Fire of London are probably historical reasons for this British phobia, and the United Kingdom was much faster to comply with EU standards than the Italians and the Spaniards: not only would the implementation of this regulation in all public buildings involve massive investment that Italian and Spanish state budgets cannot afford, but also in Latin countries stone is more common than wood in construction and the anguish caused by building fires has been rare.

Drinking a beer

Individuals invest meaning into their consumption experiences. Whereas aggregate data seem to demonstrate quantitative convergence, they also conceal huge qualitative divergence as far as experiences, context, perceptions and interpretations are concerned. For instance, beer is consumed in greater quantities in southern Europe than in the past, but the very experience of drinking beer still has a different meaning from that in the north of Europe: the meaning differential has not yet diminished in the same proportion as the volume differential.

Shared situations, habits and stories around beer differ across Europe. This is most obvious in the type of beer, glass preference and environment in which it is consumed. Beer differs in terms of the bitterness, froth, bubbles, sweetness and alcoholic content. For instance, most British beers are high-fermentation beers with lower alcohol content than beers on the Continent. The Bavarian *Krug* (a large jar) does not give the same 'taste' to beer as the French *demi* (a quarter-litre stemmed glass), the English pint glass or the Australian middy.

Drinking beer in Germany has a different meaning to drinking beer in the United Kingdom or in France. In Germany, beer is consumed in a *Kneipe* (tavern) or bought from a *Getränkeshop* (a nice combination of German and English to refer to a side-store to a supermarket entirely dedicated to beverages). Local beers play a dominant role on the German beer scene. In the region of Cologne, for instance, the *Kölsch* beers, comprising some ten high-fermentation brands of beer, are seen as a reference to the place, a little like wines in France. The German returnable half litre bottles suit a densely populated country where people are concerned with recycling glass. German beers always refer to the purity law (*Reinheitsgebot*) of 1516.

In a British pub, drinking a pint (0.57 litres) or half-pint of beer is a different experience; the pub is a comfortable place that invites people to stay and feel at home. Since people often drink more than a single pint of beer, it must be low in alcohol. This beer can be drunk without 'getting plastered', especially if one stays for quite a long period of time. A pub is a totally different world from the French *café-bar*, with its tiled floor and its rather cold interior design. In France regular customers invest the place with their own sense of comfort and human warmth. But non-regular customers will never find in a *café-bar* the immediate comfort that they find in most British pubs.

This contrasts the Australian experience. Pettigrew (pp. 162–4)[46] interviewed patrons at local pubs to uncover the basic symbolic values of leisure, freedom and solidarity, at least for men:

Older Male: 'What you are is a person when you walk into a pub. No matter where it is in Australia, automatically you can get into such a situation where you can just be friends with a person you have never met before. It doesn't matter from one state, one pub, one environment to another.'

Older Male: 'You are in my home. This pub is my home. This place is about socialized drinking. People come down here to enjoy themselves, talk to their workmates after work, have a couple, and then go home. Kiss the dog and feed the missus. You go to work and you go to the pub, and that is home.'

Male: 'It is probably perceived that men are allowed out for beers basically and the women still stay home and look after the family, which sounds a very old attitude. Although everybody says they have changed, and things have changed, maybe they haven't.'

Another contrast is Finland where, until recently, supermarkets were only allowed to sell low-alcohol beer. All other types of alcoholic drinks, including standard beer, are sold only in the state chain, Alko, which has a monopoly. Alko stores have limited opening hours and are generally removed from central shopping areas. This symbolizes the effort one must make to buy beer (apart from the low-alcohol type), indicating a level of societal disapproval.[47]

6.5

Local consumer cultures and resistance to change

The Danes dominate the world market for blue cheese with their Blue Castello, a decontextualized product with an Anglo-Italian name. It is a pasteurized, inoffensive, white soft cheese, palatable for every germphobic cheese-lover. As such, it is a good candidate for promotion as a global product, and a typical progeny of Fordist consumption. The British Stilton, the French Roquefort or the Italian Gorgonzola, all traditional blue cheeses, may in the long run be under threat from this global alternative.

You may wonder how much autonomy consumers have in encouraging or limiting the movement towards globalization. Naturally, we may or may not buy globalized products and services, and to this extent we 'vote with our feet'. But we also have little choice but to buy what is available, as goods are astutely brought to stores by sophisticated merchants. In this respect, there could be some resistance to change, not at the level of the individual buying decision, but at more of a macro-level.

Even though we win as consumers, we may lose from globalization as citizens and workers, which leads to a preference for buying locally made products. Holt et al.[48] in a study of consumers in 12 countries (US, UK, Brazil, China, Egypt, France, India, Indonesia, Japan, Poland, South Africa and Turkey) found that one in ten would not buy global brands if given a choice. This is despite the widespread belief that global brands are associated with high levels of quality. What this amounts to is people asking to have their 'way of life' preserved.

While some products may be global, there are strong arguments against the existence of a global consumer per se. The concept of cosmopolitanism has been oversimplified and used to depict a privileged universal, impartial and objective individual, who is above 'localism'.[49] According to Levy and colleagues (p. 240):[49] 'cosmopolitanism does not denote an intrinsic value, but represents a state of mind that is manifested as an orientation toward the outside, the other, and which seeks to reconcile the global with the local and mediate between the familiar and the foreign'. Thus, cosmopolitans are not global, in the sense of being the same worldwide; they are still anchored in their local culture, and their behaviour depends on their purchase motivation, personality and past experiences.[50] As shown above, consumers' motivations do not easily globalize.

Consumers always 'construct' the identity of brands, even for 'global products' and they do so on the basis of their local culture and identity. One way of examining the symbolic meaning of brands is to identify the human characteristics that consumers associate with a brand. While brand personalities include some universal elements, such as competence, trendiness, excitement, sincerity and sophistication, they also include some culture-specific elements.[51,52] For instance, for more collectivist Japanese and Spanish respondents the products were associated with characteristics of peacefulness (e.g., dependence, naiveté, mildness and shyness), whereas for the more individualist US respondents, ruggedness (e.g., outdoorsy, masculine, Western, tough and rugged) emerged.[51] In addition, in the Spanish group, products were also associated with the characteristic of passion (emotional intensity being fervent, passionate and intense) and spirituality (being spiritual, mystical and bohemian), which is certainly descriptive of Spanish culture. It is also interesting to note that even

BOX 6.4

Consumer resistance to McDonald's?

France, where cultural resistance to fast food and hamburgers exists as a matter of national pride, is one of McDonald's leading markets in Europe. Having first achieved great success with a limited number of successful 'luxury' (high end of the market) fast-food stores located in the centre of major towns in France, McDonald's has now expanded to the suburbs and motorway junctions, and offers breakfast service. Anti-fast-food consumer associations have resisted the fast-food movement. Anti-globalization activists such as José Bové have caused material damage to restaurants. Nutrition specialists have shown that traditional French meals, based on diverse foods, eaten over a longer time (one hour or more), are much better for the digestion and may prevent cancer of the digestive tract. Despite all this, McDonald's is popular with the young generation, especially children who will be tomorrow's adults and parents.

McDonald's has been responsive to criticisms of nutritionists in the United States. It has reduced fat, salt and sugar in its products and introduced a lean Deluxe burger with only 10 grammes of fat and 310 calories, against 20 grammes of fat and 410 calories for the Quarter Pounder. The French weekly *Femme Actuelle* carried a McDonald's advertorial advising families not to eat at the restaurant more than once per week for health reasons.[53] McDonald's has also responded to attacks from environmentalists and animal rights activists by replacing the Styrofoam hamburger box with paper or a new starch-based alternative, and enforcing strict guidelines for animal husbandry. In northern Europe, McDonald's now insists on sorting its own refuse so that it can be appropriately recycled. McDonald's is also responsive to localized demands, as stated on page 11 of the 2010 Annual Report: 'Our business in Europe will continue to be guided by three strategic priorities: increasing local relevance, upgrading the customer and employee experience, and building brand transparency.' Resisted or beloved, fast food is now an institution.

the apparent universal elements of brand personality show differences in their emphasis. For instance, the characteristic of excitement (young, contemporary, spirited and daring) also contained imaginativeness, uniqueness and independence in the US and Spain, while in Japan it included talkative, funny and optimistic. This emphasizes the ability of consumers to perceive and interpret the same information differently in each culture.

'Global brands' in this sense are portfolios of local marketing assets, federated under a common, lexically identical name. Although Blue Castello builds on both an American referential (blue-cheese dressing) and an Italian image, it is doubtful whether people in all countries have the same kind of buying motives, product use and product image. False 'global' consumers buy false 'global' products, which they re-invest with their own culture-bound motivations and purposes. This suggests that most of the resistance will be hidden from global marketers. Box 6.4 illustrates this point.

Will consumers resist the globalization process?

Globalized consumption assumes that consumers are pleased with it because it means cheap, good-quality products. The 'globalness' of a product is a cue for quality across cultures.[48] Perceptions of 'globalness' is positively related to perceptions of quality and prestige and, through them, to purchase likelihood in the United States and Korea, but only for consumers with low ethnocentrism.[54] Those with higher ethnocentrism resist globalization by paying a premium for locally made goods, voting for protectionist governments, or acting as consumer lobbyists to support public action (e.g., against fast food) in order to maintain or re-create entry barriers that protect local consumption. They may, nonetheless, be self-contradictory – for instance, drinking Coke while complaining about the Americanization of society.

Globalization obviously has some drawbacks. Some have denounced the de-humanizing process in post-Fordist consumption, and the possible decrease in consumption diversity which may result from the progressive replacement of local consumption by globalized offerings.[28] Others have wondered whether globalization is just going a bit too far. For instance, the continual opening up of national markets through the WTO has resulted in increased worldwide competition across countries that have widely different levels of social security. These countries cannot compete on a fair basis because social insurance may raise the cost of goods subject to global competition. Globalization favours the consumer, not the worker, and raises complex issues when these combine in one single citizen. As Rodrik (p. 30) argues:[55]

Globalization is exposing a deep fault line between groups that have the skills and mobility to flourish in global markets and those who either don't have these advantages or perceive the expansion of unregulated markets as inimical to social stability and deeply held norms. The result is severe tension between the market and social groups such as workers, pensioners, and environmentalists, with government stuck in the middle.

There are two different issues here. The first, is knowing whether there are intellectual, ethical and practical reasons for protecting local cultures and consumers from the globalization of consumption patterns. As Ger (p. 122)[56] points out, opening up markets is not necessarily desirable: 'goods can delight or frustrate, cultivate or impoverish, empower or alienate, and nourish or destruct social relations for individual people and contribute to societal, cultural, health and environmental problems'.

The second issue is whether mechanisms resisting globalization actually occur at the individual and/or social level. For this issue we can see a growing network of loosely associated individuals and groups opposed to globalization. Activists fall into sometimes dissonant categories, including Marxists, environmentalists, trade unionists, anarchists, cultural preservationists, advocates of fair trade, and, more recently, anti-war activists. But not all opposition to globalization is based in identifiable groups. In a recent study we found that 15 per cent of adult consumers in the USA and 10 per cent in China had a high level of animosity towards global companies, on the basis of their economic power, cultural impact and environmental harm to the consumer's country.

Website link 6.3

Search for information about globalization, such as the following Index of Globalization: **http://globalization.kof.ethz.ch/static/pdf/ rankings_2011b.pdf.**

Global marketing is often presented as a powerful tool for promoting economic development. For instance, those countries higher on the Index of Globalization (see Website link 6.3) tend to have greater income equality, even when we contrast emerging economies. This illustrates one of the benefits of globalization. However, in emerging consumer culture, there is often and emphasis on status and hedonistically conspicuous consumption, even when basic utilitarian needs have not been met.[5] Thus, it is important to emphasize a marketing system that designs, produces and delivers products and services that increase the populations' material welfare without damaging tradition.[57] This clearly means avoiding some of the uglier consequences of globalization, such as the problems caused by supplying infant formula to developing countries.

Corporate social responsibility (CSR) programmes are becoming increasingly important to companies. Companies are using CSR programmes not only address the unintended consequences of their own processes, such as Coca-Cola's partnership with World Wildlife Fund, but also opportunities to apply their specific capabilities to solve societal and environmental issues (see the IBM example in Website link 6.4) and philanthropic donations to local causes. Rather than a one size fits all focus, many companies are addressing specific local issues, such as Wal-Mart's Global Care programme which invests in local social infrastructure, such as the provision of care for mentally ill children in India, rebuilding homes and drinking water facilities in Africa and the Middle East and rebuilding schools destroyed by earthquakes in China.[10]

Website link 6.4

Search for global company corporate social responsibility actions, such as those from IBM: **http://www.ibm.com/ibm/responsibility/.** Also, research opportunities for public–private partnerships, such as those promoted by the World Bank Group: **http://www1.ifc.org.**

Preference for national products

In most developed countries domestic products are more popular than foreign-made products. In contrast, many developing countries preferred products from well-known developed nations, especially when local companies are limited in skill and reach.[58] However, it is important to note that this is not static. The preferences of Hong Kong and Chinese consumers changed, since the handover of Hong Kong from the United Kingdom to China, to a greater preference for their own products than foreign products, including UK-made.[59] Further, as local companies improve on style, design, quality and pricing, their knowledge of the local market, coupled with consumer's national pride, has challenged international brands.

Many consumers throughout the world have deep-rooted nationalistic feelings that extend to purchasing situations. There are different explanations for this preference for national products, especially in developed countries. For instance, ethnocentrism, patriotism, collectivism, and a lack of openness to foreign cultures are all significantly related to a preference for national products. Consumer ethnocentrism, which is defined as beliefs about the appropriateness or morality of buying foreign-made products,[60] has been studied extensively. Ethnocentric consumers are more likely to buy domestic than foreign products[61,62], and have negative attitudes towards global brands.[63] In addition, some consumers have deep-rooted feelings toward specific countries, because of past events, such as wars or economic histories between countries.[64] Whereas ethnocentrism is related to a tendency not to purchase any foreign products, animosity is related to the tendency not to purchase products from specific countries.

Tapping into nationalism, 'Buy National' campaigns have been used in many countries including the United States, Portugal, Japan, France, Canada, and Mexico, as well as Australia.[65] 'Buy National' campaigns have again increased in frequency in the aftermath of the recent global economic downturn; however, they should be used very cautiously as they are affected by country of origin (COO) perceptions, product categories and situations. First, we should consider the possible opposing influences of ethnocentrism and COO perceptions. Attitudes towards foreign products are negatively affected by ethnocentrism and positively affected by COO perceptions.[66] These campaigns are less likely to be effective when other countries' products are seen to have a COO appeal, such as Italian shoes or Swiss watches. The influence of nationalism is likely to differ by product category. It depends on country competencies and capabilities. Second, the influence is also likely to differ by usage situation or context. Ger and colleagues found that coffee type differs by situation in Turkey, especially when convenience may be a factor (p. 167):

I have Nescafé all the time, all day, when I am studying. Nescafé is more practical, you can easily make it, but it takes time to prepare Turkish coffee. Turkish coffee is usually consumed after the meals. Turkish coffee reminds me of being with friends and chatting together. When you go to a neighbour or a friend, she prepares Turkish coffee and you chat while you drink. I almost always drink it with my mother or my friend. I never drink it alone (Zehra, female, 18).[67]

The effectiveness of 'Buy National' advertising was brought into question when it was found that American consumers' attitudes towards domestic products did not correspond with their purchasing behaviour.[68] Consumers are fairly rational in their product evaluations. Attempts to artificially enhance the relative quality perceptions of locally made products are likely to be ineffective. The best approach may be to reinforce nationalistic feelings, and not to attempt to influence consumers in their product evaluation.

6.6

Emergent patterns of mixed local/ global consumer behaviour

What emerges from the confrontation of global and local consumption is a complex pattern, where the variety of consumption experiences reaches unprecedented levels. Global consumption patterns are reflected in local kaleidoscopes where myriad pieces of coloured glass are constantly rearranged into innumerable pictures.

Positioning the local vis-à-vis the global: patchworks and kaleidoscopes

As Firat (p. 111)[33] rightly observes, 'In an overwhelmingly marketized existence, individuals experience practically all aspects of their lives as consumers'.

> ## BOX 6.5
>
> ## 'European' beers
>
> Typical of the diversity of the European brewing industry is how different brands in their segments are viewed from country to country. Brands which do not have their origin in a country, which are 'foreign', are invariably viewed as premium segment products. A good example of this is BSN's Kronenbourg 1664, which is sold in France as an ordinary segment beer, but is viewed in almost all other (European) markets as a premium product. As an Italian brewer puts it: 'Foreign brands command a premium price for their image of higher quality.' However, potential hazards exist for brewers in pursuing this policy: 'In
>
> Great Britain, (Belgian) Stella Artois is a premium beer, one of the most expensive beers you can get there, and people buy it because it is expensive. It is marketed and promoted that way. The British are travelling people, so now when they come to Belgium, they discover that Stella Artois is a cheap beer. So they ask themselves if it is justified to pay so much for it in Great Britain' (French brewing manager).
>
> (Source: Steele,[69] p. 58. Reproduced by permission of Sage Publications, London, Los Angeles, New Delhi and Singapore, from European Brewing Industry, Murray Steele, *The Business of Europe: Managing Change*, Roland Calori and Peter Lawrence (eds), copyright © Sage Publications, 1991.)

Whereas consumption was not always highly regarded by modern consumers, the postmodernist consumers pursue, with little thought, the construction of their self-image. Further, Firat (p. 115) states:

Because the postmodern consumer experience is not one of committing to a single way of being, a single form of existence, the same consumers are willing to sample the different, fragmented artifacts. The consumer is ready to have Italian for lunch and Chinese for dinner, to wear Levi's 501 blue jeans for the outdoor party in the afternoon and to try the Gucci suit at night – changing not only diets and clothes but also the personas and selves that are to be (re)represented at each function.[33]

Whether people really change their self-image so quickly may be debatable. However, most consumers assemble diverse consumption items in a very opportunistic, fragmented and idiosyncratic way, not hesitating to mix local products and ways with global products and services. There is high degree of pragmatism in postmodern consumption, in particular because budgetary constraints are still very meaningful. Fordist consumption items have their place in the patchwork: they offer good value and are often shrewdly advertised so that the potentially negative aspects of standard offerings on the consumer's self-image are largely erased. High-touch products and luxury brands play a complementary role, being the shiniest and most colourful squares of the harlequin tights of postmodern consumption. Local products are also present: they make up the bulk of the patchwork with more discreet and less shiny pieces of

fabric. As shown by Box 6.5, featuring our favourite example (beer), local products are candidates for promotion at a higher level of image in other countries where they are opportunistically re-interpreted, precisely because their foreignness allows it.

A process of creolization takes place when foreign goods are assigned new meanings and uses by the buyers' culture, even if they are transferred to it without change. For instance, Kragh and Djursaa (p. 1306)[70] observe that 'traditional furniture such as English furniture of the eighteenth century Chippendale and Hepplewhite mould is found in a number of especially elderly Danish homes and kept alive as a cultural expression through the exposure to English upper-class interiors depicted in television series and films'. In this sense, one can contrast the creolization paradigm, where attention focuses on the reception and domestication process of global goods in local contexts, to the Cocacolonization paradigm, where emphasis is on uniformity.[71] A good example of such localization of consumption is Disneyland Tokyo, which is a perfect replica of the American model, yet is completely 'Japanized', i.e., fully reinvested by local cultural codes.[72,73]

Central and peripheral consumption contexts

In the emergent consumption patterns the consumption context is an important aspect of how consumers combine global 'Fordist' goods and services, high-touch luxury brands and local items. Consumption contexts involve a certain space (i.e., certain rooms in a home), as well as particular time periods and people. A family dinner in a British dining room or a ski holiday in the French Alps are examples of consumption contexts. Djursaa and Kragh[74] studied the fragmented nature of globalization by distinguishing central and peripheral consumption contexts, based on in-depth, direct observation for two highly culture-bound product categories: furnishings and food. The consumption contexts of furnishings are Britain and Denmark, and the consumption contexts of food are three Arab cities: Riyadh, Jeddah and Dubai. Centrality for food is defined in terms of time of the day when a meal is consumed whereas centrality in the case of furnishings is defined in spatial terms as the room where traditional cultural values are respected because this room carries a strong culture-bound meaning. British informants clearly express the dining-room as a central consumption context and, when presented with modernist furniture for dining-rooms, indicate that:

. . . they were pleasant enough and would be OK for kitchens or breakfast rooms, but not for 'proper' dining rooms, which for the majority of English respondents clearly had to be traditional to carry the proper cultural message of identity. In Denmark, by contrast, modernism is the cultural norm and carries our notions of identity perfectly adequately, in central rooms as well as in main homes (p. 28).[74]

In peripheral consumption contexts, it is easier for a consumer to innovate by borrowing from foreign cultural contexts. Informants from the three Arab cities note that dinner, a peripheral meal, is increasingly taken in fast-food outlets, unlike their lunch, which for Arabs is the 'central' meal. A common pattern is to go out for dinner at Pizza Hut, McDonald's or Harvey's, which have compartments for male and female members of the family to eat together, separated from other guests. In the case of dinner taken at home, 'global products also play a very significant part in the meal; as one respondent said, "Dinner is pizza and Pepsi"' (p. 30).[74]

Kaleidoscopic borrowing and the assemblage of local and global items is only possible if marketers are flexible enough to introduce some adaptations to their offerings, ignoring the Levittian criticism of adjustment to local ways.[7] For instance, when McDonald's in Egypt suffered an anti-American boycott for its support of Israel in 2001, the company introduced the McFalafel, promoted by the singer of the hit *I Hate Israel* by Sha'ban Abdel Rahim.[75] Since then, McDonald's has been proactive about incorporating local tastes into the standard menu.

Global marketers should first target peripheral consumption contexts to successfully introduce foreign products that are not grounded in the local culture. In China, McDonald's is appropriate for a date, but not for a celebration.[76] McDonald's is not appropriate for a celebration because the prices and seating arrangements are standardized and offer no opportunity to make a special display of face to the guest of honour. Conversely, it is the standardized offering that makes it more appropriate for a date, as the man does not need to worry about the lavishness of a meal.

Borrowing can also be progressive: McDonald's has started in many countries without being open at breakfast time, as it is in most Western countries. It is now introducing breakfast offerings worldwide, which brings – from a Fordist perspective – increased efficiency in terms of covering overhead costs by prolonging demand patterns over 14 or more hours. McDonald's and other fast-food outlets have succeeded in extending Fordist consumption throughout the world because they have been pragmatically adaptive, partly tailoring their offering to local habits.

Complexity and ambivalence in globalized consumption patterns

Consumers search for and create meaning because they need constantly to re-build their self-image. For this reason, their search for identity through consumption must be a key concern for marketers. In a globalized world, identity-seeking consumers can pick up products from two different shelves: one that favours the locality and the ingroup orientation and another that displays desirable values, meanings and signs offered by foreign, outgroup cultures. How consumers combine local and global meanings is complex. There is much ambivalence in the search for identity in a radically modern world where local diversity based on linguistic and religious differences will not disappear for centuries.

Globalized consumption has a threefold pattern. The first component is based on modernity and on

Fordist consumption; it corresponds to low-cost/fair-quality, weakly differentiated, utilitarian products, embedded in fairly low-context consumption experiences. Its highest potential for success is reached when products and consumption experiences are culture-free, or consumption contexts are peripheral. Examples range from the film *Titanic* to Camay soap. Families, because they often face stricter budgetary constraints than singles, are likely to be adept in modern Fordist consumption. Despite appearances and discourse, fordist marketers show major adaptations and flexibility in facing local consumption. They display much more sensitivity to local ways than is described in textbooks, and their success is more pragmatic than ideological. The second element is a postmodernist type of consumption: fragmented, continually re-assembled and re-interpreted. This can be particularly true for big brands, conspicuous consumption, younger people and yuppies. The third element corresponds to people who are aware that consumption is now a key driver for culture and that their choices as consumers will influence their culture. This radically modern type of person behaves both opportunistically and critically, with a willingness to display diversity in consumption.[28] For these consumers, McDonald's is an ethnic, American restaurant.

In concluding this chapter, it may be wondered why companies ignore local diversity. Rather than being a liability, it can also act as a superb opportunity for building competitive advantages based on differentiation, which are easier to defend against competitors than low-cost advantages.

Questions

1. Take mineral water as a product example and outline how 'global' mineral waters such as Perrier or Evian can coexist with quite local ones.

2. Is there a 'modern' lifestyle, common to many cultures around the world? How could it be described? What could be its principal *raisons d'être*?

3. 'Dating' is a very curious concept for many people. It cannot be fully translated into many languages and in some cases simply means 'making an appointment'. Compare what dating means to Americans with what it means in other cultures, demonstrating how the complex process of finding a partner for life can be commercialized in different contexts.

4. List some arguments and evidence that may show that globalization of consumption and lifestyles is under way. Outline the limitations and discuss the counter-arguments.

5. To what extent are 'modern culture' and individualism primary inputs in the process of globalization of consumer preferences and lifestyles?

6. Discuss to what extent 'Buy National' advertising campaigns are effective. What can they achieve? What can they not achieve?

7. The FDA (US Food and Drug Administration) prohibits the import of traditionally prepared French *foie gras*. FDA inspectors visit French *foie gras* laboratories and refuse most of them the right to export to the United States since hygiene standards are not met. For the French, too much antiseptic would kill the taste, and for the Americans, such unpasteurized products are dangerous to one's health. Discuss the difference in understanding of what 'good food' is.

8. Compare a global film (e.g., *Spiderman* or *Lord of the Rings* or *Titanic*) and a local film on a number of aspects: story, characters, situations, atmosphere, key appeals for the viewer (action, love, violence, etc.), combination of music and sound, rhythm, type of ending, etc.

Explain why local films are most often not good candidates for reaching a global audience.

References

1. *Euromonitor* (2011), 'In Focus: The Biggest Global Trends Influencing Consumer Markets', retrieved 11 Feb 2012 from http://www.euromonitor.com.
2. Douglas, Susan, P. and C. Samuel Craig (2011), 'Convergence and Divergence: Developing a Semiglobal Marketing Strategy', *Journal of International Marketing*, 19 (1), 82–101.
3. Bell, David and Gill Valentine (1997), *Consuming Geographies*. London: Routledge.
4. Ricardo, David (1817), 'On the Principles of Political Economy and Taxation', in *Bounties on Exportation and Prohibitions on Importation*, Piero Sraffa (ed.) (1951 edn). Cambridge: Cambridge University Press.
5. Ger, Güliz and Russel W. Belk (1996), 'I'd Like to Buy the World a Coke: Consumptionscapes of the "Less Affluent World"', *Journal of Consumer Policy*, 19 (3), 271–305.
6. Crumley, B. (2009), 'Protectionism on the Rise in Europe', *Time*, Wednesday, 4 Febuary. Retrieved 10 Jan 2012 from http://www.time.com/time/world/article/0,8599,1876944,00.html.
7. Levitt, Theodore (1983), 'The Globalization of Markets', *Harvard Business Review*, 61 (May–June), 92–102.
8. *Collins English Dictionary* (2003), 6th edn. London: Collins.
9. Daft, Douglas N. (2000), 'Connecting with Global Consumers', *Executive Excellence*, 17 (10), 11–12.
10. Cavusgil, S. Tamer and Erin Cavusgil (2012), 'Reflections on International Marketing: Destructive Regeneration and Multinational firms', *Journal of the Academy of Marketing Science*, 40(2), 202–17.
11. Leefang, Peter, S. H. and W. Fred Van Raaij (1995), 'The Changing Consumer in the European Union: A "meta-analysis"', *International Journal of Research in Marketing*, 12, 373–87.
12. Hofstede, Geert (1991), *Cultures and Organizations: Software of the Mind*. Maidenhead: McGraw-Hill.
13. Lovelock, Christopher and Jochen Wirtz (2007), *Services Marketing: People, Technology, Strategy* (6th edn). Upper Saddle River, NJ: Prentice Hall.
14. Smith, David E. and Hans Stubbe Solgaard (2000), 'The Dynamics of Shifts in European Alcoholic Drinks Consumption', *Journal of International Consumer Marketing*, 12 (3), 85–109.
15. de Mooij, Marieke and Geert Hofstede (2002), 'Convergence and Divergence in Consumer Behavior: Implications for International Retailing', *Journal of Retailing*, 78 (1), 61–9.
16. de Mooij, Marieke (2001), 'Convergence–Divergence', Unpublished doctoral dissertation, Universidad de Navarra.
17. de Mooij, Marieke (1998), 'Masculinity/Femininity and Consumer Behavior', in *Masculinity and Femininity: The Taboo Dimension of National Cultures*, Geert Hofstede (ed.) Thousand Oaks, CA: Sage.
18. Huszagh, Sandra M., Richard J. Fox and Ellen Day (1986), 'Global Marketing: An Empirical Investigation', *Columbia Journal of World Business*, XX (4), 31–43.
19. Agarwal, Sanjeev and R. Kenneth Teas (2002), 'Cross-National Applicability of a Perceived Quality Model', *The Journal of Product and Brand Management*, 11 (4/5), 213–36.
20. Dawar, Niraj and Philip M. Parker (1994), 'Marketing Universals: Consumers' Use of Brand Name, Price, Physical Appearance, and Retailer Reputation as Signals of Product Quality', *Journal of Marketing*, 58 (2), 81–95.
21. Zaichkowsky, Judith L. and James H. Sood (1988), 'A Global Look at Consumer Involvement and Use of Products', *International Marketing Review*, 6 (1), 20–33.
22. Nicholls, J. A. F. and Sychey Roslow (1999), 'Oceans Apart: The Influence of Situational Factor in Grenada and Cyprus', *Journal of International Consumer Marketing*, 12 (1), 57–72.
23. Woods, Walter A., Emmanuel J. Chéron and Dong Han Kim (1985), 'Strategic Implications of Differences in Consumer Purposes in Three Global Markets', in *Global Perspectives in Marketing*, Erdener Kaynak (ed.) New York: Praeger.
24. Jain, Subhash C. (1989), 'Standardization of International Marketing Strategy: Some Research Hypotheses', *Journal of Marketing*, 53 (January), 70–79.
25. Belk, Russel W. (1988), 'Third World Consumer Culture', in *Marketing and Development: Toward Broader Dimensions*, E. Kumçu and A. Fuat Firat (eds). Greenwich, CT: JAI Press.
26. Prahalad, C. K. and K. Lieberthal (1998), 'The End of Corporate Imperialism', *Harvard Business Review* (July–August), 70–79.
27. Ritzer, George (1999), 'Contemporary Urban Japan: A Sociology of Consumption/the Sociology of Consumption: An Introduction/Golden Arches East: Mcdonald's in East Asia', *Contemporary Sociology*, 28 (1), 68–70.
28. Ritzer, George (1993), *The Mcdonaldization of Society*. Newbury Park, CA: Pine Forge Press.
29. Anderson, Patricia M. and Xiahong He (1999), 'Culture and Fast-food Marketing Mix in the People's Republic of China and the USA: Implications for Research and Marketing', *Journal of International Consumer Marketing*, 11 (1), 77–95.
30. Sheth, Jagdish N. and S. Prakash Sethi (1977), *A Theory of Cross-Cultural Buyer Behavior*. New York: North Holland Publishing.

31. Bouchet, Dominique (1994), 'Rails without Ties: The Social Imaginary and Postmodern Culture: Can Post-Modern Consumption Replace Modern Questioning?', *International Journal of Research in Marketing*, 11 (4), 405–22.

32. Auger, Pat, Timothy M. Devinney and Jordan J. Louviere (2007), 'Using Best–Worst Scaling Methodology to Investigate Consumer Ethical Beliefs across Countries', *Journal of Business Ethics*, 70 (3), 299–326.

33. Firat, A. Fuat (1995), 'Consumer Culture or Culture Consumed?', in *Marketing in a Multicultural World*, Janeen Arnold Costa and Gary J. Bamossy (eds). Thousand Oaks, CA: Sage.

34. Nguyen, Thus-Doan and Russell Belk (2012), 'Vietnamese Weddings: From Marx to market', *Journal of Macromarketing*, 32(1), 109–20.

35. *Euromonitor* (2012), 'Vietnam: Country Pulse', 12 Jan 2012, downloaded 11 Feb 2012: http://www.euromonitor.com.

36. Bagozzi, Richard P., Nancy Wong, Shuzo Abe and Massimo Bergami (2000), 'Cultural and Situational Contingencies and the Theory of Reasoned Action: Application to Fast Food Restaurant Consumption', *Journal of Consumer Psychology*, 9 (2), 97–106.

37. Han, Sang-Pil and Sharon Shavitt (1994), 'Persuasion and Culture: Advertising Appeals in Individualistic and Collectivistic Societies', *Journal of Experimental Social Psychology*, 30, 326–50.

38. Lee, Julie Anne (2000), 'Adapting Triandis's Model of Subjective Culture and Social Behaviour Relations to Consumer Behavior', *Journal of Consumer Psychology*, 9 (2), 117–26.

39. Wong, Nancy and Aaron Ahuvia (1995), 'From Tofu to Caviar: Conspicuous Consumption, Materialism and Self-Concepts in East-Asian and Western Cultures', in *Proceedings of the Second Conference on the Cultural Dimension of International Marketing*. Odense, 68–89.

40. Kopytoff, Igor (1986), 'The Cultural Biography of Things: Commoditization as Process', in *The Social Life of Things, Commodities in Cultural Perspective*, Arjun Appadurai (ed.) Cambridge: Cambridge University Press.

41. Mick, David Glen (2008), 'Degrees of Freedom of Will: An Essential Endless Question in Consumer Behavior', *Journal of Consumer Psychology*, 18 (1), 17–21.

42. Geertz, Clifford (1983), *Local Knowledge*. New York: Basic Books.

43. Thogersen, John (2010), 'Country Differences in Sustainable Consumption: The Case of Organic Food', *Journal of Macromarketing*, 30 (2), 171–85.

44. Kurzer, P. and A. Cooper (2007), 'What's for Dinner?: European Farming and Food Traditions Confront American Biotechnology', *Comparative Political Studies*, 40, 1035–58.

45. Triandis, Harry (1994), *Culture and Social Behavior*. New York: McGraw Hill.

46. Pettigrew, Simone (2006), 'Symbolic Double-coding: The Case of Australian Pubs', *Qualitative Market Research*, 9 (2), 157–69.

47. Vrontis, Demetris and Claudio Vignali (1999), 'Bass Plc, an Assessment, Evaluation and Recommendations for Their Strategic Approach in Entering Foreign Beer Markets', *International Marketing Review*, 16 (4/5), 391–405.

48. Holt, Douglas B., John A. Quelch and Earl L. Taylor (2004), 'How Global Brands Compete', *Harvard Business Review*, 82 (9), 68–75.

49. Levy, Orly, Schon Beechler, Sully Taylor and Nakiye A. Boyacigiller (2007), 'What We Talk About When We Talk About "Global Mindset": Managerial Cognition in Multinational Corporations', *Journal of International Business Studies*, 38 (2), 231–58.

50. Cannon, Hugh M. and Attila Yaprak (2002), 'Will the Real-world Citizen Please Stand-Up! The Many Faces of Cosmopolitan Consumer Behavior', *Journal of International Marketing*, 10 (4), 30–52.

51. Aaker, Jennifer, Veronica Benet-Martínez and Jordi Garolera (2001), 'Consumption Symbols as Carriers of Culture: A Study of Japanese and Spanish Brand Personality Constructs', *Journal of Personality and Social Psychology*, 81 (3), 492–508.

52. Sung, Yongjun and Spencer F. Tinkham (2005), 'Brand Personality Structures in the United States and Korea: Common and Culture-Specific Factors', *Journal of Consumer Psychology*, 15 (4), 334–50.

53. Dolbeck, Andrew (2002), 'A Quick Taste of the Fast Food Industry', *Weekly Corporate Growth Report*, 11 November.

54. Steenkamp, Jan-Benedict E. M., Rajeev Batra and Dana L. Alden (2003), 'How Perceived Brand Globalness Creates Brand Value', *Journal of International Business Studies*, 34 (1), 53–65.

55. Rodrik, Dani (1997), 'Has Globalization Gone Too Far?', *California Management Review*, 39 (3), 29–53.

56. Ger, Güliz (1997), 'Human Development and Humane Consumption: Well-Being Beyond the "Good Life"', *Journal of Public Policy & Marketing*, 16 (1), 110–25.

57. Dholakia, Ruby Roy, Mohammed Sharif and Labdhi Bhandari (1988), 'Consumption in the Third World: Challenges for Marketing and Economic Development', in *Marketing and Development: Toward Broader Dimensions*, E. Kumçu and A. Fuat Firat (eds). Greenwich CT: JAI Press.

58. Newburry, W., N. A. Gardberg and L. Y. Belkin (2006), 'Organizational Attractiveness is in the Eye of the Beholder: The Interaction of Eemographic Characteristics with Foreignness', *Journal of International Business Studies*, 37 (5), 666–86.

59. Yu, Julie H. and Gerald Albaum (2002), 'Sovereignty Change Influences on Consumer Ethnocentrism and

Product Preferences: Hong Kong Revisited One Year Later', *Journal of Business Research*, 55 (11), 891.

60. Shimp, Terence A. and Subbash Sharma (1987), 'Consumer Ethnocentrism: Construction and Validation of the Cetscale', *Journal of Marketing Research*, 26 (August), 280–89.

61. Klein, Jill Gabrielle, Richard Ettenson and Balaji C. Krishnan (2006), 'Extending the Construct of Consumer Ethnocentrism: When Foreign Products Are Preferred', *International Marketing Review*, 23 (3), 304–21.

62. Yang, Zhilin, Nan Zhou and Jie Chen (2005), 'Brand Choice of Older Chinese Consumer', *Journal of International Consumer Marketing*, 17 (4), 65–81.

63. Alden, Dana L., Jan-Benedict E. M. Steenkamp and Rajeev Batra (2006), 'Consumer Attitudes toward Marketplace Globalization: Structure, Antecedents and Consequences', *International Journal of Research in Marketing*, 23 (3), 227–39.

64. Klein, Jill Gabrielle, Richard Ettenson, and Marlene D. Morris (1998), 'The Animosity Model of Foreign Product Purchase: An Empirical Test in the People's Republic of China', *Journal of Marketing*, 62 (1), 89–100.

65. Granzin, Kent L. and John J. Painter (2001), 'Motivational Influences on "Buy Domestic" Purchasing: Marketing Management Implications from a Study of Two Nations', *Journal of International Marketing*, 9 (2), 73–96.

66. Moon, Byeong Joon and Subhash C. Jain (2001), 'Consumer Processing of International Advertising: The Roles of Country of Origin and Consumer Ethnocentrism', *Journal of International Consumer Marketing*, 14 (1), 89–109.

67. Ger, Güliz, Søren Askegaard and Ania Christensen (1999), 'Experiential Nature of Product-Place Images: Image as a Narrative', *Advances in Consumer Research*, 26, 165–9.

68. Ettenson, Richard, Janet Wagner and Gary Gaeth (1988), 'Evaluating the Effect of Country-of-origin and the "Made in the USA" Campaign: A Conjoint Approach', *Journal of Retailing*, 64 (1), 85–100.

69. Steele, Murray (1991), 'European Brewing Industry', in *The Business of Europe*, Roland Calori and Peter Lawrence (eds). London: Sage.

70. Kragh, Simon Ulrik and Malene Djursaa (2001), 'Product Syntax and Cross-cultural Marketing Strategies', *European Journal of Marketing*, 35 (11/12), 1301–21.

71. Howes, David (1996), 'Commodities and Cultural Borders', in *Cross-cultural Consumption*, David Howes (ed.) Vol. 1–18. London: Routledge.

72. Brannen, Mary Yoko (1992), '"Bwana Mickey": Constructing Cultural Consumption at Tokyo Disneyland', in *Re-Made in Japan*, Joseph J. Tobin (ed.) New Haven, CT: Yale University Press.

73. Van Maanen, John and André Laurent (1992), 'The Flow of Culture: Some Notes on Globalization and the Multinational Corporation', in *Organization Theory and the Multinational Corporation*, S. Ghoshal and D. E. Westney (eds). New York: St Martin Press.

74. Djursaa, Malene and Simon Ulrik Kragh (1998), 'Central and Peripheral Consumption Contexts: The Uneven Globalization of Consumer Behaviour', *International Business Review*, 7 (1), 23–38.

75. Dabbous, Dalia (2001), 'Sing a Song of Conflict', *Cairo Times*, 5 (20), 19–25.

76. Eckhardt, Giana M. and Michael J. Houston (2002), 'Cultural Paradoxes Reflected in Brand Meaning: Mcdonald's in Shanghai, China', *Journal of International Marketing*, 10 (2), 68–82.

Teaching materials

A6.1 Case

Setting the stage – Disneyland Resort Paris

Disney is the biggest entertainment company in the world with a market value of US$41.5 billion in May 2011,[1] and one of the oldest, continuously operating since 1923. Today it comprises filmed entertainment businesses, major media networks, publishing, theme parks, resorts, a cruise-line, real estate, and consumer products. Disney's first international park opened in Tokyo, Japan in 1983. Tokyo Disneyland opened with a flourish and continued to do well until the softening of Japan's economy in the 1990s, from which it has yet to recover. In an effort to boost attendance, the older male-oriented Tokyo DisneySea Park opened in 2001.[2] Hong Kong Disneyland opened in 2005 – about the time that Universal Studios opened China's first world-standard theme park in Shanghai. There has been criticism of value-for-money at Disney parks, which total ten worldwide, with an average admission fee of US$50. The company recently spent US$5 billion to address this concern and to build new rides and attractions to bolster falling attendance at the parks. The parks account for US$1.2 billion in operating income, which is 41 per cent of Disney's total – a significant business unit for the company.[3]

After their initial success with the Japanese park in the mid 1980s, Disney entered into negotiations with the Spanish and French governments. The French bid 'won' by enticing Disney with tax breaks, loans, and below-cost land. Disney was determined to profit more from the Paris park than they did in Tokyo, where a local operator, Oriental Land, took most of the initial risk and currently takes most of the profits. Therefore, the company staked a 39 per cent ownership in EuroDisney to operate the park, and to receive 10 per cent of admission fees, 5 per cent of food and merchandise sales, and 49 per cent of the profits.

EuroDisneyland opened in April 1992 to a host of problems, which were to continue until Disney loosened corporate constraints to fit the desires of local and European visitors. Disney's admissions and pricing policies were in the 'premium' bracket, even higher than US parks. At first, spending per visitor was half that of Japan, and hotel occupancy rates were 37 per cent.[4] French intellectuals and artists had criticized the park since its embryonic planning stages.[5] Notably, theatre director Ariane Mnouchkine coined the term 'Cultural Chernobyl' in the early 1990s, an enduring sobriquet applied to the park and other Disney ventures even today. Cries of cultural imperialism were heard from the intelligentsia, the media, and farmers who protested at the expropriation of agricultural land by the government for the park. However, the French had enjoyed Disney cartoons for more than 60 years, and some supporters of the project were very enthusiastic, such as film-star/singer Yves Montand who declared: 'T-shirts, jeans, hamburgers – nobody imposes these things on us. We like them'.[6]

It's a small world – or is it?

The EuroDisney park lost US$515 million during its first year.[7] In the early days of EuroDisney, the management structure was rigid, and little provision was made for local or employee participation, the prevailing Disney attitude formed by their self-ascribed 'infallible experience'.[8] Many American managers in Paris were unaware of the many local and Asian adaptations made in Tokyo, and accepted at face value the relatively short psychic and cultural distance between the US and France as signifying that the two cultures where similar.[9] Therefore, Disney implemented the same amusements, policies and plans in France as they did in the US with some architectural changes to allow for the cooler weather.[10] In response to local criticism, Disney took steps to 'Europeanize' the park by adding a Discoveryland based on the writings of nineteenth-century French author Jules Verne, and by emphasizing characters of European origin such as Pinocchio (Italian), Cinderella (French), and Peter Pan (British). French managers were recruited as the issues became increasingly critical, such as the disputes with French employees, who being rather individualistic resented strict codes of conduct and dress. After a series of adaptations to the local and European markets, Disneyland Paris first became profitable in 1995, going on to become the 'number one tourist destination in Europe' in 2001, with 12.3m visitors.[11] Disneyland Resort Paris (http://disneylandparis.com) follows Tokyo, Orlando, Florida, and Anaheim, California, to rank fourth place in terms of attendance per year, which was 12.3 million in 2001.[12] French visitors currently make up 40 per cent of the park's total, while 18 per cent come from the UK, 8 per cent from Germany, 8 per cent from Belgium, 8 per cent from the Netherlands and Luxembourg, 8 per cent from Spain and Italy, and 10 per cent from other countries.[13]

There are seven on-site themed hotels with occupancy averaging 86 per cent in 2001,[14] and about 22 others in the local area. Disneyland Resort Paris concluded joint ventures for the construction of the three hotels that opened in Spring 2003. The hotel partners were Airtours UK Leisure Group (tour operator), Holiday Inn, and the French hospitality group Envergure. These hotels added 1100 more rooms to the 5800-room capacity currently within the resort's seven Disney hotels. The design and décor of the new hotels draws its inspiration from the many châteaux of the local region.[15]

Learning from mistakes

As EuroDisney's CEO Jay Rasulo admitted, 'We had not yet had an on-the-ground experience in a multicultural environment. It was really the first park that had the majority of its guests coming from very diverse cultural backgrounds.' After near-catastrophic losses, Disney was quick to respond customers' demands. The company reversed its ban on alcoholic beverages, adding wine to the menu. They developed more table-service restaurants, of which two employ chefs with '*Meilleur Ouvrier de France*' status. Restaurants open earlier in the evening for early-bird German guests, and stay open later for Spanish night owls. Disneyland Paris is now working closely with French and European tour operators, travel agents, and transport operators who were formerly disregarded.[16] The company has forged better relations with the local and national government, to the point where it is Mickey Mouse who concludes the French national tourism advertisement with the declaration, '*J'aime la France!*' The resort still needs to exercise great care in setting its prices, because continental Europeans with six weeks' paid holidays per year are necessarily more thrifty on holiday expenditures than Americans with their two-week, often unpaid holidays. Europeans therefore have less to spend at the park than Disney would like. As Milhomme emphasizes: 'In short the theme park is a short duration recreational means, with a high density spending pattern at the opposite of the recreational European pattern which aims at long duration recreational means with low density spending pattern'.[17]

Act Two: Disney Studios

Disney Studios opened in March 2001 after a three-month 'soft opening' to test the reactions of visitors. The park is divided into four areas: the Front Lot, Animation Courtyard, Production Courtyard, and Back Lot, the whole comprising ten attractions. Front Lot includes a studio mock-up, complemented by film props, a restaurant, and boutiques. Animation Courtyard offers visitors the chance to learn about animation, while 'Animagique' showcases clips from Disney films, and 'Aladdin' is the backdrop for a magic carpet ride. Production Courtyard is the home of Disney Channel and allows visitors a backstage glimpse of production through the Studio Tram Tour, while Catastrophe Canyon puts visitors through an imaginary film shoot. Back Lot includes notably the Rock 'n' Roller Coaster Starring Aerosmith and the Stunt Show Spectacular featuring Rémy Julienne. Visible efforts were made to adapt the primarily American material to local and European tastes. In the Tram tour, for instance, the following actors lend their voices to the eight languages used during narration: Jeremy Irons (English), Irène Jacob (French), Isabella Rossellini (Italian), Inès Sastre (Spanish), Famke Janssen (Dutch) and Nastassja Kinski (German). An effort was made in the décor and content to include European references, for instance to the French classics 'Les Enfants du Paradis' and 'Les Parapluies de Cherbourg'.

Aims of the new park

Disney Studios expected to attract guests from further away, such as Scandinavia and Spain, more likely to consider the distance traveled as offset by the increased benefits. According to EuroDisney Chairperson Jay Rasulo, the Studios should increase visitor counts to 17 million yearly, up 36 per cent from 12.3 million in 2001. The park should increase the average length of stay per visitor from today's 2.4 days to 3.4, and increase return visits from 41.5 per cent.[18] The visitors attending the opening of Disney Studios could observe the improvements implemented over the past decade, including the expansion of Disney Village, and the dedicated rail station (with RER and TGV trains)[19] bringing Paris within 20 minutes and Belgium or the UK within less than three hours. Within the immediate vicinity is an outlet mall that is open seven days per week. Disney Studios was not designed to deal with the SARS epidemic, the Iraq conflict, fears of terrorism, a disastrous summer heat wave, massive strikes, and destructive forest fires, all of which increased cancellations and prompted holidaymakers to go elsewhere.[20]

Financial matters: Some day my prince will come . . .

EuroDisney is still plagued with troubles. In September 2003 *The Times* reported that the park was asking one of its major investors, Saudi prince Alwaleed bin Talal, for a refinancing deal. Due to low park admissions the company was expecting to have difficulty meeting its debt payments in 2004.[21] Walt Disney Studios reportedly cost the company US$600 million. The company reported a profit of 30.5 million euros for the financial year ending September 2001, 20 per cent less than the previous year.[22] Stock analysts do not appear to be interested in Disney stock. Contributing factors include a debt load that is two times equity at US$13 billion,[23] and a stock price of about 1 euro – one-tenth of its value a decade ago.[24] There are concerns that a debt-loaded park that is managing approximately 50 per cent more capacity in a time of slowing economies and a fast-growing theme park sector may be putting itself in danger.[25] The average visitor spends 43 euros per day at Disneyland Resort Paris, which is 20 per cent lower than the figures for Orlando or Anaheim. This figure is worrying, given that theme parks make their profits from their hotels and their merchandise.[26] In addition, France began in 2001 to see a slowdown in GDP growth (down to 1.9 per cent that year), caused by a climate of uncertainty and softer global economic conditions that slowed exports. At home, this has translated into higher unemployment (up to 9.8 per cent in 2002), lower inventory levels, and a lower level of business confidence.[27] Analysts are concerned with the park's launch during an economic downturn; however, some point out that as an accessible, full-service, short-break destination, Disney Studios could even benefit from a softer economy.[28]

Marketing the studios

A massive campaign for Disney Studios started in December 2001 with the slogan 'Come and live the magic of cinema'. Advertising agency Publicis focused on television, print, billboard, and online advertising. The ads were rolled out in the UK, Germany, France, Belgium, the Netherlands, Spain and Italy and were designed to differentiate the new park from the resort, which was accordingly renamed 'Disneyland Resort Paris.' According to Disneyland Paris central marketing director, Christian Darquier, Disney Studios is positioned as 'a journey behind the screen to understand how the magic of movies, television, and animation is made', whereas the resort was 'designed to make guests live out the stories behind Disney entertainment'. In an unusual move, Disney used direct marketing in the UK and the Netherlands.[29] The Disney Channel, with its headquarters within Disney Studios, is working to raise awareness of the park, just as the channel successfully did for the resort in the 1990s.

Not everybody loves Disney Studios

Disney Studios has drawn criticism from visitors, who claim that the ten attractions are not enough to keep a family entertained for one half-day. Other criticisms stemmed from the three rides cloned from Walt Disney World, as well as the 'tame' nature of some of the other rides. Other journalists refer to the new park as 'dull', and boring for children.[30] In addition, there is continuing wider criticism of 'Hollywood' and American culture by French intellectuals and the media. A new wave of concern is sweeping France regarding American imperialism, cultural or otherwise, at a time when geopolitical considerations have focused scrutiny on the global actions of the US. Anti-globalization activist José Bové, who went from destroying a McDonald's restaurant in the south of France to global fame as a leader of the 'altermondialiste' movement, considers himself a spokesperson for France's ambivalent attitude towards globalization. Even for those within the globalization camp, France and the US have had several rancorous disputes over trade and foreign policy, most recently over Iraq. On a smaller scale, a journalist voiced his concern for the impacts of a tour operator's decision to change from 'Paris and the Chateaux de la Loire' to 'Paris and Disneyland'.[31] Placed within the framework of more quantitative terms, however, according to an international comparative study, the French give the US the lowest ratings in Europe. Other nations whose citizens have flocked to the park in the past have been equally alienated by the policies of the US government.[32] This may give cause for concern that the Disney complex continues to operate in a culturally sensitive environment.

Competing with a better mousetrap

There is stiff competition among amusement/theme parks throughout Europe, of which France has its share. Parc Astérix, located 30 minutes away in Plailly, offers a unique blend of humour, thrills, history, and French and European culture. Parc Astérix shas doubled its attendance, from 950,000 in 1992 to 2 million in less than a decade.[33] Two Astérix films and the release of a new Astérix album have fuelled the enduring popularity of the character in Europe, to the likely benefit of the park. The identification of Astérix as a plucky Gallic villager, standing up to the evils of empire, may even inspire goodwill towards the park in times of complex international politics. Planète Futuroscope, a unique park in Poitiers, is an intense audiovisual and amusement experience themed on high technology run by a former EuroDisney executive (see **www.futuroscope.com**). Three other large regional parks are slated to open in 2003.[34] The French company Vivendi-Universal owns Universal Mediterranea, two clustered theme parks near Barcelona, Spain. The new water-themed park, Costa Caribe, boasts a new ride that attracted 1.5 million new visitors within its first four months.[35] The addition of the new park and two new hotels are part of the positioning of the park as 'the most complete family resort in Europe',[36] thereby bringing the park into more direct competition with Disneyland Resort Paris.[37] Paramount Parks owns Terra Mitica, a history- and mythology-themed park near Benidorm, Spain. There are two Warner Bros. Movie World parks featuring Looney Tunes and Superheroes like Batman – one in Madrid, Spain and the other near Bottrop-Kirchhellen, Germany. There are two European Six Flags parks, located at Flevo, Netherlands and Wavre, Belgium. Growing competition may not be a threat in itself, however, because it is likely that tougher competition in Europe may benefit Disney in the long term, by habituating Europeans to Disney-style parks.

Early in 2011, the Euro Disney share on the Paris stock exchange took a sudden start. At the end of April 2011 the Euro Disney share traded at 8.6 euros, a 108 per cent increase over 1 January 2011. All company-specific information and additional information can be found at the Disneyland Resort Paris corporate website: **http://www.Disneylandparis.com/uk.**

Questions

1. More than a decade later, has Disney's top management completely addressed the lack of cultural sensitivity observed at the opening of the first park in 1992?

2. Comment in more detail on the issue of holiday regulations in Europe, the US and Japan (duration, paid versus unpaid holiday) and their impact on leisure consumption.

3. How will changing geopolitical situations affect park attendance? What can be the repercussions of a US-led conflict in the Middle East or Far East?

4. Taking the case study, use cultural factors to explain why visitors from Germany make up only 8 per cent of total Disneyland Resort Paris visitors. Do you think that Disney Studios will attract more Germans than the other park? What steps could management take in order to increase the German share of the market?

5. Do you consider that the company made a wise decision in incurring debt to develop Disney Studios? Given the state of the economy, the need to continually spend on new attractions, and the rapid rate of development for other competing theme parks in Europe, do you believe this investment is justified in the long term?

Saskia Faulk and Jean-Claude Usunier prepared this case solely to provide material for class discussion. The authors do not intend to illustrate either effective or ineffective handling of a business situation. The authors may have disguised certain names and other identifying information to protect confidentiality.

A6.2 Case

Papa Ingvar's worries

Who can successfully market products around the world with names like 'Lillången', 'Tofteryd', 'Ljusås Ysby', 'Bestå', 'Bjursta', 'Slugis' or 'Aspelund'? In 2011 IKEA, the world's biggest home furnishings retail chain, can use names that break some 'rules' of branding, and make a healthy profit out of it. Quirky and identifiably Swedish, the names mirror the company's image.

Small-town entrepreneur Ingvar Kamprad founded IKEA as a furniture mail-order company in Almhult, Sweden, in 1943. Since then, IKEA has expanded far from its pastoral headquarters to worldwide sales of 23.5 billion euro[38] from 301 outlets in 37 countries and territories (see Table 6.2).[39] IKEA is now one of the world's largest family-owned companies. Although well past retirement age, Kamprad remains active in the business, reportedly travelling to IKEA stores by economy class and public transport, in order to listen to the concerns of the common people – and to save a little money. His three sons have worked at the company.[40] The annual growth rate is about 15 per cent and a new IKEA store is opened, on average, each month. Today, IKEA operates retail stores in countries as diverse as Austria, Japan, France, Hungary, Iceland, Israel, Malaysia, Russia and Saudi Arabia, with 45 outlets in Germany, and 37 in the USA.[41]

At the insistence of founder Kamprad, IKEA expanded rapidly, without adapting its core concept to local conditions. Starting in the early 1960s, IKEA took a foothold in Sweden, then Denmark. In 1973 the company took its high-design, good-quality, reasonably priced goods throughout Europe and Australasia. Today, four out of IKEA's top five markets are in Europe, the fifth is the USA (see Table 6.1). Although IKEA has concentrated on company-owned, larger-scale outlets, franchising has been used in 16 countries[42] and all stores operate on a franchising basis, regardless of ownership.[43]

Table 6.1 Top individual geographic markets, according to percentage of sales

Country	Percentage of sales generated
Germany	16
UK	7
USA	11
France	10
Italy	7

(Source: Inter IKEA Systems B. V., 'Facts and figures'.[44])

During 2003 store openings were scheduled in Germany, Australia, Hungary, and Spain.[45] There are currently three IKEA stores in Moscow, and two in St Petersburg.[46] In Moscow, IKEA has developed a mega-shopping mall (including an Auchan hypermarket) and hotel complex adjacent to its southern Moscow store.[47] Over recent years IKEA has opened more than ten stores in Russia, with the majority in provincial cities.[48] In 1974, the North American expansion began, a venture which continues with plans to open 70 stores in the US by 2013.[49]

Recent expansion in Asia Pacific is projected to continue at a significant rate. IKEA aims to double its stores in China from the current eight by 2015.[50] After an initial failure in Japan in the mid 1970s, IKEA opened a new giant store in Tokyo in 2006.[51]

Table 6.2 Turnover for all IKEA outlets (in billions of euro)

1954	0.001
1964	0.025
1974	0.169
1984	1.216
1994	4.396
2000	8.22
2001	11.3
2005	14.8
2007	19.8
2009	21.5
2010	23.5

(Source: Inter IKEA Systems B.V., 'Facts and figures'.[44])

Table 6.3 IKEA turnover per region (2010)

Asia and Australia	6%
North America	15%
Europe	79%

(Source: Inter IKEA Systems B.V., 'Facts and figures'.[44])

The nuts and bolts of IKEA

Founder Ingvar Kamprad formulated IKEA's vision to 'offer a wide range of home furnishings with good design and function at prices so low that as many people as possible will be able to afford them'.[52] IKEA carries approximately 9500 different home furnishings, garden items, plants, lighting, office furniture and supplies, household textiles, decorative items, kitchen cabinetry, toys and children's equipment, crockery and flatware, and seasonal decorations.

Product strategy

IKEA follows a standardized product strategy with an identical assortment around the world. IKEA designs all of its product lines and products, then uses a bidding process among hundreds of agreed suppliers, contracts the manufacturing job out under stiff, quality-controlled conditions. Furniture and accessories have to be:[53]

- Scandinavian – simply styled, streamlined and *well designed*;
- functional;
- of high quality;
- stylish;
- safe; and
- healthy.

IKEA's office-supply division offers office furnishings that also fit into the four categories. It operates on a business-to-business as well as a retail level, in some areas publishing its own catalogue and employing its own call-centre employees. IKEA pioneered the idea of flat-pack merchandising, which means that buyers do the final assembly for most items. It has been estimated that six times more freight space would be needed if its products were shipped already assembled, a significant cost point especially when increasing numbers of items are made in the Asia-Pacific region and control of shipping times and costs becomes critical.

IKEA's shopping experience is a unique element in the marketing mix. In addition to the items they buy, shoppers have an experience at IKEA's self-contained shops. The largest stores feature a self-service restaurant with Swedish menu items, a snack bar, Swedish food boutique, and a child-care centre for customers. The restaurant and café have been given central status at newer USA stores built on a clover-leaf shape, with sales floors radiating off from the food-service facilities.

Pricing strategy

The IKEA concept is based on low price, and products are designed to offer prices that are 30 to 50 per cent lower than fully assembled competing products. Keeping within this constraint, IKEA responds to different customer needs using a three-level pricing strategy: low, medium and high. The affordability of IKEA products is the result of several business practices, including target-pricing, whereby a product is priced first then designed and sourced accordingly. Other elements of IKEA business that keep prices low are: high volume purchasing, waste reduction, low-cost logistics (hence the flat-packs and minimal packaging), and inexpensive retail space as well as strategic placement, mainly in suburban areas. IKEA's prices do vary from market to market, largely because of fluctuations in exchange rates and differences in taxation and tariff regimes, but price positioning is kept as standardized as possible.

Communications strategy

IKEA's promotions are effected mainly through its catalogues, websites, and the IKEA family loyalty programme. All stores follow a communications prototype, with catalogues, printed materials, and websites designed to conform to the IKEA look. Websites (**www.ikea.com**) are examples of tailored uniformity, featuring the same type of information on all 39 websites and some mini-sites. However, the sites feature different photos and colours, and information based on the location and market familiarity with the concept, and many feature a choice of several languages. The mini-sites are standardized, simply offering contact information and map/directions (such as IKEA Saudi Arabia).[54] The company has turned increasingly to online marketing, and has even indulged in the 'viral marketing' fad, whereby customers forwarded a promotional message to friends via facebook and SMS.[55] Primary communications are centred on IKEA catalogues, of which 56 editions are printed in 27 languages with a worldwide circulation of over 198 million copies.[56] The catalogues are uniform in layout except for minor regional differences. Other specialized publications include 'Smart Kitchen', 'IKEA View', 'Professional Office Furniture' and 'IKEA Summer'.[57]

IKEA advertising is designed to be unique and provocative. The company's communications goal is to generate word-of-mouth publicity through innovative and sometimes ground-breaking approaches. IKEA has featured ground-breaking advertising in several markets, earning the ire of some conservative groups. For instance, company ads have used homosexual couples, just-divorced women, teenage pregnancy, and marijuana as a topic in its ads. Perhaps the most controversy was sparked by IKEA's Netherlands campaign featuring a male homosexual couple with their daughter. For a view of IKEA's portrayals of lesbian and gay worlds, visit: **www.commercialcloset.org** (a review of gay advertising) or **www.gayalliance.org** (the Gay Financial Network).

According to Irena Vanenkova, IKEA's head of public relations in Russia, a good example of innovative communications by IKEA was a competition to find a handsome cat with a Swedish heritage to enter the new Russian showroom on opening day (cats are considered to bring Russians good luck), generating publicity and goodwill through 20 publications and websites that would have otherwise cost thousands of roubles.[58] IKEA's thirtieth birthday celebrations in Switzerland were characterized by a thought-provoking use of the Swiss flag on a sombre and staid background, emblazoned with '30 years of democracy in Swiss home furnishings'. The official-looking artwork was counterbalanced by pricing offers using the number '30', such as sofas normally priced at 900 Swiss Francs selling for 30 Swiss Francs.[59] On a quieter front in communications, IKEA is active on environmental and social-responsibility programmes, providing the company with exposure in the press, and a themed emphasis in their communications materials.

Target market

IKEA executives tend to be vague about their target markets, and the comment on the topic from the country manager for Japan Tommy Kullberg is typical. In an interview with *Nikkei Weekly*'s Asako Ishibashi, he stated that the company targets families with young children and young people starting a home, from virtually all social categories. These are people who tend to have a young 'mental age'.[60] Industry analysts refer consistently to first-time home buyers, young families, and people renting their homes.

Distribution

IKEA has a division devoted to business travel logistics, primarily to allow company representatives to visit manufacturers in order to ensure that working conditions are optimal, and that products are made in accordance with IKEA's code of environmental and social responsibility.[61] The primary countries of origin of IKEA products are: China (20 per cent), Poland (18 per cent), Italy (8 per cent), Germany (6 per cent) and Sweden (5 per cent).[62] Manufacturers ship the components or finished products to large warehouses, such as the central one in Almhult, or to one of the other 11 distribution centres in 16 countries. About 30 per cent of the products are shipped directly to the stores which are, in effect, warehouses.[63] The network of subcontracted manufacturers numbers nearly 1,220 in 55 different countries, with 31 trading services offices in 26 countries, for which the company uses an online suppliers' portal to negotiate bids and order supplies, such as nuts and bolts from IKEA's internal supplier-to-supplier division.[64] IKEA does not offer home delivery, but IKEA stores cooperate with local companies that offer small trucks for rent, delivery, and even furniture assembly services.[65] IKEA offers a mail order service and has introduced an online ordering facility in some countries; however, in its first stages the cumbersome system was not well received.

IKEA's competitors?

There is no global competitor for IKEA. The company has used its relatively low prices, stylish design and offbeat image, environmental performance (no PVC products, no sweatshop workers), and immediate gratification via do-it-yourself delivery in order to attain a unique positioning. No other large company in this sector has pioneered so many supply chain innovations, including long-term and online collaboration that is spiced up with civilized competition between suppliers. No other international furniture company offers such a universal appeal. Competitors are inevitably smaller than IKEA, and may be able to compete with the Swedish monolith on one of the above points, such as low price, but not simultaneously on all of them. The experience of shopping at IKEA is likewise unique: although lacking in sales people, store facilities present many opportunities for the shopper to maximize the benefits of shopping IKEA-style. Measuring tapes, pencils, handy order forms, desks to write on, realistic mini-showrooms, and user-friendly merchandising are examples of this. IKEA's day-trip dimension is also inimitable, with signature food service, children's entertainment, and even child care.

It's a big country. Someone's got to furnish it . . . IKEA in the USA

IKEA entered the US market in 1985, quickly establishing three outlets in the north-east, and experiencing such success that a major warehouse near Philadelphia was followed by others around the country. IKEA quickly learned from its early experiences in North America. Firstly, people considered their glasses to be too small in order to add ice – a singularly American habit. In addition, bed sizes needed to be changed according to standard North American measurements. Generally, furniture was made wider and larger for the US, changing IKEA's conception of a worldwide appeal. In terms of merchandising, IKEA stores tend to display easily identifiable colour and design combinations, to guide the customer a bit more than they were accustomed to doing in Europe.[66]

To gain awareness in a relatively new market, IKEA has been inventive, including among its promotions the 'Living Works of Art' exhibit as part of downtown Chicago's 'Home Suite Home' campaign. Three couples 'lived' in the heart-shaped exhibit, made up of IKEA furniture for several days, thereby earning US$15,000 for charitable causes.[67] Another example is the 'unböring' campaign in the USA that included a dedicated website, television, print, direct, outdoor, and wildpostings. The 'unböring' campaign's 'manifesto' clearly situates IKEA as an idiosyncratic company of Swedes, fighting 'for liberty and beauty for all'.[68] For more on the campaign (see **www.ikeafans.com**).

IKEA is a complex business, comprising retail businesses, franchising, product development and design, supply-chain businesses like Schwedwood, and manufacturing management, distribution using conventional channels and massive warehouse operations, real estate, food-service operations, and even the ownership of local competitors like Habitat in the UK and France. The pan-European IKANO Bank and real estate services company is also owned by the Kamprad family. In Sweden in the 1990s IKEA designed and sold houses. The 'Bo Klok Project' ('live smart' in Swedish) wood-frame houses were pre-fabricated and built with Swedish developer Skanska, in two Swedish cities. Efforts have been made to bring the project to the UK and other markets. Of course, home-buyers were given a 3000 SEK gift certificate for IKEA merchandise.[69] As a reflection of this complexity, IKEA founder Ingvar Kamprad told the Swedish newspaper *Smaalandposten* in an interview that, contrary to his earlier position as an 'engine' of growth, he now worries that the firm is expanding too quickly. In particular, he cites concern that in an economic downturn, some IKEA stores may have to close. 'Papa Ingvar', as he is known to many IKEA employees, said that he felt the responsibility for potential lost jobs was a very heavy burden.[70]

Questions

1. Furniture styles and home trends are usually thought to be linked to cultural attitudes and perceptions. How can a global company like IKEA successfully market its standardized products in so many countries? Based on your visit to IKEA websites for several familiar countries, give some suggestions for improvement to the communications director.

2. Why do IKEA products receive Swedish-sounding names? What is the role of IKEA's Swedish image, and its Swedish country of origin in the company's image policy?

3. How can IKEA continue long term to market its wares to people with a 'low mental age' around the world? Can the company remain true to its original mission, culture, and mass-appeal through so many complex changes?

4. Although IKEA successfully faced the recent economic downturn, does the company expand too quickly or into too many different sectors? Are Ingvar Kamprad's worries about the firm's expansion well founded? What marketing problems do you expect this growth will cause in the short and long term?

Saskia Faulk and Jean-Claude Usunier prepared this case solely to provide material for class discussion. The authors do not intend to illustrate either effective or ineffective handling of a business situation. The authors may have disguised certain names and other identifying information to protect confidentiality.

2011-05-24   Version: (A)

A6.3 Case

McDonald's – a global cultural icon?

McDonald's is often considered to be a symbol of globalization in its American incarnation. This case study will explore people's perceptions of McDonald's in the Middle East and other regions where religion-based ideologies are rooted and anti-globalization has spread. This is a broad attempt to document the tectonic shifts that surround globalization, and how companies like McDonald's adapt, as they fight for profits and survival.

About McDonald's

In 2011, McDonald's was the biggest fast food chain worldwide, operating more than 32,000 restaurants in 120 countries.[71] Current growth was achieved primarily through franchising.[72] McDonald's topped the market share ratings of fast food restaurants with 7.3 per cent of US market share in 2002, more than double that of the next ranked chain, Burger King.[73] The company was ranked number 29 out of the top 100 global marketers in 2008,[74] and was rated eight among 25 US 'Megabrands' in terms of domestic advertising spending.[75] In the US, the corporation developed *Chipotle* (Mexican food) and *Boston Market* ('comfort' food), while it sold *Donatos* pizzeria and closed its *Pret* chain in Japan in order to reallocate resources to McDonald's outlets. In an effort to improve the marketing of its toy, books, videos, and clothing lines, the company has rebranded them in early 2004 as *McKids* in North America, Australia, China, Japan, Korea and Taiwan with expansion planned shortly. The strategy is designed to 'connect with customers in fresh, relevant ways both inside and outside our restaurants' according to the company's marketing head, Larry Light.[76]

The company had for a long time a higher sales growth overseas than in its home market. Europe was McDonald's second biggest market after the US. France, Germany, and the UK accounted for 75 per cent of European operating income in 2002. France and Russia accounted for most of the sales growth from 2001–2 in constant currency terms.

In December 2002 McDonald's posted its first-ever quarterly loss. The company announced restaurant closings in several countries in the Middle East and Latin America, delaying new openings, and increasing layoffs through 2005. Poor business performance was blamed on weak economies, 'mad cow' disease, and increased competition. In 2003 Subway, a sandwich chain, overtook McDonald's as the largest fast food company in the US.[77] According to McDonald's late Chief Executive Officer Jim Cantalupo, writing in the company's 2002 annual report, 'McDonald's has lost momentum ... and lost what it takes to make customers feel special. We have struggled to grow our business in the face of weak and uncertain economic conditions around the world. The result has been disappointing financial performance.' He stated that 'McDonald's is in transition from a company that emphasizes adding restaurants to customers to one that emphasizes adding customers to restaurants,' adding 'McDonald's has a new boss . . . it's not me . . . it's the customer.'[78] During Cantalupo's tenure in 2003 the company's performance began to improve, with more of a focus on improving existing restaurants, new menu offerings, and attempts to improve service.

The operating environment for McDonald's has become increasingly threatening over recent years, with tougher competition from agile multi-brand rivals like YUM! (owners of Pizza Hut, Taco Bell, and KFC among others), Burger King, and increasing local competitors. Despite the increase in smaller, more regional chains, the top ten fast food leaders tend to remain the same: McDonald's, Burger King, Wendy's, Pizza Hut, KFC, and others, almost exactly in that order. An example of such local competition is Marrybrown (www.marrybrown.com.my), a Malaysia-based fried chicken and burger chain, a shiny, clean competitor with more than 250 outlets in China, India, Malaysia, Sri Lanka and the Middle East. Al-Tazaj ('fresh') at www.altazaj.com.sa, has grown from one Mecca-based grilled chicken restaurant, opened in 1992, to 100 units across Egypt, Malaysia, Qatar, Lebanon, and the US, where it is known as Taza. The company is owned by a Saudi Arabian poultry supplier, Philippines-based Jollibee (www.jollibee.com.ph), and is one of the only regional fast-food chains to outstrip McDonald's in terms of market share. The chain offers a similar menu to McDonald's, with Philippine-adjusted ingredients such as sweeter, spicier and more juicy meat-based items, locally inspired sauces, and rice. Jollibee has expanded from 686 domestic units to 57 international units, including locations in the US, Indonesia, Brunei, Hong Kong and Vietnam. Nando's, a spicy-grilled chicken chain, has grown from a strong South African base to more than 850 stores worldwide, including 33 in Malaysia and others in the Middle East, sub-Saharan Africa, Australasia, Canada and the UK. According to *Nielsen Monitor-Plus*, McDonald's global advertising expenditure totalled approximately US$2.08 billion on global advertising, of which US$1.2 billion was spent in the US.

US multinationals generally consider global advertising campaigns to be too challenging due to cultural differences. However, for the first time, McDonald's launched a global advertising campaign in 2003. The 100-country campaign's tagline, 'I'm lovin' it', was sung in many markets by internationally known American pop star Justin Timberlake. The German-designed ads had an edgy, urban feel to them and a hip-hop beat and style. The campaign accompanied Justin Timberlake's McDonald's-sponsored, 35-country tour and recent release titled 'I'm lovin' it'. The new ad campaign was viewed as 'hype' by many in the advertising world, who believed that the company should fix its operational and internal problems prior to embarking upon a new branding campaign.[79] Renowned ad critic Bob Garfield of *Advertising Age* called the campaign an 'embarrassing, pandering mess', describing its youth appeal as 'desperate'. In his analysis of the 'I'm lovin' it' ads, the ad critic believes that it violated several principles of advertising.[80]

In 2004, McDonald's planned to modify menu items and offer new benefits to customers. In the wake of lawsuits claiming that McDonald's food made people obese, and popular concerns about obesity and health, McDonald's decided to remove the 'Supersize' option from its menus, allowing extra large-sized portions. The Happy Meal, which celebrated its 25th anniversary in 2004, was redesigned to offer more variety and more healthy alternatives. In Lebanon and China greeters were hired to welcome diners at restaurants, special parking for mothers was to be introduced in New Zealand and Canada, organic milk made available in Britain, fruit cups offered in Italy, bottled water and low-fat yoghurt available in Spain, and child-care staff watched the children in Italy and the Netherlands. 'Salads Plus' was to be launched in 16 European countries in a bid to offer healthier menu offerings, although some of the salads may contain more fat than a cheeseburger. As a special offer, music downloads are planned to be offered free upon purchase of certain McDonald's menu items in a partnership with Sony's download service, Sony Connect, in which McDonald's is said to have committed US$30 million in advertising. The company stated it is considering tie-ins with companies 'in the area of music, sports, fashion, and entertainment'.

According to a survey conducted in Gulf countries during the first quarter of 2003 by Synovate, McDonald's scored higher than other chains on last visit satisfaction, market penetration, and market share. Market share actually increased during the period, but visits to McDonald's declined – possibly due to geo-political tensions. The period coincided with the recent introduction of the locally inspired McArabia, grilled chicken on Arabic bread.[81] The sandwich was launched with a powerful promotional campaign that overshadowed marketing efforts for the jealously guarded Big Mac. The campaign has been viewed as an effort to 'Relaunch McDonald's in the Muslim world'.[82] The owners of McDonald's Middle East Development Company run a 'Hamburger University' training programme in Dubai for the region to reflect local training needs.[83] As for McDonald's in Iraq, the corporation joined the vanguard of American and multinational corporations seeking business opportunities in post-war Iraq at the Madrid fund-raiser conference.[84]

Adapting to local conditions and trends

McDonald's President Jim Cantalupo said in 1991 that the company's strategy was to become 'as much part of the local culture as possible.'[85] McDonald's customizes its foods and elements of decor according to local preferences and competitive environment; however it maintains its power as signifier of that which is American and modern. The company has made major menu modifications in line with local tastes, and has modified its marketing and public relations campaigns significantly in line with local concerns. In **China**, where McDonald's plans to open between 150 and 175 new restaurants each year, McDonald's has introduced a pork burger and shrimp McNuggets in deference to local preferences. According to McDonald's China Development Company managing director Tim Lai, 'Consumers do not go to McDonald's for Chinese-style food', in contrast with primary competitor KFC which has 3,200 outlets in the country and regionally adapted Chinese-style menus. McDonald's has 1,125 outlets in China. In **India**, where McDonald's has 192 outlets,[86] the company serves no beef, in deference to Hindu principles, and no pork in deference to Muslim principles. India is primarily Hindu, with an influential Muslim minority. Due to the strictness of vegetarianism in the country, McDonald's India practises segregation of vegetarian and non-vegetarian foods from suppliers through to service.[87] Kitchen staff who cook vegetarian food are identifiable by their green aprons. With a menu that is '75 per cent different in India' from the rest of the world, McDonald's introduced the Maharaja Mac, (a version of the Big Mac made with lamb), McAlu Tikki (vegetarian) burgers, Chicken McGrill (grilled chicken with a mint sauce), Paneer Salsa Wraps, chicken tikka, and Veg McPuff (a version of Indian samosas).[88] In the context of some anti-American feeling in the country, McDonald's is not considered to be American, but Indian. In **Saudi Arabia**, with variations among Muslim other countries, the menu offers Halal items (ingredients and meat processing in keeping with Muslim regulations). McDonald's outlets close five times per day for prayers, and close during the day through Ramadan, in keeping with Muslim custom of fasting while there is daylight. The company introduced a version of a popular regional dish with the McArabia, grilled chicken and salad on Arab bread. In order to conform to local expectations, since its inception in Saudi Arabia in 1993, McDonald's has kept a strict 'apartheid' of the sexes in its operations. All workers are men. Women must sit separately in a glassed-off dining area from men. There are two separate lines for service, one for women and one for men, and two separate entrances.[89] McDonald's will not serve a woman, even a Western woman, who wants to eat alone, if she does not have the permission of her husband or male relative. According to one report, the women's seating area is not well maintained, in contrast to the lavish appointments of the men's area.[90] Gender segregation in Saudi Arabia was confirmed by McDonald's Communications Office employee Ann Rozenich, and justified as respecting and observing local customs.[91] In Saudi Arabia men and women are supposed to remain separate in public places, unless they are relations among whom marriage is not permitted, such as brothers or fathers.[92]

In **France** the company upgraded decors to compete with the ambience of local cafés. Themed restaurants near sports stadiums have sports motifs, and in the mountains have a chalet-like decoration. One concession to French tastes is the Croque McDo (a version of the ubiquitous *croque-monsieur*, a ham and cheese toasted sandwich). McDonald's outlets in areas with many Muslims, such as Marseilles, offer fish-based, promotional Ramadan menus starting late afternoon. McDonald's **Malaysia** made a donation composed of employees' individual donations to the Iraq Humanitarian Fund. In **China**, McDonald's proposes a pork burger and shrimp McNuggets. In **Turkey** the menu includes a Double Kofte burger (meat patties with onions and Turkish spices).[93] In **Israel**, McDonald's seven kosher restaurants are closed on the Sabbath and religious holidays. Israel also has more than 124 non-Kosher outlets.[94] Following lawsuits and concerns about health and obesity, McDonald's **UK** introduced Happy Meals offering more choices, including fruit juices and fresh fruit slices, as well as a wide variety of sandwiches. In **Mexico** the company reflected local preferences by increasing egg offerings such as McHuevo, and adding spicy peppers and refried beans. In **Japan**, McDonald's menu includes teriyaki burgers, corn soup, bacon potato pies, and a wide variety of milkshakes.

In terms of religious dietary restrictions, there are many resources that advise Muslims as to Muslim suitability of foods, including fast-food options. According to several Muslim websites, Muslims are advised to avoid 'most items' at McDonald's and other fast-food outlets. Some McDonald's outlets in the US, Canada, UK, France and elsewhere with many Muslim patrons purchase Halal meat, and McDonald's is experimenting with Halal chicken nuggets. In an ordinary McDonald's, however, reasons for avoiding most items include: non-Muslim staff, contamination of vegetarian burger and other vegetable/fruit offerings by unlawful (*Haram*) meats or animal fat (if cooked or prepared in common area or if touched by a utensil that previously touched non-Halal meat), and dairy products contaminated by rennet (ingredient derived from the intestine). Some sweets are banned for their content of vanilla flavouring, which is commonly conditioned by alcohol.

Common factors among McDonald's community involvement programmes include World Children's Day activities, celebrations of the anniversary of the UN adoption of the Convention on the Rights of the Child, Ronald McDonald Houses located near hospitals for families of sick children, and donations to orphanages, children's hospitals and children's health organizations.

Consumer attitudes towards McDonald's

There are many more McDonald's outlets implanted in Asia than there are in the Middle East, suggesting that, among other factors, people in the Middle East may be less willing to embrace this representative of globalization. According to brand consulting firm CoreBrand head Lawrence McNaughton, 'If you hate America, it's real easy to hate Coke or McDonald's'. For him, the primary risk criteria are 'if you're in business in the Middle East and you're a cultural icon'.[95] Two surveys conducted in the months leading up to the Iraq conflict showed that although many consumers do not use consumer choices to express political views, a sizable minority say they try to avoid buying American products. Publicis-Groupe's Leo Burnett Asia Pacific surveyed people in China, South Korea, Indonesia, India and the Philippines to uncover their beliefs about a brand's country of origin and its impact on their purchasing habits. The survey asked whether certain brands have 'my country's interests at heart'. Of all multinationals active in the region, McDonald's and Coca-Cola scored most favourably – probably a reflection of the companies' efforts to market themselves as local companies. Two-thirds of young Asian shoppers said they bought brands they liked regardless of the brand's country of origin, but 23 per cent claimed to avoid American brands. A similar study, conducted in Spain, Russia, Canada, France, Italy, Japan, Germany and the UK by Ipsos Public Affairs found that in some countries close to a third of respondents agreed with the statement 'I currently avoid US products and services'. Among the countries that ranked top with high levels of avoidance of American brands were Spain, Russia, Canada and France.

McDonald's has made many efforts to be viewed as a local company – with local menu adaptations, sports sponsorship, and community relations seen by the company as key to success in this aspect. 'We do share a common brand but we are local companies throughout Europe' according to McDonald's Europe spokesperson Louise Marcotte. Director of marketing and communications for McDonald's in the Middle East, Dubai-based Ricarda Ruecker stated in a telephone interview that, when threatened by boycotts protests, and violence, local franchisees initiated advertising campaigns. 'We educated people; we have a 100 per cent local ownership model, 80 per cent local suppliers, we do a lot of charity. Now people understand more.' According to Brandeis University's international marketing professor Shih-Fen Chen, 'Consumer attitudes toward American brands can change quickly, if a bomb lands in the wrong place.'

Protesters targeting McDonald's seem to reject the corporation's claim that it is a 'local' company. In Indonesia, for example, where much work has been done by master franchiser Bambang Rachmadi to convince local people that McDonald's is not a foreign implant (see previous section), people protesting against the war in Iraq and other American-related issues consistently targeted McDonald's outlets, in addition to boycott campaigns and an occasional KFC or other fast-food chain attack. During one protest the 1000-strong crowd chanted 'God is great' and 'USA go to hell'. Protesters also denigrated the United Nations, Kofi Annan, and George Bush.[96] In Egypt Essam Haraz, manager of local competitor Mo'men stated his belief that of all the fast-food chains in Egypt, McDonald's has suffered the most, due to its alleged close ties with Israel. He believed that many Egyptians felt the same way, because he did not perceive that other American fast-food chains were suffering, although they had featured equally on boycott lists.[97] Ahmad Bahi Al-Din Shabaan of the Arab Popular Boycott Committee said that the committee chose as a strategy to focus a boycott on a limited number of brands, including McDonald's, Marlboro, and Coca-Cola, which 'represent the American way of life and US hegemony'.[98]

Anti-McDonald's timeline

This section will detail, in a non-exhaustive manner, violent actions and protests against McDonald's between 1999 and 2009, in selected countries. Action taken by McDonald's shortly after the attacks or protests is supplied for each time period. Table 6.4 summarizes the events.

Table 6.4 Chronology of attacks on McDonald's outlets in selected countries

Location	Year	Casualties	Admitted/convicted	Weapon/means
Millau, France	August 1999	Destruction of property (McDonald's construction)	Farmers protest US agricultural tariffs in retaliation for EU refusal of US beef	Tractors, tools
Cahors, France	17 August 1999	None	Farmers against US agricultural tariffs	Blocked roads, distributed local produce
Athens, Greece	4 October 1999	Damage	Filiki Etairia group	Fire bomb
Dinan, France (Brittany)	19 April 2000	1 killed	Suspected Breton separatists	Bomb
Istanbul, Turkey	17 February 2001	None	Unknown	Bomb defused by police
Merter, Istanbul, Turkey	28 September 2001	3 wounded, property damage	Unknown	Pipe bomb
Beirut, Lebanon	Spring 2002	None	Students	Sit-ins, protests
Bahrain (2 outlets)	April 2002	'Substantial' damage	Pro-Palestinian demonstrators	Stones
Oman	April 2002	Damage	Pro-Palestinian demonstrators	Smashed windows
Moscow, Russia	25 October 2002	1 killed, 8 wounded, major damage to outlet	Presumed Chechens	Bomb
Al Kharj, Saudi Arabia	20 November 2002	None	McDonald's near US military base	Fire
Dammam, Saudi Arabia	25 February 2002	None	Unknown	Fire-bomb attempt
Jounieh (Beirut) Lebanon	23 September 2002	3 cars destroyed	Unknown	Car bomb
Bombay, India	6 December 2002	23 wounded	Unknown	Bomb
Makassar, Indonesia (Sulawesi)	5 December 2002	3 dead, 11 wounded	Islamists	Bomb
Dora, Beirut, Lebanon	5 April 2003	5 wounded	Considered to be anti-American group	Bomb; 55 kg TNT found outside outlet
Istanbul, Turkey	15 April 2003	Extensive damage	Unknown	Bomb
Thessalonica, Greece	21 June 2003	Outlet destroyed	Protesters during European Union summit	Fire
Yanbu, Saudi Arabia	1 May 2004	Damage	Five Westerners, killed, shots fired at McDonald's and Holiday Inn	Gunfire
Istanbul, Turkey	19 May 2004	Car park damage	Unknown	Percussion bomb
Rome, Italy	19 May 2004	2 bombs defused; no damage	Thought to be Red Brigades	Homemade bombs
Indonesia	2009	Minor damage	Unknown	Stones and bricks

France, 1999: Anti-globalization activist José Bové set fire to a McDonald's outlet, for which he was imprisoned for 20 days. In 2003, as the prospect of hostilities in Iraq became likely, anti-war activists smashed windows and spray-painted obscenities and 'Boycott' on McDonald's outlets.[99]

McDonald's action: The corporation adopted French comic hero Astérix as corporate mascot. Astérix is a well-loved symbol of French resistance to foreign occupation, having battled Imperial Rome in a prolific comic book series.

Saudi Arabia, 2000: boycott of American products and companies inspired by perceived US support for Israeli incursions into Palestine. The call to boycott US products included the statement 'Each dollar spent buying an American product is transformed into a bullet to kill our brothers in Palestine.' McDonald's General Manager in Jeddah said that the boycott would hurt Saudi employees more than American interests, and added that some anti-Western activists were hypocrites who drive American cars while complaining about American products.[100]

McDonald's action: Saudi franchise committed during the month of Ramadan to sending 26 cents from each Big Mac sold to the Al Quds Intifada Fund,[101] helping children's hospitals in Palestinian territories.[102] The message is 'Buy a burger and help a Palestinian child'. The BBC's Middle East correspondent termed the campaign as a 'canny marketing move, as much as a well-meaning act of charity'. Prince Mishal Bin Khalid, who heads a McDonald's licence holder, expected that the campaign should raise US$100,000.[103] The reaction to McDonald's announcement was quasi-immediate: several e-mails began circulating, calling for Jews worldwide to boycott McDonald's for the company's perceived support for the Intifada.[104] This was a similar situation to that of Burger King, which responded to Arab boycotters by removing its contentious outlet from a West Bank Israeli settlement. By doing so, Burger King triggered the anger of pro-Israel groups.[105]

Egypt, 2001: US support for Israel sparked anti-American protests and boycotts. Clerics declared in *fatwa* that Israeli and US products should be forbidden.[106] President Hosni Mubarak was quoted by his Information Minister as saying 'People are right to boycott their [Israeli] goods, but a boycott of European or American goods must be considered in a wider and more general context.'[107] US military action sparked several boycotts and violent action. Demonstrators threw bricks and rocks at some outlets. Anxious employees at the American University outlet in Cairo hung up a poster declaring their support for Palestine.[108] The Doctor's Syndicate boycott advised people to buy nothing from any country active in Iraq. A sweeping boycott, organized by a retired professor from Washington, DC, was developed at a pan-Arab conference. According to organizer Dr Al Boyoumi, the boycott criterion is that the products 'should be symbols of US globalization', not just those one would target in an anti-war or pro-Palestinian protest. The main brands targeted were: Always, Ariel, Coca-Cola, Lay's, Marlboro, and McDonald's, and activists believed the boycott is a positive tool to encourage local businesses to take the place of foreign brands that may suffer. They also attempted to educate the public about the health and environmental impact of global brands in Egypt. The boycott marked a change in Egyptian activism – this time it was focused and understandable, as well as aligned with the common causes of foreign anti-globalization organizations. Alongside McDonald's assertion that the boycott is doing nothing to harm their business, company reports suggest that Egyptians may be wary of being seen in public at a McDonald's because of the social pressure of the boycott, but online and telephone-based orders for home delivery have soared since the beginning of the boycott.[109] Despite this, McDonald's and KFC reportedly suffered 20–50 per cent fall in sales since the beginning of the second Intifada 19 months previously.[110] Businesspeople and government officials are concerned about the future of foreign direct investment in Egypt. Egypt is the second largest recipient of US aid after Israel.[111]

McDonald's action: In 2001 the company introduced the McFalafel in its 49 outlets, with an advertising soundtrack by 'I hate Israel' hit singer Shabaan Abdel Rahim, a song considered a rallying point in an anti-American and anti-Israel boycott. In the anodyne McDonald's jingle he sang, 'If you eat a bite, you can't stop before finishing the whole roll'. Following an official complaint by the American Jewish Committee (AJC) to McDonald's, the ad was dropped after running for three weeks.[112] McDonald's US corporate office stated that the marketing decision was locally made and lacking in research. The AJC stated it was 'delighted in their responsiveness'. Egyptian fast food chain Mo'men ('Believer'), launched in 1999, appears to do well from any disaffection from McDonald's. It has its own strong market share. The chain sells typical 'Western' fast food items like chicken nuggets as well as traditional Egyptian offerings.[113]

Indonesia, 2002–2003: During the unrest leading to the fall of President Suharto in 1998, several McDonald's outlets were destroyed. In the wake of US forces' strikes on Afghanistan, Indonesia's highest Muslim order called on the government to sever diplomatic ties with the US. When students demonstrated against US interests, McDonald's was a common target. Protests against US military action in Afghanistan turned against McDonald's outlets. McDonald's outlet in Makassar was bombed by a militant Islamic group affiliated with Al-Qaeda in December, 2002, killing three people and wounding 11. During the run-up to hostilities in Iraq, anti-war protesters sealed doors and plastered restaurants with signs urging people not to go inside McDonald's restaurants, as well as other US food chains.[114] Since the beginning of US military operations in Iraq, McDonald's outlets were targets of demonstrations. Demonstrators stated their belief that a portion of American profits go to Israel. Despite the highly visible local-ownership campaign by owner Bambang Rachmadi, demonstrators emphasized the American-ness of the brand. They threw away McDonald's leaflets stating how McDonald's Indonesia 'Grew in the hands of Indonesian sons and daughters'.[115]

McDonald's action: Emphasis on the local ownership of franchises, proclaimed on big green banners outside the 85 restaurants (green is the colour of Islam), proclaiming: 'In the name of Allah, the merciful and the gracious, McDonald's Indonesia is owned by an indigenous Muslim'. The company hired security staff from local Islamist organizations to guard the outlets. Such organizations include Ka'bah Youth Movement, a black-uniformed group advocating the adoption of Islamic Law in Indonesia, which has been known to close night clubs perceived to transgress Islamic codes. On Fridays staff are supplied with religious-inspired uniforms. Female employees are required to wear a headscarf. Walls are covered with photos of the Indonesian franchise owner Bambang Rachmadi on his Mecca pilgrimage. Arab music is played in outlets. In some outlets, tables are raised over straw mats so patrons can eat without shoes in the Javanese style. The menu includes the popular 'Rice Packet', rice with fried chicken, scrambled egg, and a dose of spicy Sambal sauce.[116] American-educated Bambang Rachmadi, McDonald's master franchise owner in Indonesia, described McDonald's as America's 'most significant icon'. McDonald's headquarters receives 5 per cent of revenue from the McDonald's Indonesia franchise. Food served at the outlets is mainly produced locally, and boasts a menu containing traditional ingredients like chicken and rice. 'If you destroy it [McDonald's outlet], you'll only destroy a job for a Muslim.' McDonald's Indonesia donates goats for sacrifice during Muslim Ramadan ceremonies.

Lebanon, 2002: Boycott against American goods and companies doing business with Israel. Influential Shia cleric Sheikh Mohammed Hussain Fadlallah asked Arabs to buy European or Asian products instead of American ones.
McDonald's action: Franchise owners pay for full-page newspaper advertisements declaring the franchise is fully owned and financed by Lebanese.

India, 2003: Opposition members of parliament called for a boycott of all American brands, notably Coca-Cola, McDonald's, Pepsi, and British-owned Lever. Demonstrators blocked the entrance to McDonald's outlets to protest the war and call for a boycott of American goods.

Pakistan, 2003: According to Pakistani police, an attack on McDonald's and KFC by Islamic militants was prevented by arrests. 'It's a Western cultural invasion', according to Jamaat-e-Islami representative Munawar Hasan. Jamaat-e-Islami, a powerful Islamist political party, considers the presence of the chain in Pakistan to be an 'ideological issue'. Also angering Pakistanis is the uniform requiring women to wear trousers, which is for some against Islamic principles.

McDonald's action: the company stations private security guards armed with pump-action rifles outside outlets.

Palestinian occupied territories, 2003: American-style fast-food restaurants in Ramallah were compelled to close, although the motive was not clear. Closed restaurants included US chain outlet Subway and three local copies of McDonald's and KFC.

UAE, Egypt, Jordan, 2002–2003: rumours circulated that McDonald's donates some of its profits to Israel. Boycotts against American emblems like McDonald's leave restaurants 'empty'. In Jordan, people walking into American restaurants are 'socially ostracized'.[117]

McDonald's action: Published a statement in Egyptian daily *Al-Ahram* and other publications denouncing the rumours as 'ridiculous' and stating that such rumours endanger 3000 Egyptian jobs. In other countries criss-crossed by such rumours, McDonald's franchisees issued statements that the outlets were locally owned and operated. In 2003 McDonald's introduced the McArabia sandwich, a version of a popular regional snack using Arabic bread and grilled chicken, appeasing some people by this apparent salute to local food culture. According to some reports, the introduction of the McArabia counteracted reduced sales caused by calls to boycott McDonald's. The company denied that the introduction of McArabia was related to geopolitical issues, asserting that the item had been in development for two years. McDonald's owner Rafiq Shah in Dubai pointed out that 'There is no liaison between McArabia and politics'.

Indonesia, 2009: During the night some individuals with stones and bricks smashed every window and door of a McDonald's restaurant in Makassar (Indonesia). They left a message saying: 'We are aware of what you multinationals have done to the people of Kulon Progo, Takalar, Bima, and other places. We are angry and we'll do more!'.

Other attacks during the past several years on McDonald's have occurred in Belgium, Mexico, England, Chile, Serbia, Colombia, South Africa and Xian, China. In the same time-frame, American-based Yum! brand KFC has been attacked in Pakistan, Indonesia, Lebanon and Greece, and Pizza Hut was bombed in Lebanon. Table 6.5 provides recent information about the number of outlets located in regions experiencing criticism aimed at US foreign policy.

Table 6.5 McDonald's locations in sensitive spots around the globe (2010)

Country	Locations
Bahrain	14, since 1994
Egypt	More than 70 outlets and points of sale (since 1994)
Indonesia	110 since 1990
Israel	153 since 1993
Kuwait	40 since 1994
Pakistan	25 since 1998
Saudi Arabia	60 since 1993
UAE	28 since 1994

Local ownership is emphasized on the McDonald's corporation website, where sentences like 'Bahraini-owned, operated, and proud to serve you' are repeated on practically every country page. In addition, each page dedicated to a gulf region country contains the statement: 'In the Arab nations, all McDonald's restaurants are locally owned and operated by Arab entrepreneurs' (for more information visit **www.mcdonalds.com**). Charitable actions and community campaigns are strongly emphasized on McDonald's Corporation websites, including donations to and activities with children's cancer hospitals and Red Crescent. Equally prominent on local pages of the McDonald's website are claims of the percentage of ingredients supplied locally, and the number of local workers employed.

Non-violent and violent action

Some militant Islamic websites, such as those affiliated with Al-Qaeda, have specifically designated McDonald's as a target to weaken the US economy. According to the Islamic-centered magazine *Khilafah*, McDonald's is a 'tool serving to promote the domination of the US. The chain has become an empire with fiefs around the world.'[118] 'There are people who are very, very, angry with the US and they retain their ability to strike', said Dr. Achmad Abdi, Director of criminal investigations South Sulawesi, Indonesia.[119] According to an Islamic militant held in the US camp at Guantanamo, Cuba, the South East Asian Islamic group Jemaah Islamiyah has decided to attack 'soft' targets like American-linked businesses because 'hard' targets such as military or government installations were too difficult.[120] So-called 'soft' targets thought to be desirable and easily accessible for terrorists include restaurants, hotels, shopping centres, and entertainment facilities.[121] Examples of such attacks include assaults on McDonald's, KFC and Pizza Hut outlets in several countries as well as deadly bombs at a hotel in Kenya, night clubs in Bali,[122] a J. W. Marriott Hotel in Jakarta, Indonesia, in August 2003 and simultaneous attacks on a Spanish restaurant, Jewish community centre, and a five-star international hotel in Casablanca, Morocco in May 2003.[123] In the past, 'soft' tourist targets were also deadly but were smaller in scale, such as the killing of 58 tourists at Luxor, Egypt in November, 1997 and several violent incidents in Turkey in the late 1990s.[124]

A form of non-violent protest, the boycott, has been extensively used in the Middle East to protest against McDonald's itself, American presence, cultural imperialism, the US government's stance on Israel and Palestine, and the invasion of Iraq. Although companies are understandably reluctant to discuss the economic/social impacts of boycotts, the recent boycott has cost McDonald's sales in the Middle East, according to Claire Babrowski, McDonald's former Asia Pacific and Middle East/Africa president.[125] Repeated attempts by journalists at McDonald's headquarters to hear the company's view on the topic were ignored. According to Islam Online, an 'upswing' of American and Jewish boycotts has caused losses to McDonald's, and is partly to blame for the company's ill-health. A professor of Economics at Al-Azhar University, Cairo, Egypt, stated that 'We should bear in mind that this is a form of waging economic war on the enemies, and war always necessitates sacrifice . . . as part of the positive results of the boycott, people will shift to purchasing local products and services . . . creating a form of [Muslim] self-sufficiency'.

Beliefs about boycotts

The Arab Movement for the Boycott of American and Jewish Products spokesperson Amin Iskander stated his belief that the economic damage of the Arab boycott on American companies may be very small; however it is seen to be a 'message of protest . . . [to] mobilize popular feelings and raise awareness in the streets about the US biased attitude towards Israel.'[126] Amin Iskander is also an up-and-coming Egyptian politician. Some boycotts have the force of Fatwa (religious ruling based on the Sharia,[127] the body of Islamic law) behind them. According to Muslim scholar and president of the European Council for Fatwa and Research Sheikh Youssef Al-Qaradawi, 'Each dinar, dirham used to buy their [US] goods eventually becomes a bullet fired at the hearts of a brother or child in Palestine'.

The US Bureau of Industry maintains an anti-boycott office with examples and analysis at: http://www.bxa.doc.gov/AntiboycottCompliance/Default.htm. Calls to boycott continue today, examples of which may be consulted on the Internet at: http://www.inminds.co.uk/boycott-israel.html.

Other boycotts of McDonald's

Global Boycott for Peace, an organization that has as a mission to 'pressure the US government, through its corporate sponsors, into becoming an international partner in maintaining peaceful and sustainable world peace and renounce militarism' lists McDonald's as among the 'Top 20 companies to boycott'. (For more information, go to http://www.globalboycottforpeace.org.) Hindus in India and abroad have called for a boycott of the company on the basis of its promotion of meat, and its use of beef flavouring in french fries in some markets. People for the Ethical Treatment of Animals have advocated a boycott of McDonald's for alleged cruel practices in the meat industry that supplies the fast-food company (see http://www.mccruelty.com/.)

Why McDonald's is a target

In an interview with *Foreign Policy* journal, former Chief Executive Officer of McDonald's, Jack Greenberg, was asked why McDonald's outlets were often defaced and attacked. Greenberg saw these disruptions as proof of McDonald's widespread power: 'The price of our unique success'. Greenberg added that no other service company 'touches so many people [60 million] every day in such a personal way . . . If you're going to have that kind of presence, you're going to have that kind of attention'. Greenberg stated that in his belief, many frustrations are blamed on globalization, and conveniently vented on McDonald's. 'Would I rather be the target or would I rather be number two and not be the target? . . . I'd rather be number one. . . . Because of our leadership position and our size, we are a very natural, highly visible point of discussion for good and bad.' Greenberg expressed his view that some critics of globalization should like McDonald's because it is a 'decentralized entrepreneurial network of locally owned stores that . . . adapts very well to local conditions.'[128] When *Foreign Policy* journal editor Moises Naim asked whether McDonald's could correct some misperceptions about the company, Greenberg asserted that the company is not a 'Big American company'. Rather, it is a network of local businesses owned by local entrepreneurs. 'We have become the symbol of everything people don't like or are worried about in terms of their own culture'. In 2000 more than half McDonald's sales came from outside the US. In an attempt to increase public understanding, the company has stated 'McDonald's is a global brand and is often used as a symbol in complex issues facing the world' on the McDonald's Kuwait website. Philippe Labbe, Director General of McDonald's France, stated after anti-McDonald's protests that the company was a 'Victim of its visibility'. He added that trade wars do not concern McDonald's which buys only 10 per cent of its beef outside France.[129]

Effects of the anti-US and anti-Israeli boycotts

Although companies are understandably reluctant to discuss the economic/social impacts of boycotts, the recent boycott has cost McDonald's sales in the Middle East, according to Claire Babrowski, McDonald's former Asia Pacific and Middle East/Africa president.[130]

Director of marketing and communications for McDonald's in the Middle East, Ricarda Ruecker, said that since April 2002, when Intifada-related tensions rose, 'We, like every global brand, suffered definitely'. Repeated attempts by journalists at McDonald's headquarters to hear the corporate view on the topic were ignored. According to Islam Online, an 'upswing' of American and Jewish boycotts has caused losses to McDonald's, and are partly to blame for the company's ill-health. In Jordan two out of six McDonald's outlets have closed due to lack of business, and in Muscat, Oman, McDonald's sales reportedly fell by 65 per cent.[131] An industry association representing 22 mostly American fast-food chains in Egypt, Mahmoud Al-Kaissouni, claimed that sales at most member restaurants was down 20 per cent since Israel entered the Left Bank in March. After the eruption of the Intifada in September 2000, sales reportedly fell 5 per cent.[132] Even in cosmopolitan Dubai, it was reported that business was down at McDonald's and other American fast-food chains. In another report sales at most American fast-food outlets were down by about 20 and 30 per cent around the Arab world in 2002.[133] The impact on local economies is often a concern when there is a boycott.

McDonald's as a subject for study

Why is there such rage and passion surrounding McDonald's? In his analysis of the company, *The Sign of the Burger: McDonald's and the Culture of Power*, academic author Kincheloe offers some explanations. Kincheloe argues that dramatic differences in people's perceptions of McDonald's illustrate the company's importance as a worldwide symbol. McDonald's 'all-American success story' has captured the imagination of people around the world, incarnating many roles:[134]

- rampaging cultural imperialist or actor in cultural homogenization;
- symbol of America itself;
- harbinger of free market capitalism;
- symbol of aggressive American capitalism;[135]
- exploiter of labour;
- exploiter of children;
- bellwether brand;
- sign of Western-driven economic development;
- signifier of what is 'modern';
- destroyer of the environment;
- embodiment of greedy corporatism, and so on.

José Bové, the French farmer opposed to globalization, vandalized a McDonald's under construction to protest against trade policies and bad food. Some of Bové's acclaim throughout France and in other countries came from his opposition to a widely understood symbol as powerful as a national flag, McDonald's. Kincheloe analyses the company's ability to 'produce and transmit knowledge, shape values, influence identity, and construct consciousness'.[136] Although there are limits to post-modernist analysis, the book helps in understanding how a multinational brand can inflame the passions of people everywhere.

In a similar vein, George Ritzer used McDonald's as a vehicle and as a form of shorthand to describe deep socio-cultural and economic changes in his book *The McDonaldization of Society*. Ritzer studied the manner in which McDonald's rationalized the processes involved in food production and service. He uses the word 'rationalization' in the sense that processes are examined and re-designed in a more rational manner. Four factors emerge as key to the rationalization process: efficiency, predictability (standardization), calculability (quantifiable outcomes) and control (of customers, processes, and employees). According to Ritzer's thesis,

McDonald's-like rationalization has taken root in other industries and institutions hoping to improve output and efficiency. As a result, consumers are trained to do some of the corporation's tasks, such as taking their food to the table and clearing the table when finished, filling the car tank with petrol rather than being served by an employee, and delivering furniture to their homes themselves instead of relying on a delivery service. Rationalization is described in the book to have irrational consequences for the company and society, such as employee turnover and phenomena that alienate people.[137]

The ethnographic studies in James L. Watson's book *Golden Arches East: McDonald's in East Asia* are illuminating in their portrayal of different meanings ascribed to the company and its products. The book shows how in Korea the chain did not expand quickly due to the perception that it affronted Korean culture. In Beijing the hamburger was considered to be a snack similar to a type of ravioli (*xianbing*), while in Japan a hamburger could not be considered a meal since it lacked rice. The essays appear to confirm that McDonald's is considered to be a local product by many of its loyal customers, and has supplanted local institutions (such as the tea house or street vendors) with apparent ease.[138]

Thomas Friedman, foreign affairs columnist at the *New York Times*, famously contended that McDonald's fosters peace. In his book *The Lexus and the Olive Tree: Understanding Globalization*,[139] he argued that globalization is the new economic system. After checking the facts with McDonald's headquarters, he theorized that when two countries grew middle classes large enough to justify the growth of McDonald's outlets, they were not likely to go to war. That has since been proven wrong, with India and Pakistan being notable examples; however, it is notable that he chose McDonald's as a leading indicator of globalization. The 'Golden Arches theory of conflict prevention' has been amended to *Starbucks*, Friedman's new model.[140]

Leading business publication *The Economist* selected McDonald's as a relatively stable, global institution to determine the value of currencies in foreign exchange markets. 'Burgernomics', as the publication calls the process, is about purchasing power parity or the ability to pay a similar amount of US Dollars for goods around the world. In theory, exchange rates should converge at a point where it costs the same in US Dollars and local currency to purchase a similar basket of goods in both countries. In this case the basket of goods is a Big Mac, sold in 120 countries. Former Chief Executive Officer of McDonald's Jack Greenberg said the company 'loves' the Big Mac Index, adding that 'It says something about the strength of the brand that you can do something like that and have credibility'.[141] In a similar development, the investment bank UBS created a measure of purchasing power in terms of minutes of work needed to buy a Big Mac around the world. The UBS index reflects local productivity as well as McDonald's costs in local markets, where the most time is needed in Kenya, the least in the US.[142]

Questions

1. How would you describe McDonald's global marketing strategy: are they hard globalizers or do they adjust to local contexts? What are the reasons for their choices?

2. What is a cultural icon? To what extent are McDonald's, as a corporate name, and its product brand names (e.g. Big Mac) associated with its country of origin (the US) and to large scale, standardized service operations?

3. Describe the ambivalent attitudes of consumers to McDonald's. Do boycotts really succeed in stopping the growth of McDonald's outside the US? Base your answer on actual data. Please take into account the slowdown in attacks against McDonald's in recent years (see Table 6.4).

4. How should McDonald's react to boycotts in the short run? In the long run, how could the company avoid being considered a mere cultural icon?

Saskia Faulk and Jean-Claude Usunier prepared this case solely to provide material for class discussion. The authors do not intend to illustrate either effective or ineffective handling of a business situation. The authors may have disguised certain names and other identifying information to protect confidentiality. This case was designed to present a complex marketing situation. It presents sensitive political, cultural, economic, and religious issues, and was in no way intended to offend, nor to advocate, the cause of any party.

© IRM/HEC, 2011

2011-05-11   Version: (A)

Appendix references

1. *Forbes*, retrieved 16 May 2011 from http://finapps.forbes.com/finapps/jsp/finance/compinfo/CIAtAGlance.jsp?tkr=DIS.
2. Dawson, Chester (2001), 'Will Tokyo embrace another mouse?', *Business Week Online*, 10 September 2001. Retrieved 12 May 2011 from http://www.businessweek.com/magazine/content/01_37/b3748079.htm).
3. Pulley, Brett (2002), 'Disney the sequel', *Forbes*, 9 December 2002, Vol. 170 Issue 12, pp. 106–12. Retrieved 12 May 2011 from http://www.forbes.com/forbes/2002/1209/106.html.
4. Gregerson, Hal B. (1998), 'Developing leaders for the global frontier', *Sloan Management Review*, Fall 1998, Vol. 40 Issue 1, pp. 21–32. Retrieved 12 May 2011 from http://sloanreview.mit.edu/the-magazine/1998-fall/4012/developing-leaders-for-the-global-frontier/.
5. Aupperle, Kenneth E. and Grigorios Karimalis (2001), 'Using Metaphors to Facilitate Cooperation and Resolve Conflict: Examining the case of Disneyland Paris', *Journal of Change Management*, Vol. 2,1, pp. 23–32.
6. Kauth, Robert K. Jr. (1988), 'The myth of cultural imperialism', *The Freeman*, November 1988, Vol. 38, No. 11. Retrieved 12 May 2011 from http://www.ilw.com/articles/2008,0812-rauth.shtm.
7. Pulley, Brett (2002), 'Disney the sequel', *Forbes*, 9 December 2002, Vol. 170 Issue 12, pp. 106–12. Retrieved 12 May 2011 from http://www.forbes.com/forbes/2002/1209/106.html.
8. D'Hauteserre, Anne-Marie (2001), 'Destination Branding in a Hostile Environment', *Journal of Travel Research*, February 2001, Vol. 39 Issue 3, pp. 300–307.
9. *Supra*.
10. Usunier (2000), *Marketing Across Cultures*, (3rd edn). Prentice Hall, London.
11. Disneyland Resort Paris (2002), *Disneyland Resort Paris Press Kit*, Disneyland Resort Paris. Retrieved 12 May 2011 from http://www.Disneylandparis.com/uk.
12. International Association of Amusement Parks and Attractions (2001), 'Attendance Worldwide: Top 25 most visited parks' cited from *Amusement Business*. Retrieved 12 May 2011 from http://www.iaapa.org/europe/de/documents/2009ThemeIndex.pdf.
13. Disneyland Resort Paris (2002), *Disneyland Resort Paris Press Kit*, Disneyland Resort Paris. Retrieved 12 May 2011 from http://www.Disneylandparis.com/uk.
14. *Supra*.
15. Disneyland Resort Paris (2002), 'Three new hotels set to open at Disneyland Resort Paris in Spring 2003', *Disneyland Resort Paris Press Kit*. Disneyland Resort Paris. Retrieved 12 May 2011 from http://www.Disneylandparis.com/uk.
16. Assaoui, Mohammed (2002), 'Disneyland Paris, 2ème Edition', Etude de Cas (case study), *Le Figaro Entreprises*, 11 March 2002.
17. Milhomme, Albert J. (1993), Customised or global, the strategy may not work at Eurodisney, in Tom K. Massey Jr. (ed.), Marketing: Satisfying in diverse customerplace, *Proceedings of the Southern Marketing Association*, New Orleans, Louisiana, November, pp. 91–4.
18. Koranteng, Julia (2001), 'European park owners bullish about future', *Amusement Business*, 20/8/2001, Vol. 113 Issue 33. Retrieved 12 May 2011 from Business Source Primer at http://www.epnet.com.
19. Disneyland Resort Paris (2 March 2002), *Disneyland Resort Paris Practical Guide* (16 March to 2 November 2002), Disneyland Resort Paris. Retrieved 12 May 2011 from http://www.Disneylandparis.com/uk.
20. Gentleman, Amelia (2003), 'Iraq fallout, strikes and forest fires have kept Americans and Europeans away', *Guardian*, 9 August 2003. Retrieved 12 May 2011 from http://www.guardian.co.uk/international/story/0,3604,1015132,00.html.

21. Hopkins, Nic (2003), 'Saudi Prince in talks with EuroDisney over rescue', *The Times*, 6 September 2003. Retrieved 12 May 2011 from http://www.timesonline.co.uk (lien direct avec article payant: http://www.thesundaytimes.co.uk/sto/public/sitesearch.do?querystring=Saudi+Prince+in+talks+with+EuroDisney+over+rescue&sectionId=2&p=sto&bl=on&pf=all).

22. Assaoui, Mohammed (2002), 'Disneyland Paris, 2ème edition'. Etude de Cas (case study). *Le Figaro Entreprises*, 11 March 2002. Retrieved 18 January 2003 from http://www.lefigaro.fr/etudiant.

23. Pulley, Brett (2002), 'Disney the sequel', *Forbes*, 9 December 2002, Vol. 170 Issue 12, pp. 106–12. Retrieved 12 May 2011 from http://www.forbes.com/forbes/2002/1209/106.html.

24. Chu, Jeff (2002), 'Happily ever after?' *TIME Europe*, 25 March 2002, Vol. 159 No. 12. Retrieved 12 May 2011 from http://www.time.com/time/europe/magazine/article/0,13005,901020325-218398,00.html.

25. *Supra*.

26. *Supra*.

27. U.S. Commercial Service (2002), 'Welcome to the French market', U.S. Commercial Service, France. Retrieved 12 May 2011 from http://www.buyusa.gov/france.

28. Chu, Jeff (2002), 'Happily ever after?' *TIME Europe*, 25 March 2002, Vol. 159 No. 12. Retrieved 12 May 2011 from http://www.time.com/time/europe/magazine/article/0,13005,901020325-218398,00.html.

29. Koranteng, Julia (2002), 'Disney embarks on European marketing push', *Amusement Business*, 18/3/2002, Vol. 114 Issue 11. Retrieved 12 May 2011 from *Business Source Primer* at http://www.epnet.com.

30. Chu, Jeff (2002), 'Happily ever after?' *TIME Europe*, 25 March 2002, Vol. 159 No. 12. Retrieved 12 May 2011 from from http://www.time.com/time/europe/magazine/article/0,13005,901020325-218398,00.html.

31. Guyotat, Régis (2001), 'Un grand salon au rez de chaussée', *Le Monde Diplomatique*, December 2001. Retrieved 12 May 2011 from http://www.monde-diplomatique.fr/2001/12/GUYOTAT/15971.

32. Anonymous (2002), 'What the world thinks in 2002: How global publics view their lives, their countries, the World, America', *The Pew Charitable Trust*, 4 December 2002 Retrieved 12 May 2011 from http://people-press.org/2002/12/04/what-the-world-thinks-in-2002/.

33. O'Brien, Tim (2000), 'Parc Asterix', *Amusement Business*, 16 October 2000, Vol. 112, Issue 42. Retrieved 12 May 2011 from *Business Source Primer* at http://www.epnet.com.

34. Chu, Jeff (2002), 'Room for the imagination' *TIME Europe*, 25 March 2002, Vol. 129 No. 12. Retrieved 12 May 2011 from http://www.time.com/time/europe/magazine/article/0,13005,901020325-218402,00.html.

35. Koranteng, Julia (2001), 'European park owners bullish about future', *Amusement Business*, 20/8/2001, Vol. 113 Issue 33. Retrieved 12 May 2011 from *Business Source Primer* at http://www.epnet.com.

36. Universal Mediterranea (2003), *Press Dossier*. Universal Mediterranea. Retrieved 12 May 2011 from http://www.portaventura.es.

37. Chu, Jeff (2002), 'Happily ever after?' *TIME Europe*, 25 March 2002, Vol. 129 No. 12 Retrieved 12 May 2011 from http://www.time.com/time/europe/magazine/article/0,13005,901020325-218398,00.html.

38. Armitstead, Louise (2010-10-01), 'Ikea', The *Daily Telegraph* (London), retrieved 19 May 2011 from http://www.telegraph.co.uk/finance/newsbysector/retailandconsumer/8037637/Ikea-reveals-profits-for-first-time-to-dispel-secretive-image.html.

39. 'Facts and figures', Company website, retrieved 19 May 2011 from http://www.ikea.com/ms/en_US/about_ikea/facts_and_figures/ikea_group_stores/index.html.

40. Inter IKEA Systems B. V. (2002), '*Accueil – à propos d'IKEA*'. Retrieved 19 May 2011 from http://www.ikea.com/ms/en_US/about_ikea/index.html.

41. Inter IKEA Systems B. V. (2003), 'ikea Global – Select country site'. Retrieved 19 May 2011 from http://www.ikea.com.

42. Inter IKEA Systems B. V. (2002), '*Acceuil – à propos d'IKEA*'. Retrieved 19 May 2011 from http://www.ikea.com/about_ikea/our_vision/better.asp.

43. Inter IKEA Systems B. V. (2002), 'Facts and figures'. Retrieved 19 May 2011 from http://www.ikea.com/ms/fr_CH/about_ikea/facts_and_figures/index.html.

44. Inter IKEA Systems B. V. (2002), 'Facts and figures'. Retrieved 19 May 2011 from http://www.ikea.com/ms/fr_CH/about_ikea/facts_and_figures/index.html.

45. Inter IKEA Systems B. V. (2002), 'FAQs – What new IKEA store openings are scheduled?'. Retrieved 19 May 2011 from http://www.ikea.com/ms/fr_CH/about_ikea/facts_and_figures/index.html.

46. Anonymous (2002), 'Eastern Europe's largest mall opens on MKAD', *The Moscow Times*, 17 December 2002. Retrieved 19 May 2011 from *Business Source Primer* at http://search.epnet.com.

47. Anonymous (2002), 'Auchan signs up to anchor new IKEA shopping center', *The Moscow Times* (online), 21 March 2002. Retrieved 19 May 2011 from http://www.themoscowtimes.com/business/article/auchan-signs-up-to-anchor-new-ikea-shopping-center/247624.html.

48. Anonymous (2010), 'Ikea founder "cried like a baby" over Russian bribery scandal', *The Local*, 19 February 2010. Retrieved 19 May 2011 from http://www.thelocal.se/25096/20100219/#.

49. Gilligan, Gregory J. (2002), 'IKEA on the move', *Shopping Centers Today*, April 2002. Retrieved 19 May 2011 from http://www.icsc.org/srch/sct/sct0402/page51.php.

50. Anonymous (2011), 'IKEA eyes further expansion in China', *Channel NewsAsia*, 18 March 2011. Retrieved 19 May 2011 from http://www.channelnewsasia.com/stories/afp_asiapacific_business/view/1117185/1/.html.

51. Lane, Greg (2007), 'Failed Businesses in Japan', J@pan Inc, 17 September 2007. Retrieved 19 May 2011 from http://www.japaninc.com/mgz_sep-oct_2007_issue_failed-businesses.

52. Inter IKEA Systems B. V. (2002), 'About IKEA – Our vision' (web page). Retrieved 19 May 2011 from http://www.ikea.com/about_ikea/our_vision/better.asp.

53. IKEA report (2010), 'Welcome inside – Yearly Summary FY10 IKEA Group'. Retrieved 19 May 2011 from http://www.ikea.com/ms/en_GB/pdf/yearly_summary/Welcome_inside_2010_update.pdf.

54. Inter IKEA Systems B. V. (2002), 'Global directory' (web page). Retrieved 19 May 2011 from http://www.ikea.com.

55. Boris, Cynthia (2010), 'IKEA turns Consumer Behavior into Viral Marketing', *Marketing Pilgram*, 24 August 2010. Retrieved 19 May 2011 from http://www.marketingpilgrim.com/2010/08/hide-and-seek-game-viral-marketing-ikea.html.

56. Inter IKEA Systems B. V. (2002), '*Acceuil – à propos d'IKEA*' (web page). Retrieved 19 May 2011 from http://www.ikea.com/ms/en_GB/about_ikea/facts_and_figures/index.html.

57. Hatch, Denny (2003), 'Case Study, IKEA, Sweden's Jewel', *Target Marketing* (online) 18 May 2003. Retrieved 19 May 2011 from http://www.targetonline.com.

58. *Supra.*

59. Inter IKEA Systems B. V. (2003), '*IKEA Family: Fêtez avec nous*', undated. Retrieved 19 May 2011 from http://www.ikea.ch.

60. Asako Ishibashi (2002), 'IKEA brings back Scandinavian design' (interview of Tommy Kullberg of IKEA, with Asako Ishibashi) *Nikkei Weekly Page*, published online by the Danish Furniture Promotion Center, 22 July 2002. Retrieved 19 May 2011 from http://www.denmark.or.jp.

61. Inter IKEA Systems B. V. (2002), '*Accueil – à propos d'IKEA*' (web page). Retrieved 19 May 2011 from http://www.ikea.com/ms/fr_CH/about_ikea/index.html.

62. Inter IKEA Systems B. V. (2002), 'Facts and figures' (web page). Retrieved 19 May 2011 from http://www.ikea.com/ms/fr_CH/about_ikea/facts_and_figures/index.html.

63. *Supra.*

64. *Supra.*

65. Inter IKEA Systems B. V. (2002), 'Global directory' (web page). Retrieved 19 May 2011 from http://www.ikea.com.

66. Gilligan, Gregory J. (2002), 'IKEA on the move', *Shopping Centers Today*, April 2002. Retrieved 19 May 2011 from http://www.icsc.org/srch/sct/sct0402/page51.php.

67. Anonymous (2001), 'IKEA takes art to a new height with its Suite Home Chicago entry', *Furniture World*, June–July, 2001. Retrieved 17 December 2002 from http://www.furninfo.com/news/newsindex0601.html.

68. Inter IKEA Systems B. V. (2002), 'The unböring manifesto, book one', Retrieved 19 May 2011 from http://www.ikeafans.com/ikea/ikea-history/unboering-ikeas-unboring-campaign.html.

69. Slavin, Terry (2001), 'IKEA in pre-fabs plan for low-paid', *Guardian*, 25 November 2001. Retrieved 19 May 2011 from http://society.guardian.co.uk/keyworkers/story/0,1266,606148,00.html.

70. Anonymous (2003), 'IKEA founder worried over growth', *BBC News World Edition*, 19 May 2011. Retrieved 4 January 2003 from http://news.bbc.co.uk/2/hi/business/2626387.stm.

71. Wikipedia, *McDonald's*, Retrieved 5 May 2011 from http://en.wikipedia.org/wiki/McDonald's.
72. *Supra.*
73. Stewart, Glenn, *Hamburger Wars: Burger King vs. McDonald's* (2003), The University of Tennessee at Martin. Retrieved 5 May 2011 from http://www.utm.edu/staff/johnston/mktg710/HamburgerWars.ppt#256,1,Hamburger Wars: Burger King vs. McDonald's.
74. Anonymous, 'McDonald's 2008 Ad Spending Tops $1.2 Billion', *Burger Business*, 21 June 2009. Retrieved 18 April 2011 from http://www.burgerbusiness.com/?p=1505.
75. Bruene, Jim, '*Top U.S Financial Brands*', 29 July 2006. Retrieved 5 May 2011 from http://www.netbanker.com/2006/07/top-us-financial-brands.html.
76. MacDougall, W., 'McKids: burger giant puts clothes on the menu', 26 April 2004, Retrieved 5 May 2011 from 'http://www.sevenoaksmag.com/culture/10_mckids.html.
77. Day, Sherri, 'After years at top, McDonald's strives to regain ground', *New York Times*, 3 March 2003. Retrieved 5 May 2011 from http://query.nytimes.com/gst/abstract.html?res=F30913FB34580C708CDDAA0894DB404482.
78. McDonald's Corporation, *Summary Annual Report 2002*, McDonald's Corporation, 2003. Retrieved 5 May 2011 from http://www.aboutmcdonalds.com/etc/medialib/aboutMcDonalds/investors.Par.29509.File.dat/mcdap_p01_16.pdf.
79. Davis, Scott, 'Top of mind: McDonald's strategy doesn't deliver', *Brandweek*, 10 November 2003. Retrieved 5 May 2011 from http://www.allbusiness.com/marketing-advertising/branding-brand-development/4680724-1.html.
80. Garfield, Bob, 'Why we're not lovin' it', *Advertising Age*, 8 September 2003. Retrieved 5 May 2011 from http://adage.com/garfield/post?article_id=38296.
81. Cooper, Peter J., 'McDonald's', *AME Info*, 11 June 2003. Retrieved 5 May 2011 from http://www.ameinfo.com/25009.html.
82. New York Times News Service, 'U.S. brands stand to suffer should war be declared', *New York Times News Service*, Paris, 16 March 2003. Retrieved 5 May 2011 from http://www.taipeitimes.com/News/bizfocus/archives/2003/03/16/198307.
83. Anonymous, 'McDonald's Hamburger University to train managers in the region', 24 January 2004. Retrieved 5 May 2011 from http://www.ameinfo.com/33723.html.
84. Docena, Herbert, 'Dying for a McDonald's in Iraq', 22 October 2003. Retrieved 5 May 2011 from http://www.zmag.org/content/showarticle.cfm?ItemID=4382.
85. Karon, Tony, 'Adieu, Ronald McDonald', *TIME Magazine*, 22 January 2002. Retrieved 5 May 2011 from http://www.time.com/time/columnist/karon/article/0,9565,196925,00.html.
86. Kamath, Raghavendra, 'Big Mac's new menu', *Third Eyesight*, 25 October 2010, Retrieved 5 May 2011 from http://www.thirdeyesight.in/articles/big_mac_breakfast.htm.
87. Hindu Business Line, 'Animal flavouring – McDonald's Indian arm says it's clear', *Hindu Business Line*, 8 March 2002. Retrieved 5 May 2011 from http://www.thehindubusinessline.com/bline/2002/03/09/stories/2002030901530600.htm.
88. Deshpade Vidya, 'McDonald's goes more Indian', *Financial Express*, 11 September 2000. Retrieved 5 May 2011 from http://www.financialexpress.com/fe/daily/20000911/faf10031.html.
89. King, Colbert I., 'Saudi Arabia apartheid', *Washington Post*, 22 December 2001. Retrieved 5 May 2011 from http://www.desert-voice.net/new_page_7.htm.
90. Manning, Nicole (2002), 'U.S. Companies support gender segregation in Saudi Arabia', *National Organisation for Women Times*, Summer, 2002. Retrieved 5 May 2011 from http://www.now.org/nnt/summer-2002/gender.html.
91. King, Colbert I., 'Saudi Arabia apartheid', *Washington Post*, 22 December 2001. Retrieved 5 May 2011 from http://www.desert-voice.net/new_page_7.htm.
92. Amnesty International (2000), 'Gross human rights abuses against women in Saudi Arabia' *Amnesty International Report*, September 2000. Retrieved 5 May 2011 from http://www.amnestyusa.org/countries/saudi_arabia/document.do?id=D2C1FC0DC59EC51C802569610071BFEC.
93. Ford, Peter (2002), 'McDonald's in disguise', *Christian Science Monitor*, 11 September 2002. Retrieved 5 May 2011 from http://www.csmonitor.com/2002/0911/p02s02-wogi.html.
94. Anonymous, 'McDonald's lance le Mc Falafel', *JSS*, 18 January 2011, Retrieved 5 May 2011 from http://jssnews.com/2011/01/18/mc-donalds-lance-le-mc-falafel/.
95. Cohen, Deborah (2003), 'America's corporate icons brace for war backlash', *Reuters*, 8 March 2003. Retrieved 5 May 2011 from http://www.commondreams.org/headlines03/0308-04.htm.

96. Agence France Presse, 'Indonesian protesters unswayed by McDonald's defence', *ABC News*, 28 March 2003. Retrieved 5 May 2011 from http://www.mcspotlight.org/media/press/mcds/afp280303.html.

97. Abdel-Halim, Mustafa, 'Muslims rally against U.S. products, Big Mac feels backlash', *Islam Online*, 8 February 2003. Retrieved 7 May 2008 http://www.islamonline.net/English/News/2003-02/08/article03.shtml.

98. Athanasiadis, Iason, 'U.S. products, and some Egyptian ones, still feeling boycott', *American Chamber of Commerce Business Monthly*, October 2002. Retrieved 5 May 2011 from http://www.amcham.org.eg/resources_publications/publications/business_monthly/issue.asp?sec=17&im=10&iy=2002&subsec=US%20products,%20and%20some%20Egyptian%20ones,%20still%20feeling%20boycott.

99. Kirschbaum, Erik, 'Boycott of American goods over Iraq war gains', *Reuters*, 25 March 2003. Retrieved 5 May 2011 from http://www.commondreams.org/headlines03/0325-10.htm.

100. Gardener, Frank, 'Saudi burgers to help Palestinians', *BBC News*, 28 November 2000. Retrieved 5 May 2011 from http://news.bbc.co.uk/1/hi/world/middle_east/1044998.stm.

101. Karon, Tony, 'Adieu, Ronald McDonald', *TIME Magazine*, 22 January 2002. Retrieved 5 May 2011. from http://www.time.com/time/columnist/karon/article/0,9565,196925,00.html.

102. Abu-Nasr, Donna, 'Calls to boycott U.S. sweep the Gulf', *New York Times*, 30 November 2000. Retrieved 5 May 2011 from http://www.hsje.org/calls_to_boycott_us_sweep_gulf.htm.

103. Gardener, Frank, 'Saudi burgers to help Palestinians', *BBC News*, 28 November 2000. Retrieved 5 May 2011 from http://news.bbc.co.uk/1/hi/world/middle_east/1044998.stm.

104. Emery, David, 'Big Mac and a side of lies', *Urban legends and folklore*, About.com, 17 January 2001. Retrieved 5 May 2011 from http://urbanlegends.about.com/library/weekly/aa011701a.htm.

105. Karon, Tony, 'Official sandwich of the Intifada?', *TIME Magazine*, 29 November 2000. Retrieved 5 May 2011 from http://www.time.com/time/columnist/karon/article/0,9565,89889,00.html.

106. Abu-Nasr, Donna (2000), 'Calls to boycott US sweep the Gulf', *New York Times*, 30 November 2000. Retrieved 25 July 2012 from http://www.hsje-org/calls_to_boycott_us_sweep_gulf.htm.

107. Hassan-Gordon, Tariq, 'Boycott against Israel gathers steam', *Middle East Times*, 18 May 2001. Retrieved 5 May 2011 from http://www.inminds.co.uk/boycott-news-0204.html.

108. Wax, Emily, 'In Egypt, anger replaces admiration of U.S.', *Washington Post*, 24 March 2003. Retrieved 5 May 2011 from http://www.commondreams.org/headlines03/0324-07.htm.

109. American Chamber of Commerce Egypt, 'Boycott campaign thinks bigger', *American Chamber of Commerce Egypt Business Monthly*, April 2003. Retrieved 5 May 2011 from http://www.amcham.org.eg/resources_publications/publications/business_monthly/issue.asp?sec=17&im=4&iy=2003&subsec=Boycott%20campaign%20thinks%20bigger.

110. Anonymous, *Global Summary of anti-war boycott actions*, Boycott Bush, 18 March 2003. Retrieved 5 May 2011 from http://www.motherearth.org/USboycott/global_en.php.

111. American Chamber of Commerce Egypt, 'Egypt asks Washington for war damages', *American Chamber of Commerce Egypt Business Monthly*, April 2003. Retrieved 5 May 2011 from http://www.amcham.org.eg/resources_publications/publications/business_monthly/issue.asp?sec=17&im=4&iy=2003&subsec=Egypt%20asks%20Washington%20for%20war%20damages.

112. Associated Press, 'McDonald's dumps "I hate Israel" singer', *Jerusalem Post*, 5 July 2001. Retrieved 5 May 2011 from http://www.inminds.co.uk/boycott-news-0076.html.

113. Wax, Emily, 'In Egypt, anger replaces admiration of U.S.', *Washington Post*, 24 March 2003. Retrieved 5 May 2011 from http://www.commondreams.org/headlines03/0324-07.htm.

114. Kirschbaum, Erik, 'Boycott of American goods over Iraq war gains', *Reuters*, 25 March 2003. Retrieved 5 May 2011 from http://www.commondreams.org/headlines03/0325-10.htm.

115. Agence France Presse, 'Indonesian protesters unswayed by McDonald's defence', *ABC News*, 28 March 2003. Retrieved 5 May 2011 from http://www.mcspotlight.org/media/press/mcds/afp280303.html.

116. Ford, Peter, 'McDonald's in disguise', *Christian Science Monitor*, 11 September 2002. Retrieved 5 May 2011 from http://www.csmonitor.com/2002/0911/p02s02-wogi.html.

117. Cherian, John, 'A test of resilience', *Frontline (India)*, 25 May–7 June 2002. Retrieved 5 May 2011 http://www.frontlineonnet.com/fl1911/19110610.htm.

118. Editorial staff, '*Antiaméricanismes*', *Le Monde*, 7 December 2002.

119. Murphy, Dan, 'U.S. multinational companies wary of backlash', *Christian Science Monitor*, 21 April 2003. Retrieved 5 May 2011 from http://www.csmonitor.com/2003/0421/p12s01-woap.html.

120. *Supra.*
121. Shannon, May, 'Another warning from Zubaydah', *TIME Magazine*, 11 May 2002. Retrieved 5 May 2011 from http://www.time.com/time/nation/article/0,8599,236992,00.html.
122. Crock, Stan and Michael Shari, 'Terrorism: A gulf between fear and fact', *Lifewhile*, 16 January 2003. Retrieved 5 May 2011 http://www.lifewhile.com/news/1914872/detail.html.
123. BBC News, 'Bomb carnage shocks Morocco', *BBC News*, 17 May 2003. Retrieved 5 May 2011 from http://news.bbc.co.uk/2/hi/africa/3037157.stm.
124. International Labor Organization, 'The social impact of events on the hotel and tourism sector of events subsequent to September 11, 2001', (Briefing Paper), International Labor Organization, Geneva, 2001. Retrieved 9 May 2011 from http://www.ilo.org/public/english/dialogue/sector/techmeet/imhct01/imhctbp.pdf.
125. Farkas, David, 'Risky business: Claire Babrowski runs McDonald's most volatile region, which just might be its best hope for growth', *Chain Leader*, November 2002. Retrieved 7 May 2008 from http://findarticles.com/p/articles/mi_hb5682/is_200211/ai_n23722653.
126. Adbel-Halim, Mustafa, 'Muslims rally against U.S. products, Big Mac feels backlash', *Islam Online*, 8 February 2003. Retrieved 5 May 2008 from http://www.islamonline.net/English/News/2003-02/08/article03.shtml.
127. Streusand, Douglas, 'What does Jihad mean?', *Middle East Quarterly*, September 1997. Retrieved 9 May 2011 from http://www.meforum.org/article/357.
128. Naim, Moises, 'McAtlas shrugged' (interview with McDonald's CEO Jack Greenberg), *Foreign Policy*, May 2001. Retrieved 9 May 2011 from http://www.jstor.org/pss/3183188.
129. Anonymous, 'French farmers bid to banish Big Mac', *BBC News*, 20 August 1999. Retrieved 9 May 2011 from http://news.bbc.co.uk/2/hi/europe/426141.stm.
130. International Labor Organization (2001), 'The Social Impact of Events on the Hotel and Tourism Sector of Events Subsequent to 11 September 2001', Geneva. www.ilo.org/public/English/dialogue/sector/techmeet/imhct01/imhctbp.pdf.
131. Pallister, David 'Arab boycott of American goods spreads', The *Guardian*, 8 January 2003. Retrieved 9 May 2011 from http://www.guardian.co.uk/international/story/0,3604,870412,00.html.
132. Adbel-Halim, Mustafa, 'Muslims rally against U.S. products, Big Mac feels backlash', *Islam Online*, 8 February 2003. Retrieved 7 May 2008 from http://www.islamonline.net/English/News/2003-02/08/article03.shtml.
133. MacFarquhar, Niel, 'An anti-American boycott is growing in the Arab world', *New York Times*, 10 May 2002. Retrieved 9 May 2011 from http://www.commondreams.org/headlines02/0510-02.htm.
134. Kincheloe, John L., *The Sign of the Burger*, (excerpt). Temple University Press, Philadelphia, PA, USA. Retrieved 9 May 2011 from http://www.temple.edu/tempress/titles/1599_reg.html.
135. Collins, Samuel (1998), 'Book review: James L. Watson, ed., *Golden Arches East: McDonalds in East Asia*', *H-Net.org*. Retrieved 9 May 2011 from http://www.h-net.org/reviews/showpdf.cgi?path=9287903478462.
136. Kincheloe, John L., *The Sign of the Burger*, (excerpt). Temple University Press, Philadelphia, PA, USA. Retrieved 9 May 2011 from http://www.temple.edu/tempress/titles/1599_reg.html.
137. Ritzer, George (2000), *The McDonaldization of Society*. Thousand Oaks, CA: 3rd edn, Pine Forge Press.
138. Collins, Samuel (1998), 'Book review: James L. Watson, ed. *Golden Arches East: McDonalds in East Asia*', *H-Net.org*. Retrieved 9 May 2011 from http://www.h-net.org/reviews/showpdf.cgi?path=9287903478462.
139. Friedman, Thomas (2000), *The Lexus and the Olive Tree: Understanding Globalization*. New York: Anchor Press.
140. Thrupkaew, Noy (2003), 'Big-Mac Attack, The American Prospect', January 2003. Retrieved 9 May 2011 from http://www.prospect.org/cs/articles?article=mac_attack.
141. Naim, Moises (2001), 'McAtlas shrugged' (interview with McDonald's CEO Jack Greenberg), *Foreign Policy*, May 2001. Retrieved 9 May 2011 from http://www.jstor.org/pss/3183188.
142. Anonymous, 'Working Time Needed to Buy a Big Mac', *The Economist*, 9 May 2011. Retrieved 5 May 2008 from http://www.economist.com/markets/bigmac/displayStory.cfm?story_id=2054313.

7

Cross-cultural market research

As Craig and Douglas (p. 625) state:[1]

Cross-cultural research is a complex and time-consuming undertaking, but extremely important to the advancement of knowledge about consumption behaviour and understanding of the limits and range of consumer behaviour theories.

Well-planned cross-cultural market research can be extremely insightful; however, poorly planned research can not only be a waste of time, but extremely detrimental to a company which acts on it. For instance, a European syrup maker ordered a survey of the Swedish syrup market from a large international market research company. Unfortunately, syrup, a solution of sugar dissolved in water and flavoured with fruit juice, was incorrectly translated as *blandsaft*, a Swedish term for concentrated fruit juice, a local substitute for syrup with much less sugar. Thus, when the results came in, they were of no use, because it was a local product rather than the product category at large that had been surveyed. This simple translation mistake may have cost the company the money allocated to the research, but had they not discovered the mistake and acted on an answer to the wrong question, it could have cost them dearly in market share as well.

Market research is about timely, relevant information. For instance, the simultaneous launch of new products into several different national markets requires research to be undertaken in multiple locations at the same time. Typical research questions may be similar to the following:

1. How should one undertake a market survey for instant coffee in a traditionally tea-drinking country like the United Kingdom or Japan? What information and data must be sought? How should the data be collected?
2. Which information-gathering technique should be used for personal care products in a country where, for instance, potential respondents resent interviews as an intrusion into their privacy, or female members of a household are not permitted to talk to strangers?
3. How should a questionnaire be translated and adapted to the cultural specificity of other countries when the starting point is a questionnaire that was originally designed for a specific country?

Even slight differences in the research question may require a different emphasis or even a different research technique to uncover the required answers. For instance, we might want to know how to increase market share, but we need to make sure that the problem (and not just the symptom) is correctly specified. Using instant coffee as an example, we might ask one of the following:

1. How can we recover the market share lost by instant coffee to ground coffee in a traditionally coffee-drinking country? This requires the investigation of consumption patterns in certain social and family situations, and the times at which people drink specific coffee-based beverages.
2. How can we increase the market share for instant coffee out of the total hot beverages market in a traditionally tea-drinking country? This requires an in-depth investigation of market segments that are likely to drink coffee in at least some consumption situations.

When contrasting countries or cultural regions, the objectives cannot simply be the same as those for domestic market research. Differences in cultural assumptions complicate the questions we need to ask, the methods we need to use to answer the questions and, potentially, our interpretation of the answers. Therefore, establishing the quality of research instruments, consistency of behavioural/attitudinal constructs and equivalence of samples are of paramount concern to the marketer.

The first section in this chapter discusses the local marketing environment and infrastructure (Section 7.1) that need to be considered in marketing research decisions. Then, the main limits to cross-cultural equivalency in market research are described and discussed to provide some basic insights as to how to solve these problems, including conceptual and functional equivalence (Section 7.2), translation problems (Section 7.3), measurement equivalence (Section 7.4), the comparability of samples and sampling procedures (Section 7.5), as well as potential problems with equivalence due to interviewers' and respondents' attitudes towards surveys (Section 7.6). The final section (Section 7.7) discusses whether international market research should use a different approach from traditional, positivistic market research techniques.

7.1
Local marketing institutions and infrastructures

Observers of local marketing environments need to remember the lesson of the Schrödinger's cat experiment – namely, that the observation or measurement of something in itself affects an outcome. In layman's terms, the experiment's conclusion is that a cat in a sealed box is *both* alive and dead until someone observes it. There is always a reference point that makes judgements about others implicitly comparative. For example, when local people fail to understand or appreciate the value of the interviewing process in market research, we might do either of the following: a) try to understand their viewpoint, and gain useful information about how products and services are used by local people, or b) judge them as uneducated and dismiss the value to be gained from this insight (an ethnocentric perspective).

Managers need to consider the whole marketing process, using a series of steps or processes that need to be applied locally, in preparing for decisions (market research), developing strategy, and implementing it (e.g., advertising campaigns or placing the product in distribution channels). However, the feasibility of marketing decisions and details of their execution are affected by local marketing institutions and infrastructures. Consequently, market research is needed to provide accurate information to decision-makers.

Market research can be undertaken in most countries of the world, and international marketers will find subsidiaries of major international market research organizations or local or regional companies that offer good research services almost everywhere. While the multinational firms may not offer the full range of services in developing nations, the list of services is expanding every year. In the case of China, the lead-up to the 2008 Olympics in China created a dramatic increase in the number of marketing research firms and services being offered, at least in the major cities. Since then, marketing research sales have consistently grown from an estimated $6880 million in 2010 to $7506 million in 2011 and $8589 in 2012, despite the global financial crisis.[2] Further, in almost every country around the world, companies are collecting digital information over the Internet and using this to uncover patterns in the behaviour of potential customers. However, the interpretation of this data is not straightforward.

The feasibility of marketing decisions and details of their execution are affected by local marketing institutions and infrastructures, including the socioeconomic, regulatory systems and cultural systems. Burgess and Steenkamp (pp. 341–4)[3] describe these as:

1. Socioeconomic systems including macroeconomic and demographic characteristics, heterogeneity within countries, as well as social, political and economic change.
2. Regulatory systems including formal rules, levels of conformity and sanctions.
3. Cultural systems including the shared interpretive processes and understanding that influences beliefs, attitudes, habits, norms and behaviours.

Differences in these systems need to be considered when deciding the goals of the research, the information that needs to be collected and the way in which it is collected. For instance, the socioeconomic systems influence the target markets and importance of factors, such as household income and access to consumers. Regulatory systems influence the way in which we conduct marketing research and, in a broader sense, how we implement marketing strategies, but it also influences the rights of consumers and their expectations. Cultural systems influence almost every aspect of marketing and market research, and respondents' perceptions about, and acceptance of, marketing research as an objective, anonymous process are far less flexible and rapid. The more apparent and more subtle influences of culture are elaborated throughout this chapter.

Local marketing styles

Before we discuss the technicalities of conducting market research internationally, we need to consider differences in beliefs or assumptions about its role and the type of information considered to be vital for decision making. While the sheer number of marketing research firms and expenditure on marketing research worldwide attests to the importance placed on this function, there are marked differences in the localized or predominant approach in different cultures and the associated company turnover. For instance, it is estimated that there will be almost 6,000 marketing research and public opinion polling firms in the US, turning over US$16,900 million in 2012, whereas it is estimated that there will be over 2,812 firms in Japan with a relatively smaller turnover of US$6,117 million.[4]

Website link 7.1

Search for global and local marketing research firms to examine their offerings. Explore ESOMAR, a worldwide organization promoting better research into markets, consumers and societies: http://www.esomar.org.

Quite apart from its technicalities, which are explained at great length in specialist textbooks, market research is a human activity that generally involves interviewers/researchers and informants/respondents as human beings. The kind of neutral, objective stance that is required from informants, who must speak their true mind without any influence from the interviewer, is difficult enough to find in countries

where market research, polls and panels are well established. It is all the more difficult to find in many local environments, where willingness to answer or, more generally, to deliver information to strangers is low, since interviewers are seen to be hidden sellers or impolite intruders. Similarly, motivation to answer will be low when there is no local belief that answering benefits consumers as a community, because the feedback loop that links consumer research information to product improvement and to personal interest is uncertain and complex.

The Japanese style of market research

Japanese firms use market survey techniques that are quite distinct from those used by US companies.[5] While the Japanese companies *do* survey markets, they often make decisions fairly independently of the survey conclusions. For example, research was presented to Akio Morita, founder and president of the Sony Corporation, which suggested that the Walkman would not be bought by consumers: they would not buy a tape player that does not record, even a portable one. Trusting his intuition, though undoubtedly after fairly wide consultation, Akio Morita and Sony took the decision to launch the Walkman, with the success we all know about. Japanese firms tend to take a more direct interest in the realities of the marketplace and outlets. They look for information from the actual *buyers* (not the potential consumers), who are interviewed about the products they want, and how the products themselves could be better tailored to consumers' needs. The chief executive officer of Canon USA spent six weeks visiting Canon distribution neworks, chatting to sales executives, customers and store managers, in order to find out why Canon cameras were not selling as well as the competition. As Johansson and Nonaka emphasize (p. 16):

Japanese-style market research relies heavily on two kinds of information: 'soft data' obtained from visits to dealers and other channel members, and 'hard data' about shipments, inventory levels, and retail sales. Japanese managers believe that these data better reflect the behaviour and intentions of flesh-and-blood consumers. Japanese companies want information that is context specific rather than context free – that is, data directly relevant to consumer attitudes about the product, or to the way buyers have used or will use specific products, rather than research results that are too remote from the actual consumer to be useful.[5]

This attitude is quite different from the prescriptions of traditional market research, which are as follows:

1. Market research should be representative; therefore a representative sample must be used.
2. Market research must be scientifically objective. A questionnaire should be administered by non-participating researchers, who should not be personally involved in the consequences of the responses given by interviewees.
3. Research should study the *potential* market, not the *actual* market (real buyers and real users).
4. As far as possible, the people who undertake market research should not be the same people who ultimately decide on the marketing strategy to be adopted. There is a potential danger that the boss of Canon USA could be manipulated by customers and distributors, who might take the opportunity to demand lower prices or other benefits by overstating competitors' strengths. There is also the risk that by focusing on the actual market, as yet untargeted market segments could be ignored or neglected.

Market research as images of reality: atomistic versus organic views

In fact, market surveys are, at best, 'photographs' of the market; they are not the market itself. At the Los Angeles County Museum of Art, there is a painting by the Belgian painter René Magritte, called *La pipe*. It simply shows a pipe, with a thin trail of smoke coming out of it. That is (almost) all. There is a short subtitle at the bottom of the painting, saying '*ceci n'est pas une pipe*' ('this is not a pipe'): a very 'down to earth' way of reminding us that *images of reality* should not be confused with reality itself. We may create images of reality, especially through the media (for instance, a war reported on a TV screen), but we may also ignore large chunks of reality (especially its experiential elements).

On the other hand, we should not underestimate the power of the process of designing images of reality, especially for decision-making purposes. Scientific market research provides marketing decision makers with an image of the actual and/or potential market, consumer behaviour and the competition. Large parts of reality are beyond our limited perceptual apparatus. We may derive images of the market from panels or representative samples that we will never match simply by talking with anyone who is around.

Across countries, marketing decision makers do not use exactly the same information for a similar decision process, as, to a certain extent, culture influences the scope and nature of researched information, and the use of the results in the process of marketing decision making. Two basic approaches to reality may be contrasted as archetypal: the atomistic and the organic approaches (see Table 7.1). In terms of research traditions, the atomistic view is close to the more remote positivistic research, whereas the organic view is nearer to humanistic enquiry.[6,7]

In the atomistic view, we consider ourselves as being outside the real world, as observers, able to depict with a certain degree of precision workable images of the real world (atomistic), and then use them to interact with this external world. The atomistic approach leads us to consider reality as fundamentally divisible into units that display enough

Table 7.1 Atomistic versus organic approaches

Approach to reality	Atomistic	Organic
Nature of reality	Divisibility/independence	Global/indivisible/dependent
Time	Linear/divisible	Cyclical/integrative
Communication style	Explicit/low context	Implicit/high context
Interpersonal relations	Individualist/reciprocal	Collectivist/loyal
Intellectual style	Data/measurement oriented	Intellectual modesty
Proof	Validated theory (truth)	Virtue/conviction
Space	Universalist	Localist
Decision making	Formalized	Weakly structured

independence that, we can ignore the interrelations between pieces of it, operationally.

Conversely, we may consider ourselves as an integral part of the reality, to which we belong so inextricably that it is not really possible to separate from this reality. We are so deeply immersed in it that it would make no sense. The organic approach assumes the indivisible nature of reality, its elements (if there are any) being fundamentally interdependent. Reality is global, rather than piecemeal.

These two approaches are complementary rather than antagonistic. However, one approach can be dominant among a group of people or a culture, or in an individual or an area of knowledge.[8] Table 7.1, which builds on Chapters 2 and 3, illustrates how these approaches are linked to major categories of cultural differences, although the difference between atomism and organism is not a cultural one.

The atomistic belief in *divisibility* favours the view that time is divisible, that the basic unit of interpersonal relations is the individual, and that communication can and must be explicit (that is, clearly separated, 'divided' from surrounding issues, topics and preoccupations). Separating emotions from actions, friendship from business, is typically an atomistic attitude towards reality, seen as divisible. Very naturally, the atomistic approach favours the perception that data orientation and measurement are the proof that a piece of reality is divisible and (therefore) exists. To illustrate the importance of measurement in the atomistic approach, let us think about a company trying to improve service *within* the company, so that it is not only frontline service providers who are concerned with service to customers. In addressing such an issue, a typical atomistic statement would be: 'To arrive at a position where excellent service is achieved will be a difficult enterprise. This primarily results from the lack of service measurement knowledge *within* the company.' The atomistic solution is to try and develop a measurement instrument, because the reality of within-company service cannot be tackled in the absence of measurement instruments.

On the other hand, a dominance of the organic approach favours collectivism in its strongest sense: people do not consider themselves as being separate from the group to which they belong. Their sense of belonging includes the implicit view that they are not really separable from their group. The communication

style is more implicit and contextual, because the sense of the interdependence of pieces of reality is much stronger. In interpersonal relationships, loyalty is characteristic of the organic approach. Rather than searching for proof (in terms of a measured piece of reality), the organic approach is based on observation and arguments favouring conviction.

With divisible reality, linear time and individual emphasis, the atomistic approach conceives of decision making as a highly formalized process, followed by implementation, control and feedback. It follows a time sequence, such as we see in many marketing and managerial textbooks. Conversely, the organic approach emphasises circularity in time and the integration of time horizons. Preparing, making decisions and implementing them are not easily seen as completely separated pieces of time reality, leading to a fairly unstructured decision-making process. Finally, the organic approach favours 'localism', local solutions, because solutions are built within a context and there is a difficulty in conceiving universal solutions. Conversely, the data and theory orientation in the atomistic approach favours universalism, because reality, when reduced to figures, shows a fairly high degree of universality.

7.2

Equivalence in cross-cultural research

It is not self-evident, as the Japanese style of market research shows, that research procedures and the type of data sought are completely independent of the cultural context of the researcher. However, if 'hard' or atomistic data are sought, especially across cultures, the main difference between domestic and cross-cultural market research lies in the difficulty in establishing equivalence at the various stages of the research process, to enable comparisons to be made. The complexity of the research design is greatly increased when working in an international, multicultural and multilinguistic environment.

Research approaches: emic versus etic

The classic distinction in cross-cultural research approaches is between *emic* and *etic*, which derive from linguistics, where phon*etic* is universal and depicts universal sounds that are common to several languages, and phon*emic* stresses unique sound patterns in languages.[9,10] The emic approach to market research holds that attitudinal or behavioural phenomena are expressed in a way unique in each culture. Taken to its extreme, this approach states that no comparisons are possible. This approach requires researchers to become very familiar with the target culture through the use of observation, participation and other ethnographic methodologies. The etic approach, on the other hand, is primarily concerned with identifying universals. Of course, there is middle ground, where some local adaptation is possible (adapted etics) and some common models can be found through the use of multiple emic studies (linked emic approach).[11]

Market research measurement instruments adapted to each national culture (the emic approach) may offer more reliability and provide data with greater internal validity than tests applicable to several cultures (the etic approach, or 'culture-free tests'). However, the use of such instruments is at the expense of cross-cultural comparability and external validity, as the results are not generalizable to other cultural contexts. If we want to directly compare across cultural contexts using an emic approach, we need to first examine cross-cultural equivalence at several stages in the process, and management must make decisions about which approach (domestic or international) will provide the necessary information. It is only after a clear and concise statement of the research problem that a precise plan can be outlined.

However, changes may still have to be made during the process, which highlight the importance of staged decision making. For instance, when a food-related lifestyle instrument that had been developed in Western Europe was administered in Singapore, the researchers discovered that the context was not equivalent, and changes were required to the planned etic approach. They found marked differences attributed to (a) different cooking patterns in Singapore, where the use of maids and eating out are more prevalent, (b) lower involvement in cooking, (c) a broader concept of convenience, (d) different beliefs in health properties of food, and (e) different use of information in the highly competitive Singaporean food sector.[12]

Levels of cross-cultural equivalence

Different types of cross-cultural equivalence are displayed in Table 7.2. They are explained in the following text, under the six main categories and outlined in the table.

Conceptual equivalence

A basic issue in cross-cultural research is the determination of whether the concepts have similar meaning across the social units studied. The same construct (e.g., innovativeness) may be relevant across cultures, but interpreted or expressed in different ways. Problems of *conceptual equivalence* are frequent when

Table 7.2 Categories of cross-cultural equivalence

A. Conceptual equivalence	B. Functional equivalence
C. Translation equivalence ■ Lexical ■ Idiomatic ■ Grammatical–syntactical ■ Experiential	D. Measure equivalence ■ Perceptual ■ Metric ■ Calibration ■ Temporal
E. Sample equivalence ■ Sampling unit	F. Data collection equivalence ■ Respondents' cooperation

(Source: Adapted from Craig C., Samuel and Susan P. Douglas, *International Marketing Research*.[13] *Consumer Behavior*, 4th edn, Craig C. Samuel and Susan P. Douglas, 2001, © John Wiley & Sons Limited, reprinted with permission.)

examining consumer behaviour across cultures. For instance, the hypothesis that people do not willingly behave inconsistently may hold true in the United States, but not in some other countries. For instance, in East Asian collectivist cultures, people are seen as more mature if they can overcome their internal attitudes and emotions and act in a manner that is appropriate to the situation whereas, in many individualist cultures, people are seen as more mature if they act on their internal attitudes and emotions in a consistent manner.[14]

Reaching true conceptual equivalence between cultures can be extremely difficult. As anthropologist Clifford Geertz (p. 59) notes:

The Western conception of a person as a bounded, unique, more or less integrated, motivational and cognitive universe, a dynamic center of awareness, emotions, judgement and action, organized in a distinctive whole . . . is, however incorrigible it may seem, a rather peculiar idea, within the context of world's cultures.[15]

Such basic concepts as beauty, youth, friendliness, wealth, well-being, sex appeal, and so on, are often used in market research questionnaires where motivation for buying many products is related to self-image, interaction with other people in a particular society, and social values. At first glance, they seem universal. However, it is always advisable to question the conceptual equivalence of all these basic words when designing a cross-cultural survey questionnaire. Even the very concept of 'household', widely used in market research, is subject to possible inequivalence across cultures: in Northern Nigeria, people often live in large extended family compounds or *gida*, something which is very different from the prevalent concept of the nuclear family in most western cultures.[16]

Many of the practical difficulties in dealing with conceptual equivalence are grounded in the cultural assumptions discussed in Part 1 of this book. For instance, the concept of 'waiting in line' (to be served) may be very different for cultures that see time as economic and those that do not, as the whole concept of time is very different. This may shed light on the reason Americans are willing to pay more for items that are available for immediate consumption than Singaporeans.[17] This insight would be lost if we simply compared willingness to pay, as the conceptual equivalence of several basic interrelated constructs has to be questioned.

Box 7.1 shows some construct equivalence problems in the case of life insurance policies.

Generally speaking, conceptual equivalence is an obstacle to the direct use of constructs that have been specifically designed for Western cultures. The perceived risk construct, for instance, may differ in its components across cultures. As mentioned in Chapter 5, perceived risk has to be broken down into several sub-dimensions, including psychological, financial, performance, physical, social and time or convenience risk.[18] The emphasis placed on these sub-dimensions may vary across cultures. For instance, people in some cultures may give more value to the social risk of buying a car, because their purchase and use of the car is mostly status oriented, whereas in other cultures, people may be more concerned with physical safety because death in accidents is greatly feared. Further, it would be important to know if it was the perceptions of risk in the specific situation or the more generalized attitude toward risk that differed. Chinese students are less risk-averse than Americans; however, the difference is in the perceptions of the risk, rather than the attitude towards perceived risk.[19]

It is necessary to investigate – far more frequently than is actually done – the construct validity in each target culture, when cross-cultural consumer behaviour is being studied. The construct validity is affected by both construct bias and equivalency issues. Bias occurs when the definition of the construct differs across cultures influencing construct validity (e.g., lack of consideration of the extended family in measuring intergenerational influence across countries), whereas equivalency relates to the level of comparison or measurement of the construct.[20] The validity of the underlying constructs at the conceptual level and reliability at the empirical/measurement instrument level should be tested by following recognized procedures, as outlined in the sections below.

Functional equivalence: similar products and activities performing different functions

Functional equivalence focuses on whether the concepts have the same role or function across groups. If similar activities perform different functions in different societies, their measures should not be used for the purpose of comparison. Concepts frequently used

Box 7.1

A multinational survey on life insurance: conceptual equivalence problems in Islamic countries

Muslim people do not fear death. On the contrary, they appear much less frightened by the prospect of death than most people in Western/Christian countries. The notion of destiny is of great importance, as humans do not decide about their own death, nor are they entitled to control the process of it. One cannot challenge the course of destiny, and therefore should not speculate on one's own life and death. A verse of the Koran says something like this: 'Behave each day as if your life will be very long, and for your after life, behave as if you will die tomorrow.' In Saudi Arabia, life insurance is forbidden. But some high-risk industries, such as oil production, bypass this prohibition by insuring their local employees through foreign life-insurance companies, with policies located abroad.

In the Islamic world, people are less focused on the long term. Effort must be rewarded quickly, if it is to be maintained. The concept of a financial product, such as life insurance, is less popular as it requires a long-term focus and a strong individual capacity to imagine the future. Projection towards the future is a culture-related trait (see Chapter 2). In Islam you may certainly imagine how you will be tomorrow, but not at a particular place or moment. The future tense exists, but it is not as 'accurate' or meticulous as that of the English or European languages. Moreover, protection of the family and solidarity within the extended family are highly valued and work effectively. If a man dies, his brother should care for his wife and children.

The concept of life insurance is related to culture in at least the following four aspects: protection of the family and/or the individual; future orientation; betting on one's own life and death; the degree of solidarity in the family and extended family group. In terms of doing market research on life insurance, the prevalent cultural assumptions need to be taken into consideration.

In most Islamic countries, it is important to use local interviewers (often of the same gender), who have a thorough personal knowledge of Islam and the local culture (the Islamic world spreads from black Africa to China). Local interviewers less likely to offend potential respondents and more likely to understand contextual information. In-depth, non-directive interviews and focus groups are likely to provide better information than quantitative surveys, as fewer people are familiar and comfortable with the use of scale questions to express their inner thoughts and personal opinions.

Some of the research questions that should be addressed before the preparation of a marketing strategy include:

■ What is the appropriate mix of benefits in the design of the life insurance policies offered to potential consumers (e.g., death benefits being the amount paid on death versus annuities being a series of regular payments based on the premiums previously paid)?
■ What term(s) should be proposed before policy holders receive the benefits of their life insurance policy?
■ How should the beneficiaries be designated?
■ How should the offer be communicated to potential consumers through advertisement. Which brand name should be adopted and which themes and advertising style should be favoured in the advertising campaign?

in market surveys, such as preparing a meal, are not necessarily functionally equivalent across countries. Functional equivalence problems can be illustrated taking the example of hot milk-based chocolate drinks.[21] While in Australia, the US and the UK, milk-based drinks are generally considered an evening drink, best before going to sleep, in much of Latin America a '*Chocolate Caliente*' is a morning drink. In this case, functional equivalence is not reached. This is due to differences in the consumption time period and in the purpose for use: waking/energizer versus sleep/relaxer. Similarly, functional equivalence will be a problem if we compare bicycle purchases in China, where they are used mainly for transportation, with other countries, where they are mainly used for leisure.[22]

Similarly, a watch may be used as jewellery, a status symbol, or an instrument for handling time and daily schedules. The same holds true for a fountain pen. In some countries, its function may be as a simple, general-purpose writing instrument; in others it may be regarded mostly as an instrument for signing documents. Elsewhere it may be considered purely non-functional, since it needs time and care to refill it, and often stains. Many other examples could be given, such as wine (everyday beverage accompanying meals versus beverage for special occasions), beer (summer refresher versus all-year standard 'non-water' beverage), mixed spirit drinks (a man's versus a woman's drink) and perfumes (masking bodily odours versus adding a pleasant smell after a shower).

The simple word 'coffee' covers a whole range of beverages that are enjoyed in very different social settings (at home, at the workplace, during leisure time, in the morning, or at particular times during the day), in quite different forms (in terms of quantity, concentration, with or without milk, cold or hot), prepared from different forms of coffee base (beans, ground beans, instant). The function of the Brazilian *cafezinho*, very small cups of strong coffee drunk regularly in informal exchanges with colleagues, cannot be compared with that of the weaker American coffee, which is consumed in large cups and drunk mostly at home, while in transit or in restaurants. Similarly, the meaning and even the uses of coffee in the Haya community of Tanzania are in fact significantly different to those of the global economy.[23]

Website link 7.2

Search for differences in the way food is consumed internationally, such as this site that discusses different styles of coffee drinking: http://www.talkaboutcoffee.com/coffee-culture-in-asia.html.

One of the best ways to investigate functional equivalence is to examine the social settings in which a product is consumed. Local observational methods and focus groups are commonly employed for this purpose.

7.3

Translation equivalence

Translation equivalence focuses on whether the language is understood by respondents as having the same meaning in different cultures. For the many reasons outlined in Chapter 4 on language, culture and communication, translation techniques, no matter how sophisticated, may be incapable of achieving full comparability of data. Following is a small review of potential translation equivalence problems.

Website link 7.3

Search for translations gone awry, such as this site that lists some humorous examples of translation mistakes: **http://www.clickz.com/clickz/column/2036234/marketing-translation-mistakes-learn**.

Categories of translation equivalence

Translation equivalence may be divided into the following subcategories:

1. *Lexical equivalence*: This is what dictionaries can provide us with: for instance, one may discover that the English adjective *warm* translates into the French *chaud*.

2. *Idiomatic equivalence*: The problem of idiomatic equivalence comes when you try to translate a sentence such as 'it's warm': French has two expressions for it, either '*il fait chaud*' (literally, 'it makes warm' meaning 'it's warm [today]') or '*c'est chaud*' (meaning 'it [this object] is warm'). An idiom is a linguistic usage that is natural to native speakers. Idioms are most often non-equivalent: the present continuous (i.e. I am *doing*) has no equivalent in French, except *je suis en train de . . .* , which is highly colloquial, not to be used in correct French written language. This may also be problematic for regions within a country, as Roy *et al.* (p. 207) state:

   The English phrase 'high risk' can be translated as '*qiang feng xian*' in the middle and northern China but as '*gao feng xian*' in southern China. To Chinese from the south, the word '*qiang*' has two meanings, one is related to the 'magnitude' and the other to 'strength'; as such, it can be difficult to interpret the concept '*qiang feng xian*'.[22]

3. *Grammatical–syntactical equivalence*: This refers to the way words are ordered, sentences are constructed and meaning is expressed in language. English generally proceeds in an active way, starting with the subject, followed by the verb and then the complement, avoiding abstractions as well as convoluted sentences. Many languages, including German and French, start by explaining the circumstances in relative clauses, before they proceed into the action. This makes for complex sentences starting with relative clauses based on *when*, *where*, *even though*, *although*, and so on. The Japanese language has a quite different ordering of words from Western languages: verbs are always at the end of the sentence: '*Gurunoburu no daigaku no sensei desu*' means: 'Grenoble of [*the*] university of professor [*I*] am', that is, 'I am a professor at the university of Grenoble'.

4. *Experiential equivalence*: This is about what words and sentences mean for people in their everyday experience. Coming back to '*chaud*', it translates into two English words 'warm' and 'hot': the French do not experience 'warmth' with two concepts as the English, the Germans and many others do. Similarly, the special experience of coldness in the word 'chilly' cannot be adequately rendered in French. Translated terms must refer to real items and real experiences which are familiar in the source as well as the target cultures. An expression such as 'dish-washing machine' may face experiential equivalence problems when people, even if they know what it is, have never actually seen this type of household appliance or experienced it. Another example of experiential non-equivalence

is given by the Japanese numbering system, which reflects a special experience of counting, where the numbers cannot be fully abstracted from the object being counted. Most often, the Japanese add a particle indicating which objects are counted. *Nin*, for instance, is used to count human beings: *yo-nin* is four (persons). *Hiki* is used for counting animals but not birds, for which *wa*, meaning *feather*, is used, *satsu* is used for books, *hon* for round and long objects, *mai* for flat things such as a sheet of paper, textiles, coins, etc., and *hai* for cups and bowls and liquid containers in general. Finally, some concepts have no real equivalent translation, despite how hard translators may try.

As a vivid illustration of translation problems, Box 7.2 shows the translation errors in the case of a major concept, 'reproductive health', for the UN World Conference on Population Development, held in Cairo in 1994. Despite the best efforts of the translators, there was really no way to create an equivalent, stand-alone translation.

Back-translation and related techniques

The back-translation technique is the most widely employed method for reaching translation equivalence (mainly lexical and idiomatic) in cross-cultural research. This procedure helps to identify probable translation errors. One translator translates from the source language (S) into a target language (T). Then another translator, ignorant of the source-language text, translates the first translator's target language

Box 7.2

'Reproductive health'

Cultural discrepancies are not only evidenced in factual themes, they also manifest themselves in translation difficulties: the concept of 'reproductive health' was translated into German as *Gesundheit der Fortpflanzung* (health of propagation). The Arabic translators invented the formula: 'spouses take a break from each other after childbirth', which in despair the Russian translators worded as 'the

whole family goes on holiday' and the Chinese translators elevated themselves to the almost brilliant formula 'a holiday at the farm'. This shows that the new word-monsters, elegantly coined by the Americans, are almost non-translatable worldwide; on the other hand, they provide international conferences with a lot of humour.

(Source: Bohnet.[24])

text (T) back into the source language (S'). Then the two source-language version, (S and S') are compared to prepare the final target-language questionnaire (T$_f$).

For instance, when translating *un repas d'affaires* ('a business meal' in English) from French (T) to Portuguese (S) in the preparation of a questionnaire for Brazil, it is translated as *jantar de negocios*. When back-translated (S'), it becomes a *dîner d'affaires* ('business dinner'). In Brazilian Portuguese, there is no specific expression for *repas d'affaires*. It is either a 'business lunch' (*almoço de negocios*) or a 'business dinner'. One has to choose which situation to elicit in the Brazilian questionnaire: the 'business meal' has to be either at noon or in the evening in the Portuguese version. The researcher (who preferably speaks the source language) and the two translators then discuss the final target-language questionnaire (T$_f$) to resolve any discrepancies. This stage is important, as discrepancies may be substantive, such as the example above, or due to mistakes in either of the two directions. In practice, it is advisable to have one translator who is a native speaker of the target language and the other one a native speaker of the source language. It means that they are translating *into* their native language rather than *from* it (this is always more difficult and less reliable).

However, back-translation can also instil a false sense of security in the investigator by demonstrating a spurious lexical equivalence.[25] Simply knowing that words are equivalent is not enough. It is necessary to know to what extent those literally equivalent words and phrases convey equivalent meanings in the two languages or cultures. Another technique, blind parallel translation, consists of having several translators simultaneously and independently translate from the source language into the target language.[26] The different versions are then compared and a final version is written. This is similar to the collaborative and iterative technique, which engages a committee or expert panel, both at the initial translation stage, as well as the iterative revision translation stage.[27]

Combined translation techniques and limits of translation

Parallel and back-translation can be merged, as shown in Figure 7.1. When two languages and cultures present wide variations, such as Korean and German, combining parallel and back-translation may provide a higher level of equivalence.[21] For example, two Koreans translate the same German questionnaire G into two Korean versions, K1 and K2. A third Korean translator, who is unfamiliar with the original German text G, translates K1 and K2 into G1 and G2. A final Korean questionnaire, K3, is then prepared by comparing the two back-translated German versions G1 and G2. English is used to help compare the versions, as it is widely used and more precise than either German or Korean. Depending on the importance of the issue and distance between languages, this example could be refined, by increasing the number of parallel translations, or the number of independent back-translations.[28]

A more sophisticated solution to the problem of translation is to develop research instruments in the two cultures, and generate items, questions or other survey materials jointly in the two cultures.[29] After the selected translation process is complete (e.g., back-translation), changes are made to both the source and target language wording. This technique is called *decentering*. In the previous example of the French-Portuguese 'business meal', the French version could be changed to a 'business lunch' to be consistent with the Portuguese translation. Of course, the ultimate words and phrases employed will depend

Figure 7.1 Examples of translation techniques

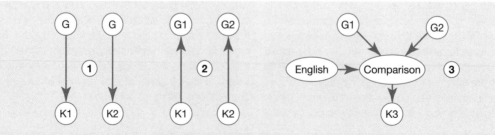

Table 7.3 Advantages and drawbacks of translation techniques

Technique	Direct translation	Back-translation	Parallel translation	Combined techniques
Process	$S \Rightarrow T$	$S \Rightarrow T; T \Rightarrow S'$ comparison S to $S' \Rightarrow$ final version T_f	$S \Rightarrow T; S \Rightarrow T'$ Comparison T to $T' \Rightarrow$ final version T_f	$S \Rightarrow T; S \Rightarrow T'T \Rightarrow S'$; $T' \Rightarrow S''$ comparison S'/S'', decentring of $S \Rightarrow$ final version T_f
Advantages	Easy to implement	Ensures the discovery of most inadequacies	Easier to implement in S country with T translators	Ensures the best fit between source and target versions
Drawbacks/ Constraints	Leads to translation errors and discrepancies between S and T	Requires the availability of two translators, one native in S and one native in T languages	Leads to good wording in T, but does not ensure that specific meaning in S is fully rendered	Costly to implement Difficult to find the translators Implies readiness to change source-language version

Key: S = source language, T = target language (translators or versions).

on which common/similar meaning is sought in both languages simultaneously, without regard to whether words and phrases originate in the source or the target languages.

In any case, it remains absolutely necessary to pre-test the translated research instrument in the target culture until satisfactory levels of reliability on conceptual and measurement equivalences are attained. Table 7.3 presents a synthesis of translation techniques as well as their advantages and drawbacks.

7.4

Measure equivalence

Variations in the reliability of research instruments

After the reliability of existing instruments has been assessed, the next step is to assess the measurement reliability across cultures. Measurement equivalence includes perceptual, metric, calibration and temporal equivalence, as depicted in Table 7.2.

Some types of questions are less likely to be plagued by measurement equivalence than others. It should be easier to obtain measurement equivalence for demographic variables than for psychographic variables such as lifestyles. For psychographic variables,

it may be necessary to use a more in-depth assessment method to gain a better understanding of the variable, as well as potential linkages to products. Semi-structured methods, such as the means-end approach has been suggested as an alternative to more structured approaches. The objective of means-ends is to link concrete product or service attributes to the positive or negative consequences of using the product or service, to personal values or goals.[30] This technique often uses laddering, as it 'guides the respondent up or down the ladder of abstraction, linking relatively concrete meanings at the attribute level, to more abstract meanings at the benefit or personal value level' (p. 706).[31] This technique often begins with the core values, where respondents are asked which values are important in their life. Then, they indicate which of a list of products make the value or feeling possible. Finally, they say how each product facilitates the value or feeling. Using this technique, the broader value of *family security* was associated with both physical safety and financial security, which were found to be associated with very different products: alarm systems through physical safety and mutual funds through financial security).[32] Further this technique is not limited to written and verbal interactions, as visual and other sensory images can be provided in the interview.[33]

Variations in knowledge and familiarity with products, concepts or attitudes also impact on the equivalence of measures. As a less familiar concept, a warranty may be perceived quite differently in China from the United States. In China it may be viewed as an extrinsic cue of little value to the potential buyer. This is caused by their lack of familiarity with, or belief in, the benefits of the concept, whereas it has a very real functional meaning in the United States.[34] Differences in the level of knowledge and familiarity across product categories, or with products from different origin countries, can also lead to differing reliabilities.[35] Parameswaran and Yaprak (pp. 45–6) suggest two alternative courses:

> Measures to be used in cross-national market comparisons may be pre-tested in each of the markets of interest until they elicit similar (and high) levels of reliability . . . Alternatively, one might devise a method to develop confidence interval (akin to statistical spreads based on sample sizes) around the value of the measure based on its reliability.[35]

Perceptual equivalence

As emphasized previously, perception varies across cultures. Colours are perceived differently according to culture – that is, not all cultures have equivalent sensitivity to the various parts of the colour spectrum, and the corresponding languages do not qualify colours in exactly the same way.[36] In addition, the symbolic interpretation of colour varies widely. The same is true for smells: the first issue in equivalence is whether people perceive them physically and mentally in the same manner; the second issue deals with the kind of interpretation they bestow to these smells. When conducting research about sensory products (e.g., perfumes for washing liquids) or sensory elements (e.g., packaging), where perceptive clues are important for product evaluation, questions must be formulated to allow interviewees to express their perceptual views on the smell or the colours. Rather than ask them whether they like a lavender smell, it is better to ask them first to recognize the smell, then to comment on what it evokes.

Metric equivalence

If the scores given by respondents do not have the same meaning, then metric equivalence is a problem. Scores may differ across cultures for a variety of reasons including differences in the interpretation of numerical or verbal anchors, the avoidance of extreme responses, humility or social desirability.[37] Unfortunately, these differences can only be checked after the data are collected, limiting the validity of cross-cultural comparisons. There are several techniques available to researchers to assess metric equivalence, including the popular multiple-group confirmatory factor analysis,[38] and the Rasch measurement approach.[39,40]

The validity of a rating scale in a cross-cultural context is affected by the equivalence of the scales and by the homogeneity of meanings. For instance, the Chinese language does not readily provide good antonyms, which will cause problems with lexical equivalence (see Table 7.4). It is also difficult to

Table 7.4 Adjectives which have the same level of meaning in two languages should provide similar distances between the points of the scale

Colloquial rating scale				Formal rating scale			
US adjectives			**French adjectives**	**US adjectives**			**French adjectives**
Fantastic	20	20	Extraordinaire	Remarkably good	17	17	Très bon
Delightful	17	17	Superbe	Good	14	14	Bon
Pleasant	14	14	Très correct	Neutral	10	10	Moyen
Neutral	10	10	Moyen	Reasonably poor	6	6	Faible
Moderately poor	7	7	Assez faible	Extremely poor			Très mauvais
Bad	4	4	Remarquablement faible				
Horrible	2	2	Terriblement mauvais				

(Source: Pras and Anglemar, p. 76.[41] © March 1978 by ESOMAR® – The World Association of Research Professionals; this article first appeared in *European Research*, published by ESOMAR®.)

Box 7.3

Correspondence analysis

Correspondence analysis can be used to examine the way respondents used the scale points in a survey. In this case, respondents answered 57 (58 for China) items from the Schwartz Values Survey. In the following table, the differences between each row, or scale point, should be equal to 1, if the scores were on an equivalent interval scale. However, this was clearly not the case, with the largest distances appearing at the bottom end of the scale (−1 to 1), and the smallest distances between important (3) and very important (6).

	Notional	New Zealand	United Kingdom	United States	South Korea	China
Opposed to my values	−1	−1	−1	−1	−1	−1
	0	1.71	1.38	0.34	1.94	−0.21
	1	3.29	2.90	1.93	3.21	2.77
	2	4.09	3.57	3.38	4.03	3.48
Important	3	4.83	4.53	4.13	4.64	3.99
	4	5.08	4.81	4.57	4.80	4.35
	5	5.6	5.5	5.32	5.22	5.01
Very important	6	6.42	6.18	6.26	5.77	5.56
Of supreme importance	7	7	7	7	7	7

(Source: Lee and Soutar.[42] Julie Anne Lee and Geoffrey N. Soutar, Is Schwartz's Value Survey an Interval Scale, and Does It Really Matter? *Journal of Cross-Cultural Psychology*, 41(1), pp. 76–86, copyright © 2010 by Sage Publications. Reprinted by Permission of SAGE Publications.)

ensure that the distances between scale points, especially verbal scales, are equivalent across languages (see Box 7.3). While scale anchors, such as 'agree/disagree' and asking about various degrees of importance, might work well for English-speaking managers, they might not work as well in other languages, such as Japanese.[42] As mentioned in the language section, it is naive to translate scales lexically (simply with dictionary-equivalent words); rather they must be translated for equivalence of meaning. Reaching equivalence of meaning may require the original wording to be 'decentred' in order to obtain reliable and valid data for all the countries under survey.

As an example, the metric equivalence of nine scale terms (from 'excellent' to 'very bad') across eight languages (English, Arabic, Chinese, Farsi, French, German, Korean and Spanish) reveals that: (1) some languages have fewer terms to express gradation in evaluation (e.g., Korean), whereas others have a multitude (French); and (2) there are large discrepancies in the 'value' of these adjectives, measured on a scale from 0 to 100. For instance, the Spanish '*muy malo*' rates 58 per cent higher than its supposed English equivalent of 'very bad'.[43] Therefore, the best solution is not to simply translate scale terms, but rather to start from local wordings based on scales used by local researchers. Further, we need to be wary about the meaning of numbers across cultures. For instance, the numbers 2, 8 and 9 are considered lucky in China and as such may be chosen more frequently.[21] Thus, it may be advisable in some cultures to number only the end points.

One promising avenue for cross-cultural research is the use of purely visual scales that avoid the verbo-centric nature of most market research instruments, which are based on words and sentences that never translate perfectly. Perhaps 'putting people back in' is best: most communication relies on images and is non-verbal, whereas thinking processes rely on metaphors to elicit hidden knowledge.[33] Instruments that allow respondents to express the mix between emotions and reason may be more useful. The use of 'smiling faces' as scales should not be limited to children, on the basis of the (unconscious) view that adults *should* use words, not pictures, and should not express their views metaphorically. Visual and verbal representations of the overlap between a person's self-identity and the identity of the group increase

Table 7.5 The SVBWS task

Most Important		Least Important
○	Successful, capable, ambitious.	●
●	Protecting the environment, a world of beauty, unity with nature.	○
○	Helpful, honest, forgiving.	○
○	Devout, accepting portion in life, humble.	○
○	Clean, national security, social order.	○

equivalence across cultures.[44] More sophisticated, visually oriented scales, such as the self-assessment manikin (SAM), allow cross-cultural measurement with less bias than verbal scales; they further enable a better apprehension of the respondents' emotions.[45]

Another promising research method is the best–worst scaling (BWS) proposed by Jordan Louviere and colleagues (see Marley and Louviere[46] for a more formal discussion of BWS, including formal proof of the measurement properties associated with different cognitive processes that respondents might use to make best and worst choices). This method was recently applied to measure Kahle's[47] List of Values and Schwartz[48] values (see Lee *et al.*[49,50]). A sample set from the Schwartz Value Best Worst Survey (SVBWS) is shown in Table 7.5.

Best Worst Scaling (BWS) simply requires a respondent to choose one item that is the best/largest/most-x and one that is the worst/smallest/least-x from a series of sets that contain different combinations of a larger master set of items. The particular combinations that appear in each set are determined by an experimental design to ensure balanced appearance and co-appearance across the sets. BWS assumes respondents behave as if they examine every pair of items or options in each set and then choose the most distinct or maximally different pair. Respondents find it relatively easy to choose the *most* and *least* within a set; however, the repetition for large numbers of items can be problematic.

Further, the BWS method has the potential to reduce response-style effects, as respondents cannot consistently use the middle points, end points, or one end of a scale. It also has the potential to reduce problems with equivalence, due to the difficulty in finding lexically equivalent verbal descriptions for a scale, metrically equivalent distances between numbers, and separating numbers from their meanings. The BWS method only has two verbal scale terms (e.g., most important and least important); it is relatively easy to find equivalent terms for 'most' and 'least' in most languages. The BWS method also has no numbers, which eliminates problems found when numbers have meanings in certain cultures, such as 2, 8 or 9 being lucky and 4 unlucky in China. Finally, the BWS method results in a relative score based on multiple measurements within different item contexts.[50]

Calibration equivalence

Calibration equivalence problems arise from different *basic* units being used as well as from *compound units* when they are based on different computation systems. For instance, a typical calibration equivalence problem relates to differences in monetary units; this is especially true in high-inflation contexts where daily prices over a year cannot be directly compared with those of a low-inflation country. Naturally, exchange rates and units of weight, distance and volume cause calibration equivalence problems. Calibration equivalence mixes with perceptual equivalence: for instance, how many colour classes are recognized by people from a particular country? This might prove useful for a packaging test or a product test. Western subjects, for example, have more colour classes than African subjects, and some primitive people have only a two-term colour language. The Bantu of South Africa, for example, do not distinguish between blue and green. Consequently they do not discriminate between objects or symbols in these colours.[51]

Website link 7.4

Search for threats to calibration equivalence, such as the following website, which lists inflation rates; Venezuela hit the highest in 2011 with almost 29 per cent: **http://www.tradingeconomics.com/ inflation-rates-list-by-country.**

Temporal equivalence

Temporal equivalence is similar to calibration equivalence, in terms of calibrating dates and time periods. Information, for instance, ages at different speeds across countries: in a country where the annual inflation rate is minimal, income and price data are comparable across years, whereas in a Latin American country such as Venezuela with a 20 per cent annual inflation rate in 2007, it is necessary to indicate on which day the data were collected and what the price indexes and exchange rates were at that time.

Temporal equivalence also deals with differences in development levels and technological advancement: certain countries are 'equivalent' to what others were 20 years ago. Assessing time lags may be useful for making analogies: such a market may develop in South Africa now as it did in the United States 15 or 20 years ago, and the product life cycle may be similar even though the two countries are at different points on the curve.

7.5

Comparability of samples

When secondary data – especially published statistical data – are sought, there may be some difficulties in comparing these data across countries:

1. Differences in categories: for instance, for age brackets, income brackets or professions.
2. Difference in base years, when some countries have no recent data.
3. Unavailable or unreliable data, the data collection procedure by the local census bureau being biased for certain reasons (non-exhaustive census, inadequate sampling procedure).
4. Sampling unit (who should the respondent be?).

Choice of respondents (sampling unit equivalence)

An important criterion for sampling is the choice of respondents. Selecting a unit of analysis is a key issue in the conceptualization of comparative research designs. The role of respondents in the buying decision process (organizational buying, family buying,

information and influence patterns, etc.) may vary across countries. Several studies have found differing parental influence over children's purchases across countries. For instance, parents have a greater influence over their children's purchasing in Fiji,[52] Japan[53] and Thailand,[54] when compared to the United States. In the United States it is not uncommon for children to have a strong influence when buying cereals, desserts, toys or other items, whereas in countries that are less child-centred, children's influence on the buying decision will be much smaller. It is therefore crucially important to first assess the basic equivalence of sampling units. This statement is as relevant for industrial markets as for consumer goods markets: when researching industrial products, it is important to compare the position, role and responsibility of industrial buyers throughout different countries.

Website link 7.5

Search for information about sampling techniques and examples of poor sampling and bias: **http://www.marketresearchworld.net/** or **http://www.aapor.org/Bad_Samples1.htm**.

The main problem in the cross-cultural sampling process is the selection of comparable samples across countries. Sampling is a basic step in most market surveys. A complete census, where the whole population of interest is researched, generally proves too costly. More often, we infer the characteristics of the whole population from a limited sample. In this process, the following tasks must be carried out:

1. Finding a sampling frame or list, where the basic population characteristics are known (a telephone directory, an electoral list, etc.).
2. Drawing a sample from this frame, by a method which may be either probabilistic or non-probabilistic.
3. Checking that the selected sample is representative of the population under study.

In cross-cultural research, there are often two levels of sampling to consider. The first level is a sample of countries or cultures and the second level is based on samples of individuals within the chosen countries or cultures. Reaching perfect comparability at either level is difficult, if not impossible, which means that results must be considered with this limitation in mind.

Representativeness and comparability of national/cultural samples

At the first level, the research question is usually focused on directly comparing across countries or cultures. While a list of countries exists, it is rare for companies to draw a random sample, from this list. More often samples are purposefully chosen to represent the markets of interest, or a selection of maximally different countries, in an attempt to compute the average influence of cultural values on certain consumption patterns. At this level country characteristics, such as socio-demographic, economic and cultural variables, may be related to the per capita consumption of a particular product or service. For instance, national wealth was found to explain most of the variance in country-level adoption of technology, such as mobile phones, cable television, computers and the Internet, across 26 developed countries.[55] Similarly, the evaluation of brand manufacturer websites was related to the countries' legal systems, individualism and their level of national identity, across 23 countries.[56] This type of information can guide strategic marketing decisions related to the selection of national target markets, including the identification of markets with low actual demand, but high growth potential, as will be discussed in Chapter 8.

A cross-cultural/cross-national design may also be useful when one tries to derive an estimated market demand figure in a country where statistical sources are scarce and unreliable. For instance, it is possible to estimate a regression equation explaining per capita annual wallpaper consumption, with explanatory variables such as income per capita, percentage of home ownership, frequency of use of other wall-covering materials, etc.[57] Estimates can be based on a cross-section sample (data for a sample of countries, for the same year), or a pooled cross-section/time series sample, when the countries' data are available for several years. It may then be possible to use the explanatory variables to compute the wallpaper consumption for a country where there is no available data.

A second issue is the representativeness of each sample in each unit of analysis, which may be a country, a culture, or a common language group that shares similar patterns of social interaction and communication.[58] Countries are often used as proxies for cultural units. In cross-cultural research it may seem logical to follow a systematic procedure, choosing the same sample characteristics in every country, to achieve reliability and comparability of data. Unfortunately, demographic definitions in secondary data (collected by someone else for another purpose, such as census data) rarely correspond exactly from one country to another. While age is one characteristic that would seem to be comparable, people may not accurately know their birth dates, or census figures, even if available, may include different age groupings. Other characteristics, such as occupation, education and socioeconomic status, often reflect quite different definitions across countries. Income may also be difficult to compare (e.g., exchange rates cannot capture income equivalence, in terms of what the money is worth). If possible, religion and tribal membership should also be added to traditional demographics, as they are of the utmost importance in some less developed countries.[59]

Finally, samples of cultures should not be confused with samples of individuals. There is a risk of gross stereotyping, when country characteristics are considered as individual characteristics. If individuals are of interest, sampling equivalence at this level must also be considered.

Representativeness and comparability at the individual level

To compare at the individual level across cultures, researchers must also carefully design the within country or culture sample. Often representative samples are chosen to reflect some characteristics of the population of interest, such as being representative of the census characteristics of the countries involved or representative of the primary purchasers of a product or product category. Holding these characteristics equal across countries can lead to inequivalence. For instance, equal gender proportions may convey a different meaning in a country where gender rights are fairly equal in comparison to countries where women are restricted from leaving the home unescorted. A sample of actual shoppers may have very different characteristics across cultures. In some places, men tend to do most of the shopping, in other countries it is mostly women; this also depends on various other factors (income level, type of product, etc.). In this case, the gender proportions might be very difference across cultures. The sampling method must be selected so that each national sample is fully representative of the *population of interest*.

Sampling frames or lists are usually unavailable at the individual consumer level across cultures.[24] Audience research for the BBC worldwide stresses the frequent lack of reliable or recent census data in many developing countries, including the former Soviet Union and in eastern Europe.[16] For instance, a sample drawn from the electoral list in Bolivia may over-represent men, since women are not as likely to vote.[60] Similarly, most sampling frames in Saudi Arabia are inadequate: there is no official census of the population, no exhaustive voter registration records, and telephone directories tend to be incomplete.[61] Non-probability sampling is necessary in many countries. Often sampling frames for businesses are of better quality, since most businesses want their number on lists, such as the telephone directory, but in China these directories are often out of date and lists are likely to include only the businesses or people associated with the list supplier.[21] Moreover, getting a list is not the only problem. As Harzing and colleagues[62] describe, the purchase of a customized commercial list of multinational subsidiaries cost them a significant amount of money ($A11,000) and time (three months), before it was usable. They experienced long delays in responses to their questions, as they had to pose all questions through a local customer relations contact. The addresses for several Asian countries (i.e., Korea, China and Japan) were in roman script rather than their character-based written form, which could not be used for mailing in China. They had to purchase additional addresses, the result of one of their sampling frame requirements not being a compulsory question in Japan. In the end, 20 per cent were undeliverable, duplicate, or addresses outside the sampling frame.

Screening criteria may also be necessary to ensure that the sample fits the characteristics of the population of interest. While this threatens representativeness, it may produce better reliability. Different screening criteria are often used in North America and China to ensure that the samples are comparable.[63]

In North America the objective may be to sample mainstream consumers with screening criteria including being a native English speaker, born in North America to North American parents. In China the objective may be to sample respondents who had access to consumer markets, with screening criteria including an education level that would allow a literate information search and an income level that would allow consumption.

Estimating sample size is also critical. The use of traditional statistical procedures, such as constructing confidence intervals around sample means, or hypothesis testing, is difficult to implement since such procedures require precise estimates of the variance of the population. This variance estimate is often unavailable in countries that have poor census data. The most frequently used procedure is, therefore, the selection of sample size, country by country, taking into account their respective peculiarities.

Ultimately, the main problem (before any statistical procedure is implemented) is to secure equivalence in meaning: we need to ask, does it make sense to represent the same populations across various countries? Do the samples actually represent these populations in the same way? The objective of the research should guide the sample choices.[64] If the objective is to examine similarities and differences across cultures, and cross-national comparability is important, purposefully chosen non-probability samples may be better, as this allows the researcher to create homogeneous samples. Conversely, when the objective is to describe attitudes or behaviour within specific countries, within-country representativeness is important, and probability samples should be used to enable the researcher to estimate the sampling error.

7.6
Data-collection equivalence

Let us assume that through any of the translation procedures described above we are able to develop equivalent national versions of a common questionnaire for a cross-cultural market research study, and that we have consistent and equivalent samples. We may still have to overcome response equivalence, including the following:

1. secrecy/unwillingness to answer (respondents' co-operation equivalence);
2. response biases (data-collection context equivalence); and
3. differences in response style (response-style equivalence).

These sources of error can create discrepancies between observed measurement and true measurement. Some basic precautions may help to avoid the generation of data with a great deal of measurement error.

Reluctance to answer: respondents' cooperation equivalence

Respondents sometimes feel that the interviewer is intruding into their privacy. They prefer not to answer or they consciously bias their answers, fearing that their opinion could later be used against them.[60] Many countries have strong privacy/intimacy patterns, where the family group is protected from external, impersonal interference. It seems the very private and reserved nature of Saudis may not be conducive to personal interviews.[61] Saudis do not want to be exposed to justifying or explaining their actions when answering a barrage of questions. In the case of Afghanistan and Mozambique, Mytton (p. 26) explains that:

Protocol demands that the most senior woman of the house should be interviewed before any other female . . . In some areas of Afghanistan, women cannot be used as interviewers. In others the reverse is the case; a male stranger coming to a house would be regarded as a possible threat . . . As in Afghanistan, many respondents in Mozambique did not know their own age or that of other members of the household . . . In several areas the presence of strangers writing down information on pieces of paper while talking to people, started rumours. One rumour suggested that the survey team was registering the number of children in each household with the intention to return later and kidnap them. Research had to be delayed for meetings to be held with the local authorities in order for them to reassure people living in the area.[16]

This may lead to differences in response rate, as well as biased responses. Business-to-business surveys are not immune to these biases, with vastly different response rates being reported around the world. For instance, industrial mail survey response rates across 22 countries ranged from over 40 per cent in Denmark and Norway to 7 per cent in Hong Kong and 11 per cent in the United States.[65] This was in spite of the efforts to motivate respondents (CEOs and Human Resource Managers),[66] including a reminder mailing, letter, photograph of the researcher and a tea bag or coffee sachet with the message 'Why don't you take a short break, have a nice cup of tea and fill out the questionnaire right now, it will only take 10–15 minutes'.[65]

Different survey methods may need to be employed in different cultures. Global opinion polls and international survey firms often use different methods, depending on the acceptability to respondents and businesses. Quota sampling is often used in most of Europe, but considered less acceptable in the United States.[67] Similarly, the use of RDD (random digit dialling) to construct phone samples, which is standard practice in the United States for telephone surveys, in order to include both unlisted people and recent movers, is not used in phone samples in many other countries, including other western countries.

Context equivalence of data collection

Questions are never culture-free: there is inevitably a social and cultural context built into them. Contextual equivalence relates to elements in the context of the data-collection process that have an influence on responses. As Douglas and Craig explain (p. 109): 'In the Scandinavian countries, for example, respondents are considerably more willing to admit overdrinking than in Latin America. In India, sex tends to be a taboo topic.'[51] Any question that deals, directly or indirectly, with social prescription needs to be worded so that people can elaborate a response without feeling too embarrassed, and responses have to be screened in order to know if the responses reflect actual reality or a view of what is socially desirable. This may mean further questioning some well-disposed and open-minded interviewees to ascertain their true view on the question.

Social desirability may also be a factor, where individuals answer questions in a way that presents themselves or their country in a more positive light. People from collectivist cultures attend to social expectations more than those from individualist cultures, and they tend to express culturally appropriate or normative responses to promote a desired social image more often than people in individualist cultures.[68] Malaysian respondents have been found to have a higher level of social desirability bias in their answers than the US or French respondents and were also more strongly influenced by personal sources, such as family and friends, than US respondents who were more strongly influenced by impersonal sources such as the media and government.[69]

Biases resulting from the relationship with the interviewer

Perceptions about the interviewer can also lead to response bias. In many traditional countries, housewives are reluctant to grant interviews to male interviewers. Local or ethnic biases may also be present, such as a traditional Chinese person feeling uncomfortable when being interviewed by a Malay.[70] Further, the interviewees may not understand that the process of interviewing them is for the purpose of generating objective data. They may perceive the purpose of research as a very long-winded form of selling, especially in developing countries.[59] In this case, the objective and the process of the interview must often be explained at the beginning.

When briefing local interviewers (management students) in Mauritania, the researchers were asked: 'What do you want us to tell the interviewee to answer?' It was necessary to explain to the interviewers that interviewing was a distanced and objective process, where interviewees had complete freedom of response. The idea of objective truth, external to personal relations, was unfamiliar to Mauritanians (also see Box 7.4). Furthermore, the Mauritanian interviewers of Arabic descent, the *Maures*, did not want to interview black Africans and, consequently, black Africans interviewers had to be used for their own ethnic group. A strong ingroup orientation implies that group membership has to be shared between interviewer and interviewee for the process to take place. However, this ethnicity-of-interviewer bias has been shown to exist even within the United States where both Hispanic and Anglo-American respondents significantly bias their responses to items pertaining to the interviewer's culture.[71] As a result, it seems more appropriate to match respondent's and interviewer's ethnicity.

Box 7.4

The weaknesses and strengths of the 'local researcher'

1. Weaknesses

(a) Often lower levels of education and research experience than his or her equivalent in developed countries.

(b) Often finds it difficult to adopt neutral, objective stance with reference to informants or clients. May want to be didactic in groups and may well prefer to distort findings to reflect a more educated picture of his countrymen than exists in reality. Alternatively, may seek to distance himself from the 'average consumer' by exaggerating their foibles and lack of sophistication. More educated interviewers may be out of touch with the average respondent.

(c) May be unwilling or unable, even for business reasons, to cross traditional barriers of class, religion or tribe.

(d) Rarely has the 'Puritan work ethic' and does not always see the value of objective truth. Delays, shortcuts and distortion are likely.

2. Strengths

(a) A better knowledge of the country and its people. Rapport is usually established more easily and has a better understanding of what is said. Can help to interpret the answers, especially if s/he has international experience.

(b) Knowledge of the language. Language can be an enormous barrier, as anyone who has tried to interview through interpreters must recognize.

(c) Physical comfort in the (research) environment. Better ability to cope, through familiarity, with common problems.

(Source: Goodyear, pp. 90–91.[59])

Response-style equivalence

Response-style equivalence is the final step. All the rest may be equivalent; yet our respondents may offer non-equivalent responses. The four main concerns in relation to response-style equivalence are:

1. yea-saying pattern (and, conversely, a nay-saying pattern) or acquiescence/disacquiescence;
2. extreme response style/response range and middle response style;
3. non-contingent responding (careless, random or non-purposeful); and
4. item non-response pattern.

Significant differences in response styles have been found across cultures and individuals within cultures. If managers interpret these differences as being substantive, they can make grave mistakes in their marketing decisions. For instance, an analysis of five-point Likert-scale questions from a 26-country study (including countries from North and South America, Asia, northern Europe, western Europe, eastern Europe and southern Europe) showed major differences in response styles that were related to cultural characteristics.[72,73]

First, 'yea-saying' or acquiescence is the tendency to agree with items and nay-saying or disacquiescence is the tendency to disagree with items regardless of content.[74] For acquiescence, the response scores tend to be inflated across items, and for disacquiescence the reverse occurs. When interviewing Greek and Italian housewives on their cooking behaviour this bias has an effect: there is a systematic tendency in the Greek sample to give more positive answers in psychographics as well as in product-related questions than in the Italian sample.[75,76] These types of response bias are related to different cultural assumptions, as follows:[72,73]

- Acquiescence is negatively related to individualism and positively related to power distance and extraversion.
- Extreme response bias is positively related to extraversion, whereas middle response bias was negatively related to power distance and individualism.

Within cultural regions and countries there were also marked differences, such as Japan having much lower acquiescence bias than most other Asian countries. Similarly, an analysis of mail survey data from 11 European countries found that all of the above forms of response styles influence some of the five-point Likert scales, but that in this case there was no evidence of more severe response styles in some countries than in others.[74] The scales with the most contamination measure health consciousness, consumer ethnocentrism, quality consciousness and environmental consciousness.[74]

Standardizing scores across cultures allows the 'yea-saying' pattern to be eliminated, although it is fairly difficult to differentiate whether people were generally striving to give answers towards the positive end of the scale or were agreeing strongly with a particular item. Thus, the 'yea-saying' pattern is diagnosed only when it is consistent across almost all the questions. Balancing the items so that some are positively worded and others are negatively worded, may be helpful,[74] but this approach may affect other aspects of equivalence across countries, as East Asians do not see positively and negatively worded items as opposites.[77]

Second, extreme response style is the tendency to choose the most extreme response regardless of content, while response range is the tendency to either use a narrow or wide range of categories around the mean.[74] This response pattern is systematically marked by a higher or lower standard deviation. For instance, in the United States people tend to respond with more enthusiasm, and therefore present a more extreme response style in answering, than the Japanese[78] or Koreans.[79] This could produce a bias in the standard deviation of data, increasing it artificially in cultures where people tend to overreact to questions, compared to other cultures where people may tend to suppress their opinions, either positive or negative. In responses given to scales ranging in format (3- to 10-point) by university students in Australia, France, Singapore and the United States,[80] the amount of extreme response differs by country, with France exhibiting the highest level, followed by the United States, followed by Australia and Singapore. The scales with the least extreme response style are 5- to 7-point response formats.[80,81]

Third, non-contingent responding is the tendency to respond carelessly, randomly or non-purposefully.[74] This may happen if respondents are not very motivated to answer the questionnaire.

Fourth, item non-response is an important source of bias in cross-national surveys. Respondents may be unwilling to respond to some questions, such as those relating to income or age. In a public opinion survey in eight European countries, there is evidence of non-response in relation to income being higher in the United Kingdom and Ireland, whereas the willingness to respond to political questions is highest in Germany and Italy.[51]

Encouraging feedback from the informant on cultural adequacy

Humans are not simple response machines. 'Criticality dissonance' is when respondents disguise and transform responses because they fear that information may be misused.[82] As previously discussed, international market research is full of criticality dissonance. The basic process affecting the truthfulness of responses is 'relevance dissonance', as Maruyama (p. 30)[82] states: 'the purpose of the questionnaire survey as perceived by the respondent differs from the respondent's own purpose. The questionnaire is perceived as irrelevant and useless. In such a case counter-exploitation takes place. The respondent looks for a way to manipulate the survey or interview to produce some benefit.' A questionnaire forced upon interviewees is unlikely to elicit useful information (see the hair shampoo exercise in section A7.2).

Informants should be neither overestimated nor underestimated. They cannot respond to a barrage of questions alien to their knowledge and frame of reference. Therefore, the content of the research must somehow be strictly controlled and must focus on really significant issues; surveys should be parsimonious and should not ask too much from informants. On the other hand, informants need to be carefully listened to because it is they who, as insiders, have the relevant pieces of information. The same care has to be taken with interviewers: they must be properly controlled (some – not all – may cheat by guessing responses or even filling in questionnaires themselves), and adequately briefed professional interviewers may not be found everywhere.

Multiple methods may be used to elicit feedback from respondents, including a preliminary study using in-depth interviews, focus groups to identify the appropriate product categories and help define the interview, and, after the main study, follow-up interviews to clarify unclear issues and investigate new issues.[63] If emic feedback is to be introduced, both interviewers (especially when they have not been personally involved in compiling the questionnaire) and interviewees must be put in a situation where they may comment on the questions themselves and explain what is culturally meaningful in their own context and what is not. Interviewees should be given the opportunity after the normal answering process to elaborate freely on what they think of the questions, the situations described, and so on. This orientation is slightly different from the traditional one where interviewed people are simply required to answer, not to 'criticize' the questions. Emic feedback allows an improvement in the adequacy of the source culture's constructs and instruments. As previously mentioned, a pre-test of the questionnaires is also necessary.

7.7

Researching internationally

Limited data availability and limited resources

International business and marketing requires a greater focus on the external environmental, since this differs more across countries than within countries. There are two levels of environmental data that must be monitored. First, the vertical environment must be monitored, including government policies, organization, and other governing structures that may affect the industry. Second the horizontal environment must be monitored, including the competitive environment, industry-specific opportunities, consumer preferences, etc. For instance, an international chemical firm commissioned researchers to interview government officials to obtain their position on a new regulation, 'China's Environmental Regulations for Chemical Products Imports and Exports', that could threatening their business operations, so that they could develop a strategy to lobby for adoption of internationally accepted practices.[83] Tan and Lui (p. 803) discuss trends in international marketing research in Asia:

There is also a growing realization that it is not enough to monitor shifts in brand perceptions or market share. It is, in fact, far more important to possess a holistic understanding of the total operating environment (including political and economic issues) and have better appreciation of the competitors' plans and activities. This understanding results in the clients' increasing dissatisfaction with traditional marketing research as being too narrowly focused on marketing issues: research techniques and an overriding concern with data rather than analysed information . . . Market research should therefore not just be conducted in response to one apparent market threat or opportunity, but rather on an ongoing basis in order to achieve a sustainable advantage.[84]

As explained in the sections above, when research is conducted internationally, the basic conditions of market research are different from those prevailing in the domestic market. For instance, the information that export managers in the United States value most highly is that which provides market potential, followed by legal, political, infrastructure, economics and, finally, culture: they want to establish that the country has the necessary demand, is open, will remain open, is conducive to entry, and is evolving, and then they can seek the cultural information that will improve on success.[85] However, market experience, market share and availability of people and resources are generally much stronger in the domestic environment than in international markets.[86] This and the limited availability of objective information, both in quantity and in quality, increase the uncertainty in international markets.[87]

Most firms in international business place less emphasis on their foreign markets, using less formal and less frequent market research procedures than in their domestic markets.[88] However, the sophistication increases with the amount of involvement (percentage of profits) in foreign markets, as measured by the percentage of export profits to total company profits.[88]

Research on the Internet

The Internet offers many opportunities to access both secondary and primary research. It is relatively easy to locate preliminary information about a region or country of interest, including the macro-environmental factors, such as political, legal, geographical, economic and cultural information, as well as the micro-environmental factors, such as market size, distribution systems, presence of local and global competition and consumer information. This infor-

mation can then be compiled into an initial industry analysis, competitive intelligence analysis, buyer behaviour analysis, and so on, that can inform the initial stages of market consideration.[89] Access to secondary information over the Internet is fast, easy and low cost, but it is also somewhat difficult to compare across countries and difficult to validate. As such, the source of the information should be considered.

The widespread availability of the Internet also allows access to detailed information about potential buyers. Blogs and other posts can be researched to examine product and competitor reputation to identify new opportunities, as well as information about customers' perceptions about a firm's current products. For instance, the Kryptonite lock company almost folded, when management ignored customer posts about a flaw in their locks.[90] Further, for established businesses, the Internet allows tracking exposure to websites, product, advertising, company information and patterns of use, such as information search patterns. The Internet's capacity for interactivity also means that it is easy to communicate directly with customers and respondents through chat rooms and bulletin boards.[84]

The Internet also provides relatively easy options for initial primary research, including traditional surveys via e-mail, online surveys and focus groups. Access to primary information over the Internet is relatively easy and cheap, but it is usually limited to Internet/e-mail users. This may be especially problematic in countries where there is low Internet access.[24]

> ### Website link 7.6
>
> Explore online survey programs, such as SurveyMonkey: **http://www.surveymonkey.com**.

7.8

Conclusion

International market surveys should not be constructed by simply replicating domestic research. The nature and scope of researched market information, the ways of collecting it, the accuracy of the data, as well as the criteria of reliability of the data, present cross-cultural variance. This holds true even when these factors are perceived as normatively quite universal. International market researchers should consider their own ethnocentric biases and give their local informants or collaborators opportunities to give feedback.

As Craig and Douglas (p. 85)[24] put it, international marketing researchers 'are being challenged to conduct research that is of the highest possible quality, as quickly as possible, in multiple diverse settings'. While a systematic search for formal equivalence, as laid out in this chapter may appear daunting, comparisons of inequivalent information are misleading, at best. As such, the final recommendation is to search for meaning, bearing in mind this advice:

1. Scientific methods provide pictures, which otherwise would not be available (the 'Mount Wilson' argument).
2. But, images of reality are not reality itself (the '*ceci n'est pas une pipe*' argument).
3. Address relevant questions (only those that can be articulated into decision and action).
4. Respect your informants and consider their competence as insiders, as superior to yours as an outsider; but interview only those people who have something to say.
5. Keep a 'hands-on' approach to market research.
6. Examine potential cultural influences, at each step of the research process: questions, survey methods, interviews and questionnaires, informants.

Questions

1. Define the following terms:
   (a) conceptual equivalence;
   (b) temporal equivalence;
   (c) sexual bias.

2. Discuss the functional equivalence of the following products or consumption experiences. For this, choose countries/cultures with which you have familiarity and experience and think in terms of benefits and those that are particularly emphasized in certain cultures:
   (a) a bicycle;
   (b) drinking a beer;
   (c) red wine;
   (d) a watch.

3. What are the obstacles for a sample of consumers to be cross-culturally representative?

4. Discuss how market size can be estimated in a country where there is little or poor statistical data available.

5. List possible benefits for a washing powder or liquid and suggest possible cross-cultural variability in the dominance of certain benefits as compared with others.

6. Suggest ways of obtaining relevant market and consumer behaviour information where potential informants are not accustomed to questionnaires and interviews.

7. How does the individualism/collectivism difference have an impact on the drafting of market research questionnaires?

8. What constraints does strong ingroup orientation put on the data-collection process?

References

1. Craig, C. S. and Susan Douglas (2011), 'Assessing Cross-cultural Marketing Theory and Research: A Commentary Essay', *Journal of Business Research*, 64, 625–7.

2. Barnes Reports (2011), 'Worldwide Mktg. Research & Public Opinion Polling' (NAICS 54191) USA.

3. Burgess, Steven Michael and Jan-Benedict E. M. Steenkamp (2006), 'Marketing Renaissance: How Research in Emerging Markets Advances Marketing Science and Practice', *International Journal of Research in Marketing*, 23 (4), 337–56.

4. Barnes Reports (2011), 'Worldwide Mktg. Research & Public Opinion Polling' (NAICS 54191) USA.

5. Johansson, Johny K. and Ikujiro Nonaka (1987), 'Market Research the Japanese Way', *Harvard Business Review* (May–June), 16–22.

6. Easterby-Smith, Mark, Richard Thorpe and Andy Lowe (1993), *Management Research: An Introduction*. London: Sage.

7. Hirschmann, Elisabeth (1986), 'Humanistic Inquiry in Marketing Research: Philosophy, Method and Criteria', *Journal of Marketing Research*, 13 (August), 237–49.

8. Usunier, Jean-Claude (1997), 'Atomistic Versus Organistic Approaches: An Illustration through Cross-National Differences in Market Research', *International Studies of Management & Organization*, 26 (4), 90–112.

9. Pike, Kenneth (1966), *Language in Relation to a Unified Theory of the Structure of Human Behavior*. The Hague: Mouton.

10. Sapir, Edward (1929), 'The Status of Linguistics as a Science', *Language*, 5, 207–14.

11. Douglas, S. P. and C. S. Craig (2006), 'On improving the Conceptual Foundations of International Marketing Research', *Journal of International Marketing*, 14 (1), 1–22.

12. Askegaard, Søren and Karen Brunsø (1999), 'Food-related Lifestyles in Singapore: Preliminary Testing of a Western Research Instrument in Southeast Asia', *Journal of Euromarketing*, 7 (4), 65–86.

13. Craig, C. Samuel and Susan P. Douglas (2001), *International Marketing Research*. Chichester: Wiley.

14. Kacen, Jacqueline J. and Julie Anne Lee (2002), 'The Influence of Culture on Consumer Impulsive Buying Behavior', *Journal of Consumer Psychology*, 12 (2), 163–76.

15. Geertz, Clifford (1983), *Local Knowledge*. New York: Basic Books.

16. Mytton, Graham (1996), 'Research in New Fields', *Journal of the Market Research Society*, 38 (1), 19–32.

17. Chen, Haipeng (Allan), Sharon Ng, and Akshay R. Rao (2005), 'Cultural Differences in Consumer Impatience', *Journal of Marketing Research*, 42 (3), 291–301.

18. Stone, R. and K. Gronhaug (1993), 'Perceived Risk: Further Considerations for the Marketing Discipline', *European Journal of Marketing*, 27 (3), 372–94.

19. Weber, Elke U. and Christopher Yr Hsee (1998), 'Cross-cultural Differences in Risk Perception, but Cross-cultural Similarities in Attitudes Towards Perceived Risk', *Management Science*, 44 (9), 1205–17.

20. Craig, C. Samuel and Susan P. Douglas (2006), 'On Improving the Conceptual Foundations of International Marketing Research', *Journal of International Marketing*, 14 (1), 1–22.

21. Marchetti, Renato and Jean-Claude Usunier (1990), 'Les Problèmes De L'étude De Marché Dans Un Contexte Interculturel', *Revue Française du Marketing*, 130 (5), 167–84.

22. Roy, Abhik, Peter G. P. Walters and Sherriff T. K. Luk (2001), 'Chinese Puzzles and Paradoxes: Conducting Business Research in China', *Journal of Business Research*, 52 (2), 203–10.

23. Weiss, Brad (1996), 'Coffee Breaks and Connections: The Lived Experience of a Commodity in Tanzanian and European World', in *Cross-Cultural Consumption*, David Howes (ed.) London: Routledge.

24. Bohnet, Michael (1994), 'Was Wurde in Kairo Wirklich Beschlossen', *Eine Welt* (BMZ, Bonn), October.

25. Craig, C. Samuel and Susan P. Douglas (2001), 'Conducting International Marketing Research in the Twenty-First Century', *International Marketing Review*, 18 (1), 80–90.

26. Mayer, Charles S. (1978), 'Multinational Marketing Research: The Magnifying Glass of Methodological Problems', *European Research* (March), 77–84.

27. Douglas, Susan P. and C. Samuel Craig (2007), 'Collaborative and Iterative Translation: An Alternative Approach to Back Translation', *Journal of International Marketing*, 15 (1), 30–43.

28. Usunier, Jean-Claude (1991), 'Business Time Perceptions and National Cultures: A Comparative Survey', *Business Time Perceptions and National Cultures: A Comparative Survey*, 31 (3), 197–217.

29. Campbell, D. T. and O. Werner (1970), 'Translating, Working through Interpreters and the Problem of Decentering', in *A Handbook of Method in Cultural Anthropology*, R. Naroll and R. Cohen (eds). New York: The Natural History Press.

30. Ter Hofstede, A. Audenaert, J. B. Steenkamp and M. Wedel (1998), 'An Investigation into the Association Pattern Technique as a Quantitative Approach to Measuring Means-end Chains', *International Journal of Research in Marketing*, 15, 37–50.

31. Watkins, Leah (2010), 'The Cross-cultural Appropriateness of Survey-based Value(s) Research', *International Marketing Review*, 27 (6), 694–716.

32. Durgee, Jeffrey F., Gina Colarelli O'Connor and Robert W. Veryzer (1996), 'Translating Values into Product Wants', *Journal of Advertising Research*, 36 (6), 90–100.

33. Zaltman, Gerald (1997), 'Rethinking Market Research: Putting People Back In', *Journal of Marketing Research*, 34 (November), 424–37.

34. Erevelles, Sunil, Abhik Roy and Leslie S. C. Yip (1998), 'Prices and Warranties as Signals of Quality: An Investigation of Chinese Consumers', Working Paper, University of California-Riverside.

35. Parameswaran, Ravi and Attila Yaprak (1987), 'A Cross-National Comparison of Consumer Research Measures', *Journal of International Business Studies* (Spring), 35–49.

36. Chattopadhyay, A., Gorn, G. J. and Darke, P. (2010), 'Differences and Similarities in Hue Preferences Between Chinese and Caucasians', in A. Krishna (ed.), *Sensory Marketing: Research on the Sensuality of Products*. New York: Taylor and Francis Group, LLC, pp. 219–39.

37. Van de Vijver, F. J. R. and Ype H. Poortinga (1982), 'Cross-cultural Generalization and Universality', *Journal of Cross-Cultural Psychology*, 13, 387–408.

38. Steenkamp, Jan-Benedict E. M. and Hans Baumgartner (1998), 'Assessing Measurement Invariance in Cross-national Research', *Journal of Consumer Research*, 25 (1, June), 78–90.

39. Ewing, Michael T., Thomas Salzberger and Rudolf R. Sinkovics (2005), 'An Alternate Approach to Assessing Cross-cultural Measurement Equivalence in Advertising Research', *Journal of Advertising*, 34 (1), 17–36.

40. Rasch, Georg (1960), *Probabilistic Models for Some Intelligence and Attainment Tests*. Copenhagen: Danish Institute for Educational Research.

41. Pras, Bernard and Reinhard Angelmar (1978), 'Verbal Rating Scales for Multinational Research', *European Research* (March), 62–7.

42. Lee, Julie Anne and Geoffrey N. Soutar (2010), 'Is Schwartz's Value Survey interval scaled and does it really matter?' *Journal of Cross-Cultural Psychology*, 41 (1), 76–86.

43. Sood, James H. (1990), 'Equivalent Measurement in International Market Research: Is It Really a Problem?', *Journal of International Consumer Marketing*, 2 (2), 25–41.

44. Bergami, Massimo and Richard P. Bagozzi (2000), 'Self-Categorization, Affective Commitment, and Group Self-Esteem as Distinct Aspects of Social Identity in the Organization', *British Journal of Social Psychology*, 39, 555–77.

45. Morris, Jon D. (1995), 'Sam: The Self-Assessment Manikin, an Efficient Cross-Cultural Measurement of Emotional Response', *Journal of Advertising Research*, 35 (6), 63–8.

46. Marley, A. A. J. and J. J. Louviere (2005), 'Some Probabilistic Models of Best, Worst, and Best–Worst Choices', *Journal of Mathematical Psychology*, 49, 464–80.

47. Kahle, L. R. (1983), *Social Values and Social Change: Adaptation to Life in America*. New York: Praeger.

48. Schwartz, S. H. (1992), 'Universals in the Content and Structure of Values: Theoretical Advances and Empirical Tests in 20 Countries', *Advances in Experimental Social Psychology*, 25, 1–65.

49. Lee, Julie Anne, Geoffrey N. Soutar and Jordan Louviere (2007), 'Measuring Values Using Best–Worst Scaling: The LOV Example', *Psychology and Marketing*, 24 (12), 1043–58.

50. Lee, Julie Anne, Geoffrey N. Soutar and Jordan Louviere (2008), 'An Alternative Approach to Measuring Schwartz's Values: The Best–Worst Scaling Approach', *Journal of Personality Assessment*, 90 (4), 335–47.

51. Douglas, Susan P. and C. Samuel Craig (1984), 'Establishing Equivalence in Comparative Consumer Research', in *Comparative Marketing Systems*, Erdener Kaynak and Ronald Savit (eds). New York: Praeger.

52. Wimalasiri, Jayantha (2000), 'A Comparison of Children's Purchasing Influence and Parental Response in Fiji and the United States', *Journal of International Consumer Marketing*, 12 (4), 55–74.

53. Rose, Gregory M. (1999), 'Consumer Socialization, Parental Style, and Development Timetables in the United States and Japan', *Journal of Marketing*, 63 (July), 105–19.

54. Viswanathan, Madhubalan, Terry L. Childers, and Elizabeth S. Moore (2000), 'The Measurement of Intergenerational Communication and Influence on Consumption: Development, Validation, and Cross-cultural Comparison of the Igen Scale', *Journal of the Academy of Marketing Science*, 28 (3), 406–24.

55. de Mooij, Marieke and Geert Hofstede (2002), 'Convergence and Divergence in Consumer Behavior: Implications for International Retailing', *Journal of Retailing*, 78 (1), 61–9.

56. Steenkamp, Jan-Benedict E. M. and Inge Geyskens (2006), 'How Country Characteristics Affect the Perceived Value of Web Sites', *Journal of Marketing*, 70 (3), 136–50.

57. Amine, Lyn S. and S. Tamer Cavusgil (1986), 'Demand Estimation in a Developing Country Environment: Difficulties, and Examples', *Journal of the Market Research Society*, 28 (5), 43–65.

58. Douglas, Susan P. and C. Samuel Craig (1997), 'The Changing Nature of Consumer Behavior: Implications for Cross-cultural Research', *International Journal of Research in Marketing*, 14 (4), 379–95.

59. Goodyear, Mary (1982), 'Qualitative Research in Developing Countries', *Journal of the Market Research Society*, 24 (2), 86–96.

60. Stanton, John L., Rajan Chandran and Sigfredo A. Hernandez (1982), 'Marketing Research Problems in Latin America', *Journal of the Market Research Society*, 24 (2), 124–39.

61. Tuncalp, Secil (1988), 'The Marketing Research Scene in Saudi Arabia', *European Journal of Marketing*, 22 (5), 15–22.

62. Harzing, Anne, B. Sabastian Reiche and Markns Pudelko (2012), 'Challenges in International Survey Research: A review with Illustrations and Suggested Solutions for Best Practice', *European Journal of International Management*.

63. Doran, Kathleen Brewer (2002), 'Lessons Learned from Cross-cultural Research of Chinese and North American Consumers', *Journal of Business Research*, 55 (10), 823–9.

64. Reynolds, N. L., A. C. Simintiras and A. Diamanto-poulos (2003), 'Theoretical Justification of Sampling Choices in International Marketing Research: Key Issues and Guidelines for Researchers', *Journal of International Business Studies*, 34 (1), 80–89.

65. Harzing, Anne-Wil (2000), 'Cross-National Industrial Mail Surveys: Why Do Response Rates Differ between Countries?', *Industrial Marketing Management*, 29, 243–54.

66. Paulhus, Delroy L. (1991), 'Measurement and Control of Response Bias', in *Measures of Personality and Social Psychological Attitudes*, J. P. Robinson and P. R. Shaver (eds). San Diego, CA: Academic Press.

67. Taylor, Humphrey (1995), 'Horses for Courses: How Survey Firms in Different Countries Measure Public Opinion with Different Methods', *Journal of the Market Research Society*, 37 (3), 211–19.

68. Lalwani, A. K., S. Shavitt and T. Johnson (2006). 'What is the Relation between Cultural Orientation and Socially Desirable Responding?', *Journal of Personality and Social Psychology*, 90 (1), 165–78.

69. Keillor, Bruce D., Deborah Owens and Charles Pettijohn (2001), 'A Cross-cultural/Cross-national Study of Influencing Factors and Socially Desirable Biases', *International Journal of Market Research*, 43 (1), 63–84.

70. Kushner, J. M. (1982), 'Market Research in a Non-Western Context: The Asian Example', *Journal of the Market Research Society*, 24 (2), 116–22.

71. Webster, Cynthia (1996), 'Hispanic and Anglo Inter-viewer and Respondent Ethnicity and Gender: The Impact on Survey Response Quality', *Journal of Marketing Research*, 33 (February), 62–72.

72. Harzing, Anne-Wil (2006), 'Response Styles in Cross-national Survey Research', *International Journal of Cross Cultural Management*, 6 (2), 243–66.

73. Smith, Peter B. (2004), 'Acquiescent Response Bias as an Aspect of Cultural Communication Style', *Journal of Cross-Cultural Psychology*, 35, 50–61.

74. Baumgartner, Hans and Jan-Benedict E. M. Steenkamp (2001), 'Response Styles in Marketing Research: A Cross-national Investigation', *Journal of Marketing Research*, 38 (2), 143–56.

75. Van Herk, Hester and Theo M. Verhallen (1995), 'Equivalence in Empirical International Research in the Food Area', in *Proceedings of the Second Conference on the Cultural Dimension of International Marketing*. Odense, 392–402.

76. Van Herk, Hester, Ype H. Poortinga and Theo M. M. Verhallen (2004), 'Response Styles in Rating Scales: Evidence of Method Bias in Data from Six EU Countries', *Journal of Cross-Cultural Psychology*, 35 (3), 346–60.

77. Wong, Nancy, Aric Rindfleisch and James E. Burroughs (2003), 'Do Reverse-worded Items Confound Measures in Cross-cultural Consumer Research? The Case of the Material Values Scales', *Journal of Consumer Research*, 30 (1), 72–91.

78. Zax, Melvin and Shigeo Takashi (1967), 'Cultural Influ-ences on Response Style: Comparison of Japanese and American College Students', *Journal of Social Psychology*, 71, 3–10.

79. Chun, Kl-Taek, John B. Campbell and Jong Hae Yoo (1974), 'Extreme Response Style in Cross-cultural Research: A Reminder', *Journal of Cross-Cultural Psychology*, 5, 464–80.

80. Clarke, Irvine III (2000), 'Global Marketing Research: Is Extreme Response Style Influencing Your Results?', *Journal of International Consumer Marketing*, 12 (4), 91–111.

81. Clarke, Irvine III (2001), 'Extreme Response Style in Cross-cultural Research', *International Marketing Review*, 18 (3), 301–24.

82. Maruyama, Magoroh (1990), 'International Meta-marketing: Strategic Judo, Foreign User Habits and Interactive Invention', *Human Systems Management*, 9, 29–42.

83. Ya-Fei, Margaret (2000), 'Putting the PR in PRC', *Asia Pacific Management Forum*, July/August, www.apmforum.com/columns/china5.htm.

84. Tan, Thomas Tsu Wee and Tan Jee Lui (2002), 'Globalization and Trends in International Market Research in China', *Journal of Business Research*, 55 (10), 799–804.

85. Wood, Van R. and Kim R. Robertson (2000), 'Evaluating International Markets: The Importance of Information by Industry, by Country of Destination, and by Type of Export Transaction', *International Marketing Review*, 17 (1), 34–55.

86. Grønhaug, Kjell and John L. Graham (1987), 'Inter-national Market Research Revisited', in *Advances in International Marketing*, S. Tamer Cavusgil (ed.) Greenwich, CT: JAI Press.

87. Cavusgil, S. Tamer and Yezdi M. Godiwalla (1982), 'Decision-Making for International Marketing: A Comparative Review', *Management Decision*, 20 (4), 47–54.

88. Cavusgil, S. Tamer (1984), 'International Marketing Research: Insights into Company Practices', in *Research in Marketing*, Vol. 7. Greenwich, CT: JAI Press.

89. Kumar, V. (2000), *International Marketing Research*. Upper Saddle River, NJ: Prentice Hall.

90. Heil, Oliver, Don Lehmann and Stefan Stremersch, (2010), 'Marketing Competition in the 21st Century', *International Journal of Research in Marketing*, 27, 161–3.

Appendix 7

Teaching materials

A7.1 Case

Mobile phones in the European Union

Questions

Using the same text as in Chapter 5 (see Section A5.3), answer the following questions:

1. Assuming that Orange has decided to undertake an in-depth market survey in order to decide whether to develop its market penetration in a southern European market (e.g., France or Spain), versus a northern European market (e.g., Germany or Denmark), how would you design such a survey?

2. What information is needed?

3. How would you collect it?

A7.2 Exercise

Hair shampoo questionnaire

You will find below a market survey questionnaire, administered by interviewers to women interviewees between the ages of 18 and 30. It was originally designed for the US market. A similar market survey, as far as the objectives are concerned, will be undertaken in other countries. Suggest cross-cultural adaptations to this instrument. In particular:

1. Review the possible problems related to the translation of the questionnaire. Suggest solutions and translate it into. . . .
2. Review the data-collection procedure, from the point of view of the interviewer as well as that of the interviewee.
3. Suggest changes in the questionnaire design and/or wording, and/or modification in survey methods, if:
   (a) the information sought is meaningless in the local context;
   (b) the required information is meaningful but the data-collection procedures are inadequate; either they will not enable you to collect the information, or else this information will be biased.

- You must do this for at least three of the following countries: Algeria, Brazil, France, Germany, Thailand.
- You should then propose a 'central' version of the questionnaire: that is, a survey instrument which enables you to collect the maximum amount of information, which could be retrieved in a reliable manner, in the largest possible number of countries. This questionnaire would then help the meaningful comparison of countries.

Questionnaire used in hair shampoo study

	Time Interview Started ....
	Ended ....
Respondent Name	Respondent No. ....
Address	
City	State ....
Telephone No	
Interviewer	
Name	
Interview Date	

Screening Questions (Part S)

'Hello, I'm .... of the Wharton School, University of Pennsylvania. We're conducting a survey on women's attitudes and opinions about hair care products.'

1. On average, how often do you shampoo your hair at home?

More than twice a week	....
Once or twice a week	....
Once or twice every two weeks	....
Once or twice every three weeks	....
Twice a month	....
Less than twice a month	....
	IF LESS THAN TWICE A MONTH, TERMINATE

2. What is your age? ....
   (IF UNDER 18 OR OVER 30 TERMINATE)

Part A

'First I'm going to show you a set of 16 cards. Each card contains the name of a benefit that a hair shampoo might provide.' (PLACE SET OF WHITE CARDS* ON TABLE IN FRONT OF RESPONDENT.)

'Please take a few moments to look over these benefits.' (ALLOW TIME FOR RESPONDENT TO STUDY THE CARDS.)

'Now, thinking about various brands of hair shampoo that you have tried or heard about, pick out those benefits that you think are most likely to be found in almost any hair shampoo that one could buy today.' (RECORD CARD NUMBERS IN FIRST COLUMN OF RESPONSE FORM A AND TURN SELECTED CARDS FACE DOWN.)

* For the wording on the cards, see CARD TEXT.

'Next, select all of those remaining benefits that you think are available in at least some hair shampoo – but not necessarily all in a single brand – that's currently on the market.' (RECORD CARD NUMBERS IN SECOND COLUMN OF RESPONSE FORM A. RECORD REMAINING CARD NUMBERS IN THIRD COLUMN. THEN RETURN ALL CARDS TO TABLE.)

'Next, imagine that you could make up an ideal type of shampoo – one that might not be available on today's market. Suppose, however, that you were restricted to only four of the 16 benefits shown on the cards in front of you. Which four of the 16 benefits would you most like to have?' (RECORD CARD NUMBERS IN FOURTH COLUMN OF RESPONSE FORM A.)

RESPONSE FORM A

(1)	(2)	(3)	(4)
Benefits available in some shampoo – card numbers	Benefits most likely to be found in almost any hair shampoo – card numbers	Remaining benefits – card numbers	Four benefit ideal set – card numbers

Part B

'Now, let's again return to some of the shampoo benefits you have already dealt with.' (SELECT WHITE CARD NUMBERS 1 TO 10: PULL OUT CARD 4 AND PLACE IT IN FRONT OF RESPONDENT.)

'Suppose a shampoo were on the market that primarily stressed this benefit – "produces hair that has body". If you could get a shampoo that made good on this claim, which one of the remaining nine benefits would you most like to have as well?' (RECORD NUMBER IN RESPONSE FORM B.)

'Which next most?' (RECORD.)

'Please continue until all of the nine benefits have been ranked.'

RESPONSE FORM B

(Enter card numbers 1 to 10 excluding card 4)
( ) Most like to have   ( )
( ) Next most   ( )
( )   ( )
( )   ( )
( )   ( ) Least most

Part C

'Now, I am going to read to you some short phrases about hair. Listen to each phrase carefully and then tell me what single words first come to your mind when you hear each phrase.' (RECORD UP TO THE FIRST THREE 'ASSOCIATIVE-TYPE' WORDS THE RESPONDENT SAYS AFTER EACH PHRASE IN RESPONSE FORM C.)

RESPONSE FORM C

(a) Hair that has body

_____   _____   _____

(b) Hair with fullness

_____   _____   _____

(c) Hair that holds a set

_____   _____   _____

(d) Bouncy hair

_____   _____   _____

(e) Hair that's not limp

_____   _____   _____

(f) Manageable hair

_____   _____   _____

(g) Zesty hair

_____   _____   _____

(h) Natural hair

_____   _____   _____

Part D

'At this point I would like to ask you a few questions about your hair.'

1. Does your hair have enough body?
Yes _____   No _____

2. Do you have any special problems with your hair?
Yes _____   No _____
If yes, what types of problems?
_____ ____
_____

3. How would you describe your hair?
My hair type is:
Dry _____   Normal _____   Oily _____

4. The texture of my hair is:
Fine _____   Normal _____   Coarse _____

5. My hair style (the way I wear my hair) is:
Straight _____
Slightly wavy or curly _____
Very wavy or curly _____

6. The length of my hair is:
Short (to ear lobes) _____
Medium (ear lobes to shoulder) _____
Long (below shoulder) _____

7. How would you describe the thickness of your hair?
Thick _____ Medium _____ Thin _____

Part E

'Now I would like to ask you a few background questions.'

1. Are you working (at least 20 hours per week, for remuneration)?
Yes _____ No _____

2. Are you married?
Yes _____ No _____

3. What is your level of education?
Some high school _____
Completed high school _____
Some college _____
Completed college _____

4. (HAND RESPONDENT INCOME CARD.) Which letter on this card comes closest to describing your total annual family income before taxes? (CIRCLE APPROPRIATE LETTER.)
(A)   Under $9,000
(B) $9,001–15,000
(C) $15,001–20,000
(D) $20,001–30,000
(E) $30,001–45,000
(F) $45,001–60,000
(G)   Over $60,000

'Thanks very much for your help.'

Card text

Text of the 16 benefits cards (original text in English + suggested translation into French):

1. Hair stays clean a long time
2. Hair stays free of dandruff or flaking
3. Hair that looks and feels natural
4. Hair that has body
5. Manageable hair that goes where you want it
6. Hair with sheen or lustre
7. Hair with no split ends
8. Hair with enough protein
9. Hair that doesn't get oily fast
10. Hair that's not too dry
11. Hair with fullness
12. Hair that's not frizzy
13. Hair that holds a set
14. Hair with texture
15. Hair that's easy to comb when it dries
16. Hair that looks free and casual

Example of a translation into French.

1. *Des cheveux qui restent propre longtemps*
2. *Des cheveux sans pellicules ni noeuds*
3. *Des cheveux respirant le naturel*
4. *Des cheveux qui ont du volume*
5. *Des cheveux souples que l'on peut coiffer à son gré*
6. *Des cheveux brillants et chatoyants*
7. *Des cheveux qui ne se cassent pas*
8. *Des cheveux assez riches en protéines*
9. *Des cheveux ne devenant pas gras trop vite*
10. *Des cheveux pas trop secs*
11. *Des cheveux qui ont de la plénitude*
12. *Des cheveux qui ne sont pas frisottés*
13. *Des cheveux tenant la mise en plis*
14. *Des cheveux ayant une bonne texture*
15. *Des cheveux faciles à coiffer lorsqu'ils sèchent*
16. *Des cheveux naturels, en liberté*

(Source: Adapted from Green *et al.*, pp. 359–62.[1])

Appendix reference

1. Green, Paul E., Donald S. Tull and Gerald Albaum (1988), *Research for Marketing Decisions* (5th edn). Englewood Cliffs, NJ: Prentice Hall.

Part 3 Marketing decisions for the intercultural environment

Introduction to Part 3

As with most international marketing textbooks, this book discusses marketing decisions and their implementation around the '4Ps' model: *product, price, place* and *promotion*. Part 3 explains how the first three Ps – product, price and place – should be managed internationally with a view to generating the best possible compromise between the cost savings that can be achieved from large-scale operations and the necessary adaptation to local markets. Part 4 focuses more directly on marketing communication (branding, promotion and personal selling), which deserves special treatment in an international context.

Multinational companies design international marketing strategies to create experience effects, within the constraint of transport costs. They also use a number of production systems, such as flexible manufacturing, to gain differentiation advantages related to the customization of product offerings to local markets. Chapter 8 first deals with the supply side by examining how cost arguments explain the emergence of global strategies and the globalization of competition. On the demand side, cross-border segments are targeted in order to generate larger-scale operations. Chapter 8 also explains how geographical and demographic segmentation criteria can be combined in order to segment international markets optimally.

Chapter 9 focuses on product strategy. It starts with a review of key arguments in favour of the standardization or adaptation of physical attributes. Physical attributes are the most sensitive to scale economies and, at the same time, they often require customization because of climate and other objective features of local markets. Service attributes also need to be tailored, because consumer expectation regarding service quality and service performance varies across national contexts. Finally, symbolic attributes linked to product design and packaging are examined in a cross-cultural perspective that highlights the diversity of cultural interpretations of symbols by looking at attributes such as colour, figure, shape, etc.

In an effort to consider price other than merely *the* objective factor in the economics of international marketing, Chapter 10 examines the role of price as a central element of relational exchange: that is, a signal conveying meaning between buyers and sellers, marketers and consumers, and between companies and their middlemen. It also presents and documents the main pricing decisions that a company has to face when it sells internationally. The first perspective developed is that of bargaining, which is still widely used in many markets and remains a key ritual in buyer–seller relationships because it mixes economics and human interaction in a subtle way. Cross-cultural variation in the way consumers use price to evaluate and choose products is then discussed. The last three sections of the chapter are devoted to managerial issues in international price policy. This includes the way in which multinational companies use price policy to conquer new markets, how to enter markets where competition is avoided through cartels and price agreements, how to fight against parallel imports by unauthorized dealers, and how prices should be managed in unstable environments, which often combine high inflation, administered prices and strict foreign exchange control.

Chapter 11 focuses on the 'place' variable in the 4Ps model and consequently deals with international distribution. It shows how relationships between channel members are deeply rooted in local patterns of human and economic relationships, and highlights the role of distribution as a cultural filter, to be carefully considered (along with other criteria) before choosing a foreign distribution channel. Direct worldwide marketing is rapidly developing, with ever-increasing access to the Internet. The section dealing with direct marketing outlines some linguistic and cultural limitations to consider carefully before designing and implementing cross-border direct marketing. The final section examines cross-national variations in sales promotion methods and explains which aspects need to be customised when transferring promotional techniques across borders.

8

Intercultural marketing strategy

The global and international marketing literature has largely focused on describing an evolutionary process, designed to mitigate the costs and risks associated with operating in international markets. This process focuses on building experience and reducing costs/risks by (1) entering culturally similar neighbouring markets, (2) expanding into the local and neighbouring markets, and finally (3) rationalizing to focus on the global market. This literature describes how to select countries or markets, how to enter each country (e.g., exporting, joint venture, or wholly owned operation), as well as the timing and sequencing of market entry. Once international operations have reached a 'substantial' level, rationalization is necessary to shift away from a large number of county-centric strategies to become a global organization and achieve substantial synergies and scale efficiencies. However, with a wider range of markets comes a greater degree of cultural, economic and environmental diversity, which may result in diseconomies.[1]

Further, as Douglas and Craig point out, a new phase of global marketing has emerged that will see a greater emphasis on emerging market economies, due to saturation and competition in developed countries.[2] They note that these markets have very different demand characteristics (i.e., customer interests, preferences, purchasing patterns and price sensitivity), competitive environments and very different infrastructure, which means a 'shift away from global integration, coordination of strategy, and issues such as global branding to development of divergent strategies geared to different customer needs, competitors, and market conditions in different geographic

locations.' (p. 86).[2] This reaffirms the need for intercultural marketing strategy, as is emphasized throughout this book.

Intercultural marketing suggests that we standardize where true cost reductions can be achieved and localize where necessary. The strategic dilemma for international marketers is to achieve both low cost and differentiation in the minds of consumers *vis-à-vis* competitors. While differentiation may result in cost increases, there are possible compromises. Cost efficiency can be obtained in production, transport and some areas of marketing. In order to minimize costs and unnecessary differentiation, and to maximize relevant differentiation, customers can be clustered into groups sharing common characteristics.

The first section of this chapter discusses *scale*, concentrating on cost arguments, as global strategies are very significant from a pure cost perspective. The second section discusses *scope*, concentrating on how global competition has progressively advanced, due to the liberalization of world trade. The third section focuses on the three major perspectives of global marketing strategy, including standardization-adaptation, configuration-coordination and integration-independence. This illustrates how companies have reacted to major changes during the past 20 years and how they have been forced by the pressure from worldwide competition to standardize marketing strategies, while keeping an eye on very dissimilar consumer environments. The final section deals with the *segmentation* of world markets and discusses the respective place of cross-border segments based on socio-demographics and lifestyles, as well as geography-based cultural segments.

8.1

Cost arguments and global strategies

Trends towards global (competitive) markets

In the 1980s Michael Porter[3] identified a widely accepted and applied distinction between multi-domestic and global markets. According to Porter (p. 18),[3] competition becomes global when 'a firm's competitive position is significantly affected by its position in other countries and vice-versa'. Conversely, when an industry is multi-domestic, separate strategies are pursued in different national markets, and the competitive scene remains essentially domestic.

Certain forces move society toward global competition, including regional integration, an ideology-free world, technological advances and borderless markets, while other forces are actively slowing the process down.[4] However, Rugman (p. 583)[5] suggests that globalization 'does not, and has never, existed in terms of a single world market with free trade . . . Government regulations and cultural differences divide the world into the triad blocks of North America, the European Union and Japan'. He argues that there has been a move to regionalization rather than globalization, as most global companies earn the majority of their revenue within their home triad and adapt their products to the local market. The WTO international trade statistics still support this argument, as 71 per cent of European exports going to Europe, 53 per cent of Asian exports going to Asian countries and almost 50 per cent of North America's exports going to North American countries in 2010.[6]

There are some fundamental reasons for industries to remain multi-domestic, including wide differences in consumer needs and attitudes across markets, legal barriers resulting from domestic regulations (which have long been in place in the case of banking and insurance), and non-tariff barriers, which artificially maintain competition between purely national competitors (food and drug health regulations, for instance). Further, the trend towards global markets differs across product categories, due to differences in:

1. national regulations and non-tariff barriers;
2. potential for experience effects (e.g., less for perishables than microchips, due to volume);

3. international 'transportability' (i.e. cost-effectiveness; and
4. cultural connectedness (i.e., culture-bound products, e.g., cheese).

Globalization may not be the most profitable route for a company to take. While research results are somewhat mixed, there is evidence that a medium global market diversification strategy performs better than a highly global strategy.[7] To understand this, it is important to examine the areas in which pure cost efficiencies can be obtained. Accordingly, cost efficiencies are first discussed in terms of production and transportation. Then, the implications of different world views within the organization are discussed.

Production and experience effects

Experience effects provide companies with the ability to reduce unit costs dramatically through an increase in product quantity. The experience effects determine the relationship of unit cost to cumulated production volume according to the following formula:

$$C_n = C_1 n^{-\lambda}$$

where Cn is the cost of the nth unit; C_1 is the cost of the first unit; n is the cumulated number of units produced; and λ is the elasticity of the unit cost with respect to the cumulated production volume.

The form of the function reflects constant elasticity. Let us call k the effect of elasticity. When production is doubled, the cost (and therefore, to a certain extent, the price) will decrease by $1 - k = 1 - 2^{-\lambda}$ per cent each time the experience effect doubles. If, for example, k equals 70 per cent, the cost will decrease by 30 per cent when doubling the cumulated production. Experience effects have been estimated for diverse products and services such as long-distance telephone calls in the United States, bottle tops in West Germany, refrigerators in Great Britain, and motorcycles in Japan. The potential for experience effects differs widely across product categories.

Website link 8.1

Search for information about the experience curve effect, such as this article in *The Economist*:
http://www.economist.com/node/14298944.

Experience effects can be found in the following:

1. *Learning by doing*. The more a task is carried out or the more a component or a product is manufactured, the more efficiently and quickly it can be done.
2. *Scale effects*. By increasing the scale of production, the average cost can be reduced. Many products, such as smart phones, require a large amount of research and development for product design, yet only a small quantity of raw material to be manufactured. Scale has become a major factor in the consumer electronics industry. Apple, for example, outsources a large proportion of their iPhone and iPad manufacturing to Foxconn in China, in large part due to their ability to scale up (or down) production rapidly.[8]
3. *Technological advances*. The increase in cumulated production leads to technological improvement to the production equipment, as well as the product itself. Production and product simplifications are usually a result of a reduction in the number of component parts, rather than a reduction in the number of functions and the degree of sophistication.
4. *Economies of scope*. The same component parts may be used in multiple products. For instance, the same basic diesel engine may be used for a fork-lift truck, a small truck, a van, a car, or as an inboard motor for a boat, with a few slight adaptations. The increase in the production scale of shared components (or shared overhead costs, or any kind of shared common inputs) results in economies of scope.

Not every product has the same potential for experience effects. The potential is clearly smaller for cheese or books than for computers or smartphones. In the world market, the Japanese have concentrated on goods that have very high experience effects, such as motorcycles, cars, photocopiers, home entertainment systems, outboard motors, musical instruments and digital cameras. Right from the start, Japanese companies opted for global markets, even though their domestic market for such products was itself very substantial. Competitors have struggled to resist the competitive pressure of Japanese companies. For instance, the motorcycle industry in Europe illustrates how a lack of experience effects can inhibit innovation. In an attempt to compete with the Japanese (Honda, Yamaha, Suzuki, Kawasaki), Motobécane, a French manufacturer, launched a 125cc motorcycle some years ago. This model had a two-stroke engine that operated on a mixture of petrol and oil, since Motobécane was unable to make a four-stroke engine, like Honda, or an 'oil lube' (a device for mixing oil and petrol automatically), like Yamaha, Suzuki and Kawasaki. The motorcycle made a thick cloud of white smoke. The range of models offered remained very limited, as with other French motorcycles. The 350cc Motobécane, which could have catered to a lucrative local market consisting of the French police, was not fast or reliable enough. The company's lack of experience effects was a barrier to technological improvements. Motobécane was renamed MBK and is now a subsidiary of Yamaha.

Local players, however, can use experience effects to maintain the upper hand over transnationals by using their local identity advantage. In developing economies, local firms are able to take advantage of a low cost based for resources and labour, as well as a deeper understanding of the local supply and demand environment.

International transportability

The unit weight, that is, dollar price per kilogramme or per pound, differs widely across categories of goods, and, by extension, across the industries that manufacture them. The price range of cement or basic ordinary steel products is much lower per kilogramme than luxury cars or vintage wine. However, shipping charges do not follow a simple tariff, which would be directly proportional to weight. They are calculated on the basis of a mix of criteria, including weight, volume, dimensions, ease of loading and unloading, perishability, packaging and speed of delivery. Of these, weight, volume and perishability are clearly the most detrimental factors to international transportation. Transportation cost factors are also influenced by the forces of competition between transportation companies.

Some markets remain almost exclusively multidomestic, because goods and services cannot be transported (e.g., very heavy goods and services, such as hairdressing). Although transportability may have a negative influence on cross-border transactions of goods and services, it does not hamper the globalization of an industry where cross-border investments are possible. For instance, the cement industry still competes on a global basis through foreign direct investment and the sale and licensing of technology, despite the markets being regionally segmented within countries, owing to the high cost of transportation in proportion to basic unit price.

Transportability also relates to consumers, who may be more 'transportable' than the products or services offered to them. Ski resorts are a good example: ski slopes, buildings and equipment are not transportable, nor is snow. However, potential skiers may be transported at low cost on charter flights, from countries without mountains, snow or ski resorts (provided they have some purchasing power). Consequently, in the international ski resort industry a twofold pattern of globalization is observable. On the one hand, some world-famous ski resorts, such as Val d'Isère in France, Kitzbühl in Austria, Zermatt in Switzerland and Thredbo in Australia cater to a global market. People come from many parts of the world, often on package holidays sold by tour operators or travel agencies. On the other hand, a large number of purely local ski resorts ('ski villages') in most ski-oriented countries compete on a more domestic basis. This part of the industry is multi-domestic. On a scale ranging from globalized at one end and multi-domestic at the other, there are in fact many intermediate ski resorts competing on a regionally globalized basis. This is the case with most medium-size ski resorts in the European Alps: in Austria, France, Germany, Italy, Switzerland and some eastern European countries, which compete for European skiers.

While the Internet cannot transport most physical products, it has the potential to lower costs across supply and demand chains, by improving efficiency in terms of speed, flexibility, and responsiveness, increasing market access and overcoming time and distance barriers.[9] Books, clothing and travel arrangement, such as airfares, appear to be the most commonly purchased goods over the Internet. Both access to the Internet and online shopping are on the increase. It is was forecast that the value of e-commerce in Europe would increase from €102 billion in 2006 to €263 billion in 2011.[10] Similarly, the value of e-commerce in the United States is forecast to be more than US$250 billion in 2011.[11] As at the end of 2011, Internet penetration was growing rapidly, especially in emerging countries. However, penetration and sheer numbers differ widely across regions of the world: over 78 per cent in America (273 million), 67 per cent in Oceania/Australia (24 million), 61 per cent in Europe (500 million), 39 per cent in Latin American (236 million), 26 per cent in Asian (1017 million), 35 per cent in the Middle East (77 million) and 13 per cent in Africa (140 million).[12] It is easy to see where the opportunities, and future growth, is emerging.

The disconnection between sourcing and marketing

When sourcing and marketing take place in geographically distant countries the most cost-efficient production sites are often export-processing zones in emerging economies (e.g., China's special economic zones). Consumer markets may be located in distant and remote places. The same brand may be 'made in' multiple countries, generating different country-of-origin (COO) images. This multinational production causes a 'blurring effect' for COO. Consumers, who still use country of origin as an information cue for comparing brands, are now becoming more and more aware of the actual disconnection between sourcing and marketing. Actual knowledge about a product's origin and its influence on preference for local products has been found to be relatively small.[13]

World views within the organization

Once a company has achieved a certain level of development in foreign markets, the 'export' view and the 'international development' view can no longer coexist effectively. The direction within an organization dependents on four different perspectives: ethnocentrism, polycentrism, regiocentrism and geocentrism, which permeate the way in which a company organizes its international activities, including the nationalities of top executives, choice of language spoken, etc.[14,15]

Two of these, ethnocentrism and geocentrism are the most irreconcilable. In terms of set theory, the domestic market is perceived as isolated from foreign markets. Ethnocentric companies view international operations as secondary to their domestic operations. A company that considers its national base as its top priority will impose its own language on its foreign subsidiaries. It will supply the domestic market first when production capacity is overstretched. It will never invite a non-national on to the board of directors unless this person shares the company's native language and culture. Conversely, a geocentric company, which considers its domestic market as belonging to the world market in the same way as any other domestic market, will make the opposite choices. It has been argued that the nine determinants of international marketing cycles are gradually declining: political stability, government policy, ideology-driven economy, fear of colonialism, marketing transfer issues, lack of infrastructure, North–South dichotomy, East–West dichotomy and product life.[16] A geocentric perspective is dependent on a truly borderless world.

Regiocentrism and polycentrism are more moderate perspectives. A regiocentric company is more open to global marketing than an ethnocentric one. However, this perspective also recognizes that regional marketing strategies may be necessary to better meet customer needs. Cultural factors still strongly inhibit the development of a homogeneous market.[17] Regional trading blocs can be used as building blocks to world trade. It is important to acknowledge differences within the bloc. Finally, a polycentric company recognizes that differences occur in overseas markets. Each country is accepted as one of many ethnocentric places which may have their own marketing policies and programmes.

When companies distance themselves from an ethnocentric attitude and adopt one of the other perspectives, by virtue of their management style and corporate culture, they develop genuinely offensive and defensive marketing strategies in foreign markets. Such a strategy manifests itself in flexible reallocation of resources from one market to another. For instance, a company will relocate to market Y, where it holds a solid position, as a reaction to a large competitor launching a price offensive in country X. This type of situation is conceivable in strongly oligopolistic markets where several (five to ten) large multinationals control the world market, as is true in the food industry or the liquefied gases industry.

Nevertheless, stiff competition may give way to forms of cooperation between large companies from developed countries. The theory developed by Kenichi Ohmae, head of the Tokyo office of McKinsey Consultants, in his book *Triad Power: The Coming Shape of Global Competition*,[18] emphasizes the need for companies that want to survive international competition to have a solid base in the market area of each of the three major industrialized regions collectively known as the 'triad': North America, Japan and Europe. Ohmae further suggests that in each of these regions companies should establish links of international division of labour with neighbouring developing countries. Companies in Latin America are natural subcontractors for North American companies. South-East Asian countries subcontract for Japanese firms. The same cooperation pattern should occur between African countries and European companies. To ensure this necessary tripolar presence, Ohmae advocates that alliances should be built between companies belonging to one of the developed market areas. Most of these companies, even if they are large, cannot individually afford to make the necessary investment that would ensure full presence in each of the three regions.

Prioritized markets often remain undisguised. To avoid the trap of 'collective unconsciousness', companies must reflect on how prioritized markets relate to corporate culture, as well as to the search for market and business opportunities, and to the decision-making process. Some European companies still supply their domestic market as a priority on the basis that this market is the 'home base'. There are consequences to this, as follows:

1. It leads to a bias in *product design*. The modest sales records of certain European cars (mainly French and Italian), in the North American market can, at least partially, be attributed to local French and Italian motor regulations which bias the design of cars, and make them inappropriate for use in America. In France the speed limits on highways and stiff road taxes that vary according to engine size have caused manufacturers to shy away from producing large cars and sports cars. The same holds true in Italy, where the high cost of petrol has led manufacturers to produce cars which are too small according to mainstream American public opinion. This has dissuaded car manufacturers in those countries from building high-speed luxury sedans, a gap in the market that was mostly filled by the Germans and the Swedes, before the Japanese.

2. Home-base oriented companies often suffer from an international reputation of being unreliable with respect to *delivery dates*. This is due to the

marginalization of foreign markets, which are considered as a provisional outlet to be approached when the home market is depressed. It leads to a consistent preference for supplying domestic rather than foreign customers. Even though a foreign customer may have ordered before a domestic customer, they will systematically be forced to wait and will only receive delivery after the domestic customer has been satisfied. A genuine respect for delivery dates would have led to a more equitable outcome.

As soon as domestic demand increases, the prioritization of national markets implies that production capacity will cease to be used for supplying foreign customers. As a consequence, there is a general risk that attempts to set up stable business relationships with customers and intermediaries in foreign markets will be hampered. Typically, foreign agents will only be visited when business at home is slack, and will be let down (as will foreign customers) as soon as the home market situation improves. This attitude fails to satisfy the essential precondition for effective international development.

Website link 8.2

Search the Fortune Global 500 for their origins: the United States lays claim to the most global giants (133), followed by Japan (68), and China (61): http://money.cnn.com/magazines/fortune/global500/2011/.

The world market share concept

Calculating its world market share helps a company to prevent itself from becoming ethnocentric when defining its position *vis-à-vis* the competition. Competition is seen from the outset as global. Box 8.1 illustrates the dangers of overemphasizing domestic market share.

Diagnosing a particular company's situation within world markets requires evaluating the following criteria (even though estimates may be only approximate):

1. size of world market (volume, units, sales figures);
2. company's production size;
3. company's share of world market; and
4. minimum world market share necessary to remain competitive, considering potential experience effects.

There is no precise rule for estimating the 'competitive' world market share. This figure depends on the optimum size of production, which in turn depends on the potential for experience effects for a specific product or service. Experience effects are enhanced by the following factors:

1. product/service is mass produced;
2. a production process with large initial fixed costs (in R & D, and/or in production facility investment, and/or in initial marketing costs);
3. added value is high, in relation to entire production cycle; and

---

BOX 8.1

Fenwick, a synonym for fork-lift

Fenwick is the leading French company for fork-lift trucks, At one point in time, the company controlled 40–50 per cent of the French market, but nearly went bankrupt because it lacked international clout. This company only produced 4,000 fork-lift trucks per year, whereas its global competitor, Toyota, produced 35,000 and its main east European competitor, Balkankar (a Bulgarian company), 70,000. This had a negative effect on Fenwick's unit costs.

Fenwick should have adapted its marketing strategy by reducing the depth of its product range, thereby increasing production size within this narrower product range. Toyota was in a position to offer a very wide product range (diesel or electric, with varying loading capacities, etc.). Fenwick, on the other hand, should have restricted its range albeit at the risk of losing customers who expect to find a single supplier capable of dealing with all their requirements.

4. market is fairly open internationally; any producer may sell throughout the world without facing prohibitive transport costs, customs barriers, statutory restrictions or market barriers (e.g., differences in taste).

The easiest empirical solution for evaluating 'competitive' market share is to examine the competitors and determine the size of those who operate most effectively. International size is limited in some industries; for example cement (very high transport costs compared to its price), pharmaceuticals (statutory restrictions), foodstuffs (taste differences), etc. As far as services are concerned, the potential for experience effects is much smaller, since in many cases services must be performed in a direct relationship with the consumer and are often intangible, which means they cannot be held in stock. In addition, their geographical market area is often fairly local, and subject to local customs and ways of life, such as the type of food and service found in a restaurant or the kind of service offered by hotels.

Global markets as learning opportunities

It is important to globalize in an efficient and controllable manner.[19] Searching out culturally similar markets can help a company learn in environments that are similar to their own. Cultural similarity has been positively related to many aspects of business, including the level of affinity,[20] communication, trust and relationship development,[21] successful cooperation,[22] a tendency to consume similar goods,[23] a more positive country of origin image[24] and a lower cost of doing business.[23] The distance to regulative, normative and cognitive levels can also be broken down.[25]

In fact, the internationalization process has been presented mostly as a learning and experiencing process in organizations. Since the cultural variable is fundamental to this learning process, some markets may be used almost purely as learning opportunities. When Procter & Gamble invaded the Japanese market for baby nappies (diapers), initially it was a great success. Its market share subsequently dropped sharply against the main Japanese competitor Kao. P & G did its best to survive against the harsh competition from Kao and other Japanese producers, to satisfy the demanding Japanese consumers and to make its way through the Japanese *keiretsu* distribution system. Among other things, the P & G nappy was just too bulky for Japanese consumers. Subsequently, their new slim-fitting nappies became a best seller in the US and P & G learnt a great deal from their experience in Japan. The company realized that it would face harsh competition if Japanese producers were to decide to expand to world markets. This has already helped it resist the internationalization of Kao, which, to date, has not succeeded in becoming a global competitor to P & G.

BOX 8.2

Stimorol and Hollywood

A Danish chewing-gum company, Dandy A/S, which produces Stimorol, encountered difficulties in selling its products in France. Dandy was particularly successful at producing chewing gum. Hollywood France (owned by the US company General Foods/ Kraft) was less successful in the production of this type of product, but had better access to the major distribution outlets (hypermarkets). In fact, only large companies are able to have their products referenced: that is, registered as products accepted for sale by the channel. Referencing requires the payment of large 'entry fees' to the hypermarkets, which are only semi-legitimate. Dandy of Denmark and Hollywood ended up forging a cross-competence alliance whereby Dandy produces Hollywood products and markets Hollywood products through Dandy's international sales organization, and Hollywood markets Dandy's Stimorol brand in France and produces the Dandy stick products.

(Source: Hollensen, 1991, p. 736, reproduced with permission.)

Global markets may also be seen as opportunities for partnership: with local consumers, with distributors and perhaps even with competitors (Box 8.2). They can also help local firms to create niche markets, where their local identity and culture is an advantage. A local company can become a global player, but it needs to think and act both locally and globally, by either creating a niche at home or an alliance as a global player.

Technology can help small and medium sized firms in targeting niche markets. According to Susan Douglas (p. 106),[26] 'firms can instantly "go global", targeting a specific market segment worldwide, or reach customers by building a network of Internet sites in different languages throughout the world'. Computer maker Lenovo (incorporated in Hong Kong) chose a map of the world with symbolic landmarks, such as the Sydney Opera House, Statue of Liberty and Eiffel Tower, to represent its vision on its Chinese language homepage, along with the slogan 'in step with global technology'.[27]

8.2

The globalization of competition

There is little doubt that the globalization of competition is driven by decreasing trade barriers and increasing glogal supply, economies of scale and experience effects, rather than by the homogenization of consumer preferences. Clear evidence from macroeconomic figures shows that competition is globalizing both worldwide and regionally.

International trade continues to expand despite the effects felt worldwide from the American subprime mortgage crisis and subsequent economic downturn, tension in the Middle East and terrorism. World exports grew (14 per cent for merchandise and 9 per cent for services) in 2010, bouncing back from negative growth in 2009, which was attributed to the economic downturn in most developed countries.[6] Since 1995 there has only been two years, 2001 and 2009, when merchandise exports increased less than the world gross national product (GNP) for the nations involved in international trade. This points to a long-term trend: an increase in the scale of production.

The economic linkage between countries and therefore competition between companies has continued

to grow. A comparable evolution may be observed, at an even greater pace, regionally. Distances are becoming less significant, and the move to worldwide globalization has its roots in regional operations. The most rapid growth has been from emerging economies, such as India and China, with the top three countries in merchandise trade now being the USA, China and Germany, respectively.[6]

Many companies have been compelled to globalize their business. One example of this is Black & Decker, which was compelled to go global thanks to fierce competition from the Japanese power tool maker Makita. The reasons for this are stated by Saporito (p. 24) in *Fortune* magazine, reporting the strategic move of Black & Decker towards globalization: 'Makita is Black & Decker's first competitor with a global strategy. It doesn't care that Germans prefer high powered, heavy duty drills, and that Yanks want everything lighter. Make a good drill at a low price, the company reasons, and it will sell from Baden-Baden to Brooklyn.'[28]

Nevertheless, globalization depends on continual efforts to dismantle, or at least reduce, trade barriers. The establishment of the WTO in 1995 was a major move towards freeing trade in products and services and improving the institutional mechanisms for solving trade disputes between countries. However, free trade can be maintained and expanded only if a reasonable equilibrium in the balance of trade between nation states makes it possible to maintain low trade barrier environments in favour of globalization within industries. Today, significant imbalances remain, with trade deficits in the US being over $690 billion, whereas worldwide trade surpluses were reported in many of their trading partners, including $183 billion in China and $76 billion in Japan, in 2010.

> **Website link 8.3**
>
> Search the World Trade Organization (WTO) for recent reports in globalization and worldwide trade: http://www.wto.org.

In the past, international businesses were mainly concerned about competition from other developed countries. However, it is clear that increasing competition is coming from medium and larger companies in emerging markets. For instance, Brazil's Embraer is the third largest in the aircraft manufacturing industry, China's Haier is increasing market share in consumer electronics and many Indian companies (e.g., Mahindra and Mahindra, Infosys and Tata) are rapidly expanding in world markets.[2]

8.3

Globalization of international marketing strategies

So how can products and marketing strategies faced with fierce world competition, as well as consumer resistance to the globalization movement, become globalized? There are three major perspectives on international marketing strategy:

1. *Standardization-adaptation* of market offerings (marketing mix elements).
2. *Geographical concentration–dispersion* of the structural or organizational aspects of the value chain.
3. *Integration-independence* of the competitive processes (planning, implementation and control).[29]

Standardization-adaptation of international market offerings

Prior to Buzzell's classic article, 'Can you standardize multinational marketing?',[30] natural entry barriers related to culture were seen as very high, requiring adaptation to national markets and offsetting the potential advantages of scale economies. Buzzell clearly showed that, with the decrease of purely artificial trade barriers, large international companies could create natural entry barriers unrelated to culture through economies of scale. Since then there have been numerous texts that have sought to advise business people how to make the best choices between standardization and adaptation of marketing policies to foreign markets.

The standardization perspective views global marketing strategy as being the same or standardized across countries, including all elements of the marketing mix, product, promotion, price and distribution strategies. There is general acknowledgement that there are some environmental constraints, owing to the physical conditions within a country, as well as legal issues, especially product standards, taxes, etc.

Consumer wants in various national markets are not really considered, as differences are either denied or treated as an external constraint. Behind the globalization debate there is a quite practical issue in terms of the everyday life of companies: the traditional dilemma between production flexibility and the (marketing) tendency to customize products to diversified needs. Factory managers prefer to be inflexible, for low-cost purposes, whereas marketing managers favour as much tailoring to customers' needs as possible. However, developments in factory automation allow for products to be customized without major cost implications, due to economies of scale and experience effects. A modular conception of products permits shared economies of scale, as far as components are concerned, whereas lagged differentiation maintains a high scale of production for as long as possible in the production process and organizes cheap final customization either in the factory or in the distribution network.[31–33]

Why is it necessary to maintain such a strong 'paradigm for action' emphasis on globalization, if consumption patterns are not clearly globalizing and if adjusting to global competition is reconcilable with tailoring products and marketing strategies to national markets?

First, many companies believe that standardization will result in higher performance. Zou and Cavusgil[34] surveyed companies in the US to assess the influence of self-reported standardization on perceived performance (both strategic and financial). The standardization of promotions and products are perceived to affect both aspects of performance. However, other studies have found that a firm's performance is indifferent to standardization versus adaptation.[35] This relationship is complicated, being dependent on the fit between strategy and context. For instance, if a firm takes a cost leadership strategy, then standardization of marketing strategy makes for a strategic fit.

Second, these beliefs are often acted upon. For example, case studies of Western European and US companies operating in central eastern European countries show that Western companies rely heavily on standardization even when market conditions seem to favour localization.[36] Managers typically underadapt their market offerings to foreign markets.[37]

Third, many companies place more importance on their home markets: Wright's interviews with managers from US and Japanese companies found the 'existence of ethnocentric orientations in both US and Japanese firms because of the prevailing assumptions by headquarter firms about the importance of their home markets' (p. 352).[38]

Subhash Jain (p. 8)[39] examined the academic papers on standardization over the last 40 years, concluding that:

- across the board standardization is inconceivable;
- the decision on standardization is not a dichotomous one between complete standardization and customization; rather there can be degrees of standardization;
- although a variety of internal and external factors impinge on the standardization decision, the product/industry characteristics are paramount;
- standardization is most feasible in settings where the marketing infrastructure is well developed.

Moreover, Schilke and colleagues (p. 38)[40] suggest that both B2C and B2B firms should 'focus relevant resources on the market specific differences that are important to the international customers and apply standardized approaches to the marketing aspects that are less critical to these customers'.

Organizational aspects of globalization

The reasons for globalizing marketing activities are largely organizational. Although there is evidence of some savings in manufacturing costs, the financial payoffs for hard globalization are, at best, dubious when one considers the financial performance of companies as a whole.[41,42] MNCs that grew fast worldwide in the 1960s and 1970s did so by granting a large degree of decision-making autonomy to their subsidiaries in their home markets. Subsidiaries were asked to replicate the corporate values and organizational practices of the parent company and also encouraged to completely adjust to the local market. Later on, subsidiary managers used the message that 'our market is unique' to defend specific, nationally designed marketing policies. Hence, they defended their autonomy even at the expense of sometimes rather fallacious arguments. In the 1980s and 1990s MNCs probably needed to shift their organizational design towards more centralization.

Parent companies wanted to have a more unified implementation scheme of new, more centrally

---

BOX 8.3

Global companies refocusing on emerging markets

Consumer goods companies are refocusing their efforts on fast-growing emerging markets to offset weakness in the European and North American markets. For instance, Procter & Gamble moved their global headquarters for beauty and baby-care (including their biggest brand Pampers) to Singapore in 2012 to be closer to Asian markets. The Reckitt Benckiser Group (RB: makers of Nurofen, Durex, etc.) moved their regional headquarters from Singapore to Shanghai and from Miami to Sao Paulo, Brazil, to focus on high-growth countries within these regions. They now have 36 percent of their management concentrates on the 6 billion consumers in emerging markets (e.g., Asia-Pacific, Latin America and Africa).

Bruno de Labarre, General Manager Reckitt Benckiser Russia and CIS, gives the following advice:[43]

There is ample opportunity for growth, as the Russian people begin to take care of themselves more and more. They will also certainly acquire greater purchasing power

in coming years. So there will be organic growth – even if such growth is, from time to time, hindered by some new governmental decision.'

However, he cautions that marketers must be very careful when they enter emerging markets:[43]

Come for two months, and do not speak – listen. Look to the people, look to the market, listen to your customers, and listen to your suppliers. Spend two months just listening! After that try to put on a piece of paper what you have understood about the market, and then decide what you must do. . . . I see too many managers come to Russia and believe that they understand everything after a week. They promptly begin making mistakes.

When we acquired BHI in 2006, I spent two months visiting pharmacies, visiting distributors, suppliers etc. I always asked them the same question: 'Tell me what you think of my company, what I need to improve, and what I do well that I should maintain. The best advice I can give is that you must understand that you do not know!'

designed international marketing strategies, responding to the globalization of competition. Procter & Gamble did this in Europe by introducing the Eurobrand concept, consisting of a common brand name and a basic marketing strategy for most western European countries. After a long period of centralization, P & G is now giving slightly more weight to localization, especially with regard to advertising and branding.

The two main elements to globalization at an organizational level include the centralization of elements of the value chain (e.g., functions such as research and development, logistics and distribution and after sales service) and the centralization of financial responsibility. Each of these is discussed below.

Geographical concentration–dispersion

The concentration–dispersion characterization of international marketing can be traced to Porter's 'design' framework,[3] which argued that multinational firms should configure the optimal value chain, so that scale and national comparative advantages are exploited, while still being responsive to local needs.[34] The focus is on the geographic 'concentration' vs 'dispersion' of the value chain activities, such as research and development, logistics, distribution and after sales service. For instance, Craig and Douglas (p. 7) describe the configural advantage of News Corporation's Fox network as follows:

In the United States, News Corporation's Fox network typically ends up fourth in the rating wars with the three established networks, ABC, NBC, and CBS. However, outside the United States, the picture is quite different. In addition to establishing a fourth television network, Rupert Murdoch is building a strong configuration of satellite and cable companies around the world. The extensive geographic network of operations allows content developed for the Fox television network in the United States to be aired on News Corporation's vast satellite network, which consists of BSkyB in the United Kingdom, Star TV in Asia, and ISkyB in India, as well as through satellite and terrestrial-based networks in other countries where News Corporation has strategic alliances. This vast network gives News Corporation a strong configural advantage over the three U.S. television networks – one that is very costly and difficult to replicate.[44]

Concentration of value-creating activities can increase economics of scale and accumulations of specialized knowledge. In contrast, geographically dispersed value-creating activities provide greater contact with both customers and competitors, which allows more rapid response to competitive innovations, market conditions (e.g., swings in foreign exchange, economic or political conditions) and tailoring of offerings to meet local customer needs.[44] As can be seen in Box 8.3, this will be especially important as companies move toward emerging markets.

Integration-independence

The *integration-independence* characterization of international marketing is concerned with the extent to which competitive moves are planned, implemented and controlled in a global manner.[44] At one end, a firm treats its subsidiaries as an *integrated network*, and, as such, may decide to cross-subsidize its competitive position across countries. At the other end, a firm treats its subsidiaries as independent profit centres, responsible for their own markets. However, the relationship between headquarters and subsidiaries in the defining of any marketing strategy is complex. Too much autonomy results in purely local solutions with few economies of scale and an absence of worldwide coordination; at that point, strong action is needed.

It is the patterns in the globalization of competition which impose changes in organizational design (recentralization), rather than the globalization of consumption patterns. In this process, negotiations and compromises between headquarters and subsidiaries are constant. Local managers naturally tend to emphasize the uniqueness of local consumption patterns and marketing environment (legal, distribution networks, sales promotion methods, and so on). The headquarters of successful global companies are flexible rather than authoritarian in dealing with their subsidiaries' assumed or real uniqueness. For instance, they commission research rather than flatly ignore a subsidiary's arguments and they take new ideas and suggestions from the most talented and dynamic subsidiaries, rather than rejecting their advice outright.

In fact, international marketing programmes have experienced a trend towards greater standardization, but this needs to be differentiated, according to: (1) the elements of the marketing mix considered; (2) the type of market, such as whether it is a developed or undeveloped country; (3) the type of product, such as consumer or industrial goods; and (4) the control exerted over the subsidiary, whether it is wholly owned or a joint venture.

The type of market and market similarities will also influence the standardization of offerings. Similarities in consumer preferences, as well as environmental factors, such as the cultural, economic, legal and infrastructure environment, will all assist in the level of feasible standardization.

The level of standardization in US multinational companies operating in Europe varies by product category.[45] There has been a decrease in the degree of standardization for consumer durables and industrial goods, and an increase for consumer nondurables. Most studies report industrial products as more standardized than consumer products and that high technology and branded premium luxury goods are more likely to be standardized. The caveat here is that there is no conclusive evidence, and common practice is not equivalent to best practice.

Culture-related experience is all the more important since natural entry barriers relating to consumer behaviour and marketing environments diminish very gradually and only in the long term. Language-related differences, for instance, remain. Therefore, global marketing strategies must be implemented cautiously, especially in emerging economies and culture-bound industries: local knowledge has to be generated, by research, by organizational learning, by hiring 'cultural' insiders or by acquiring local companies with culture-specific business experience.

8.4

Market segments

Intercultural marketing is about localizing as much as globalizing: it aims to customize product and marketing strategies to customer needs within the framework of a global strategy. Intercultural marketing tries to balance cross-national differences requiring mandatory local adaptation and cross-national commonalities, which are conducive to the development of size and experience effects. To do this, the international marketer needs to define country clusters where similar marketing policies can be followed.

Website link 8.4

Search for websites that discuss international market segmentation, such as Tourism Australia: **http://www.tourism.australia.com**.

Cultural identification: the case of cultural products

Cultural products, such as music, literature and films, are strongly suffused with local particularities. Books, music and films are, however, three products where global marketing has been successfully employed. The success of Harlequin romantic novels, Harry Potter and *The Lord of the Rings* films has been remarkable: profound attraction has bypassed the filter of national cultures. The romantic and melodramatic adventures of Harlequin heroes target a lonely female public eager for tenderness in the majority of urban centres. Similarly, the meanings conveyed by the adventures of Harry Potter extend far beyond British culture.

Cultural products that build on fairly universal feelings and lifestyles are the ones to which standardized marketing policy can be applied. In the recording industry, marketing techniques, particularly with regard to collections of popular music, have generally evolved in a similar fashion across countries with a global standardization of product presentation. However, there are differences in the platform for DVDs, which are formatted as either NTSC or PAL.

The recipe for global success is, however, less easily applicable than it seems: American country music has failed in its attempt to achieve major success in continental Europe. Its only real international development has taken place in Australia, despite some success in the United Kingdom. One reason for this is that no significant segment of the European population can identify with the images portrayed by the music from the American West and the symbols of a pioneer tradition. On the other hand, the Australian outback, with its jackaroos and jillaroos, is similar in many respects to the American West with its cowboys and cowgirls. This has given birth to an Australian musical tradition whose roots are in country music.

Intercultural marketing is facilitated when the conditions for product identification are present in the target market. Consumers buy the meaning that they find in products for the purpose of cultural identification, based on the desire to assimilate to a certain civilization, as in the case of ethnic consumption. Such identification was the reason that record companies began to market classical music on a large scale in the form of collections. Market surveys showed that owning a collection of classical music recordings, combined with a superficial knowledge of the most famous pieces, promoted a personal image of stability and respectability, projecting an image of successful integration in professional and social lives. As a result, certain record companies launched mass-market compilations of classical music. Their marketing strategy was to implement the strict rules of global marketing: same product, same packaging, same price and same type of communication. These compilations became less successful in the 1990s when classical music ceased to be a major element in the acquisition of respectability; however, they recently gained popularity with the youth market, who were exposed to classical music as background to computer games.

Apart from their utilitarian aspects, McDonald's Big Mac and Coca-Cola are sources of meanings that provide young buyers with fantasized cultural adaptation to a desired way of life. New trends in music often represent a break from reality for many young Europeans and Asians. Identification with these symbols is one of the necessary conditions for being *trendy*. The international marketing of music to youth achieves even greater success where certain values (e.g., individualism, strong desire for equality) are already present in the potential market segment.

Cultural identity involves two mutually contradictory desires: one is to identify oneself with the national or home culture, and the other is to identify with an exotic or foreign culture. This creates ambivalence and makes it necessary to cluster countries or consumers who share certain meaningful cultural characteristics. Such clusters form cultural affinity zones and cultural affinity classes.

Cultural affinity classes and zones

The intercultural marketing approach not only concentrates on geography- and nationality-based criteria but also takes into account consumer attitudes, preferences and lifestyles that are linked to age, class and ethnicity, occupation, and so on. Many studies have used these bases to identify international market segments, including demographics, psychographics and values, quality of life, attitudes, behaviour, brand loyalty and situation.

Geographical cultural affinity zones correspond to a large extent to national cultural groups, while cultural affinity classes exist in terms of other segmentation bases. For instance, people between the ages of 15 and 20, in Japan, Europe and the US, form a cultural

affinity class. They have a tendency to share common values, behaviour and interests; their lifestyles converge worldwide irrespective of national borders. As such, we see lifestyle convergence in teenagers in Europe who spend time watching MTV. Carey et al.[46] surveyed 7- to 12-year-olds around the world in the ABC Global Kids Study, tracking their lifestyle and consumption patterns. A pictorial response scale was used when interviewing children on emotions and preferences while product usage was reported more frequently by mothers, rather than children. Worldwide, children basically seem to share many common dreams and aspirations and they tend to have significant purchasing power and participate actively in family decision making for a number of product categories. Lifestyle convergence can also be observed for gender-based segments on a worldwide basis.

> ### Website link 8.5
> Search for segmentation derived from the European Social Survey, which can be found at: www.europeansocialsurvey.org/.

Cultural affinity classes are probably an ideal means of defining an international target for standardized products, in so far as they create a sense of belonging to a common age, gender or income group across different countries. However, there is practical difficulty in combining geography-based cultural affinity zones and demographics and lifestyle-segmentation criteria (cultural affinity classes). You may wonder, for instance, if consumption behaviour, values and lifestyles among 15- to 20-year-olds are more homogeneous across Europe or Asia than in relation to other age groups in the same zone. Accordingly, market research should survey consumer segments as cells in a matrix, with countries in columns and cultural affinity classes in rows. If similar behaviour is observed by market researchers for a particular row across the different cells of the matrix with regard to key consumer behaviour figures (e.g., consumption of soft drinks, organization of personal time, time spent listening to the radio or watching television, etc.), the emergence of a common consumption culture and a cross-national segment may be detected. If, on the other hand, different cultural affinity classes in different countries adopt similar behaviour across

Figure 8.1 A hypothetical map of the zones of cultural affinities in Europe

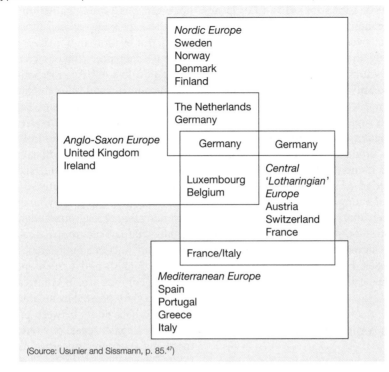

(Source: Usunier and Sissmann, p. 85.[47])

international contexts, at the very least marketing communication will have to be modified to facilitate the process of diffusion from one country to another. If a drink, for example, is popular among 25- to 30-year-olds in one country and among 50- to 60-year-olds in another country, this indicates a weak affinity of national cultures.

Attempts to market products globally also highlight cultural affinity zones in which the same marketing strategy with the same type of products can be successfully implemented. In Europe, for example, two of these zones are quite separate (see Figure 8.1) – Scandinavia and the Mediterranean countries. A third zone encompasses the central European countries and Great Britain, which serve as a bridge between northern and southern Europe, while retaining their own distinct personality. Despite the traditional isolation of the United Kingdom, there are fewer differences between the United Kingdom and Denmark or Sweden than between the UK and Italy or Spain. Accordingly, an item successfully marketed in the United Kingdom is more likely to repeat this success in the Netherlands or Denmark than in southern Europe. The long

established differences between Anglo Saxon and Latin culture are reinforced by the religious divide between Protestants and Catholics. Cultural affinity zones display similar characteristics for easily identifiable criteria such as language, religion, family life patterns, work relations and consumption patterns. Intercultural marketing begins by choosing one of the main countries from a cultural affinity zone as a 'lead country' that will be used as a base for market entry and diffusion of strategy, with only minor adaptation for other countries throughout the zone. Marketing teams can interact with each other across zones within a regional area, especially when countries lie at the border of two zones. As an example, Figure 8.1 offers a *hypothetical map* of the zones of cultural affinities for Western Europe.

The operational mapping of cultural affinity zones can be based on cultural as well as marketing criteria related to the product category, such as consumer behaviour, price levels, attitude towards innovation, opening hours in distribution outlets, etc. When a product is launched internationally, the new product will be launched first in lead countries and subsequently marketed in other countries in the zones. For instance, a new song that may be successful in Latin European countries during the summer, when waves of holiday-makers come from all over Europe, will have a greater chance of spreading into Nordic countries once visitors from those countries return home. Equally, a brand may be so successful in a single country, such as Germany, then its music spreads into neighbouring countries. It spreads rapidly in the border regions – for example, in Belgium, because of media overlap. The launch of a new product through cultural affinity zones can take from 18 months to two years, which is a relatively long period of time compared with the standard life cycle of a song, generally a few months. The concept of 'lead country' has been used success-fully by multinational companies such as Procter & Gamble when they developed the Eurobrand con-cept in the mid-1980s. However, the popularity of YouTube may dramatically speed up this process.

National versus regional differences

Sovereign states have very dissimilar sizes: China $(9,600,000 \text{ km}^2)$ is more than 232 times the size of Switzerland $(49,293 \text{ km}^2)$, even though both countries are significant international players on the world scene. Geographical location is related to culture: for instance, on average, islands tend to develop more homogeneity than continental countries. A special case is that of mega-countries such as the United States, Canada, Brazil, China and India because their internal diversity is fairly large. Even smaller countries, such as the United Kingdom, Spain, Italy, Sweden and France, exhibit a strong North/South paradigm which is reversed in the southern hemi-sphere for countries such as Argentina, Australia and New Zealand. Even tiny Switzerland displays significant internal diversity, especially between the French- and the German-speaking communities, which respectively account for 20 per cent and 75 per cent of the population. National differences are not the only source of variance in consumer behaviour across different geographical locations.

Regional differences in large countries with multi-ethnic and multicultural backgrounds can explain differences in consumer behaviour. Researchers have consistently found significant within-country differ-ences. Most of these have to do with geographical divisions where geography, a shared history and a common ethnic background has served to create homogeneous groupings within countries.[48] In the USA there are many regional differences in consumers' values, innovation and perceived risk, as well as cultural adherence, religious commitment and fate-orientation. In South America both regional differences within countries and value similarity across countries are found. Lenartowicz and colleagues[48] used the Rokeach Value Survey (RVS) to examine the import-ance of regional subcultures in Brazil and Colombia and their value similarity with consumers in Uruguay and Venezuela. They found significant differences between regions in the relative importance of values, concluding that 'geography, a shared history and a common ethnic background might be as important in defining cultural subgroups as religion and language' (p. 1006).[48] In Canada differences have been found between English and French speakers in the same location. For instance, in Montreal, Canada, there are differences in pro-environmental knowledge, atti-tudes and behaviours between primarily French and primarily English speakers. French Canadians know more and are more concerned about environmental issues, whereas English Canadians are more likely to recycle and are willing to pay more for environment-ally friendly products.[49]

However, regional differences within countries, even if perceived more clearly by nationals than by foreigners, are most often much smaller than interna-tional differences. For instance, among Belgian and Polish consumers of chocolates, at least two of the five segments were driven by nationality: the first seg-ment was made up of 87 per cent Belgian consumers and the second made up of 91 per cent Polish con-sumers.[50] It was also found that a sub-cultural design was not appropriate for Poland. Similarly, English female Quebecers were found to be more similar to French female Quebecers than to English female Ontarians (all of these being Canadian females) in the benefits they seek from a brassiere.[51] These findings support the idea of the assimilation model, where the cultural values of the immigrants tend to merge with those of the locally dominant cultural group. This supports geography as an operational basis for inter-national marketing segmentation.

However, some global segments are emerging, with increasing access to the Internet and global media, creating segments that transcend regions. Douglas and Craig (p. 89) identify some of these as: 'environmentally and socially concerned consumers targeted by companies such as the Body Shop, Aveda, fair-trade stores, and retailers selling organic products, as well as young married couples targeted by companies such as IKEA with low priced furniture and ING with financial products.[2] While local adaptation of products and services targeted to these segments (e.g., affluent, environmentally concerned, cosmopolitan individuals) may seem unnecessary, there may be very real differences in their motivations (e.g., recycling in dense populations versus water conservation in drought-ridden areas), as well as their local contexts, including regulations and cultural factors. Further, these individuals still interpret these 'global' messages within their local context. Thus, overarching strategies may be similar, but the implementation may be different (e.g., department stores versus specialty stores; culturally based message context, and the media used to reach them).

8.5

Conclusion

Intercultural marketing is based on the premise that it is wise to standardize when significant cost advantages can be achieved and localize where necessary. The increasing interest in growth through emerging and developing nations will make this even more important. Recently, international marketers have even espoused country-centric marketing for sizable emerging markets, as the demand characteristics, nature of competition and infrastructure are all likely to be very different from developed nations.[2] However, as companies learn from these new experiences, attractive emerging countries can be grouped together, in cultural affinity classes where there are common characteristics. Satellite strategies can then be developed to transfer knowledge from the Chinese market to say the Vietnamese or Thai markets.[2]

Further, when building clusters of countries ('cultural affinity zones') that can be approached with a regionally standardized marketing strategy, marketing professionals should take into account basic cultural variables such as language, institutions, membership in a regional grouping, and basic cultural traits as described in Chapters 2, 3 and 4. Socio-demographic characteristics such as sex, age and income also provide a potential basis for transnational marketing strategies in terms of 'cultural affinity classes'. International marketing segments must be defined in order to allow for the best possible compromise between national/cultural and socio-demographic characteristics.

Questions

1. Describe how experience effects induce firms to standardize products. Provide examples.

2. Select a multinational company annual report and find evidence of globalization (global decisions, global products, globalization of competition, consumption patterns, management procedures, etc.).

3. Why does globalization take place more clearly on the supply side than on the demand side?

4. For the following industries/products, discuss to what extent: (a) a world consumer exists; (b) the product or services offered are themselves global (similar worldwide); and (c) the industry itself can be considered as global:
   - airlines;
   - tobacco;
   - meat-based foods;
   - sheets and pillows;
   - pharmaceuticals.

5. What are zones of cultural affinity?

6. Discuss the relative importance, for segmentation purposes, of sociodemographic variables, such as age, sex, income, habitat, etc., in comparison with cultural variables based either on nationality or values.

References

1. Contractor, Farok J. (2007), 'Is International Business Good for Companies? The evolutionary or multi-stage theory of internationalization vs. the transactional cost perspective', *Management International Review*, 47 (3), 453–75.

2. Douglas, Susan P. and C. Samual Craig (2011), 'Convergence and Divergence: Developing a semiglobal marketing strategy', *Journal of International Marketing*, 19 (1), 82–101.

3. Porter, Michael E. (1986), 'Changing Patterns of International Competition', *California Management Review*, XXVIII (2), 9–39.

4. Sheth, Jagdish N. (2001), 'From International to Integrated Marketing', *Journal of Business Research*, 51, 5–9.

5. Rugman, Alan (2001), 'The Myth of Global Strategy', *International Marketing Review*, 18 (6), 583–88.

6. WTO (2011), 'World Trade Developments', retrieved 13 February 2012 from www.wto.org.

7. Qian, Gongming and Ji Li (2002), 'Multinationality, Global Market Diversification and Profitability among the Largest Us Firms', *Journal of Business Research*, 55 (4), 325–35.

8. Duhigg, Charles and Keith Bradsher, 'How U.S. Lost Out on IPhone Work', *New York Times*, 22 January 2012, p. A1: New York edition.

9. Prasad, V. Kanti, K. Ramamurthy and G. M. Naidu (2001), 'The Influence of Internet-Marketing Integration on Marketing Competencies and Export Performance', *Journal of International Marketing*, 9 (4), 82–110.

10. Favier, Jaap (2007), 'Europe's Ecommerce Forecast: 2006 to 2011', *Forrester Market Research*, 1, 1–7.

11. Mulpuru, Sucharita (2006), 'U.S. Ecommerce: Five-Year Forecast and Data Overview', *Forrester Market Research* (1), 1–15.

12. World Internet Users and Populations Stats' downloaded from 13 Feb 2012 http://www.internetworldstats.com/stats.htm.

13. Usunier, Jean-Claude (2002), 'Le Pays D'origine du Bien Influence-t-il Encore les Évaluations des Consommateurs?', *Revue Française du Marketing*, 189/190 (2002/4–5), 49–65.

14. Perlmutter, Howard V. (1969), 'The Tortuous Evolution of the Multinational Corporation', *Columbia Journal of World Business*, 4 (1), 9–18.

15. Wind, Yoram, Susan P. Douglas and Howard V. Perlmutter (1973), 'Guidelines for Developing International Marketing Strategies', *Journal of Marketing*, 37 (April), 14–23.

16. Sheth, Jagdish N. and Atul Parvatiyar (2001), 'The Antecedents and Consequences of Integrated Global Marketing', *International Marketing Review*, 18 (1), 16–29.

17. Malhotra, Naresh K., James Agarwal and Imad Baalbaki (1998), 'Heterogeneity of Regional Trading Blocks and Global Marketing Strategies: A Multi-cultural Perspective', *International Marketing Review*, 15 (6), 476–506.

18. Ohmae, Kenichi (1985), *Triad Power: The Coming Shape of Global Competition*. New York: Free Press.

19. Matthyssens, Paul and Pieter Pauwels (2000), 'Uncovering International Market-Exit Processes: A Comparative Case Study', *Psychology and Marketing*, 17 (8), 697–719.

20. Swift, Jonathan B. (1999), 'Cultural Closeness as a Facet of Cultural Affinity', *International Marketing Review*, 16 (3), 182–201.

21. Anderson, Erin and Barton Weitz (1989), 'Determinants of Continuity in Conventional Industrial Channel Dyads', *Marketing Science*, 8, 310–23.

22. van Oudenhoven, Jan Pieter and Karen I. van de Zee (2002), 'Successful International Cooperation: The Influence of Cultural Similarity, Strategic Differences, and International Experience', *Applied Psychology*, 51 (4), 633.

23. Yu, Chwo-Ming Joseph and Dixie S. Zietlow (1995), 'The Determinants of Bilateral Trade among Asia-Pacific Countries', *A.S.E.A.N. Economic Bulletin*, 11 (3), 298–305.

24. Wang, Chih-Kang and Charles W. Lamb Jr (1983), 'The Impact of Selected Environmental Forces Upon Consumers' Willingness to Buy Foreign Products', *Journal of the Academy of Marketing Science*, 11 (2), 71–84.

25. Xu, Dean and Oded Shenkar (2002), 'Institutional Distance and the Multinational Enterprise', *Academy of Management Review*, 27 (4), 608–18.

26. Douglas, Susan P. (2001), 'Exploring New Worlds: The Challenge of Global Marketing', *Journal of Marketing*, 65 (1), 103–07.

27. Lane, K. P., I. St-Maurice and C. S. Dyckerhoff (2006), 'Building Brands in China', *McKinsey Quarterly*, 35–41.

28. Saporito, William (1984), 'Black & Decker's Gamble on Globalization', *Fortune*, 14 (May), 24–32.

29. Lim, Lewis K. S., Frank Acito and Alexander Rusetski (2006), 'Development of Archetypes of International Marketing Strategy', *Journal of International Business Studies*, 37 (4), 499–524.

30. Buzzell, Robert D. (1968), 'Can You Standardize Multinational Marketing?', *Harvard Business Review* (November–December), 102–13.

31. Deher, Odile (1986), 'Quelques Facteurs de Succès Pour la Politique de Produits de l'entreprise Exportatrice: Les Liens entre Marketing et Production', *Recherche et Applications en Marketing*, 1 (3), 55–74.

32. Gilmore, James H. and B. Joesph Pine II (1997), 'The Four Faces of Mass Customization', *Harvard Business Review*, 75 (1, January–February), 91–101.

33. Stobaugh, Robert and Piero Telesio (1983), 'Assortir la Politique de Fabrication à la Stratégie des Produits', *Harvard-L'Expansion* (Summer), 77–85.

34. Zou, Shaoming and Tamir Cavusgil (2002), 'The G.M.S.: A Broad Conceptualization of Global Marketing Strategy and Its Effect on Firm Performance', *Journal of Marketing*, 66 (4), 40–56.

35. Theodosiou, Marios and Leonidas C. Leonidou (2003), 'Standardization Versus Adaptation of International Marketing Strategy: An Integrative Assessment of the Empirical Research', *International Business Review*, 12 (2), 141–71.

36. Schuh, Arnold (2000), 'Global Standardization as a Success Formula for Marketing in Central Eastern Europe', *Journal of World Business*, 35 (2), 133–48.

37. Dow, Douglas (2006), 'Adaptation and Performance in Foreign Markets: Evidence of Systematic Under-Adaptation', *Journal of International Business Studies*, 37 (2), 212–26.

38. Wright, Len Tiu (2001), 'Intercontinental Comparisons in Marketing Strategy', *International Marketing Review*, 18 (3), 344–54.

39. Jain, Subhash C. (2007), 'State of the Art of International Marketing Research: Directions for the Future', *Journal for Global Business Advancement*, 1 (1), 4–19.

40. Schilke, Martin Reimann and Jacquelin S. Thomas, (2009), 'When Does International Marketing Standardization Matter to Firm Performance?' *Journal of International Marketing*, 17 (4), 24–6.

41. Samiee, Saeed and Kendall Roth (1994), 'The Influence of Global Marketing Standardization on Performance', *Journal of Marketing*, 56 (April), 1–17.

42. Whitelock, Jeryl and Carole Pimblett (1997), 'The Standardization Debate in International Marketing', *Journal of Global Marketing*, 10 (3), 45–65.

43. Reckitt Benckiser (2012), Interview with: Bruno de Labarre, General Manager Reckitt Benckiser Russia and CIS, Retrieved 13 August 2012 from www.rb.com/ru/Media/BDL-Interview (downloaded 13 August, 2012).

44. Craig, C. Samuel and Susan P. Douglas (2000), 'Configural Advantage in Global Markets', *Journal of International Marketing*, 8 (1), 6–26.

45. Picard, Jacques, Jean-Jacques Boddewyn, and Robin Soehl (1989), 'U.S. Marketing Policies in the European Economic Community: A Longitudinal Study, 1973–1983', in *Dynamics of International Business*, Reijo Luostarinen (ed.) Vol. 1. Helsinki: Proceedings of the 15th Annual Conference of the European International Business Association.

46. Carey, George, Xiaoyan Zhao, Joan Chiaramonte and David Eden (1997), 'Is There One Global Village for Our Future Generation? Talking to 7–12 Year Olds around the World', *Marketing and Research Today*, 25 (1), 12–16.

47. Usunier, J-C. and Pierre Sissman (1986), 'L'interculturel au service du marketing', *Harvard-L'Expansion*, 40 (Spring), 80–92.

48. Lenartowicz, Thomasz, James P. Johnson and Carolyn T. White (2003), 'The Neglect of Intracultural Variation in International Management Research', *Journal of Business Research*, 56 (12), 999–1008.

49. Laroche, Michel, Marc-Alexandre Tomiuk, Jasmin Bergeron and Guido Barbaro-Forleo (2002), 'Cultural Differences in Environmental Knowledge, Attitudes, and Behaviours of Canadian Consumers', *Canadian Journal of Administrative Sciences*, 19 (3), 267–83.

50. Januszewska, Renata, Jacques Viaene and Wim Verbeke (2000), 'Market Segmentation for Chocolate in Belgium and Poland', *Journal of Euromarketing*, 9 (3), 1–25.

51. Calantone, Roger, Michael Morris and Jotindar Johar (1985), 'A Crosscultural Benefit Segmentation Analysis to Evaluate the Traditional Assimilation Model', *International Journal of Research in Marketing*, 2 (3), 207–17.

Teaching materials

A8.1 Case

Bollywood: selling Indian movies in the West

'*Why me?*' grumbled Nico Rogosky, account executive for Pentagram Asian films North America. In July 2011, when Bollywood producer Anjali Kumar called to ask him to take over the marketing and distribution of two new 'Bollywood' films, he suggested she contact a South Asian film marketing expert like Eros. 'No, no', she had breezily said, 'we don't want to plug the films to your Indian minority market as usual. We want to make crossover films to appeal to other ethnic groups and the general public. I called you for a different approach.'

Nico had spent the entire afternoon viewing two Bollywood hits with his Indian equivalent, just to get an idea of the genre. So, he mused, sipping a searing-hot green tea, they want us to market their movies, then DVDs and videos, and maybe cable. The company also asked for advice on producing films directly for the North American market. Nico had enjoyed talking over dinner with his Indian counterpart from Kumar Film, a sophisticated chain-smoker named Rishi, who had studied business in Florida. Now sitting comfortably at his home office, Nico listened to the conversation he had recorded.

Nico's conversation with Rishi

Nico: I could see the actors were lip-synching, it was embarrassingly obvious!

Rishi: We'll cut the singing out of the films for you. Everyone knows that actors can't sing, and a handful of back-up singers sing for all the Bollywood stars. Actually, no one cares: back-up singer Lata Mangeshkar has more worldwide sales than the Beatles. Actors Shah Rukh Khan and Aamir Khan sold out London's Wembley Arena with back-up singers singing 100 per cent of the concert!

Nico: It was incongruous, though, all those songs interfering with the story line.

Rishi: Actor and film producer Shahrukh Khan famously said that if he had produced *Gladiator*, he would have Russell Crowe singing songs in it.[1] Film star Aamir Khan said that in a movie, the songs hold an emotion, and squeeze the juice from it . . . It's just pure Bollywood.

Nico: The sexual tension between the lovers was unbearable, but the most we saw was some kissing. I would have expected them to, like, hop in bed at that point.

Rishi: Yeah, some say we're prudes, that we're censored. We're conservative, but not prudish. So metaphor, imagery and song/dance routines express sexual undercurrents. That film was quite explicit, actually. You have a lot of people here in the US who would appreciate our level of modesty in films.

Nico: The movies were fabulous, but the story and character development were weak.

Rishi: When I've spoken with film critics from your country, from England, and from France, they all say we're 'exuberant', 'melodramatic', 'earthy'. But film snobs prefer 'over the top', 'predictable', 'unrealistic', and 'superficial'. Our films are life, only more pretty. We don't pretend we're intellectuals or artists. A lot of our audiences are in far-flung villages, workers who spend a day's wage at the ticket office. We give them beauty, glamour, romance, music . . . escape. That is what your troubled people are now seeking too.

Nico had seen *Bend it like Beckham*, *Monsoon Wedding*, and other 'Asian' films that were hits in the US and the UK, like *Crouching Tiger, Hidden Dragon*, but nothing like this. They want to appeal to Americans? For the art-house crowd there shouldn't be an issue, thought Nico. Indian style is 'in', henna, piercing, yoga, ayurveda, tattoos and so on have become mainstream, and South-Asian inspired music like Bhangra and Asian Underground are played regularly in dance clubs.[2] But what will the archetypal housewife in Idaho think of Bollywood movies? On the other hand, the conservative right should love the movies. Nico smiled, remembering their recent boycotts of Hollywood stars for their political stances and the boycotts for alleged sexual and homosexual allusions in Disney children's films.

What about the growing communities of immigrants who tend to be more conservative (at least where their families are concerned) than mainstream Americans. A lot of them have felt marginalized over the past few years, and may be seeking self-affirmation elsewhere than Hollywood. *You know, Rishi and his colleagues might just stand a chance with a little help from us*, was Nico's surprising thought before sitting down to read more about Bollywood.

Bollywood: a preview

In the world of film, there are two giants: the USA and India. In terms of films produced per year, India's Mumbai (formerly Bombay, hence 'Bollywood') is the leading lady. In 2009 India produced 1325 movies, while Hollywood films numbered 463.[3] Any similarities between the two end there. It is estimated that Mumbai alone produces about 800 Hindi films per year, with other Indian cities producing the rest. Worldwide Bollywood revenues were estimated at US $2.8 billion in 2009,[3] while Hollywood totaled US$10 billion.[4]

According to the legend, Bollywood films resemble the fragrant, heady *masala* mixture of black pepper, cumin, cloves, cardamom and other spices used in cooking. *Masala* films are a mixture of elements to keep audiences interested: song, dance, action, romance and comedy. It is a film genre unto itself: the product of Indian village theatre, Victorian drama, and opera. Films commonly comprise three hours of romance, travel, courtship, marriage, tragedy, and redemption, played to the backdrop of sumptuously appointed and colourful sets. (For more information, visit **http://www.bollywhat.com**.)

The stars, like Madhuri Dixit, Rani Mukherjee and Hrithik Roshan, are gorgeous, and they express their emotions with a frantic sincerity in words and in lip-synched songs that appear to put the plot on hold. The music uses primal rhythms, and the tunes are catchy, accompanied by sinuous dances featuring dozens of costumed dancers. The plot may shift from place to place, with surprising interludes shot in beautiful locations like Scotland, Australia, Switzerland or New Zealand.

The storyline usually begins with a boy meets girl premise: however, one of the two is from the 'wrong' social background. There is a coincidence that brings star-crossed lovers together, then fate thwarts them with death. Weeping mothers, archetypal families, giggling sisters, stereotypical characters and slapstick roles complete the *masala* film recipe. That is the legend. The reality of Bollywood films has changed in recent years, for artistic and more prosaic business and marketing reasons.

Bollywood is often accused of taking 'inspiration' from Hollywood productions partly because Hollywood is India's primary recognizable reference for wealth, style and coolness. This perception only works one way, however: Bollywood films have yet to cross over from the 'ethnic' South Asian cinema to the main street cinema. Leading producer Ashok Amritraj does not believe that a Hindi film can have mass appeal in the USA.[5]

Others point to *Lagaan* and *Monsoon Wedding*, two Indian films with critical and box-office success. *Lagaan* (2001) featured a cricket game that put oppression into play between poor Indian villagers and their sneering colonial overlords. (Visit **http://www.lagaan.com** for more information.) It was shortlisted for the Best Foreign Film Award at the Oscars, nominated Best Foreign Language Film at the Academy Awards, and won seven India International Film Awards.[6] It made money also: US$2 million at US and UK box offices.[7] *Monsoon Wedding* (2001), which featured an arranged marriage in New Delhi, won a Golden Lion at the Venice Film Festival. The film earned over US$30 million worldwide The movie *3 Idiots* was the highest grossing Indian movie up to 2009 and earned US$82 million.[8]

Bollywood holds obvious potential, with an annual growth rate of 11 per cent in 2010, more than twice than the Hollywood industry's growth rate.[9] Some Bollywood hits boast of a return on investment of 25 per cent or more. Possibly the most persuasive argument in favor of Bollywood is the general claim that 'half of humanity' views Bollywood films: 3.2 billion tickets were sold in 2009 more than doubled the US and Canada together.[10] New forms of distribution are adding Bollywood's profitability. Only 40 per cent of the revenue of a typical Bollywood film today comes from the box-office; the rest comes from music, DVD, satellite and Internet rights and direct-to-home (DTH) TV services and mobile ring-tones, according to estimates in 2007 (**http://www.bollywood.com/node/843**).

Bootlegged DVDs and videocassettes inundate India's domestic and expatriate markets worldwide within days of a Bollywood film release, costing the Indian film industry US$75 million in 2002, or 60 per cent of the market value.[11] From pirated soundtracks, Bollywood lost over US$140 million.[12] According to Ernst & Young, Bollywood lost about US$959 million in 2008 (**http://www.wopular.com/mpaa-and-bollywood-team-tackle-piracy-0**).

Up until 2001 film making was not recognized as an 'industry' in India. Consequently, about 40 per cent of Bollywood's finances originated in organized crime, according to the police.[13] A string of film-worthy murders and scandals made clear that Bollywood glamour, power, and money laundering were attractive to the mob. Producers now seek funding from banks and international corporations, forcing a new professionalism that includes proper marketing plans and newer marketing tools like in-film product placements and 'marketing the film like a brand' activities and public relations, and merchandising.[14] (To get an idea of some Bollywood marketing tactics, visit **http://www.indiafm.com**).

Hollywood itself believes in the potential of Bollywood: Columbia TriStar Motion Picture Group distributed *Lagaan* and *Mission Kashmir* in the US, and is slated to distribute many more. Twentieth Century Fox has committed to marketing and distributing Hindi films by Bollywood producer Ram Gopal Verma. Hyperion Pictures is collaborating in a US–Bollywood feature called *Marigold*.[13] Columbia TriStar Motion Pictures was the first production house that started to co-produce Bollywood movies, followed by Warner-Bros and Walt-Disney Co. Hollywood sees a big opportunity in collaborating with the Indian film industry (**http://www.india-server.com/news/hollywood-production-houses-are-india-18596.html**). Bollywood film, video, and DVD distributors in the US target the 'Desi' communities (Indian, Pakistani, Sri Lankan, and Bangladeshi), and increasingly the Middle Eastern and Russian communities there where the genre has a huge following.[15]

Indian films have slowly but surely become an international commodity. An estimated 10–15 million Indian expatriates known as Non Resident Indians (NRIs) live in Britain, the

US, Asia, and Africa. Their annual income totals approximately US$ 375 billion, and they are said to account for 40 per cent of any Bollywood production's profits. The large South Asian communities in the US and Britain account for 55 per cent of international ticket sales,[16] and, understandably, Bollywood films incorporate NRIs into their stories in an effort to keep the interest of expatriates.[17] This apparently alienates the average viewer in India, however.

Hindi cinema has for years enjoyed a strong following independent of the South Asian expatriate communities in the Gulf region, Egypt, Russia and certain Eastern European countries, and some African nations. Afghanistan was once one of the biggest markets for Hindi films, and the first films to play after the fall of the Taliban were Hindi.[18] Because of their relatively modest and subtle portrayal of the female body and sexual acts, Hindi films have long had the favour of distributors in Arab countries.[16] The fact that many Bollywood stars are Muslim is also helpful. Indian films have long had a 'cult' or 'art house' following in wealthy countries as well.[19] Since 2001 the Indian government has demonstrated greater commitment to export efforts, and has participated in more film festivals and exhibitions.[20] Technological change has played a role in the 'internationalization' of Bollywood films, with satellite television beaming around the globe. DVDs may include any number of subtitles that widened marketing possibilities of many films around the world and through different channels, such as retail and e-commerce.[21]

Resembling a drama, at the moment Bollywood was poised to achieve respectability, things started to go wrong. Some reports estimate that only 7 per cent of films in 2001 made a profit. In 2002 98 per cent of films were box office failures, with the notable exception of horror film *Raaz*,[22] incurring a loss of US$ 58 million.[23] (For a survey of Bollywood's lucrative 'horror' phase, go to **http://sify.com/entertainment/movies/horror/index.php**.) The Indian government announced that it was to loosen its protectionist laws on cinema imports, opening the floodgates to Hollywood films. Across India 500 cinemas closed in 2002.[24] Bollywood appeared to be at a crucial juncture. Although 2007 was a successful year, the percentage of successful movies was only 11.1 per cent (**http://dhaka-pic.blogspot.com/ 2008/01/bollywoods-profit-2007.html**). Experts said Bollywood suffered a net loss of about $66 million in 2010. They say that it is time to focus more about the content of the movie than stars and frills. One to two movies a month is a success; all the rest fail.[25]

As actor Akshay Kumar observed, Indian audiences no longer imperatively seek *roha-dhona* (tears and family-oriented emotion) at the cinema, because they receive high doses of it from television soap operas.[26] Analysts have reported audience fatigue with re-hashed formulas and high ticket prices.[24] Producers have responded to a perception that audiences want a change by making thrillers and horror films (all containing some song and dance routines). Suspense films have all but taken over from the well-worn Bollywood romantic formula. However they are conducive to good music, and romance may be integrated into the plot to keep the audience happy, according to trade analyst Vindo Mirani.[23] In 2010 the movie *Raajneeti*, a political thriller containing a romance, found a great success not only in Asia but also in the UK, US and New Zealand.[27]

In a nod to 'Western' films, some recent films have included fewer songs or no songs at all, in addition to faraway locations, such as Los Angeles where Sanjay Gupta directed *Kaante*, a US$2.2 million thriller featuring four Bollywood idols and an all-American cast and crew. The film, recorded in English and Hindi, opened to mixed reviews in India. The film was closely modelled on Hollywood hits *Usual Suspects* and *Reservoir Dogs*. Because of the length of these movies producers sometimes plan two releases: the full-length version for South Asian expatriates and a shorter one for the general public. For example, *Asoka*, the story of the emperor turned Buddhist monk is an example where songs and dances have been cut for European release.[28]

Questions

1. What is culture specific and what is universal in Indian movie films? Which features of Indian films may not fit with a Western audience?

2. Is there a market for Indian movies in the United States? In Europe? What are the target audiences (ethnic groups versus general audience)?

3. Should Nico Rogosky and Pentagram accept the offer of Anjali Kumar to take over the marketing and distribution of two new 'Bollywood' films? If yes, what should Nico ask from Anjali and Rishi if he wants to minimize the risk of a failure?

For images and profiles on some major Bollywood stars, go to the following sites:

http://www.amitabh4u.com
http://www.bollywhat.com/Biographies/RANI_bio.html
http://www.khoj.com/Entertainment/Films/Hindi/Actresses/Madhuri_Dixit/
http://www.iifa.com/web07/cntnt/theindianfilmindustry.htm

Saskia Faulk and Jean-Claude Usunier prepared this case solely to provide material for class discussion. The authors do not intend to illustrate either effective or ineffective handling of a business situation. The authors may have disguised certain names and other identifying information to protect confidentiality.

© IRM/HEC, 2011

2011-09-05

Version: (A)

A8.2 Case

Muslim Cola: cola wars or cola crusades?

During the prelude to the 2003 American-led invasion of Iraq some consumers worldwide boycotted American products and brands. In the Philippines, ten leading products were targeted, notably Coca-Cola, McDonald's, Citibank and Starbucks. Among the reasons given by boycott leaders were 'disgust and revulsion' at the invasion.[29] In some Russian and German cities restaurant patrons were told that Coke was unavailable because of the current political situation.[30] Other countries with active boycotts discussed in the press included Argentina, Egypt, France, Greece, India, Indonesia, Italy, Malaysia, Pakistan, Saudi Arabia, Tunisia and Yemen. Almost without exception, Coca-Cola figures prominently in the boycotted product lists. Coca-Cola has itself been targeted in a longstanding boycott over its bottling plant in occupied Palestine.[31,32] For years boycotts in support of the Palestinian Intifada have been in effect, as well as boycott threats in opposition to the Bush Administration's international trade stance on biotech foods and other issues.[33] What is more, Coca-Cola has been accused of pollution[34] as well as dangerous levels of pesticides in soft drinks sold in India.[35] Boycotts and protests have been vivid in the US as well. In 2005 some university campuses have chosen to stop selling coke products.[36]

Coca-Cola's prominence on boycott lists points to its paradigmatic status as an American brand. Variations on the Coca-Cola logo have often been misused in anti-war and anti-globalization posters, and in puns, as in 'COLA-teral Damage' by the Belgian group STOPUSA (**www.stopusa.org**, a website that does not exist anymore).

Online boycott lists that prominently feature Coca-Cola

■ http://www.krysstal.com/democracy_whyusa_boycott.html (UK)
■ http://www.ethicalconsumer.org/Boycotts/currentboycotts.aspx (UK)
■ http://www.boycott.hpg.ig.com.br/index.html (Brazil)

- http://www.alterinfo.net/PAS-D-ARGENT-POUR-LA-GUERRE-BOYCOTT-DES-ETATS-UNIS_a174.html (France)
- http://killercoke.org/ (USA)

Muslim Colas

Mecca Cola (http://mecca-cola.com/) was launched by Tunisian-born entrepreneur Tawfik Mathlouthi in November, 2002. Its packaging is similar in colour and style to that of Coca-Cola; however, its philosophy is diametrically opposed to the drinks monolith: its logo is 'No more drinking stupid – drink with commitment!', and 'Don't shake me, shake your conscience!' The French company claimed that 10 per cent of its net profits will be sent to Palestinian children's charities, plus another 10 per cent to European charities favouring international peace and Palestinian causes. Mecca drinks (including Tonic, Classic, Mentha, and Vanilly) are now distributed in 64 countries, among them Australia, Belgium, Canada, France, Germany, Great Britain and even the US.[37] In Great Britain orders were brisk at over 2 million bottles per month[38] Mecca Cola 'sponsored' the million-strong peace march in London in February, 2003, handing out 'Not in my name' T-shirts and Mecca Cola.

Across the Channel, Qibla Cola made its appearance in February 2003. According to the Qibla Cola website (www.Qibla-cola.com), British entrepreneur Zahida Parveen founded the company to offer 'real alternatives to global consumer brands that support unjust policies'.[39] Like Mecca Cola, Qibla's offerings resemble those of Coca Cola, and Qibla is the Arabic word for the direction to pray to Mecca, but the company is more than a nod at Mecca Cola. The company promotes Qibla Cola, Qibla Diet Cola, Qibla Fantasy Orange, Qibla Mango, Qibla Guava, Qibla 5 (lemon-lime – named for the five pillars of Islam) and spring water to 2.5 million Muslims in Britain, with an eye on Indonesia, Pakistan and Bangladesh.[37] The company works with Islamic Aid, a registered charity that is to receive 10 per cent of net profits. Qibla noted that it broke even after only two months, an exceptional performance for a start-up.[40] In an interview, Qibla CEO Zafer Iqbal proffered that the products' packaging and taste parallels with Coca-Cola were intended to 'leverage' Coke's global image and make consumers aware of Islamic alternatives like Qibla.[40] Company spokesperson Abdul Hamid Ebrahim stated that the company's inspiration came from Iran's ZamZam Cola, a company that profited from a leading Iranian cleric's ruling that Coke and Pepsi were 'un-Islamic'.[37]

ZamZam cola (http://www.zamzamrefreshment.com/) has a leading market share of 47 per cent in its home country Iran, a net income of US$176 million last year and more than 7000 employees in 17 factories.[41] It is distributed throughout the Middle East, and some African and European countries, notably Denmark. The company was Coke's long-term partner in Iran, prior to the Islamic Revolution. In the autumn of 2002 ZamZam produced more than 10 million bottles to meet rising demand in Saudi Arabia, spurred on by anger over American support for Israel.[42] As a consequence of boycotts and the advent of competitors like ZamZam, sales of Coca-Cola and Pepsi Cola fell from 20 to 40 per cent in some Middle Eastern countries in 2002.[43]

There are other so-called 'Muslim' Colas dedicated to taking market share from Coca-Cola, including French brand Arab Cola (http://www.arab-cola.com) and Star Cola from the United Arab Emirates. All these cola companies face similar problems. They are up against the world's most valuable brand, Coca-Cola, valued at more than US$68 billion in 2009.[44] For all but ZamZam, securing capacity contracts with bottling plants has proved difficult. Distribution is often a problem, with supermarkets reluctant to take on a new 'niche' product with an unsure future, although in France Arab Cola can proudly make the claim that it has the 'trust' of its national super/hypermarket distributors Carrefour and E. Leclerc.[45] Distributors are also concerned about the capacity of cola suppliers to meet demand at a consistent quality level, which is often an issue in the Middle East where ambient temperatures may be excessive for many packaging and ingredient formulations. As a result, these alternative colas are often sold in small, family-owned shops in areas populated by immigrants.[46] They may ride the wave of temporary consumer sentiment against US brands, but people tend to revert to predictable quality brands over time.[47] It is unlikely that any of the Muslim colas poses a real and sustainable threat to the entrenched hegemony of Coke and Pepsi, however. As one consultant has put it, if the market for Muslim colas gets too big, Coke will simply buy them up, just as it did with upstart cola company Thumbs Up[48] in India.

Questions

1. Some analysts believe that companies like Qibla, Mecca and Arab Cola are not capable of long-term market share, and that their initial success is due to publicity that will quickly fizzle out. Is this a likely scenario, given the competitive environment in which they operate?

2. Some Muslims object to the 'commercialization' of Islam, as represented by these cola companies' marketing strategies. Should these Muslim cola companies target a wider audience? If so, how? Give them some marketing ideas.

3. If you were the CEO of the leading company (Coca-Cola) how would you react to the emergence of Muslim colas? In non-Muslim countries? In Muslim countries? Consider the same question if you were the CEO of the longstanding challenger (Pepsi-Cola)?

Saskia Faulk and Jean-Claude Usunier prepared this case solely to provide material for class discussion. The authors do not intend to illustrate either effective or ineffective handling of a business situation. The authors may have disguised certain names and other identifying information to protect confidentiality.

2011-05-11

Version: (A)

A8.3 Case

Odol

When Manfred Hansen took over as marketing director of Lingner and Fischer, the company held a meagre 15 per cent of the oral care market in Germany – half of what the leader, Procter & Gamble, could claim. Known since 1997 as SmithKline Beecham, the company now commands a 30.4 per cent share of oral care while P&G's slice has shrunk to 13.8 per cent, according to AC Nielsen. And Mr Hansen has kept his promise to be the leading oral care company in Germany, while becoming No. 1 in Switzerland and Austria as well.

SmithKline managed this turnaround through savvy marketing, including extending the familiar Odol and Dr Best brand names, bringing a fresh positioning to whitening products and paying close attention to consumer needs in areas such as packaging, where it eliminated wasteful wrapping entirely. The company also achieved its success in Germany by keeping an eye on global strategies while giving local managers some autonomy. 'SmithKline Beecham is acting much faster and takes greater risks than P&G,' said a marketing manager at the now pacesetting company. 'We are in constant touch with headquarters in order to understand market situations in other countries, [but] fortunately headquarters leaves us freedom to act in our market, taking into consideration the local situation.'

Becoming the market leader in toothpaste, a $545 million category in Germany and hotly contested by rivals P&G, Colgate-Palmolive Co. and Elidda-Gibbs hasn't been easy. Newcomers barely get a chance to survive; Henkel's thera-med, is a rare exception. So SmithKline and Mr Hansen proceeded cautiously, testing its toothpaste in a year-long test in two German cities, Bad Kreuznach and Buxtehude, of the names Odol med 3, Aquafresh med 3 and – extending the name of its existing toothbrush line – Dr Best med 3. It soon became evident that consumers favoured Odol med 3, a brand name under which the company had marketed a mouthwash concentrate since 1893. Not coincidentally, Odol is category leader in mouthwash with a 70 per cent share in Germany, 80 per cent in Austria, and 60 per cent in Switzerland. 'Odol's brand name is extremely strong; consumers have had confidence in the product for 100 years,' Mr Hansen said. 'We used this name because of the brand capital it has. Our head-quarters ensures that each subsidiary uses international experience, but if we can be more successful with a local brand name, we use it.' For example, in Spain, the Aquafresh brand is marketed under the name Binaca Med 3.

SmithKline's eventual success in toothpaste was an even harder-won fight considering Odol med 3's premium price. The toothpaste was marketed for 25 per cent more than the average in Germany, but the price was justified by its attributes, such as three-prong protection against cavities, plaque and periodontal disease. After notching a 4 per cent market share, its first year, Odol med 3 climbed to 6 per cent the following year with the introduction of a mint line extension. Four years later, share was still climbing despite the fact that SmithKline was spending only $8 million to $10 million on advertising – half of what P&G was laying out for its Blend-a-Med brand. Odol also got a boost from SmithKline's move to strip away cumbersome packaging and sell the tubes without an outer box. 'We take our consumers very seriously,' Mr Hansen said 'When we noticed that consumers were reacting to unnecessary packaging, we acted immediately.'

The stripped-down package was touted in an amusing campaign from Grey Advertising, Düsseldorf, SmithKline's agency of record in oral care for 15 years. The spot mimicked a strip-tease act with the toothpaste unburdening itself of its outer wrapper as an audience of animated teeth yelled out cheers and catcalls. Mr Hansen, in fact, said its close relationship with Grey was a major reason for its conquest of German-speaking countries. 'We are one team,' he said. 'We have integrated the agency – the account people as well as the creative team – totally in our marketing, and we discuss with them everything from product policy to marketing strategy, prices and distribution.' Grey, then, was part of SmithKline's decision to create a special package shaped like a tooth for Odol med 3 in Germany. This development also helped the base brand reach its current 9 per cent market share in Germany, neck-and-neck with Blend-a-Med. The package is being used as a template in other markets, Mr Hansen said.

What put SmithKline finally over the top was its whitening line extension, Odol med 3 samtweiss. At the time of its introduction, whitening toothpastes were considered an also-ran in the category, used mainly by smokers and coffee and tea drinkers, and they claimed only a 5 per cent segment of the total toothpaste market in Germany. Mr Hansen and his team aimed to change that with advertising that argued against consumers' notions that whiteners damage teeth and are abrasive. Further, the message was that everyone with yellowing teeth should try Odol med 3 samtweiss. In a single year the strategy propelled the toothpaste's German share to 6.8 per cent share and rocketed SmithKline's overall toothpaste share to 15.8 per cent. That sent competitors, including Henkel and Colgate, scrambling to introduce whiteners, which are just now about to hit store shelves.

But SmithKline wasn't finished yet. There were still toothbrushes to consider. Although the company had sold a toothbrush under the Dr Best name for many years, the brand's share languished at 5 per cent of the German market, and Mr Hansen said the company was considering spinning it off. 'We even discussed selling the brand,' he revealed, 'but I fought for its survival because market research showed us the Dr Best name had a recognition level of over 70 per cent. What we needed was a product advantage.' The break came in the form of a new brush with a floating neck and a flexible handle that massaged the gums without injuring them. Grey then set to work: the agency sought, and found, a real Dr Best, a dental professional from the United States who appeared in TV ads that showed the toothbrush working on a tomato without damaging its delicate skin.

Not surprisingly, P&G and Colgate followed with products of their own; but not until SmithKline had leapt into the leadership position in toothbrushes with a 39.8 per cent share, up from a mere 5 per cent when Mr Hansen began his initial assault.

(Source: Adapted from Mussey, 1997.[49])

Questions

1. Which aspects of the German marketing environment explain the success of Odol med 3 in terms of consumer response to the brand's innovations?

2. Why can a market like Germany be a lead market for packaging innovation in general?

3. Discuss the issues involved in transferring part of Odol's recipe for success to near national markets (France, the United Kingdom), especially the tooth-like packaging.

A8.4 Exercise

Dangerous Enchantment

First read the short extract from *Dangerous Enchantment*, the evocative title of the novel by Anne Mather (1966). Harlequin books are worldwide bestsellers. They have been translated into 15 languages and read by countless people in many countries. Therefore, they can be considered a truly 'global' cultural product. This short extract has been chosen for its capacity to illustrate the Harlequin style.

The next day Julie had collected herself. She was glad in a way that she had seen the woman with Manuel. At least it brought home to her more strongly than any words could have done the completely amoral attitude he possessed.

Marilyn had seen the television as well, however, and said: 'I say, Julie, did you see that Manuel Cortez is back in England?'

Julie managed a casual shrug. 'So what?'

'Darling, really!' Marilyn gave her an old-fashioned look. 'Surely you aren't as indifferent as all that! I know you refused a date with him, but I'm sure that was more because of Paul Bannister than anything else.'

Julie tossed her head. 'I really can't see what all the fuss is about. Paul would make four of him!'

'You must be joking!' Marilyn giggled. 'Get you! I didn't know Paul was becoming such a dish all of a sudden. Why? What's changed him?'

Julie refrained from replying. She had no desire to get involved in an argument about Paul when it meant her stating things that in actual fact were not true. It was no use pretending about Paul's attractions; he was handsome, yes, and tall, yes, and young; but there was nothing particularly exciting about him and Julie could never understand girls who thought men's looks were enough. She had known many men, and in her small experience personality mattered far more than mere good looks.

However, during her lunch break she did borrow a newspaper from Miss Fatherstone in the hope that there might be more particulars about the woman with Manuel, but there was not. There was a picture of him at the airport, and a small article, and that was all.

When they left the building that evening it was snowing, and an icy wind was blowing, chilling them to the bone. Julie, wrapped in a loose dark blue mohair coat, hugged her handbag to her as she started along towards the main thoroughfare accompanied by Donna and Marilyn. She wore knee-length white boots, but between the place where her boots ended and the place where her skirt began she felt frozen, and she wondered whether for the winter at least she should go back to normal-length skirts.

Her hair was blowing about her face, for she was wearing no hat, and she walked straight into the man who stood purposely in her way.

'I'm sorry . . .' she began hastily, a smile lightening her face, and then: 'You!'

Manuel smiled, and her heart leapt treacherously into her throat. She had let go of Donna's arm in her confusion, but both Marilyn and Donna were staring open-mouthed. Manuel took Julie's arm, and said smoothly: 'You will excuse me, ladies,' in a mocking tone, and drew Julie across the pavement to the familiar green Ferrari.

'No, wait!' began Julie, but it was no use. Manuel had the car door open and was propelling her inside, his hard fingers biting cruelly into her arm.

'Don't argue,' he said, for all the world as though it was a natural occurrence that he should meet her from work.

Julie did not want to create a scene in the street, so she climbed into the luxurious warmth of the car and sliding across out of the driver's seat, she allowed him to slide in beside her. He slammed the door, flicked the ignition, and the car moved silently forward, purring like a sated panther.

She stole a glance at him as they turned into the main thoroughfare, and saw, with a sense of inevitability, that far from changing he was much more attractive than she remembered. He turned for a moment to look at her as they stopped at some traffic lights, and said: 'How have you been?'

Julie contemplated her fingernails. 'Fine. And you?'

He shrugged, and did not reply, and she felt like hitting him. How dared he sit there knowing that she must have seen him with that girl yesterday! She looked out of the car window, suddenly realizing that she was allowing him to drive her heaven knows where, and she was making no comment.

'Where are you taking me?' she asked in a tight little voice.

'Home,' he said lazily. 'Where do you think? I thought I would save you the journey on such a ghastly night. Tell me, how do you stand this climate? It's terrible. Me, I like the sun, and the sea, and warm water to swim in.'

'Don't we all?' remarked Julie dryly. 'This will do.' They had reached the end of Faulkner Road.

Manuel shook his head. 'What number?'

'Forty-seven. But please, I'd rather you didn't drive along there. It would only cause speculation, and if you should be recognized . . .' Her voice trailed away.

'That's hardly likely tonight,' remarked Manuel coolly, and drove smoothly to her gate where he halted the car.

'Thank you, señor.' Julie gave a slight bow of her head, and made to get out, but Manuel stopped her, his fingers biting into her arm.

'Aren't you pleased to see me?' he asked mockingly. Julie looked at him fully. 'No, not really.'

'Why?'

'Surely that's obvious. We have nothing to say to one another.'

'No?'

'No.' Julie brushed back her hair as it fell in waves over her eyes. It glistened with tiny drops of melted snow and she was unaware of how lovely she was looking.

Manuel shrugged, and lay back in his seat. 'Go, then.'

Julie felt furious. It always ended this way, with herself feeling the guilty one. Well, he wasn't going to get away with it! She swung round on him.

'Don't imagine for one moment that I've been brought home believing your little tales', she cried angrily. 'I know perfectly well that the reason you have brought me home is because you could hardly take me to the apartment when you already have one female in residence!'

Manuel stared at her, a dull flush just visible in the muted light of the car rising up his cheeks.

(Source: Mather, pp. 89–92.[50] Text copyright © 1966 by Anne Mather; permission to reproduce text granted by Harlequin Books S.A.)

Questions

1. Identify the main sociodemographic characteristics of the target audience for such books.

2. Identify from the text (situation, characters and the relations between them) how, and to what extent, this text effects people in such a way as to manipulate feelings and emotions that are widely shared by the world population.

3. Define the target audience for Harlequin books, in terms of cultural affinity class(es).

Appendix references

1. Rose, Steve (2001), 'Sheer Khan', *Guardian*, 20 October 2001. Retrieved 20 July 2003 from http://film.guardian.co.uk/bollywood/story/0,11871,683296,00.html.

2. Kaushal, Raj (2003), 'The rise and rise of "desi" beats', *Telegraph*, 13 September 2003. Retrieved 9 May 2011 from http://www.telegraph.co.uk/arts/main.jhtml?xml=/arts/2003/09/13/bmasia13.xml.

3. Retrieved 9 May 2011 from http://www.2point6billion.com/news/2010/05/21/bollywood-productions-double-the-views-of-hollywood-5737.html.

4. Retrieved from http://www.usatoday.com/life/movies/news/2009-12-09-hollywood_N.htm.

5. Chabra, Aseem (2002), 'How original is Bollywood?', *Rediff on the Net*, 31 October 2002. Retrieved 9 May 2011 from http://www.rediff.com/entertai/2002/oct/31bolly.htm.

6. BBC News (2002), 'Lagaan scoops Bollywood awards', *BBC News*, 6 April 2002. Retrieved 9 May 2011 from http://news.bbc.co.uk/1/hi/entertainment/film/1915331.stm.

7. BBC News (2002), 'Bollywood's hopes for Oscar dollars', *BBC News*, 13 February 2002. Retrieved 9 May 2011 from http://news.bbc.co.uk/1/hi/business/1818660.stm.

8. Retrieved 9 May 2011 from http://calcuttatube.com/aamir-khan-film-3-idiots-is-highest-grossing-indian-movie-in-usa/59441/. http://www.boxofficeindia.com/showProd.php?itemCat=127&catName=MjAwMC0yMDA5.

9. Retrieved 9 May 2011 from: http://articles.timesofindia.indiatimes.com/2011-03-25/news-interviews/29188047_1_film-industry-film-fraternity-raj-kapoor; http://www.uos-hp.com/hollywood-vs-bollywood.

10. Retrieved 9 May 2011 from http://english.alrroya.com/content/hollywood-goes-bollywood-us-studios-target-india-filmgoers.

11. Sternstein, Aliya (2003), 'Bully for Bollywood!', *Forbes Global*, 28 April 2003. Retrieved 9 May 2011 from http://www.forbes.com/global/2003/0428/047.html.

12. Mathur, Arti (2003), 'India looks to UK to stem piracy', *Variety*, 29 May 2003. Retrieved 9 May 2011 from http://www.variety.com.

13. Kripalani, Manjeet, and Ron Grover (2002), 'Bollywood: Can new money create a world-class film industry in India?', *Businessweek*, 2 December 2002. Retrieved 9 May 2011 from http://www.businessweek.com/magazine/content/02_48/b3810013.htm.

14. Anonymous (2002), 'Movie marketing comes of age', *Business Standard* (New Delhi), 21 March 2002. Retrieved 9 May 2011 from 'Movie marketing comes of age', http://www.responservice.com/archives/apr2002_issue1/feature/feat02.htm.

15. Amdur, Meredith (2003), 'Koch Lorber lines up Bollywood DVD series', *Variety*, 10 July 2003. Retrieved 9 May 2011 from http://www.variety.com.

16. Dentsu Young and Rubicam, Inc. (2000), 'New York marketing information. The Indian Influence.' Dentsu Young and Rubicam, Inc. (Japan), 10 July 2000. Retrieved 9 May 2011 from http://www.dyr.co.jp.

17. Shah, Deepa (2002), 'Hooray for Bollywood', *Observer*, 24 March 2002. Retrieved 9 May 2011 from http://observer.guardian.co.uk/screen/story/0,6903,672784,00.html.

18. BBC News (2001), 'Bollywood eyes Afghan market, *BBC News*, 27 November 2001. Retrieved 9 May 2011 from http://news.bbc.co.uk/1/hi/entertainment/film/1679115.stm.

19. Gahlot, Deepa (1999), 'Why the world loves Hindi movies', *Himal: The South Asian Magazine*, September, 1999. Retrieved 9 May 2011 from http://www.imdiversity.com/villages/asian/Article_ Detail.asp?Article_ID=809.

20. Episcopo, Jo (2001), 'Bollywood comes to Cannes', *BBC News World Edition*, 15 May 2001. Retrieved 9 May 2011 from http://news.bbc.co.uk/1/low/entertainment/film/1331700.stm.

21. Chawda, Aniruddh (2001), 'Bollywood goes global', *Indian Currents*, Vol. 15, No. 9, 31 January 2001.

22. Cooper, Louise (2003), 'Bollywood struck by horror', *BBC News*, 23 April 2003. Retrieved 9 May 2011 from http://newswww.bbc.net.uk/2/hi/business/2969101.stm.

23. Pearson, Bryan (2003), 'Love, song, dance . . . and suspense', *Variety*, 16 February 2003. Retrieved 9 May 2011 from http://www.variety.com.

24. Pearson, Bryan (2003), 'Analyst sez Bollywood's on track to bounce back', *Variety*, 23 March 2003. Retrieved 9 May 2011 from http://www.variety.com.

25. http://articles.timesofindia.indiatimes.com/2011-03-25/news-interviews/29188047_1_film-industry-film-fraternity-raj-kapoor.

26. Jha, Subhash K. (2002), 'Hollywood, Bollywood-style!' *Rediff on the Net*, 28 March 2002. Retrieved 9 May 2011 from http://www.rediff.com.

27. Retrieved 9 May 2011 from http://entertainment.oneindia.in/bollywood/box-office/2010/raajneeti-international-market-160610.html.

28. Malcolm, Derek (2001), 'A song and a dance', *Guardian*, 25 October 2001. Retrieved 9 May 2011 from http://film.guardian.co.uk/bollywood/story/0,11871,683300,00.html.

29. BusinessWorld (2003), 'Anti-war, consumer groups launch boycott of 10 leading US products', *BusinessWorld (*Manila), 27 March 2003, p. 1.

30. O'Flynn, Kevin (2003), 'Americans and Dollars not welcome', *The Moscow Times* (online), 26 March 2003. Retrieved 10 January 2010 from http://www.themoscowtimes.com/article/americans-and-dollars-not-welcome/239550.html.

31. Anonymous (2003), 'Qibla shows its bottle', *The Publican* (online), 7 May 2003. Retrieved 10 January 2010 from http://www.thepublican.com/cgi-bin/item.cgi?id=9604&d=11&h=24&f=23&dateformat=%25o-%25B-%25Y.

32. Anonymous (2002), 'Coca-Cola to build plant on stolen Palestinian land', *Innovative Minds*, 19 July 2002. Retrieved 10 January 2010 from http://www.inminds.co.uk/boycott-news-0226.html.

33. Cowen, Richard (2003), 'EU official sees boycotts if US files biotech suit', *Forbes* (online), 6 May 2003. Retrieved 10 January 2010 from http://www.foodmarketexchange.com/wp/news_archive.php?p=394.

34. Bond, Sam (2005), 'Coca-Cola ousted by Indian pollution regulators', *Edie Newsroom*, 26 August 2005. Retrieved 10 January 2010 from http://www.edie.net/news/news_story.asp?id=10466&channel=0.

35. Smad, Bari (2006), 'Kerala, India Kicks Out Coke and Pepsi', *Global Exchange*, 1 September 2006. Retrieved 10 January 2010 from http://www.globalexchange.org/update/publications/4203.html.

36. Warner Melanie (2005), 'U. of Michigan Becomes 10th College to Join Boycott of Coke', *The New York Times (online)*, 31 December 2005. Retrieved 10 January 2010 from http://www.nytimes.com/2005/12/31/business/31coke.html.

37. Viboonchart, Nalin (2008), 'Mecca-Cola introduced to Thailand', *The Nation Business (online)*, 21 January 2008. Retrieved 10 January 2010, 2010 from http://www.nationmultimedia.com/2008/01/21/business/business_30062839.php.

38. Jeffery, Simon (2003), 'Is it the real thing?' *Guardian*, 5 February 2003. Retrieved 10 January 2010 from http://shopping.guardian.co.uk/food/story/0,1587,889470,00.html.

39. Qibla Cola (2003), 'Qibla Cola Company Ltd. . . . Liberate your taste', Qibla Cola website homepage (undated). Retrieved 10 January 2010 from http://www.Qiblacola.co.uk.

40. Datson, Trevor (2003), 'Muslim Cola – idealism or marketing froth?', *Reuters* (online), 30 April 2003. Retrieved 10 January 2010 from http://www.reuters.co.uk.

41. Fernandez-Fanjul, Eufrasio (2002), '*ZamZam* Cola crece con la ola Antiyanqui', *El Mundo* (online), 8 September 2002. Retrieved 10 January 2010 from http://www.el-mundo.es/nuevaeconomia/2002/139/1031386792.html.

42. Anonymous (2002), 'Iran takes on cola giants', *Asia Times*, 17 October 2002. Retrieved 10 January 2010 from http://www.atimes.com/atimes/Middle_East/DJ17Ak06.html.

43. Theodoulou, Michael, Charles Bremner, and Daniel McGrory (2002), 'Cola wars as Islam shuns the real thing', *The Times Online*, 11 October 2002. Retrieved 10 January 2010 from http://www. timesonline.co.uk/article/0,,3821-443269,00.html.

44. Interbrand (2010). Retrieved 10 January 2010 from http://www.interbrand.com/best_global_brands_ intro.aspx?langid=1000.

45. Supermarket company sites: *E. Leclerc*: http://www.e-leclerc.com and *Carrefour*: http://www. carrefour.com/.

46. Majidi, Nassim, and Christina Passariello (2003), 'After Iraq, Cola wars heat up', *BusinessWeek Online*, 17 April 2003. Retrieved 10 January 2010 from http://www.businessweek.com/bwdaily/dnflash/ apr2003/nf20030417_5930_db039.htm.

47. AME Info (2004), 'Coke and Pepsi battle it out', *AME Info*, 8 April 2004. Retrieved 10 January 2010 from http://www.ameinfo.com/37492.html.

48. Go to http://www.coca-colaindia.com/.

49. *Advertising Age* (1997), November.

50. Mather, Anne (1966), *Dangerous Enchantment*. London: Harlequin.,

9

Product strategy: physical, service and symbolic attributes

Chapter 8 argued that standardization should be considered where true cost reductions can be achieved and localized where necessary. Some of the main considerations in making this decision include the type of market, the type of product, and the element of the marketing mix being considered. The product strategy is an element that should be considered, as production is one of the areas in which cost efficiencies can be obtained. That is, the average cost can be reduced by increasing the scale of production, especially for products that require a large amount of research and development. However, technological advances can also be used to simplify production and allow mass customization to occur. To this end, it is important to consider whether and which elements of the product strategy (physical, service and symbolic attributes), can be effectively standardized.

The implications of decisions around standardization or adaptation are enormous for firms operating on an international or global scale. However, it is not a decision that has to be universal. It may be possible to have a higher level of standardization in developed markets, where competition is intense, and a higher level of adaptation in attractive emerging markets, where growth potential is substantial. As noted in Chapter 8, emerging markets have very different demand characteristics (including customer interests, preferences, purchasing patterns and price sensitivity), very different competitive environments, and very different infrastructure.[1] Most companies, in fact, include some standardization and some adaptation of their products.[2] For instance, Coca-Cola and McDonald's customize the non-core elements of their products when required. The effectiveness of the strategy depends on many factors related to the four elements of the marketing mix.[3]

This chapter proposes a decision-making framework for the adaptation-standardization of various product attributes, including the *physical characteristics*, in terms of design, form, colour, function, packaging, brand name and 'made-in' label. It also assesses the potential for adaptation-standardization at different levels of *product attributes*, including physical attributes, service attributes and symbolic attributes (through colour, shape, country of origin, brand name and so on).

The first section of this chapter sets out a systematic model to clarify the choice between adaptation and standardization of product strategy. It can be applied successively to each existing national market, as well as to markets where a company intends to set up new business. The second section is devoted to the physical attributes of the product. The third section deals with the standardization/adaptation of service attributes. The fourth section relates to symbolic attributes.

The ancient Greek word 'symbol' refers to an object cut into two halves. Both the host and the guest kept their halves and later passed them on to their children. When the two halves were reunited, the owners could be recognized by their halves, as these were proof of the previously established hospitality bond. The symbol therefore replaces, represents and denotes another entity by means of a conventional relationship or a suggestion, the evidence of which has usually been lost. The connotative meanings of symbols are culture based and, as such, are interpreted differently across countries.

Other important symbolic attributes include the brand name and the national images linked to the product and its country of manufacture. Chapter 12 elaborates on the linguistic issues in converting a national brand into an international brand. It also discusses issues with global brands, either worldwide or regionally based.

9.1

Adaptation or standardization of product attributes

The product element of the marketing mix is often cited as the most standardized element, but within the product element there are various attributes that have more or less need for adaptation. From a company point of view, Table 9.1 lists the proportion of 500 large multinational UK companies across five sectors (including manufacturing, services, transportation and communication, construction, and retail and wholesale) that reported the standardization of various product aspects, as well as reasons for adaptions.[2]

As can be seen in Table 9.1, the more abstract aspects (e.g., quality, brand name and image) were more often standardized and the service elements (e.g., pre- and post-sales services, warrantees, delivery and installation) were least often standardized. Further, the most important reason for adaptions

included culture, followed by market development, competition, laws and economic differences. It is important to note the large differences in the percentage of companies standardizing different product elements.

From a consumer point of view, Hult and colleagues[4] compared the importance consumers place on 16 product attributes in France (a developed market) and Malaysia (an emerging market), finding that only two attributes (product quality and appearance) received high emphasis for both samples. In Malaysia consumers relied more on the core product attributes and in France on the image and service attributes when evaluating grocery products and clothing.[4] In reality, consumers do not buy the product itself; they buy the benefits they hope to derive from the product.

A product can be defined as a set of attributes that provide the purchaser or user with actual benefits. In some cases, these benefits may be fairly universal, at least across cultural affinity segments. For instance, consumers appear to appreciate similar product attributes from IKEA furniture (i.e., low cost, reasonable quality, Swedish aesthetics), regardless of whether the buyers are in China, Australia or the United Arab Emirates. Notably, IKEA is one of the strongest proponents of product standardization in the global marketplace. You can find the same 'Boksel' coffee table in their Australian stores as you can in China, the UAE and basically everywhere else they

Table 9.1 Reported level of standardization of product strategies and reasons for adapting

Percentage standardizing	Reasons for adapting the marketing mix
78% product quality	92% culture
72% brand name	87% market development
71% image	84% competition
67% performance	82% laws
54% size and colour	78% economic differences
52% packaging and styling	74% sociological consideration
48% variety, design and features	71% customer perceptions
45% pre-sales service	60% technological consideration
43% after-sales service and warrantees	53% political environment
42% delivery and installation	49% level of customer similarity
	44% marketing infrastructure
	39% differences in physical conditions

(Source: Vrontis.[2] Integrating adaptation and standardisation in international marketing: the adaptstand modelling process, Demetris Vrontis, *Journal of Marketing Management*, copyright © Westburn Publishers Ltd, reprinted by permission of Taylor & Francis Ltd, www.tandfonline.com on behalf of The Westburn Publishers Ltd.)

have a presence. The Boksel range might vary in consumer *popularity*, depending on cultural and physical difference across countries, but the product is identical, resulting in both production and design efficiencies for IKEA. However, for many other products, consumers from different countries assign quite different weights to various product attributes. For instance, German consumers value ecological attributes more than British consumers.[5]

There are three layers of product attributes that are more or less applicable to standardization:

1. *The physical attributes* (e.g., size, weight, colour). Standardization of these attributes provides the greatest potential for cost benefits, since economies of scale are mostly gained at the manufacturing stage. Therefore, any customization of physical attributes must be carefully weighed against the lost efficiencies.[6]
2. *Service attributes* (e.g., maintenance, after-sales service, spare parts availability). These attributes are fairly difficult to standardize, as expectations and circumstances for service delivery differ widely from one country to another. Furthermore, most services are performed in direct relation to *local* customers, so service attributes are more dependent on culture.
3. *Symbolic attributes*. These often comprise the interpretive element of the physical attributes. A

colour is simultaneously a chemical formula for a painting or a coat, and also the symbolic meaning conveyed by the material. However, symbolic attributes affect the choice to adapt and/or standardize in a fairly ambiguous manner. It can be quite confusing when consumers show a strong liking for domestic goods, based on nationalism, and also show a fascination for foreign cultures and their goods. Therefore, when adapting or standardizing symbolic attributes, the requirements for national identity symbols will sometimes intermingle with those for symbols of exoticism.

Table 9.2 proposes a systematic description of the arguments in favour of adaptation on the one hand and standardization on the other. Distinctions can be made according to the different levels of physical, service and symbolic attributes. Some arguments originate from within the company, which can benefit from changes to their operations. Other arguments are related to external constraints imposed by the environment, product lifecycle, competition, physical or communication infrastructure, and consumer behaviour.[6] The influence of these factors may require a company to either adapt or standardize its offerings. In Table 9.2 each internal cell is numbered and this number will be referred to throughout this section.

Table 9.2 Factors influencing adaptation or standardization of product attributes

Product attributes	Arguments in favour of adaptation	Arguments in favour of standardization
Physical attributes	1 Cost-reducing adaptations Local standards, hygiene and safety regulations, local marketing knowledge, consumer behaviour, marketing and physical environments	2 Experience effects Economies of scale International standards International product use
Services attributes	3 Limited savings related to scale Local peculiarities in service, maintenance and distribution	4 Significant learning effects 'Mobile' clientele
Symbolic attributes	5 Unfavourable image of imported products, company, nationality or brand name Inadequate meaning conveyed by colour, shape, etc.	6 Favourable image of imported products, company, nationality or brand Exotic or ethnic appeal Demands for 'universals'

Website link 9.1

Search for an iconic global company, to see if they offer customized elements in different countries. For instance, McDonald's Hong Kong includes a range of noodle dishes: **http://www.mcdonalds.com.hk/english/**.

9.2

Physical attributes

Chapter 8 discussed experience effects and, accordingly, the potential for cost reductions related to cumulated production clearly weigh in favour of standardization (Table 9.2, cell 2). Despite this, current empirical evidence finds that neither standardization nor adaptation is inherently superior. The decision depends on the type of markets (e.g., similarity in culture, economic development, laws, marketing infrastructure, competition, technology, competition, the type of customer and their preferences), the type of product (the potential is clearly smaller for cheese or books than for computers or smartphones) and compatibility with the firms' strategic direction. Further, there are more opportunities for standardization across developed countries, as more of the market factors will be similar, at least across some segments.

In the case of the emerging economies the opportunities for standardization are vastly reduced. There is likely to be a range of necessary product modifications including the use of cheaper components, simpler packaging, fewer product features, all of which enable the product to be sold at a lower price.[1] Major phone manufacturers, such as Nokia have used these techniques to developed inexpensive phones targeted at low-income consumers. While some of the more abstract product elements, such as quality, brand name and image, may be easier to standardize, even this standardization may not be as effective. For instance, product quality, which is the most highly standardized product element, does not clearly support a positive relationship between standardization and performance.[7]

In fact, cost-reduction adaptations may be transferable to other markets, which may compensate for the loss of cumulated volume through adaptation (Table 9.2, cell 1). The success of Japanese pick-up trucks in developing countries is due to product simplifications in suspension, engine and gearbox, which lowered their cost. However, this situation is rare, as it is common for product simplifications to fail to achieve their goals. Historically, Ford and General Motors developed a 'bare bones' model T type of vehicle to sell in developing countries. They both failed. Similarly, recent attempts to design low cost, low performance computers have also failed in emerging markets, where the advantages resulting from 'simplifications' did not sufficiently reduce costs and the product functionality was not adequately appreciated by consumers. Since simplified products may not be advantageous in terms of cost, the learning process for local consumers and the effect of the local context on this learning process may become the central concerns for the international marketer.[8,9]

Compulsory adaptation

Compulsory adaptation of physical attributes is often related to national regulations and standards (Table 9.2, cell 1). Certain countries use standards which seem to operate as non-tariff trade barriers. For instance, Germany is known for its use of an exhaustive system of over 30,000 industrial standards (DIN), which are determined by standard-setting committees. German manufacturers are strongly represented on the boards of these committees. Nevertheless, DIN standards are by no means intended as non-tariff barriers.

Some examples of compulsory adaptation include:

1. *Industrial standards for supply of electricity*: voltage, frequency of alternating current (50 versus 60 Hz), shape of plugs, and so on, differ by region, if not by country. Apple, among other firms, has attempted offset the voltage issue by producing most of the products with dual-voltage capabilities. This has added advantages for travellers, who can take their computer anywhere in the world, as long as they buy the appropriate and relatively inexpensive adapter, rather than a costly step-down converter.
2. *Safety standards*: in the motor industry lighting, brake systems and vehicle safety often differ by country. For instance, the Corsa is one of the most

widely sold cars of all time. It is sold in approximately 80 countries and manufactured on five continents. Its name, body style, suspension and/or engine are modified to meet local standards. The Corsa is called Vauxhall/Opel Corsa in Germany, Chevrolet Chevy (Corsa) in Mexico, Buick Sail in China and Holden Barina in Australia. However, these variations on a theme lead to increased production costs, documentation and country-specific spare parts. Consequently, it is difficult to control marketing management.

3. *Hygiene regulations*: the food processing, chemicals and pharmaceutical industries adapt to comply with hygiene legislation. Producers of *foie gras* exporting their produce to the United States have to obtain FDA (Food and Drug Administration) hygiene certification. For this they have to allow the FDA to inspect their laboratories for bacteria as well as method of production. FDA inspectors often require *foie gras* to be pasteurized and the laboratories disinfected with an antiseptic detergent. This inevitably affects the taste and conflicts with the traditional image of a home-made quality product. French *foie gras* producers have set up laboratories in the USA where the product is prepared according to US hygiene standards. Even a product as common as Coca-Cola faces different regulations, including very different requirements for the use of artificial sweeteners across countries and the necessity to include an expiry date in some countries (e.g., France), but not others (e.g., Holland).[10]

Countless regulations influence the need for adaptation (packaging, labelling, sizes, advertising, sales promotion, and so on). In many countries public or mutual bodies offer to assist companies by examining the issues of conforming to the technical aspects of foreign standards. Despite this, a good number of companies fail to consider the issue of adapting products to foreign markets for ethnocentric reasons. Newcomers to the export business often do not start by considering the loss of standardization; their first concern is being forced to adapt to technical standards.

In fact, obligatory adaptations are often minor in comparison to the required adaptations to differences in consumer behaviour and in the national marketing environment. Three main issues should be considered:

1. *Consumption patterns*: consumer tastes, frequency of consumption, the amount consumed per helping, and so on, differ. The size of a cereal box and the style of packaging that preserves the product depend in part on whether consumers eat 50 grammes of cereal a day, or if they consume larger amounts but less frequently. Even products which are supposed to be the epitome of international standardization are subject to customization for local tastes (see Box 9.1). Not only does Coca-Cola add different levels and types of sugar in different countries to account for differences in taste, but consumers also treat the product differently. For instance, Coke is served in the US with lots of ice, whereas in Tromso, Norway, it is kept in warmers.[10] Similarly, Starbucks introduced the 31oz (917ml) 'Trenta' sized cup in the US in 2011 in response to their consumer's demand for larger iced beverages. However, the global chain is not introducing this size cup elsewhere, as consumer preferences do not support the American 'supersize' culture.[11]

In contrast to these examples of adaptation, luxury fashion products offer a different perspective. High-end brands such as Louis Vuitton and Gucci typically make few (if any) concessions to local usage patterns or cultural differences, in terms of product design. This is because the main utility of their products is not in the use of them, but in the actual possession of the product. Chinese luxury consumers may desire these items out of a need to show status,[12] while at the same time US consumers might be driven by self-expression . . . but the product itself is exactly the same in either country.[13]

While there are definite national trends, it is also important to remember that market segments exist within and across countries. Allio and Allio[14] described the successful introduction of Coors beer in Puerto Rico, after using local market research knowledge to identify the segment with the most potential (young, upper income, urban). Their major competitor, Budweiser, lost market share because it continued to target the entire market, and ignored unique aspects of local Hispanic culture. In fact, van Mesdag[15] argues that food is part of a group of products (visual art, music, architecture, social behaviour, clothing, etc.) that are not easily globalized. He proposes the 'duration-of-usage' hypothesis, where products

---

Box 9.1

'Pizza relativity'

'Pizza relativity' is a reality in today's world. During in-depth interviews at Hewlett Packard in Grenoble, France, several American expatriates mentioned they occasionally travel to Geneva, Switzerland (100 miles/160 km away) just to eat at Pizza Hut (although, unfortunately for them, Pizza Hut has since ceased operating in Switzerland). There are many traditional pizzerias in Grenoble (the town has a very large Italian population), and yet these American expatriates prefer the taste, crust, toppings and style of American pizza. When attending a congress in Milan, I discovered that Italian pizza (at least at the restaurant where I ate it) is very different from what I am used to eating in Grenoble even though they are made by Italian cooks in both contexts: the crust is much thicker and there is less topping. My most recent pizza experience is that of the oily Brazilian pizza (which I have only tried twice).

Conclusion: Pizza, like 'Chinese' food, is largely local. This is often because of the lack of genuine ingredients, but also because taste is local. Local views of what is genuine and traditional are mostly based on fantasies about the 'true' pizza or the 'genuine' Peking duck.

---

that evolved in times when countries did not readily communicate are more difficult to standardize.

2. *Climate and the physical environment* are often important, and sometimes neglected factors that cause necessary adaptation (Table 9.2, cell 1). Motor vehicles must be specifically designed to withstand the harsh Scandinavian winters or the warmth and humidity of the Ivory Coast. The diversity of physical environments is often the cause of unexpected failure (Box 9.2). The range of elements that constitute potential demands for adaptation need to be taken into consideration at the strategic design stage. This is not always an obvious step to take. Ethnocentrism is often the rule in product design.

3. *Adapting products to local product usage.* The uses of seemingly standard products can vary subtly from country to country, in ways that might not be evident to the ethnocentric designer. For example, Indian consumers don't typically freeze left-overs for later consumption and prefer the freezer section at the bottom of the fridge. In Japan increasing dual-income families have created a desire for larger fridge-freezers to accommodate less frequent grocery shopping. In Norway, the rising costs of electricity and extremely cold winters combined with environmental consciousness have led to a strong preference for extremely energy efficient designs. Although awareness of differing product usage is crucial, it is still important to execute customization well. Take, for instance, Whirlpool who, knowing the types of clothing common in India, produced a washing-machine with an ultra-delicate mode, labelled 'Sari Cycle'. Unfortunately, the particular interior design of the washer meant that these fine garments were often snagged and subsequently destroyed, resulting in a costly failure.[16]

Adaptation to possible misuses is related to the issue of product liability, where quite different legal solutions are found from one country to another. In his book, *Remove Child before Folding*, Jones[17] lists 101 'wacky warning labels' on products designed by litigiously paranoid American businesses, including 'Do not use while sleeping' on a hair dryer; 'May cause drowsiness' on sleeping tablets, 'Harmful if swallowed' on a fishing lure, and 'If you do not understand, or cannot read, all directions, cautions and warnings, do not use this product' on a bottle of drain cleaner.

Website link 9.2

See examples of remarkable warning labels such as 'Danger: Avoid Death', 'Do not iron while wearing shirt' etc: **http://www.mlaw.org/wwl/photos.html**.

Box 9.2

Adaptations to the physical environment

A European drinks manufacturer decided to widen the range of one of its product lines with a giant-size version, to actively promote it in several markets, the United States in particular. After completion of production facilities, the new model was launched. The company then realized to its horror that it had forgotten one small detail: the giant-size bottle was a couple of inches too tall for the shelves in the vast majority of American stores. You can imagine the result: the sales promotion activities that were planned had to be cancelled, there was discontent among the distributors and the sales force lost a great deal of motivation while a new mould was hastily manufactured.[18]

Quaker Oats has an established share of the Cameroon market: it has been carefully adapted in line with consumption habits. It is easily made into the gruel that the Cameroons call *paf* or *pap*. It is usually eaten with maize or tapioca. In addition, Quaker uses metal packaging which is perfectly suited to the preservation of the product in the Cameroon climate. The shelf life of the can is about ten years, even in a tropical country. Cameroon itself is not a wholly typical tropical country since in Douala, for instance, there is an annual rainfall of 7 metres. The can ensures that the product is preserved despite the humidity. It does, however, rust, and even though the product itself is not affected, certain retailers refuse to repurchase Quaker Oats because their previous stock may have partially or completely rusted.

(Sources: Adapted from Giordan, p. 110;[18]Camphuis.[19])

Requirements for international standardization

Sometimes national requirements lean toward international standardization (Table 9.2, cell 2). This may occur in four situations:

1. There are industries where *international standards* tend to develop from technical standards originating in individual countries. For instance, in the field of oil drilling, the API (American Petroleum Institute) standards are enforced worldwide. Every oil company, whether American or not, must follow the API standards. Oil-drilling equipment manufacturers are also obliged to design their products in accordance with these standards. However, the number of industries with worldwide standards remains limited. The adoption of foreign/international standards can even prove to be problematic for selling in the country of origin. For instance, a European iron and steel company obtained certification from ASME (the American Society of Mechanical Engineers) for the very thick steel plate used in nuclear and petrochemical plants. In this small industry the company had

a quite substantial world market share. ASME certification was recognized worldwide since most nuclear plants use licensed American technology. When the company subsequently sold its heavy steel plates for use in German and French electricity utility plants, the American standards were not considered acceptable and it was forced to adapt to German and French standards.

2. Some products achieve *international usage* such as aircraft suitcases (Samsonite of Belgium and Delsey of France), portable computers, duty-free articles, etc.

3. *Innovative products* often experience an international diffusion process. High R & D costs are initially incurred for many innovative products, and the benefits from many technical products are not greatly affected by culture (e.g., DVDs). The pace of innovation diffusion is largely enhanced by the strength of 'early adopter' groups. These groups may also have a high level of exposure to international travel and to new products in the countries where they are first launched. By word-of-mouth communication, they transfer knowledge of the product to their non-travelling compatriots. They facilitate positive reactions from other

consumers, who are not exposed to these new products, in the first phases of the adoption process: awareness, interest, evaluation, testing. More generally, international travel accelerates the process of diffusing standardized innovation. There is also some evidence that consumer innovativeness is higher for people from countries with lower uncertainty avoidance, higher individualism and more masculinity.[21]

4. The final point in cell 2 encompasses the basis of Levitt's[22] assertions about the globalization of markets. According to Levitt, certain aspects or ways of life would tend towards uniformity with differences in cultural preferences, national taste, standards and the institutional business environment being remnants of the past. Levitt argues that the so-called 'ethnic' markets are a good example: Chinese food, country music, pizza and jazz now tend to be found worldwide. Although Levitt claims that he does not advocate systematic disregard for local or national differences, he overestimates the worldwide convergence of taste for global products, as emphasized in Chapters 5 and 6. Whatever value judgements are made about the all-inclusive tendency towards homogenization of world cultures, consumer segments and product categories, this issue must be raised for each company, on the basis of careful research in relation to its product, consumers and markets. For instance, Schuh[23] points out that while market conditions favour customization in Central Eastern Europe, the extra cost may not pay off as many of these countries have small markets which are rapidly changing due to massive investment from Western retailers, media, banks, etc.

Trend towards international standards

The costs required for adapting to national standards are very high, since adaptation also implies the replication of test and certification procedures in many countries. In the pharmaceuticals industry the cost of bringing a new drug onto the market is estimated at US$230 million in the United States, $150 million in Europe and $125 million in Japan. Countries still follow somewhat different routes for granting market entry to new pharmaceuticals. For instance, Japan, requiring only 18 months, appears liberal in contrast

with the US Food and Drug Administration, but given the relative brevity of initial trials in Japan, approval covers only the first six years, after which the manufacturer must reapply.[24]

Fortunately, there is a definite trend towards common standardization worldwide, especially with ISO (International Organization for Standardization) standards; some of these are now widely applied, such as the standards on quality, the ISO 9000 series. European technical standardization is participating in this movement, which stems from the EC Treaty, especially Article 30, which prohibits quantitative restrictions on imports from other member states and measures having an equivalent effect (that is, this is mainly a form of protectionist standardization). For instance, the *Cassis de Dijon* ruling firmly established the 'home country rule', whereby a product should not be barred from being imported into an EU country when it conforms to the standards of the EU country in which it is produced. The EU countries are engaged in a European standardization process through three Brussels-based organizations: CEN (Comité Européen de Normalisation), CENELEC (Comité Européen de Normalisation pour les produits Electriques et Electroniques) and ETSI (European Telecommunications Standards Institute). This largely stems from the 1985 EC White Paper, which identified technical barriers as one of the main obstacles to the achievement of a single market in Europe.

Product standards are in fact a very complex strategic issue (much more so than depicted here), since they have a definite influence on the competitive strategy of the firm.[25] Issuing compatibility of standards over time (multi-vintage compatibility) and across competitors is very important in high-technology industries (e.g., computers, consumer electronics and telecommunications). There are examples where promoting a standard and licensing it to competitors (Matsushita's VHS) proved a better strategy than keeping a monopoly on one's own standard (e.g., Sony's now defunct Betamax VCR). Interestingly, it appears that Sony has learned from its costly Betamax VCR defeat. In early 2008, Toshiba was forced to abandon its HD-DVD rival to Sony's Blu-ray high-definition DVD standard. This time around Sony licensed its Blu-ray technology to competitors, while Toshiba largely kept the HD-DVD technology in-house. Other examples show that it was more efficient to keep the technology under total control, as Xerox did for its proprietary photocopying technology before the patent expired. However, technology products are not the only items for which product standards need to be considered as part of their marketing strategy. For instance, Vertinsky and Zhou (p. 250)[26] examined forest product firms, finding that their choice to obtain Forest Stewardship Council (FSC) certification 'was to defend or create market access to markets with influential buyers' groups (e.g., the UK) or markets where environmental groups have strong influence on public opinion and the government (e.g., The Netherlands and Germany)'.

Website link 9.3

See how Sony won the High Definition DVD format war: **http://money.cnn.com/2008/02/28/technology/siklos_sony.fortune/**.

9.3

Service attributes

World export in commercial services decreased by 11 per cent in 2009, but increased by approximately 10% each year since then.[27] There are many factors driving this expansion including the WTO, protective measures (intellectual property rights, copyrights, trademarks, etc.), changing government attitudes, trading blocks, technology and changing demographics (e.g., more women in the workforce).[28]

Despite this, there are still many barriers for companies that wish to export services. In fact, the export of services is more highly regulated than the export of products. Managers regard regulatory barriers as more important than barriers internal to the firm (e.g., limited resources) or unfavourable markets (e.g., competitive environment or weak demand).[29] Many of these barriers are not transparent to outsiders and are difficult to negotiate. Informal barriers, such as official harassment to support local policy objectives (e.g., delays in delivery of work permits or excessive administrative fees to ease local unemployment), private harassment for personal gain (e.g., customs delays alleviated by 'fees' and 'donations'

to family members of high ranking civil servants) and red tape for no apparent reason (e.g., inefficient public administration) are more problematic to managers than formal barriers.[29] In light of this, service exporters should adopt 'world class' practices from corporate structure and process to information networks and public relations strategies in order to comply with the regulatory environment.

Services may stand alone, or be part of a product offering. Service attributes include the following:

1. repair and maintenance, after-sales service;
2. installation;
3. instruction manuals, information and guidance on how to use item;
4. other related services (demonstrations, technical assistance);
5. waiting time, delivery dates (and respect for them);
6. guarantees (repair or replacement of goods);
7. spare parts availability; and
8. return of goods, whether defective or not.

Adaptation of service in light of local conditions

The extent of service attributes differs according to the type of good being serviced. Service attributes are essential for industrial equipment and many consumer durables. Although it might not seem so, they also have a significant role to play in the field of consumer non-durables. Service requirements differ widely from country to country (Table 9.2, cell 3) because they are related to environmental factors such as:

1. Level of technical expertise.
2. Level of labour costs, which is decisive in the balance between durability and reparability. For instance, Africans are experts at repairing and even revamping totally worn-out cars.
3. Level of literacy (this may render instruction manuals useless).
4. Climatic differences: certain climates increase difficulty of performing maintenance operations because of temperature, humidity, etc.
5. Remoteness of locations, which can render services difficult and costly to perform (e.g., servicing a gas turbine in the middle of the Amazonian forest).
6. Different ways of performing a seemingly identical service (see Box 9.3).

Box 9.3

Who's afraid of injections?

What is more standard in appearance than a syringe and an injection? There are, however, significant differences in the methods used to avoid causing pain to the patient. For intramuscular syringes, there are two different ways of administering an injection. They correspond to two basic service attributes (correct injection of the substance, avoidance of pain):

1. Only the needle itself is stuck in, then the body of the syringe (the cylinder containing the substance and the plunger driving it) is fixed into the base of the needle, in accordance with a technique known as *luerslip* (this method is used in America). The first question asked by an American nurse is: how does it come apart? (Service attribute.)
2. French, Italian and Spanish doctors and nurses prefer (and are used to) using the fully assembled syringe. The American method would probably involve the risk of causing the patient more pain when connecting the two parts of the syringe after the needle has been implanted (an operation they are not used to doing). The service attribute required of the syringe is therefore based on its lightness and being in one piece, which is provided by a bolt system (*luerlock*). The first question asked by a French, Italian or Spanish nurse is: does it hold tight?

Further service attributes relate to who is legally permitted and professionally qualified to administer an injection and where it is possible to buy syringes. In Italy – in contrast to other European countries – syringes are on general sale, even in corner shops. They are available in blister packaging at the supermarket. Traditionally, many housewives actually give injections to members of their family.

(Source: Excerpt from a discussion with Beckton Dickinson, a world leader in single-use medical items – consumables.)

Actual services in developing countries are more traditional and of a limited technical level, at least when viewed by technologically developed countries. In societies where shortages are common, recycling is essential: African shoemakers, for instance, are experts at making shoe soles from used tyres. There is no lack of technical expertise and craftsmanship in developing countries; it is expressed differently, and relates to the prevailing economic conditions. In many African countries for instance, a lot of maintenance is done by small mechanical workshops, which succeed in repairing cars but take a long time to do so; although their repair methods may not be orthodox, they do work. Service instructions issued by car manufacturers naturally need some adaptation. It is better to show mechanics how to do a job than to send them a free 800-page book on maintenance operations. Services are generally delegated to distribution channels. The shortage of available and/or adequate channels and the small size of distribution outlets are obstacles to services, particularly in developing countries.

Even across developed countries differences in the service offered by distribution channels are much greater than may be expected. The daily and weekly shop-opening hours vary widely. They may range from less than 60 hours per week total opening time in northern Europe and Australia to more than 100 hours per week in southern Europe and the United States. This affects attitudes towards distribution services; for example, where weekly store-opening hours are limited, people tend to turn to the Internet or mail order. Where a husband and wife are at work during shop-opening hours, an elderly parent with different service requirements may have to do the shopping for them.

From a customer perspective, differences have been found in service expectations, service evaluations and service reactions.[30] Service expectations are the reference points from which consumers judge performance. The SERVQUAL is the most commonly used framework to assess service quality, as it measures the gap between expectations and evaluations of performance, which influences satisfaction.[31]

It includes five dimensions: tangibility, reliability, assurance, responsiveness and empathy. From an etic perspective, these dimensions have been found to be important across cultures. From an emic perspective, additional dimensions have been found. For instance, Raajpoot[20] found that personalization, formality and sincerity were also important in some cultures. Generally, it has been found that US consumers have higher overall service quality expectations than consumers from other countries, which is commonly explained by the service environment and level of individualism.[30]

Service perceptions and evaluations also appear to differ across countries. For instance, Japanese (high context/collectivist) consumers rated service perceptions, in the same superior service condition, lower than US (low context/individualist) consumers.[32] Similarly, Canadians (low power distance/low uncertainty avoidance) rated banking service quality higher than the French (high PD/high UA).[33] Some differences have also been found in the factors that influence service evaluations. For instance, consumers from low-context Western cultures placed more emphasis on the tangible cues, whereas those from high-context Eastern cultures placed more emphasis on the intangible cues.[34] Similarly, collectivists have been found to be more susceptible to positive WOM when making service quality evaluations about their current bank than individualists.[35] Additionally, in high-social interaction contexts (e.g., bookstores) collectivism has been shown to increase the importance of relationship and service quality on behavioural intentions, such as positive word-of-mouth and repurchasing, but in low-social interaction (e.g., supermarkets) there was no such affect.[36]

People also react differently to service failures across cultures. For instance, consumers from Eastern cultures are less likely to complain than those from Western cultures, particularly when there is some kind of prior relationship.[37,38] Whereas compensation from a service failure positively influenced Western and Eastern consumers, it only influenced repurchase intentions and word of mouth for the US sample.[39] Customers from more collectivist or uncertainty-avoidant countries have a greater intention to give positive word-of-mouth after a positive service encounter, but if they receive a negative service encounter they tend not to give negative word-of-mouth, complain, or even switch.[34] The reverse is true for consumers from more individualist and lower uncertainty-avoidant countries. According to Zhang and colleagues (p. 219): 'Northern Americans may be more result-focused and pragmatic in their reactions to service experiences.'[30]

In a business setting, word-of-mouth may be more important in Japan than in the United States: when searching for a service in Japan and in the United States, buyers from Japanese and US firms use a number of personal information sources. Japanese companies have been found to use 340 per cent more referral sources than US firms when purchasing services in the United States. While US firms use more referral sources when purchasing in Japan, the Japanese firms still use 78 per cent more referral sources overall.[40]

Culture and the waiting experience

An important aspect of service is waiting to be served: to obtain maintenance or spare parts, to receive cash in a bank or to be served in a restaurant. In waiting, people have to deal with time, rules and power. The cultural assumptions concerning time are central to the waiting experience: people with a strong economic time pattern (see Chapter 2) may experience waiting as a waste of time, a painful moment with negative emotions. For instance, Chen and colleagues (p. 291)[41] found that 'people from Western cultures are relatively less patient and therefore discount the future to a greater degree than do people from Eastern cultures, and thus Westerners value immediate consumption relatively more'.

Waiting is organized in queues to varying degrees and the rules concerning the waiting process are more or less respected according to culture (see Chapter 2 and 3). Another important aspect of waiting is power: where power distance is strong, it seems almost legitimate to let the least powerful wait, with jumping the queue as standard behaviour for the most powerful. In fact, rather than jumped, the waiting line is bypassed: important consumers have direct access to the service. On the contrary, in the US, where low power distance and strong economic time prevail, waiting lines are well organized and everybody is treated fairly, following the principle of 'first come, first served'. Matters can be further complicated by priority-lines (where consumers can pay extra for no or shorter queues) as, perhaps paradoxically, these are very popular in the US despite the potential activation of power distance. However, the strong economic time orientation and perceived 'fairness' of paying more for lower waiting times explains this. Box 9.4 presents the Japanese attitude towards waiting in various service situations.

Waiting time can be reduced or increased according to the level of service personnel available; it can therefore be adapted according to the locally prevailing assumptions about time. In Europe, where time is, on average, slightly less economic than in the US, fast-food outlets are not as quick. People are not as preoccupied with waiting time. In the US many pizza restaurants give a free pizza to customers who have waited more than a set amount of time (e.g., 10–30 minutes) for their order; in most European countries this practice is not necessary, because people do not resent waiting and may even value waiting time in a restaurant as a sign of careful preparation. Similarly, Rowley and Slack (p. 375) discuss differences in airport departure lounge environments across countries:

US airports have much more of a sense of urgency and activity (or a 'buzz') than airports in other parts of the world. Elsewhere the sense is more one of leisure and luxury, calm and relaxation. These messages are subtly conveyed through the way in which retail outlets are arranged, the attitudes of service agents and the nature of promotional messages.[42]

Another service attribute is the type of rules that apply to waiting and the degree to which the waiting lines are organized. In many countries waiting is not organized at all and the principle 'first come, first served' finds no translation. Since people are used to unorganized waiting, they know that they will have to fight those who jump the queue, by shouting, threatening them or jumping the queue themselves. For instance, the contrast between French and Swiss ski resorts, especially at peak time, is striking: whereas in France the absence of waiting corridors results in untidy crowds, in Switzerland the waiting process remains fairly peaceful and organized even if the waiting time is slightly longer. It comes as no surprise that American tourists travelling to Europe see the service quality image of French ski resorts as significantly lower than that of the Swiss and Austrian ski resorts, particularly as concerns honesty and friendliness.[43]

Cultural assumptions and service encounters

The service encounter implies a person-to-person relationship, in maintenance as well as in restaurant or other services. To this extent, the prevailing cultural norms apply in service encounters as they apply in any social interaction. Even though much is shared, especially from a normative point of view (availability, courtesy, willingness to give information), social codes concerning adequate service vary according to culture. Edward Hall (pp. 58–9), for instance, explains how, when staying in a hotel in downtown Tokyo, he was completely mystified by a problem with his room:

I had been a guest for about ten days and was returning to my room in the middle of an afternoon. Entering the room I immediately sensed that something was wrong. Out of place. Different. I was in the wrong room. Someone else's things were distributed around the head of the bed and the table . . . I checked my key again. Yes, it really was mine . . . At the desk, I was told by the clerk, as he sucked in his breath in deference (and embarrassment?) that indeed they had moved me. My particular room had been reserved in advance by somebody else. I was given the key to my new room and discovered that all my personal effects were distributed around the new room almost as though I had done it myself.[44]

Later Hall was to discover that, in contrast to the United States where being moved in such a way is almost an insult, in Japan it was tangible evidence that, after some days, he was treated as a family member, somebody belonging to the group of familiar clients, who can be treated in a relaxed and unceremonious way.

There are many situations where 'good' service is not self-evident. A case in point is when people are asleep on a plane when a meal is served. As far as the Japanese are concerned, the steward must wake those who are asleep so that they do not miss the meal, whereas Westerners prefer not to be disturbed in their sleep.[45] Naturally, the best solution, whatever the culture, would be for the steward to wait and serve the person sleeping as soon as he or she awakes; but such treatment is rarely possible because of schedule constraints. Instead, some international airlines (e.g., Emirates) provide passengers with sticky labels to indicate their individual preferences for being woken for food service or being left undisturbed.

An important cultural aspect of the service encounter is the *doing/being* divide. Hall (p. 109),[44] contrasts the French and the Americans: 'The French as a rule are much more involved [than the Americans] with their employees and with their customers and clients as well. They do not feel they can serve them adequately unless they know them well.' The first sentence is questionable to many foreigners, service quality in France (as in other Latin countries): appears poor in comparison with the United States. Many American visitors perceive the commitment of French service providers towards their clients as quite low. The real key is in Hall's second sentence: '*unless they know them well*'. In societies where *doing* is strongly emphasized, as in the United States, waiters and other service providers are task-centred rather than person or relationship-centred. It is no real problem for them to serve *unknown* people. To many French or Latin eyes, North American service appears the exact opposite of Hall's judgement; friendlier, more attentive and more dedicated than in European countries, especially in southern Europe. So, in a *being*-oriented

---

Box 9.4

Sabisu (Japanese concept of service)

Misako Kamamoto, chief of the Japan Travel Bureau, recounts her experience guiding Japanese tourists overseas:

'When I take a group of Japanese tourists to a restaurant in Europe for the first time, I make a point to advise them in advance as follows: "Quite apart from the problem of whether the food suits the Japanese palate, you must be resigned to the fact that it takes a good deal of time to have a meal in a European restaurant." . . . Some members of the party are bound to start complaining despite the warning that I have given them. "Why are European restaurants so slow in serving us? Please ask them to speed up the service." Some get so impatient that they stand up and leave, saying, "I don't want to wait for dessert or coffee. I can't stand a restaurant which gives such bad service." In a European restaurant, the essence of good service is to give the guests plenty of time to enjoy conversation together with the meal. So it makes sense that dishes are served with long intervals in between.

Japanese tourists who go shopping in Paris invariably return full of complaints because they were not treated like "gods" as in Japan. "The sales clerks take the attitude that they are doing you a favor by 'allowing you to buy'. They are so curt. What do they think customers are, anyway? The sales clerks have absolutely no interest in doing business. When I asked a clerk to show me something of a different color or different size, she acted annoyed and said brusquely, 'We have none.' She didn't even try to search."

In a Japanese bank the clerk counts the notes by himself and puts them all together in a tray for the client, . . . few Japanese take the trouble of counting the notes on the spot . . . The Japanese usually consider that it is impolite to distrust anyone and believe that the other party will most naturally live up to the trust placed in him. In restaurants and hotels Westerners do not make payment until they have thoroughly examined the bill, item by item and make sure that the sum is correctly totalled. In contrast the Japanese have always believed that restaurant and hotel bills are correct. Therefore, even when they are overseas, they assume the same and make payment without examining the bill. This habit sometimes becomes a trouble.

When they travel by train in Europe, the Japanese are struck by the quietness of the stations which are so unlike the noisy Japanese stations. There is no bell or loudspeaker signaling the departure of a train. Their first reaction is, "It's so nice and quiet." But this soon gives way to anxiety. "Why is it that there is no bell notifying us of the departure? It would be a lot of trouble if we missed the train," some say. . . . Whereas European railways give priority to silence and their rule is to have travelers enjoy a quiet journey, Japanese railways seem to think that their mission is to provide passengers with all kinds of information via blaring loudspeakers.'

(Source: Kamamoto, pp. 26–7.[45])

Table 9.3 Cultural dimensions and automated service

Dimensions		High	
		Being	Doing
Dimensions	Affectivity	1. Strong preference for personnel in contact	3. Like(s) the machine but would like personnel also
	Neutrality	2. Do(es) not like the machine but do(es) not like people either	4. Strongest preference for purely automated service

society, known customers are shown attentive and friendly service, whereas unknown customers may well be neglected.

Another interesting question is whether customers prefer automated service, which is widely expanding (e.g., automatic teller machines, ticket machines, etc.), or to be served by real, flesh-and-blood people. A *being* orientation implies a preference for personnel in contact whereas the *doing* orientation favours automated service, which is purely task oriented. The dimension of affectivity versus neutrality (see Chapter 3), an important aspect of Trompenaars'[46] relational orientation, can be combined with the *doing–being* divide for describing possible preferences, as in Table 9.3: affectivity creates a preference for personnel in contact, because human relationships in the service encounter are preferred to service automation. Naturally, all this is based on cultural ideal types; other factors, such as age and level of education, have a strong influence on individual acceptance of automated service; older people and less educated persons have more difficulties in dealing with automated service devices, which they do not consider user friendly.[47]

Factors in favour of service standardization

The decision to adapt services to diversified international requirements implies little cost (Table 9.2, cell 3), since it is far easier to reach increasing returns from economies of scale for a product's physical attributes than for its service attributes. On the other hand, there can be substantial learning effects with service attributes. For example, various management

procedures such as stocking spare parts or hotel laundering may be standardized.

In certain cases (Table 9.2, cell 3) adapting service attributes leads to cost savings because locally supplied services are far less comprehensive than in the country of origin. This is feasible either when local service requirements are less demanding or when the product has been intended to be almost maintenance free. In this case, it will also be designed to stand up to 'untrained' users. Physical attributes will then interact with service attributes within the product as a whole.

However, service standardization (Table 9.2, cell 4) is required when the clientele are internationally 'mobile'. Customers move with their service requirements. The global success of truck manufacturers from northern Europe (DAF, Volvo, Scania, Mercedes) is due in part to their ability to offer a standardized service in a range of countries and on sites along the routes that are most commonly taken by international truck drivers. For instance, an engine or a gearbox can be completely overhauled within a specified period of time at any location on the route. The same holds true for McDonald's restaurants where service is to a large extent standardized worldwide: customers know what they will find in terms of service, whether they enter a McDonald's in Tampere, Finland, Osaka, Japan or Montauban, France.

9.4

Symbolic attributes

The symbolic aspects of consumption are important to consumers: the social meaning of many products is more important than their functional utility or at least as important, e.g., clothes or perfumes. As Solomon emphasized (p. 320): 'Symbolic interactionism focuses on the process by which individuals understand their world. It assumes that people interpret the actions of others rather than simply react to them.'[48]

In terms of product adaptation/standardization, two different issues should be addressed:

1. The relationship between symbolic attitudes and national product images, with respect to product category, company and brand names and country of manufacture.
2. Divergent symbolic interpretations. Meanings are principally conveyed by the packaging and outward appearance of a product. If a symbolic attribute which was ethnocentrically conceived has a very different and highly negative interpretation in the target culture, adaptation is required (Table 9.2, cell 5). For instance, symbolic associations linked to objects or colours may vary considerably across countries and cultures. Carlsberg had to add a third elephant to its label in Africa, since two elephants seen together are considered an ominous sign.[49]

Images diffused by symbolic attributes

The interpretation of symbolic messages conveyed by attributes, such as colour, shape and consistency of products may differ significantly between the marketer's culture and the consumer's culture. Williams and Longworth[50] cite the case of the Coral Sea tuna fishery in Australia, where the government spent money to develop exports to Japan. The fishing operation was unable to obtain a high price for its fresh tuna airfreighted to Japan, because the Japanese had a problem with the colour of the fish. After investigations were conducted in the Tsukiji central wholesale market, it appeared that the negative interpretation was related to the meat colour, which was identified as a non-Japanese origin; this resulted in the Australian tuna consistently being sold at a discount. Today, Australia selects and sends only the more compatibly coloured Southern Bluefin tuna into the highly priced sashimi (raw fish) market in Japan. Australia is the second largest exporter of Bluefin Tuna to Japan with 21 per cent of the market in 2006.[51]

Ethnocentrism is instinctive in all symbolic thought. It is therefore quite inevitable, especially when it is present in the consumer's culture. In the case of ethnic products, it may even be of some use to marketers in order to maintain genuineness. However, inappropriate (or even poor) use of backgrounds that diffuse symbolic images that are not adapted to the local consumer presents a danger for international marketers. Inappropriate use of symbolic meanings may be based on the best possible intentions on the part of the marketer but may result in the worst consequences for users: for example, the skull and crossbones symbol, used in most Western countries to represent lethal dangers posed by electricity, poison, steam, etc., is a symbol of potency in many African countries.

Symbolism of colours, shapes, numbers, etc.

White is the colour of birth and in the West usually refers to a happy life event, whereas in China it symbolizes mourning. Conversely, the colour black symbolizes death in the West, perhaps because its darkness suggests fears that the sun will not return, whereas it is an everyday colour in China.

Hidden behind each symbol is one or more material support. Red, for example, is the colour of blood: it can evoke and suggest meanings that differ widely depending on the culture (see Figure 9.1). Every culture has an image of blood, which feeds part of the symbolic content of the colour red. Naturally, the colour red can be linked to substances other than blood – certain flowers, for instance. Use of red as the dominant colour on a product or its packaging must therefore be very carefully considered beforehand (Table 9.2, cell 5).

Website link 9.4

Search for information about the symbolic meaning of different colours, such as the following: **http://www.globalization-group.com/edge/ resources/color-meanings-by-culture/**.

Associating symbols

Symbols which are diffused by the design of a product or its packaging may be associated with the

Figure 9.1 An example of diverging symbolic interpretations

intrinsic qualities of the product itself. For example, the Italian company Olivetti produced a typewriter that was such a beautiful object that a New York museum displayed it in its modern art collection. This typewriter proved to be a commercial failure in the United States even though the Americans liked its appearance. Potential purchasers found that its design did not inspire an image of robustness (Table 9.2, cell 5). Furthermore, in Anglo-Saxon societies there is often a puritanical attitude that work is an activity required by duty, which is sometimes arduous and should be more painful than enjoyable. This beautiful and enjoyable object was incompatible with such an attitude.

In many cases symbolic associations may work even though, from a rational point of view, individual symbols are somewhat contradictory: consumer interpretation of symbolic associations take the form of an impressionistic halo rather than a detailed content analysis. An example is a German *Weissbier* (a beer brewed with wheat instead of barley), called Oberdorfer. It claims on one side of its label to be brewed according to the Bavarian purity law dating back to 1516, whereas the other side of the label boasts 'ice-rifing' (*sic*), 'our new *coole* art to brew beer' (*coole* is a germanification of 'cool', which evokes positive values of quietness and relaxation in many non-English-speaking cultures, and 'ice-rifing' probably evokes a late crop of hops which provides a more bitter taste). Associating (local) tradition and (foreign) modernity is in general no major problem: in daily life, consumers themselves experience the complex mix of modern and traditional, local and foreign values and behaviours.

A French company exported a cheese from the Pyrenees to West Germany. A shepherd surrounded by his sheep was depicted on the packaging. This picture was directly related to what was shown in the television commercial. In France this image conveyed the idea of a natural manufacturing process and home-made qualities. A consumer test carried out in Germany, after the initial failure of the product, showed that the Germans associated the shepherd with dirt. The shepherd was withdrawn and subsequently replaced with a picture of mountain scenery. The product was then able to undergo a successful relaunch. In this example the problem stems from the association of symbolic opposites: country/mountain, dirty/clean, natural/artificial. Clearly, in this case, the symbolic associations of the French and the Germans are very different.

Colours may also be associated with particular product categories or product attributes. Purple, for instance, is perceived as expensive in Asian cultures, but inexpensive in the United States. Black is perceived as demonstrating trustworthiness and high quality in China.[52] Colours may also be associated with countries, the products of which are supposed to be the most likely to have this colour dominant on their packaging. By gathering data in four countries (China, South Korea, Japan and the United States), Jacobs and colleagues[52] show that Asian nations associate red with the United States, but US people do not associate their country with red; purple is associated with France, and the four cultures reviewed associate both France and Italy with the colour green.

Madden and colleagues[53] explored the extent to which students from East Asia, Europe, North America and South America like various colours, the meanings they associate with colours and how they would match colours for a logo by testing. They found that blue, green and white share similar meanings and are well liked across countries, while black and red, although also liked, hold different meanings across countries. For instance, red was perceived as active, hot and vibrant across all countries, but in the PRC and Taiwan it was also perceived as pleasant. In addition, when students were asked to match colours for a product logo, the colours paired with red differed considerably. It was paired with black (for the United States and Brazil), with white (Colombia, Hong Kong, China and Taiwan) and with yellow (Austria, Canada and China).

Exotic, ethnic and universal appeals

Certain factors weigh in favour of the standardization of symbolic attributes (Table 9.2, cell 6): favourable perception of imported products, positive association with the country of origin (perfume with France, fast food with the United States, etc.) and other factors are examined in detail in Chapter 12. Many people buy a small slice of American life when they enter a McDonald's restaurant, a touch of French romance when they buy Cacharel perfume, or an instant of German *Gemütlichkeit* when they drink a Löwenbräu beer. In these consumption experiences ethnic product symbolism is associated with exotic appeal for the consumer; thus, symbolic attributes must be kept standardized even though the product or its surrounding services are to a certain extent adapted to local markets.

Website link 9.5

View symbols from all over the world: **http://www.whats-your-sign.com/index.html.**

A good example of a purely standardized product is the 'Classic Christmas Cake' sold worldwide through mail order by Collin Street Bakery from Corsicana, Texas. The advertisement, sent by mail worldwide, emphasizes that they still bake the 'Deluxe cake true to the Old-World recipe brought to Corsicana, Texas from Wiesbaden, Germany in 1896, by master baker Gus Weidmann'; it boasts the richness of the ingredients ('a full 27 per cent rich pecans') and claims to deliver in 196 countries. Associating symbols of tradition (Old World), genuineness and American richness, they have a full register of images that work worldwide (and claim to do so!). Some brands also try to build on universal symbols: Coca-Cola has always successfully avoided being associated too strongly with an American image by creating a strong brand association with youth, sports and leisure situations, all universal themes. Packaging consistency is a solution for products that want to diffuse a universal image and build on a highly standardized offering: Coke uses the same red and white logo in each country, and its bottle design is consistent across markets. Similarly, McDonald's never strays from its yellow arches. The symbolic interpretation then shifts from the parts to the whole: rather than relating to interpretations of yellow and arches in particular cultures, it diffuses a message about McDonald's worldwide.

For the designer of product attributes that convey appropriate symbolic meanings, the following recommendations can be made:

1. When conducting research on possible standardization before a product launch, it is preferable to choose symbols that have a universal or near-universal value (as far as they exist).
2. Since there is very great diversity in the interpretations and associations of symbols, product and packaging standardization must be systematically preceded by product and packaging tests carried out in each national market, using local informants.

Questions

1. List basic attributes of a perfume at the three levels (physical, service and symbolic). Indicate how the interpretation of symbolic attributes of perfumes may differ cross-culturally.

2. What are basic attributes of Coca-Cola (physical, service and symbolic) in its original US context? Coca-Cola is adapted to suit local tastes and its advertising, although based on core advertising themes and guidelines, is customized for local audiences. Why?

3. How can a company make compromises between worldwide product standardization and customization to local markets?

4. Why is service adaptation across markets necessary? Outline basic reasons.

5. People in a queue may be told how long they still have to wait before being served. What are the possible interpretations by consumers of such information?

6. You have been asked to choose a colour and a design for a fire extinguisher. What are the standard colour and signs used in your native culture? Assess whether they are cross-culturally transferable. Answer the same question for a coffee packet.

7. Are there universal, or near-universal, symbols? To what extent can they be used in a marketing strategy? Provide examples.

References

1. Douglas, Susan P. and C. Samual Craig (2011), 'Convergence and Divergence: Developing a Semiglobal Marketing Strategy', *Journal of International Marketing*, 19 (1), 82–101.

2. Vrontis, Demetris (2003), 'Integrating Adaptation and Standardization in International Marketing: The Adaptstand Modelling Process', *Journal of Marketing Management*, 19, 283–305.

3. Baalbaki, Imad B. and Naresh K. Malhotra (1995), 'Standardization Versus Customization in International Marketing: An Investigation Using Bridging Conjoint Analysis', *Journal of the Academy of Marketing Science*, 23 (3), 182–94.

4. Hult, G., Tomas M., Bruce D. Keillor and Roscoe Hightower (2000), 'Valued Product Attributes in an Emerging Market: A Comparison between French and Malaysian Consumers', *Journal of World Business*, 35 (2), 206–20.

5. Diamantopoulos, A., B. B. Schlegelmilch and J. P. Du Preez (1995), 'Lessons for Pan-European Marketing? The Role of Consumer Preferences in Fine-Tuning the Product-Market Fit', *International Marketing Review*, 12 (2), 38–52.

6. Powers, Thomas L. and Jeffrey J. Loyka (2010), 'Adaptation of Marketing Mix Elements in International Markets', *Journal of Global Marketing*, 23, 65–79.

7. Shoham, Aviv (1996), 'Marketing-Mix Standardization: Determinants of Export Performance', *Journal of Global Marketing*, 10 (2), 53–73.

8. Amine, Lyn S. (1993), 'Linking Consumer Behavior Constructs to International Marketing Strategy: A Comment on Wills, Samli, and Jacobs and an Extension', *Journal of the Academy of Marketing Science*, 21 (1), 71–7.

9. Wills, James A., Coskun Samli and Laurence Jacobs (1991), 'Developing Global Products and Marketing Strategies: A Construct and a Research Agenda', *Journal of the Academy of Marketing Science*, 19 (1), 1–10.

10. Dana, Leo-Paul and Brenda M. Oldfield (1999), 'Lublin Coco-Cola Bottlers Ltd', *International Marketing Review*, 16 (4/5), 291–8.

11. Bates, Daniel (2011), 'How much Caffeine can one Person Take? Starbucks Unveils the 1.5 PINT Trenta Coffee Cup', *Daily Mail*, 17 January. Available from: http://www.dailymail.co.uk/news/article-1347958/Starbucks-unveil-1-5-pint-Trenta-coffee-cup-bid-satisfy-US.html#ixzz1lYwzKz99.

12. Zhan, Lingjing and Yanqun He (2011), 'Understanding Luxury Consumption in China: Consumer Perceptions of Best-known Brands', *Journal of Business Research*, in press.

13. Bian, Qin and Sandra Forsythe (2011), 'Purchase Intention for Luxury Brands: A Cross Cultural Comparison', *Journal of Business Research*, doi:10.1016/j.jbusres.2011.10.010.

14. Allio, David J. and Robert J. Allio (2002), 'Coors Light in Puerto Rico: Battling for Local Dominance in a Global Market', *Strategy and Leadership*, 30 (6), 13–17.

15. van Mesdag, Martin (2000), 'Culture-Sensitive Adaptation or Global Standardization – the Duration-of-Usage Hypothesis', *International Marketing Review*, 17 (1), 74–84.

16. Charvan, Apala Lahiri, Douglas Gorney, Beena Prabhu and Sarit Arora (2009), 'The Washing Machine Ate My Sari – Mistakes in Cross-cultural Design', *Interaction*, Jan–Feb, 25–31.

17. Jones, Bob Dorigo (2007), *Remove Child Before Folding: The 101 Stupidest, Silliest, and Wackiest Warning Labels Ever*. New York, NY: Grand Central Publishing.

18. Giordan, Alain-Eric (1988), *Exporter Plus 2*. Paris: Economica.

19. Camphuis, Pierre-Arnold (1984), 'Launching a Product on the Cameroon Market', Internship report, Ecole Supérieure De Commerce De Paris.

20. Raajpoot, Nusser (2004), 'Reconceptualizing Service Encounter Quality in Non-Western Context', *Journal of Service Research*, 7 (2), 181–201.

21. Baumgartner, Hans, Jan-Benedict and E. M. Steenkamp (1996), 'Exploratory Consumer Buying Behavior: Conceptualization and Measurement', *International Journal of Research in Marketing*, 13 (2), 121–37.

22. Levitt, Theodore (1983), 'The Globalization of Markets', *Harvard Business Review*, 61 (3), 92–102.

23. Schuh, Arnold (2000), 'Global Standardization as a Success Formula for Marketing in Central Eastern Europe', *Journal of World Business*, 35 (2), 133–48.

24. Pahud de Mortanges, Charles, Jan-Willem Rietbroek and Cort MacLean Johns (1997), 'Marketing Pharmaceuticals in Japan: Background and the Experience of US Firms', *European Journal of Marketing*, 31 (8), 561–82.

25. Shapiro, Carl and Hal R. Varian (1999), 'The Art of Standard Wars', *California Management Review*, 41 (2), 8–32.

26. Vertinsky, Ilan and Dongsheng Zhou (2000), 'Product and Process Certification: Systems, Regulations and International Marketing Strategies', *International Marketing Review*, 17 (3), 231–52.

27. World Trade Organization (WTO) (2012), Grade growth show in 2012, after strong deceleration in 2011. Available at: www.wto.org/english/news_e/pa658_e.pdf. Retrieved on 12 August 2012.

28. Javalgi, Rajshekhar G. and D. Steven White (2002), 'Strategic Challenges for the Marketing of Services Internationally', *International Marketing Review*, 19 (6), 563–81.

29. Kostecki, Michel Maciej and Marcin Nowakowski (2002), 'Regulatory Barriers to Export of Services: A Managerial View from Poland-based Export Firms', *Argumenta Oeconomica*, 12 (1), 17–51.

30. Zhang, Jingyun, Sharon E. Beatty and Gianfranco Walsh (2008), 'Review and Future Directions of Cross-cultural Consumer Services Research', *Journal of Business Research*, 61 (3), 211–24.

31. Parasuraman, A., Valarie A. Zeithaml and Leonard L. Berry (1988), 'Servqual: A Multiple-item Scale for Measuring Consumer Perceptions of Service Quality', *Journal of Retailing*, 64 (1), 12–40.

32. Laroche, Michel, Linda C. Ueltschy, Shuzo Abe, Mark Cleveland and Peter P. Yannopoulos (2004), 'Service Quality Perceptions and Customer Satisfaction: Evaluating the Role of Culture', *Journal of International Marketing*, 12 (3), 58–85.

33. Ladhari, Riadh, Frank Pons, Grégory Bressolles and Michel Zins (2010), 'Culture and Personal Values: How They Influence Perceived Service Quality', *Journal of Business Research*, 64, 951–7.

34. Mattila, Anna S. (1999), 'The Role of Culture in the Service Evaluation Process', *Journal of Service Research*, 1 (3), 250–61.

35. Schumann, Jan, H. Florian, V. Wangenheim, Anne Stringfellow, Zhilin Yang, Vera Blazevic, Sandra Praxmarer, G. Shainesh, Marcin Komor, Randall M. Shannon and Fernando R. Jiménez (2010), 'Cross-cultural Differences in the Effect of Received Word-of-mouth Referral in Relational Service Exchange', *Journal of International Marketing*, 18 (3), 62–80.

36. Ozdemir, V. Emre and Kelly Hewett (2010), 'The Effect of Collectivism on the Importance of Relationship Quality and Service Quality for Behavioral Intentions: A Cross-national and Cross-contextual Analysis', *Journal of International Marketing*, 18 (1), 41–62.

37. Liu, Ben Shaw-Ching, Olivier Furrer and D. Sudharshan (2001), 'The Relationships between Culture and Behavioral Intentions toward Services', *Journal of Service Research*, 4 (2), 118–29.

38. Hui, Michael K., Candy K. Y. Ho and Lisa C. Wan (2011), 'Prior Relationships and Consumer Responses to Service Failures: A Cross-cultural Study', *Journal of International Marketing*, 19 (1), 59–81.

39. Wong, Nancy Y. (2004), 'The Role of Culture in the Perception of Service Recovery', *Journal of Business Research*, 57 (9), 957–63.

40. Money, R. Bruce, Mary C. Gilly and John L. Graham (1998), 'Explorations of National Culture and Word-of-mouth Referral Behavior in the Purchase of Industrial Services in the US and Japan', *Journal of Marketing*, 62 (October), 76–87.

41. Chen, Haipeng (Allan), Sharon Ng and Akshay R. Rao (2005), 'Cultural Differences in Consumer Impatience', *Journal of Marketing Research*, 42 (3), 291–301.

42. Rowley, Jennifer and Frances Slack (1999), 'The Retail Experience in Airport Departure Lounges: Reaching for Timeless and Placelessness', *International Marketing Review*, 16 (4/5), 363–75.

43. Ofir, Chezy and Donald R. Lehmann (1986), 'Measuring Images of Foreign Products', *Columbia Journal of World Business* (Summer), 105–8.

44. Hall, Edward T. (1976), *Beyond Culture*. New York: Doubleday.

45. Kamamoto, Mitsuko (1984), 'Japanese Concept of Service', *Dentsu Japan Marketing/Advertising* (January), 26–9.

46. Trompenaars, F. (1993), *Riding the Waves of Culture: Understanding Diversity in Global Business*, New York: Irwin.

47. Simon, Françoise and Jean-Claude Usunier (2007), 'Cognitive, Demographic, and Situational Determinants of Service Customer Preference for Personnel-in-contact over Self-Service Technology', *International Journal of Research in Marketing*, 24 (2), 163–73.

48. Solomon, Michael R. (1983), 'The Role of Products as Social Stimuli: A Symbolic Interactionism Perspective', *Journal of Consumer Research*, 10 (December), 319–29.

49. McCornell, J. D. (1971), 'The Economics of Behavioral Factors in the Multinational Corporation', in *Combined Proceedings of the American Marketing Association*, Fred E. Allvine (ed.), p. 260.

50. Williams, Stephen C. and John W. Longworth (1989), 'Factors Influencing Tuna Prices in Japan and Implications for the Development of the Coral Sea Tuna Fishery', *European Journal of Marketing*, 23 (4), 5–24.

51. Infofish (2007), Tuna Market Report – Bluefin – January 2007. Available from: www.infofish.org/marketreports/tuna-bluefin0107us.html.

52. Jacobs, Laurence, Charles Keown, Reginald Worthley and Ghymn Kyung-Il (1991), 'Cross-cultural Colour Comparisons: Global Marketers Beware!', *International Marketing Review*, 8 (3), 21–30.

53. Madden, Thomas J., Kelly Hewett and Martin S. Roth (2000), 'Managing Images in Different Cultures: A Cross-national Study of Color Meanings and Preferences', *Journal of International Marketing*, 8 (4), 90–107.

Appendix 9

Teaching materials

A9.1 Case

Movies worldwide

The world market for feature films has been dominated by the United States for more than 60 years. Hollywood, 20th Century Fox, Warner Bros, and the roaring MGM lion are names, images, and sounds with worldwide recognition. Examples of 60 years of creative work by US studios may be seen on *TCM/TNT Turner Classic Movies* (**www.turnerclassicmovies.com**). Despite the criticism that films are too commercialized, with scenarios overly influenced by focus groups, the average Hollywood release remains a worldwide success. *The Lord of the Rings, Star Wars* and *Titanic* are examples of global hits that have done more than sell tickets around the world. They also reached the status of artistic myths in their categories (epic, science fiction, and disaster, respectively). The *Harry Potter* films (released by Warner Bros), are a more recent example of Hollywood's massive impact around the world. The six films are included in the 25th highest international grosser in history.[1] In Norway one in five people saw the second film, having booked weeks in advance of the opening night. Twelve million Germans have seen the film. In Japan adults, to whom the film is primarily marketed, are as fanatical about it as children.[2] *Harry Potter*, as a franchise, is more profitable than blockbusters *Star Wars, Titanic*, and *Matrix*.[3] (See **www.harrypotter.warnerbros.co.uk/**.)

What many non-American US movie viewers ignore is that some films succeed at home but not abroad, and vice versa. Robin Williams did very well globally in *Good Morning Vietnam, Mrs. Doubtfire* and *The Dead Poets Society*. However, his US health system drama *Patch Adams* failed overseas. According to Duncan Clark, international theatrical department head at Sony, certain formats are thought to fail abroad, such as black, urban and historical themes, as well as baseball and football films.[4] At home, film makers try to target different ethnic markets in addition to the mainstream. Since marketers are targeting youth, English now is the language of ethnic-oriented films (Spanish or Chinese subtitles may be available, so as not to alienate older viewers); however, the theme of the screenplay may differ. Action and adventure movies are more successful among Asian-American audiences, for example.[5] Film makers tend to select their cast, and particularly their stars, with a view to attracting international interest in their films. A respected source for directors is the *Hollywood Reporter's* 'Star Power' classification for the international box office. In 2008 the top-earning actors were Harrison Ford, Adam Sandler, Will Smith, Eddie Murphy and Nicolas Cage.[6] Non-white actors are thought to hold little attraction for overseas markets,[4] apart from Will Smith, Denzel Washington and Jackie Chan.[4]

Movie imports

In most cinema markets around the world the majority of films are imported, reaching 96.8 per cent in Canada and 52.3 per cent in Japan.[7] The market share of American films is very high (most often above 50 per cent). In 2008, it reaches 63.8 per cent[7] in the European Union as a whole in comparison to 78 per cent in 2002,[8] and 66 per cent in 2001.[9] In France, a 'resistant' country, the share of American films amounted to 44 per cent in 2008, which represent approximately four times more in value than the combined imports of films made in other European countries.[7] In Spain, domestic film production is stagnant, accounting for 13.3 per cent of admissions, while American films accounted for 71.5 per cent.[7] Films from Central and Eastern Europe, Mediterranean Basin, and Latin America generally account for a market share of about 1 per cent in the European Union, making the EU more impenetrable to filmmakers other than those from the US, Canada, Australia and Japan. It is likely that a combination of cultural protectionism and poor distribution systems create conditions for market dominance of US films in Europe.[9] Interestingly, there are historical differences. In the 1950s, German, French and Italian audiences had a marked preference for their own national productions. Up until the 1980s it was rare that the same film would share top ten status in Germany, France and Italy. However, since that time, 40 per cent of the top ten films in these three continental European countries are the same Hollywood films.[10] Between 1996 and 2007 the top five films in terms of box office receipts were either British or American including sometimes co-productions from a third (or more) country: *Harry Potter and the Order of the Phoenix* (2007, UK+ US), *Pirates of the Caribbean: At World's End* (2007, US), *Casino Royale* (2006, UK+US, DE, CZ), and *Star Wars III: Revenge of the Sith* (2005, USA).[7]

Hollywood's hegemony

Hollywood's hegemony was won primarily thanks to its massive home market, which allowed studios to recover their costs domestically, freeing up resources for expensive stars, special effects, and marketing (which averages US$65 million per film[11]). Having recovered production costs in their home markets, Hollywood studios can sell their films relatively cheaply to foreign distributors. In fact, three-quarters of film distributors around the world are American-owned,[12] making the top ten film studios also the top ten global distributors. Around the world US distributors have the leverage to do what is illegal at home: 'Blockbooking', forcing theatres or distributors they do not own to buy packages of lower-quality films in order to obtain a desirable hit film.[13] The appeal of Hollywood films around the world is not so surprising considering that Hollywood producers have always had to appeal to different ethnic, religious and social groups in their heterogeneous home market. In addition, many 'Hollywood' directors of the present and past are not American at all. Examples are many, including Taiwanese Ang Lee (*Hulk, The Wedding Banquet, Brokeback Mountain*), British Sam Mendes (*American Beauty, Revolutionary Road*), German Roland Emmerich (*Independence Day, The Patriot, The Day after Tomorrow*), British Ridley Scott (*Gladiator, Alien, Body of Lies*) and Swiss Marc Forster (*Monster's Ball, Finding Neverland, The Kite Runner, Quantum of Solace*). Another element that increased acceptance of US films among non-native speakers of English was the adoption of an introspective, non-verbal style in interpreting roles. This style (known as the 'Method') originated in nineteenth-century Russian theatre and is diametrically opposed to the Shakespearean tradition that emphasizes eloquence. As a by-product of the 'Method' style of Marlon Brando, James Dean, Robert DeNiro, and others, Hollywood films are easily understood even when one's knowledge of English – or the quality of subtitles – is poor.[14] It is helpful that Hollywood's American-ness can tap into the most prominent country-brand equity in the world, to increase its potency.[15]

Table 9.4 Top two films by gross box office receipts per country/region in 2008[7]

Country	Top grossing film	Second grossing film
Australia	*The Dark Knight* (USA/UK)	*Mamma Mia!* (USA/UK)
European Union	*Mamma Mia!* (USA/UK)	*Quantum of Solace* (UK/USA)
France	*Bienvenue chez les Ch'tis* (FR)	*Astérix aux Jeux Olympique* (FR/DE/ES/IT)
Italy	*Kung Fu Panda* (USA)	*Madagascar: Escape 2 Africa* (USA)
Germany	*Keinohrhasen* (DE)	*Madagascar: Escape 2 Africa* (USA)
Japan	Gake no ue no Ponyo (JP)	Hana yori dango: Fainaru (JP)
South Korea	The Good, the Bad, the Weird (KR)	Chugyeogja (KR)
Brazil	*The Dark Knight* (USA/UK)	*Kung Fu Panda* (USA)
Spain	*Inidana Jones and the Kingdom of the Crystall Skull* (USA)	*Hancock* (USA)
USA	*The Dark Knight* (USA)	*Iron Man* (USA)

US concerns about declining share of global movie market

Although American film productions account for about 85 per cent of world film audiences,[16] some in Hollywood are increasingly concerned about dependence on world markets. The market share of American films tends to decrease against local films around the world, and local films are sometimes bigger hits than US films in Korea, France, India, and other countries. Hollywood has its sights trained on the Asian markets (Japan, India, and China) and related markets (Arab countries, North Africa, East Africa, Indonesia, Iran and South Asia), comprising over 75 per cent of the world's population.[17] Hollywood is actively seeking to acquire films from around the world with a more global appeal and to this end Sony and Miramax have acquisition executives seeking Chinese-language films in Hong Kong.[18] More and more Hollywood studios are giving a more international flavour (and appeal) to their films by co-producing abroad or by filming extensively on location in target markets. Africa, for example, is considered to be a safe bet by some Hollywood studios thanks to an almost total lack of cultural protectionist measures, and little resentment of America and the concept of an 'American Hero'. *Tears of the Sun* and *Emma's War* were filmed on location, and Disney's *Lafiya* is intended to interest Africans and Black Americans.[19]

Cultural protectionism

American film marketers need to take into account the cultural protectionism in some European countries and others, including Indonesia, Brazil, and Korea. Protective duties, import quotas, and screening time quotas are common tools used to protect local film production.[10] The French film industry receives approximately US$400 million per year in subsidies, an amount that has been growing each year. Other European countries with a cultural subsidy structure, such as Spain and Italy, are with France the most prolific of Europe's film producers.[20] In an effort to preserve the smaller, fragmented film industries around the world, Canada and 35 other countries have joined trailblazing France to negotiate a 'cultural exception' within the World Trade Organization, and the adoption of UNESCO's global convention on cultural diversity.[16] Hollywood has paid for protectionism of its own, too. The massive motion picture industry lobbying of Washington pushed hard for a decision favouring copyright extensions for creations like Disney's Mickey Mouse in *Steamboat Willie* (soon to expire). The US Supreme Court recently upheld a law extending to a total of 70 years after the creator's death, or 95 years in the case of creations owned by corporations.[21]

Non-American films are beginning to attain better acceptance in the United States. *Crouching Tiger, Hidden Dragon* won the second highest number of Oscar awards, grossed US$100 million in North America despite American's traditional dislike for subtitled films. *Crouching Tiger Hidden Dragon* is one of the 'breakthrough' films signalling the increasing acceptance of foreign films in the US. Another such film is *Life is Beautiful*, the surprising humorous drama directed by Italian Roberto Benigni, where again a subtitled, foreign-language film succeeded in mainstream cinemas across North America to become the top grossing foreign language film in history, with more than US$ 43 million in receipts.[22]

The film's key cultural components

Traditionally the film industry is local. It is a multi-domestic industry, dealing with local actors, local scripts, and the indigenous language. Most films produced worldwide are targeted for local or regional audiences. Egypt and India are major movie film producers. Indian films are viewed from the Middle East to East Asia. Apart from the work of well-known film-makers, like Satyajit Ray, the majority of Indian films are unknown to a non-Asian audience. Films essentially reflect the local cultural scene of the country where they were made. The local scene means familiar landscapes, clothing, institutions, scenes, urban sites, and ways of interacting between people. A film also features products, because product placement has become a way of increasing film budgets everywhere, resulting in the presentation of local products or global ones distinguished by a local touch. In Hong Kong films feature the names of companies that have purchased product placement more prominently than they do the names of the film stars themselves.[23] Local cues portrayed in films, such as the US legal system inherent to courtroom dramas, are most often unfamiliar to foreign viewers and generate an impression of the unknown, which may be positive (exoticism) but is usually viewed negatively. Films that are popular usually reflect the values held by the audience. In Germany, for instance, a rather collectivist and duty-oriented society gradually evolved post-war into one that valued self-determination and pleasure-seeking. This change in value orientation was reflected in increasing popularity of the *James Bond* series, John Wayne films, *Jaws* and *Superman* where the protagonist drives the narrative to fulfil his own goals and the main values of the work are 'fun'.[10]

Films are about storytelling (e.g., drama, comedy), through a visual and spoken narrative based primarily on language. This causes one of the key problems when selling films worldwide: how will speakers from other linguistic contexts understand a Mexican or a Japanese film if it is still in its original language. Generally, when Hollywood studios produce films intended for international markets, they intentionally minimize the dialogue and simplify it, so translations are easier to make, and narrative cues are embedded in the context.[24] Partly for this reason, film-makers emphasize the visuals of a film when the overseas market is targeted. Most countries either use dubbing or subtitles. Dubbing is more costly to implement because it requires specialized professionals to draft a text that fits, as well as actors to dub the voiceover that replaces the original voice soundtrack. In the case of Dreamworks animated films like *Shrek 3*, dubbing may bankroll international stars like Cameron Diaz, Mike Myers and Eddie Murphy, with local stars doing the dubbing in smaller markets, like Alain Chabat in France. Dubbing is very popular in most European countries, where industries have grown up around the activity in large countries like Italy, Germany, France and Spain. Dubbing is also popular in Asia. Viewers of dubbed films are accustomed to the inevitable mismatch between actors' lips and their dubbed pronouncements. Smaller countries tend to use subtitles, because the dubbing process is too costly. In Finland, for instance, most films are subtitled in Finnish and Swedish, the two official languages. US viewers have never accepted dubbed films, with *Crouching Tiger, Hidden Dragon* and *Amélie* being notable exceptions. They also dislike watching subtitled foreign language films. Perhaps, more important, US distributors consider foreign-language films as more suited to the niche 'art-house' cinema circuit than the mainstream. This, among other factors, explains the very low market share of foreign films on the US market where, in 2008, 91.5 per cent of the films viewed were locally produced.[25]

Story-telling is also culturally meaningful, whether scripts put the emphasis on fine-grained psychological relationships between characters (e.g., Swedish films by Ingmar Bergman), historical topics, action films, mob and gangster films, kung fu, or any kind of drama that is meaningful to the audience. The film script may finish with a happy ending or not. According to Czech-born Hollywood director Milos Forman (*One Flew over the Cuckoo's Nest, Ragtime*), the main difference between US and European films is that Hollywood likes happy endings and 'macho fairy tales', while Europeans prefer more ambiguity and realism.[26]

There are also a number of other components for a film, including music, soundtrack, and images. The most significant cultural component in a film is in the interaction between the key characters: their communication style typically reflects a context-bound interaction style. When people with Al Pacino interact in *The Godfather*, it cannot at all be compared with people interacting with Toshiro Mifune in the *Seven Samurai*.

The global film: the exception rather than the rule

The market for films is not *per se* a global market. There still will remain some important market barriers related to language and culture. However, the market is far from being a purely multi-domestic one. As noted above, imports are considerable and viewers are eager to watch foreign films. Many spectators like both national films (identity enhancing) and foreign (mostly American) films. There are greater chances that a film reaches a worldwide audience, if a story is rather simple and universal, relatively context-free and easy to capture. An example of this is Japanese filmmaker Akiro Kurosawa's *Seven Samurai*, a global success later adapted by Hollywood as *The Magnificent Seven*, a Western deprived of its Japanese context, with a larger global reach than the original film. Filmmaker Jean-Jacques Annaud (**www.jjannaud.com/**) has produced films that reached a worldwide audience because, apart from their artistic quality, they eluded certain cultural obstacles (such as *La Guerre du Feu*, devoid of language, as was an interpretation of Jack London's *The Bear*. The popularity of animated films, such as *Finding Nemo* and *Ice Age*, may in part be due to their lack of particularistic cultural cues. *The Lord of the Rings* series (**www.lordoftherings.net/**), although filmed on location in the Southern Island of New Zealand, has no context-bound cues for the spectator apart from those from J. R. R. Tolkien's fantasy works. Appeals are also important to establish when targeting wider audiences: violence, action, science fiction, sex and eroticism, and suspense are likely to appeal broadly and in different cultures. In an international business analysis of film, six characteristics of American films were identified as: a fast pace, sexual tension, graphic violence, repetition of a fable or storyline, and a happy or spectacular ending.[13] Less likely to appeal worldwide are family intrigues, psychological dramas, social criticism, and moral narratives – more likely to characterize European films.

Questions

1. Why have American films been so successful over the last half century? Outline what you consider to be the key success factors for a film (type of story and genre; actors; directors, pace, music, and so on). Was the fascination for the American culture and way of life the prominent reason for that success? What was the contribution of the American melting pot with its huge diversity of migrants' origins to the creativity and global outlook of the American film industry?

2. What is the future of local films? Should they still target a local language and culture audience? Is there any future for local movie industries? Why? Take country examples if you wish.

3. If you were a ROW (rest-of-the-world – that is, non-US) film director, willing to reach a wider audience, how would you go about increasing your chances to be accepted by the audience in a larger number of countries?

4. Are films primarily artistic pieces or are they mere commodities? Should filmmaking be seen as an industry or as an art? If compromises are possible, how would you devise them?

In order to answer the questions, you may use the Web-based information listed below. If you want more information you may conduct a keyword search on **www.google.com**, *and generally you will find it.*

General: **http://www.screendigest.com/**: the pre-eminent source of business intelligence, research and analysis on global audiovisual media.

Box office data for films: **http://boxoffice.com**.
Research guide in film studies (from Yale University, with links to industry data for many countries): **http://www.library.yale.edu/humanities/film/industry.html**.

On the US film industry: **http://www.mpaa.org/**.
On US/EU market shares: **http://www.obs.coe.int/oea_publ/market/focus.html**.

On French films: **http://www.cnc.fr/Site/Template/Accueil.aspx?SELECTID=614&&t=3**.
http://www.unf.edu/groups/spinnaker/archives/2002/feb27/french.html.

About Jean-Jacques Annaud: **http://www.rottentomatoes.com/celebrity/JeanJacquesAnnaud-1040523/**.

On Finnish films: **http://www.preview-online.com/jan_feb/feature_articles/focus_on_finland/**.

About Chinese, Asian and Australian films:
http://www.heroic-cinema.com/www.htm.
http://www.expatsinchina.com/culture/movies/.
http://www.the-trades.com/column.php?columnid=622.

About Japanese films: **http://www.lisashea.com/japan/movies/mov_main.html**.
http://www.cdjapan.co.jp/movie/jmovie/.
http://www.jref.com/entertainment/japanese_movies.shtml.

About the pros and cons of dubbing:
http://www.cnn.com/SHOWBIZ/Movies/9908/26/life.is.beautiful/.
http://www.film.com/features/story/to-dub-or-not/17540523.

About Iranian films:
http://www.film-international.com/.

A9.2 Case

Fast food – Halal or Haram?

It was a crowded table at this noisy North African KFC outlet in the Spring of 2011. Kader and four of his friends lounged comfortably in their chairs, eating and talking at a leisurely pace. After a range of references to France, films, friends and cars, the lunch companions launched into a discussion of the calls for an American boycott.

'I've been boycotting Israeli products for ages, that's why I don't drink Coke', stated Ahmed. 'Oh, come on: that's just one of a million rumours going around by e-mail. You can look at any "rumours" website to find out the truth', retorted Fadi. 'As for me, I drink Pepsi because they refused to go into Israel while others did.'

Kader sensed an opportunity: 'Look at you both, if you really are so politically aware, why are you wearing Nike shoes and smoking Marlboros? You should be embarrassed!' Ahmed laughed as he answered 'Mr. Kader, my friend, what are you doing enjoying your KFC food, then? It's an American company isn't it?' 'We all know that. What a lot of people don't realize is that everyone in that kitchen is an Arab, all the food comes from Arab suppliers, all . . .' Fadi interrupted, 'How do you know? How do any of us know? You believe what they say in their ads? Did you check with their suppliers? My friend, you, and all of us, are in the dark.' Taking a deep puff on his cigarette, Ahmed stated emphatically: 'I agree with all the calls to boycott, I don't want to support the Americans. As they say "by buying American products you cause Palestinian blood to flow", but what would I smoke, what would I wear, where would I eat? You tell me where there are some good local "light" cigarettes.' He squashed the cigarette in the ashtray. 'And where are the great Arab clothes designers and shoe manufacturers? When I'm at home I like Starbucks even though the head of the company's a Zionist, and THAT's not a rumour, bro'. Let's face it, we don't have a choice. Look, my shoes are counterfeit Nike's, and at least I don't go to McDonald's.'

Fadi snorted, and pointed his finger at Kader. 'Look, Ahmed, you are my friend, I wouldn't say anything bad about you, but you think that not going to McDonald's is going to help the Palestinians? The Iraqis? You know I don't normally eat here, you invited me. I don't believe that by wearing a Tommy Hilfiger shirt I'm oppressing Palestinians. Why don't you start your own clothes and shoes company, then I would know it's really "Arab",' he added quietly. Kader shook his head, and said 'Come on guys, let's not wear each other out. It's true, though, that instead of Hilfiger you could choose a European company, at least they're not as bad. Diesel is cool. Puma is cool. I read that the guy who runs Hilfiger is a racist, did you know that? Marlboro addicts should switch to smokes like Gauloises Blondes.' Then he lightly touched each friend on the arm, adding 'Guys, guys, we can do better. The point is we don't have to be slaves to American marketing. What's the big deal? We can make a little sacrifice on favourite brands compared with the price that Palestinians pay in blood.' Fadi had been quiet for a while. Suddenly, he spoke out 'You know, I heard this Lebanese girl speaking, she started a pro-boycott organization. She said that boycotting American products isn't just about hurting the American economy, she said it's more about getting the Americans to understand that their interests lie with us, 200 million Arabs, instead of the four million Israelis!'[27]

Fast-food restaurants in the Middle East and other sensitive parts of the world have been hit by boycotts, criticism and direct violence. Starbucks, McDonald's, Pizza Hut, KFC and others are pawns in the global game of traditionalists versus progressives, of conservatives versus liberals, of protectionism versus globalization. Fast-food companies have been the target of religious edicts, protests, vandalism, and aggressive competitive tactics, some of which have been openly supported by governments.

Globalization in the Middle East

The Middle East is a particular case of development. Most economies in the Middle East are state-controlled. Many are young states with a colonial legacy, and some were Cold War battlefields. The concept of Arab nationalism restricts some countries in an inflexible frame of reference. In some cases, the legitimacy of Middle East governments is challenged by their peoples' perception that they are passive in the face of the regularly televised humiliations of Palestinians, and foreign influence in countries like Afghanistan and Iraq. Various conflicts have justified large expenditures on arms, reducing resources for education and social benefits. These factors combine to create a polarized ideological environment where pro-globalization pragmatists may be in opposition to Islamists. Such conditions are not conducive to good business.[28]

As Arab nationalism has worn thin over the last two decades, the opposing forces in Arab societies have become more visible. Those likely to welcome globalization and its manifestations like McDonald's into their countries tend to be more affluent. Those on the lower end of the social scale are more likely to embrace ancient identities based on cultural, religious, ethnic, or linguistic differences.[29] In his book *Jihad vs. McWorld*, Benjamin Barber attempts to understand these opposing forces. 'McWorld', or globalism, offers integration into a larger economic system, and access to credit, markets and technology. 'Jihad', a term Barber uses loosely to describe tribalism, represents the fragmentation of societal identities, with 'Jihad' offering its proponents a local identity, sense of community, and solidarity against perceived outsiders.[30] Jihad being the compelling ideology of the 'losers' of a capitalist economic system, it is also the ideology of the majority, of the masses. With the cosmopolitan exception of Dubai, these two axes describe the tensions within which foreign-owned or foreign-influenced businesses must operate in the Middle East,[29] representing a complex marketing environment.

Fast food has quickly established itself as a growing trend in the Middle East. In Saudi Arabia, for example, fast-food outlets account for 15 per cent of all foodservice sales, compared with 32 per cent in the US. However, sales by fast food outlets have grown by 10 per cent per year over five years. Table 9.5 gives an idea of the fast growth rate of the fast food market in Saudi Arabia.

Table 9.5 Number of fast food outlets in Saudi Arabia (1990–2002)

Food type	1990	1997	2002
Burger	95	181	268
Chicken	17	70	151
Coffee/baked goods	16	61	244
Ice cream	24	174	309
Pizza	49	136	209
Sandwich/Arabic	11	50	112

(Source: IMES Research (2002), *The food service market in Saudi Arabia*.[31])

In Egypt fast food has become a part of daily life. According to a recent study done in Cairo, 23 per cent of the city's population buy foreign-branded fast food at least twice per week. The main consumers were teenagers and adult males, and consumption mainly took place via home or office delivery.[32] Fast-food outlets have become ubiquitous in the Middle East, with the exception of Syria. Table 9.6 gives an idea of the degree to which fast-food outlets have become part of the landscape.

Table 9.6 Non-exhaustive list of fast-food outlets in predominantly Muslim countries.

Name of food-service chain: Domino's (US) **www.dominospizza.com**

Country	Outlets in 2004	Outlets in 2009
Saudi Arabia	36	53
Turkey	32	114
Malaysia	19	42
Egypt	8	14
United Arab Emirates	6	10
Kuwait	5	18
Bahrain	4	0
Lebanon	4	14
Pakistan	1	6
Jordan	1	4

Name of food-service chain: Hardee's (US) **http://www.hardees.com/**[33]

Country	Outlets in 2004	Outlets in 2009
Saudi Arabia	24	42
United Arab Emirates	21	26
Egypt	14	30
Lebanon	10	8
Bahrain	6	7
Qatar	4	9

Name of food-service chain: Subway (US) **www.subway.com**[34]

Country	Outlets in 2004	Outlets in 2009
United Arab Emirates	32	72
Kuwait	16	34
Saudi Arabia	13	31
Pakistan	9	29
Turkey	3	10
Lebanon	3	3
Oman	1	7
Qatar	6	14
Malaysia	2	36

Table 9.6 (cont'd)

Name of food-service chain: Burger King (US) **www.bk.com**[35]

Country	Outlets	Outlets in 2009
Turkey	98	266
Kuwait	47	54
Saudi Arabia	35	51
Malaysia	21	20
United Arab Emirates	21	52
Lebanon	8	8
Qatar	6	6
Jordan	5	5
Bahrain	3	3

Name of food-service chain: McDonald's (US) **www.mcdonalds.com**[36]

Country	Outlets	Outlets in 2009
Turkey	111	127
Indonesia	108	180
Saudi Arabia	71	83
Egypt	More than 50	59
Kuwait	34	52
United Arab Emirates	25	25
Pakistan	21	20
Bahrain	8	10

Other foodservice chains with significant presence included at the time of writing KFC with 275 units in Indonesia,[a] 390 in Malaysia,[b] and 85 in Egypt;[c] Pizza Hut with 64 units in Saudi Arabia[d] and a strong presence elsewhere. Allied-Domecq-owned Baskin Robbins developed 89 units in Saudi Arabia.[e] According to the website, Subway has 20 units in Iraq.

[a] http://www.kfcindonesia.com/index.php?option=com_storefinder&Itemid=41.
[b] http://www.kfc.com.my/about-malaysia.html.
[c] http://www.americana-group.net/Default.aspx?Id=1140.
[d] http://www.pizzahutsaudia.com/location.cfm?Loc=WE.
[e] http://www.baskinrobbinsme.com/stores_SA.aspx.

Religious edicts (fatwa)

Prominent Muslim scholars have issued religious edicts (fatwa) against the consumption of American products in Egypt, Qatar, Syria, Kuwait, and other countries. Sheikh Youssef Al-Qaradawi, Muslim scholar and president of the European Council for Fatwa and Research, has issued several fatwa calling for a Muslim boycott of Israeli and American products, stating that 'To buy their goods is to support tyranny and oppression. It's a duty not to do that'.[37] The Grand Imam of Islam's highest authority, Al-Azhar, stated that it is 'forbidden' not to follow the boycott of Israel and the supporters of Israel ('America is a second Israel'[38]), issuing a fatwa on the subject.[37] In a more precisely worded fatwa regarding franchises, Dr Mohammad Saeed Al-Bouti of Damascus University's Sharia school said that 'American products which must be boycotted are those whose revenues go to the US such as American cigarettes and restaurants. There are too many of these companies in our countries'. He specified that products produced in Islamic countries according to franchise agreements were forbidden, because a portion of revenues from these products was given to the American company.[38] Other fatwas issued regarding the anti-Israel/anti-US boycotts have been issued by Dr Fu'ad Mukhaymar, head of the Egyptian Sunni Egyptian Institutions, and Dr As-Sayed

Nuh, Kuwait University professor.[38] The International Union for Muslim Scholars (IUMS) lately revive the economic boycott of US and Israeli products, stating that 'each dirham or dinar earned by these peope turns into a bullet in the chests of our brothers'.[39]

Vandalism, protests and violence

The destruction of a fast-food outlet, defacing of its facade, breaking windows and graffiti are common ways of expressing one's disagreement with all that is represented by US fast-food operations. McDonald's windows were broken by angry pro-Palestinian demonstrators in Oman, and an outlet in Bahrain was defaced by stone-throwing youths.[40] KFC was attacked in Pakistan, Indonesia, Lebanon and Greece.[41]

Burger King, McDonald's and Starbucks were the sites for sit-ins and protests in Beirut where they blocked access to the counters and held pro-Palestinian messages.[40] Pizza Hut was bombed in Lebanon.[41] KFC was bombed in 2001 in Makassar, Indonesia.[42] In 2003, in central Sulawesi, students from the State Institute of Islamic Studies [STIAN] protested in front of a KFC to express their resistance to a war in Iraq.[42] A bomb exploded outside KFC in Pakistan in December 2001, causing no injuries.[43] A KFC outlet was destroyed in Cairo by anti-American protesters.[37] Mobs attacked several KFC outlets in Karachi, Pakistan in 2003. The company decided against further expansion in Pakistan in the short term, preferring to invest in less risky locations.[43] At McDonald's in New Delhi, protesters closed the outlet, screaming 'America off our soil'![44] In 2005, bombs hit a KFC and a McDonald's restaurant in Pakistan.[45] Recently, in 2009, activists protested in front of Starbucks outlets and handed out leaflets to inform people of Starbucks' chief executive's pro-Israel stance.[46]

Muslim food prescriptions

'Halal' is the Arabic word for 'lawful', being food that is produced in the manner stipulated in Muslim Holy texts. In the case of restaurants, 'Halal' mainly applies to meats, dairy products, and other items contaminated by meat.[g] Halal directives pertain mainly to slaughter, when the animal should be killed by a Muslim who invokes the name of Allah as the animal dies. Death should be caused by a slit throat causing the animal to bleed to death. The slaughter-house should be supervised by a pious Muslim man.[47] In Europe, the largest Halal meat processing plants are in Belgium.[48] Some Muslims insist that meats be Zabihah in addition to Halal: that the owner of the meat-processing business is a Muslim, that the animal was fed exclusively on a vegetable diet and not treated with growth hormones, that the animal be hand-slaughtered and not stunned.[49] Devout Muslims are generally advised by Muslim organizations to avoid 'Most items' at fast-food outlets, although some fast-food chains attempt to purchase some Halal ingredients.[50] Muslims are advised particularly to avoid non-Halal pizza restaurants where there is a 'high risk' of contamination from pork products and meat by-products in cheese toppings.[50] In France the many Muslim patrons often justify KFC purchasing Halal meat, although the company does not publicize the fact, nor do they display their Halal certificate (which is on hand in the kitchen if a Muslim wanted to inspect it), for fear of alienating other customer segments.[48] The Halal market was estimated at US$150 billion in 2002. Food industry experts have predicted that the Halal food trend will grow, with demand rising and increasing numbers of food suppliers and restaurant operators seeking Halal certification.[51] Table 9.7 puts Muslim food restrictions in the context of the world's other major religions.

---

[g] For more information about Halal foods and the food industry go to: http://www.eat-halal.com/ and http:// www.zabihah.com/ (the global directory of Halal restaurants. Try also: http://www.ifanca.org/index.php (Islamic Food and Nutrition Council of America).

Table 9.7 Food restrictions of Muslims compared with other major religions

Religion	Ingredients	Preparation	Consumption
Islam Food guidelines stem from the Koran, the Hadith, and cultural traditions	No pork or pork by-products, such as gelatin; No carnivorous animals with fangs or claws; No donkeys, elephants or monkeys; No alcohol.	Meats should be from animals slaughtered by a Muslim who invokes Allah; Slit throat/bleeding is the preferred slaughter method; Stunning animal prior to slaughter is not proper; Halal foods should be prepared separately from *Haram* foods, with different utensils.	The daylight fasting period must be respected during Ramadan (one of the 'Pillars of Islam'); According to tradition, women should eat separately from men, particularly when guests are present (some regions); According to some traditions men should eat first, and a sacrifice should be made at the time of Ramadan.[52]
Judaism Food guidelines established in the Old Testament (Leviticus)	Ruminants with cloven hoofs are fit for consumption ('Kosher'); No pork or pork by-products; No animal hindquarters to be eaten; No horsemeat, no seafood lacking fins and scales.	Separate preparation of meat and dairy products; No food preparation work or washing up to be done on the Sabbath; Animals should be slaughtered rapidly by a God-fearing man.	Meat and dairy products should not be consumed at the same meal; There are clear traditions about foods to be consumed on certain feast days.[53]
Christianity Bible and the Pope (Catholics), the Patriarch (Orthodox) or denominational authority	Catholics should avoid meat on Fridays; Orthodox fasting may prescribe avoidance of olive oil or other ingredients.	Fasting or deprivation should be practised during Lent; The Orthodox Church has prescriptive rules for extended and frequent fasting (more than other Christians).[54]	
Hinduism Regulations stated in the Code of Manu	Meat is not encouraged but allowed according to cultural traditions; No beef; In the case of Jainism, no living creatures should be consumed.		
Buddhism	It is accepted that people can and often must take lives of other living creatures in order to continue living. It is desirable to reduce the extent of the slaughter as much as possible, however. Serious Buddhists avoid meat.		

New Muslim-based competition

In some countries local Muslim and Halal operators have stepped in to attract Muslim customers, responding to the expressed reluctance of some Muslims to frequent fast-food outlets. Reasons cited by Muslims for avoiding fast food and prepared foods generally include preparation and service by non-Muslim staff, contamination of vegetarian and vegetable/fruit offerings by unlawful ('Haram') meat products, animal fat, gelatin, wine vinegar, enzymes, emulsifiers, non-Halal rennet (as used in cheese and other dairy products), and vanilla-laced sweets (because vanilla essence may contain alcohol).[55,56] In France, there is a definite trend towards offering Halal fast food on the American fried chicken and hamburger model. The kitchen equipment and menu at outlets named among others ChickenSpot and 'Paris Fried Chicken' resemble that of KFC and McDonald's, and the equipment identical to that used by KFC.[48] A similar phenomenon is visible in Canada, Singapore, Australasia, and the UK. In the UK, for example, Chicken Cottage, a Halal fast-food chain, had 62 outlets in 2004 and is currently opening one new store every month.[57] In Egypt a local entrepreneur started Mo'men ('believer' in Arabic) in 1998 as a substitute for McDonald's. The chain, reported to be 'doing well' with outlets that are 'always packed' serves burgers and chicken nuggets, along with some traditional Egyptian items.[58] All machines and equipment used by Mo'men restaurants are American-made.[59] Mo'men offers vegetarian items that cater to Christians fasting for Lent, and a variety of festive menu items following the Muslim Eid festival.[60] In other countries, such as Malaysia and Singapore, restaurants apply for Halal certification from an official Muslim organization. In Malaysia, for example, KFC and Pizza Hut are advised by a 'Syariah Council' that oversees the supply chain and food production and service to ensure that all are Halal (http://www.kfcholdings.com.my/English/Flashsite/Home/Home.asp). In Singapore the Majlis Ugama Islam Singapura inspects and provides certificates for Halal products and services (http://www.muis.gov.sg).

Boycotts targeting fast food chains

As stated in several reports, fast food is often a target of boycotts because it is far from being a necessity, particularly when there are local brands as alternatives. Recent Arab boycotts are considered to be an extension of the original anti-Israel boycott, which is still technically in force in some countries.[h] Boycotts intensified and took on different forms in the run-up to the hostilities in Iraq, with Malaysians focusing on Coca-Cola and Pepsi, Thai Muslims setting up 'US product free zones', Moroccans calling for a US dollar boycott, and Egyptians boycotting McDonald's specifically for its alleged Jewish ties.[38] In Bahrain a major supermarket chain removed American products from the shelves, replacing them with alternatives produced by companies not affiliated with the US.[61] In Pakistan, KFC chief executive Rafiq Rangoonwala said that during the beginning of hostilities in Afghanistan and Iraq, sales at KFC outlets dropped by 5 to 10 per cent, but soon regained earlier levels.[43] In Egypt, Jordan, and some Gulf countries, in-store sales were down but home delivery stayed the same or even rose, suggesting that some customers were simply avoiding the social pressure of being seen at the restaurant.

Some people supported boycotts for their perceived cultural benefits, such as protecting local culture from 'American culture'. Regarding fast-food franchises, Muslim economist Dr Monzer Kahf bemoaned American fast food, replacing 'our traditional hommos, fool,

---

[h] For more information on politico-religious activism against fast food companies go to: http://www.proislam.com/muslim_boycott.htm and http://www.petitiononline.com/sb2002/petition.html.

sharwerma, falafel/ta'miyyah, kebab, booza, and other traditional fast food you see all over the Muslim land from Morocco to Malaysia and Indonesia'.

The context of fast-food chain boycotts

In its original form the anti-Israel boycott was initiated on 2 December 1945, as a means of refusing any kind of Arab support to Israel. The original goal of the boycott was to isolate Israel from other countries, particularly its geographic neighbours.[62] The boycott originally operated on three levels: companies trading directly with Israel, companies that do business with Israel, and companies that do business with companies trading with Israel.[62] Companies allegedly operating on all or some of these three levels were listed by Arab governments to facilitate their identification by local traders. 'The boycott of Israel was designed to destroy the state,' according to Yoram Sheni, Israeli Foreign Ministry division head. Companies were forced to choose between trading with Israel or the more populous Arab countries.[63] In one example, Coca-Cola traded with Israel starting in the mid-1960s (earning blacklist status in the Arab world until 1992), while Pepsi-Cola traded with the Arab world and was barred from trading with Israel until 1992.[63] In 1977, during the Carter Administration, the Congress made it illegal for US companies to participate in the boycott.[62] Since then, contrary to expectations, trade between Arab countries and the US continued to improve.

In 1994, six Gulf Cooperation Council states announced that they would no longer follow the secondary boycott. The beginnings of the peace process reduced the power of the boycott, and indeed dismantling the boycott was one of the conditions set out in peace treaties between Israel, Egypt, Jordan, and the Palestinian Authority. The boycott was estimated to have cost Israel some US$40 billion in lost trade as well as a 'psychological impact'.[63] As a result of Israel's violent response to the Intifada in 2001, the Arab League's Boycott Office revived its activities at the behest of Arab leaders in Damascus, with the notable absence of influential Arab countries like Egypt and Jordan.[62] The statement they issued said that the boycott was a 'peaceful, legal and noble' action to support Palestinians.[64]

Why do they care? The transnational aspect of Muslim cultures

When the French government declared in January 2004 that Muslim headscarves were to be banned from schools, there were vocal demonstrations all over the world. Muslim women and men in Egypt, Indonesia, Lebanon, Palestinian territories, Syria, UK, and the US joined French demonstrators to protest against the ban.[65] This recent event illustrated the solidarity felt by Muslims around the world on certain issues, particularly where Islam meets the 'West'. In what some thinkers have referred to as the 'transnational' nature of Islam, or 'active pan-Islamic consciousness',[66] Muslims tend to be concerned for the welfare of Muslims in other countries. Founder of Pakistan and poet Sir Muhammad Iqbal wrote on the topic: 'Our essence is not bound to any place; . . . Nor any fatherland do we profess except Islam'.[66] Partly for this reason, there is widespread concern among Muslims everywhere about the Palestinian issue, and the US-led conflict in Iraq.

The Muslim world, which will comprise one third of humanity by 2025,[66] is far from monolithic. Ethnic, racial, and nationalist differences often bedevil efforts at unity. Within Islam the religious distinctions, such as those between Sunni and Shi'a, are divisive. Differences aside, Muslims generally hold themselves to be members of a global community, or Ummah.[67] Despite the manifold historical, regional and national differences in Islamic institutions and interpretations of the Koran, Shari 'a (Islamic Law) and Hadith (Traditions of the Prophet), there are commonalities in the stated beliefs of politicized Islam centred on the rejection of material capitalism. The rise of Islamist beliefs and the search for an Islamic foundation for political and economic life is very likely a reaction to the perceived secularization brought on by 'Modernity'.[68]

Political Islamic movements appear to agree on protesting the invasion of foreign capital, culture and goods. The founder of the internationally active Muslim Brotherhood and father of political Islam, Egyptian Hasan Al-Bana, declared in 1928 that Europeans were using materialism and other devices to foster atheism among Muslims. Today, the Muslim Brotherhood is considered to represent mainstream Islam in Egypt and Jordan, providing a credible opposition.[69] In a similar vein, the Iranian Ayatollah Khomeini said that the pro-capitalist policies of the Shah allowed American capitalists to enslave Iranians and aimed to destroy Islam and its sacred laws.[70] In his book *America and the Third World War* Osama Bin Laden challenged Muslims to rise up against the intentional spread of Westernization, which he said destroys Muslim rights.[66] Organizers of anti-American boycotts, such as activists, religious leaders, and students, argue that Israel is the beneficiary of taxes paid by US corporations via US foreign aid.[40]

An issue that appears to unite Muslims the world over is support for the Palestinians,[8] hence their vocal, political, and economic support for Palestinian and anti-Israeli causes. Both rejection of Western material culture and support for Palestine have been important in understanding a backlash against McDonald's and other overtly 'Western' and American brands which intensified during Israeli campaigns in the West Bank and Gaza following the beginning of the so-called 'Second' or 'Al-Aqsa' Intifada, initiated on 29 September 2000.[71] Support for the Palestinian struggle is often cited by Muslims around the world as reasons to reject Israel and perceived supporters of the state of Israel. The Palestinian issue has united the 23 members of the Cairo-based League of Arab States (known as the Arab League) for years, notably through its support of the Israel boycott.[i] Apart from media reports of Muslim statements to this effect, official sources confirm this view, such as the pronouncements of clerics and political leaders in Iran. The Egyptian State Information Service published a report in English, for example, making economic arguments that the best way to condemn Israel is via a boycott.[72] In the United Arab Emirates and elsewhere in the Arab world, phrases like this are common on websites, leaflets and e-mail messages: 'The penny you spend to buy these products amounts to another [Israeli] bullet for the body of our brave Palestinian brothers'.[40]

As a result of Israel's response to the Intifada and the Arab League's call for boycott, a boycott was announced in Saudi Arabia and lists were circulated of American products and their non-American substitutes. As in many recent boycotts, news of the boycott spread via the Internet, e-mail messages, SMS, voicemail messages, newspaper editorials (even in state-run newspapers) mosque sermons and fliers.[61] In a related development Burger King opened an outlet in the Ma'aleh Adumim Mall in 1999. The mall was located in a settlement in the occupied territories. After an Arab boycott and letter-writing campaign to Burger King, the company closed its controversial outlet. McDonald's has so far refused to open branches in the West Bank.[73]

Questions

1. Why have fast-food restaurants been so successful outside their country of origin, the United States? Consider basic, universal aspects of consumer behaviour in your arguments.

---

[i] See for instance, the Palestinian Initiative for the Promotion of Global Dialogue and Democracy (MIFTAH), headed by Dr Hanan Ashrawi, Palestinian Member of Parliament. Contains news, research studies, historical documents, social and economic information on the Middle East. **http://www.miftah.org**.

2. How does religion affect consumer behaviour, especially concerning eating habits, food products and beverages? Take examples from different great religions. What kinds of problems do fast-food restaurants need to take into account when considering religious prescriptions concerning food? What kinds of responses are given by fast-food companies in terms of product and service adaptation?

3. To what extent are fast food in general and fast-food restaurants in particular associated with a) globalization; b) Westernization; c) modernization; d) threats to local cultural identities? How could fast-food restaurant chains handle their marketing communications in order to avoid boycotts and reduce violence against their outlets?

4. Comment about the ambivalence of Muslim-based, fast-food competition.

Saskia Faulk and Jean-Claude Usunier prepared this case solely to provide material for class discussion. The authors do not intend to illustrate either effective or ineffective handling of a business situation. The authors may have disguised certain names and other identifying information to protect confidentiality. This case was designed to present a complex marketing situation. It presents sensitive political, cultural, economic, and religious issues, and was in no way intended to offend, nor to advocate, the cause of any party.

2011-5-10   Version: (A)

Appendix references

1. The Internet Movie Database (n.d.), 'All-Time Box Office: World-wide'. Retrieved 23 September 2009 from http://www.imdb.com/boxoffice/alltimegross?region=world-wide.
2. Hooper, John *et al.* (2002), 'World Wide Wizard (Harry Potter)', *Guardian*, 8 November 2002. Retrieved 23 September 2009 from http://www.guardian.co.uk/culture/2002/nov/08/artsfeatures. harrypotter.
3. Arlidge, John (2003), 'Harry Potter and the crock of gold', *Observer* (London), 8 June 2003. Retrieved 23 September 2009 from http://www.guardian.co.uk/books/2003/jun/08/harrypotter.harrypotter.
4. Waxman, Sharon (1998), 'Hollywood attuned to world markets', *Washington Post*, 26 October 1990, p. A1. Retrieved 30 July 2003 from http://www.washingtonpost.com/wp-srv/inatl/longterm/ mia/part2.htm.
5. Fitzgerald, Kate (2003), 'Hollywood and the demographic revolution', *AdAge.com*, 15 July 2003. Retrieved 30 July 2003 from http://www.adage.com.
6. Pomerants, Dorothy (2009), 'Hollywood top.earning actors', *Forbes,com*, 10 June 2009. Retrieved 29 September 2009 from http://www.forbes.com/2009/06/09/movies-sandler-depp-business-media-hollywood.html.
7. The European Audiovisual Observatory (2009), 'Focus 2009 World Film Market Trends'. Retrieved 29 September 2009 from http://www.obs.coe.int/online_publication/reports/focus2009.pdf.
8. Anonymous (2003), 'In 2002 European films were unable to repeat the exceptional performance achieved in 2001', *LUMIERE* press release, 21 March 2003. Retrieved 30 July 2003 from http://www.obs.coe.int/about/oea/pr/lumiere_mar03.html.
9. Lange, André (2003), 'Harry, Billy, Amélie . . . and the others?' *Focus 2002 – New: Focus 2003*, Marché du Film, Cannesmarket.com, undated, 2003. Retrieved 30 September 2009 from http://www.obs.coe.int/online_publication/reports/focus2002.pdf.
10. Garncarz, Joseph (2002), 'Germany goes global: Challenging the theory of Hollywood's dominance on international markets', Media in Transition, Globalization and Convergence: An international conference, 10–12 May 2002. Retrieved 30 July 2003 from http://web.mit.edu/cms/Events/mit2/ Abstracts/Garncarz.pdf.
11. The Numbers, Box Office Data, Movie Stars, Idle Speculation (n.d.), *Glossary of Movie Business Terms*. Retrieved 30 September from http://www.the-numbers.com/glossary.php.
12. ABN Amro (2000), *Filmspace: Behind the Scenes*, ABN Amro, 12 September 2000. Retrieved 30 July 2003 from http://www.ey.com.
13. Fuma Shapiro, Simona (2000), 'The culture thief', *The New Rules*, Fall, 2000. Retrieved 30 September 2009 from http://www.newrules.org/banking/article/culture-thief.
14. Pells, Richard (2002), 'American culture goes global, or does it?', *The Chronicle Review*, 12 April 2002, p. B7.

15. Anholt, Simon (1999), 'Getting on the brandwagon', International Finance Corporation (presentation), Fall, 1999. Retrieved 30 July 2003 from http://www.ifc.org.

16. Riding, Alan (2003), 'Filmmakers seek protection from US dominance', *New York Times*, 5 February 2003. Retrieved 20 July 2003 from http://www.nytimes.com/2003/02/05/movies/filmmakers-seek-protection-from-us-dominance.html?scp=1&sq=Filmmakers%20seek%20protection%20from%20US%20dominance&st=cse.

17. Kapur, Shekhar (2002), 'Dying cowboy, pouncing tiger', *Mail & Guardian online* (South Africa), 30 August 2002. Retrieved 20 July 2003 from http://www.chico.mbweb.co.za.

18. Anonymous (2001), 'Hey, world! Hollywood's coming!', *Telegraph* (London), 31 March 2001. Retrieved 20 July 2003 from http://www.telegraph.co.uk/culture/4722542/Hey-world-Hollywoods-coming.html.

19. Kariuki, John (2003) 'Africa at large: Hollywood goes to war in Africa', *The East African* (Kenya), The Norwegian Council for Africa 23 June 2003. Retrieved 20 July 2003 from http://www.afrika.no/Detailed/3748.html.

20. Dollt, Andreas (2003), 'Cinema Statistics', *Statistics in focus: Industry, trade, and services*, Eurostat, Theme 4-8/2003.

21. Freedman, Michael (2003), 'Supreme court upholds copyright extension', *Forbes.com*, 15 January 2003. Retrieved 20 July 2003 from http://www.forbes.com/2003/01/15/cz_mf_0115copyright.html.

22. Wattenberg, Ben and Daniel Wattenberg (2001), 'Hollywood is sharing the spotlight', *Jewish World Review*, 13 April 1999. Retrieved 30 July 2002 from http://www.jewishworldreview.com/cols/wattenberg041399.asp.

23. Chew, Eugene (1999), 'Life goes on: The 1999 Hong Kong Film Festival', *Toto Cinema Matters*, undated, 1999. Retrieved 30 July 2003 from http://www.cse.unsw.edu.au.

24. Anonymous (2001), 'Interview with Howard Stringer, Chairman and CEO of Sony America', *Frontline*, Public Broadcasting Service (USA), undated, 2001. Retrieved 30 July 2003 from http://www.pbs.org.

25. Center for Strategic and International Studies (2001), 'Culture and globalization', *Global Connections*, undated, 2001. Retrieved 30 July 2003 from http://www.csis.org.

26. Gaydos, Steven (2000), 'Forman brings Euro touch . . .', *Variety*, 10 January 2000. Retrieved 30 July 2003 from http://www.variety.com/article/VR1117760682.html?categoryid=13&cs=1&query=Forman+brings+Euro+touch....

27. Fast food scenario created from compiled articles including:
    Smucker, Philip, and Nicholas Blandford (2002), 'Arab states vent rising wrath', *Christian Science Monitor*, 22 April 2002. Retrieved 31 January 2010 from http://www.csmonitor.com/2002/0422/p01s04-wome.html.
    Kilani, Hala (2002), 'Grassroots campaign takes aim at U.S. economy', *The Daily Star* (Beirut), 13 April 2002. Retrieved 31 January 2010 from http://www.lebanonwire.com/0204/02041306DS.htm.
    Blandford, Nicholas (2002), 'Arab citizens seize boycott banner', *Christian Science Monitor*, 7 May 2002. Retrieved 31 January 2010 from http://www.csmonitor.com/2002/0507/p06s01-wome.html.

28. Henry, Clement (2003), 'Clash of civilizations', *Harvard International Review*, Vol. 25, Issue 1 (2003).

29. Springborg, Robert (2003), 'Identity in crisis: Egyptian political identity in the face of globalization', *Harvard International Review*, 25 (3): 18–24. Retrieved 31 January 2010 from http://www.questia.com/googleScholar.qst?docId=5007942733.

30. Barber, Benjamin R. (1992), 'Jihad vs. McWorld', *The Atlantic Online*, March 1992. Retrieved 31 January 2010 from http://www.theatlantic.com/politics/foreign/barberf.htm.

31. McNulty, Brian (2002), 'The food service market in Saudi Arabia', *IMES Ireland*, 16 February 2002.

32. Zayed, Dahlia (2004), 'Fast food still sells in Egypt', *AME Info*, 26 August 2004. Retrieved 31 January 2010 from http://www.ameinfo.com/news/Detailed/42253.html.

33. Americana Group (n.d.), retrieved 31 January 2010 from http://www.americana-group.net/%5CDefault.aspx?Id=960.

34. Subway (n.d.), retrieved 31 January 2010 from http://www.subway.com/subwayroot/Applications/Reports/CountryCount.aspx.

35. Burger King (n.d.), retrieved 31 January 2010 from http://www.burgerking.com.tr; http://www.kfg.com.kw/burgerking/; http://www.burgerking-me.com/saudi/eng/index.asp; http://www.burgerking.com.my/about_us.php; http://www.burgerking-me.com/uae/eng/locations.asp; http://www.

burgerking-me.com/lebanon/eng/locations.asp; http://www.burgerking-me.com/qatar/eng/index. asp; http://www.burgerking-me.com/jordan/eng/index.asp; http://www.burgerking-me.com/ bahrain/eng/locations.asp.

36. McDonalds (n.d.), retrieved 31 January 2010 from http://www.mcdonalds.com.tr/McDonaldsTurkiye. asp?mainId=0&subId=1; http://www.bkpm.go.id/index.php/main/newsdetail/1029; http://www. mcdonaldsarabia.com/english/ksa/about_story.asp; http://www.mcdonaldsegypt.com/loader.html; http://www.mcdonaldsarabia.com/english/kuwait/locations.asp; http://www.mcdonalds.com/ content/countries/uae.html; http://mcdonalds2.rozee.pk/content.php?lid=TWpJd09BPT0rQQ==; http://www.mcdonaldsarabia.com/english/bahrain/about_story.asp.

37. Abdel-Halim, Mustafa (2003), 'Muslims rally against U.S. products, Big Mac feels backlash', *Islam Online*, 8 February 2003. Retrieved 31 January 2010 from http://www.islamonline.net/English/ News/2003-02/08/article03.shtml.

38. Taja, Waheed (2002), 'Buying locally made U.S. products not permissible: Scholar', *Islam Online*, 3 July 2002. Retrieved 31 January 2010 from http://www.islamonline.net/English/News/2002-07/ 03/article09.shtml.

39. International Union for Muslim Scholars (2008), 'Statement on the horrific massacre against the people of Gaza', *Islam Online*. Retrieved 31 January 2010 from http://www.islamonline.net/ servlet/Satellite?c=Article_C&pagename=Zone-English-Living_Shariah%2FLSELayout&cid= 1231223503984.

40. Cox, James (2002) 'Arab nations seek boycotts of U.S. products', *USA Today*, 26 June 2002. Retrieved 31 January 2010 from http://www.usatoday.com/money/world/2002-06-26-arab-boycott. htm.

41. Murphy, Dan (2003), 'U.S. multinational companies wary of backlash', *Christian Science Monitor*, 21 April 2003. Retrieved 31 January 2010 from http://www.csmonitor.com/2003/0421/p12s01-woap.html.

42. *Asia Times* (2003), 'Indonesia braces for economic battle', 20 March 2003. Retrieved 31 January 2010 from http://www.atimes.com/atimes/Southeast_Asia/EC20Ae01.html.

43. Zia, Amir (2003), 'U.S. food sells fast in Pakistan despite boycott', *Reuters U.K. Top 100*, 31 July 2003.

44. Kennedy, Miranda (2003), 'America off our soil', *The Nation*, 19 May 2003. Retrieved 31 January 2010 http://www.thenation.com/docprint.mhtml?i=20030602&s=kennedy.

45. *The Sydney Morning Herald* (2005), 'Fast food terror as bombs hit Karachi KFC and McDonalds'. Retrieved 31 January 2010, http://www.smh.com.au/news/world/fast-food-terror-as-bombs-hit-karachi-kfc-and-mcdonalds/2005/09/09/1125772666931.html.

46. Abizeid, Marc (2009) 'Activists protest against Starbucks, drive off customers', *The Daily Star*, 17 March 2009. Retrieved 31 January 2010 from http://www.dailystar.com.lb/article.asp?edition_ID=1&article_ID=100121&categ_id=1.

47. Eliasi, Jennifer R. and Johanna T. Dwyer (2002), 'Kosher and Halal: Religious observances affecting dietary intake', *Journal of the American Dietetic Association*, July 2002.

48. Mathiot, Cédric (2004), 'L'éclosion fulgurante du poulet Halal', *Libération*, 14 February 2004. Retrieved 31 January 2010 from http://www.liberation.fr/economie/0101478320-l-eclosion-fulgurante-du-poulet-halal.

49. Muslim Consumer Group (2003), ' KFC Chickens at Lombard, Il store are not halal according to MCG's Zabiha criteria', *News Alerts*, Muslim Consumer Group for Food Products, 10 August 2003. Retrieved 31 January 2010 from http://www.muslimconsumergroup.com/Events.do?menu=Events &eventAction=eventdetail&eventId=82.

50. Eat-Halal.com (undated), 'Eating out', *Eat-Halal.com*, undated. Retrieved 31 January 2010 from http://www.eat-Halal.com/eatingout.shtml.

51. Eurofood (2002), 'Western food firms eyeing slice of growing Halal food market', *Eurofood*, 1 August 2002. Retrieved 31 January 2010 from http://findarticles.com/p/articles/mi_m0DQA/ is_2002_August_1/ai_90216943/.

52. Brown, Kerry and Martin Palmer (1990), *The Essential Teachings of Islam: Daily Readings from the Sacred Texts*. London: Arrow Books.

53. Rosten, Leo (1975), *Religions of America: Ferment and Faith in an Age of Crisis*. New York: Simon & Schuster.

54. Ware, Timothy (Bishop of Kallistos of Diokleia) (1993), *The Orthodox Church*. London: Penguin Books.

55. Eliasi, Jennifer R. and Johanna T. Dwyer (2002), 'Kosher and Halal: Religious observances affecting dietary intake', *Journal of the American Dietetic Association*, July 2002.

56. Islamic Food and Nutrition Council of America (undated), 'What is Halal?', Islamic Food and Nutrition Council of America. Retrieved 31 January 2010 from http://www.ifanca.org/halal/.

57. Chicken Cottage (undated), 'About Chicken Cottage' (web page), Chicken Cottage International, undated. Retrieved 31 January 2010 from http://www.chickencottage.com/.

58. Wax, Emily (2003), 'In Egypt, anger at U.S. displaces admiration', *Washington Post*, 24 March 2003. Retrieved 31 January 2010 from http://www.commondreams.org/headlines03/0324-07.htm.

59. Abdel-Halim, Mustafa (2003), 'Muslims rally against U.S. products, Big Mac feels backlash', *Islam Online*, 8 February 2003. Retrieved 31 January 2010 from http://www.islamonline.net/English/News/2003-02/08/article03.shtml.

60. Mo'men The Sandwich Company (n.d.), retrieved 31 January 2010 from http://www.momen-restaurant.com/.

61. MacFarquhar, Niel (2002), 'An anti-American boycott is growing in the Arab world', *New York Times*, 10 May 2002. Retrieved 31 January 2010 from www.commondreams.org: http://www.commondreams.org/headlines02/0510-02.htm.

62. Bard, Mitchell (2007), *The Arab Boycott*. American-Israeli Cooperative Enterprise, undated, 2007. Retrieved 31 January 2010 from http://www.jewishvirtuallibrary.org/jsource/History/Arab_boycott.html.

63. Arnold, Michael S. (1999), 'Boycott wars with burgers', *Jerusalem Post*, 13 September 1999.

64. Anonymous (2002), 'U.S. warns companies over Israel boycott', *BBC News*, 5 November 2002. Retrieved 11 January 2004 from http://news.bbc.co.uk/2/hi/business/2403303.stm.

65. Anonymous (2004), 'Minister blasts headscarf protest', *BBC News*, 18 January 2004. Retrieved 31 January 2010 from http://news.bbc.co.uk/2/hi/europe/3406969.stm.

66. Robinson, Francis (2002), 'Islam and the West', *Asian Affairs*, Royal Society for Asian Affairs, October 2002. Retrieved 31 January 2010 from http://eprints.rhul.ac.uk/333/1/OUPIslamWest1.pdf.

67. Modood, Tariq (2003), 'Muslims and the politics of difference', The Politics of Migration. Managing Opportunity, Conflict and Change *The Political Quarterly*. USA MA: Blackwell Publishing.

68. Zubaida, Sami (1998), 'Muslim societies: Unity or diversity?' *International Institute for the Study of Islam in the Modern World Newsletter*, October 1998. Retrieved 31 January 2010 from http://www.isim.nl/files/newsl_1.pdf.

69. Shadid, Anthony (2003), 'Old Arab friends turn away from U.S.', *Washington Post*, 26 February 2003. Retrieved 31 January 2010 from http://www.washingtonpost.com/ac2/wp-dyn/A2452-2003Feb25?language=printer.

70. Friedland, Roger (2001), 'Money, sex, and god: the erotic logic of religious nationalism', *Sociological Theory*, Vol. 20 (3), pp. 381–425.

71. Aide Sanitaire Suisse aux Palestiniens (undated), *Chronologie 2000–2001*, Aide Sanitaire Suisse aux Palestiniens, undated. Retrieved 11 May 2011 from http://www.assp.ch/page/history/hist11.html.

72. Egyptian State Information Service (2002) 'Economists say boycott best weapon against U.S., Israel', *Egyptian State Information Service*, 13 April 2002.

73. Maranz, Felice and Evan Greenstein, Bloomberg (1999), 'Maleh Adumim outlet elicits U.S.-Arab boycott threat', *Jerusalem Post*, 6 August 1999.

10

The critical role of price in relational exchange

At first sight, price appears to be anything but 'cultural'. In appearance, it is usually a figure, a number or a unit, and so price is often assumed to be an intrinsically objective element of exchange and an issue reserved for rational economic factors. But price has a more subjective element. It is a signal that conveys meaning and as such is perceived in quite different ways across cultures and across individuals. The subjective and perceptual aspects of price are examined in Section 10.1.

Price is an important component of communication between buyers and sellers. It is also an element in short-term or long-term bonding. Price is a decisive element of social interaction between buyer and seller; it is a way of evaluating offerings, it endorses their agreement and shapes their relationship, whether short or long term. In Section 10.2 bargaining is examined as a classical, primitive and widespread relationship between buyer and seller; particularly prevalent where there is no compulsory price labelling. In modern mass markets, the primary influence wielded by customers on price usually takes the form of a 'take it or leave it' bargain with quasi-anonymous sellers. This all or nothing attitude contrasts with the more 'friendly' concept of price in bargaining and relational exchange, where each party wants both parties to make a good deal, ending with a 'win–win' outcome: economic transactions inevitably have a human relations component. Section 10.3 deals with situations where the price is clearly marked and hence known by customers, who are then in a position to appraise the price–quality ratio.

The last three sections of the chapter present company attitudes in international market pricing decisions.

An anthropomorphic approach is used whereby companies and markets are considered as interacting parties to an exchange. Companies are led to distort and manipulate prices between domestic markets, either to increase consumer brand loyalty in certain markets through offensive strategic pricing, or to avoid parallel imports which undermine their local distribution system (see Section 10.4). Price can also be used as a tactical weapon *vis-à-vis* competitors in particular national markets (see Section 10.5). Finally, price can be manipulated because of an inflationary environment or by over- or under-invoicing in order to close price-sensitive deals (see Section 10.6).

This chapter does not consider the strictly economic aspects of price, such as the relationship between price and costs in international marketing or the law of one price, which states that, in the absence of transport, transaction-related costs and price discrimination, trade takes place in only one market and only one price prevails. Nor does it discuss the influence of exchange rate variance on price strategies in international marketing. However, you will find some information on these issues on the Internet, including indices of international price comparisons, such as the Big MAC Index and the iPod index.

Website link 10.1

Search for various country indices, such as the iPod Index, indicating which countries have the best price for an identical iPod: **http://www.comsec.com.au/public/news.aspx?id=809.**

Table 10.1 Price-based signals

Meaning conveyed by price in . . .	by . . .	Section
Buyer–seller interactions	Bargaining rituals, price offers and relationship development	10.2
Consumer behaviour	Differences in consumer price-mindedness across cultures	10.3
Product evaluation	To what extent is quality inferred from price?	10.3
(Tough) competition	Signalling willingness to compete by dumping prices	10.4
Target market(s)	Showing commitment to customers in a target market through attractive pricing	10.4
Distributors (grey markets)	Signalling desire to avoid parallel imports from opportunistic distributors who disturb international price policy and may damage brand image	10.4
(Peaceful) competition	Signalling willingness to enter a market with cartels 'peacefully'	10.5
Price increase policy	Meaning conveyed by price in high-inflation contexts	10.6
Relationship to suppliers	Overcoming barriers for supplier to receive real price by over- or under-invoicing	10.6

10.1

Price as a signal conveying meaning

Prices may be considered to be fairly objective in most consumer goods and consumer durables markets where goods are sold in mass distribution outlets that allow price comparison between stores. In such cases, the meaning conveyed by the price evolves mostly around the value of the good and the money transfer.

Prices become more central to the relationship between buyers and sellers, and to companies and their customers, distributors or competitors in the following conditions:

1. Price is not displayed.
2. It is not necessarily the seller who announces the first price.
3. There is no clear market reference for what would be a 'fair price'.
4. A particular price is understood by both the seller and the buyer as taking place within a series of transactions (i.e., past, present and future).
5. Prices for particular transactions are not necessarily meant to cover even marginal cost.
6. Prices may be distorted by inflation and government price regulation.
7. Total price is a combination of direct and indirect prices (e.g., product price plus price of maintenance, spare parts, updates, etc.).

These seven points are examples of situations where price is more 'relational' than 'economic'. As shown in Table 10.1, price can convey meaning and be an object of interaction between the various participants of the market situation, that is, manufacturers, distributors, consumers and competitors.

10.2

Bargaining

Limits of price as an element of social relations: bargaining versus no bargaining

The importance of bargaining is often underestimated because, in many countries, consumers are used to prices that are clearly displayed. If the price is not right, the product will not be bought. In most cases, people no longer bargain – or at least they appear not to. Bargaining is either legally prohibited or strictly controlled in most developed countries. Most sales of consumer products take place within oligopolistic distribution channels offering merchandise from producers also organized in oligopolies. In direct relations with customers, prices are unilaterally set by vendors and are therefore non-negotiable. Bargaining at the supermarket checkout is rare and liable to result in confusion or embarrassment.

However, once the price reaches a substantial level, people in developed countries return to bargaining as a way to maximize the value to both consumer and retailer. In many retail contexts, exchange still takes place through bargaining – for example, new and second-hand cars, furniture, property, construction activities and industrial machinery.[1] Bargaining is also common in informal retail contexts, such as garage sales or flea markets, where the value of the transaction is often insignificant to both vendor and consumer.[2,3] Bargaining in these contexts is not just motivated by rational economics; as Hermann (p. 56) writes, 'the practice of small-scale bargaining is significant for a number of reasons ... it provides a degree of empowerment, both pecuniary and psychological, in that individual actors can influence the price of goods through their knowledge of consumer goods and skill in negotiation'.[2] The recent downturn in the global economy appears to have sparked a renewed interest in bargaining amongst increasingly price-conscious Western consumers and is becoming more accepted by retailers.[4]

In most developing countries, for example Thailand, India, the Philippines and the Middle East, bargaining is still the rule, even for items of low value or little vital interest. Weak purchasing power considerably increases the importance of bargaining. In certain African markets (e.g., Mauritania), where sugar is sold by the 'lump' and carrots by the 'slice', and island economies (e.g., Marshal Islands), where cigarettes are sold by the 'stick', bargaining is essential for survival. Moreover, people may not be pressed for time; the rewards of bargaining in relation to its cost are fundamentally different in developing and industrialized nations. Finally, bargaining has a fun dimension as well as a human one, possibly because of its similarity to role-playing. The human dimension exists because bargaining and commerce generally are contemplated with more seriousness in developing countries than in industrialized ones where commercial interaction has been largely 'depersonalized', particularly in the case of consumer goods. This is in fact one of the major reasons that bargaining is either legally prohibited or socially restricted in developed countries. As stated by Allen (p. 49):

It has conventionally been supposed that bargaining is socially disadvantageous, on the grounds that it breeds hostility, rivalry and distrust ... While it is true that there is always an element of suspicion as to the real value of the

commodity (and subsequently of the price), this suspicion never turns into an open conflict if the bargainers intend to conclude the sale. Any bargainer, whether seller or buyer, is careful not to offend his partner for fear of putting an end to the transaction. Thus, though initiated by suspicion, bargaining tends rather to eliminate it, instituting instead an atmosphere of common interest and trust, which often leads to a lasting client relationship. In this way it cements community relations, rather than subverts them.[5]

Website link 10.2

Search for information on haggling and tips for getting better prices: **http://abcnews.go.com/ business/story?id=4610552.**

Ritual aspects of bargaining

Brand marketing is, by definition, not conducive to bargaining. Self-service and other non-personalized services do not allow people living in modern societies with advanced distribution systems to experience the rituals involved in bargaining. These rituals pose challenges to the uninitiated. They are independent of, yet complementary to, price negotiation. People who bargain more are no less rational – they are rational in a different way.

A Lebanese anthropologist, Khuri (p. 701), described the rituals involved in bargaining in the Middle East by emphasizing that such interaction always begins with standard signs of respect, affection, common interest and trust. As soon as a potential buyer shows interest in an item and requests information, the seller replies vaguely:

Between us there is no difference; we share the same interest, price is not what pleases me, what pleases me is to find out what pleases you; pay as much as you want; brothers do not disagree on price; for you it is free; it is a gift.[6]

Nothing in the above quote should be taken literally. No potential customer from the same culture would do so. This introductory incantation signals a social bond of mutual interest and trust through metaphorical kinship, likely to create an impression of friendliness and fraternity. The potential customer then insists that a price be indicated. The vendor hesitates and, perhaps, proposes a price after having presented and lauded the merits of his product at great length. Contrary to Western bargaining, potential customers should not pretend to doubt the qualities of the item, because that could make them seem ignorant and therefore more vulnerable. The discussion continues with each party holding a price (i.e., maximum for sellers and minimum for customers) below or above which no transaction can take place. The potential buyer suggests a price, but is not necessarily willing to pay it. After an agreement has been reached, the transaction then takes place and the buyer purchases the item for cash. However, the bargaining operation could have been conducted just to seek information on the price. This is one instance where the bargaining activity is partly disconnected from the sales activity.

Bargaining may be disconcerting for people who are used to displayed prices and who, as a result, do not envisage entering into any sort of pleasant economic interaction merely to obtain information. When prices are not displayed, it may be embarrassing for potential buyers to ask for them, because doing so may latently signal their difficulties in affording the purchase, thus exposing their low purchasing power. Roeber (p. 49) explains how asking the price is associated with class perception in the context of Zambia:

Working people, I was told, were 'sufferers'. The meaning of that word was best explained by the man who stated vehemently, 'If you have to ask the price of something, you are automatically a sufferer' . . . there was another category of people, the *apamwamba* or 'big shots', who did not have to ask for the price of commodities. They always had money to buy what they needed.[7]

The relationship between bargaining and price display is obvious. Wherever the law forces the vendor to display prices clearly, the practice of bargaining will diminish. It is understandable that people who have lost the habit of personalized commercial relations – if indeed they ever had it – may be embarrassed in these situations where affection and economics, and friendship and self-interest, are implicitly communicated, almost simultaneously. The novice bargainer also risks provoking the seller's hostility if the seller gets the impression or wishes to give the impression of being 'taken for a ride' by the buyer. It is for these reasons that bargaining can cause anxiety and tension for novice bargainers, often to the point where they will completely avoid bargaining.[8] This fear of bargaining can be side-stepped by 'rational', and non-confrontational, arguments for better deals, such as quantity and cash

discounts, stock liquidation operations and auctions of discontinued items. Moreover, bargaining could smear the image of the distribution channel as well as that of the goods it sells. Prus (p. 146) quotes certain remarks made by Canadian vendors:

'We're flexible, where if they're getting a larger order and they suggest it, we'll give a little . . . Some customers feel that they have to have a discount to buy it.' (*Sales manageress, luggage.*)

'You can dicker in furniture, appliances, carpeting, something like that, here. But not on the smaller things, like clothing, giftware, shoes.' (*Department store salesman.*)

'Normally I try not to dicker. I am quite firm on the prices. I've found that dickering can be rather awkward. It is awkward for the merchant and the customer. And it is especially awkward if other people are around. If you can stay away from dickering, you can also avoid an image as someone who will go down. I have been known to dicker, but it is something I try to avoid.' (*Women's clothing.*)[9]

Declaring prices

Cavusgil[10] noted that international pricing is not a topic that lends itself to easy generalisation. Export pricing must first address the unique nature of the individual firm or buyer with whom one is dealing. He takes the example of the Middle East where 'Regal Ware, a producer of kitchen appliances and cookware, uses a higher list price in such markets to leave a margin of discretion' (p. 505).[10]

In a culture where bargaining is expected, proposing a price is a tug-of-war exercise. Who will give way, the seller or the customer? Who should be the first to make concessions by virtue of the position of strength that is internalised within the society? At least four items play a major role in answering these questions:

1. Initial power position of each party.
2. Degree of urgency for either buyer or seller to close deal.
3. Importance of then negotiation margin from start. The initial suggested price must leave room for further discussion. It could be in the vendor's interest to exaggerate the first price in order to leave the customer some room to manoeuvre. For instance, when dealing with a buyer whose performance is subject to confirmation by superiors, that buyer is supposed to obtain a discount. The buyer's job is to reduce the price, so, ironically, the vendor

Box 10.1

Price levels and buyer–seller relationship

Scenario 1

The seller wishes to offer a fair price from the start, close to the final price, expecting it will win the customer's loyalty. This should convince the buyer of the vendor's honesty, openness and genuine desire to do business. If the customer shares these European, American or Australasian values and decides to cooperate, an agreement is quickly reached and each party is satisfied.

Scenario 2

The same vendor suggests the same price, close to the final price, as a sign of goodwill towards the buyer. The buyer who comes from a different culture (such as India or Pakistan) is embarrassed: his boss expects him to obtain the greatest possible discount from the seller. His role centres on

the price rebate rather than on the price level. The announced price, close to the final price, leaves buyer and seller with little satisfactory negotiating room, therefore no deal is made.

Scenario 3

The vendor announces a much higher initial price, leaving room for negotiation from the start. This allows the buyer to demonstrate skill in a mutually beneficial bargaining exercise and enables both parties to increase the long-term value of their social relationship. The final agreed price is very close to that in Scenario 1. With the buyer interested mostly in the rebate and the seller in the price level, both can achieve greater satisfaction than in Scenario 1.

would be wise to open negotiations with an exaggerated price (see Box 10.1). This strategy is well appreciated by the local souvenir vendors in tourist havens such as the Caribbean, where if you pay more than 25 per cent of the initial asking price, you certainly overpaid.

4. Type of social process by which buyer and seller progressively adjust their price. In the case of competitive bidding situations based on a tender offer, an excessively high price would eliminate that vendor from the shortlist of pre-selected candidates.

10.3

Price and consumer evaluations

Culture-based appraisal of quality and price

Consumers tend to use price as a proxy or cue for quality, especially when other criteria are absent. Price plays a major subjective role in the assessment of quality when:

1. It is very difficult to measure quality objectively. There is no generally accepted method of measuring the objective quality of a product, and much less so for a service.
2. Perceived quality of a product is even more difficult to measure than quality itself. The concept of quality is subjective but not irrational. It is based on an evaluation of both intrinsic product attributes, such as taste or physical characteristics, and extrinsic product attributes, such as advertising, brand, and price.
3. Perceived quality combines with other evaluation criteria (e.g., perceived monetary and non-monetary prices) to form a perceived value that shapes and determines the consumer's decision to buy or not.[11]

Price perceptions include both monetary and non-monetary aspects. Perceived monetary price means that consumers may not recall the exact price, but may have framed in their minds a simplified, general impression (i.e., 'it is expensive' or 'it is not that expensive after all') in comparison to a reference price range. This price impression needs to be sufficiently close to consumer expectations if they are to buy.[12] Maxwell[13] found support for this in India and the United States.

In both countries, the perceived acceptability of price influenced the probability of purchase by increasing the perceived value of the product (i.e., jeans).

Consumers' perception of a non-monetary price may be better understood in terms of Becker's[14] conclusion that the objective price is not the only *sacrifice* accepted by consumers when purchasing a product. Other *sacrifices*, such as time spent shopping or cooking, are often included in the perceived price. Maxwell[13] also measured the acceptability of other costs, including discussing the purchase with friends and travelling on buses for long periods of time. Interestingly, these other costs were less acceptable to Indians than Americans.

Consumers do not build these subjective evaluations of quality and monetary and non-monetary price through irrational individual idiosyncrasies but through unconscious submission, in their everyday lives, to social representations dictated by their cultural upbringing. For instance, Erevelles and colleagues[15] examined the influence of price on perceived risk as part of a larger study with students from Hong Kong and the United States. They found that price perceptions had more influence on risk perceptions in the United States in relation to a car purchase. Becker's[14] model is firmly rooted in American society and culture. Therefore, some elements are not cross-culturally equivalent; a costly 'sacrifice' in one country may be true enjoyment in another. To cite a few examples of common aphorisms (note: the reverse of each is also defensible):

1. 'It is important to measure time, time is money' (see Chapter 2): therefore, perceived non-monetary price will be higher in general for economic-time minded consumers.
2. 'Home-made food is the best': this saying could, for instance, influence the perceived quality of frozen foods even though there is no reason why their objective qualities (e.g., taste and nutritional value) should not be better.
3. 'Where there is pleasure, time doesn't count' (French proverb).

Certain representations directly influence the perceived non-monetary price of a product, particularly the desirability/non-desirability or the convenience/inconvenience of an element of the perceived non-monetary price. Put simply, the price of a nail is not easily separable from the non-monetary price involved in driving it in, including the risk of hitting one's finger in the process. Non-monetary price reflects costs related to time spent, the search itself, psychological risk, etc. These costs shape the consumer's perception of the sacrifice involved in the consumption experience in exchange for the satisfaction to be derived from it.

Non-monetary price varies a great deal across cultures. A trip to buy a product or the preparation of meals may be perceived as enjoyable in certain cultures and reflects no perception of sacrifice or non-monetary price awareness. However, the same task may be perceived as being tedious in other cultures. Ackerman and Tellis[16] argue that Chinese consumers place more importance on the monetary sacrifice and less on the time sacrifice than US consumers, owing the Chinese social norm of frugality and sophistication in money. It is also likely that time is more important than money to many US consumers, especially for small purchases like grocery items. Similarly, the rapid expansion of the 'do-it-yourself' market is related to a marked preference for doing small jobs oneself instead of requesting the services of a professional. In France this preference can be traced to a social representation in a high power distance society, where being served is negatively valued. The French concept of *égalité* tends to associate service with servitude and humiliation. The French fiscal system has long corroborated this by offering tax rebates to people engaging in 'do-it-yourself', while restricting the opportunity of hiring domestics to the very upper classes.

Relationships between objective quality and price, and choice strategies

It is to be expected that price and quality strongly correlate in a competitive market. However, many empirical studies show that the actual relationship between price and objective quality is fairly low, probably because consumers are imperfectly informed about the price and quality of competing products (for a review, see Fauld *et al.*[17]). Quality is often revealed through product use: that is, through post-purchase rather than pre-purchase information cues. Objective quality is based on characteristics that can be measured by consumer tests like those carried out by *Consumer Reports* magazine, such as durability, performance and safety features. Measures of the objective price–quality relation are based on correlations between quality evaluations, carried out by consumer magazines, and the price of the product.

Website link 10.3

Search the Consumer Reports website for information about the objective quality of products: http://www.consumerreports.org/cro/index.htm.

In the United States Oxenfeldt,[18] in the earliest study on the topic, ranked 35 products from best to worst based on two dimensions (price and quality) in comparative product tests in *Consumer Reports* between 1939 and 1949. Price and objective quality were rather weakly related with a rank correlation of 0.25. Sproles[19] found a positive correlation for 51 per cent of the 135 products retained in the study. In other words, high price was not necessarily related to high quality. For 35 per cent of the products he found no correlation and for 14 per cent a higher price was related to lower objective quality. Similarly, Riesz[20] found a positive rank correlation of 0.26 between price and objective quality among 685 categories of products. Curry and Riesz[21] studied price quality over product life cycle for 62 durable products. Their findings indicate that when both low-quality/high-price and high-quality/low-price brands were introduced early in the product life cycle, the inconsistent relationship between price and quality tended to stabilize over time.

The same conclusion has been found in a wide variety of countries. For instance, in Japan the mean price–quality relationship reached -0.06[22] and -0.18 in the automobile industry.[23] In the case of consumer durables, a slightly positive price–quality correlation was found across five countries (Australia, Canada, New Zealand, the United Kingdom and the United States), ranging from 0.18 to 0.35.[15] This illustrates that there generally exists a positive but weak correlation between objective price and objective quality. Price is a variable, but generally positive indicator for quality.

Obviously, there are differences in the price–quality relationship across product categories, as some products are more difficult to assess prior to purchase than others. For instance, it is not possible for consumers to assess whether a German Miele washing machine, which is three times more expensive than a machine branded by Zanussi (Italian arm of the Swedish Electrolux group), lasts three times longer before they purchase one. To take account of this, Nelson categorized products as having search attributes that are relatively easy to evaluate prior to purchase, and experience attributes that are only evaluated after purchase. Darby and Karni[24] extended this to include credence attributes that cannot be confidently evaluated even after purchase. Further, the purchase situation can also impact the price–quality relationship. For instance, Yan and Sengupta found that the more psychologically distant the product is from the consumer (e.g., something that is very unfamiliar or purchased for someone else), the greater the effect of price on perceptions of quality.[25]

The ability – due to the availability of information, experience and access to expertise – to judge objective product quality is likely to differ across cultures and individuals. For instance, for urban Chinese, the price–quality relationship is stronger for durables than for non-durables (which are easier to judge prior to purchase), and inexperienced consumers tend to infer more quality from price than experienced ones.[26] Similarly, in Turkey, where objective quality information is less commonly available to the general population, price is considered a good or fair indicator of quality for 75 per cent of the consumers Yucelt and Firoz[27] surveyed; a high price is relied upon as an indication of higher quality.

A recent meta-analysis on the price-*perceived* quality relationship conducted by Völckner and Hofmann[28] showed some interesting differences between countries. European countries showed a stronger positive relationship between price and perceived quality compared to North American countries. Similarly, less developed countries such as India and China also showed a stronger relationship compared to the North American countries. However, across all countries the relationship was relatively weak. Similarly, Jo and Sarigollu[29] found that Japanese consumers had a much stronger positive relationship between price and perceived quality compared to Australian consumers.

Consumers generally have difficulty establishing a clear price–quality relationship, especially when quality is only revealed after the purchase, as in the case of products with experience and credence attributes. Consumers often need to use other cues to make inferences, such as associating attractive, elaborate packaging with a higher price-quality relationship.[30] Furthermore, in order to form their perceptual evaluation of total price (monetary as well as non-monetary) consumers need a better understanding of the costs involved in using the product.[11] Often, in the absence of information based on actual product use, they are forced to resort to simplified formulae to guide their choice. The results of an experiment by Schindler and Kibarian[31] illustrate a simplified influence of price by varying the price endings (using 99 or 00) in a controlled advertising experiment. They found that consumers were more likely to perceive the price as relatively low if it had a 99 ending versus 00 ending. However, the 99 ending also had a negative effect on perceptions of quality, especially for those who are not price-driven.[32] Accordingly, higher-priced products may do better if they avoid 99 endings.

Schindler[33] found that the use of 99 endings are more common when the price is framed as a discount, and when such a number reduces the value of the left-most digit in a price (e.g., $7,999.99 instead of $8,000 might be effective, while $7,899.99 instead of $7,900 would be less so). He also found an interesting cross-cultural difference, in that Japanese price advertisements use an 8-ending price in the same situation, as the number 8 has auspicious connotations.

Tellis and Gaeth[34] depict three basic choice strategies when the consumer has a better knowledge of price than of quality. In the first strategy, *best value*, people use a rational standpoint to choose the brand with the least overall cost in terms of price and expected quality to maximize the utility that will be derived. In the second strategy, *price seeking*, price is used as a proxy for the unknown quality, leading the consumer to choose the highest-price brand (i.e., the consumer makes an attribution of quality from the price). In the third strategy, *price aversion*, people choose the lowest-price brand in order to minimize immediate costs (i.e., they are risk averse). The salience of these three models depends on the consumer's situation – that is, the amount of information they have, their capacity to establish price–quality relations, and their experiences. These relations and strategies were observed in the US, but different attitudes in making strategic choices are to be expected according to the consumer's national culture.

Cultural dimensions of price–quality evaluation and consumer choice strategies

Some dimensions of price appear to be fairly universal, including price–quality relationships, prestige sensitivity, and value-consciousness.[35] It is generally accepted that consumers are reasonably rational and, if sufficiently motivated, they attempt to evaluate, as objectively as they can, the price–quality relationship. Yet this idea of the best price–quality relationship is depicted in various ways: for example, by minimum levels of quality and maximum levels of price, below or above which consumers will eliminate a product from the set of products they will consider.

1. *Northern European consumers*: The price levels in Northern European shops and also the robustness and durability of products may be surprising. A possible explanation is that these countries are primarily Lutheran, a form of Protestantism that favours a lifestyle imbued with a certain austerity in terms of material well-being. Goods should be expensive in order to limit their consumption (see Box 10.2) and people prefer them to last, in line with an austere, thrifty and utilitarian outlook on life. For instance, furniture for homes should be sturdy and long-lasting. This means that people rarely buy furniture and, when they do, they are looking for the best price–quality relation, where the minimal level of quality is relatively high, thus eliminating a range of possibilities even where the price is low enough to enhance the price–quality relationship. IKEA's strategy corresponds to this type of choice (see the case study A6.2 at the end of Chapter 6).

2. *Southern European consumers*: Purchasing power in southern Europe is somewhat lower than the north European average. People stay outdoors more because the climate is warmer. Social life often takes place outdoors and is materially much less austere, hence the more pronounced taste for seasonal fashions and for appearance and show. In addition, the Catholic doctrine is rather ambiguous about money, and has little to say about the price–quality ratio. Moreover, the Catholic Church has never been preoccupied, either explicitly or implicitly, with the price and quality of material possessions. The Catholic religion is not a 'lover of money' and could therefore be said to implicitly support spending. Like all idealistic systems with a worldly dimension, the Catholic doctrine manages to sustain the paradox of being anti-money but not anti-expenditure. This is the complete opposite of the Protestant paradox of thrift that considers expenditure as a catalyst for poor morality but still favours the accumulation of wealth. The difference exists in where the shame lies:

Box 10.2

The Puritan paradox

I fear, wherever riches have increased, the essence of religion has decreased in the same proportion. Therefore I do not see how it is possible, in the nature of things, for any revival of true religion to continue long. For religion must necessarily produce both industry and frugality, and these cannot but produce riches. But as riches increase, so will pride, anger, and love of the world in all its branches. How then is it possible that Methodism, that is, a religion of the heart, though it flourishes now as a green bay tree, should continue in this state? For the Methodists in every place grow diligent and frugal; consequently they increase in goods. Hence they proportionately increase in pride, in anger, in the desire of the flesh, the desire of the eyes, and the pride of life. So, although the form of religion remains, the spirit is swiftly vanishing away. Is there no way to prevent this – this continual decay of pure religion? *We ought not to prevent people from being diligent and frugal; we must exhort all Christians to gain all they can, and to save all they can; that is, in effect, to grow rich.*

(Source: Speech by Methodist minister John Wesley at the end of the eighteenth century, a few years before the Industrial Revolution in Britain. Quoted by Weber;[36] last sentence italicized by Weber. By permission of Oxford University Press, USA.)

for the Catholic, spending is not really shameful, but money is, and the religion rejects money while accepting its pleasures. For the Protestant, excessive or conspicuous spending is shameful.

Max Weber (p. 31)[36] emphasized the relative benevolence of the Catholic Church, 'punishing the heretic, but being lenient with the sinner', in contrast to the Reformed Church, which imposes stricter rules and regulations. The Catholic influence lacks the austerity and rigour of Protestantism. In a way, it accords free will to material choice, as in the famous quotation from the Bible, 'Render unto Caesar the things that are Caesar's' (Matthew 22:15). Consequently, the Latin (Catholic) consumer is more diverse, particularly in relation to displaying social class. In Latin society social classes are more distinct, and buying has the function of reinforcing one's social image. Given that there are marked differences in buying power, one would expect diversified choice strategies among consumers. For example:

1. Snobbish consumers who, by definition, buy the most expensive foods (i.e., the Veblen effect of preferring high prices).
2. Consumers who are more concerned about price and who would automatically buy the least expensive items (i.e., price-averse consumers).
3. Consumers who use price–quality relations, in line with the Latin temperament that includes a propensity for intellectual logic and rationality.

10.4

International price tactics

Price manipulation

Vendors may use pricing to serve three interrelated objectives: (1) profits, (2) sales, and (3) market interactions. While profits and sales objectives are clear, marketing interactions are also profit objectives as their focus is on relations with other market actors (i.e., customers, distributors, competitors, regulatory authorities) in order, ultimately, to make a profit. Table 10.2 identifies 11 pricing objectives under these three categories.

Price is a tactical tool in local markets and a strategic tool in face of global competition. Price tactics in domestic markets must take their place within a global strategy of cost domination based on the search for economies of scale and experience effects (see Chapter 8) or differentiation, which is obtained by designing a product offering that has been differentiated from competitors or tailored to local markets (see Chapter 9).

Keegan[37] described three possible positions for international strategic pricing:

1. *The extension/ethnocentric position*: a single global price based on the factory price of the goods, with the customer being charged for insurance, freight and customs costs.

Table 10.2 Pricing objectives

	Objectives
Profit	(1) Maximize company profits
	(2) Reach target profits
Sales	(3) Increasing unit volume
	(4) Attain sales figures
	(5) Increase cash flows
Interaction	(6) Develop new markets
	(7) Maintain customer loyalty
	(8) Achieve greater market stability
	(9) Attain price parity with competitors
	(10) Eliminate competitors
	(11) Promote the image of the company and/or its products and/or brands

2. *The polycentric adaptation position*: local subsidiaries fix their own prices according to local market conditions.
3. *The intermediate geocentric inventive position*: the subsidiary takes into account local competition and seeks to maximize the firm's total income through international coordination of tactical pricing.

These positions can be related somewhat simplistically to Stöttinger's[38] results. Stöttinger interviewed 45 seasoned European international business managers to assess 'best practices', finding that all but three firms set international prices centrally, in line with an extension/ethnocentric position. The others decentralized pricing decisions for different reasons. Stöttinger (p. 49)[38] explained that one company holds different strategic positions in their domestic and international markets: 'domestically the firm is known as a low-price, mass market manufacturer, internationally it is positioned in the premium segment', in line with the intermediate geocentric inventive position. The other two companies are mainly active in Eastern Europe, 'as respondents put it – in-depth knowledge of the market situation and the customer's financial conditions govern the pricing policy' (p. 50),[38] in line with a polycentric adaptation position.

Price can also be used against competitors. Prices can be manipulated and distorted between markets as long as customer or distributor disputes can be avoided. In fact, consumers cannot always arbitrate, because of transaction costs, complexities of international trade operations for private people, customs regulations and technical standards. However, agents are often tempted to arbitrate for consumers. Agents can reduce the transaction costs and rapidly gain experience in such practice. For example, certain agents may specialize in re-importing products sold at lower prices in a neighbouring market.

Suppliers face many difficulties in pricing goods and services. For instance, large international customers place increasing pressure on suppliers to offer them global-pricing contracts to reduce inefficiencies in obtaining prices in multiple locations.[39] This poses many problems for suppliers, who may have difficulty in passing on their full costs, especially when parts or services are also transferred among divisions that may be located in different countries. Stevenson and Cabell (p. 81)[40] suggest a two-stage approach that first identifies the cost drivers which cause costs to increase or decrease and then allocates costs to products, or regions, by the drivers: 'For example, in marketing a cost driver would be the number of shipments made to a particular region, number of orders entered, or sales calls made in a region; these drivers are used to allocate costs'. After all of the costs are accumulated, they can then be allocated to products and regions.

Signalling willingness to compete: domestic markets, export markets and dumping

Who gets the lowest prices? This question requires consideration when a company operates in different national markets, where the opportunity exists to increase profits through price discrimination. It naturally presupposes that buyers or distributors have no possibility of arbitrage: that is, buying where cheapest, either for consumption or for resale at a higher price in another national market. Other reasons for price discrimination across national markets may be found among the 11 pricing objectives in Table 10.2.

A basic international pricing issue is price discrimination between domestic and foreign markets, which depends on the positions of the respective markets on the company's cost curve. For a firm to maximize its profit, it must sell its products at a price greater than or equal to the marginal cost (i.e., in addition to the total cost of producing one extra unit). In practice, people refer to the cost price based on total costs. However, in industries where overheads are high – such as aerospace, chemicals and steel – direct costing (i.e., variable costs directly related to production) may be used.

When a completely new aircraft is launched with initial fixed expenses of US$5 billion, or a new car with overhead costs of US$1 billion, is the domestic market or the export market supposed to 'pay' for the depreciation of these sunk costs? This is a very important question and calls for a number of subjective considerations. Should the domestic market or other exclusive markets pay for its loyalty or, on the contrary, should it benefit from price cuts as compensation and encouragement for loyalty? If potential car purchasers in Britain were aware of the surcharge they pay, about 20 per cent higher than the European average, perhaps they would show less loyalty to their national carmakers.

Figure 10.1 addresses the problem of where to situate the domestic and export markets respectively on the horizontal axis of the cost curve. Because sales, whether domestic or export, usually take place simultaneously, the problem is one of subjective (but stable) conceptualization of the bases of the cost curve, as it corresponds to exported quantities. It is this concept that leads directly to the practice of dumping.

Figure 10.1 Dumping and the relationship between unit costs and cumulated production

Article Vl of the General Agreement on Tariffs and Trade (GATT) prohibits dumping where it prejudices the production of one of the contracting parties.

Website link 10.4

Search the WTO website for anti-dumping restrictions: http://www.wto.org/english/tratop_e/adp_e/adp_e.htm.

It allows certain countries to impose anti-dumping taxes on dumping prices. The United States has regularly exercised this clause, especially on European and Japanese steel exports. Dumping is based on the following assumptions:

1. One role of the domestic market or other exclusive markets is to recover sunk costs. These markets should therefore be situated on the ascending part of the cost curve in relation to the x-axis signifying quantity.
2. In placing the home market in this zone, the remaining zone where marginal costs decrease would be reserved for foreign markets where competition is supposed to be more open or where prices that are more attractive are offered. It is, however, worth remembering that the company's home market is its competitors' foreign market.
3. Dumping assumes that foreign markets are like rubbish bins. This is true except in the situation where the aim is to assume the role of a predator, momentarily flooding the market with the intention of raising prices after a sizeable market share has been secured.

Showing commitment in a target market: gaining market share through pricing

Slashing prices in the short term may appear to be an attractive strategy for obtaining new clients, building customer loyalty, and increasing market share. This could even result in the consumer being trapped if prices are subsequently raised and if competitors, who have lost market share, are not prepared to engage in a price war to regain their previous share. Competitors will therefore often accept the new status quo and products will be priced high.

Slashing prices is a price tactic when viewed from the perspective of a single market. Across markets, however, it is the implementation of a global strategy. The Japanese are unsurpassed in the art of initially penetrating a market through price rebates in order to obtain a sizeable share in it. Johansson and Nonaka (p. 592) described the pricing strategies of Japanese firms as follows:

The general theme was one of seeing the entry into a market as a long-term 'investment' and market penetration was accordingly a much more important pricing objective than quick profit taking with a skimming approach. Several of the firms employed a version of the 'experience curve pricing strategy' where a relatively low price was expected to lead to large volume and future cost savings. It became rather clear that individual markets were not seen as 'profit centres' but rather as pieces in one large global puzzle. By generating sufficient funds at home and in selected country markets where the share positions were strong, the lower returns emanating from a low price penetration strategy in newer markets could be sustained over a relatively long period.[41]

As an example, Japanese car manufacturers entered the European-dominated African markets about 30 years ago offering relatively cheap, reliable, air-conditioned cars. Because their objective was not to eliminate competitors, the Japanese left room for European cars after having acquired the lion's share of the market, which they did by raising prices. The benefits of this strategy were threefold: they calmed hard-pressed rivals, raised their profit margins, and finally avoided the risk that their relatively low pricing would lead to a lasting unfavourable image of their products.

Avoiding parallel imports: combating grey markets and opportunistic distributors

According to Palia and Keown (p. 37)[42] a grey market occurs when an 'exporter knowingly or unknowingly sells to an unauthorized agent who competes directly with the sole agent appointed by the exporter within the same territory'. Grey markets are based on parallel imports that hamper the effectiveness of marketing strategies in certain national markets. For instance, if a company sells at a discount to a Central American distributor, because local consumers cannot afford European or US price levels, goods risk being shipped back from Central America to the United States and sold there through unofficial channels.[43]

Fragmented national markets are geographically proximate in regions, including Europe, West Africa,

Latin America, and South-East Asia. Once different price levels are set in neighbouring countries, consumers and some distributors seek cheaper supplies across the border, making the manufacturer compete with its own products. If the price differential is large enough to offset transaction costs, unauthorized intermediaries may compete with sole agents or exclusive dealers in national markets where a specific marketing strategy has been defined (see Case A10.2). They therefore benefit from brand advertising and marketing strategies carried out by the company and its regular dealers, without having to contribute to cover these costs and are thus able to cut their own prices and margins.[44]

Interestingly, Myers[45] found that the number of markets served and monetary issues, such as the form of currency and inflation rate fluctuations, did not impact grey market activity. However, internal and external control issues, such as distribution control and integration of channels, centralization of decision making and product standardization (i.e., a lack of interesting adaptations) were all related to lower grey market activity. After reviewing the legal controls for grey marketing, Clarke and Owens suggest that (p. 285): 'Marketers may be best served by minimising the conditions which create gray markets or looking for nonlegal response alternatives.'[46]

Many companies that manufacture home appliances and consumer durables struggle to control the ultimate destinations of their products. For instance, Belgian, Dutch and French agents in cities close to the German border sometimes buy from German wholesalers instead of their domestic distributor, who may sell at a higher price. When price policies implement country-specific prices, they should consider all the opportunities that may exist for consumer and/or distributor arbitrage. As Weigand (p. 53)[43] emphasized, consumer arbitrage is often affected through holiday travel: 'An English tourist taking a holiday in Miami bought a place setting of bone china made in Britain. She didn't pay Britain's substantial value added tax. Further the dollar was cheaper that day.' Weigand also noted that British manufacturers recognize that these personal imports affect their domestic sales. However, they have not found a way to stop them.

The same problem applies to products whose novelty is their major selling point. For example, a new DVD movie may be released in the US prior to its European release, thereby creating a potential grey market in Europe. In such cases this will be difficult to avoid because a segment of European movie buffs will know when the DVD becomes available and will happily pay a premium to be among the first to own it. Opportunists who organize the parallel market pocket the inflated profit margin. To combat this, distributors place region-specific code restrictions on DVDs, although this has been only marginally successful due to the introduction of multi-region DVD players.

In China, censors' restriction of the import of foreign music increased the opportunity for grey markets. In 2001, censors only approved about 700 titles.[47] It has been reported that more than 90 per cent of CDs sold on mainland China may be illegal copies.[47] In this case the music industry is partly responsible, as most of the CDs are not pirated but resold old stock that did not sell in the US.[47] While several companies, including Warner and Atlantic, now destroy all unsold albums in-house, piracy continues to be an issue.

Piracy is extremely difficult to combat worldwide.[48] Brand counterfeiting of consumer goods not only costs the brand owners monetary sales, but also has the effect of eroding the brand's value as the counterfeit products are of inferior quality.[48] The entertainment industry has been one of the most affected by piracy in the past few years, predominantly due to the ease of obtaining pirated media via the Internet. Ironically, illegal digital downloads (the vast majority of which are done at no cost to the consumer) have more or less wiped out the aforementioned grey markets in developed countries; however, this does not put the money back in the pocket of the producer. The Motion Picture Association of America estimates that the US motion picture industry collectively lost US$6.1 billion to piracy in 2005, and 38 per cent of that was to Internet piracy.[49] A recent analysis of cross-national piracy rates indicated that piracy of American movies was higher in collectivist countries, but is not affected by income.[50]

While the costs of lost sales are obviously enormous, the industry has only just begun to find cost-effective ways of restricting online digital duplication of their intellectual property. For the most part the combination of punitive action against uploaders and legislative attempts has failed to have a noticeable impact on this form of piracy. What is beginning to have an effect is the willingness of companies to provide cost-effective *legal* options for consumers who wish to download entertainment media. For instance,

the Apple iTunes platform is now the biggest music retailer in the world, and has not sold a single physical item. Instead, the success lies in the ability of the consumer to pay a reasonable price (slightly cheaper on average than a physical medium) and, more important, to pick and choose. For instance, a commonly cited justification for online music piracy is that music companies force consumers to pay full price for an album when only one or two tracks might be desired.[51] iTunes and other similar platforms allow the selection of any number of tracks, therefore appealing to these consumers. Perhaps the most innovative attempt at combating piracy has been pioneered by rock groups such as 'Nine Inch Nails' and 'Radiohead'.[52] In 2007 Radiohead offered their album *In Rainbows* as a download from their website, giving fans the option to pay whatever they wanted for the music, or even pay nothing at all.[53] Similarly, Nine Inch Nails offered nine tracks of the album *Ghosts I-IV* as free downloads from their website. The effectiveness of this new business model at combating piracy remains to be seen.

The objective of monitoring product price positioning across markets is a difficult issue. In some countries agents may be forced to sell at prices lawfully dictated by producers. In others legislators may consider such practices contrary to effective competition. Resale price maintenance laws prohibit the producers from imposing prices on agents, even though this may be required by marketing strategy. Firms then manoeuvre around these laws through recommended retail price labelling, thus controlling an agent's discretionary margin. Even so, the agent could still sell the product at an offer price (e.g., to promote the agent's store) and conflict with the producer's pricing strategy.

Exclusive distribution agreements in home markets would appear to be a plausible solution to the grey market issue. But the implementation of such exclusivity clauses is somewhat difficult. In the US there is some reluctance to limit competition by granting enforceable exclusivity rights to dealers, as this limits their control. Parallel importers, competing with authorized dealers in leading brands, like Cartier and Seiko, were accorded an almost complete victory by the K-Mart ruling handed down by the US Supreme Court (*Kmart Corp. v. Cartier, Inc.*, 486 U.S. 281 [1988]). However, in 1998 the Supreme Court clarified its opinion in the *L'Anza* case, where it ruled that after the first legal sale, the copyright owner no longer has the right to control distribution, which means they cannot prevent unauthorized importation of products bearing their brand name.[46]

European Union legislation also restricts exclusive distribution agreements. EU competition rules (e.g., Article 85 of the Treaty of Rome) prohibit any kind of market-sharing agreement by which a company could limit the sales of its distributors exclusively to a domestic market. In order to increase competition across EU countries, Article 85 and several jurisdictional decisions of the European Court of Justice have legitimized parallel imports. A company cannot prevent its 'exclusive' German distributor from selling to Italian customers, even if the company has also appointed an 'exclusive' distributor in Italy. Because it is difficult to prevent distributors from seeking arbitrage opportunities, grey markets have developed in Europe and other areas, seeking to overcome the many non-tariff barriers whenever price differentials offset the costs of parallel importing. Chaudhry and Walsh (p. 18)[54] reviewed the price and legal environments of the pharmaceutical industry in the EU, concluding that the European Court of Justice 'will continue to use Article 30 and the Exhaustion of Rights Doctrine to support the gray market'. In general, we expect that grey marketers will be able to continue to obtain their licences.

Possible solutions to the grey market issue, that is, solutions that may counter parallel imports, are as follows:

1. *Reduce the price differentials between markets*: lower the price in a national market where it is too high and/or inflate it where it is too low, in order to offset enough of the price differential, so that there is little profit in parallel importing. This, however, may be at the expense of the global coherence of the marketing strategy in either one or both countries. Authorized dealers, provided that they have a cost advantage, could be encouraged to engage in a price war with parallel importers in order to drive them out of the market.[41] Similarly, authorized dealers could scale down their promotional expenses in order to regain advantage over the grey dealers.
2. *Materially alter the product*: the official product should be favourably differentiated against the parallel imported product. If changes are only superficial, importers and consumers will not be fooled. If changes are more significant, economies of scale are lost. Other possibilities entail changing minor product attributes: extended warranties can be granted only to authorized dealers, so that parallel importers will offer products with little or no after-sales service and guarantee.[44] A label 'not for export' or 'for domestic sale only' may be attached to the packaging (which also clearly identifies the national origin). This may prevent some dealers from re-exporting, but the effectiveness of these labels is very limited, since in most countries it is not legal for a manufacturer to prohibit the export sales of its own products.
3. *Educate the dealer*: weaker dealers may be prime targets for grey market attacks and may, at first, react with an outburst of anger, because it may seem to them that the manufacturer is making excess profit at their expense. Explaining why such price differences exist is part of the manufacturer's role although the dealer may not consider such explanations to be credible.[55]
4. *Terminate the dealer agreements* (or threaten to do so) when the dealer buys from unauthorized parallel sources. Weigand (p. 59) cites the case of Apple, which prints the following statement: 'Any Apple dealer or VAR (Value Added Retailer) found to be in violation of the mail-order or transhipping prohibitions will be stripped of its authorized status.'[43]
5. *Buy back the grey market goods*: this is positively perceived by authorized dealers, who feel actively protected by the brand owner. Generally, this solution is possible only when a permanent solution to parallel imports has been found and is quickly implemented after a short – and costly – buy-back period.
6. *Sell products under a different name*, leaving the foreign distributors to promote the products, or develop a unique trademark in each country.[46] The danger here is loss of benefits from a global trademark.
7. *Target different consumer segments*, determined on the basis of degree of risk aversion.[41]

Finally, it is important to emphasize the risk that consumer perceptions of product positioning may be adversely affected by discrepancies in price for the same good across markets. Ibison (p. 13) described the problem for Daimler Chrysler in Japan:

There was surprise at Daimler Chrysler Japan when executives saw a television advertisement promoting a model they were not due to launch in Japan for another four months. The advertisement – for the C-class Mercedes – was not part of the German/US auto group's planned marketing strategy. Nor were the prices, which were 30 per cent cheaper than they were planning to charge. In fact, the commercials, the press conference and the news stories were all generated by a savvy Japanese car dealer who had latched on to one of last year's most tempting arbitrage opportunities: the weak euro. The dealer had travelled to Europe, where C-classes had already been launched, bought 20 from a dealer in Germany, shipped them back to Japan and put them on his forecourt.[56]

Not only has the perception of the reference price and positioning for Mercedes changed, but there will be real difficulties if there is a product recall, as there will be no way to trace the purchasers. In addition, it is estimated that it reduced the potential sales by up to 12 per cent, decreasing profitability and potentially the services that can be offered.

For informed consumers – currently a rather rare species – buying in the home market is no longer attractive when they become aware that home market prices are artificially inflated. Despite the ubiquitous Internet, average consumers tend to be ignorant of international price differentials, and even when informed, they resign themselves to the tariff and non-tariff barriers that 'imprison' customers in their home market. This situation is changing rapidly, however, as regional integration speeds up in South America, Europe and South-East Asia. Consumers are slowly becoming aware of the price levels for similar goods and services in neighbouring countries. They are also being offered increased opportunities for buying abroad, with no customs duties or clearance formalities.

Pricing and the Internet

It has been estimated that the value of global online retailing in 2010 was US$317 billion, with the US accounting for US$110 billion, and the EU US$105 billion (Euromonitor 2011).[57] The industries that have taken the most advantage of this new economy include consumer electronics, media (including news and entertainment), apparel, and increasingly food and drink.

Undoubtedly the Internet offers consumers easier access to comparative information than do retail stores, especially with the growth in mobile-Internet devices (e.g., tablets and smartphones); however, tales of the demise of the retail store appear to be exaggerated.[57]

As a recent study demonstrates, more money is spent in retail stores than Internet stores.[57] Increasingly it is becoming apparent that retailers that can successfully operate within a combined 'bricks-and-clicks' framework, where appropriate (e.g., Walmart, Apple, etc.), will thrive, while those who fail to adapt (e.g., Blockbuster Video, Borders) will struggle. Furthermore, despite the ease of comparing information online, the vast majority of online consumers purchase from the first site they visit, including 89 per cent for books, 84 per cent for toys, 81 per cent for music and 76 per cent for electronics.[58] In addition, the price is not the main consideration for business buyers, as only 30 per cent of business buyers reported lower prices as the key benefit of online purchasing; other key factors include lower transaction search costs and automating information to track inventory and make better decisions.[58]

The Internet has become almost a necessity, rather than an advantage for firms. According to Porter (p. 78): 'The more robust competitive advantages will arise instead from traditional strengths such as unique products, proprietary content, distinctive physical activities, superior product knowledge, and strong personal service and relationships.'[59] Similarly, Ancarani[60] cautions firms to avoid the 'commodity trap' by taking advantage of the increased information and advances in technology rather than being pressed by the potential power of consumers. These factors will allow firms to better differentiate their products. For instance, the increased ability to track and profile online customers presents the opportunity for firms to refine market segmentation, and use 'price discrimination, dynamic and smart pricing, product and price versioning, price bundling and unbundling' (p. 680).[60]

10.5

Market situations, competition and price agreements

Ideal versus actual competition

The status of price in the exchange process may be viewed in different ways: (1) as an objective equilibrium point of a contract between two parties, or (2) as the instrument of a social relationship, a subjective equilibrium resulting from the interaction between buyer and seller. In classical economic terms, the social exchange relationship disappears behind Adam Smith's 'invisible hand' of the market. However, it is debatable whether human nature tends more to alliance or competition; both are aspects of human nature. The invisible hand assumes that the nature of competitors is to battle each other fiercely; however, human nature may well tend, at least sometimes, more towards agreement to divide territory between companies and sign pacts, albeit of limited duration.

On the worldwide market for household care products, five main firms compete strongly against each other: Procter & Gamble, Colgate-Palmolive, Unilever, Henkel and the Kao Corporation of Japan. They compete head-to-head for market shares on some segments, brands and national markets, whereas in other areas and for other brands armistices have been implicitly signed. Competition patterns should therefore be analysed on a per case basis. A complex reality hides behind the normative position 'it is essential to be competitive'. To varying degrees, competition and alliances between companies will always occur.

The code that constrains newcomers to the competitive scene (e.g., a national market) is even more complex, as it determines how they should behave towards already established players. Large newcomers frequently face a combined attack from all the firms, whether domestic or foreign, already present in a national market. The current incumbents may, for instance, lower their prices or spread rumours about the newcomer's product/service policies and long-term commitment to local customers. This results in poor competition, which may be detrimental to customers. An example of such hidden agreements existed in the French fire safety market, where a norm stricter than the European standard (EN 54) barred outsiders from entering the market. As a result, prices for fire detectors in France are double those in Britain. For all these reasons, the customization of marketing strategies must be carried out according to *actual* rather than *ideal* competition patterns.

Market situations and competition-avoidance patterns

Competition is not necessarily self-perpetuating. The dynamics of competition may lead to the concentration of supply amongst a limited number of companies and therefore to an actual decrease in the sum total of competing forces. For instance, the trend towards concentration has been seen throughout Western Europe, with the combined market share exceeding 50 per cent for the top three in grocery retailing.[61] In Finland, a high market share locally and an increasing number of industry-wide stores were associated with higher mark-ups.[61]

Conversely, in the US effective institutions were introduced at an early stage (e.g., the US antitrust legislation and the Sherman Act) to oversee the proper functioning of competition, to discourage dominant positions and the establishment of monopolies through mergers and acquisitions. However, as Cateora (p. 128)[62] emphasized, perhaps with some exaggeration: 'Except in the United States, 20th century orientation toward competition has been to avoid it whenever possible.'

Website link 10.5

Search for antitrust cases, such as the USA versus Microsoft: http://www.justice.gov/atr/cases/ms_index.htm.

Conversely, DeMarco[63] argues that while monopolies should be monitored for exclusivities and discrimination including prices and supplies, we have insufficient evidence to condemn them. Prior to the Second World War, one of the large German cartels, Interessen Gemeinschaft Farben, brought together three major chemical and pharmaceutical companies, Bayer, BASF and Hoechst, which now operates under the Sanofi-Aventis logo. All three are now at the forefront of the world chemical and pharmaceutical industry. Japanese *zaibatsus*, such as Mitsui and Company, Mitsubishi Group and Sumitomo Group have existed for centuries. Typically, one extended family controls groups of companies that may encompass businesses as diverse as banking, car production, trading and shipbuilding. The Americans prohibited *zaibatsus* after their victory over the Japanese in 1945, which simply caused them to evolve into today's *keiretsus*.

Competition between companies in Japan is often savage. Abegglen and Stalk[64] demonstrated this using the motorcycle industry as a case in point. Honda was far behind Tohatsu in the 1950s but completely overtook them; in 1964 Tohatsu went bankrupt. After

Table 10.3 Basic forms of markets according to Von Stackelberg[66]

		Sellers		
		One	Some	Many
Buyers	One	Bilateral monopoly	Contradicted monopsony	Monopsony
	Some	Contradicted monopoly	Bilateral oligopoly	Oligopsony
	Many	Monopoly	Oligopoly	Pure competition

entering the motor vehicle sector during the 1960s, Honda's motorcycle business suffered a relative loss of competitiveness because of Yamaha, which achieved almost the same market share in 1981. At the beginning of the 1980s Honda decided to attack Yamaha. Whereas Honda introduced 81 new models and ceased production of 32, reflecting 113 changes in product range in all, Yamaha 'only' introduced 34 new models and withdrew three, reflecting 37 changes. This strategy, in combination with a fierce attack on prices and distribution, led to the collapse of Yamaha at the start of 1983. In addition to substantial losses, Yamaha announced redundancies and a restructuring programme, as well as a reduction in stocks. Yamaha's chairperson was forced to publicly acknowledge his failure.

Foreign companies seeking to establish themselves in Japan often underestimate this fierce domestic competition (for illustration see Tsurumi and Tsurumi,[65] for the case of Fujifilm and Kodak). This competitive strategy is one of the principal sources of Japanese strength when they enter foreign markets.

An industrialist's vocation is not to enjoy competition as an end in itself. Competition is imposed by the public sector opening up frontiers and ultimately by competitors themselves. If companies possess the legal and informal means to reduce competition, they will do so. This perspective remains true as long as the type of agreement is stable and the conditions remain mutually beneficial.

A German economist, Von Stackelberg[66] had the idea of combining supply and demand situations to construct a typology of markets. He distinguished buyer and seller according to whether they number one, several or many (see Table 10.3).

Every country has a few monopolies and some markets where pure and perfect competition reigns. In addition, each country has a large number of oligopolies that are usually producers of large-scale consumption and durable consumer goods, and oligopolies, and bilateral oligopolies that are usually producers of industrial input goods, such as steel, chemicals, rubber, and capital goods. What varies, as a function of culture, is the social approval or disapproval of these market forms. Local decision makers need to determine whether monopolies may be desirable or dangerous for the community. Foreign intruders will be seen positively, from the consumer's point of view, or negatively, from the local competitor's point of view, because ultimately consumers are often also employees whose employment may be put at risk by the competition.

Americans are often shocked by the amount of protection European governments provide to their flagship companies. The Airbus–Boeing saga is typical of conceptual differences that partly derive their roots from culture. The Europeans consider that government loans – often viewed as sunk costs – were used wisely in view of the success of the Airbus aircraft, the number of jobs created, the positive effects on the trade balance and the preservation of a previously threatened European civil aeronautic industry. However, for the Americans it was a costly mess that helped no one: Boeing's success was challenged by disloyal competition, European taxpayers were burdened and international trade rules were distorted. Without Airbus, Boeing would be in quasi-monopoly situation, exacerbated by the McDonnell Douglas merger in 1997; a potential problem caused by lack of competition.

10.6

Managing prices in highly regulated environments

Over the past 20 years or so, the annual inflation rate has attained double digits in some countries, sometimes exceeding 100 per cent per year, causing monthly or daily changes in prices. In 2007 the country with the highest inflation rate was Zimbabwe; in July 2007 it hit 7,634.8 per cent. High inflation may constrain pricing policies, because prices cannot be increased daily or weekly to adjust for inflation.

The case of high-inflation countries

At the national level, price stability is based on macroeconomic policies as well as cultural values. The requisite discipline is based on: (1) future time orientation, which provides the monetary authorities with a perspective of continuity in fighting inflation; (2) control of the creation of money and credit; and (3) a belief in free market forces that may keep price increases under control because of active competition. Such a belief is, in general, related to individualism and low power distance.

One of the main reasons for persistently high inflation is that it benefits some actors in the economic system. Inflation transfers wealth fairly smoothly from some social strata to others. It appears that high inflation countries are also high in power distance (see Chapter 3). With some notable exceptions (such as Japan), the higher a country's power distance, the higher its inflation rate. The typical case for high inflation is a developing country with a semi-authoritarian government and heavy financial regulation (e.g., price controls on most goods, foreign exchange control, strict import controls and high duties). High power distance at the societal level is expressed in bureaucratic controls and restricted freedom for businesses, unless they have the appropriate connections at the top.

High inflation rates cause the local non-convertible currencies to weaken systematically against stable and convertible foreign currencies, because of constantly decreasing nominal purchasing power. Furthermore, the exchange rate is maintained at unrealistic levels. This results in a parallel foreign exchange market;

illegal but generally tolerated by the authorities. In comparison with official exchange rates, parallel rates are favourable to foreign currency sellers and unfavourable to buyers. In Iran, in 1993, following a period of very high inflation, the official exchange rate was about 1,500 rials more than the grey market exchange rate, before it was decided to align the official rate. In such situations, foreign exchange controls serve the purpose of enriching the most powerful who can buy foreign currencies at the favourable official rate, while restricting the capacity of local exporters to receive a real price, because exporters are obliged to sell export receipts in hard currencies at the usually overvalued official rate.

Inflation is supposed to be combated by price control, an expression of the power of regulatory authorities over companies. Where there is high power distance, there tend to be oppressive rules (see Chapter 3). Price increases, so vital for a company's survival, may be delayed by public authorities even though last month's or last week's inflation rate may have caused the entire industry to go into the red – costs soared while sales stagnated because of controlled prices. For instance, the Brazilian automobile industry was subject to 'staircase' price increases by which Volkswagen, Fiat or Ford are suddenly allowed to increase their price by 50 per cent or more. The strong present orientation of the Brazilian public authorities' action favours high inflation, as is the case in many Latin American countries.

Such countries possess a high-inflation culture, where consumers and companies adapt to the changing situation. Consumers delay buying after price increases occur and buy very large quantities just before they are thought to occur, because price increases are not officially announced. If possible, they stock up with items bought during favourable periods. The threat of an imminent price increase is used to motivate customers to buy 'now'. Customers must also have a present orientation and a readiness to buy at the best possible moment, for instance purchasing 'inflation bargains' because they are currently cheap, rather than because they are actually needed. Such customer opportunism may be problematic for the consumers themselves, because they tend to be too price-minded, neglecting other important criteria in their decision-making process. Companies, by contrast, do not depend on consumers for defining prices. The key for price policy, which is mostly short term, is to negotiate price increases with public authorities. Pricing depends more on government authorization than on customers and competition.

The terms of discussion with price regulatory authorities is highly relational and manipulative, rather than strictly economic. In order to obtain optimal price increases, companies argue about losses incurred because of price limitation for which they have to be compensated. Cost prices declared to regulatory authorities tend to be systematically overestimated and losses exaggerated in order to obtain as favourable a new price as possible. A company will argue for a substantial price increase so as to have a 'reserve' before the next increase. Naturally, this whole process fosters inflation rather than slows it down. Another way of obtaining the necessary price allowances – although illegal and unethical – is to propose a 'baksheesh' (i.e., kickback) or some favours to the civil servants in charge of price control within the public administration.

Over- and under-invoicing

As explained above, many high-inflation countries have legislation aimed at controlling prices. The control may take effect at retail, wholesale or production levels, or at several levels simultaneously. Price increases may be curbed, limited or even frozen. Trade profit margins may be monitored. The rationale for price control is usually a basic mistrust of free market mechanisms, often augmented by a long-established tradition of state intervention in the economy.

Foreign exchange regulations also influence the practice of over- and under-invoicing. When countries experience balance of trade and balance of payments problems, they often use administrative decrees aimed at stopping the outflow of foreign currency. Local exporters are often forced to repatriate their earnings in foreign currencies as soon as possible and to exchange them for local currency at sometimes derisory exchange rates. Local importers are also under close scrutiny. The necessity of purchasing abroad is assessed before they may receive foreign currency to pay suppliers. Furthermore, they are often obliged to deposit a guarantee that may be more than the equivalent of their foreign purchase. This sum is deposited at the central bank for a specified period prior to payment, with little or no interest. Where strict foreign exchange controls are enforced, local currency may not be converted into foreign 'hard' currencies.

Two reasons induce firms to practise under- or over-invoicing. First, where there is a high level of political risk, as is the case with many developing countries, local businesspeople seek to transfer funds to foreign banks as fears of political upheaval increase. Second, local businesspeople may wish to expatriate money through under-invoicing, simply because they need cash to buy a prohibited or scarce product or equipment for their production facilities and particularly for the manufacture of products for export.

Verna[67] described various cases of over- and under-invoicing in international trade, relating to differences in currency convertibility. A totally convertible currency may be used in all international commercial and financial operations, irrespective of the object, place, or sum. Only a limited number of countries enjoy total convertibility of their currencies. Where the local currency is non-convertible, over- and under-invoicing is likely to occur,[67] whereas when quantitative restrictions are enforced, smuggling is more likely. Local businesspeople ask foreign customers to under-invoice, foreign suppliers to over-invoice, and then wait for the extra money to be paid into their bank account abroad.

Currency black markets thrive in countries where the national currency is totally non-convertible. For this reason, there may be huge discrepancies between the black-market exchange rate and the official central bank rate. Exporters who are obliged to go through official channels lose major benefits from their transactions. Either they must sell foreign currency at the abnormally low official rate, or they must buy foreign currency for their purchases at the abnormally high parallel rate. Hence the temptation for local exporters to under-invoice and have the fully convertible balance transferred to a foreign bank account. To ensure these machinations work smoothly, the local exporter should have complete confidence in the foreign customers or an effective means of pressurizing them.

Website link 10.6

Search for information about the black market of Zimbabwe: http://www.pbs.org/wnet/wideangle/episodes/underground-zimbabwe/life-lines/4189/ and http://ipsnews.net/africa/nota.asp?idnews=40734.

Over-invoicing works in a symmetrical way for imports. When local importers ask for an import licence from their national authorities, the face value should be as high as possible to increase the allowance for buying foreign currency. Importers ask their suppliers to over-invoice and to transfer the extra money into a convertible foreign account to maximize their overall profits. For example, Verna (p. 115) noted:

An import licence will authorize the importer to order goods from a foreign supplier; a specified amount in foreign currency is paid by the local authorities in the name of the importer. In return, the importer should refund the authorities in local currency, at the official rate, and also pay customs duties on arrival of the goods. To obtain such an import licence may be a sort of 'windfall' because it allows the importer to buy foreign goods at a better price than is offered on the free market, mainly through the (favourable) exchange rate differential between the official and black markets . . . import licences can sometimes be transferable. They then become objects of exchange and even the subject of an auction . . . to the extent that some governments, which have become aware of this trade, sell import licences to the highest bidder.[67]

Questions

1. To what extent does price bargaining involve friendship?

2. What is the relationship between bargaining and 'modern culture'?

3. Discuss 'economic rationality' from a cultural point of view.

4. How may price levels reflect Protestant as opposed to Catholic values?

5. What are the limitations on a consumer in displaying obvious price-mindedness when shopping? How do these limitations relate to culture?

6. In certain countries, smuggling is fairly legitimate: customs officers are not very concerned with arresting smugglers, consumers buy smuggled products knowingly, and smugglers are known by everyone for what they do. Why and under which circumstances is this so? What are the consequences of smuggling being accepted as a legitimate activity?

7. With the abolition of duty-free shopping in 1999, increasingly rapid travel to France by car (including train–car travel by Eurostar), and the loosening of import 'allowances' for wine and spirits, UK citizens continue to buy massive quantities of drinks in Calais, France. In Calais, just 33 km (20 miles) from Dover, French stores have special areas for these British day-trippers. Excise duties on alcohol are higher in the United Kingdom than in France. What are the consequences for the UK brewing industry and its distribution channels? How could the brewing industry respond?

8. Is over- or under-invoicing legal? Why is it sometimes unavoidable?

References

1. Sharma, Varinder M. and Krish S. Krishnan (2001), 'Recognizing the Importance of Consumer Bargaining: Strategic Marketing Implications', *Journal of Marketing Theory and Practice*, 9 (1), 24–37.
2. Herrmann, Gretchen M. (2004), 'Haggling Spoken Here: Gender, Class, and Style in US Garage Sale Bargaining', *Journal of Popular Culture*, 38 (1), 55–81.
3. Sherry, John F., Jr (1990), 'A Sociocultural Analysis of a Midwestern American Flea Market', *Journal of Consumer Research*, 17 (1), 13–30.
4. Euromonitor International (2009), 'The rise of haggling during the global downturn', available online: http://www.portal.euromonitor.com.
5. Allen, David Elliston (1971), 'Anthropological Insights

into Customer Behavior', *European Journal of Marketing*, 5 (3), 45–57.

6. Khuri, Fuad I. (1968), 'The Etiquette of Bargaining in the Middle-East', *American Anthropologist*, 70 (4), 693–706.

7. Roeber, Carter A. (1994), 'Moneylending, Trust, and the Culture of Commerce in Kabwe, Zambia', *Research in Economic Anthropology*, 15, 39–61.

8. Trocchia, Philip J. (2004), 'Caving, Role Playing, and Staying Home: Shopper Coping Strategies in a Negotiated Pricing Environment', *Psychology and Marketing*, 21 (10), 823–53.

9. Prus, Robert C. (1989), *Making Sales: Influence as Interpersonal Accomplishment*. Newbury Park, CA: Sage Publications.

10. Cavusgil, S. Tamer (1990), 'Unravelling the Mystique of Export Pricing', in *International Marketing Strategy*, Hans B. Thorelli and S. Tamer Cavusgil (eds) (3rd edn). Oxford: Pergamon.

11. Zeithaml, Valarie A. (1988), 'Consumer Perceptions of Price, Quality and Value: A Means–End Model and Synthesis of Evidence', *Journal of Marketing*, 52 (3), 2–22.

12. Jacoby, Jacob R. and Jerry C. Olson (1977), 'Consumer Response to Price: An Attitudinal, Information Processing Perspective', in *Moving Ahead with Attitude Research*, Y. Wind and P. Greenberg (eds). Chicago: American Marketing Association.

13. Maxwell, Sarah (2001), 'An Expanded Price/Brand Effect Model: A Demonstration of Heterogeneity in Global Consumption', *International Marketing Review*, 18 (3), 325–43.

14. Becker, Gary S. (1965), 'A Theory of the Allocation of Time', *Economic Journal*, 75 (299), 493–517.

15. Erevelles, Sunil, Abhik Roy and Stephen L. Vargo (1999), 'The Use of Price and Warranty Cues in Product Evaluation: A Comparison of U.S. and Hong Kong Consumers', *Journal of International Consumer Marketing*, 11 (3), 67–91.

16. Ackerman, David and Gerard Tellis (2001), 'Can Culture Affect Prices? A Cross-Cultural Study of Shopping and Retail Prices', *Journal of Retailing*, 77 (1), 57–82.

17. Fauld, David J., Orlen Grunewald and Denise Johnson (1994), 'A Cross-National Investigation of the Relationship between the Price and Quality of Consumer Products: 1970–1990', *Journal of Global Marketing*, 8 (1), 7–25.

18. Oxenfeldt, Alfred R. (1950), 'Consumer Knowledge: Its Measurement and Extent', *Review of Economics and Statistics*, 32 (4), 300–316.

19. Sproles, George B. (1977), 'New Evidence on Price and Quality', *Journal of Consumer Affairs*, 11 (Summer), 63–77.

20. Riesz, P. (1978), 'Price Versus Quality in the Marketplace', *Journal of Retailing*, 54 (4), 15–28.

21. Curry, David J. and Peter C. Riesz (1988), 'Price and Price–Quality Relationships: A Longitudinal Analysis', *Journal of Marketing*, 52 (1), 36–51.

22. Yamada, Yoshiko and Norleen Ackerman (1984), 'Price–Quality Correlations in the Japanese Market', *Journal of Consumer Affairs*, 18 (2), 51–65.

23. Johansson, Johny K. and Gary Erickson (1985), 'Price–Quality Relationships and Trade Barriers', *International Marketing Review*, 2 (3), 52–63.

24. Darby, Michael R. and Edi Karni (1973), 'Free Competition and the Optimal Amount of Fraud', *Journal of Law and Economics*, 16 (1), 67–86.

25. Yan, Dengfeng and Jaideep Sengupta (2011), 'Effects of Construal Level on the Price-Quality Relationship', *Journal of Consumer Research*, 38, 376–89.

26. Veeck, Ann and Alvin C. Burns (1995), 'The Formation of Beliefs in a Price–Quality Relationship: A Study of Urban Chinese Consumers', *Asian Journal of Marketing*, 4 (1), 47–61.

27. Yucelt, Ugur and Nadeem M. Firoz (1993), 'Buyers' Perception of the Price–Quality Relationship: The Turkish Case', in *Proceedings of the 6th World Marketing Congress*. Istanbul: Academy of Marketing Science, 564–68.

28. Völckner, Franziska and Julian Hofmann (2007), 'The Price-Perceived Quality Relationship: A Meta-Analytic Review and Assessment of Its Determinants', *Marketing Letters*, 18, 181–96.

29. Jo, Myung-Soo and Emine Sarigollu (2007), 'Cross-Cultural Differences of Price-Perceived Quality Relationships', *Journal of International Consumer Marketing*, 19 (4), 59–74.

30. Orth, Ulrich R., Daniela Campana and Keven Malkewitz (2010), 'Formation of Consumer Price Expectation Based on Package Design: Attractive and Quality Routes', *Journal of Marketing Theory and Practice*, 18 (1), 23–41.

31. Schindler, Robert M. and Thomas M. Kibarian (2001), 'Image Communicated by the Use of 99 Endings in Advertised Prices', *Journal of Advertising*, 30 (4), 95–99.

32. Kleinsasser, Sabine and Udo Wagner (2011), 'Price endings and tourism consumers' price perceptions', *Journal of Retailing and Consumer Services*, 18, 58–63.

33. Schindler, Robert M. 2009, 'Patterns of price endings used in US and Japanese price advertising', *International Marketing Review*, 26 (1), 17–29.

34. Tellis, Gerard J. and Gary J. Gaeth (1990), 'Best Value, Price-Seeking, and Price Aversion: The Impact of Information and Learning on Consumer Choices', *Journal of Marketing*, 54 (2), 34–45.

35. McGowan, Karen M. and Brenda J. Sternquist (1998), 'Dimensions of Price as a Marketing Universal: A Comparison of Japanese and U.S. Consumers', *Journal of International Marketing*, 6 (4), 49–65.

36. Weber, Max (1958), *The Protestant Ethic and the Spirit of Capitalism*. New York: Charles Scribner's Sons.

37. Keegan, Warren J. (1984), *Multinational Marketing Management*. Englewood Cliffs, NJ: Prentice-Hall.

38. Stöttinger, Barbara (2001), 'Strategic Export Pricing: A Long and Winding Road', *Journal of International Marketing*, 9 (1), 40–63.

39. Narayandas, Das, John Quelch and Gordon Swartz (2000), 'Prepare Your Company for Global Pricing', *MIT Sloan Management Review*, 42 (1), 61–70.

40. Stevenson, Thomas H. and David W. E. Cabell (2002), 'Integrating Transfer Pricing Policy and Activity-Based Costing', *Journal of International Marketing*, 10 (4), 77–88.

41. Johansson, Johny K. and Ikujiro Nonaka (1990), 'Japanese Export Marketing: Structures, Strategies, Counterstrategies', in *International Marketing Strategy*, Hans B. Thorelli and S. Tamer Cavusgil (eds) (3rd edn). Oxford: Pergamon.

42. Palia, Aspy P. and Charles F. Keown (1991), 'Combating Parallel Importing: Views of Us Exporters to the Asia-Pacific Region', *International Marketing Review*, 8 (1), 47–56.

43. Weigand, Robert E. (1991), 'Parallel Import Channels: Options for Preserving Territorial Integrity', *Columbia Journal of World Business*, 26 (1), 53–60.

44. Tan, Soo J., Guan H. Lim and Khai S. Lee (1997), 'Strategic Responses to Parallel Importing', *Journal of Global Marketing*, 10 (4), 45–66.

45. Myers, Matthew B. (1999), 'Incidents of Grey Market Activity among U.S. Exporters: Occurrences, Characteristics and Consequences', *Journal of International Business Studies*, 30 (1), 105–26.

46. Clarke, Irvine III and Margaret Owens (2000), 'Trademark Rights in Gray Markets', *International Marketing Review*, 17 (3), 272–86.

47. Gough, Neil (2003), 'Zombie Discs: Retail Companies and Retailers Dump Them on Scrap Dealers, but Unwanted "Saw-Gash" Music Cds Find a Ready Market in China', *Time Asia*, 161 (4), www.time.com/time/magazine/article/0,9171,409647,00.html.

48. Green, Robert T. and Tasman Smith (2002), 'Executive Insights: Countering Brand Counterfeiters', *Journal of International Marketing*, 10 (4), 89–106.

49. Motion Picture Association of America (MPAA) (2005), '2005 U.S. Piracy Fact Sheet', www.mpaa.org/USPiracyFactSheet.pdf.

50. Walls, W. D. (2008), 'Cross-Country Analysis of Movie Piracy', *Applied Economics*, 40 (5), 625–32.

51. Shanahan, Kevin J. and Michael R. Hyman (2010), 'Motivators and enablers of SCOURing: A study of online piracy in the US and UK', *Journal of Business Research*, 63 (9–10), 1095–1102.

52. Leeds, Jeff (2008), 'Nine Inch Nails Fashions Innovative Web Pricing Plan', *The New York Times*.

53. Tyrangiel, Josh (2007), 'Radiohead Says: Pay What You Want', *Time*, 1 October.

54. Chaudry, Peggy E. and Michael J. Walsh (1995), 'Managing the Gray Market in the European Union: The Case of the Pharmaceutical Industry', *Journal of International Marketing*, 3 (3), 11–33.

55. Cavusgil, S. Tamer and Ed Sikora (1988), 'How Multinationals Can Counter Grey Market Imports', *Columbia Journal of World Business*, 23 (4), 75–85.

56. Ibison, David (2001), 'Weak Euro Lets Top Car Dealers Go Far in Japan: Parallel Imports Luxury Prices Cut', *Financial Times*, 10 (January), 13.

57. Euromonitor (2011), 'Internet Retailing Blazing Growth Path', Available at: http://www.euromonitor.com/internet-retailing-blazing-growth-path/report.

58. Baker, Walter, Mike Marn and Craig Zawada (2001), 'Price Smarter on the Net', *Harvard Business Review*, 79 (2), 122–7.

59. Porter, Michael E. (2001), 'Strategy and the Internet', *Harvard Business Review*, 79 (3), 63–78.

60. Ancarani, Fabio (2002), 'Pricing and the Internet: Frictionless Commerce or Pricer's Paradise', *European Management Journal*, 20 (6), 680–87.

61. Aalto-Setälä, Ville (2002), 'The Effect of Concentration and Market Power on Food Prices: Evidence from Finland', *Journal of Retailing*, 78 (3), 207–16.

62. Cateora, Philip R. (1983), *International Marketing* (5th edn). Homewood, IL: Richard D. Irwin.

63. DeMarco, C. W. (2001), 'Knee Deep in Technique: The Ethics of Monopoly Capital', *Journal of Business Ethics*, 31 (2), 151–64.

64. Abegglen, James and George Stalk Jr (1986), 'The Japanese Corporation as Competitor', *California Management Review*, 28 (3), 9–27.

65. Tsurumi, Yoshi and Hiroki Tsurumi (1999), 'Fujifilm–Kodak Duopolistic Competition in Japan and the United States', *Journal of International Business Studies*, 30 (4), 813–30.

66. Von Stackelberg, H. (1940), *Die Grundlagen Der Nationalökonomie*. Berlin: Springer Verlag.

67. Verna, Gérard (1989), 'Fausses Facturations et Commerce International', *Harvard-l'Expansion*, 52 (Spring), 110–20.

Appendix 10

Teaching materials

A10.1 Case

Saito Importing Company

Some years ago, Saito Importing Company, located in California, US, brought in a shipment of wood carvings from Bali, Indonesia. At the time, the official exchange rate was 78 Indonesian rupias per US dollar. The 'black market' rate (as viewed by the Indonesian government), or 'free market' rate (as viewed by most of the rest of the world), was approximately 1300 Indonesian rupias per US dollar.

The seller requested a letter of credit for one-half the value of the shipment, to be provided by a US bank and confirmed by an Indonesian bank, and stipulated that the balance be wired to a New York bank account.

Obviously, the 'half' that was received in New York had many times the value of that received in Indonesia. The money in the bank account in New York was available for the seller to invest, to purchase goods for shipment to Indonesia or elsewhere, or to use if leaving Indonesia. Money held in Indonesia at that time could be used for such purposes only with the approval of the government. What the Indonesian exporter did was, of course, illegal under Indonesian law.

Saito Importing Company did not receive the goods until over a year later. Since Bali does not have a port which will accommodate ocean-going vessels, the letter of credit specified that transhipment was allowed. In the process of transhipment, the goods travelled around much of the world and were delayed while waiting for on-going vessels at points of transhipment.

When the wood carvings finally arrived in the US, Saito Importing Company declared the actual price paid for the goods, and indicated to customs why there was a discrepancy between purchase price and the value shown on the documents. The American company did not do anything illegal under US law.

(Source: Duerr, p. 310.[1] Reproduced with kind permission from *International Marketing and Export Management*, Mitsuko Saito Duerr, Pearson Education Limited, © Pearson Education Limited 1989.)

Questions

1. Should the US company have refused to agree to make the payments as requested by the Indonesian exporter? What would have been the expected effect on the Indonesian exporter's price?

2. What effects would you expect the unrealistic official exchange rates had on Indonesian exports?

A10.2 Case

Riva International

Françoise Gain, the *directrice du marketing* at Riva in Brussels, Belgium, received astonishing results from the consumer panels and distributor panels for September and October 2012. It appeared that sales in Belgium and France of one of its main products, the Nutrifying Complex Crème Riva, were 20 per cent lower than the production level in the Belgian factory, which supplied both markets. No signs of excess inventories in the distribution in France or Belgium were noticed by the sales force during visits to the distributors.

Riva Belgium was the subsidiary of Riva Products Corporation, a large US-based multi-national, whose main business lines were related to the cosmetics and beauty care industry. The Belgian subsidiary was in charge of both the French and the Belgian markets. In 2007, a scientific breakthrough by the corporate R&D laboratories had led to the development of a new skincare cream. Several patents had been filed and registered to protect the property. In Europe the industrial use of these patents had been licensed to Riva Belgium, which began producing and selling the new skincare cream in February 2009. Sales increased quickly, and Belgian and French consumers received the new product, liking both its efficiency and good price–quality ratio. Following instructions from international headquarters, the output of Riva Belgium was intended exclusively for supplying the Belgian and French markets as well as the markets of French-speaking Africa.

In January 2012, the English subsidiary of Riva, UK Riva Ltd, started producing the same Nutrifying Complex Crème product. Hefty investments had been made in the English factory to ensure the best quality and a large production capacity. This product had been launched at the top end of the market for skincare cream. It was priced high and supported by heavy advertising and promotional expenses. After a promising start, deliveries had been falling off since August 2012. Actual deliveries to English distributors steadily diverged from target sales.

Françoise Gain knew about this situation as she had been engaged as an internal consultant in the launch of Nutrifying Complex Crème Riva in the United Kingdom. However, what worried her most in November 2012 was the gap between sales to consumers in France and Belgium and ex-works shipments. She informed Jacques Graff, chief executive of Riva Belgium and a member of the international board.

At first he did not seem to be bothered by such a gap, and showed little interest in the issue: 'Françoise, you know: panel data, what does it mean really? Our product sells well and that is all that matters! Tell your panel company to reconsider their samples and their data collection procedures, and you will see that everything is in fact normal.'

Françoise Gain nevertheless took the decision to undertake an audit by an external consultant. His findings exactly confirmed those of the panels and brought evidence of no sizeable excess inventory at the distribution level. It followed from the auditor's investigations that deviations were ascribed mostly to deliveries to two large wholesalers, which ranked among the five largest customers of Riva Belgium.

One month after his talks with Françoise Gain, Graff received a confidential note, issued by the chief executive of UK Riva Ltd. It stated that a member of his sales force had accidentally seen, at an English wholesaler, a carton containing Nutrifying Complex Crème Riva with country-of-origin label 'Made in Belgium'. The wholesaler had been evasive if not reluctant to tell the sales representative where it came from. Jacques Graff asked Françoise Gain to come to his office, and handed her the note without comment.

'I am not surprised by this note', answered Françoise. 'On the contrary, it is evidence for my suspicions about parallel imports of our Belgian products to England. I have noticed that the sales figures that vanished from Belgium and France precisely equalled the drop in deliveries of UK Riva Ltd. It is now quite clear that some of our wholesalers export to English distributors and that, before doing this, they do not warn our sales and marketing group. I examined the cost structure of UK Riva production and found that our product made in Belgium could be sold by Belgian wholesalers to English distributors at a profit. Belgian distributors may price it at 15 per cent below the English list price, even though there are transport costs.'

'How is that possible?' asked Graff, amazed.

'The English Nutrifying Complex Crème Riva was launched with heavy production and promotion costs', explained Françoise Gain. 'It is positioned at the high end of the market. It is priced higher than any of the competing products. I told them, before the launch, that this retail price level was too high. They disapproved. The finance department at UK Riva Ltd wanted a quick return on investment, taking into account the large cash outflows at the start. The marketing people, backed by the advertising agency, claimed the opportunity to seize a segment which was at the very top end of the market and which had been, up to then, neglected by competitors. Consequently my opinion was put aside.'

Jacques Graff started to pace back and forth. 'As a chief executive of the Belgian subsidiary, I am delighted. Our plant works at full capacity. But, as a member of the international board, I cannot let the English subsidiary plunge. What can we do?'

'One thing is certain', answered Françoise Gain. 'We cannot prevent our customers, namely independent wholesalers, from exporting to England if they wish to do so. As for the English distributors, one cannot blame them for seizing a better-priced offer and simultaneously taking advantage of the promotional effort of UK Riva! I know it is more easily said than done, but you should have defined, a long time ago, an international pricing strategy at the international board level.'

'It is never too late to do the right thing! Françoise, please prepare a report on your suggestions to cope with this parallel import problem of Nutrifying Complex Crème Riva', said Graff in conclusion.

Questions

1. What are the reasons for these parallel import problems?

2. What can be done to stop wholesalers exporting to the UK?

3. Is it necessary to change the marketing strategy of Nutrifying Complex Crème Riva, particularly its price? If so, where and how should it be implemented?

4. How should one organize a coordinated international marketing strategy across national markets? Prepare the report requested by Graff.

(Source: Adapted from a case written by Alain Ollivier, Ecole Supérieure de Commerce de Paris.)

A10.3 Case

Taman SA

At Taman SA, a Spanish company, orders systematically exceed production. Is this a result of the marketing and sales department's expertise, the lack of production capacity, or the inability of the production department to plan demand peaks effectively? Nobody knows the exact answer.

To tell the truth, one should excuse both the production department and the sales department. The market for high-technology products, in which Taman has built a strong European share, is growing rapidly, at about 50 per cent per year. Taman's competitors face similar problems.

In spite of a rather elaborate cost accounting system, accountants may endlessly argue about the real direct and total cost price of a given order. Diverse and changing factors tend to blur the calculation of costs, such as the allocation of R&D expenses, the cost of components, shared expenses between different orders, the price–volume relation, etc.

The director of marketing and sales and the director of production and operations are constantly in conflict. Conflicts focus on such cases as that of Magnusson AB. Magnusson AB is a new customer from whom Taman has never, up to now, received an order. Following technical tests of Taman products by Magnusson people at their factory, and after a successful certification procedure, Magnusson is ready to place a fairly large order.

The marketing and sales director argues that getting a new client is something you have to pay for. The director of production and operations considers that the largely positive margin that this order brings is smaller than that of other orders. Besides, he fears that it could disturb the production schedule for the coming weeks and consequently that it could result in numerous delivery delays.

Question

Describe this problem in about 30 lines. What ways and means would you suggest to these two directors for solving their conflict and/or serving their customer base better?

A10.4 Case

AIDS – Global ethics and the pricing of AIDS drugs

The text for this case is located on the book's website (**www.pearsoned.co.uk/usunierlee**) in Chapter 10.

Appendix reference

1. Duerr, Mitsuko Saito (1989), *International Marketing and Export Management*, Gerald Albaum, Jesper Strandskov, Edwin Duerr and Lawrence Dowd (eds). Reading, MA: Addison-Wesley.

11

International distribution and sales promotion

This chapter considers two of the three elements of the marketing mix that help 'push' the product towards the consumer (the third being personal selling, covered in Chapter 14). There is no doubt that in today's business climate getting the right product to the right place at the right time is crucial to success. The primary focus of this chapter is to examine distribution from a cross-cultural perspective, beginning with the choice of distribution channel (Section 11.1), and the role of distribution as a 'cultural filter' (Section 11.2). Section 11.3 relates to the considerable expansion of direct marketing worldwide; it explains how catalogues and direct marketing tools (including information on the Internet) must be adapted for cross-border use. The final section of this chapter (Section 11.4) examines the range of techniques that fall under the sales promotions umbrella. These actions are usually designed to create short-term interest or sales, and are most often in the form of price discounts, bonuses, rebates, coupons, contests, and samples. Sales promotion has developed a number of techniques, which have been well documented. Although this whole range of techniques is known in most countries, there is wide variation in their degree of local legitimacy and legal acceptance.

11.1

Criteria for choosing foreign distribution channels

The decision to choose one distribution mechanism over another when entering a foreign market comes down to finding an acceptable balance of control versus risk. Dawson[1] outlines five basic ways in which a retailer can enter a foreign market:

1. *Internal expansion.* This involves the firm opening their own store/s within the foreign markets. This has the advantage of high control and a relatively low risk; however, it requires a very strong understanding of the market, and can take a long time to build a presence (see Box 11.1 for an examination of the success that Burberry has, using internal expansion). This strategy is most vividly demonstrated by the 'flagship' method of retailing, which is prevalent in the luxury fashion market, when a firm opens a 'showcase' store as an attraction (e.g., the Louis Vuitton flagship store in South Korea is promoted by the Korea Tourism Organization), rather than simply being a retail outlet. Louis Vuitton is one of the most successful proponents of the flagship method, with 13 flagship stores located in various fashion capitals, such as London, Paris, New York, Tokyo, Hong Kong and Sydney. These stores often project exclusivity, with private invitation only shopping suites and publicity generating fashion shows. The major advantage of the internal expansion method is that it enables strict and total control over the brand within country.

2. *Merger or takeover of a host country firm.* This strategy is essentially buying existing retailers in the host country and rebranding them, which allows quick and substantial access to the market with a structure already in place. US retail giant Walmart (previously branded as Wal-Mart) used

Box 11.1

Burberry international distribution success

Burberry (est. 1856), a British luxury fashion brand, is currently rated as one of the most valuable fashion brands in the world. However, only a decade and a half ago Burberry was facing dramatic declines in sales and consumer sentiment. They were operating under relatively haphazard wholesaling, retailing and licensing arrangements, which resulted in inconsistencies in the image of the brand at the different levels of distribution in which they operated. Burberry in essence discovered that the degree of difficulty associated with managing a global brand was difficult enough, without having retailers, franchisees and wholesalers putting out different or even contrary messages. In light of this, management reconfigured the distribution network, at great expense, including buying back distribution licences. This resulted in a strictly controlled, four-tier approach to retailing, which is the foundation for their current success:

1. Burberry own and operate 11 flagship stores in their major fashion markets, including London, Beijing, New York City, Milan and Sydney.

These serve the dual role of retailing and public relations, as they are often host to fashion shows and generate significant attention in the fashion media.

2. They own and operate 174 stand-alone regular price stores, typically located in affluent areas and carrying the full Burberry range.

3. Burberry directly operates 199 concession stores within major upmarket department stores, such as Neiman Marcus. Although these concessions carry a reduced range, they serve the important purpose of servicing the department store-oriented shoppers of the US and Europe.

4. They own 44 outlet stores, which serve as a way to maintain control over out-of-season merchandise, while still allowing it to be sold off effectively.

By maintaining strict internal control over their retail network, Burberry is able to dictate the placement of their brand and keep a consistent, and clearly successful, global image.

(Source: Based on Burberry 2010–2011 annual report;[3] Moore.[4])

---

this method successfully in countries, such as the United Kingdom, where it bought the then third biggest retailer ASDA, giving Walmart instant access to the market through an established brand name (later co-branded), which shared strategic synergies with Wal-Mart. However, this is a costly and risky: Walmart also experienced a spectacular failure in Germany using the same method.

3. *Franchising.* This strategy involves granting local groups or entrepreneurs the right to market a company's products within a certain location. Franchising allows the home firm to enter a country at a relatively low cost, with the risk shared with the franchisee. The use of local franchisees gains the firm access to local knowledge, as well as some commitment from locals to do what they can to help the firm succeed. However, franchisees must be carefully chosen as strong ambassadors of the firm, and the individuals involved are crucial

to the overall success. For example, according to Inter IKEA's website (the owner and worldwide franchisor of the IKEA concept), they assess potential franchisees on the basis of: '1) thorough retail experience, 2) extensive local market knowledge and presence; 3) corporate culture and values; and 4) financial strength and ability to carry through the investment, penetrating a country in full and in a large-scale retail environment format.'

4. *Joint ventures.* This strategy can take a wide variety of forms, but always involves some aspect of joint operations, be it retailing, promotions or technology sharing. Ideally the choice of joint venture partner is a strategic one, taking into account the firms strategic goals, resources, and capabilities. Research suggests that firms with less international experience, less R&D capabilities, and a higher need for complementary assets are more likely to choose a joint venture strategy over internal

expansion.[2] Many emerging economies have fairly strict regulations limiting direct foreign investment, which make joint ventures an attractive alternative (e.g., India, with alliances between firms, such as Tata Motors with Fiat, Mahindra with Renault, Bharthi with Walmart, and Modi with Xerox).

5. *Non-controlling interest in a host country firm.* This strategy is a relatively passive entry into a market that is a way of gaining the in-depth knowledge and experience necessary to be successful in a market without taking on direct responsibility. For instance, Walmart obtained non-controlling interest in yihaodian.com in order to get a foothold into the difficult Chinese online retailing sector.

Decisions about which of these strategies is more appropriate should be based on many factors both inside (e.g., ethnocentric versus geocentric perspectives) and outside a firm (e.g., market potential versus infrastructure), in terms of other companies and relationships.[5,6] However, a survey of Canadian firms with export sales, found that 63 per cent simply used the same channel as in their home market.[7] Nonetheless, firms should evaluate alternatives fully before extending their activities into a new market, because what worked in a firm's home country will not necessarily work in a new market. For instance, in 2008 Starbucks closed 61 of its 84 stores in Australia, after rapid internal expansion in a very competitive and mature café market that clearly favoured franchising.[8]

One method for strategically selecting channels abroad is based on a checklist of issues that have to be dealt with, prior to the choice of foreign distribution channels.[9,10] The '9-Cs' criteria as it is known, provides a holistic framework from which to assess foreign channel viability. The 9-Cs are as follows:

1. *Consumers and their characteristics.* Some geographical segments in a foreign market may be more import oriented. Channels serving these segments should be preferred. For example, the French beer Kronenbourg entered the US and was initially available only in the centre of New York City, then expanded to the whole metropolis including the suburbs. People within the centre of NYC consume large quantities of imported, as well as US, beer so they were seen as an easier entry target. Five years, later Kronenbourg became

available throughout the US. Regional roll-outs can be chosen on the basis of cultural similarity or focusing on countries with low uncertainty avoidance.[11] Groups of countries may also differ in their preference for certain retail functions.[12] For instance, one of the consequences of long-term orientation is being sparing with resources. This leads to a preference for self-serve merchandise and may lead to lower acceptability of e-commerce.

2. *Culture.* Distribution is the element of the marketing mix most deeply rooted in culture, because it is closely related to everyday life and human relationships (even in large-scale, self-service, apparently depersonalized stores). For instance, Griffith[13] studied the meanings of the market bazaar in Amman, Jordan. He found that the ties to culture and self-identification were so strong that this created a barrier to newer distribution techniques.

3. *Character.* It is important that the image projected by the channel, its sales methods, shop locations and clientele, should correspond to the image and character that the product is intended to convey. The success of Louis Vuitton Malletier is based on the large-scale investment in a global network of exclusive retail outlets, located in high-profile areas in major cities throughout the world. However, local consumers may also remain faithful to their traditional distribution outlets for specific segments of consumption. In Spain, despite the continuous development of hypermarkets, consumers make a clear distinction and prefer to purchase perishable goods such as fish, fresh fruit and vegetables, meat and bread in traditional stores.[14]

4. Necessary *capital* relates to the issue of the financial resources that are necessary to start and maintain a channel (e.g., fixed capital, working capital, possible initial losses will need to be financed).

5. *Cost.* This criterion is strongly linked to capital, but relates more to trade margins than to overhead costs. It depends largely on the respective positions in relation to the strength of producers and distributors. In the UK, for instance, food distribution is in the hands of a very limited number of large store chains, such as Tesco, Sainsbury and Walmart-Asda.[15] These giants exert pressure on

major manufacturers to bear part of the costs, particularly those relating to storage. They request small, frequent deliveries with mixed items. A similar situation exists in France where the powerful hypermarkets impose constraints on producers, which increase their overheads. For instance, they often impose payments of fixed commissions in return for the right to carry the brand. They may also require the producer's own staff to design the layout of the displays and assist with sales promotions, etc.

6. *Competition* arises in channels either through competing products being placed side by side on shelves, or through competitors refusing other producers access to the distribution channels. For instance, American manufacturers of caustic soda (used in the manufacture of glass, steel and chemical products), were incapable of successfully entering into the Japanese market despite their price advantage.[16] The Japanese union of caustic soda manufacturers formed a cartel that apparently set the level of imports, specified which trading company was to work with which American supplier and bought up the cheap American imports in order to sell them with the assistance of its members. The success of the operation was twofold. They received the profit in place of the American exporter and still managed to keep control of their market. The American exporters were also unsuccessful in their attempts to deal directly through small distributors, since the industrial users of the product were concerned about the risk of isolating themselves from their main source of supply (the Japanese) if they ordered directly from American exporters. This illustrates the power of competition, which is likely to differ across cultures, as it is often related to the concentration of retailers. For instance, in Australia two department stores account for 82 per cent of the market, while in the US the top five account for 65 per cent, whereas in Japan the top three only account for 32 per cent.[17,18] When large retail groups hold more power in the channel it often leads to higher prices.

7. *Coverage* is another significant consideration. It is important to cover markets, many of which may be widely scattered. Markets that are very concentrated also tend to concentrate competition, since

demand attracts supply. The coverage decisions, in terms of product range, size and options must also be considered, especially when channel members look for complementary products, spare parts and so on. Product coverage varies across countries according to channel type. For instance, a French *droguerie* does not sell the same products as a US *drugstore* or a German *Drogerie*, or an Australian *pharmacy*, although there is overlap between product ranges.

8. *Continuity*. It is vital that the chosen channels do not turn out to be unusable for some reason (e.g., bankruptcy or financial difficulties, recapture of market share by more aggressive competition, introduction of legal prohibitions on sale of products through the channel, etc.). Continuity may be hampered by seasoned competitors, who persuade distributors to lock out the newcomer. Threats to continuity makes initial channel choice that much more important.

9. *Control*. The ideal situation may be one in which the company creates its own distribution network. This ensures maximum control. Large companies should consider integrating their own distribution abroad, particularly when the product differentiation is large (i.e., where there are few substitutes) or where the network assets are transaction specific, such as a product which requires lengthy training for the consumer as well as the seller.[19] Another alternative is to control by equity, via a carefully drafted contract (the written base; lower context cultures), or preferably through long-established trusting relationships with the local distributor (personal verbal base; higher context cultures). For example, Caterpillar sells worldwide without sales subsidiary companies, by using a dealership system. Some Caterpillar dealers have been in business for more than half a century. If ownership is not practical, control of marketing may be maintained through a hybrid channel strategy, where sales and distribution are managed by foreign channels, but sales promotion is managed by the producer.[20] This is the most favoured option in the personal computer industry in Europe.[20]

Box 11.2 applies the 9-Cs to Starbucks in Australia, as an illustration.

Box 11.2

Starbucks versus the 9-Cs in Australia

1. *Consumers and their characteristics.* When Starbucks surveyed the café market in Australia they should have seen a consumer preference for individually owned local boutiques, with personalized service, as opposed to giant, foreign chain restaurants. Failure to recognize this meant that Starbucks severely misjudged the culture, and in fact positioned themselves in the market against the prevailing consumer sentiment.

2. *Culture.* While the US and Australia are culturally similar in some ways (e.g., high individualism and masculinity), there are some important differences, Australians tend to resent overconfidence and arrogance (tall poppy syndrome), which Starbucks demonstrated when they opened a large number of stores rapidly and aggressively took on the local market.

3. *Character.* While the image of Starbucks as a prestigious 'coffee experience' may be projected similarly across many countries, this cannot be taken as a given. Australia already had a well-established, high-quality café culture. Unfortunately for Starbucks, their coffee was not perceived as being of higher quality. Further, they decided not to advertise, assuming that Starbucks would be already known. They quickly became viewed as an American brand bully, with overpriced and low-quality service and products.

4. *Capital.* Starbucks clearly had the necessary capital to launch in several cities in Australia in a short period of time, and to this day continue to use the US base to support the small number of remaining Australian stores. 'The chain, which has accumulated losses of $204 million in Australia since opening its first store here in 2000, conceded that it was only able to continue as a going concern because of the financial support of parent Starbucks Corporation.'[21]

5. *Cost.* Starbucks opened themselves up to undue costs by managing all of their new Australian stores internally, rather than allying with a local firm with local knowledge, or by franchising out to local entrepreneurs who would have been invested in their stores success. Additionally, high inner-city rents, and very high labour costs meant that it was always going to be more difficult for Starbucks stores to turn a profit.

6. *Competition.* While Starbucks is the clear market leader in its home country, it entered an Australian market with already extremely heavy competition and low profit margins. With several successful chains offering comparable convenience service experiences (e.g., Gloria Jeans, Coffee Club) and thousands of independent retailers offering high-quality products, Starbucks entered a mature market that didn't have an open niche for them.

7. *Coverage.* Starbucks entered into highly concentrated population areas, with many substitute products available. While they offered a larger range of coffees than most local cafés, they did not actually offer coffees that the local customers favoured.

8. *Continuity.* The closure of over 60 of their 87 stores demonstrates the lack of continuity, with store closures completely removing the brand from major markets such as Adelaide, the Gold Coast, Canberra and Tasmania.

9. *Control.* Starbucks certainly maintained strict control over their Australian venture. Branding, training and marketing were all supported and managed by the US arm of the company. Starbucks said the decision to close the 'underperforming' stores was made 'to concentrate its attention and resources on profitable growth, operational efficiencies and an enhanced experience for customers and partners globally'.

(Sources: Patterson, Scott and Uncles;[8] Emerson and Tibbitts;[22] Speedy.[21])

11.2

Role of distribution as a 'cultural filter'

Culture at the interface between shoppers and stores

Distribution channels form subtle relationships with consumers through direct contact. People get into the habit of buying certain products, which are backed by fixed services, at clearly defined times, in particular shops. Table 11.1 presents guidelines for exploring how distribution is affected by the prevailing cultural patterns in a country or culture context. The table refers to specific sections in other chapters, where some of the underlying rationales have already been discussed. Naturally, culture explains only part of the variance in distribution systems; the prevailing socioeconomic and macro-economic factors also play a major role.

Shopping behaviour differs in many ways according to culture. The first point to consider is whether the shopping experience is a cost or benefit. Is it viewed as a cost in terms of using precious time (strong economic view), or as a benefit in terms of the whole shopping experience. The differences in opening hours in northern and southern Europe clearly illustrate the influence of culture on the distribution system. In northern Europe Sunday is sacred and a prevailing

feminine orientation strives towards protecting store employee quality of life (which would be spoilt by long opening hours). Product scarcities can also influence the utility of the shopping experience. For instance, in Eastern Europe people seem less concerned about the shopping environment, than in Western countries.[23] Similarly, Chilean consumers mostly focus on the utilitarian aspect of making purchases, whereas US consumers are more likely to visit malls for the hedonistic purpose of social interaction.[24] The Chinese government has recently encouraged consumers to engage in shopping for leisure, in an attempt to replicate the consumer demand levels previously seen in the US. Aspects of culture also influence store loyalty. For instance, consumers are, on average, more loyal if they come from a strong uncertainty avoidance or collectivist culture, or if they are male.[25]

Religious or social beliefs may lead to some products being legally banned from particular outlets. For instance, in France basic drugs, and more generally used drugs, such as aspirin, can be sold only through pharmacies; in the US, as in many countries, drugstores sell basic medicines. These practices correspond to differing views on whether people can be trusted to self-medicate. French legislators do not trust patients and require them to proceed through doctors and pharmacists, whereas the US system assumes people can distinguish between common

Table 11.1 Influence of culture on some aspects of distribution *vis-à-vis* shoppers

Selected aspects of distribution	Traits that *may* differ according to country/culture
(1) Shopping behaviour	Is time spent shopping experienced as wasted? (economic time; Chapter 2) Is return of goods standard behaviour? (complaining behaviour; Chapter 5) Who is the shopper? (gender roles, age, etc.; Chapter 2) Degree of loyalty to the shop and the shopkeeper (Chapter 5)
(2) Opening hours	Religion-based arguments in favour of restricted opening hours; Femininity-based arguments (store personnel should not be exploited) (Chapter 3)
(3) Product range	Products may be banned because of religious or legal prescriptions
(4) Willingness to service consumers	Human nature is good (friendliness towards shoppers) versus bad (indifference)/negative view of service to others (Chapter 2)
(5) Waiting lines	Compliance with rules (Chapter 3)
(6) Thefts by consumers or personnel	Ethical behaviour – ingroup orientation (Chapters 2 and 3)
(7) Self-service versus personnel in contact	See service attributes (Section 9.3)

ailments and serious afflictions. Another example concerns the distribution of beer in Turkey, a Muslim country. Prior to June 1984, beer was considered a non-alcoholic beverage and sold in coffee-houses. When beer consumption increased sixfold between 1969 and 1983, religious authorities placed pressure on the government to reclassify beer as an alcoholic beverage (which it undeniably is). Beer was banned from being advertised on radio and television and its sale was prohibited in outlets that did not have the required permit to sell alcohol. Prohibiting the sale of this beverage in coffee-houses resulted in a dramatic drop in beer sales in Turkey.[26] Similarly, in the US the sale of liquor is restricted to state-owned stores in some states; the most restrictive being Utah with its large Mormon population.

Wide differences also exist in perceptions of waiting and service. In the US and Japan it is standard practice in supermarkets for staff at cash registers to help customers pack their purchases. In many cases an employee is specifically assigned to packing and often offer to help get your groceries to the car. In most of Europe, where mass distribution is oriented towards low price rather than service, customers pack their things as they pay. Wal-Mart discovered that they had dramatically misunderstood existing perceptions of service when they entered the German market. By using 'excellent customer service' as a point of differentiation, Wal-Mart failed to realize that this ran counter to the German retail personality. In fact, the helpful clerks were viewed as intruding on the shoppers personal space, and the door greeters were often mistaken for strangers harassing the customers.[27,28]

Theft by customers or store employees is also an important consideration in distribution, which is likely to differ on a country by country basis. Naturally, economic constraints (purchasing power per capita) play a certain role, but they do not explain everything. For instance, in France and Italy theft is more common than in Greece, which has lower per capita income. In some countries theft is not a problem, because it is clearly understood as evil by everybody. The kind of consensus which brings about this result is hard to explain, and probably even harder to replicate. Where the rate of theft to sales amounts to several per cent, it cannot be explained simply by poverty. Theft is regarded by some as a sport and is implicitly understood as a legitimate way of social redistribution. Another explanation is strong ingroup orientation in which ethical behaviour is limited to the ingroup. For instance, in countries where retailers are immigrants belonging to a particular foreign group, shoplifting in these stores may not be considered to be evil, but rather as recovering one's own goods from the outsider. Theft may also be situation specific, as in the case of illegally downloading digital music and video via the Internet. Generally, taking a music CD from a store would be considered stealing, while, in contrast, downloading the same CD illegally off the Internet is considered acceptable by many. The only difference is in the method of obtaining the product rather than the principle.

Website link 11.1

Search for the most pirated video games: http://torrentfreak.com/top-10-most-pirated-games-of-2011-111230/.

Influence of culture on relationship between channel members

The relationships between domestic producers and distributors may be stronger, more loyal and collaborative, or weaker, more unstable and conflictual, depending on the country. Strongly established links between members of domestic channels generally make entry more difficult for foreign firms. The French invented the concept of the hypermarket and benefit from a distribution set-up that is effective, powerful and strongly independent of producers. It is so strong that products bearing the store name compete head to head with producer brands, creating an atmosphere of conflict between producers and distributors, where loyalty is difficult to maintain. The system is inherently susceptible to penetration by imports, as foreign suppliers are perceived as more flexible and a good alternative to domestic producers. At the other extreme, Japan is the place where links between producers and distributors are traditionally very strong and positive. Central to this are the *keiretsus* of distribution, true vertical relationships, mixing business and emotion in typically Japanese fashion. These networks are based on a powerful sense of loyalty, with many services being rendered by one party for the other, and therefore more difficult for foreign companies to penetrate. This is influenced by a long-term orientation, which positively affects distributor commitment.[29] It is also influenced by the focus on interdependence rather than dependence, discussed in Chapter 3. Stronger performance of Western importers has also been linked to higher levels of interdependence, investment, relational norms and trust.[30]

Kale and McIntyre[31] posit a series of hypotheses on channel relationships based on Hofstede's[32] four cultural dimensions. First, during the initiation phase, companies from high uncertainty avoidance (UA) societies will be biased in favour of finding partners with solid reputations and who can offer written performance guarantees. Conversely, in the case of weak UA, partners will be sought more informally, and more flexibility will be shown in negotiations. In addition, firms in highly individualist and masculine cultures (e.g., the US) will tend to choose partners on objective criteria, negotiate the terms of the agreement from an adversarial standpoint, and engage in new relationships as well as relinquish old ones on the basis of economic criteria. Conversely, partners from collectivist and relatively feminine societies (e.g., South Korea, Taiwan, Thailand) will be more relationship centred and will expect more harmony in the partnership, and dissolution will be less aggressive and less frequent. Next, during the implementation phase, high power distance (PD) will lead firms to use coercion in their influence attempts, whereas low PD firms will avoid coercion, prefer face-to-face communication to memos and engage in consultative rather than unilateral decision making.[31] High individualism and masculinity will result in more frequent and manifest conflicts between channel members, as well as lower levels of cooperation. It is, therefore, important to manage cross-cultural communication differences. This is illustrated by a senior Coca-Cola executive in Japan explaining that: 'Once the partnership was in place, it wasn't just the Coca-Cola company selling in Japan; it became a family, a spirit of togetherness, of common purpose.'[31]

Relationship elements also affect direct selling effectiveness (e.g., Amway), but they are more important and coherent in collectivist countries, such as China, than in Western countries, such as Australia.[33] Even firms who establish distribution relationships in similar countries will experience different value systems. For instance, Canadian retailers have to face different values when they enter the nearby US market. Americans are significantly more competition-oriented (i.e., more achievement oriented, more risk

taking) and more oriented towards a Protestant work ethic than Canadians. Canadian retailers are less individualistic and masculine and higher in power distance and risk avoidance than American distributors.[34] These findings are largely consistent with the Kale and McIntyre's[31] hypotheses in distinguishing competitive/confrontational distribution scenes from collaborative scenes: 'The executives frequently commented that Americans were found to be much more competitive than Canadians. Frequently the executives voiced comments typically used to describe battles, such as "It was all out war" or "Their arsenal was impressive"' (p. 8).[34]

Conflict is more likely when channel members belong to different cultures and are separated by cultural distance. However, high-quality support systems, including frequent visits, tend to reduce decrease this conflict.[35] In addition, a large expatriate population may help to smooth the process. In the case of Greek exporters (collectivist/high UA and PD) and their British importers (individualistic/low UA and PD), relationships are fairly stable with a low degree of conflict and few communication issues, except on pricing issues.[36] This is reinforced by the fact that, among the British importers, there are a good number of Greeks or Cypriots.

There is also evidence that leadership styles are not transferable across cultures. For instance, in the US a supportive leadership style leads to higher cooperation and reduced conflict between channel partners, followed by a participative and directive style. So, a channel leader who is clear about expectations, goals and requirements might expect less conflict from their channel members. In Finland the participative style leads to the most cooperation, and the greatest reduction in conflict, followed by supportive and directive leadership styles. Finally, in Poland a supportive leadership style is positively related to cooperation, while a directive style is negatively related to cooperation. In Poland the directive style may be too closely related to the previous Communist system.[37,38]

11.3

Direct marketing and the Internet

As mentioned, Jean-Claude is one in several million direct marketing purchasers who annually buys a Christmas cake (a Deluxe medium, $2\frac{3}{4}$ pounds) from

Collin Street Bakery in Corsicana, Texas. The product is baked following the traditional recipe of Gus Weidman, a Bavarian who immigrated to the United States at the end of the nineteenth century. Jean-Claude buys it by credit card and it is delivered to his home in Switzerland within a month. This is just one simple example of worldwide direct marketing. Lands' End, one of the leading US direct marketers worldwide, sends its products to more than 170 countries, while large European mail-order companies such as Otto Versand, Quelle, Bertelsmann and La Redoute have developed important cross-border operations, especially in Europe. The development of international credit cards and the consequent facilitation of international payment have greatly decreased the transaction costs for both consumers and cataloguers. Restricted opening hours for stores may be an incentive for consumers to buy direct: Germany and Austria, two countries where store opening hours have been historically strictly limited in comparison to other developed countries, are strong direct marketing sales per capita.

Direct marketing increasingly uses the Internet as a global medium. Many companies (e.g., Urban Outfitters) use their website to provide detailed product information, along with the ability to make online purchases. Some companies are entirely Internet based, with no bricks-and-mortar shopfronts at all. Amazon.com is perhaps the most widely recognized of these companies. Amazon started as an online bookstore and is now more like an online *everything* store which will deliver almost anything around the world. Lands' End, like many other direct mail companies, has a website from which anything in the catalogue can be ordered fast and efficiently with the click of a keyboard. 3M's website sells products, and provides access to detailed information on its products and worldwide operations.

Website link 11.2

Make your own *Marketing Across Cultures* T-shirt on Zazzle: http://www.zazzle.com.

The concept of mass-customization and user-designed content has flourished on the Internet. One example of this is Zazzle.com, a website that allows its users to create their own merchandise (e.g., posters, clothing, mugs, etc.) or buy merchandise created by others. Content creators receive a commission for every one of their items sold, which naturally encourages them to get more people to buy, effectively making them a salesperson for the company. Recent research indicates that individualist cultures are more likely to purchase customized products online, compared to collectivist cultures.[39] Interestingly, those collectivist consumers who do purchase customized products online are less price sensitive than individualistic consumers.[39]

The Internet is not limited to its purchasing potential. It offers great benefits in terms of instantaneous information exchange, sending company information to internal customers (employees and intermediaries), sending product information to customers, allowing instantaneous transactions with customers, and providing marketing and sales support and information to internal users.[40] Perhaps one of the most impactful elements of the Internet in terms of global marketing is the access to customer information that is now available to marketers. For instance, Amazon.com has opened its 257,000,000 customer database to sellers who use the Amazon storefront.[41]

In the past, Internet sales were generally focused on specialty consumer goods, or other fast-moving consumables such as books, music and movies, all of which the consumer could trial or have a strong idea about before purchasing. While it took some time, now virtually everything is available and has the potential to be successful online, depending on the country. Clothing used to be difficult to order online, because of not being able to try things on first, no tactile trial or other formerly important brick-and-mortar attributes. However, stores like ShopBop.com which offer postage paid no-questions-asked returns as well as elaborate interactive sizing charts and modelling shots have dramatically increased the acceptance of fashion purchasing online. Similarly, the advent of high-speed Internet in the majority of developed countries has made music and movie shopping download focused. In 2008 the Apple iTunes store surpassed Walmart as the number one music retailer in the US, and is currently the largest seller of music globally.

The separation or integration of traditional stores and online stores, or 'bricks versus clicks', has created some unique issues, however. From an international perspective, different copyright laws exist across national boundaries, making truly international digital stores very difficult to establish. Similarly, there is the issue of local retailers being undercut by large multinational online distributors. Recently, Internet taxation issues have been attracting more attention.[42] Such is the case in Australia, where the local 10 per cent Goods and Services tax as well as import duties are not assessed on purchases worth less than $AU1000 made online from a foreign retailer. This means that these purchases are essentially tax-free for Australian consumers, a fact noted by US department store Sears who offered a further 20 per cent discount to Australians who ordered from their website over the Christmas period of 2010. Malaysia has also shown concern about losing tax revenues from e-commerce transactions,[43] while California, home of Silicon Valley, is currently trying to pass a tax making it possible to collect sales tax from online purchases made by its residents.

Even when the website is largely global, there are issues with different rules and regulations for conducting business over the Internet. Cox (p. 64) highlights logistic hurdles within the EU:

The challenge for the EU is to come up with meaningful rules for financial services and e-commerce without strangling the nascent Internet economy in the cradle. A case in point: if a company wants to set up accounts with the same bank in different EU countries, as many as 900 signatures are required.[44]

Website link 11.3

Search for global Internet statistics for websites, such as: **www.Internetworldstats.com.**

Both domestic and international legal issues are difficult to manage on the Internet, including the content of cyberspace contracts, collecting taxes for online transactions on a national basis, protecting intellectual property, stopping certain types of information from appearing, protecting consumers, location of legal jurisdiction, location of buyer, seller, or both.[45]

As an article in *The Economist* (p. 18) put it:

Here is this amazingly useful, if disruptive, thing, built from the bottom up by idealists, largely self-regulated and beyond the reach of governments or big companies. It is a nice idea. Sadly, the Internet is neither as different nor as

'naturally' free as wired Utopians claim. The sheer pervasiveness of the Internet makes it impossible for even the best-intentioned of regulators to keep out. Such issues as privacy, consumer protection, intellectual property rights, contracts and taxation cannot be left entirely to self-regulation if e-commerce is to flourish. And, as the judge's ruling in favour of a break-up of Microsoft has just confirmed . . . antitrust action may be even more important online than off.[46]

Other issues in direct marketing across borders

There are several issues involved in direct cross-border selling, whether it be via catalogue or Internet. First, logistics issues: direct mail and purchased goods can be sent from the domestic country, from within the target country, or from a third country to reduce mailing costs while keeping speed and security of delivery at a fair level. Although it may seem the easiest solution to mail from within the target country because the local language and culture will be understood better, there may be constraints in the local postal service that make it more advantageous to mail from a third country. This can prove cheaper in terms of mailing costs.[47]

Further, cross-border direct marketing and Internet commerce involves regulation, mainly postal regulations, customs and privacy issues, all of which are largely country specific.[48] However, regulations are becoming more and more standardized at the regional level, as in the EU where a European Union Postal Service was implemented in 1998 after six years of preparation. Customs may also be a problem, since goods intended to reach the foreign customer by a specific date (e.g., Christmas) can be delayed by customs authorities; this is less likely when goods are shipped to industrialized nations. Ethics are a problem in international direct mail. Concerns with privacy, and the possible fraudulent uses of mailing lists, are major concerns in a number of countries. Germany and New Zealand have very strict privacy regulations, but other countries are more lenient. Even in neighbouring countries, such as the US and Canada, ethical views on direct marketing differ. Canadians tend to have more power distance than Americans and resent letters written in too direct a style; therefore, letters have to be written differently for Canadian audiences.[49] In fact, all, direct and

Internet marketing communication need to be adapted for language and cultural reasons (see Chapter 4 for a discussion on this).

11.4

Sales promotion: other customs, other manners

Sales promotion techniques are fairly universal, but their use and the conditions of implementing them vary cross-nationally and depend on cultural variables (see Box 11.3). Sales promotion targets some basic marketing objectives that are cross-culturally valid. It aims to engage the consumer in any of the following: (1) initial trial; (2) initial purchase; (3) an immediate purchase; (4) re-purchase; (5) an increase in frequency of purchase; and (6) entering point of sale. Promotional techniques combine the sales proposal with the following:

1. Discounts or rebates of various kinds: time-limited price discounts, coupons, 'in-pack' money-off, reimbursement offers, etc., mostly directed at immediate purchase.
2. Competitions: games, contests, lotteries, sweepstakes, etc.
3. Collection devices of various kinds (membership reward and stamps), oriented towards increasing

the frequency of purchase and building consumer loyalty.

4. Free samples or some kind of cross-product offer, for the purpose of consumer trial especially.
5. Gifts: 'in-pack' gifts, purchase with purchase, reusable packaging, product bonus, etc.

Cross-national differences in use of sales promotion techniques

The first question to be addressed is: who is the target? Often the target is not only the end consumer. Sales promotions may also be targeted at store personnel, to encourage them to stock a product, display it in a favourable position, or promote the product to the end consumer. This may be especially relevant to low-cost, commodity-type products that consumers need reminding to buy, such as batteries. Gifts (e.g., camera or vacation) may be offered from the battery producer, which encourage personnel to place them in a favourable position within the store. Directing promotions at the store may be more effective in less developed countries, where the final buyers are limited to the choices offered within a store. Similarly, it might be advisable to target the purchaser, rather than the end user, where people have servants who shop for food and household supplies.

Box 11.3

Global transferability of sales promotions: Lego examples

A case in point is Lego A/S, the Danish toy marketer which undertook American-style consumer promotion in Japan some years ago. Earlier, the company had measurably improved its penetration of US households by employing 'bonus' packs and gift promotions. Encouraged by that success, it decided to transfer these tactics unaltered to other markets, including Japan, where penetration had stalled. But these lures left Japanese consumers unmoved. Subsequent investigation showed that consumers considered the promotions to be wasteful, expensive, and not very appealing. Similar reactions were

recorded in other countries. Lego's marketers thus got their first lesson on the limitations of the global transferability of sales promotions.

Lego was involved in a global promotion with Shell Oil, since promotional Lego toys were designed exclusively to be distributed at Shell's 44,000 service stations worldwide. The material for this global promotion was the same worldwide but the tactics used, including giveaways, cash-back coupons and discount coupons, were decided locally.

(Source: Kashani, pp. 92–3;[50] Koranteng.[51])

A second question is whether a technique is considered ethical. Sales promotion regulations differ cross-nationally according to various assumptions about what is moral or immoral and what is fair or unfair in the relationship between a merchandiser/sales promoter and a customer/shopper. Most developed countries regulate sales promotion in order to prevent abuse. There is also some fear that sales promotion costs could result in overpricing of products. However, the EU appears to be reducing country level restrictions in promotions (see Box 11.4).

The areas in which ethical issues are mostly raised are competitions, gifts and cross-product offers. The UK and the US are the most favourable countries for sales promotions.[52] Anglo-Saxon countries are generally more liberal than other countries, especially for competitions: most kinds of lotteries, free draws and sweepstakes are legally permitted. In most Anglo-Saxon countries, private betting (bookmakers) organizations are permitted, whereas in most other countries, betting (horse races, lotteries) is state controlled, since it is seen as immoral for private individuals to benefit from organizing lotteries and betting games.

While the European Court of Justice is working to reduce restrictions on promotional marketing in the European Union (see Box 11.4), many countries have differences in their regulation of these lotteries and sweepstakes. For instance, Italy placed restricted lotteries and sweepstakes where prizes were in cash, The Netherlands restricted cash prizes to small amounts, and France restricted purchase limitations, so that people could enter a promotion without making a purchase. Many national regulations also prohibit gifts or limit their value. In France the value of a promotional gift could not be higher than 7 per cent of the retail price. The idea behind this prohibition is that consumers should buy products, not gifts. Collectors' items, such as gifts, are subject to the same kind of regulatory ceiling: the value of the collector's item associated with the purchase is often legally limited, especially those targeted at children. Further, sales promotions that encourage an initial trial, such as cross-product offers and purchase-with-purchase offers, are often controlled by national legislation. It is more difficult for consumers to judge value when they pay for two products at the same time.

Some sales promotion techniques are fairly consistent cross-culturally, since they appear less questionable. For instance, (a) free samples as a way to induce people to try the product, (b) discount on the next purchase as a way to induce consumers to repeat their purchase, (c) point-of-purchase materials and product demonstrations as a way to increase consumer

---

Box 11.4

European Court dismissed promotional bans in member countries

The European Court of Justice has been working to reduce restrictions on promotional marketing in the European Union, under consideration of the EU Unfair Commercial Practices Directive (UCPD) which was passed in 2005. In this case, European law takes precedence over national law.

Case 1: Under German law, a retailer cannot offer points for purchases, which go into a draw. However, the Court ruled that German law could not prevent such schemes as the national law cannot be harsher than the restrictions in the UCPD.

Case 2: In Austria, a general prohibition of bonuses was overturned, as offering a prize competition,

linked to the purchase of a newspaper, does not constitute an unfair commercial practice within the meaning of the Directive.

This clearly supports the UCPD and anything that goes further than the requirements of this Directive are likely to be invalidated. However, companies may want to consider more than the legal requirements. National authorities may still attempt to enforce their countries restrictions on sales promotion and the media may see this as an opportunity to portray global companies as being inconsiderate of local laws.

Table 11.2 Cross-cultural adequacy problems for selected sales promotion techniques

Technique	Culture-related features that may affect implementation
Coupons	Level of literacy, consumer and retailer sophistication/low social status implied
Contests and sweepstakes	Legal requirements/prizes must suit target market tastes
Price offers	Absence of price labelling and display/bargaining/trade misuse
Stamps and collections	Future orientation needed/high inflation/level of channel sophistication
Free samples	Interpretation of gratuity/trade misuse/theft of sampled products
Gifts (in, on or near packs)	Legal requirements/theft by channel employees or customers

knowledge of the product, (d) free food tasting to induce trial, (e) loyalty reward systems, etc. Additionally, some countries object to sales promotion techniques in general because of the risk of consumers being misled. Whereas some countries believe in personal responsibility and trust consumers to seek and evaluate information (e.g., Australia, the UK, the US), others have less confidence in the capacities of individuals to make free and responsible choices (Latin-European and northern European countries). In Scandinavian countries sales promotions face the greatest obstacles, since every promotion has to be approved by an official body.

Sociocultural factors influencing implementation of sales promotion techniques

Table 11.2 presents a series of sociocultural factors that influence the implementation of sales promotion techniques. The level of literacy is obviously an important variable since promotion often includes important text. For instance, if the target market is largely illiterate, people are unlikely to respond to coupons. The level of literacy becomes crucial when the purpose of the campaign is consumer education.

In this case, visual and oral promotion should be given preference. Promotional campaigns in some African countries travel from village to village showing promotional films, while the operator distributes free samples of the product. Conversely, where there is increasing education and political awareness, promotional campaigns should emphasize this.

Retailer sophistication is required when the promotional techniques need some follow-up, such as redeeming coupons, loyalty reward programmes or dealing with stamps or collectors' devices. In this case the retailer is the intermediary between manufacturer and the final consumer. They need to be organized in terms of stocking coupons, reckoning, ordering premiums, etc.

If prizes are given, they must suit the target market's tastes (e.g., cars or bicycles, small or large household items, sporting equipment or more practical appliances). This is especially important in competitions where the prizes are advertised. Whenever legally possible, cash is the most universally acceptable prize, since it allows further free spending. However, in many countries cash prizes are not allowed, or are limited to small amounts. Some competition formats might be more or less be transferable across countries, for instance the McDonald's Monopoly sweepstakes has been run in a diverse range of countries with great success, such as the US, Canada, Germany, France, Spain, Australia, Singapore, Hong Kong and Portugal among many others.

Unethical trade behaviour *vis-à-vis* the manufacturer is possible in a number of ways, which may be especially important to monitor in developing countries. For instance, retailers can decide to sell what were supposed to be free samples, or they can pocket money-off offers by increasing prices. Retailers' employees can remove samples, gifts or premiums for themselves or others. Strict control of the retailers involved in a promotion is required wherever such opportunistic attitudes are foreseeable.

Promotional techniques can be associated with images of social status. In Hong Kong the response to coupons is positive, whereas the use of stamps is more popular in Thailand; both of these locally popular techniques being associated with middle-class status.[53] In other countries, coupons or discounts can be associated with low-class status (e.g., in Australia), because the implied price consciousness suggests an image of low purchasing power. In France consumers tend to associate frequent sales promotions with lesser-valued brands.[54] On the other hand, promotional techniques based on a price reduction cannot be implemented in countries where consumer bargaining is common, as basic prices are not displayed. A rebate only has meaning in relation to a clear market price. In such cases, it is better to target channel members rather than the end user. For instance, retailers can be offered a rebate for quantity sold over a certain period of time.

Some promotional techniques require extended involvement, such as collectors' devices, loyalty reward programmes, refunds after a series of purchases, etc. Cultures with a present-time orientation respond poorly to these techniques, which require delayed gratification.[53] This can also be affected by the society itself: for instance, in the busy city of Hong Kong instant win promotions were preferred by consumers over delayed-gratification technniques.[55] The attractiveness of the benefits associated with loyalty reward programmes, such as those offered by airlines and department stores, also might vary across countries. So, while shoppers from Malaysia and Singapore might focus on informational benefits, as well as financial benefits, shoppers from Hong Kong, Thailand and Taiwan make no such distinctions.[56] Similarly, high inflation is very detrimental to any sales promotion whose rewards are not immediate. For instance, the face value of coupons, discounts and other rebates may have little meaning after a few weeks have gone by (necessary for printing, distribution and claiming the rebates).

Finally, it is necessary to check that the purpose of the promotional technique is understood locally (the problem of conceptual equivalence). For instance, in countries where much of the population grew up under Communism, it may be difficult to understand the motives behind free samples. The basic rationale, that a producer wants consumers to try a product in order to have them buy it, is not self-evident. A free sample is understood either as a sign of poor quality ('they give it because they cannot sell it') or as a sign of the naivety of the manufacturer ('let's take as much as possible'). P & G experienced major problems with free samples in Poland, where some people ignored them, and others broke into mailboxes to take them. It is noteworthy that price reductions are by far the most popular sales promotion technique.[52]

Questions

1. A distribution formula is successful in the United States; you are asked to extend it through a franchise system to several countries around the world. How would you devise a policy for those franchisees who want the standard recipe to be adapted for their home market in the following areas: size of the store, personnel recruitment, servicing, stocking, brands represented, display and store name?

2. What are the ways in which retailing know-how is transferred internationally?

3. Discuss the distinguishing features of the Japanese distribution system.

4. Why do exporting firms tend to have somewhat different distribution channels abroad compared to their domestic markets, apart from the peculiarities of the local distribution systems?

5. Until recently, the typical store in Germany was open every day, from Monday to Friday, 9 a.m. to 6.30 p.m. They closed at 2 p.m. on Saturday and all day Sunday. Once a month there was a special shopping Thursday when stores were open until 8.30 p.m. Conversely, opening hours in the United States are much longer and some supermarkets are open 24 hours a day, seven days a week. Store employees in Germany are highly unionized and unions are traditionally opposed to any increase in opening hours. To what extent do time-related cultural differences explain the huge difference in store opening hours between Germany and the United States?

6. Using a local catalogue (from your own country), explain how (in terms of language, size, photographs, prices, product information, delivery and payment conditions, etc.) it should be adapted to a culturally remote market with a similar level of economic development (choose the target market) if it were to be sent to potential customers in that context.

7. Discuss how store size can be related to culture.

8. Explain how cultural values can have a negative impact on self-service and automated service in general (that is, without personnel in contact with the shopper/consumer).

9. Based on available statistics, review key differences in the retailing systems in EU countries.

References

1. Dawson, John A. (1994), 'Internationalization of Retailing Operations', *Journal of Marketing Management*, 10 (4), 267–82.

2. Chiao, Yu-Ching, Fang-Yi Lo and Chow-Ming Yu (2010), 'Choosing Between Wholly-owned Subsidiaries and Joint Ventures of Mncs from an Emerging Market', *International Marketing Review*, 27 (3), 338–65.

3. Burberry (2011), *Burberry Annual Report 2010–211*. Available from: http://201011.annualreport.burberry.com/.

4. Moore, Christopher M. and Grete Birtwistle (2004), 'The Burberry Business Model: Creating an International Luxury Fashion Brand', *International Journal of Retail & Distribution Management*, 32 (8), 412–22.

5. Alexander, Nicholas and Hayley Myers (2000), 'The Retail Internationalisation Process', *International Marketing Review*, 17 (4/5), 334–53.

6. Ford, David (2002), 'Solving Old Problems, Learning New Things and Forgetting Most of Them: Distribution, Internationalisation and Networks', *International Marketing Review*, 19 (3), 225–35.

7. McNaughton, Rod B. and Jim Bell (2001), 'Channel Switching between Domestic and Foreign Markets', *Journal of International Marketing*, 9 (1), 24–39.

8. Patterson, Paul G., Jane Scott and Mark D. Uncles (2010), 'How the Local Competition Defeated a Global Brand: The Case of Starbucks', *Australasian Marketing Journal*, 18 (1), 41–7.

9. Cateora, Philip R. (1993), *International Marketing* (8th edn). Homewood, IL: Richard D. Irwin.

10. Czinkota, Michael R. and Illka A. Ronkainen (1990), *International Marketing* (2nd edn). Hinsdale, IL: Dryden Press.

11. Lee, Julie Anne, Ellen Garbarino and Dawn Lerman (2007), 'How Cultural Differences in Uncertainty Avoidance Affect Product Perceptions', *International Marketing Review*, 24 (3), 330–49.

12. de Mooij, Marieke and Geert Hofstede (2002), 'Convergence and Divergence in Consumer Behavior: Implications for International Retailing', *Journal of Retailing*, 78 (1), 61–9.

13. Griffith, David A. (1998), 'Cultural Meaning of Retail Institutions: A Tradition-based Culture Examination', *Journal of Global Marketing*, 12 (1), 47–59.

14. Nueno, José Luis and Harvey Bennett (1997), 'The Changing Spanish Consumer', *International Journal of Research in Marketing*, 14 (1), 19–33.

15. Child, Peter N. (2002), 'Taking Tesco Global', *The McKinsey Quarterly*, www.mckinseyquarterly.com.

16. Czinkota, Michael R. and Jon Woronoff (1991), *Unlocking Japan's Markets*. Chicago, IL: Probus Publishing.

17. Euromonitor (2003), 'Department Stores in Japan', *Euromonitor International*, www.marketresearch.com.

18. *Supra.*

19. Anderson, Erin T. and Anne T. Coughlan (1987), 'International Market Entry and Expansion Via Independent or Integrated Channels of Distribution', *Journal of Marketing*, 51 (1), 71–82.

20. Gabrielsson, Mika, V. H. Manek Kirpalani and Reijo Luostarinen (2002), 'Multiple Channel Strategies in the European Personal Computer Industry', *Journal of International Marketing*, 10 (3), 73–95.

21. Speedy, Blair (2010), 'US Parent Company Keeping Starbucks Australia Alive', *The Australian*, 18 February. Available from: http://www.theaustralian.com.au/business/us-parent-company-keeping-starbucks-australia-alive/story-e6frg8zx-1225831544786.

22. Emerson, Daniel and Alex Tibbitts (2008), 'Starbucks Closes 61 Shops, Cuts 700 Jobs', *The Sydney Morning Herald*, 30 July. Available from: http://www.smh.com.au/business/starbucks-closes-61-shops-cuts-700-jobs-20080729-3mt1.html#ixzz1jsLrxaoK.

23. Griffen, Mitch, Barry J. Babin and Doan Modianos (2000), 'Shopping Values of Russian Consumers: The

Impact of Habituation in a Developing Economy', *Journal of Retailing*, 76 (1), 33–52.

24. Nicholls, J. A. F., Fuan Li, Carl J. Kranendonk and Tomislav Mandakovic (2003), 'Structural or Cultural: An Exploration into Influences on Consumers' Shopping Behavior of Country Specific Factors Versus Retailing Formats', *Journal of Global Marketing*, 16 (4), 97–115.

25. Straughan, Robert B. and Nancy D. Albers-Miller (2001), 'An International Investigation of Cultural and Demographic Effects on Domestic Retail', *International Marketing Review*, 18 (5), 521–41.

26. Miller, Fred and A. Hamdi Demirel (1988), 'Efes Pilsen in the Turkish Beer Market: Marketing Consumer Goods in Developing Countries', *International Marketing Review*, 5 (1), 7–19.

27. Saporito, Bill (2003), 'Can Wal-Mart Get Any Bigger?', *TIME Magazine*, 5 January. Available from: http://www.time.com/time/magazine/article/0,9171,404212,00.html.

28. Pioch, Elke, Ulrike Gerhard, John Fernie and Stephen J. Arnold (2009), 'Consumer Acceptance and Market Success: Wal-Mart in the UK and Germany', *International Journal of Retail & Distribution Management*, 37 (3), pp. 205–25.

29. Kim, Keysuk and Changho Oh (2002), 'On Distributor Commitment in Marketing Channels for Industrial Products: Contrast between the United States and Japan', *Journal of International Marketing*, 10 (1), 72–97.

30. Skarmeas, Dionisis A. and Constantine S. Katsikeas (2001), 'Drivers of Superior Importer Performance in Cross-Cultural Supplier–Reseller Relationships', *Industrial Marketing Management*, 30 (2), 227–41.

31. Kale, Sudhir H. and Roger P. McIntyre (1991), 'Distribution Channel Relationships in Diverse Cultures', *International Marketing Review*, 8 (3), 31–45.

32. Hofstede, Geert (2001), *Culture Consequences* (2nd edn). Thousand Oaks, CA: Sage Publications.

33. Luk, S., L. Fullgrabe and S. Li (1996), 'Managing Direct Selling Activities in China: A Cultural Explanation', paper presented to EIRASS, Third Recent Advances in Retailing and Consumer Sciences Conference. Telfs, Austria, 1–18.

34. O'Grady, Shawna and Henry W. Lane (1992), 'Culture: An Unnoticed Barrier to Canadian Retail Performance in the United States', paper presented at Academy of International Business Annual Conference. Brussels.

35. Shoham, Aviv, Gregory M. Rose and Fredric Kropp (1997), 'Conflicts in International Channels of Distribution', *Journal of Global Marketing*, 11 (2), 5–27.

36. Katsikeas, Constantine S. and Nigel F. Piercy (1991), 'The Relationship between Exporters from a Developing Country and Importers Based in a Developed Country: Conflict Considerations', *European Journal of Marketing*, 25 (1), 6–25.

37. Mehta, Rajiv, Trina Larsen, Bert Rosenbloom, Jolanta Mazur and Pia Polsa (2001), 'Leadership and Cooperation in Marketing Channels: A Comparative Empirical Analysis of the USA, Finland and Poland', *International Marketing Review*, 18 (6), 633–66.

38. Mehta, Rajiv, Rolph E. Anderson, Alan J. Dubinsky, Jolanta Mazur and Pia Polsa (2011), 'Managing Channel Partner Relationships: A Cross-National Study', *Journal of Global Marketing*, 24 (2), 105–24.

39. Moon, Junyean, Doren Chadee and Surinder Tikoo (2008), 'Culture, Product Type, and Price Influences on Consumer Purchase Intention to Buy Personalized Products Online', *Journal of Business Research*, 61 (1), 31–9.

40. Quelch, John A. and Lisa R. Klein (1996), 'The Internet and International Marketing', *Sloan Management Review*, 37 (3), 60–77.

41. Murphy, Dennis (2012), 'Digital Marketer's New PRO Level Gives Marketers Access to Top Marketing Experts', *PRWeb*, available from: http://www.prweb.com/releases/prweb2012/1/prweb9108799.htm.

42. Waltner, Charles (1999), 'Web's Days as Tax-Free Zone Are Numbered – as E-Commerce Booms, the Battle over Internet Taxation Standards Starts Heating Up', *InternetWeek*, 6 (December), 26–30.

43. Kasim, Sharifah and Anuja Ravendran (2001), 'Tackling Tax Issues in E-Commerce Activities (Hl)', *Computimes Malaysia*, July, 1.

44. Cox, Anthony (2000), 'Europe EU Faces Tall Task in Regulating E-Commerce', *Bank Technology News*, 13 (6), 63–64.

45. Zugelder, Michael T., Theresa B. Flaherty and James P. Johnson (2000), 'Legal Issues Associated with International Internet Marketing', *International Marketing Review*, 17 (3), 253–71.

46. *The Economist* (2000), 'Leaders: Regulating the Internet', 10 June, 18–20.

47. Desmet, Pierre and Dominique Xardel (1996), 'Challenges and Pitfalls for Direct Mail across Borders: The European Example', *Journal of Direct Marketing*, 10 (3), 48–60.

48. Rawwas, Mohammed Y., David Strutton and Lester W. Johnson (1996), 'An Exploratory Investigation of the Ethical Values of American and Australian Consumers: Direct Marketing Implications', *Journal of Direct Marketing*, 10 (4), 52–63.

49. Graves, Roger (1997), ' "Dear Friend" (?): Culture and Genre in American and Canadian Direct Marketing Letters', *Journal of Business Communication*, 34 (3), 235–52.

50. Kashani, Kamran (1989), 'Beware the Pitfalls of Global Marketing', *Harvard Business Review*, 67 (5), 91–8.

51. Koranteng, Juliana (1997), 'If the Web Is So Worldwide Why Is It Mainly in English?', *Advertising Age International* (May), 16.

52. Boddewyn, J. J. and M. Leardi (1989), 'Sales Promotion: Practices, Regulation and Self-Regulation around the World', *International Journal of Advertising*, 8 (4), 363–74.

53. Foxman, Ellen R., Patriya S. Tansuhaj and John K. Wong (1988), 'Evaluating Cross-National Sales Promotion Approach Strategy: An Audit Approach', *International Marketing Review*, 5 (4), 7–15.

54. Valette-Florence, Pierre, Haythem Guizani and Dwight Merunka (2011), 'The Impact of Brand Personality and Sales Promotions On Brand Equity', *Journal of Business Research*, 64, 24–8.

55. Yang, Lin, Wah-Leung Cheung, James Henry, John Guthrie and Kim-Shyan Fan (2010), 'An Examination of Sales Promotion Programs in Hong Kong: What the Retailers Offer and What the Consumers Prefer', *Journal of Promotions Management*, 16, 467–79.

56. Steyn, Peter, Leyland Pitt, Arien Strasheimc, Christo Boshoff and Russell Abratt (2010), 'A Cross-Cultural Study of the Perceived Benefits of a Retailer Loyalty Scheme in Asia', *Journal of Retailing and Consumer Services*, 17, 355–73.

Appendix 11

Teaching materials

A11.1 Case

ComputerLand in Japan

ComputerLand recognized that it would need a Japanese partner in order to enter the Japanese market. Because of government regulations and attitude, it probably would not have been possible to obtain permission to establish a wholly owned subsidiary. Additionally, the complexities of the Japanese market would have made development of franchises there very difficult. (Both McDonald's and Kentucky Fried Chicken entered the market with Japanese partners.)

ComputerLand wanted a partner who had experience in both procurement and distribution of computer products. Following talks with a number of companies, Kanematsu-Gosho Ltd emerged as the top candidate. Kanematsu-Gosho was a major trading company, had experience in the desired areas, and already had business dealings with IBM. ComputerLand entered into negotiations with the Japanese company in order to try to develop a joint venture. The discussions, which lasted for nine months, were detailed and difficult. The Chairman of ComputerLand was concerned that if his Vice-President went to Japan to negotiate, he would be at a disadvantage trying to operate in a different culture. He therefore insisted that the negotiations be held in the United States by telephone from Japan.

This made it difficult for the Japanese to negotiate. The Japanese decision-making process requires much more consultation and agreement with the company than would normally be necessary in European and American firms. There were long delays and a lot had to be done through e-mail and fax. Among other things, the Japanese government had to be persuaded to allow the American partner to have a 50 per cent ownership rather than the customary (at the time) minority position. The agreement was finally concluded, with ComputerLand contributing knowledge, trade mark and technology and Kanematsu-Gosho contributing cash to start the joint venture, ComputerLand Japan Ltd. The Vice-President of ComputerLand then went to Japan to head the operation as Vice-President and Resident Director. A number of policy and operational problems had to be solved.

In the United States franchisees were required to pay cash before merchandise would be shipped to them. An attempt was made to follow this policy in Japan. Retailers in Japan, however, are used to receiving credit from wholesalers – often for 90 days or even longer. A cash-in-advance policy proved to be impossible in Japan, so the company eventually went to a 10-day-open-credit policy.

In the United States, franchises were given only to individuals, not to corporations or other businesses. This was done so that the stores would be personally managed by the owners. ComputerLand Japan was not able to find sufficient individuals who had or could obtain the necessary cash. Eventually the policy was changed to allow a company to own a minority interest. As in Europe store locations and format were also a problem. Within the United States ComputerLand insisted that the minimum size for a store was 2000 square feet (185 m^2), a busy location accessible and visible to a large amount of traffic, and with a parking lot in the rear. This was simply not possible in most locations in Japan.

It was also difficult to attract top-quality employees to work for a foreign company in Japan. Finally, there were simple coordination issues between proprietor-owned ComputerLand and large, publicly owned Kanematsu-Gosho. In spite of these difficulties, ComputerLand Japan was very successful, growing to 50 franchises with annual sales of US$50 million. It was assisted greatly by the fact that, for the first two years of operations, ComputerLand had exclusive distribution rights for the IBM PC in Japan.

Over the years, Kanematsu-Gosho found it increasingly difficult to continue to accept elements of ComputerLand's policy. Additionally, it felt that the American partner was simply exercising too much control. When ComputerLand offered to buy the company out, Kanematsu-Gosho agreed. The operation then became a wholly owned subsidiary of the United States corporation. Eventually, this subsidiary was sold to one of the franchisees, who continues to operate it under a licence agreement with ComputerLand.

(Source: Written by John T. Sakai, former Vice-President of ComputerLand.)

Questions

1. Was it wise for ComputerLand to insist on holding the negotiations in the United States? What were the advantages and disadvantages for each of the parties? Why did Kanematsu-Gosho agree to the location?

2. Analyse the differences between the Japanese and American distribution systems as they appear in this case. Which elements of the 'ComputerLand model' are transferable to Japan?

3. When exporting to another country or setting up a joint venture there, how can you decide which of the local customs and business practices should be accepted, and which of your home country practices should you introduce?

A11.2 Case

Virtual beehive – online marketing of US honey

The first official record of beekeeping stretches back five thousand years, to Ancient Egypt, where beekeepers navigated their bees up or down the Nile, depending on the season. Today, itinerant Chinese families and their bees track blooming flora for thousands of kilometres across the country in rented vans. Rural poor women in Malaysia cultivate the bees that pollinate coffee plantations and provide pungent honey. American beekeepers winter with their bees in Texas, and summer with them in the North Dakota plains. Argentinian landowners use low-cost labour to keep bees on their extensive lands.

Beekeeping has always been a specialized business. The demand for bee products, including honey, bee pollen, royal jelly, propolis (adhesive used for comb placement and repair), and beeswax has been quite steady throughout history. In the past beekeeping was prized because of the sweetening and medicinal properties of honey, medicinal uses for other hive products, as well as the wax used in a myriad of ways, including candles, adhesive, and hairdressing. The beekeeper's life today is in some ways more difficult than it was in the past, without the steady patronage of the religious and medical orders. Today, there are more competing products, such as corn syrup and aspartame. There are more low-cost producers, many in developing countries. The rationalized business practices of international retail conglomerates demand massive quantities, making packers and intermediaries necessary for small producers. However, now in their fifth millennium, beekeepers may finally have found through the Internet a way to keep more of their scanty margins for themselves, instead of profiting packers, agents, and exporters.

Beekeeping, a fragmented sector

Supply is subject to weather, the length of the flower blooming season, and bee disease control. Smaller beekeepers tend to leave the field because costly technology is increasingly needed for pest control, management of newly immigrated bees, and pesticide use in the environment.[1] For these reasons, among others, beekeepers tend to consolidate, however they remain a small agricultural grouping with little political muscle and low bargaining power. Under these conditions, prices tend not to be stable: US prices more than doubled between 2000 and 2003, from 60 cents per pound to 138.7 cents per pound, and are currently following a downward trend. In 2007, US average price per pound amounted to 103.2 cents, whereas the price in 2008 rose to an average of 141 cents. Yet, in the USA, 40 per cent of honey produced comes from smaller beekeepers, hobbyists and part-timers and they account for about 50 per cent of bee colonies.[2] Smaller producers may improve their chances for survival by joining a cooperative, like the almost 90-year-old Sioux Honey Association, from Sioux City, Iowa.

Risk management in a risky business: the cooperative

The oldest beekeepers' cooperative is best known under its 'Sue Bee' brand (from 'Sioux'), and is the second largest honey marketer in America with a market share of 24.1 per cent right behind the Dutch Gold Honey with a 25.3 per cent market share.[3] In addition to continuing sales to retail outlets and online, the cooperative is focusing on manufactured food plus the food service segment.[4] By featuring the Sue Bee logo on its label, a food-processing company is likely to boost the image of its sauces, prepared foods, condiments, or beverages. Use of honey in these products is at an all-time high.[4] (Visit Sue Bee Honey at **http://www.suebeehoney.com/**).

Biggest importers of US honey

The US National Honey Board (NHB) is concerned with promoting sales of US honey abroad. It has collected the following data concerning the ranking of US honey export (metric tons):

1. Canada
2. Guatemala
3. Antigua and Barbuda
4. Belgium
5. Belize
6. Netherlands

(Source: United States Department of Agriculture.[5])

The marketing environment for honey

Before the rise of the Internet, buyers and honey processors/packers spent a great deal of time negotiating their bulk honey contracts. What may have then taken up to 30 days may now be concluded during a 30-minute online bidding process.[6] Increased consolidation of retail businesses and food suppliers has placed bulk honey sellers at a disadvantage. For instance, retail buyers often demand slotting fees (to get the product on the shelf and, often, to keep competitors off) and pay-to-stay fees (to keep the product on the shelf). It is estimated that some Canadian packers pay ten per cent of their total costs on these fees.[6] Retail buyers expect to pay a low price for high volume, with accompanying food safety assurances in writing.[6]

The honey market is diverging between a high-end, specialty product and a low-end, low-cost, relatively undifferentiated, 'generic'-type product.[6] Honey is assailed by direct and indirect competitors for sweeteners (such as sugars, fruit concentrates, rice sweetener, and molasses) and spreads (such as fruit-based, nut-based, or chocolate-based spreads) which often make their own health- and nutrient-related claims. The entry of low-cost producers like China, Argentina and Mexico onto the honey stage has made retail buyers even more cost-conscious, as has the increased market share of countries like India, Vietnam, Turkey, and Hungary. The participation of China and Argentina in the US market has lessened due to fees that raise prices. Both countries were allegedly dumping honey on the US market within the past decade and had to pay anti-dumping fees, and, in the case of Argentina, countervailing fees. These anti-dumping orders largely decreased Chinese and Argentinean imports of honey in the US during three to four years, but in 2006 China and Argentina were again the biggest honey exporters in the US. During 2007 and, more important, 2008 imports for these two countries as well as Mexico dropped significantly, whereas it kept rising for Canada or Vietnam, for example.

Table 11.3 USA honey imports in metric tons from Argentina, China, Canada, Mexico and Vietnam

Country	2004	2005	2006	2007	2008
Argentina	3,620	22,776	28,878	20,379	10,043
China	26,916	29,366	32,149	17,755	11,234
Canada	10,172	10,252	11,576	13,961	17,305
Mexico	3,254	1,452	2,580	3,192	1,411
Vietnam	9,792	13,582	13,263	15,707	19,379

(Source: United States Department of Agriculture.[5])

The positioning of honey in the USA

The US National Honey Board (NHB at **http://www.honey.com/honeyindustry/**) used in-depth, face-to-face interviews to determine the positioning of honey in the US. Respondents were asked questions regarding factors such as interest/intent, believability, and uniqueness relating to three positioning statements, 'Livens up the Flavor of Any Meal', 'Nature's Healer', and 'Nature's Original Sweetener'. The top performer in the tests was 'Nature's Healer',[7] a positioning that successfully differentiates honey from other options due to respondents' beliefs in its 'healthiness' (35 per cent), 'providing more benefits than artificial sweeteners' (27 per cent) and 'promoting healing' (25 per cent).[7] Despite performing well otherwise, the 'Nature's Healer' positioning elicited the lowest 'believability' score of the three positioning statements tested. However, media reports of scientific findings relating to honey should increase believability over time. The findings show that, on average, honey is used in US households once or twice a week and that most honey consumers buy honey two to three times per year. It appears that many consumers would like to use honey more often, but do not know of ways to do so. Based on the research findings, the positioning strategy was refined. The new statement was 'Honey: the natural daily choice to enhance health and well being',[8] a positioning concept designed to address food and 'pharmacological' uses. To support this, the NHB committed its resources to encourage research on honey-related issues (including honey's antimicrobial, antioxidant, and healing properties, and its nutrient content) to communicate the findings to targeted consumer segments as well as the food-processing industry.

Whatever the positioning of the product, online marketing may help smaller and biggest producers alike, particularly in challenging marketing conditions. In the US the National Honey Board (**www.honeylocator.com**) offers the potential honey purchaser more than 150 types of US honey on its menu, while the producers' sub-sites offer even more. The types of honey depend on the flora where bees collected nectar. This determines the colour (white to dark brown), taste, and aroma. Thus, nectar collected from mesquite results in a different honey from that collected from lavender. A search for 'orange blossom', for instance, returned 90 companies.

Buyers may search the site using floral source, name of supplier, state/country of production, forms of honey, sizes offered, other honey products/services, targeted markets and export markets. The pages located display among others contact information, product lists (usually pollen, royal jelly, kosher honey, organic honey), markets (bakery, retail, foodservice, wholesale, for export, brewery, food manufacturing), and export markets. Canadian cooperative *Beemaid Honey* is Canada's biggest and one of the oldest honey marketers. The company maintains a large site in its worldwide marketing efforts at **www.beemaid.com**.

Honey exporters may list themselves on online commercial directories, such as usaexporters.net, where company profiles and links may be provided. Honey producers or marketers may opt for banner advertising on other related sites, such as the US-based **http://www.honey.com/**, or even a cooking or tourism site. In addition to export-oriented sites, the Web boasts many informative beekeeping sites, some of which offer advice on apiculture problems, such as **www.gardenweb.com**, where beekeepers may solicit comments about how to clean a hive or which queen bees to purchase. A vast resource for beekeepers and honey purchasers is **www.beehoo.com**, a site in English and French with linked directories to exporters and hive suppliers. Another resource in English, French, Spanish and German is Apiservices at **www.beekeeping.com**, where one may access academic journals, exporter directories, classified ads, and a honey web-ring. With all the possibilities offered online, rural Spanish beekeepers, beekeeping apprentices in Nepal, and isolated Australian apiaries have the potential to sell directly to buyers, anywhere in the world . . . or do they?

Questions

1a. Visit sites in at least four different languages from the list below, or from your own searches. Comment on the obstacles of selling honey internationally online, in terms of language, shipping, trust, hygiene and import regulations, etc.

1b. Of the sites you visited, which did you consider to be most effective at selling honey long-term? Discuss the reasons for your choice, keeping in mind that, in the long run, the site is only as good as its suppliers.

France	Argentina	Italy	USA
www.lunedemiel.fr www.abeillestore.com www.ruchersdelorraine.com	http://www.cipsahoney.com.ar/ http://www.apicultura.com.ar/ http://www.parodiapicultura.com.ar/	www.montioni.com	www.honeylocator.com www.suebee.com www.burlesonshoney.com

Austria	Mexico	New Zealand	
www.gourmetpantry.com/ honey	http://www.natura.com.mx/ subsex/mielyderiv.html	www.honeynz.co.nz	

Canada	Germany	Spain	Greece
www.intermiel.com	www.honig.de www.schwarzwaldhonig.de	www.naturalhoney.es www.hispamiel.com	http://greekproducts.com/

2. Discuss whether the National Honey Board's (NHB) positioning concept, 'Honey: the natural daily choice to enhance health and well being' would be effective outside the US. Use one country as an example, as well as the NHB's criteria (believability, interest/intent and differentiation) in your answer.

3. Which honey markets are targeted by honeylocator.com? How could the site be modified to effectively target other potential markets? Consider the role of marketing the site on the Internet as part of your answer.

Saskia Faulk and Jean-Claude Usunier prepared this case solely to provide material for class discussion. The authors do not intend to illustrate either effective or ineffective handling of a business situation. The authors may have disguised certain names and other identifying information to protect confidentiality.

© IRM/HEC, 2011

2011-05-11   Version: (A)

Appendix references

1. Foreign Agricultural Service (1998), 'Honey situation and outlook in selected countries', Foreign Agricultural Service, November 1998. Retrieved 18 May 2011 from http://www.fas.usda.gov/htp2/sugar/1998/98-11/honey.htm.
2. National Honey Board (2008), 'Honey industry facts', Press release, National Honey Board. Retrieved 18 May 2011 from http://www.honey.com/media/presskit/industry.asp.
3. Agriculture and Agri-food Canada (2009), 'The U.S. Honey Market: Opportunities for Canadian Honey Exporters', April 2009. Retrieved 18 May 2011 from http://www.ats.agr.gc.ca/amr/4697-eng.htm.
4. Karg, Pamela J. (1999), 'Taking flight', *Rural Cooperatives*, 10888845, September/October, 1999, Vol. 66, Issue 5. Retrieved 18 May 2011 from http://www.uwcc.wisc.edu/info/farmer/pre2001/091099k1.html.
5. United States Department of Agriculture (2009), *Statistics of cotton, tobacco, sugar crops and honey, 2009*. Retrieved 18 May 2011 from http://www.nass.usda.gov/Publications/Ag_Statistics/2009/chp02.pdf.
6. Alberta Agriculture, Food and Rural Development (2001), *Competition for World Honey Markets: An Alberta Perspective, Report Two*, prepared by Competitive Intelligence Unit, April 2001. Retrieved 18 May 2011 from http://www.alimentosargentinos.gov.ar/miel_comisiones/COMISIONES/honey_book-Alberta_Canada.pdf.
7. National Honey Board (2001a), *National Honey Board positioning report phase II*, report prepared by rose research (r2), Boca Raton, FL, September 2001.
8. National Honey Board (2002), *Health positioning of honey as a marketing strategy*, N. Holleman, 2002. Retrieved 18 May 2011 from http://www.apimondiafoundation.org/cgi-bin/index.cgi?sid=&zone=download&action=download_file&file_id=239&categ_id=111.

Part 4 Intercultural marketing communications

Introduction to Part 4

Language plays a central role in marketing communications when they take place in an international and multilingual context, since communication styles as well as world views are deeply influenced by the structure of languages. This section reviews and examines some of the major types of marketing communication tools, including branding, promotions, personal selling and public relations. These tools not only aim to communicate with customers, but also with all stakeholders in the market, including middlemen, business partners, public authorities, and even competitors.

Country of origin and brand name are two of the greatest symbolic attributes that diffuse meaning. Chapter 12 explores how both brands and national images are infused with symbolic attributes. It reviews how consumers evaluate products according to their country of origin, taking into account perceived risk related to goods produced in other countries, which may be cheaper or less prestigious in terms of design and/or manufacturing, as well as the nationalistic tendencies of consumers who prefer to buy products made in their own countries. The final section deals with the linguistic constraints of transferring national brand names onto the international scene and outlines the managerial limitations involved in the development of global brands.

The main tool for communicating marketing messages to customer audiences is advertising. For reasons of image consistency, many companies want to promote their products globally through standardized advertising campaigns that use the same advertising strategy and execution worldwide. Thus, the question to be answered before transferring campaigns cross-nationally is: which elements should be localized and which ones can be similar worldwide? Chapter 13 first examines the general influence of culture on attitudes towards the social utility of advertising, especially when advertising adopts a comparative stance. International companies have to make decisions in two main areas, advertising strategy (information content, advertising appeals, etc.) and advertising execution (characters and roles represented, visual and textual elements, etc.). Based on a review of cross-cultural studies of advertisements, the chapter explains the extent to which both strategy and execution can be standardized or should be localized. The focus is then on the development of global media resources and the globalization of advertising agencies.

A lot of marketing information is also communicated directly to market stakeholders: that is, presented and explained directly by the sales force or indirectly through intermediaries or business partners in foreign markets. Chapter 14 starts by explaining what 'commerce' means from an intercultural perspective – that is, the ways and means to effectively communicate with the market in both directions, rather than in a one-sided exchange as is largely the case with advertising. This chapter develops a number of issues that are central to personal selling in an international perspective, including how to network in business markets, buyer–seller interactions, how cultural differences affect the management of the sales force, public relations across cultures and, last but not least, the issue of bribery and business ethics in an international context.

12

Branding: managing meaning

Brand equity is a measure of the overall value of a brand.[1] The set of associations that surround a brand is referred to as customer-based brand equity. Thus, a name can convey a great deal of information and make a substantial contribution to brand equity, as Leclerc and colleagues (p. 263) point out:

What do Klarbrunn waters, Giorgio di St Angelo design wear and Häagen-Dazs ice cream have in common? All three are successful brands, and all are not what they seem. Klarbrunn is not the clear mountain-spring mineral water from the German Alps that its brand name suggests; it is American water bottled in Wisconsin. Giorgio di St. Angelo design wear is not the latest fashion from Milan but the product of U.S. designer Martin Price. And Häagen-Dazs is not Danish or Hungarian ice cream; it is American ice cream made by Pillsbury with headquarters in Minneapolis.[2]

This chapter deals with the symbolic attributes that are linked to brands and national images. These issues are more significant for a company that is planning to establish a brand on the international market, as it is easier to avoid basic errors in relation to the choice of a brand name when starting from scratch. Correcting mistakes once brand goodwill has been created can prove a costly and tricky operation. However, a brand, even one that has a poor impact, may be an asset due to marketing that resulted in brand awareness and associations. Further, consumers are often confused by changes in a brand name. Changes to brand names, if they are possible, risk wasting time and incurring expenditure.

This chapter begins by discussing the interplay of images, including the product's country of origin, the company name and/or the brand name of its products. This complex interplay of images warrants closer analysis, as it is possible to choose favourable images that transfer across cultures, and are suitable for the product category and the national segments being targeted, when beginning with an unestablished brand.

Consumer evaluation of product quality has been documented by a great number of empirical studies, as has been the perception of certain product attributes, according to their country of origin (COO). While the impact of COO has often been overestimated, it is still an important variable that can be used to convey information about a brand. The second section of this chapter reviews studies dealing with the country-of-origin paradigm. These studies suggest consistent answers to such questions: Are 'Buy British' or 'Buy American' advertising campaigns successful? Do consumers have strong preferences for their national products? Which countries are best perceived and on which attributes? Do countries' images change over time?

Section 12.3 addresses the issue of the conversion of national brands into international brands. The linguistic obstacles that are met in this conversion are examined. The question of 'global' brands is also documented, since this has become a significant issue in international marketing.

12.1

National images diffused by product origin and brand name

Complexity of national images diffused by product

There is an important relationship between images of products and the symbols based on by their nationality. For instance, purchasers of motorcycles in Vietnam are now beginning to shift to the slightly more expensive domestic models, because the market-leading 'Made in China' motorcycles have become associated with poor quality and lack of reliability. The influence of a product's nationality on consumer evaluations was first studied with respect to the 'made in' label: that is, the origin label put on products. But the 'made in' label is not the only element that contributes to consumer perception of product nationality. The following elements all contribute to such perceptions (Figure 12.1):

1. image of national products versus imported or international products;
2. national images of generic products (e.g., yoghurt calls to mind the Balkans, perfume evokes France, a pair of jeans the United States);

Figure 12.1 Several layers of country-, company- and brand-related product image

3. image diffused by brand name;
4. image of 'made in' or 'designed in' label depicting manufacturing origin; origin labelling is mandatory in international trade; and
5. national image of manufacturing company.

In most cases a product category is not clearly associated with only one country. For example, wine may first bring to mind France, but also many other countries have strong associations with one or more varieties, including other European countries (e.g., Germany, Italy, Spain and Portugal), as well as Australia, Argentina and Chile. There are also regional associations with wine, such as Burgundy, Bordeaux, Rhone, Sonoma Valley, Napa Valley and Margaret River. In fact, many products, especially those based on local natural resources, have strong associations with countries and regions. For instance, in Europe, furniture made of natural pine wood is often associated with Scandinavia.

The desirability of products associated with a country or region differs by product category and consumer group, so companies must be careful about the image they wish to convey. For example, Loeffler[3] found that, for France, Germany, Italy and Spain, the quality of foreign cars are judged to be significantly lower than for corresponding domestic cars. However, foreign cars are evaluated in a different way to domestic cars in Germany: they are seen as lower quality, but superior in emotional aspects (more interesting and fascinating). This may help explain why Americans prefer German-named burger restaurants to American ones.[4] A recent trend is to label products with hybrid country-of-origin information. For instance, Apple's iPad 2 features the more complex label 'Designed by Apple in California, assembled in China' to mitigate the relatively poor consumer perceptions in industrialized countries of Chinese-made products.

The stereotypes associated with national images are not confined to Western cultures. For instance,

Table 12.1 Some examples of the combined influence of brand name and country of origin on product image

Product	National image of generic product	National image of manufacturer	Country evoked by brand name label	Country image diffused by 'Made in' label
Shalimar (perfume by Guerlain)	French	French	India/Orient	French
Kinder (milk chocolate bars made by Ferrero)	Swiss and other countries	Italian (but manufacturer's name, Ferrero, rarely appears)	German (means 'children' in German)	'Made in' hardly visible – often Italy
National (vacuum cleaner made by Matsushita)	Neutral	Manufacturer's name (Matsushita) does not appear	National brand makes people believe that product is local	'Made in' label hardly visible – different national origins
Coca-Cola	International	American	America	Neutral
Kremly (yoghurt by Chambourcy, part of Nestlé)	Balkan/Bulgarian Slav	Looks French, but is a worldwide brand of Nestlé Switzerland	Kremly (name and graphics) evokes Kremlin, a Slavic image	'Made in' label is local
Brother (typewriters by Brother)	Neutral	English/American (in fact a Japanese company)	International	'Made in' label indicates origin

Japanese consumers associate Germany and France with long history and tradition, Switzerland and Australia with rich nature, California and Brazil with abundant agricultural products, the United States and Germany with advanced industrial technology, and France with sense of design and high-class products.[5] These associations can lead to higher perceptions of quality for compatible products. Going back to the wine example, country image leads Chinese consumers to be more likely to purchase French wine, compared to American, Australian and, especially, Chinese.[6] This perhaps accounts for French wine dominating the prime retail shelf space in Beijing and Shanghai.

As can be seen from Table 12.1, national images operate on multiple levels and as such can send confusing messages to consumers. The following broad normative guidelines for management of a product's national image are developed for the four levels illustrated in Table 12.1:

1. *National image of generic product*: images that correspond to what is locally valued in each country should be diffused (imported or national) for the product category concerned. This can lead to the adoption of a name from the target country, due to strong nationalistic feelings.
2. *National image of manufacturer*: if the product category is generally associated with a specific country of origin, the brand name should be designed accordingly. For example, a manufacturer of machine tools should not be reluctant to adopt a German name, because of the favourable association of German-sounding names with technical reliability.
3. *Country evoked by brand name label*: the visibility of the company name, the brand name and the 'made in' label should be adjusted depending on their respective ability to convey the desired symbolic meanings.
4. *Country image diffused by 'made in' label*: it is often advisable to reduce the physical size of the 'made in' label, if the perception of the country of origin proves negative for local consumers (provided such reduction is permitted, or ignored, by local regulations). On the other hand, it should be enlarged in cases where the opposite perception prevails.

12.2
Consumer product evaluation according to country of origin

The use of 'country of origin' attribute

Consumers use the manufacturer's country of origin (COO) symbolically. In other words, they use it as an associative link: Germany = robustness, France = luxury, Italy = beauty, etc. The French pronunciation of a brand name positively affects the perceived hedonism of the product and negatively affects its perceived utility.[2] In an actual product taste test, where consumers have direct sensory experience of the product, foreign branding changes consumers' perceptions of the product (such as yoghurt).[2] When Reuben and Rose Mattus started the Häagen-Dazs ice-cream company, they felt that Scandinavian foods had a positive image regarding quality in the US and, accordingly, made up two Scandinavian-sounding words to leverage this perception.

More than 300 articles have been published on COO over the last 45 years, with a great deal of diversity in countries (as origins), product categories and consumers surveyed (in terms of demographics and nationality).[7] In the early years, COO effects were often assessed in isolation, and it was the only factor that differed between product choices in early experiments. The basic objective of many of the early studies was to demonstrate that the COO cue actually influenced consumer evaluations. Attempting to determine in which direction, and why, was only a secondary objective in these first studies.[8] This made the effects seem stronger than they would be under more realistic circumstances.[8] During the early 1980s to early 1990s, researchers began to review the effects of COO in relation to other extrinsic and intrinsic product attributes, such as price, perceived risk, etc.[8-10] By the early 2000s, several integrative reviews provided some important insights regarding the transfer of influence to the real world.[11-14] In the real world, consumers are likely to be influenced by multiple intrinsic and extrinsic cues, only one of which is COO. As expected, the influence of COO is lower when other cues, such as brand name, product, price, and warranty information are included in the information presented to consumers, and this holds true for both luxury and utilitarian products.[14,15] In fact, the average effect of COO on perceptions of quality and reliability halves when multiple attributes or cues are added to the COO information.[13]

Some key COO influences have been established:

1. COO has a stronger influence at the earlier stages of the decision-making process. The effect is stronger on perceptions of brand quality than on attitude towards the product or purchase intention.[13,14] For instance, based on a meta-analysis of 52 COO studies, Peterson and Jolibert[13] reported that the average effect of COO on quality/reliability was 0.30, whereas its average effect on purchase intentions was 0.19 for single-cue studies and only 0.03 for multi-cue studies. Thus, as the consumer moves closer to a choice COO has less impact.

2. COO is more often used as a reliable cue of brand quality than to infer quality.[16] For instance, Agrawal and Kamakura[16] examined the objective quality of 13 products (chosen from US Consumer Reports) to assess whether perceived differences were due to actual differences in objective – consumer-report-ranked – quality across firms representing different countries or to a halo effect in favour of products made in some countries. First, they found that countries differed in the objective quality of their durable consumer electronic goods: products originating in Japan had significantly higher objective quality than those originating in the US and Europe, and also Korea, which had significantly lower objective quality than the other counties. They used this information to re-examine 12 previous COO studies that reported the perceived quality of similar products, adding the objective quality scores. They found that COO had no significant impact on the prices companies charged, after controlling for the objective quality of the goods. This gives support to COO being used as a reliable cue or summary for brand quality, rather than as a halo effect.

3. COO also functions as a symbolic cue, with emotional value: It can be seen as the right or normative way to do things.[14,17–20] This perception is being leveraged when governments or industries promote 'Buy [country name]' campaigns. Developing nations have started to realize that encouraging consumers to buy local can be important to their economic success. Some recent examples from Africa include 'Buy Kenyan, Build Kenya', 'Proudly Nigerian', 'Proudly South African' and 'Produce, Consume, Export Mozambican'.

Stereotypical country images

Throughout COO studies one finds a relatively small number of stereotypical images that are fairly consistent across consumer nationalities. For instance, the image of the robustness of German products, the image of France as associated with luxury goods, the image of Korean products as being cheap. However, even these shared perceptions are restricted and unstable, depending on the countries being surveyed.

There are many perceptions of COO that are not shared by consumers of different national cultures. Often, differences in relationships between countries (similarity of culture and language, past colonial links, etc.) lead to differences in the perceptions of the others products.[21] The image of a country, in political, economic, cultural and social terms, may influence the willingness of foreign consumers to purchase that country's products independently of their perceived quality.

Animosity toward another culture, which has been defined by Klein and colleagues (p. 90)[22] as 'the remnants of antipathy related to previous or ongoing military, political, or economic events', has been found to influence the purchase of products from that country. For instance, Chinese consumer animosity toward Japan negatively influenced consumers' purchase of Japanese products.[22] In a series of studies, animosity has been found to influence purchase intentions, but not product quality judgements.[19,22] Those high in consumer animosity chose not to purchase goods from a specific country because of past events, such as wars or economic histories between countries. However, some recent studies have found that consumer animosity can also negatively impact consumer perceptions of product quality, resulting in lower purchase intentions such as in the cases of Taiwanese animosity towards China or Japan[23] and Arab Israelis animosity towards the UK.[24]

Consumers may also be unwilling to purchase products originating from a country under a dictatorship or one that acts in contravention of certain internationally recognized rules (as with countries that use child workers), even if these products fit their needs. Wang and Lamb[25] asked 94 US nationals about their readiness to purchase products from different countries (36 in all). They also asked them to identify the political, cultural and economic environment of each country. In this way they were able to demonstrate that variables related to the sociopolitical image of a country partially explained consumer readiness to purchase products from that country. American consumers were more prepared to buy products from politically democratic countries, such as those in Europe, Australia and New Zealand. However, country images may become partly divorced from the image of their products. Imagine, for instance, the case of a country under a non-democratic governing regime that nevertheless produces some excellent goods which are exported to democratic countries, as is the case with China.

Further, the overall level of industrial development of a country also influences the evaluations of its products by foreign consumers. Consumers from developed countries (e.g., Canada) evaluated products from other developed countries more positively than from developing countries.[26] Similarly, consumers from a range of developed and developing countries from Asia (e.g., Japan, Taiwan, South Korea and India) evaluated products from the same four countries, finding that India (the least developed country) had the poorest image in terms of quality, creativity, design and technological level.[27]

Industrial buyers are also influenced by the level of development of the country from which they buy products. For instance, US industrial buyers were found to be more willing to source from developed (e.g., Japan, Sweden, Taiwan, West Germany) than developing countries (e.g., Brazil, China, Poland), except in the case of Mexico where buyers experienced with this trade partner rated it much better than for other developing countries.[28] US purchasers were also more ready to buy from foreign suppliers who had established warehouses or sales offices in the US, irrespective of the COO. The very fact of having already done business with industrial suppliers from less favourably perceived COOs, such as Latin American countries, causes experienced purchasers to hold a higher image of their products and quality than that held by inexperienced industrial importers.[29]

Nevertheless it remains clear that vendors located in less favourable foreign environments may be cheap and reliable suppliers, as long as they are carefully evaluated and given a fair opportunity to perform. In sum, the cost of their *learning* should be shared with their customer, and subsequently both will benefit.

Website link 12.1

Search for information on brand naming difficulties, such as this article: http://www.deseretnews.com/article/705388343/Wannabe-exotic-brand-names-can-fail-when-returning-to-their-country-of-origin.html?s_cid=s10.

How does product image change over time?

Another important issue in relation to COO image is whether there are changes in these images over time and, if there are, at what rate they occur. The response to this question seems to be yes, and the rate seems to be fairly rapid. This was particularly true of products originating from Japan and new industrial Asian countries, such as Korea and Taiwan.[30] Many studies confirm the dramatic improvement of the image of Japan as a COO. At the beginning of the 1970s, Japanese products were seen as being of dubious quality; they were backed by rather restricted guarantees and poor after-sales service. By the end of the 1970s, however, they were seen as having improved significantly as far as quality was concerned.[31–33] Today, there are many prestigious products from Japan, including the Lexus automobile.

Haier, a Chinese consumer appliance manufacturer with a German name, is grappling with the problem of differing COO reputations in different markets. In Asia-Pacific markets, such as Thailand, Haier's appliances are widely regarded as a quality 'made-in-China' option. However, it remains a relatively poorly regarded product in developed markets, such as North America, in part due to negative Chinese COO association. One of the company's major challenges going forward is to increase their quality reputation, which given their relatively low brand recognition in these markets might be achieved by emphasizing the German-sounding brand-name rather than the Chinese origin.

Perceptions of COO

Many factors may moderate the influence of COO on consumer evaluation, including customer awareness of COO, their knowledge of and familiarity with the product, their consumer ethnocentric tendencies and the product category and risk perceptions. As a result of the expansion of multinational firms and the increase in the use of international supply chains, the actual COO of products has become increasingly difficult to define, owing to the number of countries involved in the manufacture of many products, which has led to substantial market ambiguity.

Apple was considered by Interbrand to be the eighth most valuable brand in the world in 2011. The brand name 'Apple' is very much a globally known American brand, and most of the design for the iPhone is carried out in Cupertino, California. Components for the iPhone are predominantly sourced from Taiwan, China and Thailand, while the majority of manufacturing occurs in China. This varied supply chain makes the origin of the product itself difficult to truly define, which has led to COO information becoming increasingly ambiguous to consumers. Apple label their iPhone 4s with 'Designed by Apple in California – Assembled in China', although ask Siri, Apple's iPhone 4 personal assistant app, 'where do you come from?' or 'where were you made?' she replies 'I, Siri, was designed by Apple in California' or something similar, with no mention of China. This is in line with the current trend to avoid informing consumers about the origins of products when there might be an unfavourable association. Further examples of this deliberately ambiguous tactic include labels such as 'made in Europe' or 'made in Asia'.

The result of COO ambiguity means that consumers are largely unaware of the COO of many products and find it increasingly less important to accurately assess where their purchases come from.[34] For instance, only 49 per cent of 40 American brands and 22 per cent of 44 non-American brands were correctly classified as to their origin by a national sample of adult Americans.[35] Some brands are also more susceptible to misclassification. For instance, UK consumers were only able to correctly identify the origin of Whirlpool (USA) 20 per cent of the time, while incorrectly attributing it as a domestic brand 39 per cent of the time.[36] Similarly, Samsung was more likely to be attributed to Japan (44 per cent) than to its actual COO Korea (28 per cent).[36] On the other hand, the majority correctly classified Sanyo (76 per cent) and Panasonic (59 per cent) as Japanese. In light of these types of findings, some authors have suggested that COO might contain elements of country of branding

(COB) in which the *actual* origin of a product is less important than the *perceived* origin, otherwise referred to as 'country of branding'.[37,38] Balabanis and Diamantopoulos further caution that, when brands are misclassified, consumers may hold lower brand image perceptions and purchase intentions, suggesting that emphasizing country of origin is an important strategic decision for brand managers.[36]

Consumer ethnocentrism and COO

Consumer ethnocentrism represents the beliefs held by consumers about the appropriateness, or even morality, of purchasing foreign products.[39,40] Thus, highly ethnocentric consumers are likely to believe that purchasing imported products harms the domestic economy and causes unemployment. Consumer age significantly correlates with ethnocentrism, with older consumers being much more ethnocentric than their younger counterparts.[41] Similarly, older consumers are also likely to have more animosity toward specific countries.[22,42,43]

Consumer ethnocentrism has been shown to influence consumers' attitudes and perceptions about foreign products.[40,41,44,45] Generally, there is a positive relationship between ethnocentrism and domestic products, and a negative relationship between ethnocentrism and foreign products.[44,46–51] However, the relationship between ethnocentrism and foreign products has been less consistent, as preference depends on the product category.[44] Different products coming from the same country produced varying patterns of acceptability.[40,52] For example, people from Australia might like French perfume, but dislike French cameras, or even French wine, as Australia generally produces fuller bodied wines. Certain products are considered more 'ethnic' or more typical of certain countries;[53] consumers tend to associate certain countries and products: Italy and pizza, Germany and machine tools, Britain and puddings. Thus, domestic companies may benefit from ethnocentrism, but foreign companies may not necessarily find resistance to their offerings. There is also evidence to suggest that some countries are more biased towards domestic products than others, for instance South Korea has been found to be particularly susceptible.[54]

A sound hypothesis which has been forwarded by several studies is the mediation of perceived risk to explain the influence of the COO on consumer evaluations. Either consumers perceive a lesser risk for national products, which would explain the preference for national products, or they perceive a lesser risk for the products of certain countries with a favourable image.

Consumers who come from high versus low uncertainty avoidance countries may also use COO information differently. Consumers from high uncertainty avoidance countries evaluated 'uncertain' COO quality images (Russian cameras and Japanese Vodka) less positively and had weaker behavioural intentions than those from low UA countries, but for 'certain' COO quality images (high quality = Russian vodka and Japanese cameras) there was no difference.[55]

12.3

National, international and global brands

Branding is an important tool used to differentiate products. The recognized benefits from differentiation include expanding sales, increased profits, greater longevity, greater power with distributors and the ability to survive adverse economic conditions.[56] However, there are also possible negative consequences that need to be acknowledged. For instance, Naomi Klein in her book *No Logo: No Space, No Choice, No Jobs*[57] argues that the focus on branding has led to significant downsizing and outsourcing that is displacing manufacturing with the service sector and reshaping the world of work. She cites this as one of the reasons behind the backlash against the 'brand bullies' such as McDonald's and Nike. Interestingly, she also comments on the branding of activism and the need to point out that: 'there are more than two worlds available, to expose all the invisible worlds between the economic fundamentalist of 'McWorld' and the religious fundamentalism of 'Jihad' (p. 10).[57]

The majority of brands throughout the world were originally conceived on a national level and not as international brands. Even among US brands, only a small number have achieved international recognition. For instance, Rosen and colleagues studied 650 US brands and their international scope (e.g., availability internationally) and their general conclusion is that 'despite all the talk about the internationalisation of

marketing efforts, the international diffusion of US brands is actually rather limited and . . . that most US brands are not marketed abroad' (p. 17).[58] That being said, the US has produced 50 of the top 100 global brands (including the top 10 brands) according to Interbrand's Best Global Brands list of 2011.[59]

Even within companies there are different levels of international branding. For instance, General Motors sells Chevrolet and Cadillac as close to global brands, Buick is sold in North America, some parts of Asia and Israel, the GMC brand is marketed in North America and the Middle East, while Opel is sold everywhere but North America and the UK (having just launched in Australia in 2012). Additionally, GM use Vauxhall as their British brand and Holden for Australia and New Zealand. Clearly managing this diverse stable of brands requires a high level of coordination coupled with regional autonomy.[60]

Most brands are related to a specific linguistic context, their evocative power being dependent on the language of the country and markets where they were originally launched. In Europe the vast majority of all brands are still national, if not purely local, in their appeal.[61] However, certain brands are launched as international brands, right from the start. In the 1960s a Japanese car manufacturer with increasing export sales decided it was necessary to have a name suitable for international markets: Toyota, with its three syllables which can be pronounced in any language, was the name finally selected.

International companies face three situations in terms of international brand names:

1. *Ex nihilo* creation of an international brand name for new products with high global potential. It must be pronounced and understood in a similar way across diverse linguistic and cultural contexts.

2. *Selection of potential international brand names from a large brand portfolio*, resulting from both external growth by acquisitions of local players and multiple layers of branding (e.g., corporate names, category brands, product names). Such brand portfolios are increasingly being simplified, in order to avoid spreading brand advertising budgets too thinly over a large number of names. Only a few of these names will become transnational brands. The appropriate course of action is to nominate the best applicants in translinguistic terms, taking into account local brand equity and the attachment of

both local consumers and local marketing teams to brands that often have a rich history.

3. *Assessment of the potential for an international extension of regional brands*, developed by a subsidiary based in the lead country for a region.

Transposition of national brand name for international purposes

The brand name of a given product is often the name of the company that manufactures it. Since the brand name is historically related to the founders of the company, it is difficult to change. Companies such as Procter & Gamble (with names that are difficult to pronounce in many languages) have followed a twofold brand strategy. Product brand names, such as Ivory, Camay, Pampers, Vizir and Tide, have been promoted almost independently from the Procter & Gamble company name (look at the respective sizes of the names on the packaging) and the Procter & Gamble name has been colloquially simplified so that it can be more easily memorized and verbalized, either to simply Procter, or to P & G.

Website link 12.2

Search for international companies with many different brand names, to see which you know, such as P&G: http://www.pg.com/en_US/brands/all_brands.shtml.

An example of lack of adaptation is the leading French company for iron and steel and heavy mechanical equipment during the 1970s and 1980s, Creusot-Loire. It branded and sold its products under the company's name in many countries in the world, including the United States. Unfortunately, American customers found this name difficult to pronounce, for the following reasons:

1. Throaty French 'CR' sound hardly exists in English.
2. 'EU' is a typically French diphthong, unpronounceable for Americans.
3. 'S' must be pronounced 'Z' because it is located between two vowels (French rule!).
4. 'O' is a very open sound.
5. 'T' is, in this case, a mute consonant and must therefore be ignored in pronunciation.

6. 'OI': once again a typically French diphthong (unknown in English).
7. 'R' is a hard 'r', almost unused in English.
8. 'E' is a mute vowel at the end of the word, and therefore must be ignored in pronunciation.

Naturally, such a brand name is difficult to memorize for most customers in many countries. Moreover, such difficult brand names can be a serious obstacle to clear communication between buyer and seller, creating confusion when discussing business on the phone. It is therefore essential to be prepared to carry out the necessary brand-name modifications.

While there may be limited benefits from global standardization for many aspects of communication, there seem to be strong arguments for corporate branding, including increased market efficiency, reduced advertising and inventory costs, and convenient identification for people travelling internationally.[62] For instance, Melewar and Saunders[63] examined the benefits sought from a global corporate visual identity system (CVIS), which consists of company name, symbol/logo, typography, colour and slogan. They surveyed British MNCs with subsidiaries in Malaysia, finding that the perceived benefits of CVIS standardization include increased sales, consumer goodwill, consumer familiarity, consumer awareness and market share. However, the diversity of national regulations and the rarity of brands with similar spellings in most national markets make it difficult to register a standardized brand across a large number of countries.

The options for the transposition of an existing name range from translation, to transliteration, to creating a new transparent brand are as follows:

1. *Simple translation* is rarely used as it may result in a disaster in relation to meaning,[64] scattered brand image, and inability to create international brand recognition.
2. *Transliteration* is better as it attempts to reconstitute the connotative meaning in the target language that exists in the source language (i.e., language of brand's country of origin). For example, the American hair-care product Silkience (Gillette) is sold under the same brand name in Germany, under the brand name Soyance in France and under the brand name Sientel in Italy.[65]
3. The best type of brand is the *transparent* brand, such as Sony, which is suitable everywhere. The

name Sony arose from a real 'shooting down' of the company name by the brand name of its products.[66] The original name of the firm (Tokyo Tsuhin Kogyo – Tokyo Industrial Telecommunication Company) was changed to Sony, as soon as the brand name of its products proved to be successful.

In China, for example, special consideration must be given to the complexity of the language and culture when deciding how to represent a global brand. The advantages and disadvantages of maintaining the original foreign-language brand name (rarely used), as compared to a Chinese translation must be weighed. One example of successfully using a Chinese transliteration is Reebok's *Rui Bu*, which means 'Quick Steps' in Chinese, thereby resulting in a name that sounds phonetically similar and also portrays the desired image.[67] Liu and colleagues suggest that the combination of the English name and a Chinese version might be most appropriate, at least when targeting educated Chinese consumers.[68]

Linguistic aspects of brand

Brands are signs based on sounds, written signs (letters or pictographs) and visual elements (logotype, brand design). The linguistic content of a brand name has an influence on its verbal, auditory and intellectual meaning, and its interpretation by consumers.[69] The brand name is often associated with a copyrighted design. Visual elements also include how a brand is written (alphabet, characters, ideographs). Table 12.2 shows which branch of linguistics should be used to appreciate how the sound, spelling and design of a brand name travel from a source to a target-linguistic context. A brand name should generally be relatively easy to pronounce. A simple rule is that the brand name should not exceed three syllables, each composed of one consonant and one vowel. Chinese mostly has such simple successions of one consonant and one or two vowels,[70] whereas German and Dutch often have many successive consonants (up to seven in a row in German) and French sometimes has long strings of vowels.

When considering the sound or phonological aspects of an international brand, one should check that the sound pattern corresponds to phonemes that are pronounced in all major languages (phonetics) and that it does not use unique sound patterns of the source language (phonemics). The name Hewlett-Packard, for instance, is far from perfect and is better when shortened to HP. The English 'th' or the French nasalized triphthong '*oin*' (don't try it!) are among

Table 12.2 Brand cues and meaning transfer

Brand cue	Element of meaning		Branch of linguistics concerned
Sound		L	
– Assemblage (vowels and	⇨ Pure sound	I	Phonology (phonemics/phonetics)
consonants)	⇨ Denotative meaning	N	Etymology
– Tonality	⇨ Connotative meaning	G	Semantics/Rhetoric
		U	
Written name		I	
– Alphabetic letters ⇨ sounds	Sounds ⇨ words ⇨ ideas	S	Semantics
– Pictographic writing	Pictograph design ⇨ ideas	T	Semiology
	Pictograph design ⇨ symbols	I	
		C	
Design		F	
– Assemblage of words (brands	– Descriptive	I	Grammar
and slogans)	– Suggestive	L	Rhetoric
– Icons (causal and analogous sign)	– Humorous	T	Semantics
– Symbols (untraceable linkage)	– Claim supportive	E	Semiology
	– Oneiric	R	
	– Ethnic		

such difficult combinations. Japanese, on the other hand, is a formidable language for international brands because it is composed exclusively of phonemes that are recognized by virtually all languages in the world, and it eschews successive consonants.

Denotative meaning, such as that of Milka chocolate, which directly relates to milk, is lost in most other languages; understanding of this meaning is limited to Anglo-Saxon and Germanic languages which use this root (etymology) and to speakers of English as a second language. Similarly, connotative meaning is generally lost when a product crosses borders: the detergent Tide was once sold in France (the name being pronounced *teed*) but nobody had the slightest knowledge of the idea of powerful tidal waves washing clothes that was evoked by the brand in English-speaking markets. Evidence suggests that meaningful names are easier to recall than meaningless ones.[71]

Written brand names are generally based on the alphabet: people first read sounds, then decode words and finish with ideas. A third of the world's consumers use ideographic writing systems; they go directly from pictographs to ideas. Sounds for a definite written item vary: people in various parts of China and Japan use similar ideographs which they recognize as having the same meaning, but which are pronounced quite differently. However, even with the Roman alphabet, the use of identical letters may result in a brand sounding different, according to the linguistic context: the Danone brand of yoghurt is spelled Dannon in the US, because consistency of pronunciation is preferred to consistency of spelling.[72] Given the wide differences in tonicity across languages, a brand such as Coca-Cola cannot be considered global as far as sound patterns are concerned: many languages, such as French have little tonicity, whereas others like Mandarin need tonicity to be understood.

Brand design also has an influence on its verbal, auditory and intellectual meaning. For instance, Whiskas (a Mars brand) has a translinguistic iconic value because it uses a cat's head to suggest its favourite user; but the colours are likely to be interpreted differently across cultures. In fact, many aspects of brand design have a suggestive power, especially natural elements, such as colours, shapes, locations, materials, everyday objects, animals, countryside and so on. Many brand backgrounds appear to be fairly arbitrary, due to their original link with meaning being lost or transformed.

Brand names are usually associated with a copyright design and the graphic composition of a logo conveys as much meaning as the letters of the brand name. The imagery of the IBM brand logo is translinguistic, and therefore offers a truly international ability to convey meaning. The link between brand and drawing is an intimate one. As Cabat (p. 344) notes, the IBM trademark is inseparable from its graphics in its evocative ability to communicate with the consumer:

The letters of the IBM logo are actually obtained by the superimposition of characters known as 'Mecanes' and of a 'blind' (alternate slats of coloured bands). The blind is in this case the informative image of the letters IBM, their morphological determinant . . . It thereby becomes the sign of computer language, binary-based. The 'Mecanes' are typesetting characters whose square serif evokes industrial production and rooting in the mechanical world.[64]

In contrast, think about how the Coca-Cola brand name stored in consumers' minds: as eight letters, as the traditional design of the Coca-Cola words or the Coke bottle, or as a combination of all three? Trademark legislation around the world varies in this respect. In some countries trademarks can only be composed of alphabetic letters and their design must be separately registered under the design and patent laws if they are to be effectively protected, whereas in the US a trademark may be bereft of any linguistic content and can be registered solely under trademark laws. There is no systematic need in the US and many other countries for additional registration of a trademark's design.

> **Website link 12.3**
>
> Search for trademark information from different countries, such as that found on the following website: **www.worldwide-trademark.com**.

Linguistic devices for brand names

Table 12.3 shows various linguistic devices that can be used in creating brand names. Whether by accident or design, advertisers and marketers strive to give some punch and evocative capacity to their brand names. Of course this is done, as much as possible, in line with the symbolic connotations that they intend to communicate in relation to product attributes and,

Table 12.3 Linguistic characteristics of brands

Characteristics	Definitions and/or examples
I Phonetic devices	
1. Alliteration	Consonant repetition (Coca-Cola, Cocoon)
2. Assonance	Vowel repetition (Kal Kan, Vizir, Omo)
3. Consonance	Consonant repetition with intervening vowel changes (Weight Watchers, Tic Tac)
4. Masculine rhyme	Rhyme with end of syllable stress (Max Pax)
5. Feminine rhyme	Unaccented syllable followed by accented syllable (American Airlines)
6. Weak/imperfect/slant rhyme	Vowels differ or consonants similar, not identical (Black & Decker)
7. Onomatopoeia	Use of syllable phonetics to resemble the object itself (Wisk, Cif, Wizzard)
8. Clipping	Product names shortened (Chevy for a Chevrolet, Deuche for a Citroen Deux Chevaux, Rabbit for a Volkswagen)
9. Blending	Morphemic combination, usually with elision (Aspergum, Duracell)
10. Initial plosives*	/b/, /c-hard/, /d/, /g-hard/, /k/, /q/, /t/, (Bic, Dash, Pliz, Pim's)
II Orthographic device	
1. Unusual or incorrect spellings	Kool-Aid, Decap'Four
2. Abbreviations	7-Up for Seven-Up
3. Acronyms	Amoco, Amro, DB, Cofinoga, Lu, BSN
III Morphological device	
1. Affixation	Jell-O, Tipp-Ex
2. Compounding	Janitor-in-a-Drum, Vache-qui-rit
IV Semantic device	
1. Metaphor	Representing something as if it were something else (Arrid); simile was included with metaphor when a name described a likeness and not an equality (Aqua Fresh, Longeurs et Pointes, Head and Shoulders, Tendres Promesses)
2. Metonymy	Application of one object or quality for another (Midas, Ajax, Uncle Ben's, Bounty)
3. Synecdoche	Substitution of a part for the whole (Red Lobster)
4. Personification/pathetic fallacy	Humanizing the non-human or ascription of human emotions to the inanimate (Betty Crocker, Clio, Kinder)
5. Oxymoron	Conjunction of opposites (Easy-Off, Crème de peinture)
6. Paranomasia	Pun and word plays (Hawaiian Punch, Raid – insecticide, Fédor – orange juice)
7. Semantic appositeness	Fit of name with object (Bufferin, Nutella)

* An initial is said to be plosive if, to produce this sound, one needs first to stop the flow of air completely, then audibly release the air previously compressed.

(Source: Adapted from Vanden Bergh *et al.*[73] Reproduced with permission.)

inevitably, it is done in a particular source language. There are four main categories of linguistic device: phonetic devices (sound, perceived orally), orthographic devices (relating to writing, perceived visually), morphological devices (adding morphemes to the brand-name root) and semantic devices (the figure produces meaning, perceived through culture-based interpretations).

The linguistic devices set out in Table 12.3 make it possible to understand what constitutes the pure linguistic capacity of a brand; independently of the established goodwill (brand recognition may be high for linguistically unadapted but longstanding brand names). The issue for brand marketers is whether a brand and its associated elements are transposable into other linguistic contexts. The alliteration of Coca-Cola transposes well, but the composition of the words Janitor-in-a-Drum, or even the juxtaposition of opposites (Easy-Off), do not. This is because Coca-Cola does not require a basic comprehension of the words that make up the brand name. Where understanding of complex linguistic features is required, brand names are difficult to translate and, more generally, to transpose. As a rule, the linguistic devices in categories I and II are the more 'translinguistic'. A good number of the devices in category IV are not at all translinguistic, especially # 1, 4, 5, 6 and 7.

Semantic issues: intended versus unintended meaning

As described in previous sections, meaning can be lost when a brand crosses borders. Nestlé (*Nestele*: 'little nest' in the Alemanic dialects of the southern German-speaking area) is lost in most of the world's languages, which causes confusion as to why the logo presents a bird in a nest. Beiersdorf's 'Uhu' brand for glue sticks is based on the German name for eagle owl. Most intended meaning does not extend much beyond the source language area. It is, however, not a major problem if consumers in other linguistic areas memorise the sound of brand names easily and invest them with new, positive meanings.

Unintended negative meaning is the most dangerous. The brand name should not have an unfortunate meaning in a different linguistic/cultural context. However, checking the translinguistic capacity of a brand name is by no means universal practice. There is no shortage of examples: the German hairspray Caby-Net launched on the French market (*cabinet* is a toilet in French); the Japanese gun, *Miroku*, the name of which has several meanings including 'look at your bottom' in French. The examples of certain American cars in South American markets are also famous. The Chevrolet (Chevy) Nova (the intended meaning was 'new') translates into Spanish as 'does not work'. The Ford Pinto meant 'tiny male genitals' in Brazil. Kellogg's renamed its Frosted Flakes as Sucrilhos for Brazil, and its Cocoa Krispies as Crokinhos; similarly it had to change its Bran Buds brand name in Sweden, so that Swedish people did not read that they were to be served 'grilled farmer' in their breakfast bowls.[74] The type of research that must be carried out is straightforward: it is necessary to interview a group of consumers from the target country about the perceptual effects of the intended names and sometimes it is necessary to interview several different groups depending on the number of dialects with potential for unintended meanings.

The case of Asian ideographic writing systems

The scope of the discussion has thus far been limited to the framework of languages based on the Roman alphabet where letters correspond to sounds and sounds to ideas, but almost one-quarter of the world's population reads logographic characters, including Chinese, Japanese and Korean.[75] Reading logographs relies more on visual processes, which affects consumer memory,[75–77] as well as brand attitudes.[78–80] Recall is better when Westerners speak the words and Chinese write the words down, suggesting that verbal information is encoded in a visual manner in Chinese and a phonological manner in English.[79] Similarly, visual branding is more easily integrated in memory for Chinese speakers, while auditory branding is more easily integrated for English speakers.[75] Thus, certain types of translations are likely to work better in different cultural contexts.

Zhang and Schmitt[80] put forward a framework to examine issues for creating or translating English to Chinese brand names. They explored the boundaries by examining the effects of the degree of emphasis on the English name compared with that placed on the Chinese name in a dual writing situation and the presence of prior types of brand translations in the same product category. Similarly, Hong and colleagues[81] explored the effect of phonetic translations into Mandarin for familiar and unfamiliar brands on perceptions of quality in Singapore. They found that the phonetic translation performed better for an unfamiliar brand, but for a familiar brand it was better to keep the original name.

Global brands wanting to reach these markets face a difficult task. Even Coca-Cola is not known exactly by this name in China, since the simple translated name would have a negative connotation: Coca-Cola has been transliterated as 'ke kou ke le' in Mandarin and 'ho hau ho lohk' in Cantonese (in terms of approximate sound equivalence), which conveys the meaning of 'tasty and enjoyable/happy'.[82] In fact, Chinese characters are pronounced differently according to the dialect spoken (Mandarin, Cantonese, Hokkien, etc.), and there are a large number of homonyms (same pronunciation, but written differently to indicate the distinct meaning). For instance, 'gong' corresponds to many different meanings, ranging from work to attack to palace, depending on the characters.[76] Thus, there are many possibilities to select from when transposing Roman-letter brand names into Chinese characters.

In East Asia, and especially in China, calligraphy and meaning become much more important than in standard Western branding. Schmitt and Pan[76] list the factors needed for a brand to have a positive connotation in China:

1. characters with favourable sounds, which can be pronounced in about the same way in as many regions as possible, while avoiding the pitfalls due to tonality;
2. characters that convey favourable meaning, if possible related to the brand's advertised qualities;
3. a balance between *yin* (even number of strokes) and *yang* characters (odd number of strokes). Note: an analysis of 1,202 Chinese brand names found that 715 contained a lucky number of strokes;[83]
4. a favourable content in terms of lucky numbers, such as 8;
5. suitable calligraphy for the brand – the calligraphy must convey certain visual signs that fit with the brand imagery, such as in the case of the Volkswagen 'Cheep', where a character was used that evoked an imaginary slope that the jeep had to climb.

Consequently, Pepsi-Cola is transposed into Chinese characters meaning 'hundred happy things' and Mercedes-Benz becomes 'Benchi', with two characters meaning 'striving forward fast'. However, such transposition is not possible for all brands. In some cases, when the transposition of sounds is deemed more important than the transposition of meaning (it may be difficult to find a chain of characters that do both), the brand name may sound very similar to the sound of the Western version, such as 'nifeya' for Nivea, but the meaning level may be very poor.[82]

Francis and colleagues[84] examined brand names used by 49 *Fortune* 500 companies that manufactured consumer products available in China or Hong Kong. They found that most brands were leveraged in some way: that is, 44 per cent sounded similar, 22 per cent had similar meanings, and 10 per cent used their English brand names. In addition, while most brand names attempted to convey benefits (74 per cent), only 11 per cent shared the same benefits across languages. Thus, firms appear to localize their brand names in China. Localization may be necessary when there are large linguistic and cultural differences. Data from an AC Nielsen Retail Audit in China suggest that domestic brands are increasing in sales and, while the average price is lower than for multinational brands, the gap is narrowing.[85]

In Japan the issue is both less and more complicated since the Japanese are familiar with the Western alphabet (*Romaji*), but they also use the Chinese characters (*Kanji*), and two syllabaries, the *Hiragana* for Japanese words and the *Katakana* for foreign loanwords (which use the same syllables as the *hiragana*, but with a slightly different calligraphic style that signals the foreign origin). These alternative writing systems carry different associative meanings which must be carefully monitored in order to convey appropriate subliminal messages: (1) as to the origin of the product: *kanji* and *hiragana* will look more Japanese while *Romaji* and *Katakana* signal foreignness; (2) as to the product category: high-tech products will best be written in *katakana* which connotes modernity, whereas traditional products are best served by *Kanji*; (3) as to the consumer universe implied by the writing style: *hiragana* have a feminine image and are used frequently for beauty products and cosmetics.[76]

Functions of brands according to national contexts

Brand name has a number of functions for the consumer such as *identity* (it guides consumers when making their choice), *practicality* (it works as a summary of information about product characteristics), *guarantee* ('signature of the manufacturer'), *personalization* (brand name allows consumers to express their individuality through their purchases) and an *entertainment* function because the brand allows the exercise of free choice and enables consumers to satisfy their needs for freshness, arousal, and surprise.[86] For the producer, the brand fulfils two essential functions: *positioning* within the competitive scene and *capitalization* of image and advertising expenditure over the long term.

These functions are very differently valued across countries, to the extent that some functions of the brand can be almost non-existent in certain national contexts. Accordingly, in France there is a certain social mistrust of brands, especially by public authorities: they supposedly increase prices, constituting entry barriers to possible competitors, thereby limiting competition.[87] Furthermore, being set up on the basis of large cumulative advertising expenditure, they are said to increase the price of the product to the detriment of the consumer. Contensou (p. 249)[87] shows that, in fact, these fears are groundless, and further points out that 'inflationary tendencies have no connection to brand development and the multiplication of products sold under brand names'. Kapferer, taking the same defensive attitude towards brand names, has shown that they support the actual intentions of the manufacturers and their achievements to the benefit of consumers and that without effective attempts to foster product quality, brand images cannot be sustained.[88]

In contrast to France, Japan seems to be a country where brands are very highly valued. Yoshimori (pp. 277–8) explains this:

In feudal Japan, the brand was not distinct from the name of the ancestral house itself. This name had great importance, to the extent that everything was done to protect its good image, and above all to perpetuate it. Anyone who tarnished that reputation even through mere carelessness was obliged to rectify the damage through dying . . . [Yoshimori then gives examples of Japanese executives who have recently committed suicide because they believed that through their actions or negligence they had tarnished the reputation of their company] . . . a trading company, or any such firm, was not merely an economic entity; it also constituted a religious community which transcended the physical life of the family that controlled it. Ancestors occupied an almost divine place: it was therefore believed that the preservation and advancement of kamei, the name of the ancestral house, was an almost religious obligation since it (kamei) was the concrete translation of the presence of ancestors.[66]

The brand in Japan is a real figurehead of competitive struggle. Abbeglen and Stalk[89] show how, during the 1950s, the Honda brand name destroyed the Tohatsu brand (which today is completely unknown). They also describe in great detail the episodes in the Homeric quarrel between Honda and Yamaha at the start of the 1980s, which ended with a victory for Honda. In the US, as in Japan, brands are central to competition. Brand marketing occupies a stable position in the strategies of US companies, but also one which is constantly changing, as are market shares. The vigour of the brand can only be built on 'tidal waves' of sales promotion and advertising as well as on consistent efforts towards improvement of product quality. Dupuy and Thoenig[90] compared brand

status in the US, France and Japan, noting that brands in France have a much weaker status than in Japan and the US.

Differences in national distribution systems explain to a large extent the degree of brand-related competition. In Japan, the *keiretsu* distribution system enables producers to control distribution channels and therefore to direct the brand name principally towards the relationship with the consumer. Alpert and colleagues[47] surveyed buyers in relation to their behaviour towards pioneer and me-too follower brands. While they found that both Japanese and US buyers accepted about the same proportion of pioneer brands (~63 per cent), they reported being offered dramatically different numbers by the manufacturers: in Japan, about half of all new brands offered were pioneer brands, while in the US only 14 per cent were pioneers. A possible explanation is that the Japanese suppliers better understand the retailers' preferences and try to meet them.

In France, where large-scale distribution is involved in conflicts with producers, the channels develop their own brands. For instance, large-scale retailers in France (hypermarkets) have created their own private labels over the past 20 years. Distributors' brands do not need any product-related advertising expenditure and tend to compete with manufacturers' brands. This leads to an inflation of distributors' brands and private labels, which compete against established manufacturers' brands. Private labels are growing worldwide.

Website link 12.4

Search for distribution channels store brands in your country, such as this list of private label manufacturers: **http://www.privatelabelmanufacturers.com.au/ directory.php**.

International and global brands

International brands share a common trait of long-term orientation. The main objective of the brand is to establish brand goodwill or equity over time through consumer brand awareness and recognition. When products share very similar attributes and performance, a well-known brand may have the edge by virtue of its reputation and the consumer loyalty it has created. Accordingly, Procter & Gamble has retained some brands, such as Ivory soap, for more than a century. Camay soap is also nearing this age: the brand's name, that is, not the formula of the product, which has been regularly updated. Thus, public recognition of international brands is usually based on *considerable cumulative advertising expenditure*. They are often supported by the history of a prestigious company (for cars, Mercedes, Jaguar, Ferrari, Cadillac, etc.).[91]

Website link 12.5

Search for the Top 100 global brands: http://www.interbrand.com/en/best-global-brands/best-global-brands-2008/best-global-brands-2011.aspx.

Brands can be aligned with the local consumer culture, a foreign consumer culture or a global consumer culture. Alden and colleagues[92] examined ads from India, Thailand, Korea, Germany, the Netherlands, France and the United States, finding that most associate the brand with the local consumer culture (59 per cent), or global consumer culture (22 per cent), while only 4 per cent aligned the brand with a foreign consumer culture. Their definition of foreign consumer culture is fairly strict, in the sense that an association was only classified in this category if it was clearly from an identifiable country. If it was seen as 'Western', for instance, it would be classified as a global association, as it was 'not associated with a single country (local or foreign), but rather a larger group generally recognized as international and transcending individual national cultures' (p. 80).[92] Which associations are more effective is a more difficult question. Consumers may value localized international brand names, as well as international brands that convey foreign benefits.[93] For instance, Reebok customizes its image to national differences with a meaningful name (translated as *dashing step*) which has no foreign image; while Nike maintains a standardised image of 'fitness and performance' in all markets.[93] The brand name Nike has no special meaning in Chinese, but it does have a distinctly Western image which sounds appealing. Similarly, Apple maintains its iPod, iPad and iPhone brand names as-is in all of their markets, allowing efficiencies in production,

promotion and distribution. Apple even maintains their English brand names on their foreign language consumer websites.

In order to be successfully aligned with a foreign consumer culture, brands need to have a *basic credibility which is based on a national image*.[94] Chanel No. 5 is based on the image of French *luxe* and *haute couture*, conveyed by the character of Gabrielle Chanel (Coco) and their associated film star ambassadors. Buitoni is understood as Italian pasta and Johnny Walker as whisky from Scotland. Despite this, in each country, consumers 'repaint' the international brand image with their own local images.[95]

As noted in the introduction to this chapter, the interplay between brands and national images is a game of complex meanings (Table 12.1): there must be some degree of caution prior to making the affirmation that a brand is universal. Coca-Cola's name is adapted in Chinese to avoid negative connotations. Coca-Cola further decided to adapt the name 'Diet Coke' to 'Coke Light' or 'Coca-Cola Light' when it found that in some countries the word *diet* or *diète* connoted the need for weight-reduction rather than minimizing weight gain.[96] In other countries legal issues with the word *diet* have diminished its use as a label.[97] Now Coca-Cola uses the word 'Light' in almost one-third of countries, including Germany, Spain, Argentina, Mexico and Brazil.

Brand images combine with the product's origin and the manufacturer's name, which is also a brand. A name like Brother offers a fairly good combination of interpretive meanings because the Brother name diffuses an English/international image that hides the Japanese origin of the manufacturer. Brother manufactured electronic typewriters and items with no 'ethnic' relation to a specific country. LG is another example of ambiguous naming, with the majority of UK consumers unable to attribute the Korean brand to any particular country.[36]

A basic condition for belonging to the very narrow club of global brands is to have built brand equity over a number of years by considerable advertising spending based on consistent core themes (consistent both over time and across countries). Building a global brand is expensive, but valuable. The value of the Coca-Cola brand is estimated at US$72 billion, Microsoft at $59 billion, and the McDonald's brand name at $36 billion.[59] Advertising remains the key investment for developing brand awareness, although advertising spending has been claimed not to be an absolute necessity for creating brand equity, with such examples as the Body Shop or Häagen-Dazs having developed their brands through events, sponsoring and retail shops.[98]

The second condition is that the brand's image must have been carefully monitored over time. This requires considerable sophistication in the management of meaning. For instance, PepsiCo assesses its brand by examining recognition (awareness) and regard, which is made up of four components (brand reputation, affiliation, momentum and differentiation).[99] In Spain the company found that awareness is increasing and among those who are aware regard is growing (i.e., a healthy brand), but in Australia there is little increase in awareness, even though regard is growing among those who are aware.[99] Thus, using this model, Pepsi can identify the aspects of the brand they need to address, such as increasing brand awareness in Australia.

Although some people try to defend the idea of global brands,[100] it is a somewhat blurred and probably even deceptive concept. There can only be a limited number of brands known by consumers in several countries throughout the world simultaneously (a few dozen, perhaps one or two hundred at most). As Kapferer (p. 169)[101] notes, there is still hope for local brands: 'The essence of local brands' strength is their being local, which means a considerably-felt proximity that goes far beyond the local brands' advantage to an extensive and well-known distribution network developed through time, by canvassing the country and delivering a faster service to customers'.

Many companies promote both global and local elements. Contrary to the global-brand building of McDonald's, Ronald McDonald is used as a point of differentiation in each market: he celebrates Christmas in Europe, Chinese New Year in Hong Kong, promotes wine in France and fish fillets in Australia.[102]

However, it is the perceptions of globalness that often drive consumer behaviour. For instance, Steenkamp and colleagues[103] surveyed consumers in the US and Korea to assess perceived brand globalness (PBG). They found that PBG influences the likelihood of brand purchase through three sets of beliefs, that 'globalness' (a) signifies better quality, (b) provides status and prestige, or (c) provides a way to become part of a global consumer culture. More recently, Steenkamp and de Jong[104] investigated attitudes towards

global products (AGP) and attitudes towards local products (ALP) across 28 different countries. Overall, they found that there is a wide variation across and within countries in these attitudes, and that they are not mutually exclusive, meaning that 'a carefully crafted portfolio of local and global brands may be preferable to an over emphasis on global brands' (p. 36).[104] One strategy that a local brand could use to appear both local and global is to simultaneously emphasize the 'localness' of the company, whilst using foreign-oriented marketing appeals. Zhou and colleagues give the example of Tsingtao beer and Lenovo notebooks in China, both definitively Chinese brands that use combinations of foreign package design, international celebrities in advertising and sponsorship of international events to appear both domestic and foreign at the same time.[105]

Global brands are more likely to be portfolios of basically localized marketing assets (consumer franchise and goodwill based on images which are in fact heterogeneous); a mere collection of local brands, federated under a *lexically equivalent single name*. The brand name may not even be pronounced similarly in different linguistic areas, a factor which can be critical for radio advertising, for example.

The management of global brands is complex. Douglas and colleagues[106] propose a brand architecture framework, based on the geographic scope, product scope and the level in the organization at which the brand is used. This framework is designed to search for ways to reduce the number of brands and improved efficiency and harmonize brand strategy across product lines and country markets. Matanda and Ewing[107] examined the global brand management structure of Kimberly-Clark, a *Fortune* 500 company in the health and hygiene market responsible for such brands as Huggies and Kleenex. The company recently changed their overall structure from one of regional silos to a dual-layered system wherein there is a global brand management division which provides centralized guidelines and support to regional brand management teams. The global teams come up with the overall brand meaning and strategy (ensuring global brand consistency and learning efficiencies), while the regional teams decide how to best execute the broad strategy within the cultural, infrastructure and language nuances of their local market.[107]

The global brand, like the global campaign, requires a large amount of creative time and investment. A brand is a *sensitive asset of symbols*, suggested and maintained by diversified marketing communications, including sponsoring, advertising, communication, public relations, communication through the product itself or even the style of outlets. This mix of marketing communications must be carefully managed, so that the public never feels betrayed in those beliefs that have been invested in the brand. Alain Etchegoyen (p. 55) describes the Louis Vuitton brand image in the following way:

There is no mythology without gods or demigods. That is why one must not expect gods to collapse into the melting pot of the market. Some products have to keep at a distance so that other products appear to come from somewhere else. The brand can only remain influential at the expense of maintaining a sacred fire. The imaginary Eden of carefully tended [brand] images will not withstand the boorish hell of bar codes [products].[108]

Furthermore, the complexity of trademark law must be considered on an international level. Despite the move towards a standard of foreign trademark protection which binds WTO member countries, there are still many differences across countries. Gillespie and colleagues[109] examined the patterns of protection internationally. They found that groups of countries differed in their treaty participation and varied in their local trademark legislation. For participation in foreign treaties, developed countries (83 per cent) and transitional economies (79 per cent) had a higher rate (83 per cent) than NICs (newly industrialized countries) (53 per cent) or LDCs (less developed countries) (45 per cent). There were also differences in trademark legislation, such as procedures to contest the application before it is approved, the legitimacy of prior use to stop a potential preempter, and the necessity to use the product to maintain the trademark after approval. Developed countries and newly industrialized countries (NICs) rated higher than less developed countries (LDCs) and transitional economies.

> **Website link 12.6**
>
> Search for information about emerging issues in intellectual property from the World Intellectual Property Organization: **http://www.wipo.int/about-ip/en/studies/**.

In short, the costs and the legal complexity of managing a global brand remain extremely high. Creating an international brand is an undertaking that should be considered as a long-term target, especially when starting from scratch. Yoshimori (p. 279) quotes Akio Morita's (Sony Chairman) 1955 reply to an American client who requested that Sony manufacture transistor radios for him as a subcontractor. Morita refused to manufacture 100,000 of them and, allegedly, said:

Fifty years ago your brand name was probably as unknown as ours is today . . . Today I decide the first stage for the next fifty years of my company. In fifty years I can promise that our name [Sony] will be just as famous as your company's is today.[66]

Questions

1. Discuss the international transferability of the following assemblages (product, company, country of manufacture, brand name).

Generic product	Company name	Brand name	Made in
Pizza	Dr Oetker	Pizza Rustica	Germany
Computer chip	Intel	Pentium	United States
Drilling tool	Bosch	Fuchsschwanz	Spain
Car	Daewoo	Daewoo/Nexia	South Korea
Tomato sauce	Mars	Dolmio	The Netherlands
Insecticide	Bayer	Baygon	Germany

2. A very large German food company, Dr Oetker, still sells its products in France under the name Ancel (the brand name of a French company taken over many years ago). Why?

3. Discuss the relationship between a country's image (through its people, its history, its political and social situation, etc.) and the image of products known to be made in this country.

4. Discuss the possible international extension of the following companies and/or brand names:

- Müller (German yoghurts)
- Barilla (Italian pastas and cookies)
- Procter & Gamble
- Teysseire (French syrups)
- Kuoni (a Swiss tour operator)
- Schimmelpenninck (Dutch cigars and cigarillos)
- Ishikawajima Harima Heavy Industries (a Japanese industrial equipment company)
- Roi des Montagnes (French dried mushrooms)
- Hewlett-Packard
- Douwe-Egberts (a large Dutch food and tobacco company)
- Club Méditerrannée (a French tour operator)

5. Given the increasing importance of China as a consumer market, Nestlé has decided to stop using the Chambourcy category brand name for milk-based products used worldwide, which is a brand with great recognition in Europe and Latin America. The name was deemed too difficult to transfer into the Chinese linguistic context. Furthermore, Nestlé maintained advertising spending at three levels (corporate name, category name and product name) and decided to use the Nestlé name directly for all its milk-based products in addition to a brand name for the particular product in some cases. Discuss the marketing and management implications of such a decision.

References

1. Keller, Kevin Lane (1998), *Strategic Brand Management: Building, Measuring and Managing Brand Equity*. Upper Saddle River, NJ: Prentice Hall.
2. Leclerc, France, Bernd H. Schmitt and Laurette Dubé (1994), 'Foreign Branding and Its Effects on Product Perceptions and Attitudes', *Journal of Marketing Research*, 31 (2), 263–70.
3. Loeffler, Michael (2002), 'A Multinational Examination of the "(Non-)Domestic Product" Effect', *International Marketing Review*, 19 (5), 482–98.
4. Harris, Richard Jackson, Bettina Garner-Earl, Sara J. Sprick and Collette Carroll (1994), 'Effects of Foreign Product Names and Country-of-origin Attributions on Advertisement Evaluations', *Psychology and Marketing*, 11 (2, March/April), 129–44.
5. Nishina, Sadafumi (1990), 'Japanese Consumers: Introducing Foreign Products/Brands into the Japanese Market', *Journal of Advertising Research*, 30 (2), 35–45.
6. Wang, Hainan and Jill McClusky (2010), 'Effects of Information and Country of Origin on Chinese Consumer Preferences for Wine: An Experimental Approach in the Field', paper presented to *Agricultural & Applied Economics Association, Joint Annual Meeting*, Colorado, Denver, 1–29.
7. Nebenzahl, Israel D., Eugene D. Jaffé and Jean-Claude Usunier (2003), 'Personifying Country-of-origin Research', *Management International Review*, 43 (4), 383–406.
8. Bilkey, Warren J. and Erik Nes (1982), 'Country-of-origin Effects on Product Evaluations', *Journal of International Business Studies* (Spring–Summer), 89–99.
9. Papadopoulos, Nicholas and Louise A. Heslop (1993), *Product and Country Images: Research and Strategy*. New York: The Haworth Press.
10. Samiee, Saeed (1994), 'Customer Evaluation of Products in a Global Market', *Journal of International Business Studies*, 25 (3), 579–604.

11. Jaffé, Eugene D. and Israel D. Nebenzahl (2001), *National Image and Competitive Advantage: The Theory and Practice of Country-of-Origin Effects*. Copenhagen: Copenhagen Business School Press.

12. Nebenzahl, Israel D., Eugene D. Jaffé and Shlomo I. Lampert (1997), 'Towards a Theory of Country Image Effect on Product Evaluation', *Management International Review*, 37 (1), 27–49.

13. Peterson, Robert A. and Alain Jolibert (1995), 'A Meta-analysis of Country-of-origin Effects', *Journal of International Business Studies*, 26 (4), 883–900.

14. Verlegh, Peeter W. J. and Jan-Benedict E. M. Steenkamp (1999), 'A Review and Meta-analysis of Country of Origin Research', *Journal of Economic Psychology*, 20, 521–46.

15. Godey, Bruno, Daniele Pederzoli, Gaetano Aiello, Raffaele Donvito, Priscilla Chan, Hyunjoo Oh, Rahul Singh, Irina I. Skorobogatykh, Junji Tsuchiya and Bart Weitz (2011), 'Brand and Country-of-origin Effect on Consumers' Decision to Purchase Luxury Products', *Journal of Business Research*, in press.

16. Agrawal, Jagdish and Wagner A. Kamakura (1999), 'Country of Origin: A Competitive Advantage?', *International Journal of Research in Marketing*, 16 (4), 255–67.

17. Askegaard, S. and Guliz Ger (1998), 'Product-country Images: Toward a Contextualized Approach', *European Advances in Consumer Research*, 3, 50–8.

18. Batra, Rajeev, Venkatram Ramaswamy, Dana L. Alden, Jan-Benedict E. M. Steenkamp and S. Ramachander (2000), 'Effects of Brand Local and Nonlocal Origin on Consumer Attitudes in Developing Countries', *Journal of Consumer Psychology*, 9 (2), 83–96.

19. Klein, Jill Gabrielle, Richard Ettenson and Marlene D. Morris (1998), 'The Animosity Model of Foreign Product Purchase: An Empirical Test in the People's Republic of China', *Journal of Marketing*, 62 (1), 89–100.

20. Smith, N. (1990), *Morality and the Market*. London: Routledge.

21. Yaprak, Attila (1987), 'The Country of Origin Paradigm in Cross-national Consumer Behavior: The State of the Art', in *World Marketing Congress*, Kenneth D. Bahn and M. Joeseph Sirgy (eds). Blacksburg, VA: Academy of Marketing Science.

22. Klein, Jill Gabrielle (2002), 'Us Versus Them, or Us Versus Everyone? Delineating Consumer Aversion to Foreign Goods', *Journal of International Business Studies*, 33 (2), 345–63.

23. Huang, Yu-An, Ian Phau and Chad Lin (2010), 'Consumer Animosity, Economic Hardship, and Normative Influence: How do they Affect Consumers' Purchase Intention?', *European Journal of Marketing*, 44 (7/8), 909–37.

24. Rose, Mei, Gregory M. Rose and Aviv Shoham (2009), 'The Impact of Consumer Animosity on Attitudes Towards Foreign Goods: A Study of Jewish and Arab Israelis', *Journal of Consumer Marketing*, 26 (5), 330–9.

25. Wang, Chih-Kang and Charles W. Lamb Jr (1983), 'The Impact of Selected Environmental Forces Upon Consumers' Willingness to Buy Foreign Products', *Journal of the Academy of Marketing Science*, 11 (Winter), 71–84.

26. Ahmed, Sadrudin A., Alain d'Astous and Jelloul Eljabri (2002a), 'The Impact of Technological Complexity on Consumers' Perceptions of Products Made in Highly and Newly Industrialised Countries', *International Marketing Review*, 19 (4), 387–407.

27. Khanna, Sri Ram (1986), 'Asian Companies and the Country Stereotype Paradox: An Empirical Study', *Columbia Journal of World Business* (Summer), 29–38.

28. Thorelli, Hans B. and Aleksandra E. Glowacka (1995), 'Willingness of American Industrial Buyers to Source Internationally', *Journal of Business Research*, 32, 21–30.

29. Saghafi, Massoud M., Fanis Varvoglis and Tomas Vega (1991), 'Why US Firms Don't Buy from Latin American Companies', *Industrial Marketing Management*, 20, 207–13.

30. Jaffé, Eugene D. and Israel D. Nebenzahl (1989), 'Global Promotion of Country Image: The Case of the 1988 Korean Olympic Games', in Reijo Luostarinen (ed.), *Dynamics of International Business*, vol. 1, Proceedings of the 15th Annual Conference of the European International Business Association. Helsinki, Finland, 358–85.

31. Darling, John B. and F. Kraft (1977), 'A Competitive Profile of Products and Associated Marketing Practices of Selected European and Non-European Countries', *European Journal of Marketing*, 11 (7), 519–37.

32. Kamins, Michael A. and Akira Nagashima (1995), 'Perceptions of Products Made in Japan Versus Those Made in the United States among Japanese and American Executives: A Longitudinal Perspective', *Asia Pacific Journal of Management*, 12 (1), 49–68.

33. Kraft, Frederick B. and Kae H. Chung (1992), 'Korean Importer Perceptions of US and Japanese Industrial Goods', *International Marketing Review*, 9 (2), 59–73.

34. Usunier, Jean-Claude (2006), 'Relevance in Business Research: The Case of Country-of-Origin Research in Marketing', *European Management Review*, 3 (1), 60–73.

35. Samiee, Saeed, Terence A. Shimp and Subhash Sharma (2005), 'Brand Origin Recognition Accuarcy: Its Antecedents and Consumers' Cognitive Limitations', *Journal of International Business Studies*, 36 (4), 379–97.

36. Balabanis, George and Adamantios Diamantopoulos (2011), 'Gains and Losses from the Misperception of Brand Origin: The Role of Brand Strength and Country-of-origin Image', *Journal of International Marketing*, 19 (2), 95–116.

37. Magnusson, Peter, Stanford A. Westjohn and Srdan Zdravkovic (2011), ' "What? I thought Samsung was Japanese": Accurate or not, Perceived Country of Origin Matters', *International Marketing Review*, 28 (5), 454–72.

38. Prendergast, Gerard P., Alex S. L. Tsang and Cherry N. W. Chan (2010), 'The interactive influence of country of origin of brand and product involvement on purchase intention', *Journal of Consumer Marketing*, 27 (2), 180–8.

39. Shimp, Terence A. and Subash Sharma (1987), 'Consumer Ethnocentrism: Construction and Validation of the Cetscale', *Journal of Marketing Research*, 24 (August), 280–89.

40. Sharma, Subash, Terence A. Shimp and J. Shin (1995), 'Consumer Ethnocentrism: A Test of Antecedents and Moderators', *Journal of the Academy of Marketing Science*, 23 (1), 26–37.

41. Witkowski, Terrence H. (1998), 'Consumer Ethnocentrism in Two Emerging Markets: Determinants and Predictive Validity', *Advances in Consumer Research*, 25, 258–63.

42. Klein, Jill Gabrielle and Richard Ettenson (1999), 'Consumer Animosity and Consumer Ethnocentrism: An Analysis of Unique Antecedents', *Journal of International Consumer Marketing*, 11 (4), 5–24.

43. Nakos, George and Yannis Hajidimitriou (2007), 'The Impact of National Animosity on Consumer Purchase: The Modifying Factor of Personal Characteristics', *Journal of International Consumer Marketing*, 19 (3), 53–72.

44. Balabanis, George and A. Diamantopoulos (2004), 'Domestic Country Bias, Country-of-Origin Effects, and Consumer Ethnocentrism: A Multidimensional Unfolding Approach', *Journal of the Academy of Marketing Science*, 32 (1), 80–95.

45. Mascarenhas, Oswald A. J. and Duane Kujawa (1998), 'American Consumer Attitude toward Foreign Direct Investments and Their Products', *Multinational Business Review*, 6 (Autumn), 1–9.

46. Alden, Dana L., Jan-Benedict E. M. Steenkamp and Rajeev Batra (2006), 'Consumer Attitudes toward Marketplace Globalization: Structure, Antecedents and Consequences', *International Journal of Research in Marketing*, 23 (3), 227–39.

47. Alpert, Frank, Michael Kamins, Tomoaki Sakano, Naoto Onzo and John Graham (2001), 'Retail Buyer Beliefs, Attitude and Behaviour toward Pioneer and Me-Too Follower Brands: A Comparative Study of Japan and the USA', *International Marketing Review*, 18 (2), 160–87.

48. Javalgi, Rajshekhar, Khare Virginie, Andrew Gross and Robert Schere (2005), 'An Application of the Consumer Ethnocentrism Model to French Consumers', *International Business Review*, 14 (3), 325–44.

49. Klein, Jill Gabrielle, Richard Ettenson and Balaji C. Krishnan (2006), 'Extending the Construct of Consumer Ethnocentrism: When Foreign Products Are Preferred', *International Marketing Review*, 23 (3), 304.

50. Reardon, James, Chip Miller, Irena Vida and Irina Kim (2005), 'The Effects of Ethnocentrism and Economic Development on the Formation of Brand and Ad Attitudes in Transitional Economies', *European Journal of Marketing*, 39 (7/8), 737–54.

51. Yang, Zhilin, Nan Zhou and Jie Chen (2005), 'Brand Choice of Older Chinese Consumer', *Journal of International Consumer Marketing*, 17 (4), 65–81.

52. Herche, Joel (1992), 'A Note on the Predictive Validity of Cetscale', *Journal of the Academy of Marketing Science*, 20 (3), 261–4.

53. Usunier, Jean-Claude and Ghislaine Cestre (2007), 'Product Ethnicity: Revisiting the Match between Products and Countries', *Journal of International Marketing*, 15 (3), 32–72.

54. Auger, Pat, Timothy M. Devinney, Jordan J. Louviere and Paul F. Burke (2010), 'The Importance of Social Product Attributes in Consumer Purchase Decisions: A Multi-Country Comparative Study', *International Business Review*, 19, 140–59.

55. Lee, Julie Anne, Ellen Garbarino and Dawn Lerman (2007), 'How Cultural Differences in Uncertainty Avoidance Affect Product Perceptions', *International Marketing Review*, 24 (3), 330–49.

56. Kotler, Philip, Ang Swee Hoon, Leong Siew Meng and Tan Chin Tiong (2003), *Marketing Management: An Asian Perspective* (3rd edn). Singapore: Pearson.

57. Klein, Naomi (2002), *No Logo: No Space, No Choice, No Jobs*. London: Macmillan.

58. Rosen, Barry Nathan, Jean J. Boddewyn and Ernst A. Louis (1989), 'US Brands Abroad: An Empirical Study of Global Branding', *International Marketing Review*, 6 (1), 7–19.

59. Interbrand (2011), '2011 Rankings of the Top Global Brands', retrieved from http://www.interbrand.com/en/best-global-brands/best-global-brands-2008/best-global-brands-2011.aspx.

60. Townsend, Janell D., Tamer S. Cuvusgil and Marietta L. Baba (2010), 'Global Integration of Brands and New Product Development at General Motors', *The Journal of Product Innovation Management*, 27 (1), 49–65.

61. Wilsher, Peter (1992), 'Diverse and Perverse', *Management Today* (July), 32–5.

62. Onkvisit, Sak and John J. Shaw (1989), 'The International Dimension of Branding: Strategic Considerations and Decisions', *International Marketing Review*, 6 (2), 22–34.

63. Melewar, T. C. and John Saunders (1998), 'Global Corporate Visual Identity Systems: Standardization, Control, and Benefits', *International Marketing Review*, 15 (4), 291–308.

64. Cabat, Odilon (1989), 'Archéologie De La Marque Moderne', in *La Marque*, Jean-Noel Kapferer and Jean-Claude Thoenig (eds). Paris: McGraw-Hill.

65. Czinkota, Michael R. and Illka A. Ronkainen (1990), *International Marketing* (2nd edn). Hinsdale, IL: Dryden Press.

66. Yoshimori, Masaru (1989), 'Concepts et Stratégies de Marques au Japon', in *La Marque*, Jean-Noel Kapferer and Jean-Claude Thoenig (eds). Paris: McGraw-Hill.

67. Wines, Michael (2011), 'Picking Brand Names in China is a Business Itself', *The New York Times*, 11 November available from: http://www.nytimes.com/2011/11/12/world/asia/picking-brand-names-in-china-is-a-business-itself.html?pagewanted=all.

68. Liu, Fang, Jamie Murphy, Jianyao Li and Xiangping Liu (2007), 'English and Chinese? The Role of Consumer Ethnocentrism and Country of Origin in Chinese Attitudes towards Store Signs', *Australasian Marketing Journal*, 14 (2), 5–16.

69. Usunier, Jean-Claude and Janet Shaner (2002), 'Using Linguistics for Creating Better International Brand Names', *Journal of Marketing Communications*, 8 (4), 211–28.

70. Huang, Yue Yuan and Allan K. K. Chan (1997), 'Chinese Branding Name: From General Principles to Specific Rules', *International Journal of Advertising*, 16 (4), 320–35.

71. Robertson, Kim (1989), 'Strategically Desirable Brand Name Characteristics', *Journal of Consumer Marketing*, 6 (Fall), 61–71.

72. Colombat, Catherine (1997), 'Danone Imprime sa Marque sur la Planète', *L'Essentiel du Management*, April, 74–80.

73. Vanden Bergh, Bruce, Keith Adler and Lauren Oliver (1987), 'Linguistic Distinction among Top Brand Names', *Journal of Advertising Research*, 27 (4), 39–44.

74. Giordan, Alain-Eric (1988), *Exporter Plus 2*. Paris: Economica.

75. Tavassoli, Nader T. and Jin K. Han (2002), 'Auditory and Visual Brand Identifiers in Chinese and English', *Journal of International Marketing*, 10 (2), 13–28.

76. Schmitt, Bernd H. and Yigang Pan (1994), 'Managing Corporate and Brand Identities in the Asia-Pacific Region', *California Management Review*, 36 (4, Summer), 32–47.

77. Tavassoli, Nader T. (1999), 'Temporal and Associative Memory in Chinese and English', *Journal of Consumer Research*, 26 (2), 170–81.

78. Pan, Yigang and Bernd H. Schmitt (1995), 'What's in a Name? An Empirical Comparison of Chinese and Western Brand Names', *Asian Journal of Marketing*, 4 (1), 7–16.

79. Schmitt, Bernd H. and Shi Zhang (1998), 'Language Structure and Categorization: A Study of Classifiers in Consumer Cognition, Judgement and Choice', *Journal of Consumer Research*, 25 (2), 108–22.

80. Zhang, Shi and Bernd H. Schmitt (2001), 'Creating Local Brands in Multilingual International Markets', *Journal of Marketing Research*, XXXVIII (August), 313–25.

81. Hong, F. C., Anthony Pecotich and Clifford J. Schultz (2002), 'Brand Name Translation: Language Constraints, Product Attributes, and Consumer Perceptions in East and Southeast Asia', *Journal of International Marketing*, 10 (2), 29–45.

82. Wilke, Margaritha (1994), 'Der Werte Name – Die Marke auf Chinesisch', *Der Neue China*, 21 (3, September), 15–16.

83. Chang, William Li and Peirchyi Lii (2008), 'Luck of the Draw: Creating Chinese Brand Names', *Journal of Advertising Research*, 48 (4), 523–30.

84. Francis, June N. P., Janet P. Y. Lam and Jan Walls (2002), 'Executive Insights: The Impact of Linguistic Differences on International Brand Name Standardization: A Comparison of English and Chinese Brand Names of Fortune-500 Companies', *Journal of International Marketing*, 10 (1), 98–116.

85. Ewing, Michael T., Julie Napoli, Leyland F. Pitt and Alistair Watts (2002), 'On the Renaissance of Chinese Brands', *International Journal of Advertising*, 21 (2), 197–216.

86. Lambin, Jean-Jacques (1989), 'La Marque et le Comportement de Choix de L'Acheteur', in *La Marque*, Jean-Noel Kapferer and Jean-Claude Thoenig (eds). Paris: McGraw-Hill.

87. Contensou, François (1989), 'La Marque, L'efficience Économique et la Formation des Prix', in *La Marque*, Jean-Noel Kapferer and Jean-Claude Thoenig (eds). Paris: McGraw-Hill.

88. Kapferer, Jean-Noel (1989), 'La face cachée des marques', in Jean-Noel Kapferer and Jean-Claude Thoenig (eds), *La Marque*, McGraw-Hill: Paris, pp. 9–44.

89. Abegglen, James and George Stalk Jr (1986), 'The Japanese Corporation as Competitor', *California Management Review*, XXVIII (3, Spring), 9–37.

90. Dupuy, François and Jean-Claude Thoenig (1989), 'La Marque et l'Échange', in *La Marque*, Jean-Noel Kapferer and Jean-Claude Thoenig (eds). Paris: McGraw-Hill.

91. Hsieh, Ming H. (2002), 'Identifying Brand Image Dimensionality and Measuring the Degree of Brand Globalization: A Cross-National Study', *Journal of International Marketing*, 10 (2), 46–67.

92. Alden, Dana L., Jan-Benedict E. M. Steenkamp and Rajeev Batra (1999), 'Brand Positioning through Advertising in Asia, North America and Europe: The Role of Global Consumer Culture', *Journal of Marketing*, 63 (January), 75–87.

93. Fan, Ying (2002), 'The National Image of Global Brands', *Journal of Brand Management*, 9 (3), 180–92.

94. Shalofsky, Ivor (1987), 'Research for Global Brands', *European Research* (May), 88–93.

95. Clark, Harold F. Jr (1987), 'Consumer and Corporate Values: Yet Another View on Global Marketing', *International Journal of Advertising*, 6, 29–42.

96. Dana, Leo-Paul and Brenda M. Oldfield (1999), 'Lublin Coco-Cola Bottlers Ltd', *International Marketing Review*, 16 (4/5), 291–8.

97. Coleman, Zach (1999), 'Foreign Markets Develop Taste for Coke Light', *Atlanta Business Chronicle*, 10 May.

98. Joachimsthaler, Erich and David A. Aaker (1997), 'Building Brands without Mass Media', *Harvard Business Review*, 75 (1, January–February), 39–50.

99. Kish, Paulette, Dwight R. Riskey and Roger A. Kerin (2001), 'Measurement and Tracking of Brand Equity in the Global Marketplace', *International Marketing Review*, 18 (1), 91–6.

100. Peebles, Dean M. (1989), 'Don't Write Off Global Advertising: A Commentary', *International Marketing Review*, 6 (1), 73–8.

101. Kapferer, Jean-Noel (2002), 'Is There Really No Hope for Local Brands?', *Journal of Brand Management*, 9 (3), 163–70.

102. Lindstrom, Martin (2000), 'Global Branding Versus Local Marketing', *Clickz Network Solutions for Marketers*, 23 November, www.clickz.com/showPage.html?page=832711.

103. Steenkamp, Jan-Benedict E. M., Rajeev Batra and Dana L. Alden (2003), 'How Perceived Brand Globalness Creates Brand Value', *Journal of International Business Studies*, 34 (1), 53–65.

104. Steenkamp, Jan-Benedict E. M. and Martijn G. de Jong (2010), 'A Global Investigation into the Constellation of Consumer Attitudes Toward Global and Local Products', *Journal of Marketing*, 74 (Nov), 18–40.

105. Zhou, Lianxi, Zhiyong Yang and Michael K. Hui (2010), 'Non-Local or Local Brands? A Multi-Level Investigation into Confidence in Brand Origin Identification and its Strategic Implications', *Journal of the Academy of Marketing Science*, 38 (2), 202–18.

106. Douglas, Susan P., C. Samuel Craig and Edwin J. Nijssen (2001), 'Executive Insights: Integrating Branding Strategy across Markets: Building International Brand Architecture', *Journal of International Marketing*, 9 (2), 97–114.

107. Matanda, Tandadzo and Michael T. Ewing (2012), 'The Process of Global Brand Strategy Development and Regional Implementation', *International Journal of Research in Marketing*, in press.

108. Etchegoyen, Alain (1990), *Les Entreprises Ont-Elles Une Âme?* Paris: Editions François Bourin.

109. Gillespie, Kate, Kishore Krishna and Susan Jarvis (2002), 'Protecting Global Brands: Toward a Global Norm', *Journal of International Marketing*, 10 (2), 99–112.

Appendix 12

Teaching materials

A12.1 Exercise

Interpreting symbolic attributes

Below are physical attributes for different products; try to imagine how they could be diversely interpreted symbolically in different cultures (you do not need to indicate which interpretation corresponds to a particular culture, but simply to emphasize probable divergence of interpretation across cultures in general).

- a car/colour black;
- orange juice/thick (pulpy);
- blue cheese (*Penicillium glaucum*);
- beer/frothy;
- orange juice/colour deep orange;
- car/automatic;
- apple juice/vitamins added;
- refrigerator/ice dispenser;
- cheese/packed in a wooden box; and
- car/diesel engine.

For further guidance, see Zeithaml[1] and also Solomon (pp. 67–73).[2]

A12.2 Case

Soshi Sumsin Ltd

Sammy Soshi's first assignment for his new job with Soshi Sumshin Ltd was to recommend a new name for the firm's line of electronic products. Sammy had completed his MBA at Emory University in May 2007 and had returned to Seoul, Korea, to work in his father's firm. Soshi Sumsin manufactured a line of electronic products which included VCRs, stereos and televisions. Mr Soshi (Senior) got involved in electronics manufacturing when he agreed to manufacture television components for an American manufacturer in 1990. Eventually, he was producing a full line of television sets, as well as hi-fi and stereo equipment for three American firms. In addition, he had been marketing his own line of products in the Korean market starting in 1992 under the Sumsin brand name.

Mr Soshi felt that his firm was now ready, both in terms of manufacturing know-how and capital, to enter international markets under his own brand name. The American market was chosen as the first target because of its size and buying power, and an introduction date of April 2009 was tentatively set. Being unfamiliar with the American market, Mr Soshi relied heavily on his son, Sammy, to help with marketing decisions.

The first problem Sammy tackled was the selection of a brand name for the line. His father had planned to use the Sumsin name in the American market. Sammy pointed out that failing to carefully consider the effect of a brand name in a different culture could cause major marketing difficulties at a later stage. He cited the Tatung experience as a case in point. Tatung was a Taiwanese maker of televisions, fans and computer terminals. When the company entered the American market it did not even consider changing its brand name. The Tatung company had a favourable connotation in Chinese and was known in the company's oriental markets. However, in the United States, not only was the name meaningless, but it was difficult to know how to pronounce it.

Because of these difficulties, Tatung's American advertising agency finally decided to emphasize the strangeness of the name, and it launched a campaign based on a play on words to help customers pronounce Tatung. Each ad carried the query, 'Cat Got Your Tatung?' Sammy believed that a lot of effort that should have been placed on the product itself had been spent on overcoming a bad trade name.

Sammy cited a second example of problems resulting from a poorly chosen brand name. Another Taiwanese company, Kunnan Lo, introduced its own brand of tennis rackets in the American market. Recognizing that their own name would present problems in the American market, they decided to select an American name. Ultimately, they decided on the name Kennedy; it was quite similar to their company name, and it was certainly familiar in the United States. However, after initial promotional efforts, it quickly became apparent that Kennedy was not a neutral name. Many tennis players were Republicans, and for them the Kennedy name had negative connotations. As a result, the name was changed to Kennex, a neutral, artificial word that was still similar to the company name. However, Kennex also quickly proved to be unsatisfactory, because of some confusion with the name Kleenex. To eliminate this confusion, the name was finally changed to Pro-Kennex, which provided both a tennis tie-in and retention of a root similar to Kunnan Lo. The waste of resources in the series of name changes would have been better avoided.

Determined to avoid the mistakes of these other companies entering the American market, Sammy Soshi carefully evaluated the alternatives available to his company. The first was his father's preference – to use a company family name. However, Sumsin was somewhat difficult for English-speaking people to pronounce and seemed meaningless and foreign. Soshi was equally unfamiliar and meaningless, but he was also afraid that Americans would confuse it with the Japanese raw fish, *sushi*.

A second alternative was to acquire ownership of an existing American brand name, preferably one with market recognition. After considerable research, he chose the name Monarch. The Monarch company had started manufacturing radios in Chicago in 1932, and Monarch radios had been nationally known in the 1940s. The company was badly hurt by television in the 1950s, which reduced the size of the radio market appreciably. The company was finally wiped out by the invasion of inexpensive transistor radios from Asia in the 1960s. The company filed for bankruptcy in 1972. Sammy found that he could buy the rights to the Monarch name for $50,000. The name was tied in with electronic products in the public's mind, but he wondered how many people still remembered or recognized the Monarch name. He also wondered whether this recognition might be more negative than positive because of the company's failure in the market.

A third alternative would be to select a new name and build market recognition through promotion. Such a name would need to be politically and socially neutral in the American market and ultimately in other foreign markets. It had to be easy to pronounce and to remember with a neutral or favourable meaning to the public. The possibilities might be considered.

The first was Proteus, the name of an ancient Greek sea god. This name would be easy to pronounce in most European languages, but was almost too neutral to help sell the product. The other alternative was Blue Streak, again, an easy name in English, but not necessarily in other European languages. Sammy felt that the favourable connotation of speed and progress might provide a boost for the products to which it was applied.

(Source: Adapted from Cundiff and Hilger, pp. 440–42.[3] Cundiff, E. W. and Hilger, M. T., *Marketing in the International Environment*, 2nd edn, © 1988, reproduced by permission of Pearson Education, Inc., Upper Saddle River, NJ.)

Questions

1. Evaluate the alternative names being considered by Sammy Soshi. Which name would you recommend?

2. Whatever new name is chosen, should Soshi Sumsin adopt the same name in the Korean market?

3. What are the advantages of selecting different brand names, as appropriate, in each foreign market?

4. Enumerate the characteristics that should be possessed by a good international brand name.

A12.3 Case

Derivados de Leche SA

Derivados de Leche SA, founded in 1968, was the first firm to market yoghurt in Mexico. It distributed yoghurt under the brand name Delsa only in Mexico City, primarily in a limited number of upper-income areas. The company was family owned, and the capital was all local. For the first five years, Delsa was sold in food stores, particularly in the newly developing supermarkets, without any advertising or other promotion. Yoghurt was a new, unfamiliar food product in the Mexican market, but Delsa depended primarily on word of mouth to provide product recognition.

In 1983, a number of laws regulating foreign investment in Mexico were modified under a single new 'regulation of foreign investment' law. According to this law foreign investors were welcome in Mexico on a joint labour basis so long as the foreign ownership share did not exceed 49 per cent. Labour-intensive industries that helped to decentralize population were particularly welcome. It was many years before this affected the yoghurt market, but eventually three multinationals entered on this joint venture basis, changing the structure of the market dramatically.

The first new brand, Chambourcy, was introduced by a joint venture subsidiary of Nestlé which had operated in Mexico since 1935. This company, Industrias Alimentacias Club SA, was a major Mexican food producer with 7,000 employees. Chambourcy was launched with a strong promotional campaign and wide distribution. In 1993, a subsidiary of the French food firm Danone launched its Danone yoghurt in the Mexican market. Danone was also heavily supported with promotion. Finally, in 1998, a third multinational entered the market. Productos de Leche SA was 51 per cent owned by Mexican capital and 49 per cent by the

Borden Company of the United States; it entered the Mexican market with two brands of yoghurt, Darel and Bonafina.

By 2005 the management of Derivados de Leche SA was becoming concerned about its future position in the yoghurt market. All three multinational competitors were aggressive marketers and promoters and were strong financially. Although the foreign ownership was a minority (49 per cent), management was dominated in each case by the minority ownership, so that management was competent and professional. In the short term, Delsa benefited from the primary demand creation activities of the multinationals. In 1998 Delsa sales reached almost 16,000 tons, and by 2005, grew to 38,000 tons. But Delsa's market share had dropped from over 75 per cent in 1985 (there were some other, very small, Mexican-owned competitors) to only 15 per cent in 2005.

The three multinationals shared 77.5 per cent of the market. If the trend continued, it was feared that Delsa's share of the market might drop so low that it would provide very little product recognition. And it was possible that ultimately sales volume would stabilize and perhaps even decline.

By 2005, Delsa management was faced with the grim reality of competition from financially strong and aggressive, professionally managed multinationals. Delsa managers felt that pricing could not be blamed for this loss in market share; the sales price of Delsa was slightly below that of its competitors. A major handicap for Delsa was its failure to promote recognition of its brand name. Although Delsa had been pulled along in the market by the initial marketing efforts which were designed to create a primary demand for yoghurt, the marketing efforts of the competitors were now focused almost entirely on selective brand name promotion. Delsa management had concentrated its efforts on getting the product into retail outlets and maintaining good relationships with dealers; no effort had been made to create consumer recognition and franchises through advertising and other promotion. Management was made up of the family members who owned the company; they brought little professional training to the job.

Owner-managers of small and medium-sized firms in Mexico tended to run their businesses for quick, short-term profit rather than long-term development. New capital investment was needed to enlarge the production capacity, and serious consideration needed to be given to investing in a promotional campaign to build and maintain Delsa brand recognition.

Delsa was considering applying for a government-subsidized loan to double its production capacity. These loans were available only to 100 per cent Mexican-owned manufacturers, but were limited to the financing of manufacturing facilities. Delsa's marketing manager wanted to emphasize the local Mexican ownership of Delsa and to increase the firm's advertising budget from $100,000 to about $500,000. He also wanted to redesign the package so as to include some statement that indicated the brand was of pure Mexican origin. Delsa's owners wanted to put pressure on the Mexican government to limit the food-processing industry to 100 per cent Mexican-owned firms. It was not known what the possibilities were of getting such legislation passed.

(Source: Adapted from Cundiff and Hilger, pp. 335–6.[3] Cundiff, E. W. and Hilger, M. T., *Marketing with International Environment*, 2nd edn, © 1988, reproduced by permission of Pearson Education, Inc., Upper Saddle River, NJ.)

Questions

1. What are Delsa's strengths and weaknesses in competing with multinationals?

2. What is the impact of 'country of origin' on demand for yoghurt? Consider the following points: product ethnicity of yoghurt; image of Mexico as a manufacturer of food products; the Delsa brand name; and any other aspect that would relate country, product and brand image.

3. What recommendations can you make to strengthen Delsa's market position?

A12.4 Case

K21-tech: B2B or B2C brands for computer components?

Many industrial products are sold as OEM (Original Equipment Manufacturer), which means that they are supplied to further transformation stages in the industrial supply chain, nearer and nearer to the final stage of product end use. There often is a double market for such products. The first is a B2B market, for instance Goodyear tyres or Valeo wipers being sold to car manufacturers in large contracts for new car equipment. The same product may be sold to car owners for replacement often in a garage service, but sometimes also directly in a B2C relationship through specialized stores. As a consequence, it is a strategic marketing choice for companies primarily involved in business markets to decide whether they want their corporate brand (e.g., Intel) and/or their product brand names (e.g., Pentium) to be known by different publics in the supply chain. Some may decide to only target their direct customers in the supply chain, those with which they negotiate contracts. Other industrial companies may decide to also target end-users and/or invest in a brand that is present across the whole supply chain.

Visibility is an issue, since often the OEM component ends up being invisible by customers one step away from their integration in a product. Because buying behaviour, volume and loyalty differ massively between industrial purchasers and individual customers, a brand's positioning has to serve different purposes if it wants to reach typical branding goals such as fostering brand awareness (brand recall and brand recognition) and fostering brand image in the direction desired by the brand owner.

K21-tech is a large Taiwanese company supplying several computer components, in particular ASIC (Application Specific Industrial Circuits), but also a number of the products in Table 12.4 (hard disk, graphics card, motherboard, and power supplies). They do not know exactly what to do with their brand name, in terms of its visibility and the appropriate mix between B2B and B2C branding, given that part of the output is sold as OEM and part in computer stores. They think that the brand should convey a technological image: '21', for instance, conveys the idea of the 21st century, technological progress and a future orientation. In their view radicals such as Tech (or Tek or Tec) and figures in general convey a sense of calculation, preciseness, computation, and the like. The suffix '-ium' such as in Mendeleiev's periodic classification of elements, conveys a sense of hard science. The Pentium microchip by Intel, for instance, is a registered trademark that is included in the brand names of many of Intel's x86-compatible microprocessors, both single- and multi-core. Pentium followed a series of microchips whose brand names were based on figures ending in 86 (286, 386 and 486). When Intel decided to put an end to the series, they did it by using the Greek figure for 5 (*penta*, coming after the 4 in 486) and adding the suffix -ium to make it high tech. Greek letters, from α to ω, as they are often used in mathematical formulae, also evoke science and technology. The Greek symbolic contribution does not stop there. Mechanical endings that sound technological such as -ix, or the Greek prefixes for large (kilo, mega, giga, tera) or small sizes and quantities (micro, nano, pico) are often used in computer-related brand names. The computer vocabulary (e.g., bytes, bits, digital, virtual) and the like (min, max, etc.) are also often combined to create brand names.

K21-tech have been looking at other brand names for computer components and they wonder whether they should change their brand name, possibly keep a corporate brand name and maintain different product names (e.g., what Intel does as a corporation with

Pentium chips as products). Table 12.4 below shows examples of brand names for computer components.

Table 12.4 Brands of computer components

Component	Brands	Visibility
Computer case	*A+, Aerocool, Antec, Apevia, Asus, Coolmaster, Enermax, Gigabyte, Heden, Lian-Li, Thermaltake, Zalman*	None
Screen	*Acer, Asus, iiyama, LG, Samsung, Viewsonic*	None to excellent
Mouse	*Connectland, Logitech, Microsoft, Razer, Saitek*	High
Keyboard	*Connectland, Logitech, Microsoft, Razer, Saitek*	Very high
Power supply	*Antec, Coolmaster, Corsair, Enermax, LC Power, Thermaltake, Zalman*	None
Motherboard	*Asrock, Asus, DFI, Gigabyte, MSI . . .*	None
Processor	*Intel, AMD*	Very high
Random Access Memory (RAM)	*Corsair, Crucial, Dane-Elec, G. Skill, GEIL, Kingmax, Kingston, OCZ Technology, Patriot Memory, Samsung, Transcend*	None
Hard disk	*Hitachi-IBM, Maxtor, Samsung, Seagate, Western Digital*	None
Graphics card	*Asus, Gainward, Gigabyte, Point of View, Powercolor, Sapphire . . .*	None
Optical drive	*Asus, LG, Nec, Pioneer, Plextor, Samsung*	Intermediate

(Source: Adapted from Philippe Malaval and Christophe Bénaroya (2010), *Les Marques B to B*, Paris, Pearson, p. 214.)

As a brand consultant, you are asked to help K21-tech answer the issues below for redesigning their brand and developing a consistent brand policy given the existence of both B2B and B2C market segments. You can visit Alibaba.com and Europages.com where you will find myriads of companies and therefore a wide array of corporate names for industrial suppliers. You may also Google for brand names, especially B2B ones.

Questions

1. Which branding strategy would you suggest for K21-tech? Should it target B2B or B2C customers or a combination?

2. What brand positioning should K21-tech adopt for their corporate brand? For product brand names? Should they combine corporate and product brand names or stick to a policy of corporate name only?

3. Surf the Internet to search for brands names combining Roman letters (A to Z) and the suffixes 'tec' or 'tech' (or '-tec' or '-tech')? What does this suggest as to the remaining brand names available? Is it easy to find a new brand and register it?

4. You are asked to propose a new brand name for K21-tech. Please take into account the linguistic aspects of brand names as they are presented in this chapter and further discussed in Usunier and Shaner (2002).

Appendix references

1. Zeithaml, Valarie A. (1988), 'Consumer Perceptions of Price, Quality and Value: A Means–End Model and Synthesis of Evidence', *Journal of Marketing*, 52 (July), 2–22.
2. Solomon, Michael R. (1994), *Consumer Behavior* (2nd edn). Needham Heights: Allyn and Bacon.
3. Cundiff, Edward W. and Marye Tharp Hilger (1988), *Marketing in the International Environment*. Englewood Cliffs, NJ: Prentice Hall.

13

Intercultural marketing communications 1: advertising

Advertising, which is based on language and communication, is the most culture-bound element of the marketing mix. When Polaroid introduced its cameras to Europe in the mid-1970s, it used the same advertising strategy as it had successfully in the US. Unfortunately for Polaroid, these transplanted campaigns achieved little impact in terms of raising awareness of instant photography and ultimately failed to capture market share. Polaroid Switzerland, a small subsidiary in a very multicultural country, in the meantime had great success by specifically adapting their advertising strategy to actively promote the communication aspect of instant photography, focusing on the ability to share photos with family and friends (interestingly, this campaign was a very much ahead of its time given the recent popularity of instant photo sharing through digital media). Eventually, Polaroid was able to replicate Switzerland's success to develop very successful European campaigns on the basis of this more culturally appealing strategy.[1]

Even when companies set out to adapt their advertising to suit a foreign culture there is still great scope for miscommunication. In 2004, Toyota introduced its Land Cruiser SUV to China, using an image of the Land Cruiser towing an unbranded truck, which happened to bear a very strong resemblance to the East-West brand, Chinese-made military truck. Reports in local newspapers suggested an arrogant Toyota and implied that the Chinese government was incompetent.[2]

This chapter could be subtitled 'national cultures, technological advances and the globalization of marketing communications'. As with previous chapters, it attempts to show that globalization is not the very simple process it is often believed to be. The first sections of this chapter describe cultural differences as they pertain to various aspects of advertising. Section 13.1 addresses general attitudes toward advertising. Sections 13.2 and 13.3 explore how advertising strategy and creative standards are affected by local culture. Section 13.4 focuses on media selection, given differences in media availability and style. Finally, Section 13.5 examines the globalization of advertising.

Advertising is based on language and images. Cross-national differences continue to exist, for the simple reason that there are so many different languages. Moreover, language, via words or images, is the strongest link between advertisers and their potential audiences in marketing communications.

The management process for marketing communication is not *per se* dependent on the particular country where the advertising campaign is launched. It should follow the six steps outlined in Figure 13.1. Logically, these steps should be taken in order, although feedback at any step is often necessary, especially after testing the campaign. The six basic steps are as follows:

1. Isolate the communication problem to be solved, such as increase brand awareness, change brand image, increase sales, differentiate from rival brands, take market share from the competition, etc.
2. Identify the relevant target population, including the consumer segments to be targeted and their sociodemographic characteristics, consumption habits, psychographic characteristics (consumer lifestyles and values), etc.

Figure 13.1 Main steps in the management of advertising communication

3. Define the marketing communication objective in terms of influencing the target population, at either the attitudinal or the behavioural level. Communication objectives include persuading consumers to like a product (improve product acceptance), encouraging people to try a product again (increase sales by building consumer loyalty), enabling people to act, or educating the consumer, etc.
4. Select the advertising themes and a creative strategy, such as how the brand name will be portrayed and how the objective translates into copy.
5. Design a media plan, including which media to use, how to optimize the best media to reach the target audience, etc.
6. Implement and monitor the advertising campaign, including pre- and post-tests of advertisement effectiveness, research on different aspects (message recall, brand recall, aided brand recognition, actual influence on sales), etc.

The international dimension naturally has an influence on the implementation of each of these steps, but not an equal influence on each step. Many aspects of the local market need to be taken into consideration. For instance, before advertising a new mobile telephone in sub-Saharan Africa, we need to take into account that this market might have very different uses for mobile telephones compared to other regions, not to mention different experience with and knowledge about the product. Research might tell us that one of the common uses for mobile phones in this region is to find out market prices for commodities such as grain, without having to travel. Research also tells us that in this region, very much unlike in most developed countries, it is very common to share mobile phones as a community resource.[3] For these reasons, the advertising message in this region might emphasize the utilitarian benefits of mobile phone ownership (as opposed to the typically hedonic messages of developed nations advertising for this product category), and the benefits this could bring to ones community. Certainly culture influences the objective (step 3), such as the education of the consumer, as well as industry-level demand creation. However, the changes caused by cultural differences are most obvious with respect to the creative strategy (step 4). The complex mix of nationalities, social stratification and rapid urbanization of the region has to be considered, since the cheapest phone subscription in Kenya for instance costs half of the average monthly income in the country.[3]

The media plan will also be strongly influenced by local idiosyncrasies, including media availability, viewing habits and media regulations, which still differ greatly across countries. Conversely, the other steps in Figure 13.1 are not strongly affected by local factors: defining a communication problem or a communication objective, or testing the effectiveness of a campaign, calls for a similar approach in each country.

Although the first three sections of this chapter favour customization of advertising, Section 13.4 contrasts this. Technological advances, such as global media and the Internet, have had an undeniable impact on local attitudes and purchasing behaviour. The emergence of worldwide advertising media opens communication between cultures that previously were geographically and culturally separated, such as western and eastern Europe, or southern Europe and northern Africa. Furthermore, it opens the way to

new marketing communications in areas of the world which are culturally fragmented, for ethnic, linguistic or political reasons: Europe, South-East Asia, Central and Latin America. In this new style of international marketing communication, strictly national segments and audiences must be differentiated from cross-border regional segments and audiences. The choice of the appropriate media and language in which to advertise are therefore key success factors. It should also be noted that the large advances in accessibility to advertising via the Internet mean that advertisements intended for a local audience could well be seen globally, adding a layer of complexity to defining marketing messages. One controversial example of this was the infamous 9/11 ad campaign put together for an agency for World Wildlife Foundation Brasil, which contrasted the number of lives lost in the Asian Boxing Day Tsunami of 2004 to those in the 9/11 terrorist attacks on NYC. The creative execution in the advertisement pictured dozens of passenger planes heading towards NYC, an image that caused outrage in the US, when it went viral online, though there is some debate as to who approved or designed the ad (see Box 13.1 for another example). The final section of this chapter deals with the issue of advertising globalization.

BOX 13.1

KFC racist ad in Australia

The proliferation of websites such as YouTube and global online media outlets has created an unexpected layer of complexity for advertisers, even those not intending to be international. KFC Australia found this out the hard way in 2010 when they aired a TV ad in Australia during the West Indies cricket tour of the country. The ad featured a white Australian male situated in the middle of a raucous group of black West Indian cricket fans. He asks, 'Need a tip when you're stuck in an awkward situation?' and proceeds to share a bucket of fried chicken with the crowd, which happily calms them down. The ad caused outrage in the United States when it unofficially became available online, as it activated the sensitive, racially charged stereotype in that country regarding African-Americans and

fried chicken. Unfortunately for KFC Australia they had run into the relatively new marketing issue of unintended international segments taking different messages away from advertising intended for a specific national audience. As Stanglin (p. 1) reported, at the time the company said: 'The ad was reproduced online in the US without KFC's permission, where we are told a culturally-based stereotype exists, leading to the incorrect assertion of racism . . . We unequivocally condemn discrimination of any type and have a proud history as one of the world's leading employers for diversity'.[4] While the stereotype does not exist, is not widely known in Australia, and is culturally specific to the US, that did not insulate the company, and they pulled the ad shortly after airing it.

13.1

Influence of culture on attitudes towards advertising

Advertising, which is a large part of marketing communications, is a field that is constantly changing. On one hand, it is closely dependent on the cultural and linguistic attitudes of the local target population and it mirrors changing social behaviour. On the other hand, the relative freedom of advertising creation and the need to capture the audience imply that advertising is sometimes challenging and often innovative.

Managers and consumers seem to differ in their attitudes towards advertising. For instance, across 14 countries, the majority of managers find advertising to be more factual, provide important information about products, and to be both entertaining and informative, whereas consumers have a somewhat more negative view about these 'benefits'.[5] Cultural differences in consumer perceptions of advertising also exist. For instance, Chinese consumers have been found to have more positive attitudes towards advertising compared to consumers in the US.[6] China, as a relatively recent entrant into the global advertising arena encapsulates some of the unique challenges facing marketers in rapidly changing new economies. Within China there are also interesting differences, with younger Chinese more accepting of individualistic appeals (while retaining their acceptance of collectivistic appeals) compared to older generations, and Shanghai (where advertising regulations are lax) are less trusting of advertising than their counterparts in Hong Kong.[7]

However, the view that advertising is nothing more than wasted money is vaguely rooted in the ideas of the doctrine of St Simon, in which only production brings economic value to society. Retail sales and the service industry, including advertising, are considered to be parasitic activities. This view is often reinforced by the (misleading) argument that consumers pay for advertising costs, which are included in the price of the product they buy. In many European countries, especially in northern Europe and in France, there are still some traces of 'publiphobia'. The advertising profession in France was even forced to launch a huge poster and billboard campaign against those known as 'publiphobes'.

At the international level more attention is now being given to the idea that advertising, though undeniably useful to society, can also have negative results, such as encouraging conspicuous consumption, harmful consumption, and the creation of wants that cannot be satisfied. An example of harmful consumption that has received considerable attention recently is the advertising of junk-food aimed at children, in light of the growing childhood obesity in many countries.[8] A cross-national analysis of advertising to children in 2008 showed that the bulk of food advertising during children's shows was for non-core foods (which include products relatively high in undesirable nutrients, including fat and sodium, or energy), with healthy foods only marginally represented.[9] To combat these potential negative effects, the economic and social committee of the UN (United Nations) has proposed a resolution that would protect consumers in developing nations. Similarly, individual countries have taken action: for instance in the UK there are now restrictions placed on ads targeted towards children than promote unhealthy or junk foods.

Aside from advertising to children and advertising vice products, another major area of contention across cultures is the use of comparative advertising. The acceptance of comparative advertising depends on the responses given to the following questions in a particular society:

1. What is the social function of comparative advertising?
2. What are the prevailing arguments concerning the legitimacy of comparative advertising?
3. How should competition between brands be facilitated?
4. Does comparative advertising result in fooling the consumer by using disputable information to praise one's own brand and put down others?

Socially dominant responses to these questions directly influence comparative advertising regulations in a given country. In some countries comparative advertising is held in low esteem. This is the case in France, where it has traditionally been considered a denigration of competing brands. It was forbidden under Article 1382 of the Civil Code. In order for the advertisement to be considered comparative, there needed only to be a comparison of two competing products, even if the terms are not inaccurate, tendentious or antagonistic. For instance, about 20 years ago Lip, the top French watchmaker, was under attack by Timex, the top company in the American watch industry. The main feature of Timex's Kelton brand was its distribution through tobacconists, whereas Lip was confined to the more traditional channel of watch and jewellery stores. With the purpose of counter-attacking in order to regain market share, Lip began an advertising campaign that showed a broken watch in an ashtray surrounded by a thick cloud of smoke, with a slogan that read: 'The watches sold in tobacconists are like cigarettes: they go up in smoke.' As a consequence, Lip was forced to pay heavy penalties to Timex.

While comparative advertising is allowed in many but not all countries, it invites scrupulous attention from competitors. In some instances, it may spark an advertising war, as in the case of the Verizon and AT&T 'map for that' competing campaigns in the US (see Website link 13.1). By directly attacking AT&T by name, and specifically criticizing the key element of AT&Ts current 3G network advertising campaign, Verizon prompted an almost immediate rebuttal ad. Following a failed injunction lawsuit, AT&T hired popular actor Luke Wilson to front an aggressive campaign, this time directly criticizing Verizon for their comparative lack of data speed. After months of back-and-forth attacks, it is fair to say that neither company came out ahead in the eyes of the consumer.

Website link 13.1

Find some comparative ads online, such as the AT&T versus Verizon 'there's a map for that' comparative advertising battle on YouTube: http://www.youtube.com/watch?v=37NKnDRPFKU.

The basic arguments in favour of comparative advertising seem to make sense: it facilitates consumer information, choice and competition between brands. Hence, automobile advertising frequently gives performance statistics of competing models, such as fuel consumption, speed and comfort. Opponents of comparative advertising argue that truly objective comparisons would need to be handled by completely independent testing organizations. As a consequence, comparative advertising often ends up giving either no information at all or partly misleading information to the consumer. Opponents of comparative advertising also implicitly support the idea that it is necessary to

enforce moral business relationships between competitors. The role of marketing communications, by means of advertising, is to praise the virtues of their own product, not to put down the virtues of competing products (however indirectly).

James and Hensel (p. 55) emphasize the possibility that malicious comparative advertising can be negative. They take the example of a Kentucky Fried Chicken advertisement that made explicit reference to McDonald's:

The first ad, sponsored by Kentucky Fried Chicken, opens with a red-haired Ronald McDonald surrogate (sans clown outfit) being interrogated by a Senate 'subcommittee' rivalling the likes of that faced by Oliver North. Allegations are raised as to the defendant's lack of expertise and questionable ability to provide quality chicken (McNuggets) to the public. When pressed as to how he expects to be able to sell chicken given this lack of expertise, 'Ronald' responds, 'Toys, lots of toys!', while the man who appears to be his legal counsel buries his head in his hands.[10]

There is also evidence that the effectiveness of comparative advertising is likely to differ across countries. For instance, comparative advertising is perceived more favourably in the US than in South Korea.[11] Here, societal norms may be in play, as direct comparative ads have only been officially permitted in South Korea since 2001, while they are common in the US. The style of the comparison can also come into play. Direct comparisons between named brands combined with factual information (e.g., using statistics or research to present the point) has been shown to be more effective in France and the Netherlands, markets where comparative advertising is uncommon, while consumers in the US reacted better to indirect comparisons combined with more subjective or evaluative information.[12]

Where legislation allows comparative advertising, it usually requires that advertising be based on features of the competing products or services that are material, relevant, verifiable and fairly chosen. Comparisons should be objective and should not discredit competitors or their brands. False or misleading comparative advertising is illegal under both United States and European legislation.[13] The penalties are becoming increasingly harsh, such as in a 2009 court case in the US where Bracco Diagnostics was awarded US$11.4 million in damages because of misleading comparative advertising by General Electric (GE). GE was deemed to have deliberately misrepresented a study comparing the safety of two GE X-ray machines, making it appear that the study also included the market-leading Bracco product (it did not). By positioning their product as safer than Bracco's, by citing the study that did not include Bracco at all, GE left the door open to successful litigation.[14] A report by Romano[13] details many different examples and examined legal cases regarding comparative advertising in both the United States and France.

Website link 13.2

Search for information about advertising laws in different countries. Pick a member country and see what is new in advertising legal issues: http://www.gala-marketlaw.com/joomla4/.

13.2

Culture and advertising strategy

The function of an advertisement is to communicate a message to an audience based on two major elements: strategy and execution. While there is some overlap between these categories, advertising strategy comprises 'what is said' and execution concerns more 'how it is said'. Advertising strategy relates to the types of appeals used, the themes developed and the overall communication style, whether (1) direct or indirect, (2) explicit or implicit or (3) rational or emotional. Advertising style in communicating with the audiences of viewers, readers or listeners can be roughly divided into three basic categories: (1) persuasive, (2) informative and (3) oneiric, that is dream oriented.

Advertising appeals

A limited number of different advertising appeals can be identified based on common themes and concepts. Although all of them are used worldwide, cultural sensitivity is portrayed through the varying usage of these same appeals.[15] For instance, the same ten basic appeals are used in the US and Japan, but the Japanese preference for implicit, indirect communication is reflected by a relative lack of hard-sell appeals.[16] There

are four times as many soft-sell appeals in Japanese as in US advertisements.[16] Further, in accordance with Japanese values, there are also more advertisements that stress tradition and the veneration of the elderly.[16] The product-merit appeal, on the other hand, is dominant in US advertisements.[17] As stated by Lin (pp. 44–5), Japanese cultural values stress status symbols in advertising whereas Americans place emphasis on individual determinism:

Japanese advertisements reveal an indulgence with sensitive crafting of product image and appearance slated within a subtle frame of reference. This contrasts sharply with the American fixation on presenting facts and attributes to showcase product superiority . . . [In Japan] 'boasting' of product quality and 'bribing' consumers into submission are not in line with the custom of respectful treatment of consumers and respectable projection of company image. These same rationales explain why comparative and testimonial messages are not a desirable form of advertising in Japan.[18]

A similar pattern was found when comparing advertising in the US and various Arab countries, where the majority of appeal types were found in both countries, just to differing degrees of intensity.[19]

In terms of soft-sell and traditional appeals, similarities have been found across many Asian countries. For instance, Chinese advertising uses soft-sell appeals, elderly and tradition, oneness with nature and group consensus and status appeals more often than in the US, where there is more frequent use of the hard-sell appeal, time oriented, and individualist appeals, as well as product merit appeals.[20] However, the traditional family appeal was found to be used equally in Chinese and US food advertising, reflecting the universal importance of family.[21] Taiwanese advertising is generally more effective when traditional (e.g., consensus, soft sell, veneration of elderly and traditional) and transformational appeals (e.g., user image, brand image, usage occasion) are used than relying on informational appeals (e.g., comparative, unique, pre-emptive) and Westernized appeals (e.g., independence, modernity, product merit).[22] However, there are also many differences in these countries. For instance, Chinese magazines are also likely to use product merit appeals and status appeals,[23] which is in contrast to Japanese advertisements.

In terms of cultural dimensions, individualism and collectivism are most commonly associated with advertising appeals.[24] Individualist appeals are likely to focus on individuality, uniqueness and achievement while collectivist appeals structured around group harmony or achievement, and conformity.[24] To illustrate, we can compare hypothetical luxury car ads from the US and China. In the US you might expect to see some emphasis on the expression of individuality or the self that a new luxury car can bring. In contrast, in China the ad might focus on family safety, pride or togetherness.[25] The previously discussed horizontal and vertical elements of individualism and collectivism (see Chapter 3) have also been shown to influence the use of different advertising appeals. For example, advertising from vertical countries including the US (vertical individualist), Russia and Poland (vertical collectivist) has been shown to use more status appeals than advertising from Denmark (horizontal individualist), which in turn was more likely to use uniqueness appeals.[26] Again, using the car example to contrast the two individualist countries, in Denmark the advertising might focus on the ability of the new car to be customized, to appeal to the 'uniqueness' aspect of the horizontal dimension, while in the US the ability to confer status that a luxury car provides might be central to the ad.

Differences in the use of symbolic and informational appeals have been found in many countries. For instance, in Japan there is little relationship between advertisement content and the advertised product, only brief dialogue in TV commercials with minimal explanatory content, priority placed on company trust rather than product quality, etc.[26,27] In Taiwan more informational and obligation related strategies are employed, in contrast to argument and imitation in the US and symbolic strategies in France.[28] Swedish ads also depend more on symbolic associations than US advertisements.[29]

Italian and French advertisements often appear as very dream oriented: viewers and readers are supposedly willing to escape from the real world. This oneiric style of advertisement enhances the fantasy of the consumer and emphasizes the image of satisfaction and enjoyment. It does so in a rather holistic way (the product and its benefits tend to be implied rather than actually shown). The oneiric style does not really concentrate on actual buying and consumption experiences. The dream-like dimension that surrounds the product is favoured at any price. Relying on the dream-oriented part of the advertising audience is typical of the 'Séguéla' doctrine.

Germans, unlike the French or the Italians, are known to have a taste for highly informative advertising. A young German advertising specialist criticizes French advertising, and especially the most well-known publicist, Jacques Séguéla (co-founder of the RSCG agency, reputed for oneiric, dream-oriented copy strategies):

Certainly it [French advertising] is better than German advertising, but the French should take care not to sink in art for art's sake or in séguélomania. The message of the Citroen advertising campaign is horrible. What is the link between the Great Wall of China and Citroen? Are Citroen cars manufactured there now?[30]

A significant degree of similarity in advertising strategies only appears in culturally close countries like Australia, Canada, the US, and the UK. Overall, advertising agencies in all four use similar strategies, in a number of cases. Problem-solution is most popular, followed by USP (unique selling proposition), emotion, brand image and brand identity.[31,32] Strong similarities in appeal use has also been found across the culturally close Arab states.[19]

At least some of the differences in emphasis across cultures may be due to a difference in the diagnosticity of information. For instance, there is evidence that the informational value or diagnosticity is greater for consensus information[32] and source expertise[33] in more collectivist cultures than it is in more individualist cultures.

The information content of advertising: cross-national differences

The information content of advertising is a key issue, since it shows whether the strategy focuses on information, persuasion or dream orientation. The information content will naturally be lower when the two last avenues are followed. Ever since the first systematic evaluation of information content by Resnik and Stern,[34] the informativeness of advertising has received considerable attention all over the world. Many researchers compared their country's advertising situation to that of the US. The most important findings of these studies are that information content varies by country, but also by broadcast time, product type and medium.[35]

Overall, it appears that US television advertising is less informative than most other television advertising worldwide. US television advertising contains less information than Australian,[36] French-Canadian,[37] Spanish,[38] Ecuadorian,[39] Irish,[40] French,[41] German[41] and Japanese television advertising.[42] Only British TV advertisements seem to contain less information than US advertisements.[43] When other types of media are examined, a different pattern emerges. For instance, the US had higher levels of information cues than Japan, China and South Korea when television, radio and print advertising were considered.[44] In all countries, television and radio advertising were generally less informative than print advertising.[44]

A meta-analysis of 59 studies about information content found that advertising in developed countries is more informative than in developing countries.[45] Kaynak and Ghauri (p. 127)[46] explain that in developed countries advertising copy, in general, contains more writing and technical information, because most consumers have a high level of literacy and education: 'Unlike Canada and Sweden, most of the advertising copy used by the Turkish agencies is persuasive in nature rather than informative.' The Turkish word for advertising is *Reklam*: this corresponds to a more traditional vision of advertising, where persuasion and slogans are the key issues. Further, Callow and Schiffman[47] show that consumers from the Philippines (a higher context, developing nation) were more able to derive the implicit meaning from the visual images than consumers from the US.

A closer look at some of the many studies that compare advertising across countries offers additional valuable insights. Information content varies greatly from one country to another. Although product types and other environmental factors, such as the competitive environment and government regulation have an influence on information content, culture is the most important factor in explaining how much and what kind of information can be found in advertising. Both the types of information cues and the quantity of information are culture-bound. Whereas some targets, such as in the US, prefer rational, tangible cues, others expect emotional and more 'subjective' information. This is why many Japanese advertisements present 'company-sponsored research', an element that is much less important in Western countries. Even in nearby countries with a

similar economic environment, such as France and the UK, information content varies fundamentally. Cultures known to avoid uncertainty, such as the French, will always have a tendency to ask for more information, and seek quality assurances more than in cultures that have lower uncertainty avoidance, such as the UK.[48]

Assuming that consumers are rational information seekers (which is not true in most cultural contexts), advertising content should be related to information sought by consumers in order to improve the relevance of their choices. If for any reason consumers are not 'good' (motivated and educated) information seekers, they will be less sensitive to the information content of an advertisement. This is the case if they do not directly use advertising information in their brand evaluations in order to reduce perceived risks when purchasing. For instance, Mexicans generally display a much lower level of perceived risk related to their purchases than Americans, possibly due to the somewhat fatalistic tradition which exists in Mexican society versus the 'master-of-destiny' orientation in the US that implies a greater risk of being disappointed.[49] Thus, Mexican consumers and, more generally, consumers belonging to fatalistically oriented societies react more easily to persuasive messages (the brand name repeated numerous times) and also oneiric messages (a dream that allows one to escape from a daily life that is not always bright).

Finally, it should be noted that the types of information cues vary by country. While Japanese advertisements, for example, have very few price, warranty and guarantee cues, compared to US advertisements, they carry a much higher number of packaging cues.[16,18,42] Korean advertisements include the price 38 per cent of the time, whereas in other countries the average is between 8 per cent (India) and 16 per cent (France)[50] and the British prefer not to mention money at all.[51] French commercials present more quality information and new ideas, and in Taiwan information about product availability and special offers are significantly higher than average.[28]

As a general rule advertising strategy must fit with the local orientation concerning information content and style of advertising. Advertising strategies that follow purely informative, oneiric or persuasive routes will have to be considered cautiously as applicants for cross-border transfer.

13.3

Culture and advertising execution

Once the advertising strategy is defined, execution remains a quite significant cross-cultural 'filter', since meaning transfer is fine-tuned through executional details, most of which are strongly culture-bound. This section reviews the empirical literature in the following domains of advertising execution: (1) language; (2) humour; (3) characters and roles represented; (4) the influence of mores and religion, and (5) visual elements of advertising.

Language

Advertisements usually have several text elements (catchphrase, product description, slogan) and use colloquial language, very subtle yet precise in meaning. The character and structure of these elements heavily influence the advertisement's effectiveness, while language differences are the strongest barrier to effective communication. Duncan and Ramaprasad[52] show that companies which tend to favour standardized international advertising strategy (68 per cent) and standardized execution (54 per cent), standardize language much less (11 per cent) across all countries.

In order to be effective in a French context, 50 per cent of all words in an advertisement should be nouns and verbs, the percentage of words exceeding three syllables should not be higher than 10 per cent, most of the long words should be familiar words, and sentences should have an average length of about 10–13 words.[53] Furthermore, advertising language often uses colloquial words or slang, which are particular to local people and as such are difficult to find in dictionaries. The viewer or the listener understands messages all the more readily when colloquial speech expresses the delicate messages of daily life – sentiments, sensations, family relations, friendships, love affairs – that are reflected in advertising.

Translating colloquial speech is difficult, since it uses idiomatic expressions which change from one language to another. It can even be difficult to transpose creative ideas between countries with the same official language. In 2006, Tourism Australia launched its 'So where the bloody hell are you?' campaign, but soon discovered that the slang Australian term

'bloody hell' evoked different reactions around the world. In the UK they were forced to air the ad only after 9 p.m., due to 'bloody' being deemed an expletive. Meanwhile, in the US the conservative lobby group, The American Family Association, launched a boycott action based on the use of the 'bloody hell' phrase, despite no official concerns from the US government. Finally, in Singapore the words were removed from the ad altogether.

Website link 13.3

Search for controversial campaigns, such as the Tourism Australia 'where the bloody hell are you?': **http://www.youtube.com/watch?v=TebeNC-_VjA.**

Effective textual elements, including the use of foreign vocabulary in an advertisement, vary from one culture to another. English is the most frequently spoken second language.[54] The use of English in foreign advertising can convey cosmopolitan values,[55] or it can confuse the meaning, as English knowledge is only superficial in most countries.[54] As such, only certain elements, such as the brand and product class, are likely to be in English, whereas the body copy is more often in the local language.[56]

Website link 13.4

Search for Chinese languages website to see the use of English, such as the official Apple China website: **http://www.apple.com.cn/.**

Nelson and Paek[56] found multinational products were more likely to advertise in English than local products in *Cosmopolitan* magazine, with the highest English-language use in the US and India (where English is one official language) and the lowest in France and Brazil. Somewhere in between lies Asian advertising (e.g., South Korea, followed by Thailand and China), where English was often used by multinationals for the brand name, product class name, and slogan, but the local language was mostly used for body text.[56] There may be some recognition of global brand names,[57] but when information is conveyed it is best to use the local language.

A very large percentage of Asian advertisements contain at least some English – and in some rare cases French – words.[58,59] Since the most important function of this foreign vocabulary ultimately is to achieve a positive 'cosmopolitan' or country-of-origin positioning, its use depends on product type and product origin. Companies that wish to appeal to the more ethnocentric consumers might be more likely to use only local language words and images. Products that consumers use in a similar manner across cultures generally have more standardization in their advertising, such as high-tech goods,[60] personal care products[61] and perfume.[62] However, it would be fundamentally wrong to conclude from the heavy use of foreign words in Asian countries that there is a trend towards a globalization of advertising language. The Japanese culture in particular uses English loanwords for their symbolic weight; however, the symbolism is embedded in Japanese traditions.[59] Likewise, there is a trend in China moving away from the reliance on foreign languages to denote quality and prestige.

Since only a minority of persons worldwide can understand English, there are problems with the comprehension of foreign words. Multinational companies often translate directly from the origin copy, but there are many constraints, including local nuances and space. Differing language structures means that the textual part of advertisements grows by about 25 per cent when English is translated into Roman languages, and by 30 per cent when translated into Germanic languages.[63] This can alter the overall layout of the advertisement, and decrease the relative impact of visual elements.

Examples of translation and conceptual equivalence problems abound, especially for advertising campaigns in which message standardization has been attempted. A full rewrite is usually needed to transpose slogans from one language to another. This implies a thorough search for words that have the same intended meaning as in the source language, provided that these can be found (see Chapter 7). McDonald's recognized these difficulties in the planning stages of the successful global 'I'm lovin' it' campaign. In countries where the market was either not large enough to justify the effort of customization (e.g., Qatar), the translation became unappealing phonetically (as is the case with the Czech translation), or when the country had a sufficiently high level of familiarity with English (e.g., Norway, Malaysia) the slogan was kept as is. However, in other markets it was translated to a close approximate such as *Ich liebe es* in Germany, or the Spanish *me encanta* (literal

translation 'it enchants me'), which was used in much of South America, although interestingly not in Spain, where English was retained. In China it was even seen with both the English and Chinese versions together on the same logo.

However, even a 'good' translation of a message into each target country's language does not guarantee uniform comprehension. The meaning attributed to certain words depends on association norms that differ cross-culturally. When the English word 'quiet' is translated into German (*ruhig*) and French (*tranquille*), German consumers mostly think of a forest (41 per cent), sleep (35 per cent), church (20 per cent), but also of a cemetery (13 per cent) and a bed (8 per cent).[64] The pictorial associations of their French counterparts are fundamentally different and less homogeneous (countryside: 13 per cent; forest: 11 per cent; house: 9 per cent; library: 5 per cent, etc.).[64]

Where television advertisements must be easily transferable across countries, there should be a heavy emphasis on visual elements with voice-overs in the local language. For instance, television advertisements aimed at a European audience often use a script where the characters do not speak to the audience or to each other; a voice-over message is added to the image track. This cleverly avoids the drawbacks associated with dubbing. Most people lip-read unconsciously, at least in part. When watching a dubbed commercial, many people feel uneasy about the lag between lip movements and sounds. Along these lines, Apple implemented an interesting strategy when taking their US advertisements from their successful 'Get a Mac' campaign, featuring actors Justin Long (the Mac character) and John Hodgman (the PC) internationally. In Canada the ads were shown in their original format given that the accents of the two countries are quite similar. Similarly, in Australia and New Zealand the ads were again aired unaltered, given familiarity with American TV shows. However, to cover a large number of other markets, the original ads were dubbed into Spanish, French, German and Italian. Moreover, in the United Kingdom and Japan they completely and faithfully reproduced the series of ads using local comedians with more or less the same scripts. While Apple clearly believe in the benefits of localization of some elements of their ads, it was not without error. Unfortunately, in the UK versions the actor cast as the PC actually came across as more appealing than the Mac character (perhaps thanks to his popularity from other television roles), negating the message Apple was attempting to convey.[65]

Written communication should also be avoided in messages targeted at a multilingual audience. For instance, a commercial for a detergent where a housewife is handed a packet of *Waschpulver* will be identified by British, Italian or French viewers as foreign or German. A few years ago, IBM used the character of Charlie Chaplin and the mode of a silent film in a multinational campaign, the goal of which was to promote their corporate image. This allowed the advertisement to be used in any country of the world. Written messages can also be reduced or avoided in magazine advertisements. Occasionally we see text in its original foreign language in ads for ethnic products. Here, the text must be short and strongly support an ethnic image (French for perfume, English for a large international newspaper, Italian for luxury leather shoes, etc.). If possible, some 'borrowed' words can be included, but the text must be universally understood, although not necessarily in full detail. The message should make sense with respect to the halo of meanings around the product proposal.

The growing number of bilinguals brings in a new layer of complexity to language presention. Generally, bilinguals have been found to interpret information differently when they read in one or other language. The language tends to cue the salience of a self-concept related to one or other culture and their interpretation and behaviour changes. For instance, when bilinguals from Hong Kong were exposed to English advertisements and responded in English, their reactions were more similar to the Canadian sample than when they reacted to the Chinese version.[66] Specifically, they perceived greater source honesty, less forcefulness on the part of the source and reported a more positive attitude toward the brand than those who were exposed to the Chinese advertisement and responded in Chinese.[66] Other effects found include a high level of congruity between picture and text increasing memory for second-language advertisements for Spanish–English bilinguals.[67]

Humour

Humour can be based on gestures, situations, or words. It is sometimes involuntary. For instance, when Charles De Gaulle decided to retire from public life, the British ambassador and his wife threw a gala dinner party in his honour. At the dinner table the ambassador's wife was talking with Madame De Gaulle: 'Your husband has been such a prominent public figure, such a presence on the French and international scene for so many years! How quiet retirement will seem in comparison. What are you most looking forward to in these retirement years?' 'A penis', replied Madame De Gaulle. A huge hush fell over the table. Everyone heard her answer . . . and no one knew what to say next. Le Grand Charles leaned over to his wife and said: 'Ma chérie, I believe ze English pronounce zat word, "appiness!"'

The basic concept of humour is universal since it can be found in every culture and in any country's advertising; however, preferences for types of humour vary cross-culturally.[68] Globally, most humour has an incongruity-resolution structure: people develop expectations based on category norms that are capable of being violated, sometimes in a humorous way;[69] a naked businessman or a clothed ape speaking to the audience are examples of incongruity-based humour. Some cross-cultural support exists for a positive affect-based effect of humour in advertising, where the perceived funniness of an advertisement, liking the advertisement, and liking the product are all linked.[70] However, a closer look at the use of humour also reveals notable cultural differences.

> ## Website link 13.5
>
> Search for ads that may or may not transfer their humour across cultures, such as those features on the veryfunnyads website: **http://www.veryfunnyads.com**.

First, the percentage of advertisements intending to be humorous varies across countries. For instance, there is generally a higher percentage of humorous advertisements in television commercials in the UK than in the US and France, and even less in Germany.[31,71]

Second, although the incongruity principle can be found in the advertising of different countries, the relative importance of such humour varies. For instance, more incongruent contrasts are found in German (92 per cent) and Thai (82 per cent) than in American (69 per cent) and Korean ads (57 per cent).[72]

Third, the kind of humour preferred by each target culture differs. Whereas English people are known for their black humour, Germans seem to prefer humour based on gloating.[73] Americans use more self-defeating and self-enhancing humour than Arabs, while both Arabs and Americans use about the same amount of affiliative (jokes and anecdotes) and aggressive (demeaning others) humour.[74] The latter would not be much appreciated in Japan, where slapstick or demeaning humour is seldom seen in advertising. Instead, the Japanese make humorous dramatizations of situations involving family members, colleagues, neighbours, etc., to create a bond of mutual feelings between the advertiser and the viewer.[75] Additionally, black and earthy humour is also present in Japanese commercials. Subjects such as diseases, wars or funerals, which are taboo themes in the US, are treated with humour in some Japanese advertisements.[26] A study of the use of humour in print ads in the UK and Greece demonstrated that different types of humour are more or less appropriate across the two cultures depending on the objective (informational versus entertaining) of the ads. The highly individualistic, but low uncertainty avoidant, UK advertisers used more risky, aggressive and affective humour in their advertisements. This was in contrast to collectivist, uncertainty avoidant Greece, where relatively neutral humour, such as incongruity resolution was preferred.[76]

Finally, in countries with high collectivism scores, significantly more characters are depicted in humorous advertisements than in more individualistic countries.[72] Similarly, in countries high on the power distance dimension (e.g., Korea, Thailand) characters portrayed in humorous advertisements are much more likely to have an unequal status than in low power distance countries (e.g., US and Germany).[72]

Thus, it appears that humour can be an element of standardization in cross-cultural advertising, especially when it is based on the incongruity principle, which has a fairly global appeal. Nevertheless, the creative presentation of humour in advertisements needs considerable adaptation to be effective.[72]

Characters and roles represented in advertisements

When depicting characters, advertising must be extremely careful. Whether it is the age, dress or situation of a character that is represented, nothing should be left to chance in advertising messages. In general, target audiences prefer characters with which they can identify.[77] Since the physique of a person (and even more so a hero-like person depicted in an advertisement) is a clear manifestation of a particular culture, the choice of characters needs particular attention in cross-cultural advertising.

Advertising is often accused of perpetuating traditional social roles, sometimes even acting as a vehicle for outdated ideas. However, the real situation is much more ambiguous: in most countries, advertising acts as an agent of both social change and social maintenance. Advertising creation sometimes acts as an agent of change because social challenge is a method of capturing the attention of the audience, and because social innovators are also opinion leaders for new products and new ways of life. Advertising also reinforces traditional and sometimes old-fashioned social patterns, as it is the mirror of society as a whole. Potential dangers are brought home by Prendergast and colleagues,[78] who found that exposure to advertising was linked to eating disorders when they examined the relationship between the 'ideal woman' depicted in advertising and self-reports of eating disorders and body image dissatisfaction among females in Hong Kong.

Another important issue related to characters in advertising is the portrayal of gender roles. Several cross-cultural investigations have examined role portrayal in magazine and TV advertising. They all found that advertising is reflective of traditional stereotypes of male and female roles to varying degrees. In general, women are mostly shown in non-working roles, often in the home, and in decorative roles. When women appear in working roles, they are more likely than men to be depicted in clerical, blue-collar or secretarial roles. Eisend (p. 431) gives the following list of gender stereotyping in advertising, based on a meta-analytic review of a decade worth of research into the issue, in which women are more likely than men to be presented:[79]

- visually/not speaking;
- as product user rather than an authority;
- in a dependent role, relative to others rather than independent from others;
- at home/domestic environment rather than at work;
- younger rather than older;
- giving an opinion or a non-scientific argument rather than factual and scientific;

- associated with domestic products, such as those for the body, the home, or food; and
- against a background of mostly females.

Although studies show that sex role stereotypes are found in all cultures, differences exist. Some of the factors we expect sex role stereotyping to differ by include masculinity, tradition and religion. The effect of the masculinity and femininity dimension of culture on sex role stereotyping is a relatively complex issue. On the one hand, several researchers have found that sex role stereotyping differs between countries classed as more masculine versus feminine. For instance, in Web advertisements from South Korea (a more feminine culture) there was a greater proportion of female main characters and more depictions of relationships, compared to Web advertisements from the more masculine US.[80] Further, in masculine cultures, such as the US and Japan, women are less likely to appear in working situations.[81,82] However, there is also evidence to indicate that, while cultural values do matter, advertisers might be more influenced by the congruency between the product being advertised and the dominant gender stereotypes in the culture when selecting the gender of their models or actors.[83] So for products aimed at women, it is most likely that the ad will use female characters, and visa-versa.[83]

Website link 13.6

Search for gender targeted advertising on the UK Institute of Promotional Marketing website: http://www.theipm.org.uk.

Sex role stereotyping appears to be more prevalent in more traditional and religious cultures. For instance, a Malaysian television channel oriented towards a mostly Muslim target audience typically depicts men in exciting and independent top executive roles, and women as housewives who stay at home to look after the family.[84] In contrast, on Singapore television, men were more likely to be depicted in middle management roles, whereas women were depicted in white-collar and service occupations or in a more modern context: as young, attractive and concerned with beauty. Interestingly, the portrayal of women on a second Malaysian channel, targeted to both Malaysian and Singaporean audiences, shows a compromise between the stereotypes held by both audiences. However, this

is not always the case. For instance, no difference was found in gender stereotyping in advertising between the UK (masculine) and the Netherlands (feminine),[85] or between the US and the more traditional Arab world (comprising 12 Middle Eastern countries and 10 African countries).[86] The main difference, in the Arab world was that women were used mainly when their presence related to the advertised product.

We need to check our intuition with facts from the country. It seems that Australia and Sweden have a more balanced and non-traditional representation of men and women in their advertising than, for example, the US and Singapore. Malaysia, and to a lesser extent Mexico, where religious values and tradition are more important, display the biggest sex role differences in advertising. Whereas on Malaysian (Muslim) television the portrayal of the sexes lags behind changes in society (i.e., the number of housewives is grossly exaggerated; see Wee et al.[84]), marketers in countries like Sweden have a more proactive approach in defining sex roles, thus creating new trends. Even across countries with quite similar levels of development, stronger traditional values in the society, such as in Japan compared with the US, cause women's roles to be portrayed more traditionally.[16]

Similarly, a certain degree of standardization can be found regarding the use of Western models in Asian countries.[87] Such models can be found in more than one-third of magazine advertisements in Hong Kong, Taiwan, Japan and South Korea, and they are particularly frequent in advertisements for products from the West, notably personal care products.[61] For instance, a content analysis of Korean dieting ads in magazines (i.e., ads that promote an 'ideal' body type)[88] and adolescent fashion magazines[89] tended to contain more Western than Korean models. However, many other advertisements used completely local characters.

Website link 13.7

Search fashion covers on Eiffel: http://www.eiffelinseoul.com/.

Cross-cultural differences are also observed with regard to the portrayal of the elderly in advertising. A country's degree of orientation towards traditional values has an impact on the portrayal of the elderly in advertising messages. For instance, Japanese magazine advertisements show more respect towards the elderly than their American counterparts.[16,17] However, common stereotypes are not always confirmed. For example, in Latin America the elderly are not presented more frequently in a family setting or as celebrity endorsers, nor is there a greater proportion of elderly males than in the US.[90]

Traditional roles that are not present in the source culture may unintentionally appear when they are interpreted by the target culture. A 'spurious' meaning may appear in the target culture which was not intended by the advertiser in the source culture. For instance, Douglas and Dubois[91] give the example of a brandy advertisement that was targeted at the South African Bantu market. It showed a couple seated at a table with a bottle superimposed over them. Many Bantus thought that the woman was carrying the bottle on her head, as many traditional African women do. This created an unintended and confusing contrast between the traditional, local aspect of the characters and situation and the modern, imported aspect of the product. It therefore prevented clear and effective marketing communication.[91]

As a consequence, one should study a representative sample of local advertising messages, whether commercials or magazine advertisements. This will give a better idea of the sex roles, age roles, typical everyday situations and social relations in a particular country. It can be achieved by conducting a systematic content analysis of newspaper, magazine and television advertisements (at least several dozen of each). An advertisement should always be created in cooperation with a native of the target culture, who acts as a test audience; in the case of internationally standardized advertisements, messages in the various linguistic/cultural contexts should be reviewed by natives of each target culture or subcultures.

In order to avoid creating spurious associations, the advertising script may go so far as to avoid presenting any characters at all, especially if the target audience is not clearly defined or too large, making the choice of characters a difficult one. For instance, in a Renault advertisement, a car without a driver was shown moving in the middle of a scale-model city. This avoided the choice of a specific character, whose age, sex or appearance would influence the product's positioning undesirably. However, a car without a driver may be negatively interpreted in countries where such a situation is associated with a safety issue (runaway car) or a distortion of reality (how can a car drive without a driver?). This may inhibit a positive response to the message.

The influence of mores and religion

It is crucial to choose the appropriate symbolic elements by which cultural meanings about products and services may be communicated to the audience. Mores and religion act as filters of advertising messages, transforming factual information into culturally interpreted meaning (e.g., a naked woman washing her hair in her bathroom) into elements of culture-based meaning (it incites people to sexual debauchery). If one focuses on information rather than meaning, it is difficult to become aware of the influence of mores and religion on advertising messages. This point is illustrated by the example of advertising in Saudi Arabia (Box 13.2).

Many of us are superstitious, even though we may deny it. Rarely will advertisements show people walking under ladders, unless, for the sake of humour, something happens to them. This is proof of the force of superstition. The social habits of daily life also play a role, particularly those that are related to what is (locally) considered polite, courteous or hospitable. In this way, a well-known brand of tea alienated the Saudi public when it showed a Saudi host using his left hand to serve tea to one of his guests. Moreover, the guest was wearing shoes, which is considered in Saudi Arabia to be inappropriate.

The influence of religion on advertising, exemplified by the Muslim religion, although strong, is not uniform across countries or individual viewers within a particular country (see Al-Makaty and colleagues,[93] for the case of Saudi Arabia). Many differences depend on the religious belief or zeal held by individuals and groups. For instance, strict Muslims are more interested in, and especially have a higher recall of, non-contentious advertisements, whereas lenient Muslims show no difference between advertisement containing elements considered to be against the principles of Islam or not.[94] Furthermore, sensitive issues such as family planning can be treated successfully if creation adequately goes beyond traditional beliefs and taboos.[95]

Generally, the relationship between men and women, depicted by advertising, is a ticklish problem.

BOX 13.2

The influence of religion on advertising in Saudi Arabia

The Saudi legal system is unique in the sense that it identifies law with the personal command of the 'one and only god, the Almighty'. The Islamic laws known as *Sharia* are the master framework to which all legislation, existing and proposed, is referred and with which it must be compatible. The *Sharia* is a comprehensive code governing the duties, morals and behaviour of all Muslims, individually and collectively in all areas of life, including commerce. *Sharia* is derived from two basic sources, the Quran or Holy Book, and the *Hadith*, based on the life, sayings, and practices of the Prophet Muhammed . . . At the very minimum, an understanding of fundamental *Sharia* laws as contained in Quranic injunctions is necessary in order to gain insights into advertising regulation and content . . .

Three sets of Quranic messages have special significance for advertising regulation. First there are strict taboos (*haraam*), such as alcohol, gambling, cheating, idol worship, usury, adultery and 'immodest' exposure . . . For example alcoholic products are banned. There are no local advertisements, and foreign print media are only allowed into the country after all advertisements of alcoholic beverages have been censored. Promotions involving games of chance are illegal . . .

Other dangers for advertisers include messages which may be considered as deceptive by religious standards. According to Islam, fraud may occur if the seller fails to deliver everything promised, and advertisers may need to use factual appeal, based on real rather than perceived product benefits. Statuary should not appear in advertising, since it may be perceived as a symbol of idol worship. Since religious norms require women to be covered, international print advertisements may have to be modified by superimposing long dresses on models

or by shading their legs with black. Advertisers of cosmetics in Saudi Arabia refrain from picturing sensuous females; instead, in typical advertisements a pleasant-looking woman appears in a robe and headdress, with only her face showing . . . A second set of Quranic injunctions governs the duties a Muslim must perform, such as praying five times daily, fasting during the month of Ramadhan, giving *zakaat* (charity) to the poor, and respecting and caring for parents and the disadvantaged. Advertisers have to ensure that they do not hinder the performance of these obligations. For example, during the five prayer times, which last from 10 to 20 minutes, products cannot be promoted on radio or TV, retail shops close, and no commercial or official transactions are permitted. Advertisements should not depict, even humorously, children being disrespectful to parents and elders, whereas the image of a product could be enhanced by advertisements that stress parental advice or approval . . .

A third set of Quranic injunctions remind the faithful of God's bounties and enjoins them to thank Him for such blessings as good health, peace of mind, food, water and children. It is legal and sometimes recommended practice for advertisers to introduce their messages with Quranic words: 'In the Name of Allah, the Most Gracious, the Most Merciful'; 'By the Grace of God'; 'God is Great (Allah-o-Akbar)'; Al-Rabiah and Nasser, a manufacturer of water pumps, uses a Quranic verse: 'We made from water every living thing.' Such verses may also be used to legitimise operations or to assure that services are in accord with Islamic principles.

(Source: Luqmani *et al.*, pp. 61–4.[92] *International Marketing Review*, Musshtaq Luqmani, Ugur Yavas and Zahir Quraeshi, copyright 1989 by Emerald Group Publishing Limited. Reproduced with permission.)

For instance, advertising for beer on the Turkish market portrays men and women drinking the beer in a social setting at home.[96] The emphasis on a family setting as the consumption situation overcomes the problems with showing men and women together in the predominantly male institutions of coffee houses

and beer pubs, which would violate Turkish customs of courtship and social interaction. A study of college students in the US, Australia and China surprisingly found that the Chinese and Americans react equally as favourably towards sex appeal advertising, and more so than the Australians.[97] This highlights the importance of investigating local attitudes even when two countries are ostensibly very similar, such as the US and Australia.

Attitudes towards nudity differ from one country to another. French advertising is considered to have more nudity than most other countries. It is well accepted in French society, since the meaning conveyed by nudity is very much related to beauty, excellence and nature. An example is the advertisement for the Guy Laroche perfume Drakkar Noir in France and Saudi Arabia.[98] The original French advertisement showed a man's bare forearm, held at the wrist by a woman's hand, with the man's hand holding a bottle of cologne. The Saudi advertisement showed the man's forearm covered by a suit jacket, with only the cuff of the shirt showing, while the woman lightly touched his hand with one of her fingers. While it can be argued that it is a reasonable strategy to standardize within regions and localize across them, recent research has suggested that this is an overly simplistic view that may lead advertisers into trouble. For instance, while Asian countries are typically grouped together, a study of nudity in primetime TV advertising showed that, in fact, Thailand advertising had much greater use of nudity compared to China and South Korea. Similarly, using the Western country grouping could be erroneous as the same study showed that Germany used a much greater amount of nudity compared to the US.[99]

Respect for the existing social conventions in the target society will long remain a prerequisite for the localization of advertising messages. Furthermore, the role of advertising has never been (at least officially) to change a society's mores, but rather to sell a product.

Visual elements

Advertising copy is complex and inevitably tends to reflect the cultural background of those who have created it. Some differences in colour perceptions and usage across cultures include:

- Blue being a masculine colour in the US, whereas red is masculine in France;[100]
- Black represents mourning in France and the US, whereas purple does in Venezuela;[100]
- Green is associated with money in the US; whereas in France it is associated with pharmacies;[100]

- Yellow is favoured in Taiwanese advertising (the colour of royalty), whereas brown was preferred in US advertisements;[101]
- Black and brown are common in France and the US, whereas red, orange and green are more common in Venezuelan advertisements.[100]

Website link 13.8

Search for current trends in advertising from global advertising agencies, such as: http://www.eurorscg.com.

While pictures, as compared to language, are understood everywhere, the issue is not *whether* pictures are understood but rather *how* they are understood. As with language elements, pictures also present culture-specific association norms.[102] While rain evokes freshness for certain persons, it is associated with coldness by others. This is problematic for global advertising.[64] Further, different background themes, setting, and roles are depicted more or less frequently across cultures. For instance, Brazilian advertisements use significantly more urban and leisure themes than US advertisements.[103] Cutler and colleagues[104] found that advertising content differs significantly:

- Indian advertisements use significantly more black and white and show more children than those in any other country;
- Korean advertisements show price two or three times as frequently as those in other countries, and represent more elderly persons whose wisdom is valued in Far Eastern cultures;
- French advertisements are by far the most oriented towards aesthetics: five times more than US, Korean or Indian advertisements, but only twice as much as British advertisements.
- US advertisements appear by far the most comparative (ten times more than in France).

Furthermore, US advertisements depict children in more idealistic settings – clean and smiling – than French advertisements, where they are more likely to appear quite realistic.[105]

The standardization of magazine advertisements across the countries mentioned above will not be easy, since there are more differences than similarities for product types. Each country is unique on one or several visual characteristics. Overall, however, no systematic differences between developed and developing countries appear. As such, it is wise to analyse the current content of advertisements in specific countries.

Advertising in societies experiencing rapid change

China has witnessed a dramatic change in the place of advertising in the overall business and social scene. In societies where people have been told for a long time that advertising is simply capitalist propaganda, and as such evil and deceptive, advertisers today still face some degree of distrust and cannot just use the same approach as elsewhere. Many consumers still feel that good products sell themselves and that only bad products need advertising. Compared to the US, fewer Chinese respondents trusted the messages and believed in industry regulation.[106] In such a context, foreign companies have to target long-run acceptance, stressing product availability and building brand reputation.[107] They cannot just imitate what is done elsewhere.

Since the Chinese advertising market opened to the outside world in late 2005, the industry has grown dramatically. All of the major global advertising agencies entered China in some form in the lead-up to the 2008 Olympic Games. However, advertising in China is still heavily regulated. The government attempts to control the negative effects of advertising through regulations, certification and censorship, but its regulations are vague and difficult to understand. Zhihong Gao[108] provides a detailed overview of advertising in China, for those interested.

Cross-national transferability of advertising copy

Multinationals frequently need to transfer promotional materials to other countries, where they are adapted, as necessary.[109] When attempts are made to transfer advertising copy cross-culturally, the first issue is the grouping of countries within which cross-national transfers are easier. In broad terms, cultural similarity is likely to influence the success of standardization, as culturally similar people tend to consume similar goods and where the language is similar the transfer of copy is less problematic. However, other country-specific aspects should also be considered. For instance, Zandpour and Harich[110] grouped countries according to whether they value more rational (think) or more emotional (feel) advertising appeals.

An interesting approach is to cluster countries according to cultural values – e.g., Hofstede's[111] dimensions or Schwartz's[112] values – in order to determine whether it is possible to transfer part or the whole of an advertising creation or even a full campaign. Since Hofstede's dimensions seem to be meaningful, Sriram and Gopalakrishna[113] combined these dimensions with economic and demographic, as well as media availability indicators (televisions per 1000 people, radios per 1000 people, advertising spending per capita, etc.). They clustered countries into six groups: Japan is isolated in one group, and most other groups are fairly heterogeneous geographically, except northern Europe and a sort of central Asian area extending from Iran to the Philippines. The two Hofstede dimensions that discriminate significantly between these groups are power distance and individualism. As an example, status appeals are more often seen in advertisements in a high power distance society, such as South Korea, than in a low power distance society such as the US.[41] Masculinity in Mexico (*Machismo*) is influential in the advertisements for traditional male-oriented products such as automobiles.[114]

Similarly, Kale[115] gives the example of the promotion of India as a tourist destination for the US market. When trying to adapt, both the target (US) and the source (India) cultures have to be considered: they differ mostly on Hofstede's power distance (40 versus 77) and individualism (91 versus 48). Kale insists that the (Indian) message must be targeted to the (US) individual: the message must reflect friendliness and informality, and it must value autonomy, variety and pleasure, all positive values for highly individualistic cultures, such as that of the US. He further suggests that, since democracies are perceived as small power distance institutions, the message should emphasize that India has a democratic government, which would help bridge the gap of power distance between the source and the target country. Emphasizing cultural similarity is especially appropriate for tourism advertising, as tourists appear to seek elements of similarity, rather than difference. For example, Ng, Lee and Soutar (p. 1505) describe elements of cultural similarity that might be stressed in tourist destination advertising messages:

... religious similarity might be a strong marketing message for Muslims, as it facilitates their religious practices, which include eating 'Halal' food and praying at a mosque five times a day. In addition, stressing the presence of a 'multiethnic' culture might make potential international tourists feel more comfortable and secure, due to the presence of their ethnicity at the destination. ... stressing 'food' similarity or availability might increase the level of comfort with a potential destination (e.g., Korean tourists prefer to include their ethnic accompaniments, such as 'kimchi' with their meals.[116]

Thus, it is not just the broad country-level similarities and differences that need to be considered. While country-level information may guide strategy, more precise information should guide the executional details.

If advertising is to be transferred, the following elements should always be carefully checked to ensure the cultural adequacy of the final copy:

1. comparative advertising or not;
2. degree and type of informative content and style;
3. adequacy of basic copy themes in relation to local mores and customs;
4. execution: background themes, colour, use of words (puns, suggestive words), use of humour, use of symbols, type of characters and roles (age, sex, status), situations and types of relationship depicted; and
5. implementation constraints, such as lack of a medium available locally.

13.4

Media worldwide: technological advances and cultural convergence

Worldwide differences in advertising expenditure

One cannot help but be struck by the difference in advertising expenses across countries, even though these countries may have comparable levels of economic development. This can be partially attributed to media availability (radio, television, newspapers, magazines, film, billboards). Where some media are non-existent or their availability is limited, expenses are automatically restricted by the lack of space for advertising. According to **www.emarketer.com**

(see Weblink 13.9), the total media ad spending worldwide in 2010 was just over US$475 billion: the USA lead this with over $153 billion, followed by Japan (US$34 billion), China (US$33.6 billion) and Germany (US$25.4 billion).

> **Weblink 13.9**
>
> Search for current comparative advertising data, such as ad spending share worldwide, featured on the following website: **http://www.emarketer.com/PressRelease.aspx?R=1008479**.

Cross-cultural differences in media availability and use

The availability of advertising media is influenced by the level of a country's economic development and also by its view of the appropriate mix between business/commercial activities, on the one hand, and cultural/recreational activities on the other hand. For instance, there are no cinemas in Saudi Arabia, where traditional values do not permit the showing of films to public gatherings, although people are still able to watch films via satellite, DVD and video.[117,118] Ethical debates about whether certain products can be advertised have an influence on regulations, for instance about media space available for cigarettes and alcohol.

Today most developed and many developing countries are employing anti-smoking advertising, as these campaigns seem to be effective in curbing smoking. For instance, when US ninth graders' watched films with smokers in them, the result was enhanced perceptions of a smoker's stature and increased intent to smoke. When a similar audience watched the same film, but with anti-smoking advertisements in it, the result was negative thoughts about the movie characters who smoked.[119] Similar results have been found with other age groups in many countries (e.g., Australia and Malaysia): anti-smoking advertisements result in less favourable attitudes towards smoking.[120]

Advertising is largely based on the availability of news and entertainment media. The communication support systems, such as television and audiovisual equipment, printing presses, photographic equipment, etc. are costly and need to be balanced by sales, advertising or other sources of revenue. Financial support in countries where banks have limited lending capacity is often based on political influence (which may prove unstable). In many countries the press is even more dependent on politics than on advertisers.

Apart from purely economic factors, the availability of the media is also influenced by two social representations concerning the relationship between the media and its audience. First, what is considered a reasonable ratio between advertising and entertainment time (news and programmes) by the local audience and what is appropriate sequencing between advertising and entertainment – for instance, in terms of television movies being sliced up by advertising? Second, is advertising considered an entertainment in itself? If entertaining the target audience is a necessary condition for capturing their interest, creative effort may have to be devoted to entertainment rather than communicating the core messages. This may reduce the effectiveness of the advertisement, because the viewers' attention is attracted by the creative side of the message and diverted from the product that is being presented. Responses to the issue of how entertainment and advertising interrelate probably differ in the US and Europe.

Many countries have instituted rules that place limits on television advertising. For instance, many countries (e.g., Australia, New Zealand, Sweden, the UK) have national channels that prohibit advertising. Until recently Europe was notorious for the differences in regulations across countries. In December 2007 the Audiovisual Media Services Directive was adopted to align regulations across member countries. Some of the more important regulations include:

- Allowing product placement (previously illegal in most EU member states) provided the viewer is informed about it. Exceptions include news and current affairs programmes, children's TV, documentaries and advice programmes.
- Allowing up to 12 minutes per hour of advertising in television broadcasts, but for films more frequent breaks will be allowed (every 30 minutes, rather than the current 45 minutes).
- Limiting children's advertising with a code of conduct, which includes restrictions on junk food advertising.

Conversely, where little or even no advertising regulation exists, there can sometimes be such an invasion by advertising that viewing television programmes becomes little more than watching advertisements, a reproach frequently addressed by Europeans to US, Brazilian or Canadian television channels. The general contrast here seems to be between the Americas (the US, Mexico, Brazil and Canada), with liberal advertising regulations, and most other countries, where audiovisual media availability is more limited by regulation. For instance, while Saudi Arabia lifted the ban on commercial advertising on radio, all broadcasts are screened in order to ensure that they conform to Islamic moral and religious standards.

In many countries radio stations have flourished with extensive advertising space – that is, up to 20 minutes of commercials per hour; programmes are constantly interrupted by advertising. This hectic schedule may be resented by listeners, who constantly change stations, obliging advertisers to buy media space for the same time blocks across several radio stations. The question of finding the acceptable proportion of advertising to total time is an important one. Studies have shown that in the US an increasing number of consumers consider television advertising as less than intelligent, leading to dissatisfaction.[29] The situation is fairly paradoxical: as the number of media channels increases, it becomes more difficult to reach and monitor a target audience, since viewers' saturation with advertisements reduces their ability to listen to advertising and encourages zapping. It is surprising that the issue of whether the viewer/listener is entertained by advertising is rarely addressed, given its practical importance. Zapping has been widely studied, but most studies have only sought to demonstrate how an advertiser can avoid its unfortunate results. It is taken for granted that the audience has no saturation threshold, or at the very least an extremely high one. This assumption suggests the absolute legitimacy of mass advertising communication within a society that willingly portrays itself as being free-market oriented. In contrast, many European countries started from the opposite assumption, and advertising therefore took a long time to assert itself on television.

The emergence of global media

The previous sections placed emphasis upon differences in advertising across countries. These differences do not offset the similarities and convergence. Diverse media combine into a 'media landscape' which is primarily shaped by the freedom of choice of the audience. Some media have achieved almost worldwide recognition and a truly global audience. Among the international advertising media that have achieved the most impressive worldwide reach is the monthly *Reader's Digest*. *Readers Digest*'s 91 magazines (including 50 editions of *Reader's Digest* which are sold in more than 70 countries)[121] and are now available on tablets and e-readers. It was founded in 1920 by DeWitt Wallace and his wife Lila Acheson. The first issue came out in February 1922 (see Box 13.3).

The global media landscape has two facets: while local media survive because language differences remain a pervasive reality, a globalized supply of media is emerging which greatly serves the globalization of advertising. The best example of such breakthroughs in international telecommunications is the growth of the Internet as an advertising medium. Perhaps the biggest opportunity for global advertising going forward is the rapid growth of Internet penetration amongst emerging market economies (EMEs). It is estimated that, by 2020, consumers from the top 25 current EMEs (such as China, India, Argentina, etc.) will account for around 60 per cent of all Internet users, although with broadband rates only around 46 per cent (still well below the developed economy rate).[124]

Weblink 13.10

Search for the global reach of different media, such as Mondo Times, which lists the most circulated newspaper, worldwide, as *Yomiuri Shimbun*, Japan with over 10 million in circulation: **http://www.mondotimes.com/**.

However, the availability of the Internet and satellite television has some implications in terms of media overlap. The Internet is available across most countries. While satellite television is often by

---

BOX 13.3

The internationalization of the *Reader's Digest*

'Since the formula of the Digest is so effective in the United States, why not attempt to repeat it elsewhere?' thought DeWitt Wallace. But exporting the formula of a magazine requires that the obstacle of language be overcome. The simplest solution was to begin in England, which could serve as a gateway into Europe. Accordingly, the first foreign edition of the *Reader's Digest* appeared in Great Britain in 1937. The second foreign edition, however, did not appear in Europe. In 1940, in the midst of the Second World War, the first issue of *Selecciones del Reader's Digest*, the Spanish-American edition, came out in Cuba. Why Cuba? The long-term objective was to attack the South American market, even if sales had to be made at a loss (as indeed occurred for many years). But for the time being, DeWitt Wallace's objective was more of a missionary one, for he sought to combat the Nazi advance. In 1942 a Portuguese edition in Brazil followed. This edition reached a print run of 300,000 copies. In 1943 there was a return to Europe with the publication of a Swedish edition. The war was not yet over, but

DeWitt Wallace was already contemplating market entry into Europe. He offered cut-price subscriptions of the *Digest* to families of young Americans who had been called up. Along with chewing gum and nylon stockings, the *Reader's Digest* was to arouse the interest of young Europeans. After the war, in 1947, *Sélection du Reader's Digest* finally appeared in France under the management of General Thompson. There was an initial print run of 275,397 copies, which almost doubled for the second issue. The global expansion of the *Reader's Digest* did not stop . . . Germany, Italy, Switzerland and Belgium, as well as India, South Africa, Australia and New Zealand, were all in turn to have their edition of the magazine. Today, 39 editions of the *Reader's Digest* are published, including one for schoolchildren, another in large type for those with sight problems and an edition in Braille. It can justifiably claim the distinction inscribed on every cover of being the most widely read magazine in the world.

(Source: Adapted from *Reader's Digest*.[122,123])

subscription, these subscriptions are not always within 'intended' markets for advertisers. For instance, Astra cover a significant number of countries in Europe. This produces overlapping zones where viewers are able to receive a large number of channels with a simple dish and decoder. This phenomenon can be observed worldwide, especially in Europe and Asia. For instance, Unilever's household cleanser is called Vif in Switzerland, Viss in Germany, Jif in the United Kingdom and Greece and Cif in France. This adaptation carries the risk of being misunderstood by consumers, if these brands are seen by unintended markets. However, there are increasing numbers of standard brand names across Europe, especially within industries that are potential candidates for regional marketing globalization, such as banks and financial services for private clients, airlines, mass market consumer goods, as well as many consumer durables such as cars, household appliances, stereo and video systems and photographic equipment.

13.5

The globalization of advertising

Advertising agencies are now largely global. The largest agencies, including Euro-RSCG, WPP, Publicis, Dentsu, BBDO, McCann-Erickson, JWT, DDB, TBWA, Leo Burnett and Hakuhodo, have built up a network of subsidiaries covering most countries over the last 20 or 30 years.[125] One of the largest advertising agencies in the world, Dentsu Inc., is Japanese, and the largest Japanese agencies are now present in a growing number of countries, mostly in Asia. The Japanese advertising market is a large one: it remains very attractive to Japanese agencies, which then target South-East Asia and Australia in the first stages of their international expansion.

Large national agencies are compelled to follow the route towards the globalization of marketing communications, media and audiences. As well as having to be able to organize cross-border campaigns for advertisers, they also try to remain knowledgeable experts on local idiosyncrasies in the implementation of marketing communication strategies. In 2010 the top five advertising organizations reported the following revenues: WPP Group (US$14.4 billion); Omnicon Group ($12.5 billion); the French Publicis group ($7.2 billion); Interpublic Group of COS

($6.5 billion) and the Japanese Dentsu ($3.6 billion), according to *Advertising Age*'s 2011 *Agency Report*.[125]

> **Website link 13.11**
>
> Search for interesting information on advertising: http://adage.com/.

Relationships between advertisers and agencies

Following the internationalization of advertisers, agencies have increased their foreign operations. In large multinational corporations with diversified product lines, this can lead to a complex advertiser–agency organization. The various organizational levels (national, regional and worldwide) within both the multinational agency and the multinational advertiser must be in constant contact with each other, increasing the usual communication problems within large international organizations. Different approaches may be chosen for the organization of international marketing communication with respect to the agency/advertiser relationship (see Case A13.1). One possibility is to use just one large international advertising agency, which allows for centralization of communication; this can be implemented for each product division separately, or for large brands or for the purpose of managing the corporate image worldwide.

An opposite solution is to hire local agencies that are well acquainted with local constraints as they affect media and consumers. Intermediate solutions between these two extremes attempt to find an effective trade-off between worldwide coordination and the local tailoring of advertising campaigns. Ford has decided to regionalize its brand advertising in Europe with central coordination and five sub-regional teams which adapt advertising strategy to clusters of local European markets.[126]

Advertising standardization: feasibility and desirability

After a review of arguments for and against advertising standardization worldwide, a more meaningful question is whether standardized advertising should be used or not, even if it is feasible.[127] Harvey[128] considers the following arguments in favour of standardized advertising: (1) it provides consistent image across markets; (2) it avoids confusing mobile consumers; (3) it may decrease the cost of preparing campaign themes, copy and materials; and (4) it enables firmer control over the planning and execution of campaigns across markets. He gives a complete checklist of factors to be considered in order to assess whether the standardized approach is appropriate. These include product factors, competition, organization variables, media infrastructure, regulations and market/societal variables. Insight from experienced international marketing executives working for large multinationals based in the UK indicated that based on differences across these types of factors, not all elements of advertising were suitable for standardization.[127] The executives believed that overall advertising theme is possible to standardize, but creative executions and the media mix should usually be customized. Standardization of theme means that the firm can

present a consistent global image, which in today's Internet society is potentially very beneficial. Creative execution within this overall theme however requires a more customized approach, as differences in language, preference for humour types, education, and consumer tastes have a bearing on how well the message is received and interpreted. Finally, the media mix used to implement the execution is strongly affected by media infrastructure, consumer media and product habits, and competition, again pushing decision-makers in the direction of customization. The danger of this approach is that it does not distinguish desirability of standardization (which has to be assessed first) from its feasibility; Harvey states initially that 'given the strong economic and administrative rationale it is assumed that, if possible, advertisers would prefer to standardize advertising' (p. 58).[128] See Box 13.4 for IKEA's different execution and marketing mix strategies.

BOX 13.4

IKEA – Globalization of furniture

In 2011, IKEA won the prestigious Cannes Lions Advertiser of the Year award, an excellent result for the global furniture company out of Sweden. IKEA got to this stage by a careful mix of standardization and customization across their markets. First, IKEA has a strongly standardized brand message. IKEA's corporate website states that 'The IKEA Concept is based on offering a wide range of well designed, functional home furnishing products at prices so low that as many people as possible will be able to afford them'. This message does not change, regardless of the country or culture in which they operate, and is central to their brand and by extension their advertising messages. This allows IKEA to keep tight rein on their overall brand image and has helped them reach number 31 on the Interbrand Best Global Brands 2011 list. So, if their global image is so standardized, how do IKEA successfully penetrate so many diverse international markets, such as Australia, China, Russia, the UK and UAE (just a few among the 41 countries in which IKEA has at least one retail store)? Philip Thomas, the CEO of Cannes Lions, answered that question when he attributed IKEA's success to the firm's 'ability to localize its global target market and create

advertising campaigns that vary significantly across territories as they take on-board and adapt to unique marketing conditions and cultural sensibilities of each country'. In essence, by customizing their execution and media usage.

In Australia, consumers are encouraged by IKEA to 'have a go', positioning their products as the antithesis of boring interior designs. The phrase 'have a go' has a distinct relevance in Australia that encompasses the local cultural attitudes. In England consumers were told to 'Stop being so English' and try some modern furniture, a similar message but executed in a culturally unique way. In their home country of Sweden they have used the slogan 'Decorate the home as you want to live', appealing to the idea that IKEA is a part of the national identity. The slogan used in China 'Not for the rich but for the wise' reflects their affordability brand image, while targeting the Confucian ideal of wisdom. By retaining the overall brand message within these culturally specific executions, IKEA has maximized its promotional resources in the global market.

(Sources: Tan;[129] Interbrand;[130] Thomas.[131])

Interestingly, Norwegian exporters' knowledge of the local market led to more standardization: the more they learned about local conditions the more similarities they perceived and the more they felt able to standardize the marketing mix.[132] In the US and Japan multinational firms operating in Europe identified three overall factors that positively influenced the likelihood of using standardized advertising.[133] These included environmental factors (customer similarity, market similarity, similarity of advertising infrastructure and the level of competition), strategic factors (seeking to emphasize global orientation, cost savings and cross-border segmentation), and level of centralized control.[133] Evidence concerning advertising standardization shows a mixed picture. For instance, the clothing brand Polo tends to use the same print advertising in magazines across countries. However, an investigation based on Polo's close-to-identical ads demonstrated that US and South Korean viewers actually differed markedly on their perceptions of the brand.[134] Despite this, it seems that advertising standardization, as reported by major international agencies, has increased over the past 30 years under pressure from clients.[135]

The global campaign concept

One cannot underestimate the complexity of managing an international campaign,[136] especially in the realm of agency/advertiser relations, which are often difficult to manage even when both agency and advertiser are excellent companies. For instance, Procter & Gamble has always had a reputation as a demanding advertiser for its agencies, but also for being very loyal to them. P & G, like many large companies, has had very stable relationships (sometimes for 40 years or more) with a group of agencies; some of them have worldwide responsibility for a product line and/or a major brand.[137] However, the creative work is sometimes a source of conflict between major advertisers and their agencies when their views diverge as to the strategy to be followed. Most advertisers then try to adopt a democratic style, by discussing opinions, facts, data and drafts of potential advertising campaigns. The final say always comes when campaigns are actually launched and their impact on various objectives may be monitored (brand awareness, brand image, sales increase, etc.).

Globalization of marketing communications may be less pervasive than it seems at first sight; therefore the necessary degree of adaptation should increase over a continuum of four levels: *mission* (long-term identity and vision of the communicator), *proposition* (campaign themes), creative *concepts* (how themes are translated in the language and cultures of the target groups) and *execution*.[95] While mission can rather easily be globalized, execution will need much local tailoring. Kanso and Nelson[138] examined the role of American and non-American subsidiaries in designing and implementing campaigns for non-domestic markets. Their findings indicated '(1) the advertising theme should not be the same across countries; (2) even the use of similar appeals and symbols in advertising campaigns targeting foreign markets is ill advised; (3) the choice of illustrations and colours must tie well with consumers' aesthetic sense; and (4) the integration of local communication expertise is a necessity to overcome language and cultural barriers in worldwide markets' (p. 86).[138]

The objective of a global advertising campaign has to be clearly defined: it does not seek to save on creative costs. It aims to promote a global brand name and image. Accordingly, the creative director for McCann-Erickson worldwide, Marcio Moreira, emphasizes that an advertiser should not pursue a global advertising strategy as a way of saving money, trying to achieve in only one campaign what may in fact require 12. The correct implementation of a global campaign requires a great deal of effort and creative time, and ultimately its cost may prove higher than the sum total of individual campaigns.[139] Dean M. Peebles,[140] who was for many years the manager of international communications for Goodyear, the world's leading tyre manufacturer, recommends the following steps for the design and implementation of a global advertising campaign:

1. Choose a large advertising agency with subsidiaries all over the world; select in this agency an international account manager, who reports to the advertiser's headquarters.
2. Establish multinational planning meetings between the client and the agency, as well as a multinational creative team.
3. Brand managers and headquarters level should conduct and supervise consumer research and the pre-tests of the draft communication.

Figure 13.2 Flowchart for the management of multinational advertising campaigns at Goodyear

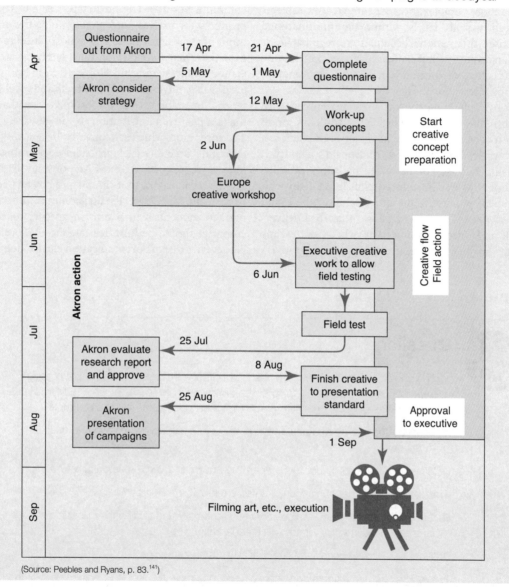

(Source: Peebles and Ryans, p. 83.[141])

4. The resulting draft global campaign should be sufficiently finalized to facilitate discussion, but flexible enough to be transposed (rather than translated) into the various cultures and lifestyles of the target audiences.

Figure 13.2 presents a flowchart of headquarters–subsidiary relations for the planning and coordination of worldwide advertising at Goodyear. This flowchart indicates the tasks to be performed and the (tight) time schedule imposed.[141]

Practical implementation of global advertising campaigns is not an easy task. The organization must be completely interactive and use both bottom-up and top-down communication flows. Communication between headquarters and subsidiaries should not be a 'sham' dialogue in which decisions already taken at the very top level would have to be accepted by local executives as if they were their own. This issue is all the more complex, because interaction problems between various levels within the multinational advertiser (international headquarters, regional headquarters, country subsidiaries) may snowball, leading to difficulties of communication and coordination with the international agency.

Global communication is primarily intended to establish the corporate image of a company or to foster recognition of one of its major brands across a large number of countries (e.g., McDonald's, Goodyear, Michelin, Nestlé). For instance, the 'subtitles' campaign of IBM was introduced globally in 1995 with the aim of promoting the universality of the brand imagery of IBM. The message was that IBM delivers simple and powerful solutions anywhere, at any time and for anyone; the use of subtitles and voice-overs allowed for both a global message and a localized communication.[142] The next step is to advertise the products themselves, and at this point the creative input of local subsidiaries and regional headquarters, as well as their influence on the advertising strategy, is much more significant. However, local campaigns, even if they advertise local products and local brand names, must be carefully coordinated so that they make a positive contribution to the global message. The core values which are conveyed by the company's corporate image (e.g., high technology, robustness, innovativeness, style, social responsibility) should also be recognizable in its brand and product advertising at the local level. Finally, communication with market segments which remain specific to certain countries should be fully delegated to the local level. Not every piece of communication can be globalized.

Questions

1. The English word 'hair' corresponds to two totally different French words: *cheveux* (of head) or *poil* (on body). Interpret the difference in concepts of what 'hair' is. What might be the consequences in terms of marketing for personal care products?

2. Describe the respective cultural adequacy of persuasive, informative and oneiric messages.

3. Why does the acceptance of comparative advertising vary cross-culturally?

4. What are the target audiences of satellite television in Europe?

5. Give examples of mores which vary cross-culturally and outline their possible consequences in terms of advertising adaptation.

6. What are the real benefits of a global advertising campaign?

7. Wella, a German giant in personal haircare, has recently decided to globalize a brand of its subsidiary Mühlens in Cologne (Germany) 4711, which is the original Eau de Cologne perfumed water. The 4711 brand, although well known in the German-speaking area, has an old-fashioned image, and Eau de Cologne seems to be associated in the minds of consumers in many countries with cheap perfume rather than tradition or luxury. How would you tackle this issue?

References

1. Kashani, Kamran (1989), 'Beware the Pitfalls of Global Marketing', *Harvard Business Review* (September–October), 91–8.
2. Li, Fengru and Nader H. Shooshtari (2006), 'On Toyota's Misstep in Advertising its Land Cruiser SUV in Beijing: A Distortion of Consumers' Sociolinguistic System', *Journal of International Consumer Marketing*, 18 (4), 61–78.
3. Aker, Jenny C. and Isaac M. Mbiti (2010), 'Mobile Phones and Economic Development in Africa', *The Journal of Economic Perspectives*, 24 (3), 207–32.
4. Stanglin, Douglas (2010), 'KFC Australia Pulls Fried Chicken Ad Called Racial Stereotyping', *USA Today*, January 8, available from: http://content.usatoday.com/communities/ondeadline/post/2010/01/kfc-australia-pulls-fried-chicken-ad-called-racial-sterotyping/1.
5. Wills, James R. and John K. Ryans Jr (1982), 'Attitudes toward Advertising: A Multinational Study', *Journal of International Business Studies* (Winter), 121–41.
6. La Ferle, Carrie, Steven M. Edwards and Wei-Na Lee (2008), 'Culture, Attitudes, and Media Patterns in China, Taiwan, and the U.S.: Balancing Standardization and Localization Decisions', *Journal of Global Marketing*, 21 (3), 191–205.
7. Jozsa, Laszlo, Andrea Insch, Jayne Krisjanous and Kim-Shyan Fam (2010), 'Beliefs About Advertising in China: Empirical Evidence From Hong Kong and Shanghai Consumers', *Journal of Consumer Marketing*, 27 (7), 594–603.
8. Hoek, Janet and Philip Gendall (2006), 'Advertising and Obesity: A Behavioral Perspective', *Journal of Health Communication*, 11 (4), 409–23.
9. Kelly, Bridget, Jason C. G. Halford, Emma J. Boyland, Kathy Chapman, Inmaculada Bautista-Castano, Christina Berg, Margherita Caroli, Brian Cook, Janine G. Coutinho, Tobias Effertz, Evangelia Grammatikaki, Kathleen Keller, Raymond Leung, Yannis Manios, Renata Monteiro, Claire Pedley, Hillevi Prell, Kim Raine, Elisabetta Recine, Lluis Serra-Majem, Sonia Singh and Carolyn Summerbell (2010), 'Television Food Advertising to Children: A Global Perspective', *American Journal of Public Health*, 100 (9), 1730–36.
10. James, Karen E. and Paul J. Hensel (1991), 'Negative Advertising: The Malicious Strain of Comparative Advertising', *Journal of Advertising*, 20 (2), 53–67.
11. Choi, Yung Kyun and Gordon E. Miracle (2004), 'The Effectiveness of Comparative Advertising in Korea and the United States', *Journal of Advertising*, 33 (4), 75–87.
12. Nye, Carolyn White, Martin S. Roth and Terence A. Shimp (2008), 'Comparative Advertising in Markets Where Brands and Comparative Advertising are Novel, *Journal of International Business Studies*, 39, 851–63.
13. Romano, Charlotte J. (2004), 'Comparative Advertising in the United States and in France', *Northwestern Journal of International Law and Business*, 25, 371.
14. Anon (2009), 'Court Rules That GE Healthcare Engaged in False Advertising Campaign Against Bracco Diagnostics', available from: http://www.reuters.com/article/2009/03/27/idUS211988+27-Mar-2009+BW20090327.
15. Agrawal, Madhu (1995), 'Review of 40-Year Debate in International Advertising: Practitioner and Academician Perspectives to the Standardization/Adaptation Issue', *International Marketing Review*, 12 (1), 26–48.
16. Javalgi, Rajshekhar, Bob D. Cutler and Naresh K. Malhotra (1995), 'Print Advertising at the Component Level: A Cross-cultural Comparison of the United States and Japan', *Journal of Business Research*, 34, 117–24.
17. Mueller, Barbara (1987), 'Reflections of Culture: An Analysis of Japanese and American Advertising Appeals', *Journal of Advertising Research*, 27 (3), 51–9.
18. Lin, Carolyn A. (1993), 'Cultural Differences in Message Strategies: A Comparison between American and Japanese TV Commercials', *Journal of Advertising Research*, 33 (4), 40–48.
19. Kalliny, Morris, Anshu Saran, Salma Ghanem and Caroline Fisher (2011), 'Cultural Differences and Similarities in Television Commercials in the Arab World and the United States', *Journal of Global Marketing*, 24 (1), 41–57.
20. Lin, Carolyn A. (2001), 'Cultural Values Reflected in Chinese and American Television Advertising', *Journal of Advertising*, 30 (4), 83–94.
21. Cheong, Yunjae, Kihan Kim and Lu Zheng (2010), 'Advertising Appeals as a Reflection of Culture: A Cross-Cultural Analysis of Food Advertising Appeals in China and the US', *Asian Journal of Communication*, 20 (1), 1–16.
22. Chiou, Jyh-shen (2002), 'The Effectiveness of Different Advertising Message Appeals in the Eastern Emerging Society: Using Taiwanese TV Commercials as an Example', *International Journal of Advertising*, 21 (2), 217–36.
23. Zheng, Lu, Joseph E. Phelps, Yorgo Pasadeos and Shuhua Zhou (2007), 'Do the Little Emperors Rule? Comparing Informativeness and Appeal Types in Chinese, American, and French Magazine Advertising', in *Advances in International Marketing*, Charles R. Taylor and Doo-Hee Lee (eds), Vol. 18: JAI.
24. Shavitt, Sharon, Timothy P. Johnson and Jing Zhang (2011), 'Horizontal and Vertical Cultural Differences

in the Content of Advertising Appeals, *Journal of International Consumer Marketing*, 23 (3–4), 297–310.

25. Zhang, Jing (2010), 'The Persuasiveness of Individualistic and Collectivistic Advertising Appeals Among Chinese Generation-X Consumers', *Journal of Advertising*, 39 (3), 69–80.

26. Di Benedetto, C. Anthony, Mariko Tamate and Rajan Chandran (1992), 'Developing Creative Advertising Strategy for the Japanese Marketplace', *Journal of Advertising Research*, 32 (January–February), 39–48.

27. Kishii, T. (1988), *Message vs. Mood: A Look at Some of the Differences between Japanese and Western Television Commercials*. Dentsu, Tokyo: Dentsu Japan Marketing/Advertising Yearbook.

28. Zandpour, Fred, Cypress Chang and Joelle Catalano (1992), 'Stories, Symbols and Straight Talk: A Comparative Analysis of French, Taiwanese and U.S. TV Commercials', *Journal of Advertising Research*, 32 (January–February), 25–37.

29. Martenson, Rita (1987), 'Advertising Strategies and Information Content in American and Swedish Advertising: A Comparative Content Analysis in Cross-cultural Copy Research', *International Journal of Advertising*, 6, 133–44.

30. Anon (1988), 'Numéro "Spécial Europe"', *Communication et Business*, 14 March, 18.

31. Appelbaum, Ullrich and Chris Halliburton (1993), 'How to Develop International Advertising Campaigns That Work: The Example of the European Food and Beverage Sector', *International Journal of Advertising*, 12, 223–41.

32. Aaker, Jennifer L. and Durairaj Maheswaran (1997), 'The Effect of Cultural Orientation on Persuasion', *Journal of Consumer Research*, 24 (December), 315–28.

33. Pornpitakpan, Chantikha and June N. P. Francis (2001), 'The Effect of Cultural Differences, Source Expertise, and Argument Strength on Persuasion: An Experiment with Canadians and Thais', *Journal of International Consumer Marketing*, 13 (1), 77–101.

34. Resnik, Alan J. and Bruce L. Stern (1977), 'An Analysis of Information Content in Television Advertising', *Journal of Marketing*, 44 (1), 50–53.

35. Stern, Bruce W. and Alan J. Resnik (1991), 'Information Content in Advertising: A Replication and Extension', *Journal of Advertising Research*, 31 (3), 36–46.

36. Dowling, G. R. (1980), 'Information Content in U.S. and Australian Television Advertising', *Journal of Marketing*, 44 (4), 34–37.

37. Johnstone, Harvey, Erdener Kaynak and Richard M. Sparkman Jr (1987), 'A Cross-Cultural/Cross-National Study of the Information Content of Television Advertisements', *International Journal of Advertising*, 6, 223–36.

38. Bigne, Enrique, Marcelo Royo and Antonio C. Cuenca (1993), 'Information Content Analysis of TV Advertising – The Spanish Case', in *Proceedings of the 6th World Marketing Congress*. Istanbul, 324–29.

39. Renforth, W. and S. Raveed (1983), 'Consumer Information Cues in Television Advertising: A Cross Country Analysis', *Journal of the Academy of Marketing Science*, 11 (3), 216–25.

40. Ward, James W. and Jim McQuirk (1987), 'Information Content in Television Advertising: Ireland, United States and Australia', in *Proceedings of the Second Symposium on Cross-Cultural Consumer and Business Studies*, C. F. Keown and A. G. Woodside (eds). Honolulu, Hawaii, 37–40.

41. Schroeder, Michael (1991), 'France-Allemagne: La Publicité. L'existence de Deux Logiques de Communication', *Recherche et Applications en Marketing*, 6 (3), 97–109.

42. Lin, Carolyn A. and Michael B. Salwen (1995), 'Product Information Strategies of American and Japanese Television Advertisements', *International Journal of Advertising*, 14, 55–64.

43. Weinberger, Marc G. and Harlan E. Spotts (1989), 'A Situational View of Information Content in TV Advertising in the U.S. and U.K.', *Journal of Marketing*, 53 (1), 89–94.

44. Keown, Charles F., Lawrence W. Jacobs, Richard W. Schmidt and Kyung-Il Ghymn (1992), 'Information Content in Advertising in the United States, Japan, South Korea, and the People's Republic of China', *International Journal of Advertising*, 11, 257–67.

45. Abernethy, Avery M. and George R. Franke (1996), 'The Information Content of Advertising: A Meta-Analysis', *Journal of Advertising*, 25 (2), 1–17.

46. Kaynak, Erdener and Pervez N. Ghauri (1986), 'A Comparative Analysis of Advertising Practices in Unlike Environments: A Study of Agency–Client Relationships', *International Journal of Advertising*, 5, 121–46.

47. Callow, Michael and Leon Schiffman (2002), 'Implicit Meaning in Visual Print Advertisements: A Cross-Cultural Examination of the Contextual Communication Effect', *International Journal of Advertising*, 21 (2), 259–77.

48. Mortimer, Kathleen and Samantha Grierson (2010), 'The Relationship Between Culture and Advertising Appeals for Services', *Journal of Marketing Communications*, 16 (3), 149–62.

49. Hoover, Robert J., Robert T. Green and Joel Saegert (1978), 'A Cross-National Study of Perceived Risk', *Journal of Marketing* (July), 102–8.

50. Cutler, Bob D., Rajshekhar G. Javalgi and Dongdae Lee (1995), 'The Visual Component of Print Advertising: A Five-Country Cross-Cultural Analysis', *Journal of International Consumer Marketing*, 8 (2), 45–58.

51. Reinhard, K. and W. E. Phillips (1985), 'Global Marketing: Experts Look at Both Sides', *Advertising Age*, 56 (15), 46.

52. Duncan, Tom and Jyotika Ramaprasad (1995), 'Standardized Multinational Advertising: The Influencing Factors', *Journal of Advertising*, 24 (3, Autumn), 55–68.

53. Tixier, Maud (1992), 'Comparison of the Linguistic Message in Advertisements According to the Criteria of Effective Writing', *International Journal of Advertising*, 11, 139–55.

54. De Mooij, Marieke (2005), *Global Marketing and Advertising: Understanding Cultural Paradoxes* (2nd edn). Thousand Oaks, CA: Sage.

55. Thurlow, Crispin and Adam Jaworski (2003), 'Communicating a Global Reach: In-Flight Magazines as a Globalizing Genre in Tourism', *Journal of Socio-linguistics*, 7 (4), 579–606.

56. Nelson, Michelle R. and Hye-JIn Paek (2007), 'A Content Analysis of Advertising in a Global Magazine across Seven Countries', *International Marketing Review*, 24 (1), 64–86.

57. Zhou, Nan and Russell W. Belk (2004), 'Chinese Consumer Readings of Global and Local Advertising Appeals', *Journal of Advertising*, 33 (3), 67–76.

58. Mueller, Barbara (1992), 'Standardization vs. Specialization: An Examination of Westernization in Japanese Advertising', *Journal of Advertising Research*, 32 (January–February), 15–23.

59. Sherry, John F. Jr and Eduardo G. Camargo (1987), '"May Your Life Be Marvelous": English Language Labelling and the Semiotics of Japanese Promotion', *Journal of Consumer Research*, 14 (September), 174–88.

60. Yip, George S. (1995), *Total Global Strategy: Managing for Worldwide Competitive Advantage*. Englewood Cliffs, NJ: Prentice-Hall.

61. Neelankavil, James P., Venkatapparao Mummalaneni and David N. Sessions (1995), 'Use of Foreign Language and Models in Print Advertisements in East Asian Countries: A Logit Modelling Approach', *European Journal of Marketing*, 26 (4), 24–38.

62. Whitelock, Jeryl and Djamila Chung (1989), 'Cross-Cultural Advertising: An Empirical Study', *International Journal of Advertising*, 8 (3), 291–310.

63. Grüber, Ursula (1987), 'La Communication Internationale a sa Langue: L'adaptation', *Revue Française du Marketing*, 114 (1987/4), 89–96.

64. Kroeber-Riel, Werner (1992), 'Globalisierung der Euro-Werbung. Ein Konzeptioneller Ansatz der Konsumentenforschung', *Marketing ZFP*, 14 (4), 261–7.

65. Evans, Jonny (2008), 'Get A Mac Ads Go Dark', *Macworld*, available from: http://www.macworld.co.uk/mac/news/?RSS&NewsID=20279.

66. Toffoli, Roy and Michel Laroche (2002), 'Cultural and Language Effects on Chinese Bilinguals' and Canadians' Responses to Advertising', *International Journal of Advertising*, 21, 505–34.

67. Luna, David and Laura A. Peracchio (2001), 'Moderators of Language Effects in Advertising to Bilinguals: A Psycholinguistic Approach', *Journal of Consumer Research*, 28 (September), 284–95.

68. McCullough, Lynette S. and Ronald E. Taylor (1993), 'Humor in American, British and German Ads', *Industrial Marketing Management*, 22, 17–28.

69. Suls, J. (1983), 'Cognitive Processes in Humour Appreciation', in *Handbook of Humour Research*, J. Goldstein (ed.) New York: Springer.

70. Unger, Lynette S. (1995), 'A Cross-Cultural Study on the Affect-based Model of Humor in Advertising', *Journal of Advertising Research*, 35 (1, January–February), 66–71.

71. Weinberger, Marc G. and Harlan E. Spotts (1989), 'Humour in U.S. Versus U.K. TV Commercials: A Comparison', *Journal of Advertising*, 18 (2), 39–44.

72. Alden, Dana L., Wayne D. Hoyer and Chol Lee (1993), 'Identifying Global and Culture-Specific Dimensions of Humor in Advertising: A Multinational Analysis', *Journal of Marketing*, 57 (April), 64–75.

73. Huth, Sabine and Fritz Unger (1988), 'Eine Vergleichende Untersuchung Zur Humorvollen Werbung: Brd vs. USA', *Planung und Analyse*, 5, 197–200.

74. Kalliny, Morris, Kevin W. Cruthirds and Michael S. Minor (2006), 'Differences between American, Egyptian and Lebanese Humor Styles: Implications for International Management', *International Journal of Cross Cultural Management*, 6 (1), 121–34.

75. Hanna, Nessim, Geoffrey L. Gordon and Rick E. Ridnour (1994), 'The Use of Humor in Japanese Advertising', *Journal of International Consumer Marketing*, 7 (1), 85–106.

76. Hatzithomas, Leonidas, Yorgos Zotos and Christina Boutsouki (2011), 'Humor and Cultural Values in Print Advertising: A Cross-cultural Study', *International Marketing Review*, 28 (1), 57–80.

77. Belch, George E. and Michael A. Belch (2003), *Advertising and Promotion: An Integrated Marketing Communications Perspective*. Columbus, OH: McGraw-Hill.

78. Prendergast, Gerard, Leung Kwok Yan and Douglas C. West (2002), 'Role Portrayal in Advertising and Editorial Content, and Eating Disorders: An Asian Perspective', *International Journal of Advertising*, 21 (2), 237–58.

79. Eisend, Martin (2010), 'A Meta-Analysis of Gender Roles in Advertising', *Journal of the Academy of Marketing Science*, 38, 418–40.

80. An, Daechun and Sanghoon Kim (2007), 'Relating Hofstede's Masculinity Dimension to Gender Role

Portrayals in Advertising', *International Marketing Review*, 24 (2), 181–207.

81. Huang, Jen-Hung (1995), 'National Character and Sex Roles in Advertising', *Journal of International Consumer Marketing*, 7 (4), 81–96.

82. Yeung, Kevin and K. F. Lau (1993), 'Gender Role Stereotyping in Print Advertisements: A Comparison of Hong Kong, Taiwan and Japan', in *Proceedings of the 4th Symposium on Cross-Cultural Consumer and Business Studies*, Gerald Albaum, Ed. University of Hawaii, 225–31.

83. Paek, Hye-Jin, Michelle R. Nelson and Alexandra M. Vilela (2011), 'Examination of Gender-role Portrayals in Television Advertising across Seven Countries', *Sex Roles*, 64, 192–207.

84. Wee, Chow Hou, Mei-Lan Choong and Siok-Kuan Tambyah (1995), 'Sex Role Portrayal in Television Advertising. A Comparative Study of Singapore and Malaysia', *International Marketing Review*, 12 (1), 49–64.

85. Odekerken-Schröder, Gaby, Kristof De Wulf and Natascha Hofstee (2002), 'Is Gender Stereotyping in Advertising More Prevalent in Masculine Countries? A Cross-national Analysis', *International Marketing Review*, 19 (4), 408–19.

86. Al-Olayan, Fahad S. and Kiran Karande (2000), 'A Content Analysis of Magazine Advertisements from the United States and the Arab World', *Journal of Advertising*, 29 (3), 69–82.

87. Frith, Katherine Toland, Hong Cheng and Ping Shaw (2004), 'Race and Beauty: A Comparison of Asian and Western Models in Women's Magazine Advertisments', *Sex Roles*, 50 (1/2), 53–61.

88. Kim, Minjeong and Sharron J. Lennon (2006), 'Content Analysis of Diet Advertisements: A Cross-National Comparison of Korean and U.S. Women's Magazines, *Clothing and Textiles Research Journal*, 24 (4), 345–62.

89. Nam, Kyuongtae, Guiohk Lee and Jang-Sun Hwang (2011), 'Gender Stereotypes Depicted by Western and Korean Advertising Models in Korean Adolescent Girls' Magazines', *Sex Roles*, 64, 223–37.

90. Bates, Constance and William Renforth (1987), 'The Elderly in Magazine Advertising: An Intercountry Comparison between the U.S. and Latin America', in *Proceedings of the Second Symposium on Cross-Cultural Consumer and Business Studies*, Charles F. Keown and Arch G. Woodside (eds). Honolulu, Hawaii, 30–33.

91. Douglas, Susan and Bernard Dubois (1980), 'Looking at the Cultural Environment for International Marketing Opportunities', in *Marketing Management and Strategy: A Reader*, P. Kotler and K. Cox (eds). Englewood Cliffs, NJ: Prentice Hall.

92. Luqmani, Mushtag, Ugur Yavas and Zahir Quraeshi (1988), 'Advertising in Saudi Arabia: Content and Regulation', *International Marketing Review*, 6 (1), 59–71.

93. Al-Makaty, Safran S., G. Norman Van Tubergen, S. Scott Whitlow and Douglas A. Boyd (1996), 'Attitudes Towards Advertising in Islam', *Journal of Advertising Research*, 36 (3), 16–26.

94. Al-Mossawi, Mohammed and Paul Michell (1992), 'The Impact of Cultural Factors on the Response of Viewers to TV Commercials in the Gulf Countries: An Empirical Study', in *Proceedings of the First Conference on the Cultural Dimension of International Marketing*. Odense, 443–69.

95. Van Raaij, W. Fred (1997), 'Globalisation of Marketing Communications', *Journal of Economic Psychology*, 18, 259–70.

96. Miller, Fred and A. Hamdi Demirel (1988), 'Efes Pilsen in the Turkish Beer Market: Marketing Consumer Goods in Developing Countries', *International Marketing Review*, 5 (Spring), 7–19.

97. Liu, Fang, Hong Cheng and Jianyao Li (2009), 'Consumer Responses to Sex Appeal Advertising: A Cross-cultural Study', *International Marketing Review*, 26 (4/5), 501–20.

98. Czinkota, Michael R. and Illka A. Ronkainen (1990), *International Marketing* (2nd edn). Hinsdale, IL: Dryden Press.

99. Nelson, Michelle R. and Hye-Jin Paek (2008), 'Nudity of Female and Male Models In Primetime TV Advertising across Seven Countries', *International Journal of Advertising*, 27 (5), 715–44.

100. Clarke, Irvine III and Earl D. Honeycutt Jr (2000), 'Color Usage in International Business-to-Business Print Advertising', *Industrial Marketing Management*, 29, 255–61.

101. Huang, Jen-Hung (1993), 'Color in Us and Taiwanese Industrial Advertising', *Industrial Marketing Management*, 22, 195–98.

102. Hung, Kineta and Marshall D. Rice (1995), 'A Comparative Examination of the Perception of Ad Meanings in Hong Kong and Canada', in *Proceedings of the 5th Symposium on Cross-Cultural Consumer and Business Studies*, Scott M. Smith (ed.) Provo, UT: Brigham Young University.

103. Tansey, Richard, Michael R. Hyman and George M. Zinkhan (1990), 'Cultural Themes in Brazilian and U.S. Auto Ads: A Cross-cultural Comparison', *Journal of Advertising*, 19 (2), 30–39.

104. Cutler, Bob D., Rajshekhar G. Javalgi and M. Krishna Erramilli (1992), 'The Visual Component of Print Advertising: A Five-country Cross-cultural Analysis', *European Journal of Marketing*, 26 (4), 7–20.

105. Hall, Edward T. and Mildred Reed Hall (1989), *Understanding Cultural Differences*. Yarmouth, ME: Intercultural Press.

106. Zhou, Dongsheng, Weijiong Zhang and Ilan Vertinsky (2002), 'Advertising Trends in Urban China', *Journal of Advertising Research*, 42 (May–June), 73–81.

107. Liang, Kong and Lawrence Jacobs (1994), 'China's Advertising Agencies: Problems and Relations', *International Journal of Advertising*, 13, 205–15.

108. Gao, Zhihong (2007), 'An In-depth Examination of China's Advertising Regulation System', *Asia Pacific Journal of Marketing and Logistics*, 19 (3), 307–23.

109. Hill, John S. and William L. James (1991), 'Product and Promotion Transfers in Consumer Goods Multinationals', *International Marketing Review*, 8 (4), 6–17.

110. Zandpour, Fred and Katrin Harich (1996), 'Think and Feel Country Clusters: A New Approach to International Advertising Standardization', *International Journal of Advertising*, 15 (4), 325–44.

111. Hofstede, Geert (1991), *Culture and Organizations: Software of the Mind*. Maidenhead, Berkshire: McGraw-Hill.

112. Schwartz, S. H. (1992), 'Universals in the Content and Structure of Values: Theoretical Advances and Empirical Tests in 20 Countries', *Advances in Experimental Social Psychology*, 25, 1–65.

113. Sriram, Ven and Pradeep Gopalakrishna (1991), 'Can Advertising be Standardized among Similar Countries? A Cluster-Based Analysis', *International Journal of Advertising*, 10, 137–40.

114. Gregory, Gary D. and James M. Munch (1997), 'Cultural Values in International Advertising: An Examination of Familial Norms and Roles in Mexico', *Psychology and Marketing*, 14 (2), 99–119.

115. Kale, Sudhir H. (1991), 'Culture-specific Marketing Communications: An Analytical Approach', *International Marketing Review*, 8 (2), 19–30.

116. Ng, Siew Imm, Julie Anne Lee and Geoffrey N. Soutar (2007), 'Tourists' Intention to Visit a Country: The Impact of Cultural Distance', *Tourism Management*, 28 (6), 1497–506.

117. Tunclap, Secil (1992), 'The Audio-visual Media in Saudi Arabia: Problems and Prospects', *International Journal of Advertising*, 11, 119–30.

118. Tunclap, Secil (1994), 'Outdoor Media Planning in Saudi Arabia', *Marketing and Research Today*, 22 (2, May), 146–54.

119. Pechmann, Cornelia and Chuan-Fong Shih (1999), 'Smoking Scenes in Movies and Antismoking Advertisements before Movies: Effects on Youth', *Journal of Marketing*, 63 (3), 1–13.

120. Quester, Pascale (1999), 'A Cross-Cultural Study of Juvenile Response to Anti-Smoking Advertisements', *Journal of Euro-marketing*, 7 (2), 29–46.

121. Jackson, Sally (2008), 'Reader's Digest Chief Shakes up Empire', *The Australian*, 27 March, www.theaustralian.news.com.au/story/0,25197,23436991-13480,00.html.

122. *Reader's Digest* (1987), 40th anniversary special edition, *Selection du Reader's Digest*, Paris, pp. 10–11.

123. *Reader's Digest* (1988), 'Products and services', news release, June 1988.

124. Euromonitor International (2011), 'Emerging Focus: Emerging Market Economies to Benefit from Robust Growth in Internet Usage and Access', available online: http://www.portal.euromonitor.com.

125. *Advertising Age* (2011), 'Agency Report', 25 April 2011.

126. *Advertising Age International* (1997), 'Brand Management Goes Regional at Ford', October, 2.

127. Melewar, T. C., D. Pickton, S. Gupta and T. Chigovanyika (2009), 'MNE Executive Insights into International Advertising Programme Standardisation', *Journal of Marketing Communications*, 15 (5), 345–365.

128. Harvey, Michael G. (1993), 'Point of View: A Model to Determine Standardization of the Advertising Process in International Markets', *Journal of Advertising Research*, 33 (4), 57–65.

129. Tan, Kathleen (2010), 'Up Close and Personal With IKEA', *The Edge Malaysia*, available from: http://www.theedgemalaysia.com/media-a-advertising/179398-up-close-and-personal-with-ikea.html.

130. Interbrand (2011), '2011 Rankings of the Top Global Brands', retrieved from http://www.interbrand.com/en/best-global-brands/best-global-brands-2008/best-global-brands-2011.aspx.

131. Thomas, Justin Ryan (2011), 'Ikea's International Marketing Strategy Recognized at Cannes Lions 2011', *Integrated Marketing News*, available from: http://mktgnews.wordpress.com/2011/05/17/ikeas-international-marketing-strategy-recognized-at-cannes-lions-2011/.

132. Solberg, Carl Arthur (2002), 'The Perennial Issue of Adaptation or Standardization of International Marketing Communication: Organizational Contingencies and Performance', *Journal of International Marketing*, 10 (3), 1–21.

133. Okazaki, Shintaro, Charles R. Taylor and Shaoming Zou (2006), 'Advertising Standardization's Positive Impact on the Bottom Line: A Model of When and How Standardization Improves Financial and Strategic Performance', *Journal of Advertising*, 35 (3), 17–33.

134. Park, Hye-Jung and Nancy J. Rabolt (2009), 'Cultural Value, Consumption Value, and Global Brand Image: A Cross-national Study', *Psychology & Marketing*, 26 (8), 714–35.

135. Rosenthal, Walter (1994), 'Standardized International Advertising: A View from the Agency Side', *Journal of International Consumer Marketing*, 7 (1), 39–62.

136. Clark, Harold F. Jr (1987), 'Consumer and Corporate Values: Yet Another View on Global Marketing', *International Journal of Advertising*, 6, 29–42.

137. *Advertising Age* (1987), 'The House that Built Ivory', 20 August, 26–27.

138. Kanso, Ali and Richard Alan Nelson (2002), 'Advertising Localisation Overshadows Standardization', *Journal of Advertising Research*, 42 (1), 79–89.

139. Hill, J. S. and J. M. Winski (1987), 'Goodbye, Global Ads', *Advertising Age*, 16 November.

140. Peebles, Dean M. (1988), 'Don't Write-off Global Advertising: A Commentary', *International Marketing Review*, 6 (1), 73–78.

141. Peebles, Dean M. and John K. Ryans (1984), *Management of International Advertising*. Boston, MA: Allyn and Bacon.

142. McCullough, Wayne R. (1996), 'Global Advertising Which Acts Locally: The IBM Subtitles Campaign', *Journal of Advertising Research*, 36 (3), 11–15.

Appendix 13

Teaching materials

A13.1 Case

Brand USA – selling Uncle Sam like Uncle Ben's

'One does not need to destroy one's enemy, one need only destroy his willingness to engage', wrote the ancient Chinese strategist Sun Tzu, as quoted on the US Psychological Operations Veterans Association website (**http://www.usapova.com/**). Using this rationale, nations throughout history have attempted to persuade potential adversaries of the justness of their cause, the certainty of their victory, or the reasons for war that do not justify the death and destruction it would cause. Although written more than 2500 years ago, Sun Tzu's thoughts are strikingly relevant in a world ever more dependent on the mass media for information. Operation Geronimo, held on 2 May 2011 to physically eliminate Osama Bin Laden, uses the branding of military operations to sell it to the US public, although it has been resented by some as dishonouring the Indian Apache leader.[1]

It appears that the US government adopted Sun Tzu's rationale in the wake of the terrorist attacks of September 11, 2001, when it appointed Charlotte Beers undersecretary of state for public diplomacy and public affairs (State Department). Charlotte Beers, the 'Queen of Branding', formerly chairperson of J. Walter Thompson Worldwide and executive at Ogilvy Mather, architect of brands ranging from IBM to top dog food and credit card brands.[2]

When facing criticism for filling the post with someone lacking diplomatic experience, Colin Powell personally defended Beers by crediting her advertising skills for his preference for Uncle Ben's brand rice. These were exactly the sales skills he thought useful in selling American policies worldwide, thereby lessening the well-documented hatred of the US.[3] The US Congress apparently agreed, granting a congressional appropriation of US$520 million for Beers' projects.[4] Upon announcing her appointment, Colin Powell advocated that the US must change from 'selling US . . . to really branding foreign policy'.[5]

Allen Rosenshine, Chairman-CEO of agency BBDO Worldwide, expressed his views about Charlotte Beers' appointment thus: branding precepts are just as appropriate for the American government as they are for commercial purposes, because they may be effective in persuading people who 'hate' America to respect America's social, economic, and political systems. The theory is that branding creates a psychological bond between user and product that enhances the value of that product. In the same manner, branding a country can create 'something people can value and aspire to with their minds and hearts'.[6] Naomi Klein deconstructed the prevailing branding emphasis in government in her article 'Brand USA' published at: **http://www.alternet.org/story/12617/**.

Beers was to hinge her campaigns on the underlying belief that Americans and foreign Muslims share fundamental values – home, family and religion – and interests like pop music and sports.[7] The most public face of her work at the State Department was the US$15 million 'shared values' campaign, designed by McCann-Erickson. According to a State Department official interviewed by the *New York Times*, the target audience for the advertising campaign was the 'non-elite', in 'disaffected countries', aged 15–59 years.[8] The ads were based on focus group research among Muslim Americans, resulting in a film of American Muslims, including a teacher, a broadcasting student, a paramedic and a banker, each speaking of the goodwill and respect for Islam they experienced from Americans (listen to video clips at **www.opendialogue.org/english/bios.html**). The video was aired during Ramadan 2002 in several Arab countries and then pulled, following criticism and the reluctance of the Egyptian, Lebanese and Jordanian governments to allow the ad on government-owned television stations. They were concerned that the video constituted propaganda.[9]

The campaign was part of an effort to address the perceived misperception of the US. Beers stated in a television interview that Muslims view the US as 'anti-Islam' and not a fitting environment for Muslims to live and work.[10] She told Congress members that 'a poor perception of the US leads to unrest, and unrest has proven to be a threat to our national and international security'.[11] Her job was publicly perceived as an effort to explain the foreign policy of the Bush administration, particularly the 'war on terrorism' to the world.[4] In a speech, Beers cited a February 2002 Gallup poll of nine predominantly Muslim countries, where less than 50 per cent of the population expressed a favourable view of the US. In the case of Kuwait, Morocco and Saudi Arabia, the numbers expressing a favourable opinion were 28, 22 and 18 per cent respectively.[11] A number of misconceptions in the so-called 'Arab Street' were also to be addressed, such as the belief held by some that Israel planned the terrorist attacks of September 11.

In support of the 'shared values' campaign, a website was launched along the lines of the video (**www.opendialogue.org**), and video characters were made available for satellite interviews. Beers' team produced a booklet on the September 11 terrorist attacks, replete with photos and Ossama Bin Laden's own admissions regarding the attacks in 1.3 million copies and 36 languages, distributed in predominantly Muslim countries, and notably as a supplement in Arab *Newsweek*.[11]

In December 2002, Beers re-branded the US government-controlled Voice of America (VOA) Arabic radio station as Radio Sawa (**www.radiosawa.com**), broadcasting so-called '*pop*oganda', complete with Western and Arab pop music and zippy news bulletins instead of the usual VOA fare.[12] The initial success was such that the station's cross-cultural and news format were soon to be copied by the army of Jordan, and other Arab countries.[12] The State Department also launched similar Radio Farda, in the Farsi language. Radio Sawa was an attempt to win the ears and hearts of those who would otherwise get their news from Al-Jazeera (**www.english.aljazeera.net**) or, in the case of Iraq, from Iranian radio stations.[13] In a similar effort and on a more traditional bent, Beers expanded the almost defunct US educational and cultural exchanges. She also started a programme to disseminate pro-American films and programming materials to Arab countries, and provided American spokespeople to work with foreign television stations to produce programming that showcases US aid to their country. She was quick to locate speakers who could rebut foreign media attacks on the US, most notably in the case of former US ambassador to Syria, Arabic-speaking Chris Ross, whom she sent frequently to speak on the pan-Arab network Al-Jazeera.

The US government is conscious that effective branding is also necessary in the military. According to Army Chief of Public Affairs, Major General Charles McClain, the perception of a military operation can be as important to its success as the execution itself.[14] Since the 1980s, military operations have been named self-consciously to please various audiences, in contrast with earlier names such as 'Operation Killer' in Korea or 'Operation Paperclip' in World War II.

Table 13.1 Names of prominent US military operations and military/humanitarian operations conducted by the military that reflect a branding emphasis

Date and location	Name of operation reflecting branding emphasis
1987–1988 – Persian Gulf	Earnest Will
1989–1990 – Panama	Just Cause
1991 – Gulf War phases I and II	Desert Shield/Desert Storm
1991–1996 – Northern Iraq	Provide Comfort
1998 – Sudan and Afghanistan	Infinite Reach
2001 – Afghanistan 'War against Terrorism'	Infinite Justice (name hastily changed after Muslim advisors warn that only Allah is 'infinite')
2001 – Afghanistan	Enduring Freedom
2003 – Irak	Iraqi Freedom (15)
2011 – Pakistan	Geronimo (elimination of Osama Bin Laden in 2011)

(Source: Norman Solomon (2002) in *Fairness and Accuracy in Reporting (FAIR)*;[15] and **globalsecurity.org**.[16])

During the past century there were two government offices dedicated to swaying opinions on war at home and abroad. The first, the Committee on Public Information, was founded at the behest of President Woodrow Wilson during World War I. J. Walter Thompson executives used pamphlets to convince German soldiers on the Western Front that their defeat was inevitable.[17] In World War Two the US Government called its wartime propaganda a 'strategy of truth' executed by the Office of Strategic Services for American allies and others. The war was portrayed in leaflets, press releases and short films as a battle between Good and Evil.[18] The Foreign Information Service broadcast news in Europe and Asia to counter the wartime propaganda run by other governments, a service called Voice of America, the precursor of today's service of the same name.[19] J. Walter Thomson continued to advise the government on the Marshall Plan, and was subsequently assigned to communications for NATO.[4] Throughout the Cold War the United States Information Agency and Radio Free Europe continued working towards the mission of understanding and influencing international public opinion – an effort culminating in the hiring of Charlotte Beers. The effort to influence the attitudes of the general public (as opposed to diplomats) in other countries is termed 'public diplomacy'. According to Harold Pachios, chair of the Advisory Commission on Public Diplomacy, public diplomacy is more important than the traditional type practised between diplomats, because all governments (whether allies of the US or not) are sensitive to domestic public opinion regarding their stance relative to American policies.[20] (For more on public diplomacy visit **www.publicdiplomacy.org/**.)

Public diplomacy activities receive a budget of US$1 billion per year. Those who believe the US faces a public relations problem in dealing with the world are advocating for more money. Richard Lugar, chair of the Senate Foreign Relations Committee, stated that for each dollar spent on the US military, seven cents are spent on diplomacy and one quarter of a cent is spent on public diplomacy.[20] Some believe that rising hostility towards the US may be a consequence of the cuts to the US$70 million spent after the September 11 attacks on US-sponsored international news services.[21] Like a marketing-minded company, the State Department's International Information Programs monitors the reaction of foreign media to US-influenced international issues. The State Department then works to correct any perceived misconceptions or biases in international media. Most other public relations efforts are carried out as in any commercial communications programme. However, there is lack of coordination between the different functions within the State Department, according to former US Information Agency comptroller Stan Silverman. Silverman also stated his belief that advertising agency tactics, like those used by Charlotte Beers in her public diplomacy campaigns, are too 'simplistic' for other cultures.[21]

Since September 11, 2001, American politicians have come to believe that hatred for the USA may come from envy, or perhaps ignorance of what their country represents. As a possible expression of that belief, September 11 is now known as 'Patriot Day' (go to **www.hallmark.com** 'browse free e-cards' to view expressions of 'Patriot Day' sentiment). However, as Naomi Klein pointed out in her article 'Brand USA', children around the world are all too familiar with America's perceived high ground in terms of 'liberty and justice for all'. Hollywood has beamed American films and television programming all over the world, while CNN and other news sources disseminate the American perspective on reality. Therefore, non-Americans are well versed in American values. They are, however, angry about the incompatibility of these stated values and United States actual foreign policy on the Israel–Palestine conflict, Iraq, and many others.[2] Charlotte Beers resigned in March 2002 due to health problems.[22] As American popularity plummeted around the world and analysts and politicians argued over the best approach to public diplomacy, the department sought a new direction. Beers and her 'shared values' campaign may have clearly communicated that the USA is a good country for Muslims to live in. Her perception that the problems between the world and the USA are simply image or branding-related problems were probably too simplistic: as with any advertised product, the world is waiting for a foreign policy 'product' consistent with advertised American values like freedom, justice, and equality. The search for a solution to the American public diplomacy problem has become urgent: a Pew Research Center study found that evaluations of the US in 20 countries and the Palestinian Authority are markedly lower than a year previously. In only seven countries did a majority of people express a favourable opinion of the US, of which the leader was Israel with 79 per cent approval ratings. In seven out of eight Muslim countries, the majority of people believe that the US is a military threat to their nation.

Following the replacement of Charlotte Beers by Margaret Tutwiler towards the end of 2003, there was much speculation as to the future of 'Brand USA'. Tutwiler, a former ambassador and State Department Assistant Secretary for Public Affairs under the first President Bush, was widely thought to be less brand-oriented than Beers. Public diplomacy continued, however, with Middle East Television Network (MTN) planned to launch in December 2003 to 'End the deafening silence from America'. Also continuing were other targeted communications efforts including *Hi* magazine, a glossy youth-oriented magazine that attempts to focus on lifestyle and avoid politics altogether.[13] The magazine's Arabic-only website offers interactive boxes for readers to 'Ask America' questions, in the spirit of promoting dialogue (**www.himag.com**). The magazine, as well as the website, have been suspended by the US Department of State since December 2005. MTN, a 24-hour news nemesis of Al-Jazeera, is designed to work harder than Fox or CNN to 'discredit' the perceived anti-American stance of Arab news networks. The network has been outsourced to an independent media company by the State Department, with the mission to 'Sell America' in the crowded media markets of the Middle East.[13]

Questions

1. It is often said that marketing is about discovering what a target audience wants and making it available. Consider what the United States could 'offer' to its 'target audience', giving three examples.

2. Is it ethical for political leaders to use marketing strategies to persuade a nation to go to war, and to persuade others, including the enemy, that war is going well?

3. Should a government market itself across cultures like Coca-Cola or Nike?

4. Is it likely that the Bush Administration, in constructing branded communications, may have increased loathing and distrust in the Arab world?

5. What is the difference between diplomacy and propaganda?

Saskia Faulk and Jean-Claude Usunier prepared this case solely to provide material for class discussion. The authors do not intend to illustrate either effective or ineffective handling of a business situation. The authors may have disguised certain names and other identifying information to protect confidentiality.

© IUMI/HEC, 2011

2011-05-11   Version: (A)

A13.2 Case

Excel and the Italian advertising campaign

Excel is a multinational company, based in northern Europe, which produces television sets, video recorders and other consumer electronics. Excel went through a phase of external growth by the takeover of the German and French subsidiaries of a large US-based company that had decided to divest itself of this industry. Within two years this Nordic company tripled in size. It changed from having a mainly Scandinavian base to having a complete European spread, with an 11 per cent share of the European market. The group, built in successive layers, inherited numerous local brands, namely those of the companies taken over. These brands are basically localized marketing assets, with only national coverage and brand recognition. Excel plans to have only one pan-European brand in the long run, with one local brand for each individual country.

The European headquarters were installed in Switzerland, near Lausanne. This location was chosen so that headquarters would be situated in central Europe but not in a country where Excel already had a plant, as this might imply some sort of 'national preference'. Over a period of two years an important reshaping of the industrial base was undertaken, with massive layoffs in some plants and industrial investment aimed at increasing productivity.

Excel wanted to minimize advertising expenses while simultaneously giving its brand a strong, similar image across Europe. In fact, it inherited some very diverse brand names, which were those of the companies most recently acquired in their home markets. Excel was therefore willing to design a pan-European advertising campaign. The national subsidiaries were invited either to join this campaign or to design their own campaign. In the latter case they would have to finance it with their own money. The campaign was scheduled for autumn. Because of the World Cup which was taking place in Italy in June, the Italian subsidiary decided that it could not wait until the autumn, as this type of sports event usually generates increased demand for television sets and video recorders. It managed to go ahead by itself: it made an advertisement which proved to be a real hit and generated a significant sales increase. A television commercial was created and a poster also. The same advertising theme was used for sales promotion. The advertisement showed a superb television set with a video recorder as an integral part, encircled by a red ribbon which largely hid the screen. The slogan was '*Venite a veder lo; dal vero*' ('Come and see it; for real').

This campaign was a success soon after it started, and was presented to the general managers of the subsidiaries, who met for a residential seminar in Switzerland with the people at European headquarters in Geneva. Reactions were very positive. They proposed the idea of using the same campaign, themes and creation in other European markets. At the beginning of March, Mr Makinen, in charge of marketing communications at the European headquarters, decided to send a memo to the marketing/advertising managers of each subsidiary. A poster and a video presenting the Italian campaign were also enclosed. This memo made a concrete suggestion to the subsidiaries that they should adopt the themes and creation of this campaign. It asked them for their opinions. Makinen invited them to study the feasibility of using such a campaign in their home market and to send their comments back quickly, so that a pan-European campaign could possibly be launched in August. The Italian advertising manager, Signor Ragoli, was available if the European headquarters or national subsidiaries wanted any additional information.

Responses from the subsidiaries (that is, the answers plus the course of action finally adopted) were as follows. It took quite a long time for answers to come back, which could be explained by the overload of work experienced by people in the subsidiaries during this period of reorganization. Some countries never answered the proposal. Otherwise reactions were quite positive, except for that of France. The Spanish answer came quickly. The advertising and public relations manager, Senor Gonzales, sent a copy of the letter to his Italian colleague at European headquarters. He wrote that Spain had decided to use the campaign created in Italy, in order to unify Excel marketing communication. The Spanish wanted to use five different television channels for a total of 22 slots. They supported this with a press campaign and sales promotion in distribution channels. They needed the original version of the Italian television commercial, with music on one track and speech on another (one image track plus two sound tracks). In Spain, the final version of the Excel campaign was launched in May. The image track remained unchanged, but the music had been modified and there were several other minor changes. What seemed, at first sight, to be a straight copy of the Italian concept finally turned out to be a greatly modified version. Nevertheless, Spain was the only country where the marketing team made the decision to use the experience of their Italian colleagues.

Sweden and Norway also responded quickly to the memo in similar terms. In neither of these two countries was advertising allowed on national television channels; furthermore, they traded under the Scandinavian brand name Scantel, rather than Excel. The Swedish response explained that the subsidiary did not advertise on television, since TV1 and TV2 did not offer any space; but with the growth of satellite television the Italian proposal might be interesting for the future. The Swedes thought that the Italian campaign was well designed and implemented. The model presented (Excel 7181) was usable with their brand name since they had the same make. The Norwegians' answer had also been very positive. They promised to keep in mind the concepts of the Italian campaign and further indicated that they would recommend its implementation for the next year.

In France, the advertising and public relations manager, Monsieur Dubois, initially contacted by telephone, expressed a positive but rather cautious opinion. He said that he had first to discuss the themes and creation with his advertising agency. He called back to make it clear that even if he had any advertising funds left (in fact, they were already entirely spent), he considered that the Italian campaign was not appropriate for Ariane (the brand name of the recently acquired French subsidiary). According to him, it did not fit in with the French criteria of what actually makes good advertising. In his opinion Ariane had a fairly traditional image in France, and French consumers would need more serious arguments to change their views. Consequently 'good' advertising for the Ariane brand had to emphasize, first of all, the high-technology image. Ultimately, he thought that the Italian campaign was not sophist-icated enough, and that French people prefer more in-depth, sophisticated and detailed campaigns.

Question

How can the failure of the European headquarters to have the Italian campaign adopted by the other European subsidiaries be explained? What is the right way to go about this in the future? What has to be changed?

A13.3 Exercise

Borovets – a Bulgarian ski resort

Compare the two short texts below (each dated the beginning of 1990). Both depict the Bulgarian ski resort Borovets. The first one is an extract from the magazine *Actuel* (no. 122), from an article entitled '*Guide des bons plans à l'Est*' ('A guide to travelling in Eastern coun-tries'), p. 69. The other is an extract from the trade brochure of the Bulgarian state tourist corporation, *Balkanturist*, entitled 'Bulgaria welcomes you', p. 10. This short exercise is not meant to serve any other purpose than as a pedagogical exercise; it does not aim to describe any real situation and should not prejudice readers concerning holidays in Bulgaria.

Text 1: a charter flight to Bulgaria

The phenomenon already exists, it never stops swelling. Bulgaria is a hospitable place for exhausted proletarians in quest of cheap snow and sun. For the time being, most of the troop comes from Britain: 75 per cent of the tourists are English, 20 per cent are German, the remaining 5 per cent are Dutch, Swedish or French.

The Bulgarian government rubs its hands. The blaze of freedom which blasts through the East has already brought hordes of capitalist tourists. Bulgaria is in urgent need of foreign currencies. The country hopes to have its holiday resorts working at full capacity. Borovets is the most famous resort: in fact, it is a concrete boil encrusted on the mountains. The eight hotels, of luxurious appearance, offer limited comfort: water shortages, telephones out of order, ghost reception desks, bad-tempered staff and rooms where the cleanliness is some-what dubious. Infrastructure, equipment and service do not meet minimum requirements.

Bulgarian tourism turns out dissatisfied customers. Like Franco's Spain of the 1970s, it is the same reinforced concrete everywhere. Varna and Burgas on the Black Sea coast look like Benidorm. The sea coast is built up with concrete rabbit hutches which swarm with Bulgarian city-dwellers, Greek spendthrifts or drunk Britons. Apocalypse! The rare night-clubs are inaccessible. Meals in the 300-seat restaurants have all the style and allure of gymnasium banquets.

Text 2: Borovets

In Bulgarian, Borovets literally means 'beautiful place'. Borovets during the winter has pure, ozone-rich air; it has 150 days of snow cover which provides exceptional ski slopes, from 1,300 to 2,500 metres high.

Each year Borovets is host to numerous international ski championships. Ingemar Stenmark, the Mahre brothers, Girardelli and many other famous skiers have spoken highly of this resort which welcomes everyone.

It is a very fashionable ski resort, with its numerous comfortable and cosy hotels, its enticing restaurants and various entertainment facilities for day and night. Borovets is located 50 miles from Sofia, and it has been enjoyed by children and adults since the end of the nineteenth century, when it was only a small holiday centre.

It is no exaggeration to say that Borovets can compete with the Swiss or the French ski resorts. Now why wait any longer to visit us? We wish only to welcome you.

Questions

1. Why is there such a difference between these two pictures? Do these two articles refer to the same reality?

2. How can one get an idea of the level of service in this resort?

3. How should the state company for Bulgarian tourism (which manages the resort) communicate? What prevents them from doing so?

A13.4 Exercise

Slogans and colloquial speech

Marketing communications (advertising copy, slogans, promotional offers, text on coupons, etc.) are language based. The quality of reception of the marketing messages by the target audience is very sensitive to the accuracy of the wording. Marketing communication is based on everyday – colloquial – speech, often very idiomatic.

The basic purpose of this exercise is fairly simple: it may be implemented with a group of people who have different linguistic backgrounds, yet have a capacity to communicate with each other since some of them speak several languages. It does not imply that total fluency is necessary. Participants should simply take care to translate *into* the language(s) which they speak fluently (not *from*).

The exercise consists of the following:

1. Collecting slogans (and, more generally, short marketing communication texts) from magazines, billboards, posters, television commercials, sponsor announcements or short texts such as those found in greeting cards; translating them into other languages, with the objective of finding the equivalent meaning and local wording. The translation techniques explained in Section 6.3 (back-translation, parallel translation and a combination of the two) should be used.

2. Collecting 'identical' slogans (again, generally any short marketing communication text) that are pushing the same international brand in different countries, then analysing and comparing how similar propositions and concepts are conveyed in the different languages. Bookshops that sell foreign newspapers and magazines will be useful places to find the basic data.

A13.5 Case

Mexicom designs a public health communications campaign for Mexico

It was late when Pilar Quiñones returned to her office after a meeting with the Director of the Centro Nacional Para la Prevención y Control de VIH/SIDA (CENSIDA), the Mexican Health Ministry's official HIV/AIDS organization. *Muy difícil*, she thought, looking at the mass of paperwork on her desk. UNAIDS reports and campaigns, Pan American Health Organization charts, internal CENSIDA statistics, and scientific journal clippings occupied the space normally taken by glowing product reviews, colour-coded consumer research reports, and shiny product samples.

Quiñones, Vice President of Mexicom, Mexico's largest advertising agency, had just agreed to design a national HIV/AIDS awareness campaign. At first, she had resisted the idea, arguing that the government should design its own AIDS programmes because an advertising agency does not have the specialized public health knowledge that is needed. Dr Perez-Bustamante of CENSIDA eventually persuaded her by saying that many governments that had successful communications campaigns on HIV/AIDS used advertising agencies. After all, was not a leading advertising agency working with the Global Coalition Against AIDS?

AIDS in Mexico[a]

As Quiñones worked on the project over the next few days, her interest deepened. She personally had never known anyone with HIV/AIDS. However, she had heard of friends-of-friends with the syndrome and had read about several high-profile cases in the media. Mexico's HIV/AIDS prevalence rate among adults was relatively low at 0.3 per cent in 2009, a little higher than Canada's (2.0 per cent) and less than neighboring Guatemala (0.8 per cent), Belize (2.3 per cent), and the USA (0.6 per cent). Adults and children living with HIV were estimated at about 220,000 in 2009, being the cause of 58,000 deaths in Mexico and the fourth leading cause of death among young men.[23] UNAIDS (2006) reported that the epidemic is concentrated among men having sex with men, sex workers and clients, and injecting drug users.[24] Among MSM the HIV prevalence rate has been estimated at 15 per cent and among drug users at 6 per cent.[25]

Policy documents commonly referred to machismo as being a factor in male sexual risk-taking, putting themselves and their female partners at risk. The very poor, of which 9 million were children living in absolute poverty, were unlikely to have access to information, testing, or antiretroviral treatment for the disease.[26] Infection rates were not stabilizing and, more worrying, the raw data on infections were probably under-representing reality, reflecting a mobile population, highly dissuasive stigma, corruption and an inefficient health-recording system.

Why were the vast majority of drug-related AIDS cases in Veracruz and in northern state Baja California close to the US border? How could Tijuana, also next to the border, have an HIV

---

[a] For more information go to NGO site Mexicovivo: **http://www.mexicovivo.org/** or the Government of Mexico Ministry of Health: **http://www.salud.gob.mx/**.

Table 13.2 Some recapitulative data about people being affected by HIV

People category	Year	Mexico	Latin America	World
Adults and children living with HIV (I-1) (Est)	2009	220,000	1,400,000	33,300,000
Adults (ages 15+) living with HIV (I-2) (Est)	2009	220,000	1,400,000	30,800,000
Women (ages 15+) living with HIV (I-3) (Est)	2009	59,000	490,000	15,900,000
Children (ages 0–14) living with HIV (I-4) (Est)	2009	nd	36,000	2,500,000
AIDS orphans currently living (ages 0–17) (I-5) (Est)	2009	nd	240,000	16,600,000
Adults and child AIDS deaths (I-6) (Est)	2009	nd	58,000	1,800,000

nd = No data

(Source: UNAIDS.[27])

infection rate three times more than the Mexican average?[28] Why were women taking up more and more of the AIDS burden? Why were homosexuals again starting to practise unsafe sex like they were in the US? Quiñones jotted down a list of 'barriers' to communication that appeared to be quite significant in Mexico, presented in Table 13.3.

Since stigma is such an important factor in AIDS prevention and treatment, what would be the best way to reduce it? Quiñones sat back in her steel-framed chair, pondering the realization that her campaign should create social norms for less risky behaviours as well as less stigma. To reduce stigma in a Catholic country where homosexuality is widely considered to be a sin was not going to be easy. It had been tried, when a director of CENSIDA launched an anti-homophobia campaign that ignited many controversies. Aren't all advertising campaigns like that, though, to create or encourage a social norm for product adoption and evaluation behaviours, she mused. To get people to value a particular brand is not so different from getting people to value safer sex practices. So, what is the need here? In any case, other countries (such as Brazil) had implemented anti-stigma campaigns.

The policy-makers at the Ministry of Health VIH/SIDA office had simply said that Mexicom's mandate was to raise awareness about HIV prevention nationally and reduce new infections. She would need to quantify those goals in order to measure the success of the campaign later on. She started making another list, influenced by her discussions with HIV/AIDS experts earlier, to be discussed later with the research department and the creative people within the agency. The list of 'needs' that should be satisfied by the country's HIV/AIDS programme is represented in Table 13.4.

Table 13.3 Informal notes on barriers to HIV/AIDS social marketing in Mexico

Language	Campaign in Spanish and some major native languages, such as Mayan or Nahuatl? There are 62 indigenous languages and many varieties of these. Indigenous peoples make up 13 per cent of Mexicans, living primarily in the following states (in ranked order): Yucatán, Oaxaca, Quintana Roo, Chiapas and others.[29] Just over the border to the south, in Guatemala, Mayan-speaking indigenous peoples are disproportionately affected by HIV – in addition to other major health problems. HIV prevalence may not be correctly diagnosed or reported, to make matters worse. HIV/AIDS has tended to establish itself among the dispossessed, the poor, and marginalized groups in other countries.
Literacy	Although Mexico has relatively high levels of literacy of 91.1 per cent (2009),[30] there are some areas and demographic groups with lower literacy levels. We need a message that sounds powerful when said on radio/tv, looks powerful when represented in image form, and can be expressed simply. Health literacy is another issue.
Religion (primarily Catholic)	The Pope has frequently condemned the use of condoms, and former First Lady, Marta Sahagun Fox, was publicly attacked by bishops for exhorting Mexicans to use condoms (their stated view was that condom use was an invitation to depravity).[31]
Demographic	Massive undocumented flows of migrants (how to reach them?) ■ From south to north, some in transit from Central America en route to the US. ■ Mexicans leaving for temporary, usually agricultural, work in the US or manufacturing work on the northern border. ■ Jobless or dispossessed farmers leaving the countryside to go to cities. ■ Migrants returning from the US, usually to homes in rural areas.
Cultural	Male value of *machismo* whereby men should be seen as invincible, not sick, and not seeking help; also, the idea that to be homosexual is not to be a 'real' man[32] (how can we break through that?).

Table 13.4 Possible needs identified for HIV/AIDS infections reduction campaign

Simply to re-open public dialogue about HIV/AIDS	A study in Peru (a country with some cultural similarities to Mexico) found that teachers and parents needed help to bring sexual issues out into the open. Doctors at CENSIDA said that many rural Mexicans have never heard of the disease, partly because it is so difficult to openly talk about sex.
Reduce stigma	There is anecdotal evidence that stigma is so strong in rural Mexican contexts that people refuse to be tested, and do not even tell their spouses if they suspect they have the disease for fear of reprisals by neighbours on their entire family.
Get tested	Pregnant women who visit clinics are tested, and in the private sector there are cases of employers who force their employees to be tested for HIV. Many young people believe that HIV/AIDS only happens to prostitutes, sexually promiscuous people, and homosexuals and, for this reason, are unlikely to request an HIV test. Another reason that people may avoid testing is that there is little publicly known about treatment options available even for low-income patients. Yet, Mexico was commended by UNAIDS for having made progress in providing antiretrovirals to those who needed them.[33] As long as resource-poor people think their likelihood of being treated is low, they will assume that testing is a useless exercise.
Behavior change communication (BCC)	Encourage men to use condoms. Condom use is dangerously low for a number of reasons, but one being related to the strong value of risk-taking and invincibility associated with masculinity.[34] In one study only 9 per cent of Mexican men with sex partners outside marriage used condoms at the last intercourse.[35]

Quiñones wondered whether to differentiate the campaign geographically to reflect the large cultural differences between the northern states, the central cities, and the south. On the other hand, it would be important to mirror the large differences in the urban and rural attitudes and access to testing, information, and treatment. There were also specific groups with shared values and behaviors in different geographic areas, such as men having sex with men. Affluent urban gay communities had often been profiled by the ad agency in the past, as a favoured target market for travel and luxury goods. She opened a new page on her laptop to list the ever-growing questions posed by this HIV/AIDS campaign, one of the major ones being *who are we trying to reach*? Potential targeted audiences are identified in Table 13.5.

Her assistant knocked at the door with his results of searching for ideas in other campaigns from around the world. He tabulated his preliminary findings in Table 13.6.

Quiñones was impressed by the range of social marketing strategies implemented in other countries, and particularly by the work in the area of international organizations and advocacy groups. The World Health Organization (WHO) provided a good example of this. Using a historical perspective in the publication 'Mobilizing for healthy behaviour', for instance, there was a comprehensive social marketing model named C.A.U.S.E. This model was inspired by the anti-apartheid movement in South Africa, the fight for civil rights in the USA, and the struggle for independence in India.

Table 13.5 Potential target audiences identified in informal study

Residents of the big cities?	Mexico City accounted for most of reported HIV/AIDS cases in 2007, other big cities having a smaller but still significant share. Urban residents tended to be affected by advertising 'clutter', with omnipresent billboards, jingles on the radio and many ads on television. Now, that environment was copied on the Internet. They would need to find a message format that would get their attention through humour, sophistication or controversy that would inspire lots of publicity. Ideally, an event should be designed to raise the profile of the ad campaign launch.
Men having sex with men?	A recent study made clear that men having sex with men (MSM) were 109 times more likely than the general population to have HIV.[36]
Rural populations?	HIV spreads much faster in rural areas than in cities[37] yet there is less awareness, testing and information about the disease, and more stigma related to it in the countryside. In rural areas, women comprise 21.3 per cent of those with HIV/AIDS, while in cities the percentage is closer to 14 per cent.[38] Rural populations may require a more conservative format for the message.
Age segments?	A particularly vulnerable group was street children, who are estimated at almost 1,900,000 in Mexico City alone by Action International Ministries.[39] Some are likely to be exploited for commercial sex and pornography, and are therefore at risk for HIV in addition to other sexually transmitted diseases.[40] According to Casa Alianza, street children's NGO, children in areas close to the US border are most at risk for sexual exploitation. About 90 per cent of such children are addicted to glue and solvents,[41] and also suffer from a low literacy level.
Gender segments?	Women comprised one-sixth of AIDS cases, whereas in the 1980s, they comprised one-twentieth. In some southern states (with high concentrations of indigenous peoples), heterosexual transmission is the predominant mode, implying that women are increasingly victims of the disease.[42]
Migrants?	Mexico is a major crossing-point for migrants in transit from neighbouring countries with higher rates of the disease. An estimated 30 per cent of all HIV/AIDS cases in Mexico are people who contracted the virus while in the US.[43]
Intravenous drug users?	These make up a relatively small portion of HIV/AIDS cases. If targeted, one geographic factor to be accounted for was that the vast majority were in states bordering the US.

Table 13.6 Non-inclusive survey of communications ideas implemented in other countries

Country/organization	Communications idea
European Commission	AIDS: Remember me? Public awareness campaign culminating in an awards-style show featuring HIV/AIDS awareness commercials where anyone can vote online or via SMS for the best. See **http://www.aids-remember-me.eu/**
UNICEF, UNAIDS 2003–2006	Unite for Children. Unite Against AIDS campaign with the then-Secretary General of the United Nations, Kofi Annan. Spike Lee, Alyssa Milano and a number of global celebrities were seen during the campaign's film festivals, photo exhibitions, workshops and televised events. See: **http://www.uniteforchildren.org/**
Several African countries	'A,B,C: Abstain, Be faithful, Condomise': simple reminder (billboard) 'Graze close to home' and cattle image: non-offensive allegory (billboard)
USA	Sharon Stone campaigns very publicly for Amfar (American Foundation for AIDS Research) as a spokesperson, fundraiser, and awareness-raiser, notably at big international meetings like the G8.[44] PSI's YouthAIDS[b] public service awareness announcements and documentaries on US channel VH1 featuring India.Arie, Adrien Brody, Ashley Judd, Avril Lavigne, and other celebrities; high-profile galas, and campaigns like 'kick me!' and Fashion against AIDS. Jamie Foxx and Queen Latifah join the National Basketball Association (NBA) to promote HIV testing. This was made possible by a partnership between the two stars, the NBA, HBO, the Global Business Coalition, and the Kaiser Family Foundation, thereby securing the campaign with multiple publicity outlets.
Various countries	Famous football players play in matches co-organized with UNICEF or other similar organization which may be combined with awareness-raising events, distribution of information materials and condoms. For an Indian example see **http://www.unicef.org/india/hiv_aids_3184.htm**
South Africa	'Soul City', award-winning 'soap opera' type edutainment series based on television episodes, supported by radio shows, press discussions of issues, and high quality booklets.[45] LoveLife, a more recent initiative, uses branding strategies to create an identity for a range of HIV prevention campaigns, initiatives like the LoveTrain, and events with celebrities such as cricket stars.[c]
Brazil	Condom use promotion: condoms emblazoned with football team emblems; carnival-themed campaigns during carnival; 'Be in the know' campaign using fashion models, among others. Significant integration of social issues and HIV awareness on TV Globo programming – a national Brazilian channel with access in most homes.
Switzerland	A billboard campaign was devised targeting migrants with provocative yet culturally sensitive HIV prevention messages in 21 languages most commonly spoken by migrants in Switzerland. Recent campaigns included controversial billboards urging people to get tested and giving specific prevention behaviors.[d]

[b] YouthAIDS site: **http://projects.psi.org/site/PageServer?pagename=home_homepageindex**.
[c] LoveLife site: **http://www.lovelife.org.za/**.
[d] See: **http://www.stopaids.ch/**.

The central idea is to roll out as many elements of C.A.U.S.E. as possible, including:

- Celebrity (such as Bono against poverty).
- Activity (such as pacifist rallies and demonstrations).
- Unexpected event/story (such as the media reports on contaminated blood).
- Symbol (such as a flag, ribbon, or logo).
- Event (such as World Aids Day).[46]

From her experience with product launches and media campaigns, Quiñones knew that more research was needed. There was no need to reinvent the wheel, much effective work already had already been done in other Latin American countries. For example, the output of ground-breaking activist communicators 'Calandria' in Peru included many ideas in media planning and products for social marketing of health and development programmes (see **www.accionensida.org.pe**).

The information she needed in order to design the campaign was of three types:

1. Profiles of targeted segments of the population. The advertising agency had many such profiles, however none that looked at sexual behavior and attitudes. Quiñones would need a clear view of who these targeted audiences are, what they believe about HIV/AIDS, and what are the themes that resonate with them that would help her get the message across.
2. Literature review of AIDS-related behavioural change intervention research. There have been many critical analyses of AIDS behavioural change programmes. Ideally, each time such a programme is carried out, the results are monitored, results that could be useful to Quiñones in designing her campaign. Because much of this work is conducted by non-profit organizations and charities, it is easily accessible and will not bite too much out of the budget. A good resource to begin with is **www.comminit.com** (The Communication Initiative).
3. The final type of information that would be helpful in designing the campaign is a survey of current and past campaigns from around the world . . . *why reinvent the wheel?* Surely, Quiñones and her creative team could find some inspiring ideas, particularly ones that already have proved their effectiveness in other settings, as those presented in Table 13.6.

Quiñones was aware that an isolated programme would get few results. It would be imperative to partner with a highly visible organization or company. She made a short list and handed it to her assistant to solicit ideas from other executives for cause-related marketing efforts, as detailed in Table 13.7.

In order to understand the best ways to reach the targeted audiences, Quiñones drew up a list of possible media and supporting vehicles to carry the message, and a quick note about the kind of information needed as portrayed in Table 13.8.

For an idea of the type of vehicle Quiñones might decide to use as one part of her campaign, go to the following sites:

- Media For Development International (mainly films): **http://www.mfdi.org**.
- Avert's collection of awareness posters: **http://www.avert.org/postershist.htm**.
- Center for Communication Programs (Johns Hopkins Bloomberg School of Public Health and USAID); fully-fledged programmes of different types: **http://www.jhuccp.org/**.
- The Communication Initiative Network which houses a collection of international case studies, campaigns and reviews of these along with communications theories and other information: **http://www.comminit.com/en/hiv-aids.html**.

Table 13.7 Potential partners for the HIV/AIDS campaign

Potential partner	Quick summary of top advantages/disadvantages
Mexican film industry	Less reach over certain target audiences than television, possibly more impact on public relations; many possible spokespeople, although costly.
Family Health International (**http://www.fhi.org**)	As one of the primary female reproductive health providers, it is well entrenched at local/community levels around the country.
Mexican NGOs like Casa Alianza (**http://www.casa-alianza.org**) or Aproase or Ave de Mexico	Prize-winning charity working with street children in Mexico and three other countries. Their 'Luna Project' focuses on HIV and AIDS. May be useful in sub-campaign targeted at street children. Aproase works with commercial sex workers primarily. These experienced organizations may imbue campaigns with more credibility than a programme run by the Ministry of Health.
US Agency for International Development (**http://www.usaid.gov**) and other similar organizations	USAID is a highly visible, credible and financially powerful organization. It is the largest donor on HIV and AIDS to Mexico, well-known for social marketing of condoms. However, with Mexicans having such high levels of 'national pride', it would be better to keep the project as local as possible.
Mexican stars	A well-known singer, Tania Libertad, has been active in promoting AIDS-related causes, notably with Frente Común in Oaxaca. A Spanish group, Mecano, was used in a Mexican HIV/AIDS prevention campaign. These are 'aging' stars, however, and if we are targeting young people we need to do more research to find out what music stars or other celebrities they would listen to and consider to be credible.
Radio stations	A multitude of radio stations, already well segmented in terms of audiences, listened to as background noise all day by many Mexicans. May lack the attention-getting power for a long message; however, may be effective for 'edutainment' formats.
MTV	MTV has a well-established track record in AIDS activism.[e]
Mexican passions	Football (everyone but mainly males), bullfighting (mainly older males) and *telenovelas*, soap-operas or social dramas (mainly females of all ages, and some gay men). A spokesperson may be found from one of these areas, or sporting events may be used to educate the 'captive audience'.

---

[e] See an example of MTV's work in the area by viewing the CNN-MTV news special on HIV/AIDS at: http://eu.staying-alive.org/stayingalive/shells/inline_watch.jhtml?article=30113633.

Table 13.8 Potential media channels to be used for HIV/AIDS awareness programmes

Media	Supporting vehicles and information type
Radio	(a) Advertising spots/public service announcements. (b) Programming including music/talk/interviews/*radionovela* (social dramas).
Printed media	Opinion pieces, regular features, even cartoons could be used. Need to know: readership (target audience) of newspaper, magazines and frequency of exposure.
Internet	(a) Dedicated sites for health, sexually transmitted infections, and public health through government and NGO sites. (b) Online presence through media releases to dedicated sites and online publications for men, women, youth, men having sex with men, and so on. (c) Weblogs (blogs) in youth, 'gay' and women categories. (d) The possibility to advertise (using click-through banners or pop-up ads) in online versions of publications and on sites. (e) Presence in chatrooms, on online forums by paid participants. (f) Presence sought after in virtual social communities (such as Facebook) (g) Direct marketing via e-mail, possibly with a viral component (inciting the receiver to send the message on to friends). (h) Internet games: e.g., online game in Swahili targeting East African adolescents titled 'what would you do?' (available at: **http://www.unicef.org/media/media_36371.html**). Information needed: access to the Internet, frequency of use, type of use for target audiences; electronic mail (e-mail): access to and frequency of use, attitudes towards direct marketing on e-mail.
Television	(a) Advertising spots/public service announcements. (b) Media releases that are timely and exciting for news and talk shows. (c) Edutainment show on the lines of Heartlines, an 8-week television series from South Africa which had measurable results in prevention and reducing stigma. (d) Insertion of HIV/AIDS issues and situations into *telenovelas* (social dramas), comedies, reality shows, or talk shows. Locate a credible celebrity spokesperson or advocate with a good media profile and frequent TV appearances.
Mobile and fixed line phones	(a) New hotline for young people, women, or men having sex with men. (b) SMS and even MMS (short and media messages) to phone users, perhaps as a game. (c) Viral marketing, inspiring users to forward the message to a number of their friends.
Public transport	(a) Minibus: the minibus being a most common means of transport, stickers could be distributed in the vehicle or by the driver. Short message ads could be displayed inside or out, such as a hotline number. (b) Similar uses could be made of buses, metro, train system, and the surrounding infrastructure: e.g., bus stations and other places frequented by migrants.
Leaflets	(a) Leaflets may support television, radio and Internet efforts. (b) These may be distributed to students and other audiences at rallies, film festivals, concerts, and so on. (c) Leaflets may be distributed through schools, labour unions, companies, and women's organizations.
Merchandise	Logo t-shirts, caps, pens, condoms, to be sold online and other designated locations, such as vending machines or retail outlets.[f]
Youth mobilization programme	Music and film festivals, street theatre, street football, beach volleyball, skate parks, popular song, video games, Internet sites.

---

[f] For a recent example of a fund-raising campaign see information about the product (red) campaign: **http://joinred.com/products/**.

HIV/AIDS communication and the theories that drive it

Cognitive dissonance and communication for HIV/AIDS

HIV/AIDS public health communication, like any communications campaign, should catch the attention of targeted audiences and carry a limited number of specific messages. Potential messages include the following:

- increase awareness of the consequences of contracting HIV;
- inform people how to reduce their exposure to HIV risks;
- adopt modified attitudes, such as stigma;
- change specific behaviours, such as the adoption of condom use or risk reduction tactics for injecting drug users; and
- incite people to seek HIV testing.

Advertising is the most prominent tool of marketing communications, although not their sole instrument. Sponsoring and public relations also play an important role in communicating messages to audiences. Originally marketing communications were a feature of market-oriented actors, mainly companies selling products or services to consumers and/or trying to promote their corporate image toward their shareholders, the financial markets, or the general public. However, marketing communications have been progressively adopted by the not-for-profit sector, including governments, public agencies, NGOs and other non-corporate organizations, in order to promote social causes, donations, responsible behaviour and, more generally, private investment in public goods based on moral altruism.[47]

The efficiency of marketing communications, especially advertising campaigns for condoms or more generally ways to protect oneself from contracting HIV, is a business communications issue surrounding HIV/AIDS. Traditional models of communication effect (such as the AIDA model) assume a linear sequence, also known as *hierarchy of effects*.[48] Where people with a message to send, such as an HIV/AIDS prevention message need to design materials that go through the following stages:

- catch people's attention before they receive information;
- develop an interest (a cognitive stage);
- build a desire (for a product, a service, a solution, an affective stage); and
- all this to culminate in a decision (action).

However, viewers need some involvement to be ready to process information; furthermore, they may try to unconsciously avoid information about an undesirable phenomenon, such as developing cancer because of chain-smoking. Persuasive processes for such sensitive topics generally cannot follow a linear and purely rational approach, where people would first learn, then appreciate the solution, and finally act accordingly.

One key issue of HIV/AIDS campaigns being attitude change, it is likely that a number of obstacles will impede information processing and acceptance of the message, the main one being *cognitive dissonance*.[g] To reduce cognitive dissonance, people have two main solutions:

1. To modify their attitudes.
2. To change their behaviour.

---

[g] The theory of cognitive dissonance (CD) by Festinger (1957)[49] explains that individuals, when confronted with new information that questions their established beliefs, will experience cognitive dissonance and consequently a psychological loss of balance. They will try to reduce the gap. Dissonance is especially activated by 1) exposure to new information incompatible with former established beliefs and 2) exposure to new circumstances and a modified social environment which questions deeply ingrained behaviour consistent with individual values.

BOX 1

A view from the field

How does Brazil keep its HIV/AIDS message fresh and appealing, and avoid 'safe sex fatigue'?

The Brazilian government has specific campaigns aimed at the delivery of the message of HIV prevention to young people. Basically, the National Programme on HIV/AIDS works in two different areas: with children and young people who are at social risk (street children and children who work) and with children and young people who are at school.

In the first group, the government works in partnership with NGOs and at community level and has been implementing measures that include information dissemination, distribution of condoms and the promotion of the so-called 'intimate visits' to young people who are in internment units.

In the second group, government action is based in the formation of the so-called 'multipliers' through three different measures: (a) capacity building of teachers through distance learning; (b) forming groups of 'multiplier adolescents'; and (c) capacity building of teachers and students through learning in the field.

In reference to 'safe sex fatigue', each year Brazilian society has the task of informing millions of adolescents and young people as they start to become sexually active. Brazilian society is young, and there is an urgent need to assess poorer regions and hard-to-reach communities with adequate information and means to prevent HIV transmission (condoms, good-quality prenatal care including HIV testing and prophylactic treatment for HIV-positive mothers and their children as well as the distribution of harm-reduction kits to avoid transmission through unsafe drug use.) There is still no 'safe sex fatigue'. This might also be due to the fact that the prevention policy is not based on prescriptive behaviour-change models, but on the idea of offering the necessary supplies and information to the population to make safer sex a possible option.

To find out more about the Brazil National Programme for AIDS and sexually transmitted diseases go to: **http://www.aids.gov.br**.

(Source: information provided by Mr Pedro Marcos de Castro Saldanha, Second Secretary, Permanent Mission of Brazil, Geneva, Switzerland, 27 June 2005.)

Changing attitudes is much easier than behavioural adaptation.[50] Typical strategies for reducing cognitive dissonance by changing attitudes are denial and substitution. In this case one can find the available information within those particular clues that help maintain the legitimacy of a behaviour or choice while discounting unfavourable information clues. As a consequence, we tend to search for information which is in line with our beliefs, preferences, and chosen behaviour. This tendency is also known as *selective exposure*.

Everything that is known about mass communications and behaviour change suggests that marketing communications for HIV/AIDS campaigns need to be properly designed, targeting specific audiences in terms of age, sex, socioeconomic status, and ethnicity, and particular communication objectives – for instance, raising awareness or aiming for attitude change. Messages have also to be crafted with the understanding that cognitive dissonance may deprive them of all desired influence.

Theories and models of communication

According to Campbell (p. 10): 'People running community programmes in various countries and contexts frequently repeat the same mistakes, or have to reinvent the wheel again and again owing to the lack of a conceptual framework for formulating and sharing lessons and findings from previous experiences'.[51] One reason for making the same mistakes is that there is no body of globally accepted theories or frameworks that underpin HIV/AIDS prevention and/or awareness programmes. Another reason is that the literature is vast and complex, and racked by disagreements between theorists.

A broad range of theories and models co-exist in the field of HIV/AIDS activism, communications and relevant social science research. The theory perspectives range from individual/psychological, such as Bandura's (1997) social cognition theory;[52] social; cultural; morality/faith-based (as reflected in the pro-abstinence policies of the US government and religious conservatives of all stripes around the world); to the social change model that acknowledges the social, community, psychological, structural barriers and enablers for health behaviours. There are also a number of specialized theories/ideas/opinions related to health communications and behaviour, which have risen to prominence along with the realization that providing information is not enough: millions of people need to be supplied with the motivation to change their attitudes and behaviour. Each theory and model has limitations: for instance, some of those commonly used in HIV/AIDS prevention programmes were designed to predict health behaviour, not change it. Examples of health communications models are provided and explained in Table 13.9 below.

Table 13.9 Characteristics of models commonly used as bases for HIV/AIDS programmes

Theory/model/ framework	Description	Example (if known)
Health belief model[53]	Attitudes, expectations and beliefs will explain a person's likelihood of adopting a less risky behaviour. The nature and relevance of the threat (susceptibility and severity) and perceived ability to avoid the threat (perceived benefits and barriers) are key concepts in the model.	Commonly used in the development of national public health programmes, such as HIV/AIDS prevention. The health belief model helps researchers to understand sexual behaviour, particularly to identify perceived benefits and/or barriers about which communication programmes may be designed.
Theory of reasoned action and planned behavior[54]	A group of theories that attempt to explain behaviour (assumed to be rational and controllable) by analysing beliefs, attitudes, intentions and behaviour.	Used in the design of HIV/AIDS interventions by identifying through research which are the behavioural and normative beliefs that influence people's intentions to behave in a specific (desirable) manner.
Stages of change (also known as transtheoretical model)[55]	Originally developed for smoking-cessation programmes, this model comprises five stages theorized to be necessary for behaviour change. Progression from one stage to the next is facilitated by viewing a model who can demonstrate skills necessary for progression.	The use of drama, talk shows and role-playing may help people to acquire skills such as condom negotiation.
AIDS risk reduction model	A three-stage theory based on the Health Belief Model and social cognition that was developed to recognize the specific nature of HIV/AIDS as a health threat. Individuals must recognize themselves as being at risk, commit to reducing risky behaviour, and action that is appropriate.	Used in television or radio dramas.
Hierarchy of effects	A series of theories, commonly used in marketing, based on the assumption that consumer behaviour progresses through specific stages – commonly from information through to adoption.	Typically used in campaigns structured around advertising.

Table 13.9 (*cont'd*)

Theory/model/framework	Description	Example (if known)
Diffusion of innovations	Diffusion of innovations theory[56] examines the communications processes involved in the adoption of behaviours by a population. People progress through a number of stages before they implement a new behaviour. In order for a behaviour to become widespread, opinion leaders should model or display it first.	The STOP AIDS programme first made available to gay men in San Francisco during the 1980s.
Social marketing	The use of business marketing principles, applied to social problems.	The use of marketing 'branding' principles for condoms distributed free of charge or at marginal cost.
Social cognition (to be discussed below)[57]	Behaviour is considered to be an outcome of perceived self-efficacy, social and environmental factors.	Many entertainment-education programmes, which meld entertaining content with deliberate educational messages using role models showing desired behaviours. Examples include 'Soul City' (S. Africa), 'Sexto Sentido' (Nicaragua), 'Malahcão' (Brazil), 'Jasoos Vijay' (India).

The ambiguous effect of fear-appeals in communication

Still commonly used in HIV/AIDS prevention programmes are fear appeals. The literature on fear appeals[h] in communication shows that there are different models to explain how messages can influence the decision to quit a dangerous behaviour, of which a selection follows.

- *An inversed U-Curve model*[58,59] There are arousal thresholds under and above which a prevention campaign is unsuccessful. Below a certain level of fear, people are not really concerned and no motivation for self-protection is generated by the message. Above a certain level people develop defensive mechanisms in line with the reduction of cognitive dissonance. Consequently, efficiency is at its maximum between the two thresholds.
- *The Protection Motivation Model*[60–62] This is based on the idea that people are motivated to protect themselves from danger when this motivation is properly aroused by both the seriousness (degree of gravity) and the probability of occurrence of a particular threat. A message will be all the more efficient if people are *also* given concrete solutions on how to avoid the danger.
- *The Extended Parallel Processing Model* This is an extension of the Protection Motivation Model that better accounts for the emotional reactions of subjects.[63] In this model, fear is a mediator of the evaluation of possible solutions to the danger. When fear emotions become too intense, the process of monitoring fear (an inner defensive mechanism) takes precedence over the rational action process to avoid danger (an action strategy that results in behavioural changes). Subjects may develop a rejection/denial of the message content in order to decrease their emotions of fear.

It is important to make a clear distinction between how subjects exposed to a risk react as compared with non-exposed subjects (e.g., smokers and non-smokers in anti-tobacco messages). The defensive reaction being small or non-existent with non-exposed subjects,

---

[h] This literature is mostly concerned with anti-tobacco campaigns (AT), but a large part of its conceptual approach and empirical findings can be transferred *mutatis mutandis* to AIDS prevention campaigns.

motivation for protection when faced with fear-arousing messages paradoxically is stronger with non-exposed than with exposed subjects. Smoking-cessation literature has been used by communications planners to model HIV/AIDS prevention programmes.

The role of perceived self-efficacy as driver of behaviour

Social cognitive theory has been considered particularly useful to underpin HIV/AIDS communications efforts thanks to its recognition of the importance of the social interaction of individuals. Because sexual behaviour constitutes a part of interpersonal relationships, interpersonal efficacy will be required to change this sexual behaviour – quite a different proposition than simply targeting behaviour change as a goal. According to Bandura (2004), only social cognitive theory offers 'principles on how to inform, enable, guide, and motivate people to adapt habits that promote health and reduce those that impair it' (p. 146).[52]

Perceived self-efficacy has a primary role in behaviour change, particularly in the domain of health. Self-efficacy is widely perceived as crucial to behaviour change, a concept gradually adapted to 'collective efficacy'.[39] Self-efficacy is the belief that 'one can exercise control over one's health habits'.[52] According to him, several determinants of health promotion and disease prevention apply, in addition to self-efficacy:[52]

- knowledge of the health risks and benefits of health behaviours;
- outcome expectations: perceived costs and benefits of likely outcomes;
- health goals: health-related outcomes people set for themselves and how they plan to attain them; and
- perceived facilitators and impediments to attaining the desired changes: social and structural limitations that may prevent whole or partial success.

In relation to the above points, the modus operandi of the HIV/AIDS virus has in effect made it difficult for people around the world to learn how to avoid infection, even though they may understand the epidemiology and prevention methods. It is difficult for people to evaluate their *risk* status for contracting HIV/AIDS from their partner, because this knowledge is necessarily incomplete: the complete and honest revelation of both sexual partners' history of sexually transmitted diseases, drug use, and sexual partner networks is constrained by social norms and potential premeditated deception, compounded by the fact that a partner may not be aware of the risks inherent in his/her own behaviour. According to Bandura, people tend to evaluate the risk of contracting HIV/AIDS by using a potential partner's physical appearance and perceived social status as guidelines. Because HIV/AIDS can be asymptomatic for a decade or more, the HIV test based on appearance is very risky and conforms blindly to stereotypes (e.g., she looks chaste and educated, therefore she probably does not have AIDS). The *outcome expectations* of practising safer sex, (i.e., using a condom and avoiding HIV/AIDS transmission) are dependent on that wholly unreliable process.

Critics of social learning theory and other individual models of behaviour change have pointed to other factors that urgently need to be considered in HIV/AIDS prevention communications, including the often unplanned and emotional nature of sexual encounters, the use of recreational drugs and/or alcohol leading up to the sex act, sex used as a form of violence against an individual or a targeted group (as in war), and the likelihood of inequality in the power status of two or more partners. Power differences (and thus differences of negotiating power) are mainly codified in gender role definitions, but may fall equally under the roles of sex buyer versus sex seller, or the power and deference commanded in many societies by age that is often gender-determined in terms of older man–younger woman. In line with these criticisms, UNAIDS declared in 1999 that, according to the research, individual behaviour change communications are likely to be ineffective. UNAIDS set out its own communications framework[64] in its report 'Communications framework for AIDS: A new direction'. In the report, UNAIDS stated that 'Seeking to influence behaviour alone is insufficient if the underlying social factors that shape the behaviour remain unchallenged.' (p. 23).[64] Reporting on the shortcomings of approaches used at that time, UNAIDS summarized the typical inadequacies of the assumptions that underpinned communications programmes:

■ There is no 'linear relationship' between people's knowledge, attitude, beliefs, and their actions, particularly when cultural, political and socioeconomic differences are considered.

■ People are not always in control of their own behaviour which itself may be determined by gender or cultural contexts.

■ Sexual behaviour is a realm where rational thinking about HIV/AIDS may be less applicable than emotions.

■ Condom promotion should be part of an holistic prevention strategy, rather than an end in itself that ignores cultural and social contexts.

■ Men should be targeted as much as women regarding issues such as condom use.

■ Condom promotion alone may not be effective without 'addressing the importance and centrality of social contexts, including government policy, socioeconomic status, culture, gender relations and spirituality' (p. 26).[64]

Questions

1. How should sensitive messages about AIDS issues be conveyed to a Mexican audience, given the cultural and social characteristics of Mexico described in this case study? What do you propose is the best strategy: direct or indirect? Emotional or rational? Informative or persuasive? Make propositions regarding the copy strategy and media planning of the campaign.

2. In order to have the biggest impact, what should be the primary target audiences of the Mexicom-designed HIV/AIDS campaign?

3. Which potential partners would you approach for this campaign? Do you recommend that Quiñones uses sponsoring and other forms of marketing communications? If yes, how would you design an integrated marketing communications plan?

4. Go to each of the three sites listed in the 'Further resources' section below. Make note of what you think is effective and ineffective in reaching the audiences you intend to target in Mexico.

Further resources

Communication Initiative: **http://www.comminit.com/en/node/119625**.

Mo Kexteya Project: Designed with the aim to reduce stigma and discrimination, the project features among other activities a photojournal – an online set of richly photographed biographies of Mexicans living with HIV/AIDS titled '*De frente a la vida*'. Available at: **http://www.policyproject.com/MoKexteya.cfm**.

Government of Mexico Ministry of health television spot campaigns for HIV/AIDS (in Spanish). Available at: **http://portal.salud.gob.mx/contenidos/sala_prensa/sala_prensa_campanas/condon/condon.html**.

Live With It: This is an award-winning campaign sponsored by Gilead Life Sciences and designed by Incendia Health Studios. The campaign features a series of short, animated, hand-drawn films that focus on the life of a person living with HIV/AIDS. Using the Live With It cartoon characters as a basis for discussion there are message boards, information and an HIV support online community. Available at: **https://www.livewithit.com**.

National HIV Testing resources: National HIV Testing Day campaigns on television, radio and podcasts. Available at: **http://www.hivtest.org/press_files/subindex.cfm?FuseAction= spotlight.psa.**

2011-05-11   Version: (A)

Appendix references

1. 'Operation Geronimo dishonors the Indian leader', Karl Jacoby, *Los Angeles Times*, 10 May 2011. Retrieved 10 May 2011 from http://www.latimes.com/news/opinion/commentary/la-oe-jacoby-geronimo-20110510,0,5625890.story.

2. Klein, Naomi (2002), 'Brand USA', Alternet.org, 13 March 2002. Retrieved 10 January 2010 from http://www.alternet.org/story/12617/.

3. Sylvester, Rachel (2003), '"*Brand USA*" campaign attempts to win over UK', *The Age* (Australia), 25 January 2003. Retrieved 10 January 2010 from http://www.theage.com.au/articles/2003/01/24/1042911549183.html.

4. de Grazia, Victoria (2002), 'Bush team enlists Madison Avenue in war on terror', *International Herald Tribune* (online), 26 August 2002. Retrieved 10 January 2010 from http://www.globalissues.org/Geopolitics/WarOnTerror/Madison.asp.

5. Teinowitz, Ira (2002), 'Charlotte Beers and the selling of America', *Advertising Age*, 23 September 2002. Retrieved 10 January 2010 from http://www.adage.com/paypoints/buyArticle.cms/login?newsId=33340&auth=.

6. Rosenshine, Allen (2002), 'Selling America to people who hate it', *Advertising Age*, 18 February 2002. Retrieved 10 January 2010 from http://www.adage.com/paypoints/buyArticle.cms/login?newsId=34046&auth=.

7. Satloff, Robert (2003), 'How to win friends and influence Arabs', *Weekly Standard*, 18 August 2003. Retrieved 10 January 2010 from http://www.theweeklystandard.com/Content/Public/Articles/000/000/002/975mvnhl.asp.

8. Perlez, Jane (2002), 'Muslim as apple pie video greeted with skepticism', *New York Times* (online), 30 October 2002. Retrieved 10 January 2010 from http://www.globalissues.org/Geopolitics/WarOnTerror/MarketingUSMuslims.asp.

9. Byrne, Richard (2003), 'Charlotte Beers goes bye-bye', *Boston Phoenix* (online), 6–13 March 2003. Retrieved 10 January 2010 from http://www.bostonphoenix.com/boston/news_features/this_just_in/documents/02740496.htm.

10. NewsHour Media Unit (2003), 'Undersecretary Charlotte Beers interviewed by Terence Smith', *NewsHour*, Public Broadcasting Service, January 2003. Retrieved 10 January 2010 from http://www.pbs.org/newshour/media/public_diplomacy/beers_1-03.html.

11. Beers, Charlotte (2002), 'Funding for public diplomacy, Statement before the Subcommittee on Commerce, Justice, and State of the House Appropriations Committee', US Department of State (online), 24 April 2002. Retrieved 10 January 2010 from http://www.state.gov/r/us/9778.htm.

12. Leonard, Mark (2002), 'Velvet fist in an iron glove' *Observer*, 16 June 2002. Retrieved 10 January 2010 from http://observer.guardian.co.uk/worldview/story/0,11581,738540,00.html.

13. Harris, Shane (2003), 'Brand U.S.A.', *Government Executive Magazine*, 1 October 2003. Retrieved 10 January 2010 from http://www.govexec.com/features/0903hs/HS0903s7.htm.

14. Solomon, Norman (2002), 'Branding new and improved wars', *Fairness and Accuracy In Reporting (FAIR)*, 29 October 2002. Retrieved 10 January 2010 from http://www.fair.org/media-beat/021029.html.

15. Solomon, Norman (2002), 'Branding new and improved wars', *Fairness and Accuracy In Reporting (FAIR)*, 29 October 2002. Retrieved 10 January 2010 from http://www.fair.org/media-beat/021029.html. and Seiminski, Gregory C. (1995), 'The art of naming operations', *Parameters*, Autumn 1995, pp. 81–98. Retrieved 10 January 2010 from http://www.globalsecurity.org/military/library/report/1995/sieminsk.htm.

16. Anonymous (2003), 'Operation Iraqi Freedom' Globalsecurity.org, 19 March 2003. Retrieved 10 January 2010 from http://www.globalsecurity.org/military/ops/iraqi_freedom.htm.

17. Wells, Robert A. (2002), 'Mobilizing public support for war: An analysis of American propaganda During World War I' paper presented at the Annual Meeting of the International Studies Association, 24–27 March 2002. Retrieved 10 January 2010 from http://www.allacademic.com//meta/p_mla_apa_research_citation/0/6/9/8/9/pages69897/p69897-1.php.

18. Public Broadcasting Service (2003), 'NOW with Bill Moyers, Politics and Economics', 31 January 2003. Retrieved 10 January 2010 from http://www.pbs.org/now/politics/propaganda.html.

19. Anonymous (2002), 'History of public diplomacy', *Gannett News Service*, 14 July 2002. Retrieved 10 January 2010 from http://www.gannettonline.com/gns/mideast/diplomacy.htm.

20. Weiser, Carl (2003), 'U.S. losing battle worldwide on public relations front', *Gannett News Service*, 31 March 2003. Retrieved 10 January 2010 from http://greenvilleonline.gannettonline.com/gns/iraq/20030331-19602.shtml.

21. Orris, Michelle (2003), 'White House: Better PR can reverse anti-American sentiment', *Austin American Statesman*, 1 August 2003. Retrieved 10 January 2010 from http://www.statesman.com/nationworld/content/news/080103/0801antius.html.

22. Tienowitz, Ira (2003), 'Charlotte Beers to resign from State Department', *Advertising Age*, 3 March 2003. Retrieved 10 January 2010 from http://www.adage.com/paypoints/buyArticle.cms/login?newsId=37278&auth=.

23. UNAIDS (2010), *UNAIDS Report on the Global Epidemic HIV/AIDS*, UNAIDS and WHO. Retrieved 1 July 2011 from http://www.unaids.org.

24. UNAIDS/WHO (2006), *AIDS Epidemic Update*. Retrieved 12 July 2011 from http://data.unaids.org/pub/EpiReport/2006/08-Latin_America_2006_EpiUpdate_eng.pdf.

25. Family Health International (2007), *Mexico Final Report October 1997 to January 2007*. Retrieved 12 July 2011 from http://www.fhi.org/NR/rdonlyres/ep53mvqacgtfazo3xhilmxmxahj56eofe4z4lcj6ptclhrmfwbl2ni7fn45unllspbyjfy3cv3iyrk/IMPACTFinalReportMexicoHV.pdf.

26. Bautista, Sergio Antonio, T. Dmytraczenko, G. Kombe and S. M. Bertozzi (2003), *Costing of HIV/AIDS Treatment in Mexico*, Partners for Health Reform Plus. Retrieved 1 July 2011 from http://www.healthsystems2020.org.

27. UNAIDS (2010), *UNAIDS Report on the Global AIDS epidemic 2010*. Retrieved 1 July 2011 from http://www.unaids.org/globalreport/global_report.htm.

28. Brouwer, K. C., S. A. Strathdee, C. Magis-Rodriguez, E. Bravo-Garcia, C. Gayet, T. L. Patterson, S. M. Bertozzi and R. S. Hogg (2006), Estimated Numbers of Men and Women Infected with HIV/AIDS in Tijuana. *Journal of Urban Health*, 83 (2), 299–307.

29. Istituto Nacional de Lenguas Indìgenas (2008), *Catàlogo de Lenguas Indígenas*. Retrieved 1 July 2011 from http://www.inali.gob.mx/.

30. UNESCO Institute for Statistics (2009), 'Education in Mexico, Education in brief'. Retrieved 12 July 2011 from http://stats.uis.unesco.org/unesco/TableViewer/document.aspx?ReportId=198.

31. Agence France Presse (2003), 'Mexico-Religion-Sex: Mexican Bishops attack First Lady for advocating condom use against AIDS' (May 9). Retrieved 12 July 2011 from http://www.aegis.com/NEWS/AFP/2003/AF030522.html.

32. Smallman, S. (2007), *The AIDS Pandemic in Latin America*. University of North Carolina Press.

33. UNAIDS/WHO (2007), *Report on the Global AIDS Epidemic*. Retrieved 12 July 2011 from http://www.unaids.org/en/KnowledgeCentre/HIVData/GlobalReport/.

34. Smallman, S. (2007), *The AIDS Pandemic in Latin America*. University of North Carolina Press.

35. Pulerwitz, J. *et al.* (2001), 'Extrarelational sex among Mexican men and their partners' risk of HIV and other sexually transmitted diseases', *American Journal of Public Health*, 91 (10), 1650–1652.

36. Baral, S., F. Sifakis, F. Cleghorn and C. Beyrer (2007), 'Elevated risk for HIV infection among men who have sex with men in low- and middle income countries 2000–2006: A systematic review', *PLoS Med* 4(12):e339. Retrieved 12 July 2011 from http://www.plosmedicine.org/article/info:doi/10.1371/journal.pmed.0040339.

37. American Foundation for AIDS Research (2002), 'AIDS in Latin America and the Caribbean', *Global Initiatives*, American Foundation for AIDS Research Special Reports. Retrieved 12 July 2011 from http://www.amfar.org/cgi-bin/iowa/programs/globali/record.html?record=139.

38. Cevallos, Diego (2002), 'Rural women with AIDS', *Inter Press Service*, AEGIS. Retrieved 12 July 2011 from http://www.aegis.com.

39. Mexico Child Link (2010), *Mexico street children statistics*, Mexico Child Link. Retrieved 12 July 2011 from http://www.mexico-child-link.org.

40. US Centers for Disease Control and Prevention (2003), 'Mexico: Street children at high risk of HIV/AIDS'. *The Body*. Retrieved 12 July 2011 from http://www.thebody.com/content/world/art29534.html.

41. Casa Alianza (2000), 'Worldwide statistics: Exploitation of children, a global outrage', *Hilton Foundation* (September). Retrieved 12 July 2011 from http://www.hiltonfoundation.org/press/16-pdf3.pdf.

42. US Agency for International Development (2004), *Literature Review of Trafficking in Persons in Latin America and the Caribbean*. Retrieved 12 July 2011 from http://www.oas.org/atip/regional%20reports/usaid%20lac%20tip%20literature%20review.pdf.

43. American Foundation for AIDS Research (2002), 'Global Initiatives Mexico', *American Foundation for AIDS Research Special Reports*. Retrieved 12 July 2011 from http://www.amfar.org.

44. Hofmann, R. (2007), 'Precious stone'. *POZ* (December). Retrieved 12 July 2011 from http://www.poz.com/archive/2007_Dec_2111.shtml.

45. Usdin, S. (2001), 'Soul City', *Urban Health and Development Bulletin*, Medical Research Council of South Africa, Vol. 3, No. 2.

46. World Health Organization (2002), *Infectious Diseases Report 2002*. World Health Organization. Retrieved 12 July 2011 from http://www.who.int.

47. Jenks, Christopher (1990), Varieties of altruism. In: Mansbridge, Jane J. (ed.) *Beyond Self-interest*, University of Chicago Press, pp. 53–70.

48. Grover, R. and M. Vriens (2006), *The Handbook of Marketing Research: Uses, Misuses, and Future Advances*. Thousand Oaks, CA: Sage.

49. Festinger, L. (1957), *A Theory of Cognitive Dissonance*, Stanford, CA: Stanford University Press.

50. Cooper, I. and R.T. Croyle (1984), 'Attitudes and attitude change', *Annual Review of Psychology*, 35, 395–426.

51. Campbell, C. (2003), *Letting Them Die: Why HIV/AIDS Prevention Programmes Fail*. Oxford: James Currey.

52. Bandura, A. (1997), *Self Efficacy: The Exercise of Control*. New York: Freeman.

53. Rosenstock, I. (1974), Historical Origins of the Health Belief Model. *Health Education Monographs*, 2 (4).

54. Fishbein, M. and I. Ajzen (1975), *Belief, Attitude, Intentions, and Behavior: An Introduction to Theory and Research*. Reading, MA: Addison-Wesley.

55. Prochaska, J. O. and C. C. DiClemente (1983), 'Stages and processes of self-change of smoking: Toward an integrative model of change'. *Journal of Consulting and Clinical Psychology*, 51 (3), 390–95.

56. Rogers, E. (1995), *Diffusion of Innovations* (4th Ed.). New York: The Free Press.

57. Bandura, A. (1986), *Social Foundations of Thought and Action*. Englewood Cliffs, NJ: Prentice Hall.

58. Janis, I. L. and I. Mann (1965), 'Effectiveness of emotional role playing in modifying smoking habits and attitudes'. *Journal of Experimental Research in Psychology*, 1, 84–90.

59. Janis, I. L. (1967), 'Effects of Fear Arousal on Attitude: Recent Developments in Theory and Research'. *Advances in Experimental Psychology*, 4, 166–224.

60. Floyd, D. and S. Prentice-Dunn (2000), 'A Meta-analysis of Research on Protection Motivation Theory'. *Journal of Applied Social Psychology*, 30 (2), 407–30.

61. Keller, P. A. and L. G. Block (1996), 'Increasing the Persuasiveness of Fear Appeals: The Effect of Arousal and Elaboration'. *Journal of Marketing Research*, 22, 448–59.

62. Rogers, R.-W. (1975), 'A protection motivation theory of fear appeals and attitude change', *The Journal of Psychology*, 91, pp. 93–114.

63. Tanner J. F., B. Hunt and D. R. Eppright (1991), 'The protection motivation model: a normative model of fears appeals', *Journal of Marketing*, 55, pp. 36–45.

64. UNAIDS (1999), *Communications framework for AIDS: a new direction*. Retrieved March 23 2005 from http://www.unaids.org/NetTools/Misc/DocInfo.aspx?LANG=en&href=http%3a%2f%2fgva-doc-owl%2fWEBcontent%2fDocuments%2fpub%2fPublications%2fIRC-pub01%2fJC335-CommFramew_en%26%2346%3bpdf.

14

Intercultural marketing communications 2: personal selling, networking and public relations

In Ghana there is a saying: 'Mouth smiles, money smiles better'. Money is always at the very center of personal selling, but so are the intricacies of human relationships. This chapter deals with the last two of the four methods of marketing communications, personal selling and public relations. (Advertising was examined in Chapter 13 and sales promotion in Chapter 11).

Cultural differences (time and space assumptions, interaction models and attitudes towards action, as described in Chapters 2 and 3) have a major impact on how relationships start and develop. It is argued in Section 14.1 that people need to be *relationship and service* centred, rather than purely *deal and product* centred. Section 14.2 develops this argument by comparing the Western view of business networks to the Chinese *guanxi*. We then discuss how culture impacts on buyer–seller interactions (Section 14.3); naturally it involves personal contact which is culture bound. Personal selling issues are then examined from an organizational perspective, focusing on how a sales force can be managed in a cross-cultural context (Section 14.4). Section 14.5 deals with public relations, which, even though it does not directly contribute to sales, may be of prime concern for defending corporate image before various publics. In the last two sections, we examine ethical issues related to selling, first by presenting facts about bribery (Section 14.6) and second by suggesting some ways of appreciating the cultural relativity of ethical attitudes (Section 14.7).

14.1

Intercultural commerce

Commerce as implementation of marketing programmes

Commerce is about personal selling and establishing continuity in the relationship with individual customers, organizational buyers and intermediaries. Commerce is defined by the *Collins English Online Dictionary* as follows: '1. the activity embracing all forms of the purchase and sale of goods and services; 2. social relationships and exchange, esp. of opinions, attitudes, etc.' Commerce favours the social interaction between vendor (producer and/or distributor) and customer. The quality of this social interaction, including marketing strategies that respect cultural integrity, influences the effective implementation of global strategies.

This view is in line with the shift from a 'goods-dominant logic' (G-D) to a 'service-dominant logic' (S-D).[1] In this context, Vargo and Lusch (p. 2)[2] define a service as: 'the application of specialized competences (skills and knowledge), through deeds, processes, and performances for the benefit of another entity or the entity itself'. In this logic, the value creation moves from production in isolation from the customer, to a collaborative process of co-creation within the exchange. The focus is on the relationship and the exchange of services, with the knowledge and skills of the providers being the sources of value creation, not the goods which may be part of the exchange.[1] Many of the changes in focus from G-D to S-D suggested by Vargo and Lusch (p. 258)[1] are relevant to the sales force function:

1. From thinking about the purpose of firm activity as *making something* (goods or services) to a process of *assisting customers in their own value-creation processes.*
2. From thinking about value as something *produced* and sold to thinking about value as something *co-created* with the customer and other value-creation partners.
3. From thinking of *customers as isolated entities* to understanding them in the context of their own *networks.*
4. From thinking of *firm resources* primarily as *operand* (e.g., tangible resources such as natural resources) to *operant* (e.g., usually intangible resources such as knowledge and skills).
5. From thinking of *customers as targets* to thinking of *customers as resources.*
6. From making *efficiency primary* to increasing *efficiency through effectiveness.*

The implications for the sales force include both an increased use of technology to reduce some traditional sales force functions and an increased concentration on relationships with the most important customers.[3] Sheth and Sharma (p. 264)[3] suggest that sales automation will reduce the sales function by allowing:

1. the exchange of detailed information instantaneously between employees, suppliers and customer 24/7 regardless of the time zones;
2. the identification of profitable customers through customer relationship management (CRM) software and activity-based accounting;
3. information on the entire set of offerings, rather than the products salespeople know most about;
4. customers the time to deliberate on decisions, especially in relation to customized products;
5. a reduction in error, as customers enter their own requirements directly; and
6. enhanced efficiency of ordering with electronic data interchange (EDI) between the customer and marketers' computers.

At the same time, there are other considerable benefits from the customer perspective. For instance, giving salespeople access to automated data helps them create more professional and personalized presentations for customers. Similarly, by enhancing the salespersons competency, efficiency and responsiveness the buyer–seller relationship can be improved.[4] Thus, technology is able to bring customers and suppliers closer, despite distance, time and cultural separation in international business. In this manner technology can serve the customer by enhancing the availability of information and allowing a higher level of service to the most important customers.[3] However, it is a support function, as cultures differ in the acceptability of initiating and managing relationships remotely: in South-East Asian countries the personal touch is still essential to build trust, while in other countries, such as Australia, people are more comfortable with remote relationships.[5] Even in low context, more individualist cultures, such as the US, the majority of people still want contact with a live customer service representative.[6]

Continuity in commercial relationships: learning from consumers

Relationship marketing focuses on customer retention, customer commitment and share of the customer's business, rather than market share.[7] According to Sheth and Parvatiyar there are three unique aspects to relationship marketing: (1) it is a one-on-one relationship between the marketer and seller; (2) it is an interactive process, where boundaries of time, location and identity between the supplier and customers are blurring; and (3) it is a value-added activity, where there is collaboration and mutual interdependence.[7]

Relationship marketing has been made easier by the availability of customer relationship management software (CRM) that helps track the records from each customer. There are two main complimentary components to CRM, the first being customer interfacing. This includes giving customers the ability to track their own orders and inventory levels, access to support services, and instant product information access. This side of CRM also keeps records of each customer which can be used to personalize direct marketing efforts, by building a customer profile and adapting offerings to best suit the customer. The second component of CRM is back-office activities, including data mining, sales quota tracking, information sharing, market analytics and administration.

This can usually be accessed by individual salespeople to provide information about when and how customers buy products, what options they choose, and whether there are any differences between first time and repeat customers. It can also be accessed at the sales manager level, allowing real-time tracking of subordinates performance, activities and efficiency. The biggest benefits of CRM are seen when the customer and office sides of CRM are implemented effectively and cohesively.[8]

While CRM is fast becoming a standard within the sales field (at least in the US), the implementation of it is not without its difficulties, particularly when considered from a global perspective.[9] Much like customers from different cultures require different approaches, so too do salespeople. A one-size-fits-all approach to CRM implementation is a common reason that the failure rate of multinational CRM implementation is high. Kumar and colleagues[9] spoke to executives from companies around the globe about their CRM experiences concluding that:

- Adoption of CRM was almost mandatory in North America, but a relatively new innovation in much of Asia-Pacific and Europe.
- North American companies were used as benchmarks by executives from other regions to indicate the success and usefulness of CRM implementation.
- Executives from Asia-Pacific and Europe were also watching North America to make sure that when they do adopt CRM, they were getting a mature and tested product.

While the use of CRM improves the information available to both customers and salespeople, it also reduces the amount of personal contact, which can be essential in many high-context cultures. As Day (p. 14) explains, a company needs to ensure that the communication flow is open and clear between the company representatives and the customer, as well as within the company:

In most organizations front-line contact people – who handle the complaints, hear requests for new services, cope with lead users, or lose sales due to competitor initiative – are seldom motivated to inform management on a systematic basis. They may fear [to] have their job load increase, suspect the information won't be used, or not know where it should be sent . . . Channels for the upward flow of information need to be established and incentives need to be offered for useful insights.[10]

Distribution channels can also act as a barrier to communication; consumers complain but there is no specific communication channel to the manufacturer and complaints are not taken seriously or are simply ignored (see Box 14.1). When the distributor is independent, located in a foreign country, and paid by commission on sales rather than rewarded for key consumer or competitor information, it is likely that the upward flow will be limited, unless specific action is taken. A product may, for instance, be refused by distribution for substantive reasons which remain ignored, such as store employees experiencing difficulties in opening cardboard boxes which are stapled in such a way that they are injured when trying to open them. Similarly, a class of potential consumers may be neglected by marketing communications, since only actual buyers are targeted and research has failed to examine alternative segments.

The example of Japanese *keiretsu*, demonstrates the value of building communication channels which help in the design and implementation of marketing strategies. Where opportunities for the return of products are liberal, distributors may warn producers about defective products that consumers are simply not happy with, as they do not want to receive these products as stock. Conversely, when producers or retailers reject consumer complaints, they will often shift responsibility for the failure on to the consumers, telling them they have not read the instructions, or have misused the product, or fixed it incorrectly.

As indicated in Chapter 5, there may be cultural differences in people's willingness to complain. The five domains of attitude toward complaining outlined in Chapter 5 differ across cultures:

1. beliefs about the effect experienced when one complains;
2. perceptions of the objective cost or trouble involved in making a complaint;
3. perception of retailer responsiveness to consumer complaints;
4. the extent to which consumer complaints are expected to benefit society at large; and
5. the perceived social appropriateness of making consumer complaints.

In general, Asian consumers are less likely than non-Asian consumers to complain directly to management, but more likely to complain privately, such as negative word of mouth.[11–13] In many Western

BOX 14.1

'Tubeless tyres', you said . . .

A consumer bought a leading European make of tyre for his car. He asked his garage to fit the tyres. In fact, they fitted tubeless tyres since they were supposed to be cheaper (as they did not need air chambers). These tyres, however, kept deflating. When complaining for the first time, the consumer was told by the garage to be slightly more careful in inflating the tyres. They had to be reinflated roughly twice a week. The customer contacted his garage again but was merely told that it 'didn't usually happen'. The customer asked if the tyre manufacturer would take back the defective tyres, but the garage told him that that was impossible and that in any case the tyres did at least stay inflated for a couple of days.

Finally, after going backwards and forwards several times, the customer had air chambers put into the tyres. The problem immediately ceased. When he spoke to his garage, they informed him that the wheel rims had warped slightly owing to the 30,000 miles (48,000 km) that the car had done. Other cars (the garage mentioned a German make) had rims made out of a thicker steel which was more resistant and therefore did not warp. Such a car could have tubeless tyres fitted successfully, whatever its age. The customer asked the garage to pass on this information to the tyre manufacturer so that it could inform tyre centres which cars were not suitable for tubeless tyres after a certain mileage had been covered. The garage said that this was impossible. The information was not passed on. Tubeless tyres continue to deflate in a fairly large number of cases. Customers either fit air chambers or buy a different car . . . or they change their make of tyre.

countries consumer rights are paramount, with external organizations, such as consumer protection, being able to intervene if a resolution between a business and purchaser cannot be reached. In many Eastern countries, this is not the case.

In addition, people from different cultural backgrounds may prefer different remedies to dissatisfaction. In many Western countries consumers perceived compensation for damages as a fair and just response, whereas consumers from Eastern countries may perceive a higher level of fairness when they are able to express dissatisfaction and someone listens.[14] The range of responses that consumers expect to receive in different countries are outlined in Chapter 5.

A human resource emphasis

Both personnel *and* clients should be seen by a company as its human resources. The frontiers of the organization should be less clear-cut: most companies develop impermeable boundaries between their 'inside' and their 'outside'. Insiders are generally people listed on the payroll. It is often claimed in company slogans that 'the customer is king' (*le client est roi, der Kunde ist König*, etc.), but in reality they are treated as *outsiders* and there is little personal knowledge of who the consumers actually are. A customer will often have a hard time getting to see the manager, even to give positive feedback.

Very often distribution channels will be used as 'shock-absorbing mattresses'. As distribution channels are in direct contact with customers, if something goes wrong, it is *their* job to deal with it. The isolation of manufacturers is too often the rule for non-commerce-oriented organizations, though they claim to be marketing oriented. In fact, consumers must be viewed as one of the key human resources of the company. They are not kings, but they are an integral part of the buyer–seller relationship. The role of the salesperson is as a consultant for the buying firm.[3] Salespeople need to be customer experts, not just product experts, who provide solutions that may require sourcing outside of the organization. They have direct relationships and communications with the both the distribution network and final customers and must convey messages in both directions, from the manufacturer to the market *and* vice versa.

BOX 14.2

The little man in rags and tatters

The story takes place in the corridor to the office of the minister of industry of the Popular Republic of Guinea at the beginning of the 1980s. Whether you had an appointment or you came to solicit a meeting, you had to be let in by the door-keeper. Besides, the door was locked and he had the key. This little man looked tired and wore worn-out clothes; his appearance led foreign visitors to treat him as negligible and to pay little attention to him. When visitors had been waiting for a long time and had watched others being given quick access to the minister, they often spoke out unrestrainedly, voicing their impatience to the old man, who seemed to have only limited language proficiency. In fact, the door-keeper spoke perfect French and was the uncle of the minister, which gave him power over his nephew according to the African tradition. It was a matter of notoriety that the minister placed great confidence in his uncle's recommendations. Thus, some foreign contractors never understood why they did not make deals although they had been developing winning arguments with the minister himself.

(Source: Gérard Verna, Laval University, Québec.)

Making contacts

Making appropriate contacts and developing relationships is an essential part of marketing. The issue is, at what level of the organization and with which people must contacts be made to maximize the chances of a successful outcome. When making contacts in a cross-cultural setting people should be aware of the following: (1) status is not shown in the same way in all cultures; (2) influential persons are not the same and individual influence is not exerted in the same way; and (3) the decision-making process differs. Box 14.2 illustrates the first two points with an African example.

Trust and commitment encourage the preservation of relationships.[15] Trust, relating to the reliability and integrity of the partner, has two basic elements in Western societies: *credibility* and *benevolence*.[16] Credibility is related to the belief that the partner will effectively and reliably perform the exchange. Benevolence is related to the belief that the partner will act in the interests of the other party. Both of these constructs differ across cultures. First, there are clearly two levels where credibility has to be established depending on cultural codes: personal and organizational. For instance, in China the concept of credibility relies on an oral commitment (personal), which differs from the Western concept which relies on a written commitment (organizational).[17] In consequence, the personal, rather than organizational,

relationship is more important in China. Second, the concept of benevolence is related to human nature orientation. In societies where a positive human nature orientation is predominant, people are viewed as capable of being trusted based on an assessment of personality traits and intentions. In societies where a negative human nature orientation is predominant, there is initial distrust. Benevolence is less relevant to trust in Chinese cultures, where *assurance* is built on the incentive structure (obligation and indebtedness) surrounding the relationship.[17]

Despite relationship marketing focusing on long-term relationships, there is necessarily a first contact. Here, the physical and behavioural attributes of people, as well as their social status, carry messages about their credibility (see Chapter 2 and 3). It is important to become personally acquainted with key decision makers in potential target companies. There may be some problems in clearly identifying the key decision makers, and establishing one's credibility with them. They may resent dealing with 'mere salespeople', especially in countries where sales status is low and power distance is high, because it conflicts with their self-image and their organizational position. Complex codes of interpersonal relationships govern the establishment of credibility: it is therefore often necessary to use sales assistants or market researchers as 'door-openers', who will quickly be succeeded by higher-ranking sales executives or sales managers (Box 14.3).

BOX 14.3

The Japanese 'message-boy'

During research into the key factors surrounding the success of Japanese engineering companies in world markets, I had the opportunity to interview several Japanese engineering specialists. One of them had worked for C. Itoh, a large Japanese trading company, on the sale and project follow-up of an oil refinery in Algeria. He explained by the use of a diagram (Figure 14.1) the Japanese 'method' for selling turnkey factories.

He stressed the central role of the *sogoshosha* (GTC: general trading company) as an *organizer*, a function that includes the responsibilities of information source, business intermediary and coordinator. An *organizer* is roughly equivalent to a 'sales prospection expert before, during and after the sale of a large and highly complex item'. One of C. Itoh's small offices in Algiers, which specialized in import–export, principally of textile products, learned of the existence of a new tender for an oil refinery which was shortly to be published. The Algiers office sent a fairly detailed fax to Tokyo – step (1) in Figure 14.1 – where the engineering

company(ies) and the manufacturing companies (MFG) who would be in a position to tender for the project were sought out – step (2).

Even at this early stage a project team will begin to assemble from among the different companies involved (3). The trading company contacts the official bodies: first, the foreign insurance division of the Ministry of International Trade and Industry (GOV) to determine whether the project has a chance of being covered for political and commercial risk (4). The Japanese Exim-Bank, the public export-finance body (BKG), will also be contacted for a preliminary study into financing options. These bodies will not make any firm commitment, but they will give a preliminary response: if the project risks not being covered by official guarantees, or receiving only limited cover, the project team instituted by the trading company may decide to abandon the tender.

While all this is going on, and even before the bid documents are available, a preliminary team will be sent to the site to examine the possibilities of water and energy supply, transport facilities, etc. Already

Figure 14.1 The role of Japanese general trading companies as 'organizers' in the negotiation and implementation of international turnkey operations: a Japanese view

Box 14.3 (cont'd)

the Japanese are gaining time (5). Once the bid documents are available to companies (6), the trading company's local representative will go to collect them personally from the future owner and dispatch the documents to Tokyo after having summarized the main points in a long and detailed fax or e-mail. The representative will not hesitate to stay up most of the night to draft this text. By this stage, the Japanese have already gained 15 days on their international competitors (7).

Once the detailed fax or e-mail has been received, a larger team will go to examine the technical and economic conditions on-site. The results of this survey, and the consultation with various engineering partners, heavy equipment manufacturers (MFG) and carriers (TRP), will enable the formulation of a detailed bid, which very often has to be submitted within a fairly short time span (30 days) after the publication of the tender. The bid will not be sent, but handed over by a young executive, who will be 25 to 30 years old: a 'message-boy' (8). His task is an important one: thanks to him, there is no risk of the documents being blocked by customs; he also has the job of 'sizing up' the people being dealt with and of discerning the people who will really make the final decision. Once more the Japanese have gained time; they are never late in submitting a tender,

whereas a number of their foreign competitors submit theirs after the deadline. Although late delivery of a bid is usually accepted (bidding times are fairly short), it does not necessarily reflect favourably on the capacity to meet delivery dates.

Now the negotiation phase begins (9). This will easily last several months and in extreme cases will stretch, with long interruptions, over several years. Much shuttling back and forth between the various levels (10) will allow the finalizing of an offer. If successful, the offer will lead to the signature of the contract for a large-scale project (11), in which the trading company and the engineering company will generally be joint contractors. As a result, the trading company will adopt the role of coordinator between the various companies carrying out the project (12).

According to my Japanese informant, Nobuhiko Suto, now a professor at Tokai University, who had been personally involved in the deal, the 'message-boy' is typical of the Japanese way of doing business. He is even requested to scrutinize the faces of the people to whom he submits the offer to determine their reaction to the Japanese bid. In the West it is difficult to conceive of such care being taken to assess subjective reactions objectively.

Any 'detail' may be of importance in establishing credibility in the absence of more profound informational cues, which come only when the relationship is more established. Business cards are important because they provide clear information on businesspersons: their family and first names, how to reach them, their status within the company, etc. A foreign-language card will also reflect sensitivity to the host culture[18] and when one is working mostly with a particular culture (e.g., a US businessperson exporting to Japan), it is advisable to have a card printed in English on the one side with the Japanese transliteration on the other side. Credibility is often based on first impressions: accent has been shown to influence the credibility and effectiveness of an international businessperson. In Guatemala, for instance, Guatemalan Spanish evokes more favourable judgements than the same sales pitch in foreign-accented Spanish.[19]

The decision-making process in the buyer's organization is a key issue for making adequate contact. Power distance (PD) plays an important role in the style of organizational decision making: the higher it is, the more centralized it is. In a French context, for instance, with high PD, individualism and uncertainty avoidance, decision making and budgetary power are located at the top of the organization. Most people cannot so much as buy a pencil without referring to the top. Thus, for personal selling, one has to target contacts at the top, while keeping friendly contacts with people at intermediate levels, because they could resent their lack of power being openly manifested by the seller's attitude and obstruct the deal. In countries where power distance is small, such as Australia, decision making is more decentralized, and there are financial thresholds for decisions at each level of the hierarchy, especially when there is also an individualistic orientation in the culture. In this context the level of contact is roughly proportionate to the financial amount of the sales contract.

The Japanese style of reaching decisions by committee can disorientate people of other nationalities who are used to decisions being made by a boss, with a great deal of power being concentrated in one person's hands. There are many examples of companies that, after protracted negotiations with Japanese firms, heard nothing more for several months. They assumed that they had lost the deal, but to their surprise they ultimately received an agreement: the process of *ringi* had been at work in the Japanese company, a procedure of written consultation that requires the input of various interested parties, meetings and careful consideration of objections and suggestions. Box 14.3 shows how the Japanese manage the process of preliminary contacts in a situation where both the seller's and the buyer's organization are complex.

14.2
Networks in business markets

Both suppliers and customers tend to develop networks. For instance, an airline builds regular relationships with an aircraft company over the lifetime of the aircraft, which is often 25 years; similarly the aircraft company is closely connected to the engine manufacturer, because the design of the aircraft includes specific engines. Industrial companies also build alliances for developing common R & D projects or to manage common assets, such as jointly developed software or a joint distribution system. Thorelli (p. 38) describes a systematic *network* between two or more organizations involved in long-term relationships:

Generically, a network may be viewed as consisting of 'nodes' or positions (occupied by firms, households, strategic business units inside a diversified concern, trade associations and other types of organization) and *links* manifested by interaction between the positions ... Networks may be tight or loose, depending on the quantity (number), quality (intensity), and type (closeness to the core activity of the partners involved) of interactions between the positions or members.[20]

The network approach to business was developed by the IMP group with the view that relationships between companies are as important as the exchanges they make.[21,22] According to Ford (p. 81),[21] personal contacts serve to reduce the uncertainty linked to complex deals: 'Mutual trust, respect and personal friendship between participants allows confidential information to be exchanged'. Social bonding (mutual personal friendship and liking) precedes the development of trust, face and cooperation.[23] Personal contacts enable partners in the network to assess each other's competence, to negotiate issues and go beyond the letter of the contract. If there is a critical problem, they offer a framework for the quick exchange of information and rapid decisions about corrective measures. However, in most Western 'doing' societies the relationship is focused at the organizational level of commercial goals. People are there to 'close the deal', not to enjoy the pleasures of social life. As Ford (p. 83)[21] points out 'some suppliers see the dangers of too close an involvement of their salesmen with customers, in that they may lose their objectivity and take actions in the interests of the social relationships, rather than in the wider interests of their company'.

While business networks are fairly universal, the relationships can be fundamentally different in other cultures. For instance, in China *guanxi* is a special type of relationship, which Wang (p. 82) describes as a mixed relationship, not as close as blood relations, but with an emotional attachment (*ganqing*) between the parties:

Guanxi marketing, however, goes beyond the commercial meaning as members in the *guanxi* network exchange both favor and *ganqing* (affection) and, at times, its affective value is more important than its monetary value in social interactions. *Guanxi* works at a personal level on the basis of friendship and *ganqing* is a measure of the level of emotional commitment and the closeness of the parties involved. It is not uncommon for a person to take his/her personal *guanxi* networks with him/her when leaving the organization. From the business perspective, people who have *ganqing* care about each other and treat each other more like friends than just business partners. *Ganqing* plays a key role in maintaining and enhancing a *guanxi* relationship and makes the impersonal business relationship more personal.[17]

Thus, in China, business relationships are more personal than impersonal and more particularistic than universalistic.[17] This type of relationship cannot be easily imitated by competitors.

Chinese *guanxi* is similar to *Kankei* in Japan and *Kwankye* in Korea. In each of these concepts after-hours socialization is important for meeting and convincing key decision makers in a more comfortable atmosphere.[18] The practice of *guanxi* translates into large sales forces for maintaining contacts and large accounts receivables. Firms engaged in a connected set of companies, called *guanxihu*, do their best to avoid embarrassing a business partner experiencing temporary financial problems. *Guanxi* enhances the performance of international joint ventures in China,[24] as well as foreign-invested enterprises in China and Chinese domestic firms.[25,26]

According to Wang (p. 86),[17] Western firms entering China need to show they are 'considerate, patient, and willing to offer assistance whenever a need is detected. In addition, being empathetic also means giving a *renqing* without expecting an immediate payback'. As Luo and Chen (pp. 3–4)[26] caution: 'many Western business people are often in danger of overemphasizing the giftgiving and wining-and-dining components of *guanxi* relationships, thereby coming dangerously close to crass bribery or to [being] perceived as "meat and wine friends" which is a Chinese metaphor for mistrust'. The emphasis should be on the concept of enhancing face. Hutchings and Murray (p. 188)[27] found that Western managers in China feel that the concept of face was the greatest difference between *guanxi* and the Western concept of networking: 'to give face, to save face, and above all, to avoid causing loss of face. They highlighted the fact that in causing loss of face to another, then they automatically lost face themselves, and thus they viewed the saving and managing of face of others as essential to their own ongoing success in China'.

14.3

Buyer–seller interactions

Seller's status and the status of trade

In many countries sales work has a low status. Even in the US, considered by many to be the home of modern selling, there is still a stigma associated with being a salesperson. Selling is implicitly associated with persuasion techniques and taking money from people rather than usefully bringing products and services to them. Trade has some negative connotations in Latin countries, where it was traditionally associated with exploitation. In this view buying for resale (i.e., distribution) is seen as economically unproductive, whereas engineering and production are noble activities. This leads to the limited view that personal selling does not require formal training, but is based rather on an innate ability to communicate, a lack of scruples and a good deal of opportunism. In actuality, the American Society for Training and Development estimates that US firms alone spend around $15 billion on sales training each year,[28] and many universities around the world have, and are launching, sales degrees.

The value placed on money is also central to the status of trade. Cultures differ in their beliefs about money.[29] In fact, most cultures have a problem with money, which is often implicitly viewed as making people *bassement intéressés* (overly self-interested). This influences the preference for pricing solutions. For instance, price bargaining may be more common in these countries (see Chapter 10); with an explicit reference to price avoided, discussions about price entering the conversation later, or a supposedly 'favourable' price being ritually associated with friendship.

In many countries, it is an absolute necessity for the seller to be personally acquainted with the buyer, and common membership in the same ingroup may also be required (see Chapter 2). In some cases, the buyer might find some personal characteristics of the seller difficult to accept, such as a European export saleswoman selling to a Saudi male buyer.

In high power distance countries, the seller's role is often reduced to conveying the producer's conditions to the customer, with very limited leeway for negotiation. The salesperson's role is persuasion; there is no consideration of the customer's needs or making these needs known to his or her company! More paradoxically, the purchaser is also in a subordinate situation to the supplying company.

Selling styles: arguments and presence

Consider the ethical position of a salesman who is asked to sell a poor-quality product or who knows the customer believes the product to be of poor quality. Should he inform the production department, or

Figure 14.2 Selling orientations

(Source: Adcock *et al.*[30] *Marketing, Principles and Practice*, Dennis Adcock, Ray Bradfield, Al Halborg and Caroline Ross, Pitman, © Pearson Education Limited 1993.)

merely stick to the role of persuasion? When preparing arguments, a salesperson has two main concerns: one is for the customers and their needs; the other is for achieving the sale or 'closing the deal'. Adcock and colleagues (p. 306)[30] combine these as shown in Figure 14.2.

If sellers are there purely to sell products, then the role of salespeople is principally that of persuasion. Cultures vary considerably in their persuasive strategies. The following questions outline possible ways of differentiating the sales persuasion technique:

1. How far can one take persuasion without becoming insistent, and irritating?
2. Is one persuasive merely by listening, where clients appreciate salespeople to whom they can talk, or by talking?
3. What arguments will be the best and the quickest for persuading the prospective purchaser?

Cateora[31] proposes some stereotypes of selling styles:

1. In Asian countries, where people are modest and offended by arrogance and extreme self-confidence, vendors should make modest, rational, down-to-earth points; they should avoid winning arguments against the buyer, who could suffer a 'loss of face', and react quite negatively.
2. In Italy a lack of self-confidence would be perceived as a lack of personal credibility and reliability; thus, one needs to argue strongly in order to be considered a serious partner.
3. In Switzerland precision is favoured; your words will be taken quite literally.

4. In the UK people do not like pushy salespersons; it is advisable to use the *soft sell* approach. The favourable position of the 'soft sell' approach in Figure 14.2 (which is drawn from British authors) adds support to this.
5. In Germany you should use the *hard sell* approach (make visits, offer trials, be very visible).
6. In Mexico the *price* should be emphasized.
7. In Venezuela the *quality* should be emphasized.

These stereotypes indicate cultural norms, but the style of selling also depends on the personality of the salesperson, the extent of the relationship, the size of the deal and the type of industry. However, culture dictates assumptions about the role adopted by the majority of sellers. For instance, if the view is that a good salesperson should be able to close the deal, then the focus will more than likely be on short-term persuasion at any price. The traditional seven-step process of selling may be followed: prospecting, pre-approach, approach, presentation, overcoming objections, close and follow-up. Conversely, if the seller is viewed as a client consultant within the company, salespeople will take a long-term approach toward problem identification, presentation of solutions and continued customer support.[3] They will work with the client to create value and even be willing to lose an order once in a while for the benefit of the customer. Selling styles also depend on which type of concrete results are expected and rewarded. Is the emphasis on winning new customers and reaching a sales target or more subjective achievements, such as building relationships and solving problems?

Table 14.1 A summary of the influence of culture on buyer–seller relationships

Cultural value	Influence on seller and buyer
Inferior status for trade	Poor status for sales; selling is reserved to a minority group
Being/doing	More personal relationship orientated; more impersonal deal orientated
Money	Price bargaining as friendship ritual
Ingroup orientation	Only people from a certain ingroup are considered as adequate for sales roles; transactions have to be made preferably across ingroup members
Family orientation	Buyer–seller relationships are viewed as an element of a larger family network
Short-term orientation	Achieving the sale is the paramount goal
Long-term orientation	Keeping the client is the paramount goal
Low/high power distance	Equality/inequality between buyer and seller
Listening versus talking	Soft sell versus hard sell

Equality in the buyer–seller relationship

Numerous empirical studies have been undertaken to determine which role, buyer or seller, holds the *ab initio* position of strength in intercultural marketing negotiations. Graham[32] suggests that one of the reasons for the American trade deficit with Japan was the difference regarding the position of strength in the representation of the buyer–seller relationship. The Japanese believe that strength lies with the purchaser, whom the salesperson must do the almost to satisfy, whereas the Americans envisage a more egalitarian position, as Graham (p. 9) points out in his examination of which party adapts to the other in the relationship of intercultural business negotiation:

Anthropologists tell us that power relations usually determine who adopts and adapts behavior in a cross-cultural setting. Japanese executives in an American setting are likely to be the ones to modify their behavior . . . However, if an American seller takes his normative set of bargaining behavior to Japan, then negotiations are apt to end up abruptly. The American seller expects to be treated as an equal and acts accordingly. The Japanese buyer is likely to view this rather brush behavior in a lower status seller as inappropriate and lacking in respect. The Japanese buyer is made to feel uncomfortable, and he politely shuts the door to trade, without explanation. The American seller never makes the first sale, never gets an opportunity to learn the Japanese system.[32]

Table 14.1 gives a summary of the influence of culture on buyer–seller interactions.

14.4

Sales force management in a cross-cultural perspective

The idea that the promotion of sales personnel is based on merit and that decisions are made on an objective basis is very strong in Western societies. This is linked with the 'master of destiny' philosophy that underlies much of the US style of management thinking.[31] People are in control of their own destiny and therefore responsible for the effective use of their own resources. In many cultures which have a more fatalistic approach to life, controlling individual performance does not seem to make sense. Uncontrollable higher-order forces largely shape our acts and future. For instance, Saudi Arabian performance and evaluation control systems often work informally, without systematic controls, established criteria or definite procedures.[33]

The influence of culture on sales force management is not considered exhaustively here, as it is based in the field of human resource management which is subject to significant cross-cultural variance. For instance, Western 'doing' societies which place value on 'affirmative action compliance programmes' ignore criteria that are considered essential to determine *who the person is* in many other societies. However, the birthplace of applicants, their marital status, age, citizenship or language competencies are standard, non-discriminatory enquiries in most cultures where there is still some *being* orientation. The 'affirmative action, equal opportunity' programme is derived from extremely strong *doing* and *outgroup* orientations, where it is seen as immoral to describe persons as they *are*.

Who to employ as sales representatives

One of the first questions that faces firms who plan to have an international sales force is whom to employ, and in which country. The most obvious decision is whether to use expatriates (i.e., employees from the firm's home country) or host country locals as sales force representatives. The major advantage of a local salesperson is that they are a cultural insider, meaning they understand the nuances of the local culture, and are more similar to the local customers. However, they also typically require more training and in some cultures will be held in low esteem. Conversely, expatriates typically have greater product knowledge and are usually more embedded in the company culture. Honeycutt & Ford[34] suggest several criteria that can be used to decide on the international sales force structure:

1. *Costs* – expatriates are significantly more expensive in terms of salary. Additionally there is a significant failure rate amongst expatriates, in that many leave before their tour is finished.
2. *Local culture* – for instance, in a high power distance culture it might be beneficial to have an expatriate sales force, as they may be accorded more status than locals.
3. *Management structure* – expatriates are generally more appropriate if the home country has centralized control, with local salespeople more useful when management decisions are made in-country.
4. *The complexity of the product* – generally the more complex or technical the product, the more benefit is gained from using expatriates, thanks to their higher levels of experience within the company and training.

Incentives for sales representatives

Hofstede's[35] cultural dimensions (Chapter 3) as well as Hall's[36] theory of communication (Chapter 4) can be used to clarify the incentives issue. Organizations

Table 14.2 Contrast models

Cultural traits	Model 1	Model 2
Power distance	Low	High
Individualism	High	Low
Uncertainty avoidance	Low	High
Context of communication	Low	High

must encourage its sales representatives and/or the sales team to attain specific objectives (e.g., turnover target, profit target, promotion of certain products, gaining market share at the expense of competitors). Many of the stages of this process are influenced by cultural differences, including:

1. setting objectives;
2. evaluation, i.e., setting up a system to calculate target-to-actual-sales deviation followed by feedback to the salespeople;
3. remunerating the sales force achievements: designing the incentive system and attempting to standardize it across countries; and
4. implementing the sales force remuneration system.

Two basic incentive systems for monitoring the sales force (models 1 and 2 in Table 14.2) are described below. They are Weberian 'ideal types', not necessarily to be found in their pure form in the real world. Model 1 is appropriate for a firm belonging to an individualistic society where communication is fairly explicit (low context, see Chapters 3 and 4), power distance is small and uncertainty avoidance is weak (e.g., the US). Model 2 is appropriate for a company originating from a society where communication is implicit (high context), power distance is high and uncertainty avoidance is strong (e.g., Japan). The masculinity/femininity dimension also influences the practical implementation of these two models of sales force remuneration, in terms of more assertive (masculine) or nurturing (feminine) feedback and corrective action to low-performing salespeople.

Attitudes towards the setting of objectives and their use in performance measurement

The first step is the setting of sales objectives. Differences in the precision and contextuality of communication style across societies influence the setting of objectives.[36] Where people communicate explicitly with low context, objectives will be precisely set, quantified and openly negotiated. In contrast, where people communicate with a high context, quantified objectives are less likely to seem accurate and, as such, do not serve the same purpose. 'Number crunching' is not a trait of high-context societies. Figures are not assumed to depict the complexities of the real world. In high-context societies, numbers are considered as efficient, but oversimplified. Despite that, some kind of quantified objectives are set, but not necessarily followed. Depending on which model (1 or 2) is appropriate, objectives may have different roles.

In model 1, formal *and realistic evaluation* is likely, where the sellers must earn their salary. In these societies, relations are depersonalized and people can be evaluated by figures. Target levels of sales are negotiated with the salesperson. Any deviation of actual sales from target is measured precisely. Corrective actions, sanctions and rewards result from monitoring the salesperson's performance.

In model 2, *internal incentives* are likely, where the context is expected to influence the outcome. In these societies, relations are personalized. The seller cannot easily be dismissed (e.g., lifetime employment and strong uncertainty avoidance, emphasizing a high level of job security), staff turnover is low and closer personal ties exist within a stable workforce. The objectives are not openly and truly negotiated. In these higher power distance societies it is assumed that the boss knows what the sales staff should achieve, rather than the salespeople themselves. Therefore, the objective cannot be as realistic as in model 1. The boss may set 'instrumental' excessively high target levels which serve as an ultimate goal. Although everybody knows (implicitly) that a lower performance level will be achieved, it is thought that the level of performance is influenced by the ambitious objective. The risk is that sellers may seek security and lack personal initiative and drive.

Accuracy of goal setting

After objectives have been set, deviation from the target must be measured. The accuracy of performance evaluation and incentive calculation is always higher in a situation of explicit communication. Model 1 rewards individual merits, as the individual is seen as the source of the performance (see the individualism assumptions detailed in Chapter 3). Conversely, in high-context/implicit communication (model 2) the evaluation phase is neither precise nor formally implemented. There is no shame in failing to attain the set objectives, as it is significantly higher than a realistic target. Despite their best efforts, the sellers would be considered as underperforming if they were evaluated by model 1. However, there is unspoken awareness in the organization that sales objectives are not realistically set. No formal and quantified evaluation is implemented. Furthermore, what constitutes a good sales performance is implicitly clear within the company, making it relatively useless to precisely assess performance.

Individualism/collectivism, uncertainty avoidance and performance measurement

The individualist or collectivist orientation in a society is a meaningful axis of cultural differentiation.[35] In the US, where individualism is very strong, the cultural emphasis is on individual achievement.[37] It implies precise and individualized sales targets, fostering competition within the sales force. Competition between the salespeople, within the sales team, is considered legitimate, even though it may undermine the coherence of collective action when this is needed (e.g., training other salespeople, transfer of experience from senior to junior salespeople, etc.).

More traditional societies tend not to engage in individual goal setting and variable commission rewarding. In Thailand family background largely determines social position; money only confers limited status.[38] Fixed salaries demonstrate social status, stability and group belonging and are more desirable than a larger income with a variable commission component, as this emphasizes individualism and instability. This is similar to Japan, as indicated by Hill and colleagues (p. 23):

Tradition is also an important determinant of Japanese compensation plans. Because their social system is based on hereditary and seniority criteria, salary raises, even for sales forces, are based on longevity with the company. Similarly commission systems are tied to the combined efforts of the entire sales force, fostering the Japanese team ethic and downplaying the economic aspirations of individuals.[39]

Precise measurement of salespeople's performance may be considered harmful in some countries. In South-East Asia the ethics of non-confrontation clearly clash with an objective performance review, as this could cause the subordinate to 'lose face', infringing a societal norm. The motivation theories which underlie sales force compensation systems are culturally bound. Because they were developed in one country (the US), they put a strong emphasis on individualism and rationalism as bases for human behaviour.

In contrast to the US system of favouring individual performance, more collectivist societies, such as Japan, tend to favour team performance. Intrinsic rewards are preferred. In the US job satisfaction is primarily driven by satisfaction with their pay, whereas in Japan it is also related to satisfaction with co-workers and happiness with work.[40,41] Similarly, in Spain (more collectivist) sales managers are more likely to give equal rewards for group effort, whereas those from more individualistic cultures (Anglo and Germanic regions, as well as France and Italy) are more likely to reward individual effort.[42]

The information used for intrinsic or extrinsic, individual or group-based reward systems will necessarily be different. In higher uncertainty-avoidant countries, such as Germany, very detailed market information will be sought in an attempt to increase their certainty in decision making.[35] In lower uncertainty-avoidant countries, especially those with high individualism and masculinity, such as the US, the same detailed information will be used for a different purpose; the precise tracking and control of salespeople.

Femininity/masculinity and ways of remedying underperformance

There are different methods to deal with the problem of sellers who are clearly underperforming. In masculine societies (e.g., Australia, Switzerland, the US), poor results will be called to attention in a fairly crude manner. Where an individual should be efficient and perform well, unsatisfactory achievements will first lead to a clear warning that performance must

improve. Then, if the salesperson fails to justify his or her performance based on uncontrollable factors and continues to underperform, the employee will eventually be dismissed.

In feminine societies (Sweden, northern European countries, France), a higher value is placed on quality of life. There is a protective and maternal attitude on the part of the organization towards its members. While these societies also strive for efficiency, a seller is entitled to more understanding. Checks are initially made to see if there are any external explanations for the weak performance (e.g., a sales territory with little potential or particularly strong competitors). When the reasons for their underperformance have been assessed with them (formally or informally), they receive assistance from colleagues and from the organization (e.g., additional training). Only after the organization has done everything within its power to help the salesperson to increase his or her performance is a final decision taken. On balance, the results from a hard-line (masculine) method do not lead to better sales performance than the softer methods employed by companies based in feminine countries.

Compensation systems based on cultural values and industry characteristics

Table 14.3 describes some basic sales force remuneration systems that are related to the type of product or service being sold and the value systems in the society. In societies with high uncertainty avoidance, employees usually prefer job security with a fixed salary and only small variable commissions. Pure commission-based salaries will only be acceptable in model 1 (Table 14.2). Of course, sellers in all countries are rewarded in different ways, dependent on the type of product. Large individual sales (e.g., desalination or nuclear plants) requiring lengthy sales efforts from a team of experts tend to be rewarded with fixed salaries, in a way preferred by the cultural values of model 2. Smaller individual sales (e.g., consumer goods) requiring individually identifiable sales efforts, tend to be rewarded with salaries that have an element of commission and the cultural values of model 1.

So far, this discussion has been about extrinsic or material rewards, which are generally in cash or in kind in the form of bonuses and commissions.

Table 14.3 Basic sales force compensation systems, sectors and the cultural values involved

Objectives/type of goods	Compensation plans	Values involved
Long-term sales efforts; equipment, turnkey sales	Fixed salary and promotions	Lifetime employment; cooperation within the sales team; collective performance
Reach precise sales quotas; consumer goods	Pure (or quasi-pure) commission	Own business: no loyalty to the company; individualistic and competitive
Achieve more precise goals (sales of certain products, new territories or segments)	Fixed salary, plus monetary and non-monetary incentives	Mixed values: contract and long-term orientation; loyalty but not unlimited commitment

Extrinsic rewards can be linear (in direct proportion to sales exceeding the objective), progressive or retrospective, or can be triggered once a single objective has been attained. The criteria and formulae for calculating variable extrinsic rewards are very varied.[43] Purely extrinsic rewards, such as variable commissions on sales, are external motivators, whereas intrinsic rewards are related to the satisfaction of inner needs. People may be intrinsically motivated by a job well done, the esteem of their colleagues or even the securing of a contract *per se*. They involve no pecuniary element and have no influence on material life.

Some rewards are on the fringe of intrinsic and extrinsic rewards. For example, medals or titles (best salesperson for the period). Rewards can be centred on the individual (e.g., gifts to seller or their family, payment of personal expenses), on the group (e.g., a leisure trip for the whole sales team) or on a mix of both (e.g., awards for the best sales teams). As is frequently the case in Japan, group rewards may take the form of a joint holiday for the sales team, which is both an individual and a group reward simultaneously and contributes to group bonding. Whereas, models 1 and 2 (Table 14.2) depict extreme characteristics, real-world remuneration systems more often combine intrinsic and extrinsic, individual and collective rewards. Rewards such as promotion and salary increases combine recognition (intrinsic) and money (extrinsic). A large range of possibilities for remuneration exists, which can be used to design a sales force remuneration system adapted to the local culture. Using innovative designs, standardization of sales force remuneration is possible at the regional

level where cultural variance is limited. It should be noted that neither model 1 nor 2 are universally 'good' or 'bad' in terms of people being treated fairly or levels of satisfaction. However, it is important that the reward structure is appropriate to the cultural values and the product category.

14.5
Public relations across cultures

Public relations (PR) consists of a set of coordinated communication programmes between an organization and its publics, designed to improve, maintain or protect a company product or image. The 'publics' can be internal, such as employees, or external to the firm, such as the general public, customers, suppliers, distributors or the media. Other PR targets include the government (e.g., lobbying for new or existing legislation), or stockholders and the financial community.

The functions of PR are twofold: (1) in normal situations, to create and enhance a favourable corporate image with the various publics concerned, with the view that a foreign firm is particularly susceptible to nationalistic criticism; (2) in crisis situations such as boycotts, accidents, strikes, product recalls, and so on, to maintain goodwill by responding to criticism, explaining remedial action to overcome the problem, and anticipating and countering messages that may damage the corporate image.

Cross-cultural differences have been noted in the way companies react to disasters such as plane crashes, major pollution, etc. They reflect the prevailing sense of responsibility *vis-à-vis* the community, but also the companies' sense of privacy and the view of what is culturally appropriate for dealing with these events. For instance, a company may choose to adopt a very low profile and wait for the storm to calm or conversely, adopt a high profile, pleading either guilty or not guilty. In some countries, such as Japan, formal apologies and explanations are expected. If the company does not step forward to do this, the government will. For instance, in 2004, when Mitsubishi Motors was found to have covered up truck defects, blamed for a series of accidents, the Japanese government made strong statements about how 'deplorable' their actions were and took steps against Mitsubishi Motors (banning purchases of vehicles for at least one year), as well as the executives involved. In other countries, where there is an emphasis on privacy and a dislike for public display (e.g., Switzerland), a company is likely to adopt an extremely low profile and engage in very little communication, even if it is clearly in the wrong.

PR is very different from advertising, in that it is focused on communications intended to build trust and relationships with key publics. PR people, whether employed by the firm or as outside consultants, have nothing to sell. They use publicity as a means of conveying messages to the public (whether by securing editorial space in the case of any kind of films, videotapes or slides), as well as the organization of events, meetings, conferences, sponsorship.

Cultural variance may occur in the following aspects of the PR process:

1. making contact;
2. managing relationships;
3. disclosing information, especially in the case of private, secret or sensitive information;
4. developing arguments, some of which cannot be understood locally; and
5. dealing with nationalistic feelings.

Thinking locally

People from Western countries do not naturally think in terms of who is a member of which group. However, the identification of key ethnic groups is important for good PR in many other contexts.

Further, the model of a free press cannot be assumed. In many countries its freedom is curtailed by the government, such as is the case in China, and often in much more subtle ways than mere censorship.

The influence of local competition should not be underestimated. The lack of antitrust laws in many countries reflects the legitimacy of agreements with competitors in regard to market-sharing or price agreements. Consequently, PR officers may be involved in talks with competing firms, a practice which would be considered unethical in most developed Western countries which have antitrust legislation. Such discussions are all the more important when the local competitors are technologically inferior to the foreign firm but are able to use their nationality as a weapon against a foreign intruder. When making agreements, PR officers should:

1. avoid disclosing information that local parties regard as secret since confidentiality is culturally relative;
2. avoid using arguments that clash with the logic of the host country, as they will not be understood; and
3. avoid conveying messages about local people and culture that are perceived as negative.

Foreign firms have to face nationalism: being foreign makes things slightly worse for a company when it is under attack. Multinational firms tend to have higher profiles and people recognize they can influence society's well-being either positively or negatively. As such, they are expected to do more for society than local firms. If the local employees of a multinational company receive better pay than the average worker in the country, this can be seen as beneficial to the recipients individually but detrimental to the community as a whole: it lures farmers to the industrial sector, or it causes merchants to raise their prices because of the purchasing power of a small affluent group. Emphasizing local citizenship is always necessary and it must be done with unambiguous arguments. As Holt and colleagues (p. 75) point out, the impact is greater if the social problems can be linked to what they sell and/or how they conduct their business:

Over a billion people in the world use unsafe water every day, leading to more than 2 million deaths a year from diarrhoea. P&G identified safe drinking water as a critical social problem that fell within its scope of expertise. It leveraged its knowledge of household sanitation to develop a water purification system that would be effective in poor countries. P&G found that people would try the product if it was easy to use and inexpensive and if they could see that the purified water was clean. Scaling down a technology used in water purification facilities, the company's engineers developed a satchel of particulate matter that consumers could stir into buckets. The particles would attract contaminants and dirt, and people could filter out the pollutants with a cloth. P&G's tests in Guatemala have demonstrated that the system can reduce the frequency of diarrhea episodes by around 25%. If the company markets the product globally, the social impact could be extraordinary. What's impressive is that P&G deployed its vast technological capabilities to tackle a problem that governments and NGOs have struggled with for decades.[44]

The case of product liability

Product liability is an area where PR is needed. As previously mentioned, there were dire consequences when Mitsubishi Motors was found to have covered up truck defects. The company was blamed for a series of accidents and its sales plummeted by 40 per cent.[45] Similarly, Nestlé, one of the largest food companies in the world, faced a boycott because its infant feeding formula had allegedly caused many deaths of babies in the Third World. In 1974 a report by a British journalist[46] and a pamphlet entitled 'Nestlé kills babies' started accusations that escalated during the mid-1970s. Nestlé withdrew its infant formula advertising and decided to participate in consumer education programmes. The key reasons for the problems experienced by Nestlé's Third World consumers' were cultural: the belief in the magic properties of Western products and the pressure to give what is the best, the most modern, as a sign of love for babies. A more down-to-earth reason was the poor use of the product, mixed with contaminated water. Nestlé should have anticipated the key reasons for misuses of its product: (1) high levels of illiteracy; (2) even when literate, people rarely rely on written materials, which have an abstract image; and (3) the inability to cope with ambiguous messages (the product is good, but can be bad). These problems are similar for pharmaceutical companies, in that most drugs have side effects. However, in many countries being explicit about the side effects may be harmful, as people may

not believe in a drug whose manufacturer clearly acknowledges the potentially adverse consequences (most of which can be avoided by proper use!).

Website link 14.1

'How to spin an oil spill'. A satirical view of PR from Australian comedians Clarke and Dawe: http://www.youtube.com/watch?v=fImVSbvS1Co.

14.6

Bribery: facts

Bribery, fraud and embezzlement are all aspects of corruption. Bribery is associated with selling, obtaining favours, and making things work. It is a practice that can be found in almost all cultures, at some level. According to the World Bank, over US$1 trillion is paid in bribes alone every year. The Germans call it *Schmiergeld* ('grease money'), the French *pot-de-vin* (literally jug of wine), in the Middle East it is a *baksheesh*, in Italy a *bastarella* (little envelope) and in Mexico a *mordida* (a bite). These practices know few borders, and even the Japanese construction industry is heavily plagued by bribery. Naturally, every country officially prohibits bribery, but laws are locally enforced (depending on the types of rules, see Chapter 3). In some cases, judges may be open to accepting a bribe.

Types of bribery

Information and data on illegal payments are very sparse and often fragmentary. Such issues are sensitive and companies remain very secretive. However, the practice is too widespread to be ignored. It takes various forms:

1. *Small and large gifts.* It could be as simple as a gift to the person or person's family. Alternatively, fully paid trips for influential foreign officials can quickly reach as much as $50,000, when it includes a prestigious hotel, a driver/guide for the duration of their stay, receptions, restaurants and potentially hostesses for the evenings.

2. *Percentages* paid based on the contract value. Here the illegal payments result in much larger sums being paid, in proportion to the size of the contract (whether it is for the sale of a squadron of fighter planes, or a turnkey plant, etc.).

3. *Tips.* When civil servants, who hold authority and responsibility (e.g., a police officer, a customs officer or a tax inspector) are poorly paid, it may be 'implicitly understood' that they will supplement their income. As such, a 'greasing' payment may be required to pass through customs or to obtain a tax form (for a mandatory declaration). The authorities are perfectly aware of the existence of such practices.

Methods

Whether illegal payments are made, and what sums are involved, varies widely from country to country. Payments are much more substantial: for example, in the construction industry or in Nigeria than in electronics or in Australia. An important caveat must be made: not everyone is corrupt. There is nothing worse than attempting to bribe someone who strongly disapproves of such immoral behaviour. This last point is clearly illustrated by Agpar,[47] who quotes the case of the managing director of a large multinational who offered 500 Saudi Riyals in cash to a Saudi police officer to ensure a favourable decision on a fairly minor offence against labour law. In a fury, the officer reported the attempted bribe to his superiors. After spending 20 days in prison, the businessman was fined 25,000 Riyals and was fortunate to escape a more serious penalty. Bribery, as with most gift exchange, follows a culturally coded etiquette that indicates who is willing to accept a bribe, where and when it can safely be given, and what to say and do when presenting the bribe to the recipient.[48] This case clearly demonstrates the danger and also the ineffectiveness of direct bribes. Accordingly, more indirect methods exist instead:

1. Slush funds are set up to effect small payments by cheque, nominally as payment for services rendered. Auditors have discovered systematically overstated expense reports where expense report copies are marked up an average of 1000 per cent from the actual expense.[49]

2. The transfer of what the English call 'brown paper packets' or 'plain brown envelopes' is often made by an intermediate consultancy company, which is involved right from the tender stage. These consultancy companies often have their head office in a tax haven, such as Luxembourg. For instance, a key decision maker may mention to the head of the negotiating team of a large engineering or construction company that it would be advantageous if his consultancy company were to carry out preliminary technical studies. These studies will in fact be largely fictitious. The fees paid for these studies will correspond to the commission. If these studies are further subcontracted to a nominee company in a tax haven, the *baksheesh* money will be transferred to a 'safe place'.

3. Nominee and local consultancy companies given 'phoney' consulting contracts may be used in different ways. For example, an adviser to the transport minister, who is well placed to influence the decision on an underground railway project, may be offered a part-time position in the Luxembourg-based nominee company. He will simply receive a salary each month which, for reasons of discretion and convenience, will be paid into an account in Switzerland. When he goes skiing with his family, he takes money out of his bank account in Geneva to spend it discreetly in an exclusive ski resort. Money spent abroad is less compromising than money brought back home.

4. Finally, two other accounting solutions can be employed, (a) over-invoicing of expenditure or receipts, and (b) the recording of fictitious transactions. For example, a foreign hospital supply company pays a 10 per cent commission to help obtain the contract for the construction of a hospital in Saudi Arabia. The artificially inflated price of the contract allows the 10 per cent commission to become tax-deductible expenditure, which looks legitimate despite being illegal.[50] Vogl (p. 30)[51] gives the example of a European supplier of pharmaceuticals negotiating with the minister of health of a developing country that has received emergency funds from an aid agency to purchase urgently reeded medicines: 'Instead of agreeing on the purchase of new drugs, the minister and the supplier conspire to use the aid funds to purchase out-of-date drugs which are far cheaper. The supplier consequently makes a handsome profit and

places a portion of it in an offshore bank account set up by the minister.'

14.7

Bribery: ethical aspects

Bribery is a key ethical issue in international marketing. More than one-third of a sample of US executives ranked bribery as the most serious of ten possible ethical problems that may arise in international marketing operations.[52] Similarly, Australian and Canadian managers rank gifts, favours and entertainment, traditional small-scale bribery, and the confusing issue of whether gifts are intended as bribes or not in different cultures, as the three key ethical problems in international marketing out of a list of ten.[53] Approximately, 45 per cent of multinational firms (which answered the question) report that they pay bribes to public officials.[54] More than 50 per cent of firms did not answer the question in the survey.

The first ethical position is that of cultural relativism: whether it is right or wrong, good or bad, depends on one's culture. This is based on the view that rules are applicable locally in the ingroup territory: when in Rome, do as the Romans do. In relativistic terms, words such as 'right' or 'wrong', 'good' or 'bad' only have a meaning within a specific cultural context. The first part of this section gives a view of cultural relativism in the case of Africa where corrupt money is largely, but not completely, redistributed in society. However, one cannot ignore the negative consequences. According to Chen and colleagues (p. 232),[54] 'corruption tends to hamper economic growth, increase income inequality, lowers investments, and reduces the level of many other economic derivers of growth (i.e., human capital, urbanization, financial depth, and foreign trade). As an example, the property of late President Mobutu Sese Seko of Zaire is said to have been equivalent to the whole of the external debt of the country.[55] A second ethical position is cultural universalism, which is based on the view that there are core ethical principles which are universally applicable, independent of territory and group membership. The US Foreign Corrupt Practices Act of 1977, revised in 1988, is an example of such a universalist approach

to ethics *and* rules. An alternative perspective is a pragmatic and respectful view of how ethical behaviour can be developed in a cross-cultural context.

Cultural relativism: the bribe as bonanza

There is a tendency to oversimplify the issue of international corruption to one of a face-to-face meeting between two people, a donor and a recipient. In reality the donor of the *baksheesh* often faces a group of recipients. An illegal payment rarely benefits one single person. As a result, bribery is intermingled with a dense network of social relationships. Bonds of fraternity and complicity develop between people of the same ethnic background or tribe. These people are necessary intermediaries to ensure that a *baksheesh* is effectively implemented. The bonds built on everyday cooperation call for redistribution of small parts of the bribe. For instance, the secretary who knows of the existence of the *baksheesh*, and the customs officer who intercepts a 'brown paper parcel', each take their share in proportion to their level of influence and power in the society (see Box 14.4).

Most of Kinshasa's residents, who were abandoned by the corrupt regime of Mobutu Sese Seko, live by roadside trading in order to feed their families. Article 15, a fictional clause in the constitution, was a general licence to do whatever you liked, or 'fend for yourself' and almost nothing was outside its ambit. A clean-up campaign spearheaded by Kinshasa governor Theophile Memba, has attempted to transform Zaire. Tom Boland[56] reports that small traders were alarmed by measures that would deny them their living: 'With Article 15 still at the back of their minds, many of the traders who have been moved on in recent weeks, have bounced back and reappeared in nearby spaces.' One senior Kinshasa banker says 'It's only when the state has provided an alternative space for trading that this kind of operation has proved successful.'

Bonds may also be forged by the possibility of retaliation. Those who have not requested a *baksheesh*, but who have a strong suspicion as to its existence, may either inform the authorities, demand their 'cut', or take no action. If they take the risk of participating in illegal remuneration they may benefit personally, or they may risk offending those in power, ultimately leading to punishment. If they inform

BOX 14.4

'Article 15'

On the banks of the large Zaire river just as in the province of Shaba, no one in Zaire is surprised to see a civil servant demanding a 'matabiche' in return for a passport or some other official document. On the contrary, people would be worried if such a request was not made. No Zairian would take offence at having to pay for an official hearing, or to have a letter sent to a department head. Seals and headed note paper are bought and are even sometimes forged. In Zaire, civil servants are 'resourceful people' and know how to supplement their income. The police set up roadblocks when they need money: drivers never have the requisite paper and are therefore obliged to put their hands in their pockets.

At the main post office in 'Kin' (Kinshasa, the capital), letters and parcels may – like anywhere else in the world – be posted in a box, but it is less than certain that they will ever arrive at their destination. The 'citizen' (in Zaire, the 'Supreme Guide' has brought into fashion this revolutionary title) greatly increases the chances of this occurring if he greases the palm of the postman. Likewise, a citizen may make a telephone call to the other end of the planet for the price of a tip. All this comes under 'Article 15', a shameful way of designating the small-scale corruption practised by civil servants. This corruption is institutionalized and widespread; it also goes under the name of 'matabiche': bribe, backhander, a 'little something', brown paper packet.

The practice is so ingrained that President Mobutu did not shy away from encouraging it in a speech on 20 May 1976: 'If you are going to steal, steal a small amount and do it intelligently, in a nice way. If you are going to steal so much that you become rich in a single night, you will be arrested.'

(Source: Excerpt from Péan, pp. 139–40.[58] *L'argent Noir*, P. Péan, © Librairie Arthème Fayard 1988, reproduced with permission.)

against the person who has accepted the bribe, they may also suffer adverse consequences.

Primitive hunter/gatherer societies, as described by ethnologists, can be used as an archetype for the redistribution of a bribe considered as plunder. While the men hunt (symbolically: those who hold power and go 'hunting' for large sums), the women, children and the elderly devote their efforts to gathering wild fruits and vegetables (symbolically: those who collaborate at a menial level, but who are still aware of what is happening). Ultimately the bribe/plunder is divided up according to fairly precise rules. Redistributing plunder and crops among the members of one's tribe is basic moral behaviour in many countries (see Box 14.5). However, the tendency to think that developing countries have 'lower' ethical standards should be resisted, even though the extent of bribery in some developing nations and evidence from research would suggest it. Many factors, including sellers' markets, high inflation, low wages and economic hardship explain questionable practices, although they do not excuse them. Very often, the bribery issue is not one of ethical standards, but a mere matter of survival. Arnould (p. 130)[57] gives the example of the consequences to West African traders who refuse to pay the bribes asked for by customs agents or policemen: 'A truck and its contents were burned at the border between Benin and Togo under mysterious circumstances when the driver working for one onion trader in Lomé refused to pay.'

Average citizens unfortunately get used to the behaviour of officials securing special privileges for themselves and their close friends. In Bulgaria a survey showed that 57 per cent of the population believed that politicians were primarily interested in taking advantage of their power position.[60] Economic power is intermingled with political influence, such as in the tradition known as *coronelismo* in Brazilian politics, which corresponds to the case of wealthy landowners who can bribe, manipulate and pressure the local electorate to vote for the candidates they choose. *Coronelismo* still flourishes in isolated and impoverished regions of the Brazilian countryside.[61]

It is sometimes difficult to distinguish between a gift and a bribe. Both obey the norms of reciprocity that are linked to the local context. As emphasized by Steidlmeier (p. 127),[62] 'phenomenologically, it is difficult to distinguish a bribe from a tip or a

BOX 14.5

A good minister in Senegal

For the man in the street, a good minister is a demagogue, someone who is adept at bypassing the law and its rulings to keep the voters from his region, his parents and his friends happy. If you try to behave like a minister acting objectively by treating your cousins, your allies, members of the branch of your party in the same way as all other citizens, even political opponents, the people will be totally confused. You will not be understood. You are not respecting the rules of the game. You will be the object of public contempt. You are not a minister for the purpose of serving the nation or carrying out the policies of a government which is in power for the good of all its citizens. You are first and fore-

most a minister for your own good, so that you may take advantage of your position, and enable your parents and allies, your friends and the members of your party to benefit too. No one will reproach you, everyone will understand. Those who are out of office are the only ones who will criticize this behaviour although if they were in office themselves they could not be sure of resisting the demands of their own tribe, family, or parents-in-law. There is nothing wrong in taking advantage of one's position to help out one's relatives; the ideal would be to consider all citizens as your own relatives.

(Source: Ndao, pp. 34–5.[59])

commission or consulting fee. In the end, moral judgment depends upon the social understanding of the meaning of the action as derived from the analysis of means and ends, consequences and intentions'.

Werner[48] also acknowledges the lack of clear boundary between gifts and bribes. She explains that in Kazakstan there are ten words for different types of gifts and ritual payments according to the context and the nature of the gift; for instance *kiit* and *minit* are gifts to in-laws, the first in the form of clothing, the second in livestock or money. However, the word for bribe, *para*, is used consistently to refer to illegal exchanges: 'a traffic policeman may extort a relatively small amount of money, the local equivalent of a few dollars, from an innocent driver. In a different context, a young man who needs a job might voluntarily pay a bribe of $500 to $1500 to a military official, who in return will forge a document specifying that the young man was exempt from military service for health reasons ($500) or a document specifying that the young man actually did complete military service ($1500)' (p. 18).[48]

The OECD convention on the fight against bribery

Since the US adopted the Foreign Corrupt Practices Act in 1977, they have been constantly fighting at the

international level to have such legislation adopted by the major industrialized countries.[63] Their efforts have been more successful since the implementation of the OECD Convention on Combating Bribery of Foreign Public Officials in International Business Transaction of 1997.[64] While all countries have laws against bribery, relatively few countries have laws against bribery abroad. This is important, as laws against bribery become more effective when they are coordinated across multiple countries.[64]

The convention was adopted on 21 November 1997. It is has now been ratified by the 36 signatory countries (the 30 OECD countries as well as six non-OECD countries). The OECD requires the implementation of legal, regulatory and policy measures to prevent, detect, investigate, prosecute, and sanction bribery of foreign public officials. It also requires countries to impose sanctions such as fines and imprisonment for bribery of foreign public officials. These sanctions apply to both individuals and companies that commit foreign bribery. The convention also requires that countries seize the bribe or property of similar value and any profits from the bribery.[65]

Website link 14.2

Search out information on bribery at the OECD website: **http://www.oecd.org/.**

The convention is not self-enforcing: countries have to modify their existing laws and enact new ones to comply with the provisions of the convention, which outlaws:[66]

1. kickbacks to obtain or retain government business;
2. the tax deductibility of bribes as business expenses;
3. off-the-books accounting practices;
4. loose public procurement procedures which facilitate bribes and collusion;
5. bribing through intermediaries, consultants and agents.

Most developed countries have now ratified the convention and modified their national legislation so as to make it locally enforceable. However, only some of the OECD countries have applied major sanctions against offenders. For instance, in 2006 the OECD recommended that Australia increase fines for foreign bribery to a maximum of A$300,000. In the same year, it recommended to Spain that liability and sanctions for companies engaging in foreign bribery and the prohibition of tax deductibility of foreign bribery be made explicit in the Spanish legal system.

Other efforts at combating bribery

The International Chamber of Commerce (ICC) has also been playing an active role by drafting a self-regulation code for companies. The ICC 'Rules of Conduct to Combat Extortion and Bribery' deal with ethical issues in international business negotiations such as payments to sales agents and other intermediaries, business entertainment and gifts, and political contributions. Contrary to the OECD convention, it covers bribery within the private sector as well as to public officials.[67]

At the corporate level, the formulation of global corporate ethics codes involves 95 per cent of CEOs and 78 per cent of company boards of directors.[67] Bribery is a topic covered by a vast majority (92 per cent) of the ethics code. Many of them provide concrete information about what a bribe is and how to deal with it. Some, not all, target compliance by providing managers involved in foreign operations with precise procedures and guidelines. In relative terms, corruption tends to deter investors from negotiating foreign direct investment in countries with high levels of corruption.[68]

There are basically two sides in bribery: that of donors, which are principally concerned with the conventions and codes previously described, and that of the recipient countries, which are less directly concerned. Corruption in international deals will not cease by the simple virtue of donors becoming suddenly honest and drying up the supply of bribes. In most potential recipient countries no strong anti-bribery code exists or, if there is one, it is not actually enforced.

The level of corruption of particular countries can be measured, based on composite indicators of perception of corruption. They are published on a yearly basis by Transparency International, an NGO considered to be the most influential global anti-corruption organization.[69] Data are based on mean scores of seven to nine surveys per country, rarely fewer. Highest scores correspond to the lowest levels of corruption. Some of the countries with lower levels of corruption based on the 2011 index are as follows:[69]

9.5 New Zealand
9.4 Denmark
9.3 Sweden
9.2 Singapore
9.0 Norway

Many developing countries and some Eastern European countries are plagued by higher levels of corruption according to the 2007 index, including:[69]

1.9 Burundi, Equatorial Guinea, Venezuela
1.8 Haiti, Iraq
1.6 Sudan, Turkmenistan, Uzbekistan
1.5 Afganistan, Myanmar
1.0 Morth Korea, Somalia

Website link 14.3

Search for more information on the 2011 corruption perceptions index on the following website: http://cpi.transparency.org/cpi2011.

A number of countries where corruption is endemic show increased severity against offenders. China, for instance, is enforcing bribery sanctions, going as far as the execution of senior officials, such as the Vice Governor of Southern Jiangxi province who was convicted of having accumulated about US$850,000 in bribes.[70] Similarly, a top banker was sentenced to 15 years' imprisonment on bribery charges in 2002. He had been found to have taken about US$500,000 in bribes from 1997 to 1999 when he was chairman of the group that controls one of China's largest banks.[71]

Comparison of ethical attitudes across industrial nations

Ethical attitudes within the major developed countries towards illegal payments are not uniform.[72] Until recently, in France, Germany and Switzerland bribery was simply seen as a cost of doing business abroad and could be claimed as a corporate tax deduction. US managers tend to adopt stronger ethical standpoints than their European and Japanese counterparts. Becker and Fritzsche[73] suggested a scenario that posed a business ethics problem linked to an illegal payment. Three sample groups of businessmen were interviewed, from the US (124 respondents), West Germany (70 respondents) and France (72 respondents). The scenario was as follows (p. 89):

The Rollfast Bicycle company has been barred from entering the market in a large Asian country by collusive efforts of the local bicycle manufacturers. Rollfast could expect to net 5 million dollars per year from sales if it could penetrate the market. Last week a business man from the country contacted the management of Rollfast and stated that he could smooth the way for the company to sell in his country for a price of US$500,000. If you were responsible, what are the chances that you would pay the price?[73]

The Americans were less likely to pay the secret payment than the French or Germans. Nearly 50 per cent of the Americans explained that it was unethical, illegal and contrary to the corporate code of conduct, whereas the Germans and French were more likely to make statements about competition forcing acceptance and 'it's simply the price you have to pay for doing business'.

France and West Germany have legislation prohibiting the bribing of public civil servants, but these regulations do not apply extraterritorially. French and German businessmen cannot be prosecuted for bribes effected outside their national territory. Conversely, the FCPA as well as numerous other American regulations (antitrust, fiscal, and so on) do have extraterritorial application.

A pragmatic and respectful view of ethical behaviour in a cross-cultural context

As noted by Berenbeim (p. 26), host country conditions have to be taken into account:

You cannot say to a country manager, 'Don't do this, don't do that, now here are your goals for country X where all of your competitors do this and that. I don't want to hear any excuses if these objectives are not met.' Under those circumstances, either rules will have to be broken or ambitious goals will not be achieved. The way to avoid this kind of impossible situation is to build a consensus among practitioners for enforceable rules . . . The example of the FCPA is a case in point. Although it would be more satisfying to punish the person who demands the bribe than the company that pays it, obtaining legal prohibitions in the major industrial countries and targeting the companies that bribe rather than the local citizens who demand payment is likely to have greater impact.[74]

The first consideration is pragmatic: businesspeople who make illegal payments take (real) personal risks for (potential) organizational benefits, either through company loyalty or personal interest (sales commission or promotion). Doing this, they (1) involve their company in the risk of being involved in a scandal; and (2) themselves risk being implicated, indicted, and ultimately imprisoned.

The payment of a *baksheesh* always involves the individual responsibility of the donor, even if his or her company, or the consortium that he or she represents, also risks being drawn into the scandal. As Graham (p. 94)[75] states: 'From a legal standpoint, the recommendation is clear – avoid questionable deals. The loss of the few "questionable" contracts is not worth the risk of indictment, prosecution, conviction . . . Moreover, if you are indicted, will your company support you or opt to plead guilty and accept the fine?' A pragmatic view for an individual requires reference to a personal norm, not a corporate one.

Useful guidelines for those confronted with this issue are provided by the definition of a 'moral personality' proposed by John Rawls in his *A Theory of*

Justice.[76] A moral personality is characterized by the capacity to conceive good and the capacity to develop a sense of justice. The first is realized through a rational project for one's life. The second implies a continuing desire to act in a just manner. Thus, for Rawls, a moral personality has chosen their own goals; and prefers conditions that enable full expression of their nature as rational, free and equal. The unity of the person is based on a higher-order aspiration to follow the principles of rational choice in a manner that suits their sense of justice. If asked to do something that violates your sense of right and wrong, it is better not to do it, even if it means not behaving as a Roman in Rome. However, Rawls' definition of a 'moral personality' remains a rather Western one, in that it emphasizes rationality,

individualism and the sense of equality with others. In many other cultural contexts, where moral personalities actually exist, these traits would not be emphasized in such a definition.

The final word may be given by Adam Smith, who describes some key aspects of the 'character of virtue' in the following terms (p. 214):

The prudent man is always sincere, and feels horror at the very thought of exposing himself to the disgrace which attends upon the detection of falsehood. But though always sincere, he is not always frank and open; and though he never tells any thing but the truth, he does not always think himself bound, when not properly called upon, to tell the whole truth. As he is cautious in his actions, so he is reserved in his speech; and never rashly or unnecessarily obtrudes his opinion concerning either things or persons.[77]

Questions

1. Indicate elements of variation in selling styles (including basic views of what is a buyer–seller interaction, the kind of arguments developed and the communication style).

2. Personal selling often plays a more important role in foreign than in domestic markets. Why?

3. Discuss the limitations to the standardization of a sales-force stimulation system.

4. Discuss how a strong emphasis on group belonging in a particular culture may influence the recruitment of salespeople.

5. Discuss the cultural relativity of the following statements about salespersons (excerpt from Hill *et al.*, pp. 68–9[78]):
   ■ Our salespersons are very achievement oriented.
   ■ Salespersons need patience to be successful.
   ■ Our salespersons consider the source of income, whether salary or commission, to be more important than the size of income.
   ■ Our sellers should have definite call schedules and planned routes.
   ■ Our salespersons are very time oriented.
   ■ Our salespersons need a lot of supervision.
   ■ Selling is a prestigious job in the country.
   ■ Salespersons are regarded as future managers.
   ■ A salesperson's social class can limit his/her contacts and effectiveness.
   ■ Family connections often help salespersons in their work.
   ■ A salesperson's religious beliefs can limit his/her contacts and effectiveness.

6. What is the borderline between a 'gift' and a 'bribe'? Outline possible criteria for defining such a border which allow for some cross-national flexibility.

7. How can bribery be related to space-related cultural assumptions?

8. WTD, a large US multinational chemical company, has recently been attacked in several large Latin American countries where it has plants. The company has been attacked by the local press for alleged pollution and poor safety conditions for employees. It has been argued that WTD has much lower standards in these areas than in the USA and that the company shows its Yankee and imperialist orientation in such choices. The company executive officers think these criticisms are largely wrong: inadequate local legislation and poor respect of safety rules by local employees have caused problems rather than a deliberate neglect on WTD's part. Advise the firm on a public relations programme.

9. Discuss the cultural relativity of the framework for a manager facing an ethical dilemma, who should ask the following questions:
   - What are the **facts**; what are my alternatives?
   - What parties will be affected?
   - What do **I** owe to each of these parties?
   - What would produce the greatest **benefits** for **all** parties?
   - What **rights** does each party have, and how can these rights best be **respected**?
   - Are all parties treated **fairly** and **justly**?
   - On balance, what is the most **ethical** alternative?
   - How do **I** best **implement** this alternative?

   The words in bold are those which offer the best route for questioning about the cultural relativity of this framework.

References

1. Vargo, Stephen L. and Robert F. Lusch (2008), 'From Goods to Service(S): Divergences and Convergences of Logics', *Industrial Marketing Management*, 37 (3), 254–59.
2. Vargo, Stephen L. and Robert F. Lusch (2004), 'Evolving to a New Dominant Logic for Marketing', *Journal of Marketing*, 68 (1), 1–17.
3. Sheth, Jagdish N. and Arun Sharma (2008), 'The Impact of the Product to Service Shift in Industrial Markets and the Evolution of the Sales Organization', *Industrial Marketing Management*, 37 (3), 260–69.
4. Boujena, Othman, Wesley J. Johnston and Dwight R. Merunka (2009), 'The Benefits of Sales Force Automation: A Customer's Perspective', *Journal of Personal Selling & Sales Management*, 29 (2), 137–50.
5. Hulnick G. (2000), 'Doing Business Virtually', *Communication World*, 17 (3), 33–6.
6. Spiegelman, Paul (2000), 'Live Customer Interaction and the Internet Join in "Internation"', *Direct Marketing*, 63 (4), 38–41.
7. Sheth, Jagdish N. and Atul Parvatiyar (2002), 'Evolving Relationship Marketing into a Discipline', *Journal of Relationship Marketing*, 1 (1), 16–94.
8. Kalaignanam, Kartik and Rajan Varadarajan (2011), 'Offshore Outsourcing of Consumer Relationship Management: Conceptual Model and Propositions', *Journal of the Academy of Marketing Science*.
9. Kumar, V., Sarang Sunder and B. Ramaseshan (2011), 'Analyzing the Diffusion of Global Customer Relationship Management: A Cross-Regional Modeling Framework', *Journal of International Marketing*, 19 (1), 23–39.
10. Day, George S. (1994), 'Continuous Learning About Markets', *California Management Review*, 36 (4), 9–31.
11. Chan, Haksin and Lisa C. Wan (2008), 'Consumer Responses to Service Failures: A Resource Preference Model of Cultural Influences', *Journal of International Marketing*, 16 (1), 72–97.
12. Liu, Raymond R. and Peter McClure (2001), 'Recognizing Cross-Cultural Differences in Consumer Complaint Behavior and Intentions: An Empirical Examination', *The Journal of Consumer Marketing*, 18 (1), 54–75.
13. Ngai, Eric W. T., Vincent C. S. Heung, Y. H. Wong and Fanny K. Y. Chan (2007), 'Consumer Complaint Behaviour of Asians and Non-Asians About Hotel Services an Empirical Analysis', *European Journal of Marketing*, 41 (11/12), 1375–91.
14. Hui, Michael K. and Kevin Au (2001), 'Justice Perceptions of Complaint Handling: A Cross-Cultural

Comparison between PRC and Canadian Customers', *Journal of Business Research*, 52, 161–73.

15. Garbarino, Ellen and Mark S. Johnson (1999), 'The Different Roles of Satisfaction, Trust and Commitment in Customer Relationships', *Journal of Marketing*, 63 (2), 70–87.

16. Kumar, Nirmalya, Lisa K. Scheer and Jan-Benedict E.M. Steenkamp (1995), 'The Effects of Perceived Interdependence on Dealer Attitudes', *Journal of Marketing Research*, 32 (3), 348–56.14.

17. Wang, Cheng Lu (2007), 'Guanxi vs. Relationship Marketing: Exploring Underlying Differences', *Industrial Marketing Management*, 36 (1), 81–86.

18. Tung, Rosalie (1996), 'Negotiating with East Asians', in *International Business Negotiations*, P. N. Ghauri and J-C. Usunier (eds). Oxford: Pergamon/Elsevier.

19. Tsalikis, John, Marta Ortiz-Buonafina and Michael S. Latour (1992), 'The Role of Accent on the Credibility and Effectiveness of the International Business Person: The Case of Guatemala', *International Marketing Review*, 9 (4), 57–72.

20. Thorelli, Hans B. (1986), 'Networks: Between Markets and Hierarchies', *Strategic Management Journal* 7, 37–51.

21. Ford, David (1990), *Understanding Business Markets*. London: Academic Press.

22. Johansson, Jan and Lars-Gunnar Mattsson (1988), 'Internationalization in Industrial Systems – a Network Approach', in *Strategies in Global Competition*, N. Hood and J. E. Vahlne (eds). New York: Croom Helm.

23. Mavondo, Felix T. and Elaine Rodrigo (2001), 'The Effect of Relationship Dimensions on Interpersonal and Interorganizational Commitment in Organizations Conducting Business between Australia and China', *Journal of Business Research*, 52 (2), 111–21.

24. Luo, Yadong (1995), 'Business Strategy, Market Structure, and Performance of IJV', *Management International Review*, 35 (3), 249–64.

25. Luo, Yadong (1997), 'Guanxi and Performance of Foreign-Invested Enterprises in China', *Management International Review*, 37 (1), 51–70.

26. Luo, Yadong and Min Chen (1997), 'Does Guanxi Influence Firm Performance?', *Asia Pacific Journal of Management*, 14, 1–16.

27. Hutchings, Kate and Georgina Murray (2002), 'Working with Guanxi: An Assessment of the Implications of Globalization on Business Networking in China', *Creativity and Innovation Management*, 11 (3), 184–90.

28. Salopek, Jennifer J. (2009), 'The Power of the Pyramid', *Training & Development*, 63 (May) 70–75.

29. Ang, Swee Hoon (2000), 'The Power of Money: A Crosscultural Analysis of Business-Related Beliefs', *Journal of World Business*, 35 (1), 43–60.

30. Adcock, Dennis, Ray Bradfield, Al Halborg and Caroline Ross (1993), *Marketing: Principles and Practice*. London: Pitman.

31. Cateora, Philip R. (1993), *International Marketing* (8th edn). Burr Ridge, IL: Richard D. Irwin.

32. Graham, John L. (1981), 'A Hidden Cause of America's Trade Deficit with Japan', *Columbia Journal of World Business* (Fall), 5–15.

33. Ali, Abbas and Paul M. Schwiercz (1985), 'The Relationship between Managerial Decision Styles and Work Satisfaction in Saudi Arabia', in *International Business in the Middle East*, Erdener Kaynak (ed.). New York: De Gruyter.

34. Honeycutt, Earl D. Jr. and John B. Ford, 'Guidelines for Managing an International Sales Force', *Industrial Marketing Management*, 24 (2), 135–44.

35. Hofstede, Geert (2001), *Culture Consequences* (2nd edn). Thousand Oaks, CA: Sage Publications.

36. Hall, Edward T. (1976), *Beyond Culture*. New York: Doubleday.

37. Kotabe, Masaaki, Alan J. Dubinsky and Chae Un Lim (1992), 'Perceptions of Organizational Fairness: A Cross-National Perspective', *International Marketing Review*, 9 (2), 41–58.

38. Still, Richard R. (1981), 'Cross-Cultural Aspects of Sales Force Management', *Journal of Personal Selling and Sales Force Management*, 1 (2), 6–9. 37.

39. Hill, John S., Richard R. Still and Ünal O. Boya (1991), 'Managing the Multinational Sales Force', *International Marketing Review*, 8 (1), 19–31.

40. Money, R. Bruce and John L. Graham (1999), 'Salesperson Performances, Pay, and Job Satisfaction: Tests of a Model Using Data Collected in the United States and Japan', *Journal of International Business Studies*, 30 (1), 149–72.

41. Hanna, Nessim and Tanuja Srivastava (1998), 'Modeling the Motivational Antecedents of the Japanese Sales Force: How Relevant Are Western Models', *Journal of Global Marketing*, 11 (4), 49–74.

42. Segalla, Michael, Dominique Rouzies, Madeleine Besson and Barton A. Weitz (2006), 'A Cross-National Investigation of Incentive Sales Compensation', *International Journal of Research in Marketing*, 23 (4), 419–33.

43. Chonko, Lawrence B., Ben M. Enis and John F. Tanner (1992), *Managing Sales People*. Boston, MA: Allyn and Bacon.

44. Holt, Douglas, John Quelch and Earl Taylor (2004), 'How Global Brands Compete', *Harvard Business Review*, 82 (9), 68–75.

45. Treece, James B. and Yuzo Yamaguchi (2004), 'Mitsubishi's Japan Sales Collapse in May', *Automotive News*, 78 (6098), 44.

46. Sethi, S. Prakash (1979), 'A Conceptual Framework for Environmental Analysis of Social Issues and Evaluation of Business Response Patterns', *The Academy of Management Review*, 4 (1), 63–74.

47. Agpar, M. (1977), 'Succeeding in Saudi Arabia', *Harvard Business Review* (January/February), 14–33.

48. Werner, Cynthia (2000), 'Gifts, Bribes, and Development in Post-Soviet Kazakstan', *Human Organization*, 59 (1, Spring), 11–22.

49. Thompson, Courtenay (2002), 'Below the Surface', *Internal Auditor*, 67–9.

50. Daniels, John D., Ernest W. Ogram and Lee H. Radebaugh (1982), *International Business: Environments and Operations* (3rd edn). Reading, MA: Addison-Wesley.

51. Vogl, Frank (1998), 'The Supply Side of Global Bribery', *Finance and Development*, 35 (2), 30–33.

52. Mayo, Michel A., Lawrence J. Marks and John K. Ryans Jr (1991), 'Perceptions of Ethical Problems in International Marketing', *International Marketing Review*, 8 (3), 61–75.

53. Chan, T. S. and Robert W. Armstrong (1999), 'Comparative Ethical Report Card: A Study of Australian and Canadian Manager's Perception of International Marketing Ethics Problems', *Journal of Business Ethics*, 12, 3–15.

54. Chen, Yanjing, Mahmut Yaçar and Roderick M. Rejesus (2008), 'Factors Influencing the Incidence of Bribery Payouts by Firms: A Cross-Country Analysis', *Journal of Business Ethics*, 77 (2), 231–44.

55. Galtung, Frederick (1994), *Korruption*. Lamuv Verlag: Göttingen.

56. Boland, Tom (1998), 'Street Vendors: Congo War on Kinshasa's Informal Sector Fwd', *CNN*, available at http://hpn.asu.edu/archives/Jun98/0081.html.

57. Arnould, Eric J. (1995), 'West African Marketing Channels', in *Contemporary Marketing and Consumer Behavior*, John F. Sherry (ed.). Sage Publications: Thousand Oaks, CA.

58. Péan, Pierre (1988), *L'argent Noir*. Paris: Librairie Arthème Fayard.

59. Ndao, Cheikh Alioune (1985), *Excellences, Vos Épouses!* Dakar: Les Nouvelles Editions Africaines.

60. CIPE (1998), 'Corruption in Bulgaria Threatens Social Stability', *Economic Reform Today* (2), 18.

61. Gallant, Katheryn (1997), 'The Art of Stealing', *Brazzil* (online).

62. Steidlmeier, P. (1999), 'Gift-Giving, Bribery and Corruption: Ethical Management of Business Relationships in China', *Journal of Business Ethics*, 20, 121–32.

63. Lewis, Eleanor Roberts (1998), 'The OECD Anti-Corruption Treaty: Why Is It Needed? How Will It Work?', *Economic Perspectives*, 3 (5), 6–9.

64. Cuervo-Cazurra, Alvaro (2008), 'The Effectiveness of Laws against Bribery Abroad', *Journal of International Business Studies*, 39 (4), 634–51.

65. Organization for Economic Co-Operation and Development (OECD) (2006), *OECD Working Group on Bribery: Annual Report*.

66. Hamra, Wayne (2000), 'Bribery in International Business Transactions and the OECD Convention: Benefits and Limitations', *Business Economics* (October), 33–46.

67. Brademas, John and Fritz Heimann (1998), 'Tackling International Corruption: No Longer Taboo', *Foreign Affairs*, 77 (5), 17–22.

68. Habib, Mohsin and Leon Zurawicki (2002), 'Corruption and Foreign Direct Investment', *Journal of International Business Studies*, 33 (2), 291–307.

69. Transparency International (TI) (2010), *Transparency International Corruption Perceptions Index 2010*. Available at: www.transparency.org.

70. ABC News (2002), 'Acting Tough as Part of Anti-corruption Stand, China Executes Official'. Available at: http://abcnews.go.com/sections/world/DailyNews/chinaexecute000308.html.

71. Xinhua News Agency (2002), 'Top Banker Sentenced on Bribery Charges (China through a lens)'. Available at: www.china.org.cn/english/2002/Oct/45463.htm.

72. Lee, K. H. (1981), 'Ethical Beliefs in Marketing Management: A Cross-Cultural Study', *European Journal of Marketing*, 15 (1), 58–67.

73. Becker, Helmut and David H. Fritzsche (1987), 'A Comparison of the Ethical Behavior of American, French and German Managers', *Columbia Journal of World Business* (Winter), 87–95.

74. Berenbeim, Ronald E. (1997), 'Can Multinational Business Agree on How to Act Ethically?', *Business and Society Review*, 98, 24–8.

75. Graham, John L. (1983), 'Foreign Corrupt Practices Act: A Manager's Guide', *Columbia Journal of World Business*, 18 (3), 89–94.

76. Rawls, John (1971), *A Theory of Justice*. Cambridge, MA: Belknap Press of Harvard University.

77. Smith, Adam (1759), *The Theory of Moral Sentiments*. London: A. Millar.

Appendix 14

Teaching materials

 A14.1 Case

When international buyers and sellers disagree

No matter what line of business you're in, you can't escape sex. That may have been one conclusion drawn by an American exporter of meat products after a dispute with a German customer over a shipment of pork livers. Here's how the disagreement came about:

The American exporter was contracted to ship '30,000 lb of freshly frozen US pork livers, customary merchandisable quality, first rate brands'. As the shipment that was prepared met the exacting standards of the American market, the exporter expected the transaction to be completed without any problem. But when the livers arrived in Germany, the purchaser raised an objection: 'We ordered pork livers of customary merchantable quality – what you sent us consisted of 40 per cent sow livers.'

'Who cares about the sex of the pig the liver came from?' the exporter asked.

'We do', the German replied. 'Here in Germany we don't pass off spongy sow livers as the firmer livers of male pigs. This shipment wasn't merchantable at the price we expected to charge. The only way we were able to dispose of the meat without a total loss was to reduce the price. You owe us a price allowance of US$1000.'

The American refused to reduce the price. The determined resistance may have been partly in reaction to the implied insult to the taste of the American consumer: 'If pork livers, whatever the sex of the animal, are palatable to Americans, they ought to be good enough for anyone', the American thought.

It looked as if the buyer and seller could never agree on eating habits.

(Source: Dun and Bradstreet Corporation.)

Questions

1. What does 'customary merchandisable quality' mean? Where? In which language and cultural context?

2. Discuss how ethnocentrism and SRC (self-reference criterion) are at work in this case.

3. In this dispute, which country's law would apply, that of the United States or of Germany?

4. If the case were tried in US courts, who do you think would win? And if tried in German courts? Why?

5. Is formal litigation justified in such a case? How can one solve this problem? How can one avoid this type of conflict in the future?

A14.2 Case

Setco of Spain

Planning sales targets for the sales force is a universal practice. Nobody questions it. So it was when Mr Gonzales, a Spaniard, was recruited by Setco of Spain, the Spanish subsidiary of a large US multinational company. Soon after his job began, he was assigned a product line, of which he had some experience, in a new sales territory. The sales manager of Setco of Spain did not know precisely the market potential of this new area. Until then, potential customers in this area had never been regularly visited. Moreover few indicators were available in order to estimate the market potential of this new area in a quantified and precise manner.

When he first met the sales manager for Spain, Gonzales was amazed by his friendly tone; dialogue within the sales team and horizontal communication were the rule. Instead of being set an objective, he was invited to give his opinion on the matter. In fact, he could set his quarterly sales target himself, after visiting the area and making some preliminary contacts with prospects. Because of the newness of this area, the sales manager made no comment. Gonzales was confronted with a new freedom: in his previous positions as sales representative, he had never fixed his own sales targets by himself. He had always been given targets by his boss. His reaction was therefore to reduce significantly the objective relative to the sales he was reasonably expecting, in order to retain some leeway.

After four months, actual sales per area were released. Gonzales was used to this kind of report, since it provided basic data for computing possible bonuses. However, he was surprised to see that his actual sales figures were compared to target sales, and the difference between actual and target sales was explicitly presented. It looked flattering. The individual achievements of the other members of the sales team were mentioned in this memo as well. They did not match that of Gonzales.

At the meeting of the sales force, quarterly sales were examined, as well as the targets for the next quarter and the marketing programme. Gonzales was surprised to see how embarrassing his 'performance' appeared to the other sales representatives. Never had any sales representative at Setco of Spain so largely overshot the mark. He was teased by his colleagues, who made some bittersweet remarks and jokes. He felt bad about it, especially because he had been trying hard. He had used all his skills as a salesman, which were considerable and had been proved in his previous positions.

During the discussions, he acknowledged that his area's market potential had been largely underestimated. His sales target was therefore revised and increased by a large amount. This was done in full agreement with all the members (including him) of the sales team, who democratically discussed targets and achievements together during the quarterly sales meetings.

In the companies for which he had worked before, sales objectives were settled in a somewhat hierarchic way. The objectives were, fortunately, too high to be achieved. Being out of reach, the objectives worked as a sort of line of sight, an ideal level. It worked as a way of forcing lazy people to do more and of motivating the achievers to surpass themselves. Logically enough, actual sales were not carefully monitored, nor were individual achievements calculated by comparisons of target sales and actual sales.

At the end of the third quarter Gonzales began to think that he had been set too high an objective. He had been working extremely hard for almost six months, pushed by enthusiasm for his new job. Moreover an unusually large order from a company in his sales area had swollen his first quarterly sales. This did not happen during the second and third quarters.

When the quarterly sales meeting took place, Gonzales once again appeared as the 'star' of the meeting: he had a record shortfall. No sales representative at Setco of Spain had ever experienced such a wide negative gap between target and actual sales. His colleagues made fun of him. They were slightly relieved to see him bite the dust. Some days later he received a personal memo from the marketing director, who made it clear that he had to adapt quickly or leave the company. 'You should know that in our company a salesman has to be able to settle his own objectives in a precise, realistic and dynamic way. Targets are the result of negotiations with the sales manager: they are based on market data. Individual sales targets are summed up, at every level in the corporation. They are the basis for the quarterly corporate sales figure forecast. The stocks of our company are registered on the New York Stock Exchange. Operators on the Stock Exchange are extremely sensitive to this kind of data. If every salesman in this company performed like you, our forecasts at the corporate level would be meaningless. Our headquarters simply cannot accept this.'

Question

What should Gonzales do?

A14.3 Case

Union Carbide at Bhopal

In 2011, 27 years after the Bhopal chemical disaster, the case is still pending between Dow Chemicals, the new owner of Union Carbide Corporation (UCC) since 2001.[1] A class action of Bhopali victims was introduced in New York in 1999 and another in 2007, which is still pending. A magistrate in Bhopal issued an arrest warrant for Warren Anderson (the CEO of UCC) on 31 July 2009, 25 years after the Bhopal disaster. However, the United States refused to extradite him, arguing that evidence was missing. UCC official declarations argue that, in 1984, the factory was owned, managed and operated by employees of Union Carbide India Limited, its local subsidiary, not by the parent company. Eight former senior employees of the subsidiary were found guilty on June 7, 2010.

In the 1970s, Union Carbide Corporation (UCC), one of America's largest chemical multinationals, had established production facilities in India. Its Indian subsidiary, Union Carbide India Limited (UCIL), under pressure from the Indian authorities, had built a new factory in 1978 to produce pesticides in Bhopal, the capital of Madhya Pradesh, a town situated 375 miles (600 km) south of New Delhi. It produced Sevin, a pesticide composed primarily of methyl isocyanate, extremely dangerous for humans and to be carefully kept in liquid form below 25 degrees Celsius. The project was plagued by problems of safety from the outset: in 1978, its year of construction, a huge fire broke out. Five major gas leaks in 1981

---

[1] For a detailed account of the Bhopal disaster chronology, see **http://www.bhopal.com/chronology** (a Union Carbide website with factual information, retrieved 10 May 2011); for an opposing view, see the Greenpeace website (retrieved 10 May 2011) at **http://www.greenpeace.org/usa/en/campaigns/toxics/justice-for-bhopal/**.

and 1983 left one dead and 47 injured. In 1982 a detailed inspection by American experts uncovered ten serious faults in the factory's safety systems. In fact, the factory's alarm system was ringing so often that people living in the vicinity of the factory treated it almost as background noise.

The Indian government imposed restrictions on foreign companies, limiting their direct participation by requiring that they negotiate local partnerships. UCC was able to continue operating in India only by agreeing to the formation of a new company, Union Carbide India Limited (UCIL), in which UCC was reduced to a majority shareholder with 50.09 per cent of the share capital. A further 22 per cent went to the government and the remainder was divided amongst 23,500 private Indian investors. Bhopal's social and political environment developed rapidly as a result of the factory. Attracted by the availability of work and the water and electricity which were supplied to the site at reduced rates, people poured into the surrounding area. As a consequence, the population grew from 385,000 in 1971 to 671,000 in 1981. By 1984 it stood at nearly 800,000. From its original position of isolation, the factory was soon totally enveloped by the town's growth. Creaking under the strain of this huge influx of population, the town struggled to accommodate everyone. In the absence of a better alternative, the poorest of the new arrivals congregated in 'Khasi Camp', a shantytown situated between the centre of Bhopal and the factory.

Links between UCIL and the local Indian political establishment were mutually rewarding in many ways. The factory's legal adviser, for instance, was a former local head of Indira Gandhi's Congress Party. The former local police chief magically won the contract to guard the factory. One of the nephews of the former state education minister was the head of public relations at the factory.

There were also financial difficulties. In 1982, a slump in sales of its products resulted in the factory suffering a dramatic reduction in profitability. UCC, the parent company of UCIL, even considered shutting the plant down completely, but the Indian government refused to countenance such a possibility for fear of frightening away potential foreign investors. To balance the books, UCIL determined to reduce the factory's overheads. They chose to make many of their most qualified personnel redundant. These vacant posts were then either filled by less experienced personnel or simply scrapped. The consequent loss of morale and expertise amongst the workforce affected work at the factory adversely. News of these unfortunate mishaps was carefully suppressed, thanks to the close working relationship between UCIL and the local authorities. The Indian authorities even extended UCIL's operating licence for a further seven years despite objections from the press and opposition members in the state parliament.

The incident took place in the night of 2 December 1984. Water in substantial quantities was mixed by error with methylisocyanate, causing high pressure, the explosion of the vessel and massive leaks of lethal gas in the surroundings of the factory. The local population had no idea of what to do in the event of a serious incident at the factory: simply putting a wet cloth on the face would have protected a great many people. Even the local doctors were completely ignorant about the effects of the product being manufactured on their doorsteps. Warren Anderson, the chief executive officer of UCC, courageously decided to go to India.

Following the disaster, the state government of Madhya Pradesh carefully drew up an initial list of the human cost of this night of horror. The toll was a heavy one: they estimated that 3828 people had been killed and 358,712 injured. Of these, 22,955 were left with a permanent disability. A single night of tragedy in Bhopal had claimed 362,540 victims. Ten years later the government believed that about 6600 people were killed in the incident. Bhopal pressure groups put the death toll at 16,000 and still rising by a few each week. They claimed that up to 600,000 people – more than half the city – suffered damage to their lungs, eyes and immune systems.

On 4 December 1984, Warren Anderson flew to Bhopal with a team of experts to try and discover the cause of the tragedy. His efforts were in vain. Anderson was arrested and imprisoned, then finally expelled. It was not until 20 December that the Indian authorities allowed a commission of inquiry to begin its work on site. They arrived to find that the factory had been closed since 6 December and was already being dismantled.

Public relations in such a context were extremely difficult to organize, since most 'hard facts' arguments might have seemed insults to the Indian management, public authorities, doctors or even to the general Indian public. The solution was found in complex litigation: each party argued that the case should be heard in the jurisdiction of the other. Finally, UCC came out with the favourable decision that the final judgements be made in India where relevant jurisprudence was almost non-existent. On 14 February 1989, the Indian Supreme Court rendered its judgement: the American defendants were found liable and ordered to pay a total of US$470 million, US$50 million was to be paid in rupees by UCIL and US$415 million by UCC; the remaining US$5 million had been paid under the previous order of the American Federal Court as first aid to the victims. Many people considered that the final award was rather low. For example, if this sum represented only those killed in the incident, it would be roughly equivalent to US$130,000 per victim. If it included those permanently disabled, the amount would represent only US$18,000 per person and if it was intended to compensate every injured person, it would represent an average of US$1350 per person.

Its reputation heavily tarnished by the Bhopal affair, UCC realized in 1986 that a great deal of time and effort would be needed to regain lost confidence. During a speech delivered to the Davos Economic Forum on 5 February 1991, the new Chief Executive Officer of UCC, Robert Kennedy, affirmed 'Care for the planet has become a critical business issue – central to our jobs as senior managers'. UCC prioritized respect for the environment and safety concerns and established a health, safety and environment committee staffed by independent outsiders and an executive vice-president was given specific responsibility for environmental issues. The global performance of UCC in tackling pollution and improving safety and respect for the environment is regularly checked by independent experts. The company has drawn up a strategic environmental plan with specific verifiable goals.

In 1994, Union Carbide sold its entire stake in UCIL to Eveready Industries India Limited and the money was used to build Bhopal hospital. Since 1998 the Madhya Pradesh State Government has taken over the facility and assumed all accountability for the site. This does not prevent further litigation from still occuring in 2011 between Bhopal victims and UCC despite the opinion of US courts that the case is now over after years of litigation in both India and the United States.

Questions

1. What are the problems involved in facing social responsibility in a culturally alien context?

2. Was Warren Anderson's trip to Bhopal a 'good' decision? Why? On the basis of which behavioural standards, home or host country's, should a company react?

3. How would you describe Union Carbide's corporate responsibility in the Bhophal case?

A14.4 Case

The *Brenzy nouveau* has arrived!

Legritte Company was founded just after the Second World War by a skilful engineer, Monsieur Legritte. Aided by the reconstruction boom which was followed by the rapid economic growth of the 1960s, the Legritte Company developed more by improving the quality of its products than by investing money in marketing and sales. The intrinsic quality of the products, namely electrical connections for industrial use, has been the strong point of the business from the very beginning.

The company is located near Lyons (France) and employs about 200 people, with an annual turnover of 80 million francs. Two years ago Legritte was taken over by a US-based multinational company, Brenzy. Monsieur Legritte, drawing near to retirement age and with no qualified successor, sold his property to the Brenzy Corporation, which now owns the full 100 per cent. Brenzy has progressively introduced more up-to-date management methods in this traditional family business. Inventory management, cost accounting and delivery systems have all been changed to fit with Brenzy's procedures.

Sales promotion in France, and Europe generally, is based on nicely printed catalogues, technical instructions and directions for use. Unit prices reduce according to the size of orders. Products are promoted through small gifts given to the purchasers. Thus, the launch of a new pre-insulated line of products, recently certified by EDF (Electricité de France, the public utility for electricity), came with a free gift (electrical pliers) for any order higher than 10,000 francs. This offer was open for six months. In order to receive the gift, the buyer simply had to fill in the gift voucher and enclose it with the order, provided the amount was sufficient.

Brenzy-Legritte was a newcomer to advertising. Being a fairly traditional medium-sized industrial company, it had not up to now invested a lot of money in advertisements. When it decided for the first time to advertise its products it did so by promoting them along with what it called '*le Brenzy nouveau*', with a play on words between Brenzy and Beaujolais, a freshly harvested red wine and a fashionable drink.

An advertisement in a specialist journal showed a bottle of Beaujolais nouveau, with the following slogan above the image: 'The Brenzy nouveau has arrived!' Text in bold characters at the bottom stated: 'You are thirsty and craving a new line of effective products! Brenzy-Legritte is happy to join you in ordering Beaujolais nouveau!' It was indicated that a minimum order of €500 entitled buyers to receive three free bottles and a minimum order of €800 entitled them to receive six free bottles. The expiry date for this offer was stipulated. The new line of Brenzy-Legritte products was shown on the label of the bottle of Beaujolais.

EDF, which is a large customer of Brenzy-Legritte, was not very happy about this humorous advertisement. It seems that EDF experienced problems amongst its personnel when the boxes of Beaujolais arrived at its offices.

Brenzy-Legritte is now undergoing drastic changes in its organization. Computers have been linked to the European headquarters in Brussels. Strictly defined management procedures have been imposed by headquarters. Brenzy has issued a professional code of conduct, the implementation of which is compulsory for the French subsidiary as well as for all the other subsidiaries around the world. It is a complete code of business ethics, comprising precise and detailed prescriptions. Below are some extracts.

Suffice it to say that this code of conduct is perceived by most people at Brenzy-Legritte, especially the salespeople, as largely inappropriate to the French context and a mere interference in their business. They prefer to disregard it.

Excerpts from the code of conduct at Brenzy-Legritte

Correct use of company funds

1. Company funds will not be used in order to make payments, or concealed loans, with the purpose of dishonestly influencing a supplier, a client or a civil servant. This prohibition applies not only to direct use of company money, but also to any kind of indirect payments, by the means of consultants/intermediaries, or by reimbursing to employees, payments made by them.
2. No payment shall be made, for and in the name of the company or one of its subsidiaries, with the intent or knowledge that part of such a payment will serve other purposes than those described in the documents related to this payment.

Gifts, favours and entertainment

Small gifts of symbolic value, minor favours and modest receptions may be offered at the company's expense only when they meet all of the following conditions:

1. They must be compatible with the rules of the company and current business practices.
2. Their monetary worth must be limited; they must be presented in such a form as not to appear as a bribe or remuneration; they must not give rise to suspicions about the impartiality of the beneficiary.
3. They must be approved by the general manager of the subsidiary or by a vice-president at Brenzy Corporation; they must be compatible with the instructions previously approved by the direct superior, the managing director and a senior vice-president at Brenzy Corporation.

Gifts and entertainment for civil servants

As indicated above, gifts, other than symbolic ones or gifts of a very modest value, whatever their nature, or a sumptuous reception, whatever its motives, are not allowed.

Issues related to these procedures and their violations

1. Any employees who want to ask questions about this code and its implementation shall discuss it with the head of the department. If it entails legal or accounting matters, they shall refer to qualified personnel from the legal services and the accounting department, who shall be consulted.
2. The discovery of a case which is fraudulent, illegal, or which violates the rules of the company shall immediately be reported to the legal counsellor. If such cases are identified which implicate senior executives in the corporation, this case shall be reported to the executive vice-president for examination by the chairman of the board, the chief executive officer, and the chairman of the audit committee.
3. No derogation to this procedure will be accepted in these matters. There will probably be some 'business opportunities' in the future, when it would be necessary to make questionable payments in order to succeed against a competitor, for one reason or another. The duty of the employee, in this case, is to reject such 'opportunities'.
4. Any infringement of the above-mentioned principles will result in disciplinary sanctions, including dismissal, a suing of the employee and a detailed report to competent regulatory authorities.

5. Moreover, disciplinary sanctions will be directed against any executive who initiates or approves such actions, or knows about them, or may have known about them, and did not quickly act to rectify them in accordance with this code. Adequate disciplinary sanctions will also be directed against any executives who neglect their hierarchical responsibilities, by not ensuring that their subordinates have been properly informed about the rules established in this code.

Questions

1. Analyse cross-cultural differences in the perception of ethical behaviour as concerns sales promotion activities. Why is this code of conduct perceived by most people at Brenzy-Legritte as largely inappropriate?

2. Why was the American company legally obliged to introduce such a code of conduct in its subsidiary?

3. Analyse the border between gifts and bribes. How can they be clearly differentiated?

A14.5 Case

Bielrohr AG

Bielrohr AG, a German company, is negotiating a licence agreement with a potential Indian licensee, Thakka Tubes Ltd. Bielrohr manufactures welded tubes for industrial use, especially for oil refineries and chemical plants. Because of the Indian import substitution policy, Bielrohr is not allowed to export to India directly, imports being forbidden in a bid to motivate foreign suppliers to transfer technology to Indian companies. Given the rapid technological development of India, Bielrohr AG has decided to grant a licence to a local industrial company.

A licence agreement provides the licensee with the right to manufacture and/or commercialize products or processes corresponding to a particular technology which is owned by the licensor. A licence agreement is often associated with patents and trademarks, not always, however. Technology is also embedded in non-patented technical knowledge (i.e., know-how) such as industrial designs, technical manuals, procedures, and pure know-how (e.g., a foreman in a plant knows how to perform a particular technical operation, how to 'make it happen', and his ability cannot be translated into words, designs, and the like). For the licensor there is a strategic risk that the licensee may become a competitor. An opposite risk exists if the licensee turns out to be industrially incompetent, does not manufacture properly, fails in quality and/or in delivery dates, and ultimately closes the market for which the licensor has granted exclusive rights. The licensor is also concerned with the spreading of know-how while protecting it from being imitated by competitors: that is, keeping know-how proprietary to the firm.

Licence agreements may be imposed by the host country in the framework of import substitution policies which target the replacement of imports by local manufacturing though transfer of technology policies. BRIC countries have historically been active in such import substitution policies which lead to restrictions on imports (i.e., full prohibitions or strict limitation for imports of a range of industrial goods and equipment). Such policies target the import and appropriate transfer of know-how by the foreign partner and the discontinuation of its product exports. This may be in the best interests of the foreign partner, especially if it fits with market trends, high levels of international competition, and limited financial resources that do not enable the foreign company to spend on foreign direct investment. This is particularly true if markets have a double digit growth in primary demand, which is the case in BRIC countries, but not at all so in older industrial nations. A licence agreement may be thought of in terms of international business strategy as a full mode of entry into foreign markets when there is a lack of financial resources to ensure quick penetration in international markets and a significant share of the world market. The search and selection of licensees is generally more active and the screening process more sophisticated when a licence agreement is considered a full foreign entry mode. Conversely, when it is associated with selling technology – or marketing-based know-how and services, the licence agreement is viewed as a business opportunity rather than a strategic move.

Licence agreements include clauses relating to products and/or services covered by the contract as well as territory clauses. A licence can be granted for manufacturing and/or commercialization. It may target the use of a brand name. There is a wide range of possibilities concerning the rights covered by a licence agreement. These rights may be granted by the licensor to the licensee in an exclusive (i.e., no other licensee is allowed on the same territory) or a non-exclusive manner (the licensor or other licensees may be allowed to operate on the same territory). The licensor and licensee may go beyond a mere licence agreement and decide to develop joint operations in manufacturing and/or commercialization. One key issue in the negotiation of a licence agreement is which brand the licensee uses: whether its own brand name mentioning that it is 'under licence of . . .' or the licensor brand (if permitted, that is), if the licensor is confident enough that the licensee will properly defend and illustrate their brand name.

Another major issue is how the licensor will be compensated for the rights it contributes to the licensee. The major choice is between a flat fee versus a commission on sales, or possibly any combination. Distrustful licensors generally prefer flat fees, while less confident licensees generally prefer a commission on sales. An opportunistic licensor may sell an almost outdated technology, not even last generation but previous versions. In this case the technology causes the licensee to be uncompetitive. Licence agreements generally include a clause about reciprocal information concerning new technological developments by both the licensor and the licensee as well as a clause of confidentiality preventing the licensee from disclosing information related to the technology to third parties. A non-disclosure agreement, which forbids the licensee to disclose information related to the to-be-licensed technology to third parties is often signed by the parties before entering into negotiation. The licensee may in fact take advantage of the negotiations (which it might not be willing to bring to an end) to gather information and learn about key details of the technology in order to later implement its own solutions without the licensor being compensated.

After a number of meetings between Bielrohr and Thakka Tubes, an initial collaboration proposal has been drafted as follows:

1. Thakka Tubes Ltd is willing to market locally in India, but wishes also to be commercially active in neighbouring markets such as Bangladesh, Burma (Myanmar), Thailand and Malaysia. Thakka Tubes Ltd always offers both products and the accompanying services: the supply of tubes (sale of goods) and technical assistance for their assembly within the complete industrial facility (services, generally about 30 per cent of total invoicing).
2. Bielrohr AG would be ready to grant exclusivity, in exchange for a guarantee of minimal sales performance from Thakka Tubes on its sales territory. The clause still has to be

drafted and accepted by both parties. In the absence of such a clause, Bielrohr AG proposes a non-exclusive licence, while committing to not granting a licence in these countries for one year (a sort of grace period for Thakka Tubes to show its capacity).

3. The duration of the agreement would be five years, tacitly renewable for the same period. Royalty payment would be in USD. Thakka Tubes Ltd is willing to use the Bielrohr brand name, in particular when being consulted and submitting bids in response to tenders launched by engineering companies or contractors. The management at Bielrohr AG wonders whether they might end up having to compete with their own licensee, and this under their own brand name through export sales of their own 'Made in Germany' products through German, European, American, or Japanese industrial contractors.

4. Market size (for both tubes and assembly services) is estimated at US$300 million per year for the five countries mentioned above, India itself representing 70 per cent of this potential. Thakka Tubes Ltd believe they hold a 20 per cent share of the Indian market and can win an additional 10 per cent market share in the other countries.

5. Bielrohr AG wants a US$1 million flat fee (in two instalments, half of it when signing the contract, half of it after delivering all technical documents), and a 4 per cent variable commission on all licensee sales figures related to the products and services under licence. The evaluation of its own negotiation costs by Bielrohr AG shows that expenses directly imputable to signing this licence agreement would amount to US$100,000 dollars (travel, preparing plans, procedures, and specific documents). All payments should be remitted by Thakka Tubes to Bielrohr in US dollars, free of any royalty tax. Thakka Tubes Ltd asks for technical assistance from Bielrohr on the basis of a full cost of US$3,000 per week for Bielrohr AG engineers working with them.

Questions

1. Which are the points (as a consequence, written clauses) which have not yet been considered in this draft licence agreement, and should be if the agreement is to work satisfactorily for both parties?

2. What additional information should each partner request of the other? Does the agreement, as presently drafted, favour Thakka Tubes Ltd or Bielrohr AG? Provide arguments indicating why it would favour one party or the other.

3. Given the relatively direct communication style of Germans and their self-awareness as concerns German technological excellence in industrial goods, what would you expect in terms of culture clash and communication misunderstandings with their Indian partners. You can elaborate both on German and Indian cultural traits and base your observations on materials found by Googling on the Internet.

4. Try to highlight the main aspects (clauses) of a balanced agreement between the two partners; write a draft proposal for their licence contract.

The Bielrohr case can be assigned either in traditional case study discussion or played as an International Marketing negotiations simulation. Company names are fictitious.

Jean-Claude Usunier prepared this case solely to provide material for class discussion. The authors do not intend to illustrate either effective or ineffective handling of a business situation. The authors may have disguised certain names and other identifying information to protect confidentiality.

Author index

Abegglen, James 305
Ackerman, David 295
Adcock, Dennis 437
Adler, Peter 17
Agpar, M. 445
Allen, David Elliston 292
Allio, David J. 255
Allio, Robert 255
Ancarani, Fabio 304
Arnould, Eric J. 447
Askegaard, Søren 105

Balabanis, George 348
Becker, Gary S. 295
Becker, Helmut 450
Belk, Russell W. 136, 140
Berenbein, Ronald E. 450
Berne, Eric 55
Berry, J.W. 114
Billikopf Encina, Gregorio 19
Blodgett, Jeffrey 112
Boland, Tom 446
Bouchet, Dominique 115
Brunso, Karen 105
Burgess, Steven 185
Buzzell, Robert D. 228

Cabell, David W.E. 299
Callow, Michael 379
Carey, George 232
Cateora, Philip R. 305, 437
Cavusgil, S. Tamer 112, 228, 293
Chaudry, Peggy E. 303
Chen, Haipeng 261
Chen, Min 436
Chen, Yanjing 446
Clarke, Irvine III 301
Condon, John C. 74
Craig, C. Samuel 184, 202, 207, 230, 234
Curry, David J. 296

Daft, Douglas N. 134
Darby, Michael R. 296

Day, George 430
DeMarco, C.W. 305
De Mente, Boye 83
De Mooij, Marieke 136
Djursaa, Malene 116, 149–50
Douglas, Susan P. 184, 202, 207, 230, 234, 385
Droit, Michael 15–16
Dubois, Bernard 385
Duncan, Tom 380

Erevelles, Sunil 295

Ferraro, Gary P. 76
Firat, A. Fuat 148–9
Fisher, Glen 80
Ford, David 435
Fritzsche, David H. 450

Gaeth, Gary J. 297
Gans, Herbert 114–15
Gauthey, Franck 18
Geertz, Clifford 5, 190
Ger, Güliz 114, 136, 147–8
Ghauri, Pervez N. 379
Goodenough, Ward H. 6
Gopalakrishna, Pradeep 388
Graham, John L. 438, 450

Hall, Edward T. 28–9, 34, 71, 74, 262–3, 439
Harich, Katrin 388
Harris, Philip 30, 76
Harvey, Michael G. 292–3
Harzing, Anne-Wil 162
Hensel, Paul 376
Hermann, Gretchen M. 292
Hill, J.S. 440–1
Hofstede, Geert 47–8, 50–4, 135, 323, 388, 439
Holt, Douglas 145, 443–4
Honeycutt, Earl D. Jr 439
Hutchings, Kate 436

Ibison, David 303–4
Ikel, C. 106

James, Karen 376
Jain, Subhash C. 229
Johansson, Johny K. 186, 301
Jo, Myung-Soo 296
Jones, Bob Dorigo 256

Kahle, Lynn R. 198
Kale, Sudhir H. 323, 388
Kanso, Ali 394
Karni, Edi 296
Kaynak, Erdener 112, 379
Keegan, Warren 298–9
Keown, Charles F. 301
Khuri, Fuad I. 292
Kibarian, Thomas M. 297
Kitayama, Shinobu 39
Kluckhohn, Florence 5, 26, 30–1, 111
Kopytoff, Igor 142
Kragh, Simon Ulrik 116, 149–50
Kumar, Rajesh 8, 57
Kumar, V. 430

Lagerlöff, S. 25
Lee, James 18
Lee, Julie Anne 358–9
Lenartowicz, Thomasz 234
Levine, Robert A. 79
Levitt, Theodore 133, 138, 258
Levy, Orly 145
Lieberthal, K. 137
Lin, Carolyn A. 377
Linton, Ralph 5–6, 13
Longworth, John W. 265
Louviere, J.J. 198
Lui, Tan Jee 205–6
Luo, Yadong 436
Lusch, Robert F. 428–9

McIntyre, Roger P. 323
McLelland, D. 54
Macleod, Marcia 81
Madden, Thomas J. 266–7
Al-Makaty, Safran 385
Malinowski, Bronislaw 5, 8
Mallard, D. 74
Markus, Hazel Rose 39
Márquez, Gabriel García 35
Maslow, Abraham H. 54, 104
Maxwell, Sarah 294–5
Mead, Margaret 14, 37
Minkov, Michael 13
Montesquieu, Charles de 15, 57
Moran, Robert T. 30

Moreira, Marcio 394
Morita, A. 186
Morschbach, Helmut 76
Murray, Georgina 436
Myers, Matthew B. 301
Mytton, Graham 202

Nelson, Michelle 380
Nelson, Philip J. 296
Nelson, Richard Alan 394
Nguyen, Thus-Doan 140
Nig, Siew Imm 388–9
Nonaka, Ikujiro 186, 301

Ohmae, Kenichi 224
Østergaard, Per 114
Owe, Ellinor 38
Owens, Margaret 301
Oxenfeldt, Alfred 296
Oyserman, D. 33, 39, 107

Paek, H-J. 380
Palia, Aspy P. 301
Palmer, David K. 29
Parameswaran, Ravi 196
Park, Seong-Yeon 114
Parvativar, Atul 429
Peebles, Dean 394
Penaloza, Lisa 116
Pettigrew, Simone 144–5
Porter, Michael E. 221, 230, 304
Prahalad, C.K. 137
Prendergast, Gerard 383
Prus, Robert C. 293

Raajpoot, Nusser 261
Ramaprasad, Jyotika 380
Rawls, John 450–1
Resnik, Alan J. 378
Ricardo, David 133
Richins, Marsha 112
Riesz, Peter C. 296
Ritzer, George 137
Rodman, Hyman 106
Rodrik, Dani 147
Roeber, Carter A. 293
Romano, Charlotte J. 377
Rowley, Jennifer 262
Roy, Abhik 192
Rugman, Alan 221

Sapir, Edward 77
Sarigollu, Emine 296

Schiffman, Leon 379
Schilke, Martin 229
Schindler, Robert M. 297
Schoorman, David F. 29
Schuh, Arnold 258
Schwartz, Simon 47–50, 53, 198, 388
Sengupta, Juideep 246
Sharma, Arun 429
Shavitt, Sharon 49
Sheth, Jagdish N. 429
Simon, Paul 83
Slack, Frances 262
Smith, Adam 451
Solomon, Michael R. 104
Soutar, Geoffrey N. 388–9
Sproles, George B. 296
Sriram, Ven 388
Stalk, George Jr. 305
Steenkamp, Jan-Benedict 208
Steidlmeier, P. 447
Stern, Bruce L. 378
Stevenson, Thomas H. 299
Stöttinger, Barbara 299
Strodtbeck, Frederick L. 5, 26, 30–1, 111
Sugimoto, Naomi 73

Tanouchi, Koichi 116–17
Tan, Thomas Tsu Wee 205–6
Tellis, Gerard J. 295, 297
Triandis, Harry C. 58
Trompenaars, Fons 47, 60

Tsurumi, Hiroki 306
Tsurumi, Yoshi 306

Vargo, Stephen L. 428–9
Verhage, Bronislaw J. 112
Verna, Gérard 308, 309
Vertinsky, Ilan 259
Völckner, Franziska 296
Von Stackelberg, H. 306

Walsh, Michael J. 303
Wang, Cheng Lu 435–6
Weber, Max 298
Wee, Chow-Hou 384
Weigand, Robert 301, 303
Werner, Cynthia 448
Whorf, Benjamin Lee 7, 78
Wilk, Richard 105
Williams, Stephen C. 265
Woodward, Nancy Hatch 82

Yan, Dengfeng 296
Yaprak, Attila 196
Yoshida, Susumu 16
Youssef, Fahti 74

Zandpour, Fred 388
Zhang, Jingyun 261
Zhou, Dongsheng 259
Zou, Shaoming 228

Subject index

acculturation model 115
acquiescence 204
activity, perceived 37
adaptation of products to local product usage 256
advertising 372–96
  agencies 392
  appeals 377–8
  characters and roles represented in 383–5
  comparative 375–7
  cross-national transferability 388–9
  expenditure 389
  global campaign concept 394–6
  humour 382–3
  information content 378–9
  language 380–2
  media 389–92
  mores and religion 385–7
  publicity and 'publiphobia' 375–6
  in rapid transition societies 388
  role and functions 376
  standardization 392–4
  visual elements 387–8
affective cultures 56, 59–60
affiliation 358
affinity, cultural 231–2
Afghanistan 202
Africa 34, 37, 225, 260, 266
  advertising 384, 388
  language and communication 79
  price and relational exchange 292, 301
age factors 37, 108, 139
Amazon 324
'American way of life' 138–9
apologies 443
Apple 348
appraisal of others 36–8
appraisal of quality and price 294–5
Arab countries 30, 150, 266, 383–4
  language and communication 76
Argentina 234, 336, 344
arguments 436–7
Asia 27, 29, 205–6, 266

advertising 377, 381, 384
  consumer behaviour 106–7, 109–11
  dynamics: interactions and behaviours 38–9, 63
  East 58, 204, 266
  language and communication 76
  marketing strategy, intercultural 227, 232
  personal selling, networking and public relations
    430–1, 437
  South-East 224, 301, 304, 374, 392
assimilation 114–5, 231
assumptions 60–3
assurance 433
atomistic versus organic views 187–8
attitudes 55–8, 108
Audiovisual Media Services Directive 390
Australia 12, 27, 296
  advertising 377, 381, 384, 389–90, 392
  branding 344, 348
  consumer behaviour 107
  distribution and sales promotion 319, 328–9
  dynamics: time and space 31–2, 35
  language and communication 74, 83
  local consumers and globalization of consumption 139,
    141–2, 144–5, 147–8
  marketing strategy, intercultural 231, 234
  market research 191, 204
  personal selling, networking and public relations 434,
    441, 446, 449
  product strategy: physical, service and symbolic
    attributes 260, 264
  Starbucks versus the 9-Cs 320
Austria 54, 135, 324
  product strategy: physical, service and symbolic
    attributes 262, 267
automated service 264
avoidance patterns 305–6

bargaining 291–4
basic units 198
Basque country 12
beer drinking 114–15, 148
behaviour, actual 62–3

'being' orientation 32–3, 57, 263–4
Belgium 19, 135, 149, 234, 257, 391
benevolence 432
best value 297
best-worst method 198
Best Worst Scaling 198
biases from relationship with interviewer 203
black markets 308
Bolivia 201
borrowing, cultural 78
bowing 76
Brahmanism 5, 8, 38, 57
brand/branding 342–60
    Asian ideographic writing systems 354–5
    brand names 350–1
    consumer product evaluation according to country
       of origin 345–9
    functions of according to national contexts 355–6
    identity 378
    linguistic aspects of a brand 351–2
    linguistic devices for brand names 352–4
    image 378
    international and global 356–9
    loyalty 110
    national images diffused by product origin and brand
       name 243–5
    personality 145
    semantic issues: intended/unintended meaning 354
Brazil 55, 145, 192, 234, 307, 447
    advertising 381, 387, 390–1
    language and communication 79–80
    product strategy: physical, service and symbolic
       attributes 267
bribery 244–51
Buddhism 29
Burberry 317
buyer–seller interactions 436–8
buy, motivation to 113
'Buy National' campaign 148

Cameroon 257
Canada 148, 234, 267, 317, 446
    advertising 377, 381, 389–90
    language and communication 71, 82
    price and relational exchange 293, 296
capital 318, 320
capitalization 355
Cassis de Dijon ruling 258
castes 37
Catalonia 12
Catholicism 19, 105, 233, 297–8
centralized control 394
character 318, 320
Chile 55, 106, 321, 344

China 10, 14, 29, 38
    advertising 372, 377–8, 381, 388–9
    branding 343–8, 351–2
    consumer behaviour 107, 109–10, 112
    distribution and sales promotion 323
    ganqing (affection) 435
    guanxi 435–6
    language and communication 68
    local consumers and globalization of consumption
       137–9, 145, 147–8, 150
    marketing strategy, intercultural 234
    market research 185, 192, 196–8, 201
    personal selling, networking and public relations 432,
       443, 449
    price and relational exchange 295–6, 302
    product strategy: physical, service and symbolic
       attributes 266–7
choice strategies 295–8
Christianity 29
climate 12, 15–16, 256
Coca-Cola 77, 131, 134, 137, 147, 232, 251, 255, 267, 352
    branding 352, 354, 357
code law 58
coffee drinking 192
cognitive styles 109
collection devices 326
collectivism 39, 48–9, 148, 188
    consumer behaviour 103, 106, 109, 117
    distribution and sales promotion 323
    dynamics: interactions and behaviours 48–9, 54, 62
    personal selling, networking and public relations 440–1
Colombia 234, 267
colours 196, 198, 265–6, 296
commerce as implementation of marketing programmes
    428–9
commitment 432
common law 58
communication 48, 57, 440
    improving effectiveness 82–5
    see also language, culture and communication
comparative/relative advantage 132
compensation systems 441–2
competence 15
competition 110, 227–8, 304–6, 319–20
competitions 326–7
complaint behaviour 112
complex products 142
compliance 33
compound units 198
Confucian Pragmatism 8
Confusion Work Dynamism 27, 30
conspicuous consumption 104
construct bias 190
consume, motivation 113

consumer behaviour, cross-cultural 102–18
 cognitive styles 109
 cultural mindsets 107
 dissatisfaction 111–13
 ethnic consumption 114–16
 exchange of meanings, marketing as 116–18
 hierarchy of needs 104
 involvement of consumer 109
 loyalty 110–11
 questioning of 113–14
 risk, perceived 109–10
 who makes decisions 105–6
consumer ethnocentrism
consumer evaluations 294–8
consumer product evaluation, according to country
  of origin 345–9
consumers and their characteristics 317
consumption patterns 255–6
contacts 432–5
context 29, 70–4
 high 69–71, 440
 low 69–71, 440
continuity 143, 319–20, 429–31
control 137, 319–20
cosmopolitanism 145
cost 318–20
cost arguments and global strategies 221–6
 learning opportunities 226–7
 production and experience effects 221–2
 sourcing and marketing 223
 transportability, international 222–3
 trends towards global (competitive) markets 221
 world market share concept 225–6
 world view/local view 223–5
cost reduction 220, 254
counterfeiting 302
country evoked by brand name label 344–5
country image diffused by 'made in' label 344
country of origin 148, 223, 257, 267, 345–9
courtesy 77
 bias 203
coverage 320
credence attributes 296
credibility 432
Creolization 149
criticality dissonance 205
Cuba 115, 391
cultural factors 105–6
cultural meaning perspective 113
cultural norms, chronically and situationally accessible 39
cultural relativism 446–9
cultural universalism 446
culture-shock 17–18
cushion theory 109

customer relationship management (CRM) 429–30
customization 218, 228, 253, 255
customs 326–9
Czech Republic 112

data availability and resources 205–6
data collection 201–5
decentring 194–5
decision making 108
definition of culture 4–6
delivery dates 224–5
demand 131–2
Denmark 106, 113–4, 135, 150
 advertising 378
 language and communication 81
 marketing strategy, intercultural 233
 market research 202
dependence 54–5
depersonalization 31–2
design 117–18
desirability bias 111
desires 59–60, 104
diets, and religion 9
dimensions, cultural 106
DIN standards 254–5
direct mail 325
direct marketing worldwide 323–6
discounts 326
disloyalty 110
display, motivation 113
dissatisfaction 111–12
diversity 133–4
divisibility 39, 187–8
'doing' cultures 32, 34, 57, 60, 203–4, 435
domestic markets 300–1
double hierarchical linkage 54
dumping 300
duration-of-usage hypothesis 255–6
dynamics, cultural: interactions and behaviours 47–63
 assumptions and actual behaviour 62–3
 attitudes towards action 55–8
 chronically and situationally accessible cultural
   norms 39
 desires and feelings 59–60
 rules, coping with 60–2
 thinking to action, how to relate 58–9
 see also interaction models; self and others, concept of
dynamics of culture 25–39
 chronically and situationally accessible cultural norms 39
 hostility, cultural 19–20
 model of action based on cultural assumptions 26–7
 self and others, concept of the 35–9
 space territoriality 31–5
 time: cross-cultural variability 27–30

eastern Europe 58, 201, 299, 321
eating habits 105
Economic Community Treaty Article 30 258, 303
economies of scope 222
educational practices 13–14
efficiency 137
Egypt 145, 150
elements of culture 7–10
emic (specific) perspective 102–3, 205
emotion 60, 80, 116–17, 377
entertainment function 355
environment, consumption and 143
environmental factors 394
equalitarianism 106
equality 49–50, 438
equivalence
    calibration 198
    conceptual 191
    context 202–3
    data-collection 189, 201–5
    experiential 193
    functional 190–2
    grammatical-syntactical 193
    idiomatic 192
    levels 189
    lexical 192, 197
    measure 189, 195–8
    metric 195–9
    perceptual 196
    respondents cooperation 202
    response-style 204–5
    sample 189, 200
    temporal 199
    translation 189, 193–5
esteem needs 104
ethics 325, 327, 446–51
ethnic appeals 267
ethnic bias 203
ethnic consumption 114–16
ethnicity-of-interviewer bias 203
ethnocentrism 17–20, 83, 146, 148, 204, 223–4, 255–6, 265
    consumer 348–9
    and self-reference criteria 17–20
etic (universal) perspective 102–3
etymology 352
EU Unfair Commercial Practices Directive (UCPD) 327
Europe
    advertising 372, 376, 384, 390–4
    branding 344, 346, 348–9
    consumer behaviour 113
    distribution and sales promotion 319, 321, 324
    language and communication 74, 76
    local consumers and globalization of consumption 136, 142

marketing strategy, intercultural 222–4, 227, 229–30, 231–3
market research 201, 204–5
    price and relational exchange 296, 299, 300–2, 304–5, 307
    product strategy: physical, service and symbolic attributes 257–8, 262–3, 266
    time 27, 30
    see also central and eastern; northern; southern; western
European Court of Justice 303, 327
European Union 135, 141, 303
    distribution and sales promotion 325, 327
    product strategy: physical, service and symbolic attributes 258
evaluation 440
exchange of meanings, marketing as 116–18
Exhaustion of Rights Doctrine 303
exotic appeals 267
export markets 300–1
extension/ethnocentric position 298
extraversion 204
extreme response style 204
eye contact and communication with eyes 76–7

face, concept of 436
facial expression 76–7
family 32–3, 38, 55, 105–6
fatalism 56–7
feelings 59–60
femininity 50, 106, 135, 384, 439, 441
Fenwick 225
Fiji 199
financial integration-independence 230–1
Finland 145, 264, 305, 323, 449
fire safety systems in United Kingdom 144
flagship method 16
food 150
Food and Drug Administration 255, 258
fordist consumption 134, 139, 149, 150–1
Foreign Corrupt Practices Act (1977) 446, 448
France 12
    advertising 375–80, 387–89, 391–2
    Alsations 12
    branding 343–6, 350, 352
    Civil Code Article 1382 375
    consumer behaviour 107, 113
    distribution and sales promotion 321–2, 327
    dynamics: interactions and behaviours 54–5, 58–9, 60–1, 63
    dynamics: time and space 32
    language and communication 68, 71, 74, 79–80
    local consumers and globalization of consumption 135, 139, 142–6, 148–9
    Lois Méline 133

France (*cont'd*)
    marketing strategy, intercultural 222, 224, 226, 232, 234
    market research 193, 197, 203–4
    personal selling, networking and public relations 436, 440–1, 444, 450
    price and relational exchange 295, 301, 305
    product strategy: physical, service and symbolic attributes 252, 255, 257–8, 260, 262–4, 266
franchising 317
free samples 326
free trade doctrine 132–4
friendship 14, 34–5, 73
furnishings 150

gender 37
General Agreement on Tariffs and Trade 300
geocentrism 224
geographical concentration–dispersion 230
Germany 4, 31, 138, 301, 306
    advertising 375, 378, 381–3, 388–9, 393
    branding 344–8, 350–2
    consumer behaviour 106, 113
    distribution and sales promotion 317, 319, 322, 325, 327
    dynamics: interactions and behaviours 54, 58, 60–1
    language and communication 68, 71, 76–82
    local consumers and globalization of consumption 131, 133, 135, 138, 141–4
    marketing strategy, intercultural 224, 232
    market research 194, 205, 207
    personal selling, networking and public relations 437, 441, 444, 450
    product strategy: physical, service and symbolic attributes 253, 255–6, 258–9, 266
gestures 74–6
Ghana 428
gifts 326–8, 444
give, motivation to 114
global approach 113
globalization of consumption and local consumers 131–51
    convergence of consumption patterns 134–6
    emergent patterns 148–51
    free trade doctrine and denial of cultural variety in tastes 132–4
    local products and consumption experiences 139–45
    'McDonaldization' consumption 137–8
    'modern' culture 138–9
    resistance to change 145–8
global perspective 102, 113
goal setting 440
goods-dominant logic 428
Greece 106, 135, 322, 383, 392, 449
greeting 74

group
    cultures 34
    influence 108
    see also ingroups; outgroups
Guatemala 434, 444
guilt 61–2
Guinea 432

habits 143–5
habitus 143–5
hand gestures 74–6
handshakes 74
hard sell approach 437
head gestures 74
hierarchy 8, 80, 104
high-inflation countries 306–8
Hinduism 29, 38, 104, 113
home country rule 258
homogeneity, cultural and relevant segmentation 12
Hong Kong 31, 135, 140, 148, 267, 295, 316, 328–9, 355
    advertising 382–4
    consumer behaviour 106–7, 114
hostility, cultural 19–20
human-nature orientation 35–6, 60–1
human resource emphasis 431
humour 382–3
hygiene regulations 255

Iceland 82
ideal types 439
identification 32, 231–2
identity 10, 116
ideographic writing systems 354–5
ideologists 56, 58–9
IKEA 393
imported perspective 102, 113
incentives, internal 440
independence 39
India 8, 10, 12, 38, 57, 73–4
    advertising 379–80, 387–8, 391
    branding 347, 357
    consumer behaviour 105, 112
    local consumers and globalization of consumption 131, 134, 137, 145
    price and relational exchange 292, 294–6
individualism 32, 39, 48–9
    consumer behaviour 103, 106, 108, 110
    distribution and sales promotion 323
    dynamics: interactions and behaviours 50–1, 54, 62
    personal selling, networking and public relations 433, 439–41
Indonesia 131, 140, 145
industrial marketing 104

industrial standards for electricity 255
industry characteristics 441–2
inequality 49–50
ingroups 18, 32–4, 38–9, 49, 61, 114–16
innovative products 257–8
institutional-collectivism 49
institutions 7–8, 185–8
intellectual styles 56
interaction models 47–55
  clashes 54
  communication styles 48
  equality 49–50
  individualism and collectivism 48–9
  management theories 54
  masculinity versus femininity 48, 50
  self-reliance versus dependence 54–5
  uncertainty avoidance 48, 50–4
intercultural marketing strategy 220–35
  competition, globalization of 227–8
  financial integration-independence 230–1
  geographical concentration–dispersion 230
  market segments 231–5
  organizational aspects 229–30
  standardization-adaptation 228–9
  see also arguments and global strategies
interdependence 107
intermediate geocentric inventive position 299
internal expansion 316
internalization 33
International Chamber of Commerce 449
international standards 256–9
international usage 258
Internet 206, 227, 234, 304, 323–6
intimate zone 34
invisible hand 305
invoicing 308–9
involvement of consumer 109
IQ test 15
Iran 307
Ireland 205
Islam/Muslims 9, 30, 37, 74, 191, 384–6
Israel 150, 349
Italy 118
  advertising 391
  branding 344–5, 350
  distribution and sales promotion 322, 327
  dynamics: interactions and behaviours 60–1, 63
  language and communication 68, 75
  local consumers and globalization of consumption 135, 144, 146
  marketing strategy, intercultural 225, 232, 234
  market research 204–5, 233
  personal selling, networking and public relations 437, 441, 444

product strategy: physical, service and symbolic attributes 260, 266
item non-response 204–5

Japan 12, 14, 16, 19, 116–17
  advertising 376, 381, 383–4, 388–9, 392
  branding 345–9, 352, 354
  consumer behaviour 106, 109
  Disneyland Tokyo 149
  dynamics: interaction and behaviours 37, 50, 58, 60, 62–3
  Kankei 436
  keiretsu 226, 305, 322, 356, 430
  language and communication 68, 70–3, 76, 81, 83
  local consumers and globalization of consumption 131, 134–5, 137, 139, 141, 143, 145, 148
  marketing strategy, intercultural 221–2, 225
  market research 186–8, 193, 197, 199, 204
  personal selling, networking and public relations 430, 433–6, 438, 440–3, 450
  price and relational exchange 300–1, 303–6
  product strategy: physical, service and symbolic attributes 254, 256, 258, 261–3, 265
joint ventures 317
judgement of ourselves 38

Kaffeetrinken 144
keiretsu 226, 305, 322, 356, 430
Kenya 76, 112, 346, 374
Kwakiutl Indians 104

language, culture and communication 6, 68–85, 141
  advertising 380–2
  context 68–74
  cultural norms and communication styles 72–3
  cultural norms: high-to-low context 69–72
  improving communication effectiveness 82–5
  Internet 81–2
  language influencing culture 77–80
  language as reflection of status, hierarchy and social relationships 80
  non-verbal communication 74–7
  role of context 69–73
  Whorfian hypothesis 82–3
language groups 7
Latin America 106, 223–4, 347, 374, 385
  language and communication 70, 73, 75–6, 82
  market research 199, 202
  price and relational exchange 301, 307
learning 108
  by doing 222
  opportunities, global markets as 226–7
Likert-scale questions 204
linearity versus cyclicity 28–30
literacy 328

localism 145, 188
local marketing institutions and infrastructure 185–8
logistics issues 230, 325
Long Term Orientation 30, 55, 109
loyalty 32–3, 110–11, 322
Lutheranism 297
Luxembourg 135, 445

'McDonaldized' consumption 137–8
McDonald's 81, 137, 146, 150–1, 232
    branding 349, 358
    product strategy: physical, service and symbolic
        attributes 251, 264, 267
macro-level convergence 135–6
Malaysia 74, 203, 252, 325, 329, 350
management theories 54
manners 326–9
marginalization 114
market research, cross-cultural 184–207
    atomistic versus organic views 187–8
    back-translation and related techniques 193–4
    biases from relationship with interviewer 203
    comparability of samples 199–201
    data availability and resources, limited 205–6
    etimic versus etic approaches 188–9
    feedback encouragement from informant on cultural
        adequacy 205
    Internet 206
    Japan 186–7
    local marketing institutions and infrastructure 185–8
    see also equivalence
market segments 231–5
Marxist doctrine 58
masculinity 48, 50, 52, 54, 106
    distribution and sales promotion 323
    personal selling, networking and public relations
        439, 441–2
material productions as element of culture 8
matrix organization 54
Mauritania 203, 292
meaning, shared 143–5
means-end concept 195
mechanical rules 61
media 389–92
Mediterranean countries 233
memory 108
mergers 316–17
Mexico 134, 148, 255, 347
    advertising 384, 388, 390
    consumer behaviour 106, 111
    personal selling, networking and public relations 437, 444
micro-level convergence 136
Middle East 10, 34, 54, 147, 223, 227, 292–3, 349, 384,
    444, 449

mindsets, cultural 107
mirror effect 18
'modern culture' 37, 138–9
modernity 150–1
modernization 138–9
monochronism 27–8
morality 33, 450–1 see also ethics
motivation 108, 113
Mozambique 202
multinational corporations 62–3, 138–9, 251
Myanmar 449

national character 13–14
national culture 13
national differences 234–5
national images diffused by product origin and band
    name 343–5
nationalism 148
nationality 10–14, 32
national products, preference for 148
native English speakers 83–4
nature orientation 25
Netherlands 60, 255
    advertising 384
    branding 351, 357
    consumer behaviour 112
    marketing strategy, intercultural 233
    price and relational exchange 302
    product strategy: physical, service and symbolic
        attributes 259
networking see personal selling, networking and public
    relations
neutral cultures 56, 59–60
New Zealand 110, 234, 296, 325, 347, 349, 381, 390
Nigeria 190, 346, 445
non-contingent responding 204
non-controlling interest 317
non-durables 142
non-equivalence 204
non-probability sampling 201
Nordic countries see Scandinavia
North America 81, 113, 201, 221, 224, 263, 296, 347, 349, 430
northern Europe 204, 233, 297, 441
    advertising 374, 388
    distribution and sales promotion 321, 328
    dynamics: interactions and behaviours 50, 53, 58, 61
    language and communication 84
    local consumers and globalization of consumption 135,
        143, 146
    product strategy: physical, service and symbolic
        attributes 260, 264
North/South paradigm 234
Norway 81, 106, 138, 202, 255–6, 381
numbers 265

occupational and professional activities principle 8
opening hours 321
openness to foreign cultures 148
operational culture 6, 11
opportunism 307, 436
organic views 106, 187–8
organizational aspects 229–30
Organization for Economic Cooperation and
    Development: Convention Combating Bribery 448–9
orthographic devices 253
outgroups 18, 31–4, 49, 439
over-invoicing 308–9
own, motivation to 113

Pakistan 32, 135
Papua New Guinea 15–16, 83
patriarchy 106
patriotism 148
people orientation *see* personalization
perceived brand globalness 358
percentages (bribes) 445
perception 108
performance measurement 438–42
personal information sources 261
personality 13
personalization 31–3, 355
personal selling, networking and public relations 428–52
    bribery 444–51
    buyer–seller interactions 436–8
    commerce as implementation of marketing
        programmes 428–9
    contacts 432–5
    continuity in commercial relationships: learning from
        consumers 429–30
    human resource emphasis 431
    networks 435–6
    public relations 442–4
    sales-force management 438–42
personal zone 34
PERT 28
pharmaceutical industry 226, 255, 258, 303
Philippines 38, 134, 292, 379
phonemics 351
phonetics 351–2
physical attributes 254–9
physical conditions 12
physical environment 141, 256, 259
physical space 34–5
physiological needs 104
physiology principle 8
piracy 302
'pizza relativity' 256
Poland 145, 234, 323, 329, 347, 378
politeness 77

polycentrism 83, 223–4, 299
polychronism 27–9
Portugal 55, 79, 132, 148, 328, 344
positioning 355
post-purchase 108
potency, perceived 38
power distance 204, 262, 388
    distribution and sales promotion 323
    dynamics: interactions and behaviours 48–50, 61
    personal selling, networking and public relations
        433–4, 436, 439–40
practicality 355
pragmatism 8, 56, 59
predictability 137
presence 436–7
price 437
price aversion 297
price endings 297
price-perceived quality relationship 296
price and relational exchange 290–309
    bargaining 291–4
    consumer evaluations 294–8
    management in highly regulated environments 306–9
    manipulation of price 298–300
    market share gain through pricing 300–4
    market situations, competition and price agreements
        304–6
    as sign of conveying meaning 291
    willingness to compete 299–300
price seeking 297
private meanings 107
probability sampling 201
problem solution 378
process, cultural 4–20
    culture, competence and stereotypes 15–17
    definition of culture 4–6
    elements of culture 6–10
    nationality and culture 10–14
Procter & Gamble 226, 229–30, 329, 350, 394
product design 224
product image changing over time 347
production and experience effects 221–2
product liability 444
product life-cycle 225
product strategy: physical, service and symbolic attributes
    251–68
    adaptation or standardization 252–3
    physical attributes 254–9
    service attributes 259–64
    symbolic attributes 264–7
products, cultural 140–2, 231–2
Protestantism 233, 297–8
provincialism 34
proxemics 34, 76

publicity 375–6
public meanings 107
public relations *see* personal selling, networking and
    public relations
'publiphobia' 374
purchase 108
Puritan paradox 298

quality 133, 295–8, 437
queues 261
quota sampling 201

racism 19–20
random digit dialling 202
rebates 326
recognition (awareness) 358
referral sources 261
Reformed Church 298
regiocentrism 224
regional differences 234–5
relational orientation 264
relationship elements 141, 323
relevance dissonance 205
religion 9, 29, 233, 321, 385–7 *see also* Buddhism;
    Catholicism; Confucian; Hinduism; Islam/Muslims;
    Protestantism
representativeness and comparability of national/cultural
    samples 200–1
reproduction principle 8
resistance to change 146–7
respondents cooperation equivalence 202
response bias 203
rewards 54, 442
ringi 109–10
risk
    avoidance 323
ritual aspects of bargaining 292–3
rule orientation *see* depersonalization
rules 56, 60–2, 262
Russia 19, 76, 112, 349, 378, 393

Sabisu (Japanese concept of service) 263
safety needs 104
safety standards 255
sales-force management 438–42
sales promotion and international distribution 316–30
    criteria for choice of foreign distribution channels 316–20
    customs and manners 326–9
    direct marketing worldwide 323–6
    role of distribution as 'cultural filter' 321–3
    see also keiretsu
Sapir-Whorf hypothesis 82
Saudi Arabia 37, 438, 445
    advertising 385–7, 389–90

save, motivation to 113
scale effects 222
Scandinavia 12, 71, 141, 202, 233, 256, 328, 344–5
search attributes 296
self-actualization need 104
self-assessment manikin 198
self-concept 37, 108
self-esteem 36, 38
self and others, concept of 35–8
    appraisal of others 36–8
    human nature 35–6
    independent 39
    individualism and collectivism 39
    interdependent 39
    judgement of ourselves 38
Self-Reference Criterion 17–20
self-reliance 54–5
self-shock 4, 17–18
semantic devices 354
Senegal 448
sensitivity 62, 116–17
sensory codes 35
separation 114
service
    attributes 253, 259–64
    dominant logic 428
SERVQUAL 260
sex roles 108
sexual biases 203
shame 61
shapes 265
Sherman Act 305
Short Term Orientation 30–1
silence 263
simplifications 254
Singapore 189, 204, 328, 354
    advertising 380, 384
    consumer behaviour 105
    market research 189–90
skills 15
smells 35, 196
social beliefs 321–2
social class 12, 37–8
social desirability bias 111
social distance 34
social needs 104
social relationships 80
social status 328–9
social zone 34
soft cell approach 437
sources of culture 11–12
sourcing and marketing, disconnection between 223
South Africa 198–99, 391
South America 35, 234, 266, 304, 354, 381

southern Europe 61, 204, 233, 374
   distribution and sales promotion 321
   local consumers and globalization of consumption
      144
   price and relational exchange 297–8
   product strategy: physical, service and symbolic
      attributes 260
South Korea 31, 266, 316
   advertising 376, 379, 384, 387–88, 394
   branding 347–48
   consumer behaviour 110–12
   Kwankye 436
   local consumers and globalization of consumption
      138
space *see* dynamics of culture: time and space
Spain 318, 328, 381
   branding 344, 357–8
   local consumers and globalization of consumption 135,
      141, 146
   marketing strategy, intercultural 233–4
   personal selling, networking and public relations 441,
      449
speech versus deed orientation 56
spend, motivation to 113
spontaneous tendency to join together principle 8
Sri Lanka: Tamils 12
standard 133, 137
standardization 228–30, 264, 392–3
Starbucks 320
status 80, 436
stereotypes 15–17, 346–7, 383, 437
superego 54
supportive leadership 323
survival needs 104
Sweden 12, 81–2, 106, 441, 449
   advertising 345, 379, 384, 390, 393
   branding 347, 354
   language and communication 81–2
   marketing strategy, intercultural 233–4
Switzerland 10–11, 223, 234, 256, 262
   advertising 372, 391–2
   language and communication 70–1, 82
   personal selling, networking and public relations 437,
      441, 443, 445, 449–50
symbolism 8–9, 253, 264–6
systematic quantification and calculation 137

Taiwan 112, 267, 323, 329
   advertising 377–9, 384, 387
   branding 346–8
takeovers 316–17
Tanzania 192
technological advances 222
temporal orientations 30–1

territoriality principle 8, 31
Thailand 38, 106, 199, 292, 347–8, 440
   advertising 380, 383, 387
   distribution and sales promotion 323, 328–9
theft 322
time
   normative 27
   orientation 27–8
   patterns revealed by language 79
   tangibility 29
   use preference 29
   see also dynamics of culture: time and space
tips 445
totality principle 8
translation 193–5, 350
transliteration 350
transparent brands 350–1
transportability, international 222–3
Treaty of Rome Article 85 303
trust 432
Turkey 114–5, 131, 134, 145, 148, 246, 322

uncertainty avoidance 13, 48, 50–1, 54–5, 110, 258, 261,
     321, 323, 383
   personal selling, networking and public relations
     439–41
under-invoicing 308
Unilever 305, 392
unique selling proposition 378
United Kingdom 32, 437
   advertising 375, 378–81, 383–4, 390, 393
   branding 346, 348–9, 357
   consumer behaviour 106
   distribution and sales promotion 318, 327–8
   language and communication 71, 75, 78, 80,
     83–5
   local consumers and globalization of consumption
     135, 145, 148
   market research 191
   product strategy: physical, service and symbolic
     attributes 252, 259
United States 10, 12
   advertising 374, 376–7, 391
   antitrust legislation 305
   branding 343, 350, 357
   consumer behaviour 106, 111–12, 115–16
   cultural dynamics 19, 35
   'cultural filter', distribution 321
   distribution, criteria for choice 317–19
   distribution and sales promotion 323–5, 327–8
   dynamics: interaction and behaviours 62, 73, 75
   Haitian population 115
   Hispanic population 114
   language and communication 71, 73–8

United States (*cont'd*)
  local consumers and globalization of consumption 141, 143, 146, 148
  marketing strategy, intercultural 221, 223–4, 226–7, 230
  market research 196–7, 199, 202, 204, 206
  price and relational exchange 294–6, 300, 305
  product strategy: physical, service and symbolic attributes 255, 257–8, 261–3, 266–7
  Supreme Court 302–3
universal appeals 267
universal approach 113
universalism, unrealistic 34
Uruguay 138, 234

values, cultural 441–2
variety in tastes, denial of 132–4
Venezuela 199, 234, 387, 437
vertical market studies 206
vertical relationships 322

waiting experience 261–2
we-intentions 105
Weissbier 266
West Africa 301, 447
western Europe 27, 53–4, 80, 131, 134, 189, 204, 228, 230, 305
willingness to compete 301
wine 144
wishes 59
wishful thinking 56, 59
word-of-mouth communication 110–12, 168
world market share concept 225–6
World Trade Organization 147, 221, 259, 359
world view/local view 223–6

zaibastus 305
Zaire 446–7
Zambia 293
zapping 390
Zimbabwe 307, 449